Global Markets and Real Economy

Muhammed Veysel Kaya (ed.)

Global Markets and Real Economy

Theoretical and Empirical Approaches

PETER LANG
Berlin · Bruxelles · Chennai · Lausanne · New York · Oxford

Bibliographic Information published by the Deutsche Nationalbibliothek
The Deutsche Nationalbibliothek lists this publication in the Deutsche Nationalbibliografie; detailed bibliographic data is available online at http://dnb.d-nb.de.

Library of Congress Cataloging-in-Publication Data
A CIP catalog record for this book has been applied for at the Library of Congress.

ISBN 978-3-631-94147-8 (Print)
ISBN 978-3-631-94060-0 (E-PDF)
ISBN 978-3-631-94148-5 (E-PUB)
DOI 10.3726/b23103

Published by Peter Lang GmbH, Berlin (Germany)

info@peterlang.com

This publication has been peer reviewed.

www.peterlang.com

Table of Contents

List of Contributors

Theodore Koutroukis
University of Thrace, Komotini, Greece

Dimos Chatzinikolao
University of Nicosia, Nicosia, Cyprus

Elenica Sofianova
University of Nicosia, Nicosia, Cyprus

Charis Vlados
University of Štip, North Macedonia

Ersi-Iliana Savvopoulou
European

Cemil Senel
Ankara Haci Bayram Veli University, Turkiye

Selinay Aygun
Ankara Haci Bayram Veli University, Turkiye

Miha Robežnik
The College of Accounting and Finance, Ljubljana, Slovenia

Vladimir Bukvič
Faculty of Entrepreneurship Ljubljana, Slovenia

Zokir Mamadiyarov
Mamun University, Khiva, Uzbekistan,
Tashkent State University of Economics, Tashkent, Uzbekistan
Alfraganus University, Tashkent, Uzbekistan

Sarvar Turabov
Tashkent State University of Economics, Tashkent, Uzbekistan

Samariddin Makhmudov
Termez University of Economics and Service, Termez, Uzbekistan
Alfraganus University, Tashkent, Uzbekistan
Tashkent State University of Economics, Tashkent, Uzbekistan

Nargizaxon Shamshiyeva
Tashkent State University of Economics, Tashkent, Uzbekistan

Bobur Mirzayev
Alfraganus University, Tashkent, Uzbekistan

Umida Salikhodjaeva
Tashkent State University of Economics, Tashkent, Uzbekistan

Alima Tleubergenova
Tashkent State University of Economics, Tashkent, Uzbekistan

Mansur Eshov
Alfraganus University, Tashkent, Uzbekistan

Jamshid Pardaev
Termez University of Economics and Service, Termez, Uzbekistan

Raya Karlibaeva
Tashkent State University of Economics, Tashkent, Uzbekistan

Shahnoza Sunatullayeva
Tashkent State University of Economics, Tashkent, Uzbekistan

Nozila Toxtayeva
Tashkent State the University of Economics, Tashkent, Uzbekistan

Sabrina Leo
Sapienza University of Rome, Department of Management, Rome, Italy

Ida Claudia Panetta
Sapienza University of Rome, Department of Management, Rome, Italy

Khayrilla Kurbonov
Center of the Engagement of International Ranking Agencies, The EU CARSI International Project Participant, Tashkent State University of Economics, Tashkent, Uzbekistan,

Akbar Jumayev
Tashkent State University of Economics, Tashkent, Uzbekistan

Mirzabek Jonuzokov
Tashkent State University of Economics, Tashkent, Uzbekistan

Bakhtiyor Klichev
Mamun University, Khiva, Uzbekistan
Tashkent State University of Economics, Tashkent, Uzbekistan

Shakhzoda Farxadova
Tashkent Management of Economic Institute, Tashkent, Uzbekistan

Siddik Sayfullayev
Tashkent State University of Economics, Tashkent, Uzbekistan

Aziza Azlarova
Tashkent State University of Economics, Tashkent, Uzbekistan

Gulshat Karlibaeva
Tashkent State University of Economics, Tashkent, Uzbekistan

Boburbek Giyosidinov
Tashkent State Transport University, Tashkent, Uzbekistan

Valentina Ninova
Tsenov Academy of Economics, Svishtov, Bulgaria

Nikolay Ninov
Tsenov Academy of Economics, Svishtov, Bulgaria

Alisher Ruziyev
Tashkent State University of Economics, Tashkent, Uzbekistan

Saodat Yuldasheva
Tashkent State Transport University, Tashkent, Uzbekistan

Feruza Bekbayeva
Tashkent State University of Economics, Tashkent, Uzbekistan

Gulnaz Aymurzaeva
Tashkent State University of Economics, Tashkent, Uzbekistan

Hakimjon A. Hakimov
Tashkent State University of Economics, Tashkent, Uzbekistan

Dilnoza Azlarova
University of Science and Technology, Tashkent, Uzbekistan

Isroilova Muhabbat
National University of Uzbekistan named after Mirzo Ulugbek, Tashkent, Uzbekistan

Gulchekhra Nigmatullayeva
Tashkent State University of Economics, Tashkent, Uzbekistan

Sultanov Makhmud
Tashkent University of Applied Sciences, Tashkent, Uzbekistan

Malika Umarova
Research center "Scientific bases and issues of economic development of Uzbekistan" under Tashkent State University of Economics, Tashkent, Uzbekistan

Gafurov Ubaydullo
Tashkent State University of Economics, Tashkent, Uzbekistan

Zaripa Akbarova
Tashkent State University of Economics, Tashkent, Uzbekistan

Odil Norboev
Tashkent State University of Economics, Tashkent, Uzbekistan

Feruza Daniarova
Mirzo Ulugbek National University of Uzbekistan, Tashkent, Uzbekistan

Matluba Abdurakhmanova
Tashkent State University of Economics, Tashkent, Uzbekistan

Mirjalol Eshboev
Tashkent State University of Economics, Tashkent, Uzbekistan

Tulkin Pardayev
Customs Institute of the State Customs Committee, Tashkent, Uzbekistan

Khaitmurat Khujakulov
Tashkent State University of Economics, Tashkent, Uzbekistan

Mukaddas Elbaeva
Tashkent University of Architecture and Civil Engineering, Tashkent, Uzbekistan

Tolib Nutfulloyev
Tashkent State University of Economics, Tashkent, Uzbekistan

Ma'mura Abdujaborova
Tashkent State University of Economics, Tashkent, Uzbekistan

Nurguzal Kabulova
Tashkent State University of Economics, Tashkent, Uzbekistan

Mohigul Murodova
Tashkent State University of Economics, Tashkent, Uzbekistan

Nuriddin Javliev
Tashkent State University of Economics, Tashkent, Uzbekistan

Nargiza Talapova
Namangan State University, Namangan, Uzbekistan

Nigora Khayitova
Tashkent State University of Economics, Tashkent, Uzbekistan

Gulzar Jumatova
Tashkent State University of Economics, Tashkent, Uzbekistan

Olmos Ochilov
Tashkent State University of Economics, Tashkent, Uzbekistan

Askarjon Samadov
Tashkent State University of Economics, Tashkent, Uzbekistan

Rasul Salayev
National Research University: "Diplomat University", Tashkent, Uzbekistan

Saidov Mashal
Alfraganus University, Tashkent, Uzbekistan

Gulizahro Turayeva
Gulistan State University, Guliston, Uzbekistan
Tashkent State University of Economics, Uzbekistan

Shoh-Jakhon Rakhmat ogli Khamdamov
Mamun University, Khiva city, Uzbekistan,
Alfraganus University, Tashkent, Uzbekistan
Tashkent State University of Economics, Uzbekistan

Fakhriddin Ikromovich Isayev
Research Center CEDR, Tashkent State University of Economics, Tashkent, Uzbekistan

Komil Rabbimovich Khotamov
International School of Financial Technology and Science, Tashkent, Uzbekistan
Tashkent State University of Economics, Tashkent, Uzbekistan

Nurbek Kadirovich Rizaev
Kimyo International University, Tashkent, Uzbekistan
Tashkent State University of Economics, Tashkent, Uzbekistan

Nafisa Mukhammadiyeva
Tashkent State University of Economics, Uzbekistan

Olgica Glavaški
University of Novi Sad, Faculty of Economics in Subotica, Subotica, Republic of Serbia

Emilija Beker Pucar
University of Novi Sad, Faculty of Economics in Subotica, Subotica, Republic of Serbia

Seda Bayrakdar
Ankara Haci Bayram Veli University, Türkiye

Constantinos Challoumis
National and Kapodistrian University of Athens

Svetlana Biloocaia
Moldova State University, Republic of Moldova

Nargiza Shaislamova
Tashkent State University of Economics, Tashkent, Uzbekistan

Alisher Sherov
Mamun University, Khiva, Uzbekistan

Umidjon Matyakubov
Mamun University, Khiva, Uzbekistan

Mukhiddin Kalonov
Navoi State University, Navoi, Uzbekistan

Toshmurod Kulmanov
Tashkent State University of Economics, Tashkent, Uzbekistan

Amina Ruzikulova
Navoi State University, Navoi, Uzbekistan

Vera Susana Nunes Amarante Ribeiro
Setúbal Polytechnic University, Setúbal, Portugal

Pedro Fernandes da Anunciação
Setúbal Polytechnic University, Setúbal, Portugal

Antonio Juan Briones Peñalver
Polytechnic University of Cartagena, Cartagena, Spain

Fernando Miguel Gonçalves
Setúbal Polytechnic University, Setúbal, Portugal

Madalena Joyce Fernandes Gaio
Setúbal Polytechnic University, Setúbal, Portugal

João David Oliveira Rocha
Setúbal Polytechnic University Setúbal, Portugal

Ivan Peronja
University of Split, Croatia

Cemil Senel
Ankara Hacı Bayram Veli University, Türkiye

Selinay Aygun
Ankara Hacı Bayram Veli University, Türkiye

List of Figures and Graphs

List of Tables

Foreword

In an era defined by rapid globalization, technological advancement, and financial integration, understanding the interplay between global markets and the real economy has never been more critical. "*Global Markets and Real Economy: Theoretical and Empirical Approaches*" offers a timely and comprehensive exploration of this dynamic relationship, bringing together rigorous theoretical insights with rich empirical analysis.

This book stands out for its multidisciplinary approach, bridging gaps between macroeconomics, finance, and international trade. It examines how financial markets influence real economic outcomes—such as investment, employment, and productivity—and, conversely, how economic fundamentals shape market behavior. Through diverse methodologies and global perspectives, the book illuminates the complexity of today's economic environment, providing valuable insights for academics, policymakers, and practitioners alike.

What makes this work especially significant is its balance between theory and practice. Readers will find in-depth discussions on topics ranging from capital flows and exchange rate dynamics to market volatility and policy transmission. The empirical sections, grounded in robust data analysis, offer practical relevance, particularly for those grappling with the implications of financial globalization in emerging and advanced economies.

As we navigate uncertain economic terrains—from geopolitical tensions to shifting monetary regimes—this book serves as a vital resource. It does not merely document trends but provides a framework for understanding the forces that drive economic outcomes in a globally interconnected world.

I commend the authors and contributors for their scholarly rigor and clarity. This book will undoubtedly stimulate informed discussion and guide future research in the field.

Muhammed Veysel Kaya

Workforce Engagement and Employee Relations in Multinationals: Insights from Greece

Theodore Koutroukis, Dimos Chatzinikolao, Elenica Sofianova, and Charis Vlados

1.1. Introduction

Multinational companies (MNCs) often provoke structural changes in the labor markets of both their home and their host countries. In practice, they function as structural transformers in the socioeconomic systems where they originate and ultimately operate across national borders (Michalet, 1999). Frequently, capital, knowledge, research and development, and high-tech production remain in industrialized nations, while labor-intensive processes are shifted to less-developed regions. This shift increases demand for skilled labor in advanced economies but can lead to job exports and structural unemployment in the country of origin (Mendola et al., 2024).

Moreover, MNCs have both positive and negative effects on host-country labor markets—especially in developing areas. On one hand, they can weaken labor-intensive small- and medium-sized production units employing large workforces. On the other hand, they often facilitate external migration, enhance local workforce training, offer improved pay and social benefits, and pressure local firms to raise compensation and working conditions, including those for top managers (Marginson & Sisson, 1994; Muller Camen et al., 2001). Overall, MNCs' indirect effects on job creation grow stronger in contexts where they cultivate tighter links with the local economy (Siegel et al., 2019).

1.2. Literature Review

In recent decades, numerous studies have examined how MNCs reshape their home and host socioeconomic systems. One of the most significant developments in the global economy has been the rapid growth of large corporations beyond national borders, fueled by foreign direct investment as they navigated profit crises in Fordist economies (Amin, 2011; Benko & Lipietz, 2000; Dardot & Laval, 2009; Redding & Venables, 2004). Although the intensity of this expansion fluctuates over time, it reflects a qualitative shift in global capitalism toward heightened internationalization (Exadaktylos et al., 2024).

Of particular interest are contributions that clarify how MNCs affect individual national and local labor markets. Indeed, the expansion of MNCs introduces a "multinational dimension" to employment relations, which can manifest through differing labor frameworks across the countries where MNCs operate (Kujawa, 1980) and through varying approaches to pay and working conditions among trade unions and labor institutions. Certain peculiarities of MNCs have a decisive influence on the formation of employee relations: (a) decisions on economic issues are made by the central administration, while labor issues are handled at the decentralized production unit level; (b) the production activities of a group of companies exhibit considerable flexibility; and (c) the economic activities of MNCs are characterized by relative opacity (Liebhaberg, 1980).

Typically, an MNC's policy on employee relations is more advanced than the prevailing situation in host countries. MNCs usually prefer to invest their capital in countries where labor laws are more flexible (Marginson & Sisson, 1994). However, a definitive, commonly accepted view on the influence of MNCs on employee relations in the economic units of their host countries does not yet exist (Ferner & Edwards, 1995; Günter, 1973). Martinez Lucio and Weston (1994) note that some MNCs tend to adapt to the traditions of national employee relations systems while others act as catalysts for change by diffusing new forms of work organization and employee relations practices. Coller and Marginson (1998) argue that employee relations practices are shaped by local factors and are not highly sensitive to the influences of a group's international management. However, the effects on employment issues and work organization through the group's supranational management practices should not be underestimated.

Furthermore, Lumley and Misra (1994) note that parent companies typically focus on the financial performance of their subsidiaries and become concerned with employee participation only when it clearly conflicts with profitability. This suggests that the degree of parent-company involvement in local employee-participation issues may be relatively limited, unless such participation practices pose a direct challenge to core economic objectives.

Other researchers consider that in most companies two opposing tendencies exist: increasing decentralization to individual business units and concentration at the European level. These trends result not only from external pressures for regulation but also from internal needs for coordination and control (Edwards, 2000; Marginson & Sisson, 1996; Turner et al., 1997). Another view suggests that employee relations in an MNC are decentralized except when central government involvement is required in cases of severe crisis (Günter, 1973), while some researchers claim that instead of fully adapting to local employee relations practices in host countries, MNCs standardize certain aspects of employee relations and diffuse them throughout the national employee relations system (Ferner et al., 2000; Muller-Camen et al., 2001).

Others, such as Hamill, have described the following influential factors as particularly important in assessing the extent to which the parent company is involved in employee relations at the host country level (Leat & Wooley, 1999:113):

- The degree of inter-subsidiary integration of production, as empirical material shows that a high degree of cross-border integration leads to a concentration of the employee relations function within the MNC.
- The nationality of the MNC, since US-owned MNCs are more centralized in employee relations decision-making than European-owned MNCs.
- How the subsidiary is established, because indigenous firms acquired by MNCs tend to enjoy much greater autonomy than subsidiaries set up as greenfield sites.
- The economic performance of enterprises. In particular, in subsidiaries with poor financial results—especially when due to problematic employee relations—MNCs tend to apply the employee relations practices of the country of origin to reduce industrial conflicts and increase productivity. In contrast, in subsidiaries with satisfactory performance and effectiveness indicators, MNCs tend to respect the particular employee relations practices traditionally applied in those units.

- The extent to which the MNC is a source of capital for the subsidiary. When the parent company must invest significant capital in its subsidiary, it tends to increase its intervention in the latter's industrial relations. Moreover, strong relationships between employees and management can lead to higher effectiveness, motivation, and productivity (Murad & Sfhea, 2023). This capacity-building allows MNCs to develop trust between themselves and their managerial staff (Fiedler et al., 2021).

1.3. Method

The empirical approach investigated two groups of companies using focus/ in-depth interviews, a method widely recommended for studying social phenomena and constructing new theory from such data (Yin, 1994). A series of Food and Beverage Enterprises (FBEs), and Oil and Lubricant Enterprises (OLEs) were contacted because these two sectors reflect different combinations of corporate culture, management style, employee voice, and industrial relations tradition. All enterprises that participated in the research project had active European Works Councils (EWCs). Thus, several focus/in-depth interviews were conducted with HR officials and EWC representatives. An interview questionnaire guided the discussions. Systematically and methodically recording all survey procedures enhanced the reliability of this research (Stake, 1994).

1.4. Findings

The main differences found between the two sectors (FBEs and OLEs) are described as in what follows:

- FBEs employ a higher average number of employees than OLEs.
- EWCs in FBEs have a shorter "life cycle" than those in OLEs.
- In FBEs, union activity is carried out by company unions, whereas in OLEs it is led by sectoral unions.
- Most FBEs are brownfield sites, while all OLEs are greenfield sites.
- The dominant forms of worker representation are company unions in FBEs and works councils in OLEs.

- Collective agreements have been signed in FBEs but not in OLEs.
- Subsidiary/local management participates in EWC meetings in FBEs but not in OLEs.
- EWC representatives have had previous experience with employee voice schemes in FBEs, whereas in OLEs they consistently bring such experience.
- In many cases, unions were involved in appointing EWC representatives in FBEs, but not in OLEs.
- Both EWC representatives reported that EWCs have a more beneficial impact in OLEs than in FBEs.
- The actions of EWC representatives were considered to improve employee relations at the subsidiary level, which did not occur in OLEs.
- The climate of mutual trust between EWC representatives and management has been stronger in OLEs compared to FBEs.
- In regular EWC meetings, local managers typically participate in FBEs but not in OLEs.
- EWC representatives are always union members in FBEs but rarely so in OLEs.
- EWC representatives transfer the information they obtain at EWC meetings to national trade unions (in FBEs) or to works councils (in FBEs).
- The actions of EWC representatives were seen as improving employee relations at the subsidiary level, which did not occur in OLEs.

1.5. Discussion

The factors influencing the expansion of EWC contributions to MNC subsidiaries in Greece that have established EWCs are particularly important (Triantafillidou & Koutroukis, 2022). The factors that emerged from the survey can be classified into two groups:

- The first group relates to the nature and character of enterprises. It includes factors such as the company's historical development (whether the EWC exists in a brownfield or greenfield site of a multinational group), administrative style (degree of decentralization/concentration of business decisions, especially on employee relations issues), company structure and intra-company decision-making levels (presence or absence of a European management structure), degree of internationalization of business functions (nation-centric or supranational approach to human resources and labor relations), and the role of local administrations (whether they are represented at EWC meetings), among others.

- The second group of factors pertains to employee relations. It includes the nature and structure of trade union organization (business or sectoral), the tradition of management–employee relations (co-operative or competitive), the degree of formalism (written/formal vs. informal agreements on working conditions), the level at which labor relations are formed (national or supranational), previous experience of workers' representatives in participatory procedures (presence or absence of national works councils), and the relationship between trade unions and participatory institutions (degree of union involvement in the election and activities of workers' representatives in EWCs, participation of EWC representatives in trade unions, among others.

Thus, the vast majority of FBEs are brownfield sites belonging to multinational groups. The local administration of these enterprises largely retains the historically shaped administrative style from the previous form of business ownership.

Within most FBEs, human resources issues are approached more nation-centrically. Local management in FBEs is usually also represented at EWC meetings with central management. It appears that the central management of multinational groups of FBEs has promoted the participation of local company representatives in EWC-central management meetings to better integrate overall management and more effectively promote a convergent management style across all subsidiaries.

In terms of employee relations, the FBE sector is dominated by company-level trade union organization, while management–employee relations—although co-operative—are sometimes characterized by reservation and suspicion. Procedures for defining employee relations are more formal (via collective or written agreements), mainly based on national criteria, and largely reflect the formalistic nature of the national employee relations system. Moreover, the relationship between (business) trade unions and participatory institutions, when they exist, presents certain overlaps without being competitive, and there appears to be a relative devaluation of works councils by the trade unions. However, the important role of business unions in selecting and controlling workers' representatives for EWC (from their union members) is clear.

In contrast, all OLEs are greenfield sites of multinational groups. The local management of these companies generally maintains the integrated management style used across the group's operations in all countries. Very few OLEs have a separate European division, while human resources issues are approached primarily from a supranational perspective. Additionally, local management in OLEs is generally not represented at EWC meetings with central management, indicating an established integrated approach to human resources and employee relations within the group.

In terms of employee relations in OLEs, sector-level trade union organization dominates, and management–employee relations have a long tradition of harmonious co-operation. Procedures for defining labor relations are more informal (with no written management–employee agreements), largely shaped by supranational criteria, and avoid the formalistic nature of the national industrial relations system whenever possible. Moreover, the relationship between sectoral trade unions and participatory institutions (works councils) is harmonious and co-operative, with clear role definitions, and sectoral unions play a supportive and guiding role toward works councils. Essentially, works councils—which are highly developed in the OLE sector—are integrated into a pyramidal form of workers' representation. At the top is the secondary trade union federation of the OLE sector, followed by primary sectoral unions in the intermediate level, and at the bottom there are the enterprise-level participatory bodies, with clearly defined roles at each level. In this context, works councils are recognized as primary representatives of company staff, and thus participatory institutions play a primary role in selecting and controlling employee representatives for EWCs (derived from works council members).

In summary, the FBE sector clearly exhibits a more nation-centric model of labor relations. In this context, EWCs—which have a shorter average duration of operation—are seen by employees as an unprecedented transnational innovation and an element of Europeanism. Consequently, employee representatives in EWCs consider themselves as playing an important role at the local level, even influencing local management decisions on corporate policy and employee relations issues to some extent. However, their ability to influence local management decisions—which is difficult to measure—is likely more related to their role as trade union members than to their status as EWC members, since the EWC primarily operates at European level. Human resources managers also seem to agree that the presence and role of an employee representative in the EWC have not improved relations between local management and employees, likely because the EWC lacks the capacity to intervene in local decision-making. Clearly, in FBEs—which adopt characteristics of the national employee relations system—managers prefer more traditional forms of employee representation, especially through business trade unions.

In contrast, the prevailing model of employee relations in OLEs is far more internationalized and supranational. EWCs essentially function as a harmonious extension of existing national works councils rather than as a breakthrough innovation in employee relations. Furthermore, in OLEs there is significant prior experience with national works councils, leading to greater familiarity among managers with these participatory institutions. Additionally, the longer operational history of EWCs in OLE companies fosters a familiarity among involved parties, which may explain their higher effectiveness.

EWCs are far more responsive to the characteristics of OLEs than to those of FBEs. Thus, employee representatives in EWC do not consider themselves as playing a significant role at the local level or influencing local management decisions on corporate policy and employee relations issues, as these matters fall outside the EWC's competence. In OLEs, HR officials confirm that the presence and role of the employee representative in the EWC have not improved local management–employee relations, likely due to the institution's inability to intervene in local decision-making. The factors affecting this differentiation are found mainly in the structure and degree of internationalization of companies in the sector, the form of collective worker representation (sectoral or business unionism, presence or absence of active works councils), and the historically shaped character or labor relations in each sector (structured on a supranational or national scale).

1.6. Conclusions

Based on these observations, one could argue that EWCs operate more effectively in highly internationalized subsidiaries of multinational groups that already have some national participation bodies, while trade unionism operates at the sector level (outside the enterprise) and serves an advisory role to the EWC. In other words, as supranational/European institutions, EWCs are better suited to highly internationalized companies and to a structure of employee representation aligned with the European trade union movement, where the roles of trade unions and participatory bodies are clearly defined and a dual collective representation of workers exists in the workplace.

The comparative analysis of the two sectors under investigation confirms a trend in many MNCs: a simultaneous move toward increased decentralization to autonomous business units and concentration at the European level. In other words, the transfer of responsibilities to autonomous business units alongside the need for internal coordination and control is achieved through a trend of glocalization at the European/global level (Marginson & Sisson, 1996). Furthermore, the results of this research confirm that local management in indigenous firms acquired by multinational groups enjoys much greater autonomy than the local management of companies that have been greenfield sites since their establishment (Leat & Wooley, 1999:113).

Therefore, the survey findings suggest that EWCs are supranational institutions consistent with internationalized enterprises, their integrated administrative functions, and the trend toward concentrating employee relations at the supranational level of Euro-companies, further fueling these developments. In these companies, EWCs are most effective in contributing added value for management and employees, as well as in beneficially influencing the Europeanization of national employee relations systems in which MNCs operate.

Additionally, in manufacturing subsidiaries of multinational groups that adopt sectoral trade unionism combined with national works councils, EWCs operate more efficiently. This is likely because pre-existing participatory experience in these enterprises, along with a clear distinction of roles among collective representation bodies at operational and supra-corporate levels, contributes to the more successful operation of EWCs. Conversely, in less internationalized companies with more autonomous management functions and decentralized, divergent employee relations practices, EWCs are less effective in contributing added value for management and employees and in positively influencing the Europeanization of national employee relations systems.

Furthermore, manufacturing companies (subsidiaries of multinational groups) that adopt an operational form of trade experience lower EWC efficiency. The lack of prior participatory experience in these enterprises, combined with possible confusion over the roles of collective representation bodies (where works councils exist), likely contributes to the less successful operation of EWCs.

1.7. Limitations and Prospects for Further Research

Future research should investigate factors contributing to the effectiveness and impact of EWCs, such as the parent company's country of origin (and its corresponding national employee relations system), mergers and acquisitions involving companies with EWCs, the role of training in the successful operation of EWCs, and the importance of language proficiency among EWC employee representatives. Additionally, investigating some other factors that may determine EWC effectiveness—such as the degree of product integration across group branches (inter-subsidiary product integration), the group's country of ownership (e.g., United States, European or Japanese), the subsidiaries' economic profitability, and their degree of capital dependence on the parent company (in fixed assets or working capital)—would be beneficial. Finally, exploring the evolving post-COVID landscape of employment relations in MNCs—including shifts toward remote work, digital transformation, and new organizational practices—could offer valuable insights into how EWCs and workforce engagement continue to adapt (Koutroukis et al., 2022, 2023).

Bibliography

Amin, A. (2011). *Post-fordism: A reader.* Wiley.

Benko, G., & Lipietz, A. (Eds.). (2000). *La richesse des régions: La nouvelle géographie socio-économique.* Presses Universitaires de France.

Coller, X., & Marginson, P. (1998). Transnational management influence over changing employment practice: A case from the food industry. *Industrial Relations* Journal, *29*, 4–17. <https://doi.org/10.1111/1468-2338.00075>

Dardot, P., & Laval, C. (2009). *La nouvelle raison du monde: Essai sur la société néolibérale*. La Découverte.

Edwards, T. (2000). Multinationals, international integration and employment practice in domestic plants. *Industrial Relations Journal*, *31*, 115–129. <https://doi.org/10.1111/1468-2338.00151>

Exadaktylos, D., Riccaboni, M., & Rungi, A. (2024). Talents from abroad. Foreign managers and productivity in the United Kingdom. *International Economics*, *177*, 100474. <https://doi.org/10.1016/j.inteco.2023.100474>

Ferner, A., & Edwards, P. (1995). Power and the diffusion of organizational change within multinational enterprises. *European Journal of Industrial Relations*, *1*, 229–257.

Ferner, A., Quintanilla, J., & Varul, M. (2000). *Country of origin effects and the management of HR/IR in multinationals: German companies in Britain and Spain*. [Paper presentation]. 12th World Congress of IIRA: Global Integration and Challenges for Industrial Relations and Human Resources Management in the Twenty-First Century, Tokyo. <https://doi.org/10.1177/095968019512004>

Fiedler, A., Casey, C., & Fath, B. (2021). Transnational employee voice and knowledge exchange in the multinational corporation: The European Company (SE) experience. *Human Relations*, *74*(7), 1033–1059. <https://doi.org/10.1177/0018726720905351>

Günter, H. (1973). *Multinational corporations and labour: A selected and annotated bibliography*. International Institute for Labour Studies.

Koutroukis, Th., Chatzinikolaou, D., Vlados, Ch., & Pistikou, V. (2022). The post-COVID-19 era, fourth industrial revolution, and new globalization: Restructured labor relations and organizational adaptation. *Societies*, 12(6), Article 6. <https://doi.org/10.3390/soc12060187>

Koutroukis, Th., Vlados, Ch., & Chatzinikolaou, D. (2023). Implications of the Covid-19 pandemic on human resource management and labor relations: Social dialogue for the new global era. In *Social and economic studies within the framework of emerging global developments* (Vol. 3, pp. 237–248). Peter Lang Publishing. <https://doi.org/10.3726/b20968>

Kujawa, D. (1980). Labor relations of US multinationals abroad. In B. Martin & E. Kassalow (Eds.), *Labor relations in advanced industrial societies: issues and problems* (pp. 14–42). Carnegie Endowment for International Peace.

Leat, M., & Wooley, J. (1999). Multinationals and employment relations. In G. Hollinshead, P. Nicholls, & S. Tailby (Eds.), *Employee relations* (pp. 93–131). Financial Times, Prentice Hall.

Liebhaberg, B. (1980). *Industrial relations and multinational corporations in Europe*. Gower-ECSIM.

Lumley, R., & Misra, S. (1994). Employee participation in the subsidiaries of multinational enterprises: Two Anglo-Indian case studies. *Economic and Industrial Democracy, 15*, 631–649. <https://doi.org/10.1177/0143831X94154006>

Marginson, P., & Sisson, K. (1994). The structure of transnational capital in Europe: The emerging euro-company and its implications for industrial relations. In R. Hyman & A. Ferner (Eds.), *New frontiers in European industrial relations* (pp. 15–51). Blackwell.

Marginson, P., & Sisson, K. (1996). Multinational companies and the future of collective bargaining: A review of the research issues. *European Journal of Industrial Relations*, *2*, 173–197. <https://doi.org/10.1177/095968019622003>

Martinez Lucio, M., & Weston, S. (1994). New management practices in a multinational corporation: The restructuring of worker representation and rights? *Industrial Relations Journal*, *25*, 110–121. <https://doi.org/10.1111/j.1468-2338.1994.tb00696.x>

Mendola, M., Prarolo, G., & Sonno, T. (2024). Curse or blessing? Multinational corporations and labor market outcomes in Africa. *Review of World Economics*. <https://doi.org/10.1007/s10290-024-00547-3>

Michalet, C. A. (1999). *La seduction des nations ou comment attirer les investissements [Seduction of nations or how to attract investments]*. Economica.

Muller Camen, M., Almond, P., Gunnigle, P., Quintanilla, J., & Tempel, A. (2001). Between home and host country: Multinationals and employment relations in Europe. *Industrial Relations Journal*, *32*, 435–448. <https://doi.org/10.1111/1468-2338.00210>

Murad, R. H., & Sfhea, R. N. (2023). Importance of a good relationship between local and international employees in an MNC: A case study on Samsung, London, UK. *Canadian Journal of Business and Information Studies*, *5*(2), 22–48. <https://doi.org/10.34104/cjbis.023.022048>

Redding, S., & Venables, A. J. (2004). Economic geography and international inequality. *Journal of International Economics*, *62*(1), 53–82.

Siegel, J., Pyun, L., & Cheon, B. Y. (2019). Multinational firms, labor market discrimination, and the capture of outsider's advantage by exploiting the social divide. *Administrative Science Quarterly*, *64*(2), 370–397. <https://doi.org/10.1177/0001839218769634>

Stake, R. E. (1994). Case studies. In N. Yenzin & Y. Lincoln (Eds.), *Handbook of qualitative research* (pp. 236–247). Sage.

Triantafillidou, E., & Koutroukis, T. (2022). Employee involvement and participation as a function of labor relations and human resource management: evidence from Greek subsidiaries of multinational companies in the pharmaceutical industry. *Administrative Sciences*, *12*(41). <https://doi.org/10.3390/admsci12010041>

Turner, T., D'Art, D., & Gunnigle, P. (1997). US multinationals: Changing the framework of Irish industrial relations? *Industrial Relations Journal*, *28*, 92–102. <https://doi.org/10.1111/1468-2338.00046>

Yin, R. K. (1994). *Case study research: Design and methods*. Sage.

Uncertainty and Crisis in Sovereign Bond Markets: A Threshold Regression Model for Greek Sovereign Spreads

Ersi-Iliana Savvopoulou

2.1. Introduction

The eruption of the Greek sovereign debt crisis in 2009, and more recently, the COVID-19 crisis turned the attention of financial news to the role of uncertainty during periods of "crisis." Often, political developments, announcement effects, and ratings changes have been associated with noise effects, news-induced sentiment, confidence crises, trading coordination failures, and other related frictions.

This chapter contributes to the literature by relating a market-based estimated measure of uncertainty to the Greek crisis timeline. More importantly, the analysis accounts for the effect of the European Central Bank's (ECB) extraordinary policy measures in response to the crisis on the Greek sovereign spread in a time series context and shows that ECB holdings of sovereign securities had an adverse effect on Greek sovereign risk pricing.

This chapter is structured as follows: *Section 2* provides a brief commentary of related literature; *Section 3* introduces the data; *Section 4* applies threshold regression to the Greek sovereign spread and provides a dating of uncertainty-regimes for the Greek sovereign spread since January 1999, and *Section 5* concludes.

2.2. Related Literature and Methodological Considerations

The empirical literature on the determinants of Economic and Monetary Union (EMU) sovereign spreads cautions that sovereign spreads are determined by economic fundamentals, market-sentiment effects (related to animal spirits and noise trading behavior), as well as by exogenous payoff-irrelevant factors (so-called '*sunspot events*') (Afonso et al., 2018). Broad categories of fundamentals include fiscal variables (the debt/GDP ratio, the budget deficit ratio, or debt-servicing metrics), the level of economic activity (economic growth, unemployment, relevant leading indicators), measures of external sector variables (e.g., external debt-to-GDP, the Current Account Balance-to-GDP), competitiveness indicators (e.g., Real Effective Exchange Rate, relative Unit Labor Costs), and liquidity risk. Global risk aversion and political uncertainty add to the risk premium, the latter usually being captured either by the economic policy uncertainty (EPU) (Baker et al., 2016), or by the *Sentix* measure of the risk of a Eurozone breakup. In addition, the impact of ratings changes or major macroeconomic events have been used. Non-linearities, time-varying coefficients, and regime switching models of bond pricing behavior (e.g., Bruneau et al., 2014) have been applied as alternative means to empirically account for uncertainty and multiple equilibria in sovereign bond markets.

2.2.1. Economic Fundamentals

Evidence on the existence of a *fiscal risk premium* for sovereigns in the EMU is mixed for the early EMU years. Later studies (Favero & Missale, 2011; Giordano et al., 2013; Schuknecht et al., 2010) agree on the significant role of fiscal fundamentals for sovereign risk in the Eurozone; yet note that their effect is heterogeneous across countries, time-varying and non-linear [*inter alia*, Hough et al. (2009), De Grauwe & Ji (2012), Bruneau et al. (2014), Giordano et al. (2013), and more recently Pamies et al. (2021)]. The most commonly used fiscal variables are the debt-to-GDP ratio (Borgy et al., 2011; De Grauwe & Ji, 2012, among others), the fiscal balance ratio (Afonso, et al., 2015; Baldacci & Kumar, 2010; Laubach, 2009), debt-service ratios, such as interest-payments-to-GDP (Bernoth et al., 2004), and fiscal track record interaction dummies (Hough et al., 2009). Empirical papers highlight the role of *expected* rather than current deficits (Attinasi et al., 2009; Hough et al., 2009).

Macroeconomic factors (e.g., unit labor costs, real effective exchange rate) or leading indicators of business activity such as the Economic Sentiment Indicator (ESI) have been used to capture the forward-looking nature of market expectations (Afonso et al., 2013, 2014, 2015, 2018; Alessandrini et al., 2012; Bruneau et al., 2014; De Grauwe & Ji, 2012; Giordano et al., 2013).

Liquidity risk encapsulates the possibility of investor capital losses in the event of early liquidation and of price reductions due to limited transactions (Afonso et al., 2015; Arghyrou & Kontonikas, 2012). The most commonly applied measures include the bid-ask spread (Barrios et al., 2009; Favero et al., 2010; Gerlach et al., 2010), turnover ratios, the average or maximum number of transactions, or outstanding government debt as a measure of depth for sovereign bond markets (Attinasi et al., 2009), as well as the ratio of transaction costs and volume available for trade, as an ask-side market depth indicator (Barbosa & Costa, 2010).

2.2.2. Uncertainty and Multiple Equilibria

Multiple equilibria are infamously possible in sovereign bond markets: A "bad" equilibrium may occur due to the perception of deteriorated fundamentals, due to the increased sensitivity to deteriorating fundamentals ("*wake-up call hypothesis*") or due to coordination effects among market players without any change in the underlying fundamentals (Afonso et al., 2018). During periods when the perception of sovereign default risk is elevated, *self-fulfilling crises* are possible as financial markets require increasing default risk premia to lend to a heavily indebted government. This adds further pressure to the government budget constraint and precipitates the shift toward a "bad equilibrium," even when the underlying fundamentals remain unchanged. The liquidity premium increases close to the crisis incident, usually to reflect the sovereign's inability to roll-over short-term debt and meet its debt-servicing obligations. Therefore, market liquidity and the presence of a Lender of Last Resort (LLR) become critical in coordinating market expectations toward a "good" equilibrium (Afonso et al., 2018). Bruneau et al. (2014) apply *smooth transition* threshold regression to indicate the presence of multiple equilibria between two regions separated by a threshold.

Since the eruption of the COVID-19 crisis, market commentaries have pointed to a substantial role for uncertainty. However, research has failed to posit a precise definition of uncertainty, as the distinction between quantifiable risk (usually proxied via the Chicago Board Options Exchange Volatility Index, or VIX index) and "radical uncertainty" in the Knightian sense (Knight, 1921) has been limited to the application of newspaper-based indices such as the EPU as opposed to the market-based VIX index (Baker et al., 2016; Hardouvelis et al., 2018; Nowzahowr & Stracca, 2020).

The choice of the metric for uncertainty to be applied in this chapter is based on the financial literature. To date, Generalized Autoregressive Conditional Heteroskedasticity (GARCH) methods have been applied in the literature to sovereign spreads *for panel data* but not as an intermediary estimation step as in this study (Caceres et al., 2012; Ribeiro et al., 2017; Sabkha et al., 2018).

2.3. Data

The selection of variables is based on Afonso et al. (2018). Figures 1–6 plot the determinants of sovereign spreads included in the analysis.

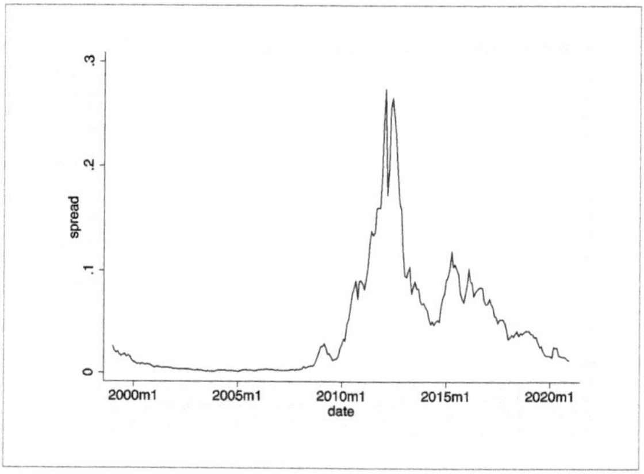

Figure 1. Plot of the Greek 10-year government bond yield spread.

Source: FRED database (2021).

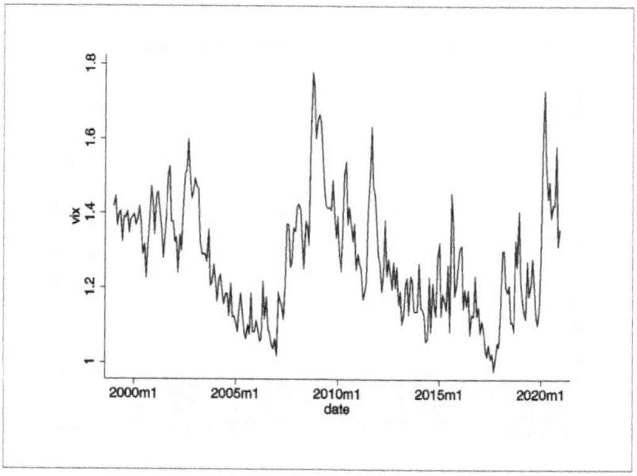

Figure 2. The VIX index.

Source: FRED database (2021).

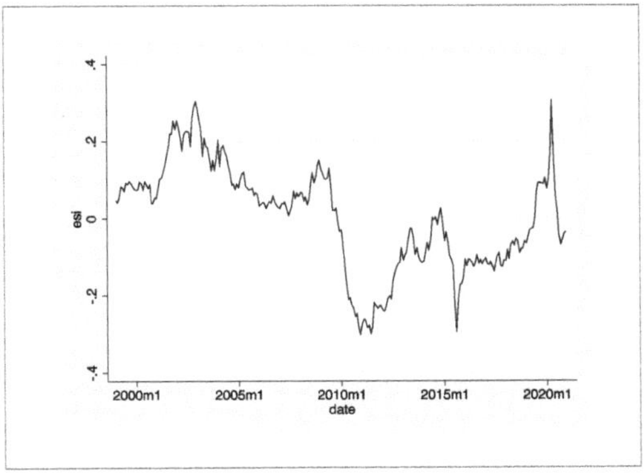

Figure 3. Economic Sentiment Indicator (ESI).
Source: Eurostat (2021).

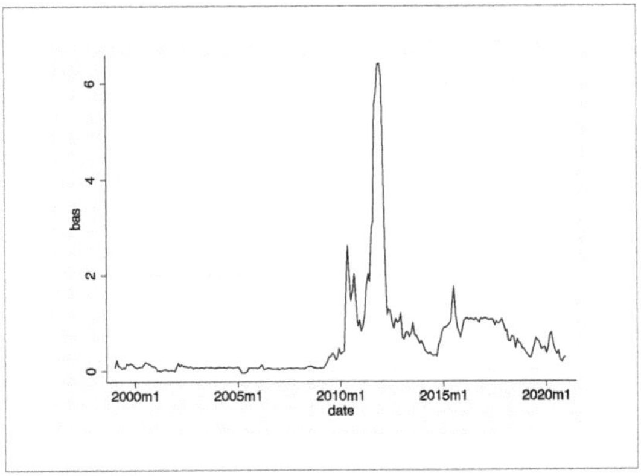

Figure 4. Bid-Ask spread (bas) for Greek government bonds.
Source: Bloomberg Terminal (2021).

Expected debt differential refers to the difference between the Greek and German debt/GDP ratio, as per the European Commission forecasts. Log transformations have also been applied, as in Afonso et al. (2018).

2.3.1. A Measure of Uncertainty

An idiosyncratic measure of uncertainty for Greece is derived, following GARCH estimation in Table 1.

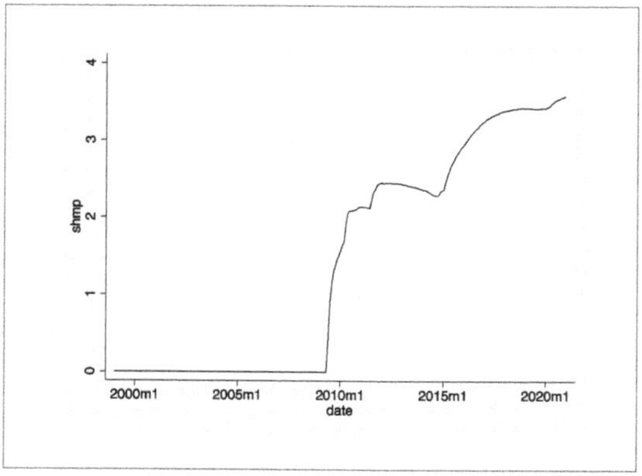

Figure 5. Securities held for monetary purposes (shmp).

Source: ECB (2021).

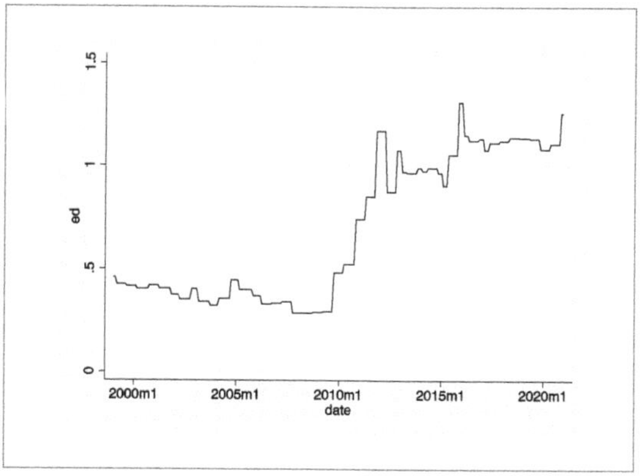

Figure 6. Expected debt differential between Germany and Greece (ed).

Source: European Commission (2021).

Uncert (Figure 7) is estimated as the time-varying conditional volatility of the Greek sovereign spread based on the GARCH(1,1) model (Table 1) (Bollerslev, 1986). The Broyden-Fletscher-Goldfarb-Shanno (BFGS) Optimization method is applied, with the Marquand step method, maximum iterations 500, and Convergence 0.0001.

Table 1. T-GARCH model results

Variable	Coefficient	Std. Error	*z*-Statistic	Prob.
C	1.84E−05	3.81E−05	0.482509	0.6294
$spread_{t-1}$	0.982420	0.008506	115.4937	0.0000
		Variance Equation		
C	5.02E−09	2.43E−09	2.063061	0.0391
$(\varepsilon_{t-1})^2$	0.441437	0.065388	6.751085	0.0000
$(\varepsilon_{t-1})^2{*}(\varepsilon_{t-1}<0)$	-0.258428	0.069363	-3.725754	0.0002
$(\sigma_{t-1})^2$	0.766920	0.023491	32.64773	0.0000
R-squared	0.958781	Mean dependent variable		0.042728
Adjusted *R*-squared	0.958623	S.D. dependent variable		0.053528
S.E. of regression	0.010888	Akaike info criterion		-9.191433
Sum-squared resid	0.030943	Schwarz criterion		-9.109939
Log likelihood	1214.673	Hannan-Quinn criterion		-9.158683
Durbin-Watson stat	1.761465			

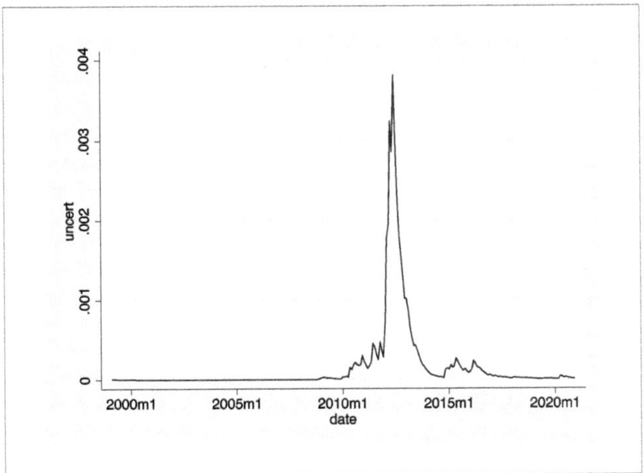

Figure 7. Estimated uncertainty measure (uncert).

The derived measure of uncertainty (Figure 7) is shown to be a good proxy of the so-called "unknown unknowns" as it is neither explained by risk aversion and uncertainty measures (VIX, EPU) nor by the fundamental determinants of spreads, while only 20 percent of the variance of this new measure is accounted for (Table 2).

$$uncert_t = \alpha^* \; vix_t + \beta^* \; bas_t + \gamma^* \; esi_t + \delta^* \; ed_t + \zeta^* \; shmp_t \\ + \theta^* \; reer_t + k^* \; epu_t + c + \varepsilon_t \tag{1}$$

Table 2. OLS regression with HAC standard errors of the estimated measure of uncertainty against other uncertainty variables and determinants of sovereign spreads

Variable	Coefficient	Std. Error	*t*-Statistic	Prob.
C	-0.007543	0.004245	-1.777016	0.0768
Vix	0.000208	0.000209	0.995894	0.3202
Bas	-4.09E-06	6.26E-05	-0.065413	0.9479
Esi	-0.001440	0.000856	-1.681347	0.0939
Ed	0.000959	0.000590	1.624530	0.1055
Shmp	-0.000266	0.000150	-1.771673	0.0776
*reer**	0.003248	0.001915	1.696269	0.0911
Epu	0.000372	0.000248	1.502944	0.1341

R-squared	0.218941	Mean	0.000157	
Adjusted *R*-squared	0.197416	S.D.	0.000490	
S.E. of regression	0.000439	Akaike info criterion		-12.59430
Sum-squared resid	4.89E-05	Schwarz criterion		-12.48535
Log likelihood	1657.854	Hannan-Quinn criterion		-12.55051
F-statistic	10.17139	Durbin-Watson stat		0.169446
Prob(*F*-statistic)	0.000000	Wald *F*-statistic		2.074345
Prob(Wald *F*-statistic)	0.046771			

2.3.2. A Measure for EMU Periphery Spillovers

Principal component analysis is performed to derive one of the data inputs to the threshold regression, capturing the relative riskiness of the Eurozone periphery to core countries (Table 3).

Table 3. Principal Component Analysis output

			Eigenvalues: (Sum = 10, Average = 1)		
Number	**Value**	**Difference**	**Proportion**	**Cumulative Value**	**Cumulative Proportion**
1	8.026805	7.052868	0.8027	8.026805	0.8027
2	0.973937	0.544430	0.0974	9.000742	0.9001
3	0.429507	0.237954	0.0430	9.430250	0.9430
4	0.191554	0.060529	0.0192	9.621803	0.9622
5	0.131024	0.024788	0.0131	9.752827	0.9753
6	0.106236	0.056684	0.0106	9.859063	0.9859
7	0.049552	0.010615	0.0050	9.908616	0.9909
8	0.038937	0.007013	0.0039	9.947553	0.9948
9	0.031924	0.011402	0.0032	9.979477	0.9979
10	0.020523	-	0.0021	10.000000	1.0000

					Eigenvectors (loadings):					
Variable	**PC 1**	**PC 2**	**PC 3**	**PC 4**	**PC 5**	**PC 6**	**PC 7**	**PC 8**	**PC 9**	**PC 10**
SPREADAUS	0.318701	0.340371	0.148615	−0.240636	−0.463347	−0.217630	−0.536497	0.919046	0.081880	0.330909
SPREADBELG	0.339638	0.029588	0.249023	−0.342807	−0.079954	−0.211574	0.161324	−0.096012	−0.603670	−0.503413
SPREADFIN	0.261565	0.632149	−0.137922	−0.111052	0.196020	0.645684	0.116582	−0.147208	−0.071671	0.069901
SPREADFR	0.337244	−0.015392	−0.328740	−0.225547	−0.163154	−0.218112	0.224954	−0.402848	0.613679	−0.251798
SPREADGR	0.314831	−0.360727	−0.054088	0.266747	−0.453595	0.525274	−0.072358	0.321365	0.058876	−0.320997

(Continued)

Table 3. (*Continued*)

Eigenvectors (loadings):

Variable	PC 1	PC 2	PC 3	PC 4	PC 5	PC 6	PC 7	PC 8	PC 9	PC 10
SPREADIRE	0.303157	−0.144806	−0.691585	−0.075972	0.468151	0.093565	−0.056788	0.100695	0.400122	−0.041029
SPREADIT	0.319201	−0.143847	−0.508020	−0.240747	0.427046	−0.151773	0.008842	0.587345	−0.063767	0.082782
SPREADNETH	0.302593	0.379599	0.035285	0.745712	0.046845	−0.367164	0.205000	0.144868	0.003836	−0.083553
SPREADPORT	0.330344	−0.305580	0.109646	0.004762	−0.179042	0.028952	0.508855	−0.140134	−0.170906	0.666914
SPREADSP	0.327604	−0.272331	−0.190373	0.265292	0.268965	0.006506	−0.558975	−0.520877	−0.224244	0.073858

Ordinary Correlations:

	SPREA-DAUS	SPREAD-BELG	SPREAD-FIN	SPRE-ADFR	SPRE-ADGR	SPRE-AIRE	SPREAIT	SPREADNETH-	SPREADPORT	SPRE-ADSP
SPREADAUS	1.000000									
SPREADBELG	0.910096	1.000000								
SPREADFIN	0.844258	0.709413	1.000000							
SPREADFR	0.852894	0.899294	0.705541	1.000000						
SPREADGR	0.687736	0.817947	0.457963	0.848254	1.000000					
SPREADIRE	0.747605	0.886131	0.524544	0.722110	0.776914	1.000000				
SPREADIT	0.729662	0.824724	0.614333	0.931960	0.829490	0.675707	1.000000			
SPREADNETH	0.868507	0.800324	0.827301	0.784250	0.646961	0.681751	0.691818	1.000000		
SPREADPORT	0.750260	0.905416	0.501311	0.887363	0.943825	0.864029	0.853077	0.692709	1.000000	
SPREADSP	0.717824	0.845562	0.533512	0.897587	0.920496	0.788352	0.910205	0.722657	0.925697	1.000000

For the second principal component (PC2), the opposite sign in the loadings of government bond yield spreads for core and periphery countries validates the interpretation provided in the literature. Whereas the first principal component constitutes contagion, the second principal component measures the relative risk and divergence between core and periphery EMU government bonds (Arghyrou & Kontonikas, 2012).

I follow Arghyrou and Kontonikas (2012) and normalize the second principal component (PC2 "normalized", *PC2N*) by taking the negative of the second principal component to ensure that it represents the relative risk of the periphery vis-à-vis core countries (Figure 8).

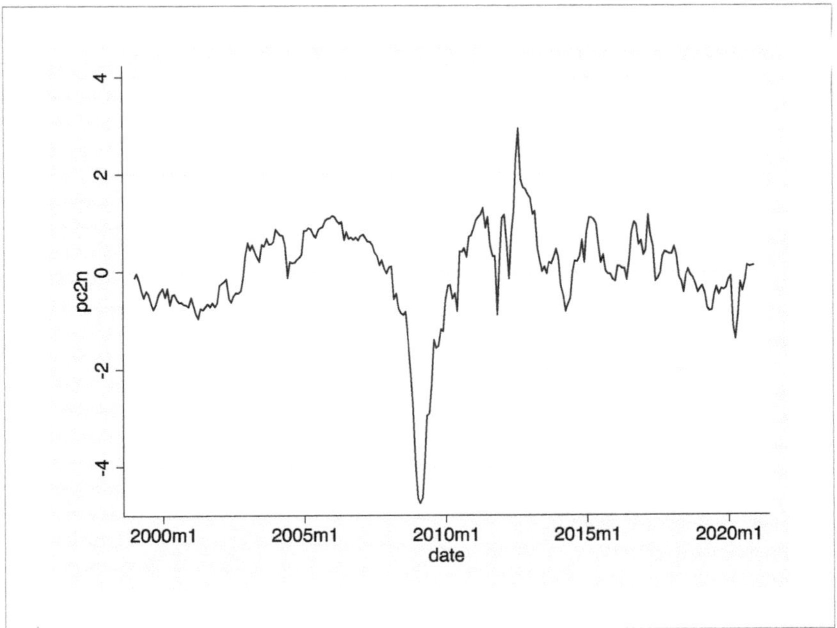

Figure 8. A PCA-based measure of Eurozone periphery spillovers (pc2n).

2.4. Threshold Regression

2.4.1. The Model

Threshold regression is applied to the Greek sovereign spread for two regions, distinguished based on the level of the uncertainty variable as follows:

$$Spread_t = \begin{cases} C_1 + a_1 * spread_{t-1} + \beta_1 * vix_t + \gamma_1 * bas_t + \delta_1 * ed_t \\ +\zeta_1 * esi_t + \theta_1 * pc2n_t + \kappa_1 * shmp_t + \lambda_1 * uncert_t + \varepsilon_t, \\ \text{for } -\infty < uncert \leq c \\ \\ C_2 + a_2 * spread_{t-1} + \beta_2 * vix_t + \gamma_2 * bas_t + \delta_2 * ed_t \\ +\zeta_2 * esi_t + \theta_2 * pc2n_t + \kappa_2 * shmp_t + \lambda_2 * uncert_t + \varepsilon_t, \\ \textit{for uncert} > c \end{cases} \quad (2)$$

where c represents the critical threshold value for the uncertainty metric (T-GARCH-based time-varying conditional variance), ε_t is zero-mean i.i.d. error term. Region 1 is the region defined by values of the parameters when *uncert* lies *below* or *at* the critical threshold (normal regime); and region 2 is the region defined by value of parameters when *uncert* is *above* the critical threshold c for uncertainty (crisis regime).

2.4.2. Results

Threshold regression

Number of obs = 263	
Full sample: 1999m2 – 2020m12	AIC = –2576.2353
Number of thresholds = 1	BIC = –2511.9366
Threshold variable: uncert	HQIC = –2550.3952

2.4.3. Analysis of Results

The estimated threshold for the variance of the Greek sovereign spread is located at 0.0002 of the uncertainty metric (*uncert*), confirming the difference

Table 4. Threshold regression estimation output

Order				**Threshold**		**SSR**
1				**0.0002**		**0.0128**
Spread	**Coeff.**	**Std. Err.**	*Z*	*P>z*	**[95% Conf.**	**Interval]**
Region 1 (Normal)						
L1.spread	0.917	0.062	14.690	0.000	0.795	1.039
vix	0.003	0.004	0.650	0.516	-0.006	0.012
bas	0.004	0.003	1.430	0.152	-0.001	0.009
ed	-0.001	0.007	-0.210	0.837	-0.016	0.013
esi	0.001	0.008	0.070	0.947	-0.014	0.016
pc2n	0.000	0.001	0.220	0.826	-0.001	0.002
shmp	0.000	0.002	0.020	0.988	-0.003	0.003
uncert	48.634	28.693	1.690	0.090	-7.603	104.872
_cons	-0.003	0.006	-0.490	0.626	-0.015	0.009
Region2 (Crisis)						
L1.spread	0.094	0.057	1.670	0.095	-0.016	0.205
vix	-0.021	0.017	-1.260	0.209	-0.054	0.012
bas	0.018	0.002	12.030	0.000	0.015	0.021
ed	-0.002	0.013	-0.130	0.898	-0.026	0.023
esi	-0.045	0.019	-2.420	0.015	-0.082	-0.009
pc2n	0.016	0.002	7.070	0.000	0.012	0.021
shmp	0.020	0.008	2.440	0.015	0.004	0.036
uncert	42.347	2.880	14.700	0.000	36.702	47.991
_cons	0.011	0.030	0.360	0.718	-0.048	0.070

*The STATA default 10% trimming percentage is applied; 200 regressions are run.

in pricing behavior above and below a threshold of uncertainty (Table 4). Below this estimated critical level of uncertainty (normal regime), the spread is highly persistent, a finding indicative of the effect of fundamentals according to the literature. No other term is statistically significant at the 5% level.

In the crisis regime (region 2), the persistence in the Greek sovereign spread declines. Liquidity effects, uncertainty, and spillover effects become statistically significant. However, although the coefficient for *securities held for monetary purposes* (*shmp*) is statistically significant, it bears the opposite sign (+0.020) to that expected: The impact of quantitative easing improved liquidity conditions in sovereign debt markets, yet due to the non-eligibility of Greek government bonds for ECB purchases, Greek spreads increased, as ECB actions lowered the yield of the benchmark German Bund. Interestingly, the effect of the VIX index (*vix*) is in the opposite direction to that prescribed by other studies and it is not statistically significant. This could be attributed to the lack of synchronization of the crisis regime for Greece to periods of high uncertainty for the United States or with respect to the global economic cycle.

2.4.3.1. Regime Dating

Equation (3) defines the binary regime dating classification for "normal" vs. "crisis" according to the critical threshold for uncertainty:

$$\mathbf{Regime_t} = \begin{cases} \mathbf{1}, \quad \text{for } -\infty < uncert \leq c \begin{pmatrix} \text{i.e. when the level of uncertainty} \\ \text{lies in the } \mathbf{normal\ regime} \end{pmatrix}, \\ \mathbf{2}, \quad \text{for } uncert > c \begin{pmatrix} \text{i.e. when the level of uncertainty} \\ \text{lies in the } \mathbf{crisis\ regime} \end{pmatrix} \end{cases} \quad (3)$$

In Figure 2, Regime2 corresponds to the months in the timeline which are classified as "crisis regimes."

According to the regime dating classification offered in this study *Regime 2* ("*crisis*") occurs at the following quarters: 2010m8; 2010m12–2011m1, 2011m5–2013m9, 2015m5–2015m6, 2016m3–2016m4. *Regime 1* ("normal") occurs at all other periods (Figure 2.13).

"Uncertainty" periods (crisis regime) correspond to bad-equilibria periods:

- *August 2010* occurs in the aftermath of the first major pension reform passed in the Greek Parliament to comply with the conditionality of the first bailout loan in July 2010. The austerity-inducing impact of conditionality was first experienced by the Greek public.

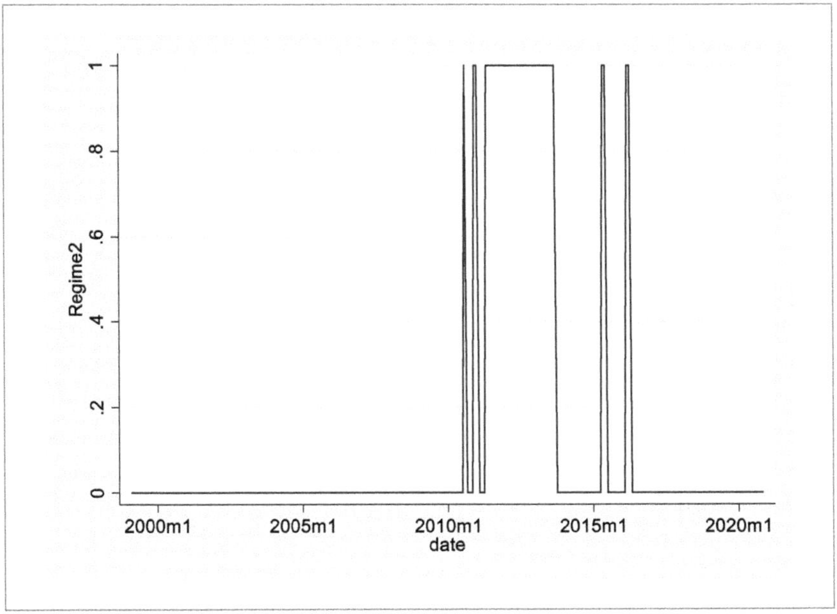

Figure 9. Threshold regression regime dating classification.

- *December 2010–January 2011*: In 2011, Fitch downgraded Greece from BBB– to BB+ and the first austerity budget was approved for 2011 in December 2010.
- *May 2011–September 2013:* This period covers the end of the First Economic Adjustment Program and the largest portion of the Second Economic Adjustment Program, also coinciding with the peak of the Eurozone debt crisis. Over the course of this uncertainty regime, markets questioned Greek membership in the EMU. This period was characterized by political instability, riots, and resistance to austerity measures. A series of rating downgrades and the largest episode of partial default in history (the Greek PSI) are included.
- *May 2015–June 2015:* This uncertainty regime covers the events that led to the Greek referendum in July 2015 and the expiration of the Second Economic Adjustment Program. In the absence of an agreed third bailout loan package, markets expected the Greek government to default on its debt servicing obligations after the second half of 2015.

- *March 2016–April 2016:* This period coincides with all-time lows in the Greek stock market, the passing of a new austerity law, and renewed market fears in anticipation of the impact of a Brexit referendum.

In contrast, the model classifies the pre-crisis era as well as the period near the expiration of the Second Economic Adjustment Program to correspond to a "good-equilibrium" regime, when Greece regained access to international capital markets and the Greek government was credible with respect to its solid progress on fiscal consolidation and structural reforms.

The onset of the Third Economic Adjustment Program is classified as a "good-equilibrium" outcome, as market fears of a Greek default and Grexit were eased by agreement with Greece's creditors. The end of the Third Economic Adjustment Program is also classified as a "good equilibrium" outcome, as earlier fiscal consolidation and the May 2018 Eurogroup Agreement on the Medium-Term measures for debt restructuring improved the Greek government debt profile and ensured the credibility of the Greek government with financial markets. The build-up of a cash-buffer also served in this direction. Similarly, the periods prior to and immediately after the contracting of the first bailout loan are classified as "good equilibria" outcomes by financial markets, as international financial assistance and conditionality measures reassured markets that Greek debt-servicing obligations would be met.

2.5. Conclusions

At negligible levels of uncertainty (below the critical threshold), financial markets price the Greek sovereign spread based on fundamentals only. Once the level of uncertainty surpasses some critical threshold, both fundamentals and market sentiment drive Greek sovereign risk-pricing behavior. The threshold regression model has offered a dating classification of the two regimes, which fits well with the narrative of the Greek debt crisis.

The finding that crisis regimes are driven by speculative liquidity effects and short-term market sentiment may be used to support the immediate and unconditional access for the Greek government to liquidity lines, such as the Enhanced Conditions Credit Line (ECCL) or the Precautionary Conditions

Credit Line (PCCL) of the ESM. Crossing the critical threshold of uncertainty proposed in this chapter could be used as an arbiter of market sentiment in relevant argumentation. Evidence that the ECB's extraordinary response to the Eurozone debt crisis worked to the detriment of non-eligible Greek bonds during peaks of the Greek debt crisis, may be used as an argument to extend the preferential access for Greece to programs such as the Pandemic Emergency Purchase Program (PEPP) in the future.

Future research could delve deeper into the long memory properties of the Greek sovereign spread and potential crisis scarring effects.

Bibliography

Afonso, A., Aghyrou, M. G. Gadea, D., & Kontonikas, A. (2018) 'Whatever it takes' to resolve the European sovereign debt crisis? Bond pricing regime switches and monetary policy effects. *Journal of International Money and Finance*, *86*(2018), 1–30.

Afonso, A., Arghyrou, M. G., & Kontonikas, A. (2014). Pricing sovereign bond risk in the European monetary union area: An empirical investigation. *International Journal of Financial Economics*, *19*, 49–56.

Afonso, A., Arghyrou, M., & Kontonikas, A. (2015). The determinants of sovereign bond yield spreads in the EMU. *European Central Bank*, *1781*(April 2015).

Alessandrini, P., Fratianni, M., Hallett, A., & Presbitero, A. (2012). External imbalances and fiscal fragility in the Euro area. *Univ. Politecnica Marche –Dept. Economic and Social Sciences*, 66, Mo.Fi.R. Working Papers from Money and Finance Research group (Mo.Fi.R.).

Arghyrou, M., & Kontonikas, A. (2012). The EMU Sovereign-Debt Crisis: Fundamentals, Expectations and Contagion. *Journal of International Financial Markets, Institutions and Money*, *22*(4), 658–677.

Arghyrou, M., & Tsoukalas, J. (2011). The Greek debt crisis: Likely causes, mechanics and outcomes. *The World Economy*, *34*(2), 173–191.

Attinasi, M.-G., Checherita, C., & Nickel, C. (2009). What explains the surge in euro area sovereign spreads during the financial crisis of 2007–2009? *European Central Bank*. Working Paper Series. No. 1131/ December 2009.

Baker, S., Bloom, N., & Davis, S. (2016). Measuring economic policy uncertainty. *Quarterly Journal of Economics, 131*(4), 1593–1636.

Baldacci, E., & Kumar, M. (2010). Fiscal deficits, public debt, and sovereign bond yields. *International Monetary Fund*, IMF Working Paper 10/184.

Barbosa, L., & Costa, S. (2010). Determinants of Sovereign Bond Yield Spreads in the Euro Area in the Context of the Economic and Financial Crisis', *Economic Bulletin and Financial Stability Report Articles and Banco de Portugal Economic Studies*. Banco de Portugal, Economics and Research Department.

Barrios, S., Iversen, P., Lewandowska, M., & Setzer, R. (2009). Determinants of intra-euro area government bond spreads during the financial crisis. *European Commission*, European Commission Papers, No. 388.

Bernoth, K., Von Hagen, J., & Schuknecht, L. (2004). Sovereign risk premia in the European government bond market. *European Central Bank,* Working Paper Series. No. 369, June.

Bollerslev, T. (1986). Generalized autoregressive conditional heteroskedasticity. *Journal of Econometrics, 31*(3), April 1986, 306–327.

Borgy, V., Laubach, T., Mesonnier, J.-S., & Renne, J.-P. (2011). Fiscal sustainability, default risk and euro area sovereign bond spreads, *Banque de France*. Document de Travail No. 350.

Bruneau, C., DeLatte, A. L., & Fouquau, J. (2014). Is the European sovereign crisis self-fulfilling? Empirical evidence about the drivers of market sentiments. *Journal of Macroeconomics, 42*(December 2014), 38–51.

Caceres, C., Guzzo, V., & Segoviano, M. (2010). Sovereign spreads: global risk aversion, contagion, or fundamentals? *International Monetary Fund*, IMF Working Papers, No. 10/120.

Caner, M., & Hansen, B. E. (2003). Threshold autoregression with a unit root. *Econometrica, 69*(6), 1555–1596.

Cole, H., & Kehoe, T. K. (1996). *Self-fulfilling debt crises. Federal Reserve Bank of Minneapolis* (Research Department Staff Report No. 211, 1996).

De Grauwe, P., & Ji, Y. (2012). *Self-fulfilling crises in the Eurozone: An empirical test*. CEPS Working Document No. 366, 2012.

De Grauwe, P., & Ji, Y. (2012). *Mispricing of sovereign risk and multiple equilibria in the Eurozone*. CEPS Working Documents, No. 361.

Favero, C., & Missale, A. (2011). *Sovereign spreads in the Euro area. Which prospects for a eurobond?* (CEPR Discussion Papers 8637), Centre for Economic Policy Research.

Giordano, R., Pericoli, M., & Tommasino, P. (2013). 'Pure' or 'Wake-Up Call' contagion? Another look at the EMU sovereign debt crisis. Temi di discussione (Economic Working Papers) 904, Bank of Italy, Economic Research and International Relations Area.

Hardouvelis, G., Karalas, G., Karanastasis, D., & Samartzis, P. (2018). *Economic policy uncertainty, political uncertainty and the Greek economic crisis*. (April 3, 2018). Available at SSRN: <https://ssrn.com/abstract=3155172>.

Knight, F. (1921). *Risk, uncertainty, and profit*. Online edition. Boston: Houghton and Mifflin.

Laubach, T. (2009). New evidence on interest rate effects of budget deficits and debt. *Journal of European Economic Association*, 7, 858–885.

Nowzohowr, L., & Stracca, L. (2020). More than a feeling: confidence, uncertainty and macroeconomic fluctuations. *Journal of Economic Surveys*, *34*(4), 691–726.

Pamies, S., Carnot, N., & Patarau, A. (2021). *Do fundamentals explain differences between euro area sovereign interest rates?* The European Commission, DG ECFIN (Discussion Paper 141, June 2021).

Ribeiro, P.R., Cermeno, R., & Curto, J. D. (2017). Sovereign bond markets and financial volatility dynamics: Panel-GARCH evidence for six euro area countries. *Finance Research Letters*, 21(May), 107–114.

Sabkha, S., Peretti, C., & Mallek, S. (2018). *Forecasting sovereign CDS volatility: A comparison of univariate GARCH-class models*. Working Paper No. hal-01769390.

Schuknecht, L., Von Hagen, J., & Wolswijk, G. (2010). *Government bond risk premiums in the EU revisited: The impact of the financial crisis* (ECB Working Paper No. 1152). European Central Bank.

Social Finance and Social Impact Investing: Investments with Social Impact and the Role of Social Bonds

Cemil Senel and Selinay Aygun

3.1. Introduction

In recent years, there has been a growing interest and need to address global economic and environmental challenges, making it imperative for financial systems to go beyond the sole objective of generating profit. In this context, concepts such as social finance and social impact investing are increasingly gaining attention as financial approaches that aim to create social benefits. Social finance is an investment approach that aims to generate not only financial returns but also social and environmental impacts. Such investments support sustainable development goals while encouraging individuals, communities, and companies to act more responsibly (Jackson, 2022).

Social impact investing, as an area where financial investments are directed to create social change, takes into account not only financial gain but also environmental and social change objectives. This type of investment typically allocates capital to projects that seek to address social problems such as education, health, the environment, and poverty, and the measurement of social benefit is of paramount importance in this process (Miller, 2021). Investors make decisions based not only on financial returns, but also on the long-term impact of these projects on society.

This study aims to examine the latest developments and trends in the field by conducting a literature review on the development, success criteria, and future of social finance and social impact investing. It will also address how social finance will evolve in the future, the impact of new technologies and regulations, and which strategies will be successful in this field. This study aims to provide a deeper understanding of the potential of social finance and its contribution to social development and to shed light on the practices in this field.

3.2. Conceptual Framework

3.2.1. Definition of Social Finance

Social finance is a field in which financial instruments and mechanisms aim to create social benefits. The term includes the use of financial capital not only to support not-for-profit activities, but also to invest in projects aimed at improving the general welfare of society (Ghosh, 2020). In contrast to traditional finance, social finance aims to achieve social, environmental, and economic impact goals in addition to the financial return on investment (Harrison & Denny, 2021). Bozkurt and Kaya (2023) investigates the foremost firm-specific factors having an impact on financial distress and bankruptcy in the acute stage of the Covid-19 crisis based on data from approximately 9,000 enterprises in 25 countries.

The main objective of social finance is to direct financial resources toward solving social problems and supporting sustainable development. It is an investment approach centered around social goals such as health, education, environmental protection, poverty reduction, and gender equality (Nicholls et al., 2018). Social finance can be adopted by both public and private actors, but the private sector, especially impact investors, have an important role to play (Wood & Green, 2021).

Social finance includes a variety of financial instruments, including microfinance, social impact investing, impact bonds, and social venture capital. These instruments are used to finance initiatives that aim to solve social problems (Cohen & Bickman, 2019). For example, microfinance helps low-income individuals start small businesses, while impact investing aims to create social good while providing financial returns (Gordon, 2021).

The definition of social finance also emphasizes the importance of measurement in the process of creating social impact. This measurement involves analyzing financial and social outcomes and helps investors understand how effectively their resources are being used (Morris et al., 2022). Social impact investing aims to deliver tangible results to solve a specific social problem, and measuring these results is critical to the success of social finance (Friedman & Miles, 2020).

However, unlike traditional financial markets, social finance evaluates risks and returns in line with social, environmental, and economic factors. Investors consider not only the financial return but also the social change that will be created when investing in social financial projects (Jackson & Adams, 2020).

Therefore, while social finance promotes economic development, it also emphasizes social responsibility (Simons & Hall, 2021).

The future of social finance will be shaped by a stronger financial ecosystem and a wider investor base. Technological advances and tools such as artificial intelligence and data analytics will contribute to making social finance more efficient (Rosen, 2022). This will facilitate wider adoption of social finance and facilitate solutions to larger societal problems (Murray & Roberts, 2023).

On the social finance side, instruments such as social impact investing, social impact bonds (SIBs), and green sukuk, and on the economic side, institutions such as self-help groups, associations, cooperatives, and foundations fall within the scope of the third sector. These institutions and activities are sometimes carried out by the private or public sector, sometimes by households, and sometimes by third-sector organizations themselves. At the same time, some of these activities are profit-oriented, while others are not. Below is an approach that comprehensively addresses institutions and activities with these very different characteristics within the framework of the tripolar relationship (Yenice, 2021).

Figure 10 reveals that activities that take social impact into account can be carried out by different sectors. In this context, area 1 represents public sector activities, area 2 represents market sector activities, and area 3 represents social activities. The lower part of the EF line indicates the private sector and the upper part indicates the public sector. The AB line positions non-profit organizations at the top and for-profit organizations at the bottom. The CD line identifies formal organizations at the top and informal organizations at the bottom. In addition, triangles 8, 9, and 10 and areas 4, 6, and 7 represent mixed organizations, while area 5 represents only third-sector organizations (Yenice, 2021).

3.2.2. Creating and Measuring Social Impact

Social impact generation refers to the process by which an initiative or investment generates social benefits. This impact is usually achieved through specific strategies and interventions to achieve environmental, social, and economic goals. Social impact investments often target activities to address societal challenges such as health, education, poverty, gender equality, and environmental protection (Gordon, 2021). Social impact generation aims

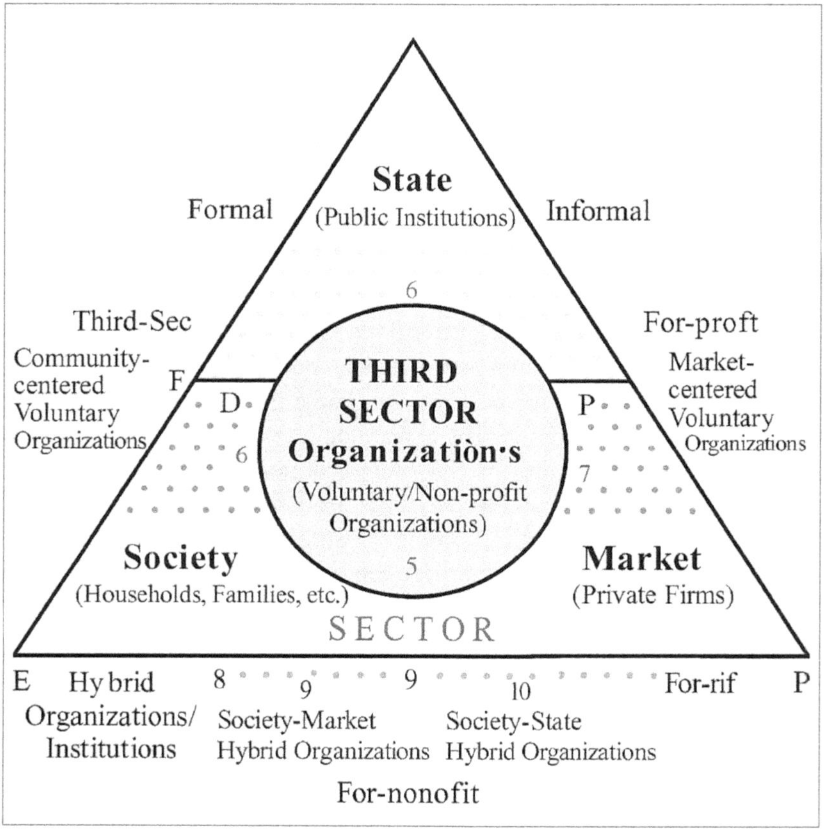

Figure 10. Third sector in a tripolar approach.
Source: Yenice (2021).

not only to generate financial returns but also to improve the well-being of society (Ghosh, 2020).

One of the most critical aspects of social impact creation is measuring that impact. Impact measurement involves assessing the tangible social benefits and outcomes of a social enterprise or investment. This measurement is not only quantitative, but also qualitative. For example, an investment in health measures an intangible social impact, such as improving people's quality of life, while an investment in education can be measured with concrete data, such as increased literacy rates (Cohen & Bickman, 2019).

The methods used in social impact measurement often require sophisticated tools and metrics to identify the social change brought about by the investment. The main objective of impact measurement is to determine how effective the activities are and to what extent they serve the purpose of providing social benefits (Morris et al., 2022). In this context, frameworks such as Theory of Change and Social Return on Investment (SROI) are widely used methods in impact measurement (Simons & Hall, 2021). These tools allow assessing both the financial and social returns on investment.

One of the challenges of social impact measurement is the intangible and multifaceted nature of social benefits. This is one of the biggest challenges when measuring social impact because traditional financial measurement methods are often limited to tangible results. Collecting the right data for social impact measurement and analyzing it appropriately requires a more complex process (Friedman & Miles, 2020). To overcome these challenges, multidisciplinary approaches and a variety of data collection tools are used in social impact measurement (Wood & Green, 2021).

Transparency, accuracy, and sustainability are essential for social impact creation and measurement to be successful. Investors and stakeholders need effective measurement methods and data-driven results to accurately assess the social benefits of an investment. In this context, social impact measurement is not only a process of assessing the success of an investment, but also of guiding future projects and increasing their potential to create greater change for society (Murray & Roberts, 2023).

3.2.3. The Role and Development of Social Investments

Social investments are financial investments that aim to create social benefits and their role is becoming increasingly critical. Social investments are strategic investments that can be made by the private sector, the public sector, and non-governmental organizations and aim to create social change as well as financial returns (Bugg-Levine & Emerson, 2011). These investments are usually directed toward projects that address social problems such as health, education, environment, poverty alleviation, and social inequality (Khan et al., 2020). The main objective of social investments is to support sustainable development by combining financial return with social benefits (Murray & Klein, 2022).

The development of social investment markets has accelerated in recent years. This development reflects the evolution of a financial approach in which investors consider not only financial returns but also social impact (Gorman, 2021). In particular, instruments such as impact investing and SIBs have become important components of social investing (Nicholls & Pharoah, 2021). These instruments enable investors to invest in projects that aim to solve social problems, while at the same time guaranteeing repayment based on the achievement of certain goals (Zimmerman & Castella, 2019).

The development of social investment has also made it an important part of the private equity sector. By providing capital to socially beneficial projects, investors not only fulfill their social responsibility, but also assume the responsibility to create and measure social impact (Gorman, 2021). Social investment instruments offer investors opportunities to spread their risk, create new business models, and bring a stronger ethical perspective to financial markets (Ghosh & Akhter, 2020). This has encouraged more investors to enter the social investment space and contributed to the growth of the markets.

The growing role of social investment goes beyond the traditional understanding in the financial sector and allows for the adoption of a sustainable development approach for societies. By combining socially responsible projects with financial investments, investors not only support economic development but also contribute to improving environmental and social impacts (Ghosh & Akhter, 2020). This transformation increases the financial sector's capacity to fulfill social responsibility, while at the same time providing opportunities to direct capital flows in a more fair and equitable manner.

The future of social investment is an area that is expected to become more diversified and comprehensive. The financial instruments used in this field are becoming more sophisticated, increasing their capacity to create impact at all levels of society (Murray & Klein, 2022). Moreover, the integration of digital technologies (blockchain, artificial intelligence) into social investment processes will help social investors make faster and more accurate decisions (Gorman, 2021). According to the study conducted by Özüdoğru and Sönmez (2024), the use of data analytics and machine learning solutions for the insurance industry is expected to increase.

3.2.4. Success Criteria for Social Impact Investments

Social impact investments are investments that aim to create social benefits in addition to generating financial returns. The success of such investments is measured not only by financial performance but also by social and environmental impacts. There are some basic criteria to be considered in determining the success of social impact investing (Friedman & Miles, 2020). A successful social impact investment supports sustainable development by combining financial returns with social benefits (Ghosh & Akhter, 2020).

First, one of the success criteria is effective impact measurement. For social impact investments to be successful, the social impact of the investment must be measured accurately and transparently. This measurement should not only be quantitative, but also be qualitative. Social impacts should be compared with the social change targeted by the investment and analyzed through certain indicators (Nicholls & Pharoah, 2021). Measuring impact in this way allows investors to better understand the social benefits they provide and to direct their resources more efficiently (Gorman, 2021).

An important criterion affecting success is financial sustainability. Social impact investments aim to create social benefits while generating financial returns. However, for these goals to be successful, the financial sustainability of the investment is of great importance. Investors should ensure that their investments are financially sustainable in the long term in order to provide social benefits (Ghosh & Akhter, 2020). Financial sustainability is a factor that will ensure that the investment maintains its capacity to create social impact not only in the initial phase but also in the long term (Simons & Hall, 2021).

Another criterion that determines the success of social impact investments is collaboration and stakeholder engagement. Social impact often requires many stakeholders to come together and work toward a common goal. Successful social impact investments should involve the participation of not only investors, but also local communities, civil society organizations, government agencies, and other stakeholders (Bugg-Levine & Emerson, 2011). These collaborations enable investments to have a broader impact and bring about more lasting changes in society (Khan et al., 2020).

Risk management is another important criterion for success in social impact investments. Social investments can often be high-risk projects, as the creation of social impact can have long-term and uncertain outcomes. Investors should carefully analyze these risks and develop appropriate risk management strategies when creating social impact. Furthermore, risk management should include mechanisms to protect the investor against negative external factors that may affect the success of the investment (Gorman, 2021).

In this context, conducting an accurate risk analysis plays a critical role in the success of social impact investing (Zimmerman & Castella, 2019).

Achievability of social change goals is also an important criterion that determines the success of social impact investing. Investors should make sure that the social changes they target are measurable and achievable before realizing their investments. Defining the social problems that the investment focuses on at a level that will create a certain impact and measuring these goals is one of the key factors that will determine whether the investment is successful or not (Morris et al., 2022). Therefore, the achievability of the set objectives is one of the cornerstones of the success of social impact investments (Simons & Hall, 2021).

3.2.5. The Future of Social Finance

Social finance will continue to play an important role in the transformation of financial markets in the future as an area where financial activities that aim to create social impact increase. Emerging technologies, changing investor expectations, and increasing pressures toward global development goals are the main factors shaping the future of social finance (Jackson, 2022). In particular, the increasing prominence of sustainability and social impact-oriented investments suggests that social finance will grow even more in the coming years (Anderson & Lee, 2023).

Technological innovations play an important role in the future of social finance. Digital tools such as blockchain, artificial intelligence, and data analytics will enable social impact investments to become more transparent, efficient, and measurable. In particular, blockchain will make it easier for investors to track the results of social impact investments, providing financial transparency and increasing investor confidence (Murray, 2023). Artificial intelligence will help measure social impacts more accurately and help investors make faster decisions on social impact projects (Zhang et al., 2022).

The role of impact investors will become increasingly prominent in the future of social finance. Investors are now focusing on projects that aim not only to generate financial returns, but also to create social change. In this context, impact investing has become an important trend in the financial world, offering investors the opportunity to not only make a profit, but also create environmental and social impacts (Miller, 2021). In particular, the proliferation of financial instruments such as "SIBs" and "green bonds" demonstrates the growing popularity and impact of such investments (Harrison, 2022).

Another important development is the impact of public policies and regulations. Governments are strengthening legal frameworks for the growth of social finance and incentivizing social impact investments. These regulations facilitate the financing of social enterprises and sustainable development projects, making them more attractive to investors (Patel, 2022). A better enabling environment for social enterprises will create significant momentum for the future of social finance.

In the future, social finance is expected to reach a wider audience. Especially in emerging markets, the growth of social finance will create more opportunities for local communities and small-scale enterprises. The future of social finance has the potential to reduce social inequality, increase environmental sustainability, and support economic development. In developing countries, microfinance and similar financial instruments will become more effective, reaching a wider audience (Choi & Lee, 2023).

The future of social finance will grow further in line with sustainable development goals and will take more place in the financial world. While investors make financial decisions with an understanding of social responsibility, the development of methods to measure and evaluate social impact will increase the impact of social finance (Thompson, 2021). In addition, opportunities provided by technology and the regulatory environment will enable social finance to grow stronger and more effective (Baker & Smith, 2022).

3.2.6. Investments with Social Impact and the Role of Social Bonds

Social impact investments are investments that aim to generate financial returns while at the same time creating impacts to solve social and environmental problems (Biancone & Radwan, 2019). This type of investment presents an important opportunity for investors seeking to generate social benefits. Social impact investments aim to strike a balance between financial returns and social change, and different instruments are used to achieve these goals (Kuzucu, 2018). In this context, SIBs stand out as an important tool (Durak & Ergen, 2016). SIBs are financial instruments in which investors make a financial contribution to the realization of certain social goals and receive a refund if they are achieved (Mazzuca et al., 2024). This mechanism is an innovative solution to achieve social goals without imposing a financial burden on the public sector (Taraktaş, 2015).

SIBs have great potential, especially in areas where public services need to be improved (Rexhepi, 2017). These bonds provide a means for investors to not only realize financial gains, but also to contribute to social good. For example, they are used to solve societal problems such as reducing crime rates, improving education systems, or fighting poverty (Sinclair et al., 2021). In this process, governments and social organizations, together with investors, commit to pay back when they achieve a successful social impact (Yenice, 2021). This model allows the public sector to create greater social impact with limited resources, while at the same time engaging the private sector in solving social problems (Biancone & Radwan, 2019).

One of the main advantages of SIBs is that they are results-oriented (Durak & Ergen, 2016). Investors are only repaid if a specific social goal is achieved. This creates a strong incentive mechanism to increase the effectiveness of SIBs (Mazzuca et al., 2024). Moreover, SIBs can often be initially high-risk, but successful projects can provide not only social benefits but also significant financial returns to investors (Kuzucu, 2018). This creates a motivation for investors to be more attracted to socially responsible projects (Rexhepi, 2017).

There are some important factors for the successful implementation of SIBs (Taraktaş, 2015). First, the accuracy of impact measurement is of great importance. Investors should be able to accurately measure social impact along with financial return expectations (Durak & Ergen, 2016). Therefore, the metrics and data collection methods developed to measure the impact of SIBs play a critical role (Mazzuca et al., 2024). Moreover, the co-operation of governments, local authorities, and civil society organizations is one of the determining factors in the success of SIBs (Sinclair et al., 2021). Policymakers need to provide incentive regulations and supportive environments to encourage investors' participation in social impact projects (Biancone & Radwan, 2019).

The growing popularity of SIBs around the world shows that these instruments offer an effective solution to global social problems (Yenice, 2021). Many countries are using these innovative financial instruments to deliver public services more effectively and increase social benefits (Kuzucu, 2018). The future of SIBs will be shaped by the wider adoption of these financial instruments and their applicability in more sectors (Taraktaş, 2015).

In light of the evident desire for SIBs, the evolution of these investments over the last 10 years is shown in Figure 11 (Konak & Demir 2023).

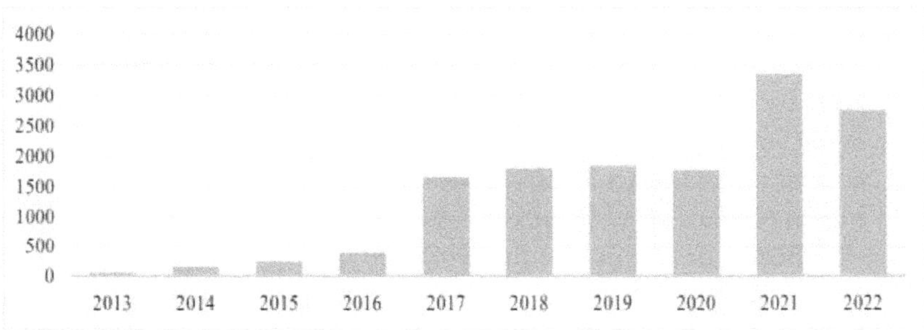

Figure 11. Total market value of SIBs over a 10-year period.
Source: Konak & Demir (2023).

Figure 11 shows that the market size of SIBs has been on a steady increase over the last decade. While the market size remained stable between 2017 and 2020, there was a significant jump in the market size with the SIBs issued in 2021. Although the data for 2022 lagged behind the previous year as the year is not yet complete, if the current trend continues, the previous year's levels can be expected to be reached at worst. In terms of market capitalization, in a ranking from the highest to the lowest level of the last decade, 2021 is at the top with $3,360 billion, followed by 2022 ($2,763 billion), 2019 ($1,851 billion), 2018 ($1,809 billion), 2020 ($1,775 billion), 2017 ($1,656 billion), 2016 ($395 billion), 2015 ($242 billion), 2014 ($158 billion), and 2013 ($59 billion) (Konak & Demir, 2023).

3.2.7. Adopt Social Finance Practices and Conduct Social Responsibility Projects

Social finance practices involve the strategic use of financial resources to solve social and environmental problems. Some examples of countries with successful practices in this field are as follows:

1. *United Kingdom*: The United Kingdom has taken a leading role in social investment. Founded in 2012, Big Society Capital is the world's first social investment bank to provide financing to social enterprises and

community projects. It aims to grow the social investment market and combine social impact with financial returns.

2. *Canada*: The Canadian government launched a fund worth 755 million Canadian dollars in 2023 to promote social innovation. This fund supports social purpose organizations to grow, innovate, and increase their social, economic, and environmental impact.
3. *India*: Social finance in India focuses on projects targeting low-income communities. Impact Investors Council (IIC) operates as a platform supporting India's social finance ecosystem. This council aims to increase the effectiveness of impact investing and inform investors.
4. *United States of America*: In the United States, social finance is used to fund environmental and social projects. Calvert Impact Capital offers investors the opportunity to take part in socially responsible projects. This organization helps investors direct their capital to projects that will create social impact.
5. *Germany*: In Germany, social entrepreneurship is supported by government and private sector partnerships. Initiatives such as Social Impact Lab contribute to the success of projects by providing financing and mentoring services to social entrepreneurs.

3.2.8. Research Related to the Subject

Biancone and Radwan (2019) emphasize that Islamic finance offers a potential alternative for financing social impact initiatives. In their study, they argue that the ethical principles of Islamic finance and social impact investing are highly compatible and discuss various financial instruments that can be used in this area. They adopt the view that Islamic finance can provide a strong alternative to support social impact investing.

Sinclair et al. (2021) examined the growing global interest in SIBs. In their study, they pointed out that while SIBs are applicable under simple conditions, they have limitations for solving complex social problems. They pointed out that these instruments are not sufficient to address more complex social conditions.

Yenice (2021) examines the developments and institutional activities in the field of Islamic social finance (ISF) and analyzes the sustainable approaches of ISF institutions in Turkey and around the world that combine people, planet, and profit. In this context, he argues that the triple bottom line approach reveals the potential of the ISF ecosystem to create a sustainable economy and social structure.

Konak and Demir (2023) stated that social finance has become widespread in recent years, especially in the post-COVID-19 period. In their study, they attributed the rise of SIBs to factors such as serving to solve global economic crises and overcoming supply chain disruptions. They also predicted that SIBs will become more widespread in the future.

Efeoğlu (2023) presented policy recommendations on the social entrepreneurship ecosystem in Turkey. In his study, he discusses the steps that governments and other stakeholders should take to support social entrepreneurship and makes various recommendations for a more sustainable development of this field.

Akça (2023) examined the potential of social impact sukuk in Turkey and focused on the advantages and disadvantages of this new financial instrument. According to his study, social impact sukuk is an important financing instrument for Turkey and the potential growth in this area can play an important role in providing social benefits.

Kuzucu (2018) discusses socially responsible investments (SRI) and impact investments, arguing that these investment types are evolving and that new financial instruments should be designed to address social needs. In his study, he emphasized the importance of innovative approaches for the future of social finance.

Durunay and Yağcılar (2024) analyzed the attitudes and expectations of socially responsible investors and identified the main reasons that lead them to such investments. They found that the most important factors that attract investors to SRIs are social and environmental concerns, while their lack of inclination toward investments can be attributed to lack of information.

Şimşek and Tunalı (2022) examined green financing instruments and analyzed the effects of financial instruments in this field, such as green bonds, green loans, green insurance, and green sukuk. The aim of their study is to evaluate the effects of green finance on economic structures.

Topbaş (2020) drew attention to the role of green bonds in financing green projects and exemplified the successful realization of the first green bond issues in Turkey. In his study, he emphasized that such issuances constitute an important model for the Turkish financial sector.

Taraktaş (2015) analyzed the processes of SIBs and the opportunities they offer for public administration. In his study, he provides examples from some countries and makes suggestions on how SIBs can be developed in Turkey.

Ergen and Durak (2016) provide detailed information on the functioning and strengths and weaknesses of SIBs. In their study, they discuss the potential of SIBs by evaluating the pilot implementation examples of these financial instruments.

Mazzuca et al. (2024) examine the factors affecting institutional investors' participation in SIBs. They also investigate the determinants of philanthropic investors' commitment to SIBs.

Kosmynin and Jack (2022) explored how SIBs can be used in the local context, especially by local governments such as municipalities. Their study addresses the impacts and implementation challenges of these instruments at the local level.

Andrikopoulos (2020) examined social finance and explained the search for social impact in financial markets. He discusses the small-scale and long-term nature of social enterprises and the shortcomings of social impact measurement, highlighting the ambiguities between impact investing and social change.

Rexhepi (2017) explained the role of social finance in the economy and examined the potential of social finance in reducing problems such as poverty, unemployment, and inequality. In his study, he evaluated the contribution of social finance to economic development.

Ela and Çoşkun (2023) provide solutions for the applicability of environmental impact bonds in Turkey. In their study, they pointed out that the use of environmental impact bonds as financing instruments has potential for Turkey.

Eren and Özçalık (2020) examined how the sustainable investment market has developed over the last two decades and the evolution of sustainable investment strategies. Their study revealed that sustainable financing and investment are becoming increasingly important.

3.3. Conclusıons and Recommendatıons

In this study, a literature review on the definitions, development, success criteria, and future of social finance and social impact investing reveals important trends and potential in this field. Social finance is increasingly being embraced by investors as a financial system that aims to generate not only financial returns but also environmental and social impacts. This financial approach takes into account the investor's goal of generating social benefits while allocating capital to projects that address social problems. Social impact investing, on the other hand, aims to promote social change and generate financial returns at the same time. Balancing these two objectives is the cornerstone of social finance's success. However, measuring social impact is one of the most critical elements of this process. By supporting their investment decisions with accurate and reliable impact measurement methods, investors can ensure more effective and efficient social impact creation. Innovative financial instruments such as SIBs and impact investments play an important role by making impact measurement transparent.

The future of social finance continues to be shaped by technological advances and growing public policy support. Technologies such as blockchain, artificial intelligence, and data analytics will increase the traceability of social impact investments and help investors measure their social impact more accurately. In addition, these technologies will contribute to the growth of social finance by making investment processes more efficient. The wider presence of social impact investing in financial markets will contribute significantly to increasing the potential of this area and to the realization of sustainable development goals. The future development of social finance will be shaped in parallel with the strengthening of the understanding of social responsibility and the emergence of more responsible investor behavior.

To implement social finance and social impact investing more effectively, several strategic steps should be taken. First, impact measurement methods need to be developed. Impact measurement is a critical element for social finance to succeed. Making existing measurement methods more comprehensive and reliable will help investors make the right decisions and ensure that social impact investments are directed more efficiently. Furthermore, impact measurement should be supported not only by quantitative data but also by qualitative analysis. Thus, the social impacts of social impact investments can be more clearly understood.

Second, the integration of technological tools is important to improve the effectiveness of social finance. Blockchain technology can enable investors to track social impact investments in a more transparent and reliable way. Tools such as artificial intelligence and data analytics will enable more accurate and faster decision-making in evaluating social impact investments. These technological innovations are expected to contribute to the growth of social finance, enabling it to reach a wider investor base. Technology will also accelerate financial processes, allowing social impact investments to become more widespread.

Public policies need to be strengthened to further maximize the potential of social finance. Governments should provide incentives for social impact investing and strengthen regulatory frameworks. Clear, sustainable, and investor-friendly legal frameworks are essential for social finance to thrive. In addition, partnerships with local governments and civil society organizations need to be increased in order for social finance to reach a wider audience. Such collaborations will make the social impact investing process more effective in creating social benefits.

Finally, training and awareness-raising activities should be increased to raise awareness on social finance and social impact investing. In order for investors to fully benefit from the potential of social finance, training programs should be organized in this area and the importance of social responsibility should be explained. Investors will better understand that it is possible to support social change while generating financial returns. Such trainings will allow social finance to grow and contribute to social development goals.

In conclusion, social finance and social impact investing are powerful tools with the potential to generate not only financial returns but also social benefits. Innovations and strategic steps in this area will greatly contribute to the realization of sustainable development goals by increasing the impact of social finance. By making more responsible financial decisions, investors can create social change and harness the power of social impact investing to build a more sustainable future.

Bibliography

Akça, E. (2023). The potential and advantages of social impact sukuk in Turkey. *Journal of Islamic Finance Studies*, *11*(2), 45–59.

Anderson, C., & Lee, J. (2023). *The future of social finance: Trends and innovations*. Springer.

Andrikopoulos, A. (2020). Social finance: Exploring the intersection of financial markets and social impact. *Journal of Financial Management, 22*(3), 98–113.

Baker, J., & Smith, K. (2022). *Financial innovation for social impact: New pathways to sustainable growth*. Routledge.

Biancone, P., & Radwan, M. (2019). Islamic finance as a viable alternative to finance social impact investment projects. *International Journal of Social Finance, 12*(3), 56–72.

Bozkurt, İ., & Kaya, M. V. (2022). Foremost features affecting financial distress and Bankruptcy in the acute stage of COVID-19 crisis. *Applied Economics Letters, 30*(8), 1112–1123. Bugg-Levine, A., & Emerson, J. (2011). *Impact investing: Transforming how we make money while making a difference*. Wiley.

Choi, S., & Lee, K. (2023). *Social finance in emerging economies: Opportunities and challenges*. Palgrave Macmillan.

Cohen, T., & Bickman, L. (2019). *Measuring social impact: Theory and practice*. Sage Publications.

Durak, S., & Ergen, E. (2016). Social impact bonds: structure, strengths and challenges in practice. *Public Administration Review, 66*(1), 112–125.

Efeoğlu, G. (2023). Policy recommendations for supporting social entrepreneurship in Turkey. *Journal of Social Entrepreneurship, 10*(1), 23–38.

Ela, A., & Çoşkun, F. (2023). Applicability of environmental impact bonds in Turkey and potential solutions. *Environmental Finance Review, 8*(2), 50–63.

Eren, A., & Özçalık, M. (2020). Development of the sustainable investment market and sustainable investment strategies. *Sustainable Finance Journal, 5*(3), 77–92.

Friedman, H., & Miles, S. (2020). *Social impact and financial returns: How to measure success*. Stanford University Press.

Ghosh, A. (2020). *Social finance and impact investing*. Springer.

Ghosh, A., & Akhter, S. (2020). *Social finance: Innovations in impact investing and social enterprises*. Routledge.

Gordon, L. (2021). *The art of social impact measurement*. Oxford University Press.

Gorman, L. (2021). *Social impact investing: A comprehensive guide*. McKinsey & Company.

Harrison, D., & Denny, J. (2021). *Social finance: A guide for practitioners.* Wiley.

Harrison, D. (2022). *Impact bonds and social finance: Transforming development*. Wiley

Jackson, P., & Adams, S. (2020). *Social impact investing: The path forward.* Harvard Business Press.

Jackson, P. (2022). *The growth of social finance: Impacts and opportunities.* Oxford University Press.

Khan, M., Khan, S., & Sultan, M. (2020). *Social investment and sustainable development: A global perspective*. Springer.

Konak, H., & Demir, S. (2023). The rapid expansion of social finance: The post-COVID-19 era and social impact bonds. *Journal of Finance and Social Impact*, *14*(1), 84–98.

Kosmynin, P., & Jack, T. (2022). The role of social impact bonds in local governance: A case study of municipal applications. *Public Finance Review*, *25*(2), 45–58.

Kuzucu, S. (2018). Socially responsible and impact investments: An evolving approach to address social needs. *Journal of Sustainable Finance and Investment*, *6*(4), 233–249.

Mazzuca, A., Panzera, A., & Ruberto, M. (2024). Factors influencing institutional investors' participation in social impact bonds. *Finance and Impact Journal*, *13*(2), 92–108.

Miller, S. (2021). *Impact investing: A strategy for social change*. Harvard Business Review Press.

Morris, R., Harper, G., & Steinfeld, R. (2022). *Impact investment: A guide to measuring social outcomes*. Routledge.

Murray, R., & Roberts, A. (2023). *Regulation and growth of social finance markets*. Wiley.

Murray, J., & Klein, D. (2022). *Financing for change: The role of social investment in sustainable development*. Palgrave Macmillan.

Nicholls, A., Thrift, N., & Haider, Z. (2018). *Social impact investing: Key drivers and success factors*. Springer.

Nicholls, A., & Pharoah, C. (2021). *Social impact: A practical guide for social entrepreneurs*. Oxford University Press.

Özüdoğru, H., & Sönmez, S. S. (2024). The impact of artificial intelligence and machine learning on the insurance industry. *Journal of Banking and Financial Research, 11*(1), 45–53.

Patel, V. (2022). *Policy and regulation in social finance*. Routledge.

Rexhepi, B. (2017). The role of social finance in reducing poverty and inequality. *International Review of Financial Studies, 25*(5), 450–463.

Rosen, D. (2022). *The future of social finance: Trends and opportunities*. Springer.

Simons, A., & Hall, C. (2021). *Investing for impact: The intersection of financial and social performance*. Routledge.

Sinclair, S., McHugh, N., & Roy, M. J. (2021). Social impact bonds: Global interest and challenges. *Journal of Social Finance*, 7(2), 100–115.

Şimşek, C., & Tunalı, M. (2022). Green financing instruments and their effects on economic structures: Green bonds, green loans and green sukuk. *Green Finance Journal*, 7(4), 133–146.

Taraktas, S. (2015). Social impact bonds: Opportunities and challenges for public administration. *Public Finance and Policy Review, 19*(3), 201–215.

Thompson, L. (2021). *Sustainable finance: Aligning capital with social goals*. Cambridge University Press.

Topbaş, B. (2020). The role of green bonds in financing green projects: The case of the first green bond issuance in Turkey. *Journal of Green Investment, 6*(1), 48–59.

Wood, D., & Green, M. (2021). *The rise of impact investing: Transforming financial markets*. Cambridge University Press.

Yenice, İ. (2021). Islamic social finance and its role in sustainable development: A comparative study of Turkey and the World. *Journal of Islamic Finance Studies, 9*(2), 34–46.

Zhang, X., Li, Y., & Wang, Z. (2022). *Artificial intelligence and social impact investments*. Elsevier.

Zimmerman, M., & Castella, L. (2019). *Social impact bonds: Theory, policy, and practice*. Routledge.

Financial Analysis of the Operations of Pošta Slovenije, d. o. o., and a Comparison with the Performance of Some European Postal Operators

Miha Robežnik and Vladimir Bukvič

4.1. Introduction

In a rapidly changing business environment, it is vital that companies constantly monitor their performance and business stability. Financial analysis enables companies to gain insight into their operations and make decisions based on accurate and relevant information. This allows them to better understand their financial challenges and opportunities and optimize their business strategies to achieve long-term growth and stability.

Financial analysis is not only a tool for retrospective evaluation of business results, but also a key aid in planning and predicting future business. With the help of various financial indicators and models, companies can identify patterns and trends that help them formulate effective business strategies. In addition, financial analysis enables the assessment of risks and opportunities, which is essential for maintaining a competitive advantage.

Pošta Slovenije, d. o. o., is a key provider of postal and logistics services in Slovenia. Its role is to provide quality public services, fulfilling its social mission by offering a universal postal service accessible to all residents. Financial stability and adapting to changes in demand, increasing the volume of logistics services due to the growth of e-commerce, and maintaining the quality of services are challenges that the company faces, but these are secondary compared to the provision of a public service.

In this chapter, we analyze the financial situation and the business performance of the company Pošta Slovenije, d. o. o., in more detail with the help of various financial indicators and models. We use a modified Altman *z*-score, which provides comprehensive insight into financial health and bankruptcy risk. In addition, we perform a comparative analysis with some postal operators from abroad to assess the performance of the Pošta Slovenije

Group in the wider international environment and to identify good practices that can be used to improve operations.

4.2. Literature Review

Financial analysis is like a beacon that illuminates the path of a company's business. The basics of financial analysis are essential to understanding how a company manages its finances, generates profits, and manages risks. They act as the cornerstone of business intelligence that enables companies to understand their financial health and plan.

Of course, financial analysis is not an end in itself. The tightening of the company's competitiveness in the environment affects the development of the needs for external and internal accounting reporting, as decision-making is increasingly demanding (Bergant, 2023). Auditing consultancy, Price Waterhouse argues that we often "measure the wrong things and prefer to behave in the old way, offering many excuses for inadequate results" (1997, 51). That is why it is so important how we carry out financial analysis in companies and what techniques, methods, and tools we use. The following factors are important: the quality of information and data (update, timeliness, credibility, and reliability) and the selected indicators, models, and schemes. According to Bergant (2023), we can design information for business decision-making, for measuring achievements in business, for protecting company assets and for sustainable orientations.

In practice, the terms "accounting analysis" and "financial analysis" are often confused or equated, even though there is a distinction between them. In English, the financial information analysis refers to the analysis of financial statements. According to Bergant (2013), the accounting analysis is limited by the source of data (mostly accounting data, past or future), and the financial analysis is not limited by data characteristics but is limited by the purpose of information (for the needs of the company's financial function). Therefore, it is necessary to distinguish the accounting analysis of the company's financial position from the financial analysis of the company's financial position. The latter is generally more comprehensive, as it also contains an analysis of the off-balance sheet financial position, which can be important for users of the analysis. The authors of this chapter rely on financial analysis to a greater extent.

Financial analysis begins with the study of financial statements, which include the balance sheet, the profit and loss statement, and the statement of financial or cash flows.

The balance sheet provides an insight into the financial position of the company at a given point in time. It tells how many assets the company has available, how it is financed, and what its liabilities are. The profit and loss statement shows how much revenue the company generated, what costs were incurred as a result, and what operating profit and net profit the company ended the studied period with. The statement of financial or cash flows shows how money flows into and out of the company, whether the company generated a positive or negative cash flow from its operations, and whether it had more inflows or receipts or more outflows or expenses during the studied period. Answers to these questions are essential to understanding a company's liquidity. In addition, financial analysis relies on financial indicators and models that measure and evaluate business performance and financial risks. Thus, liquidity indicators tell whether the company is able to settle its obligations when they fall due. Profitability indicators reveal how profitable the business is, while debt indicators show the extent to which the company finances its operations with debt, i.e., with foreign sources of financing.

Financial analysis methods, such as horizontal and vertical analysis, help us understand changes in financial statements over time. They enable comparisons with competing companies. By interpreting and clarifying the results of individual indicators, we can understand the origin and genesis of certain phenomena and events, and can make logical conclusions and come to useful conclusions that help in making key business decisions.

The results of financial analysis are the basis for decision-making, both for the company's internal and external stakeholders. Based on the findings of financial analysis, the management of the company decides on strategy, investments, etc. Investors decide on possible investments in the company, and lenders decide on approving loans to the company. "Because there are so many performance assessment tools, we need to be aware that different measurement techniques define measurement very specifically and often narrowly. One can be tempted to 'run all the numbers', especially given the speed and ease of computer spreadsheets. However, typically only a select few relationships will provide the information the analyst really needs for useful insights and decision support" (Helfert, 2001, 96).

If we quickly skim the analytical reports of our companies, we notice that the analysis of companies is mostly focused only on the display of calculated indicators. However, according to Bergant and Manohin (2018), this has certain drawbacks. There is no comparison with optimal (necessary) indicators and indicators as fundamental criteria. What these mean for the company is left to the subjective judgment of the user and there is no proper explanation of the causes (or it is wrong) for the displayed state. No guidelines are given, or they are incorrect and one-sided for business decisions and, finally, no risk assessment is given in the context of various possible measures. Therefore, the authors (Bergant & Manohin, 2018, 4) defend the thesis that business analysis should not stop only at establishing facts about situations and movements but should provide appropriate directions for further action. In doing so, the principles of internal reporting must be considered, especially in Chapter 4 of the Code of Principles of Internal Reporting (NNP Code, 2015).

We, the authors of this chapter, in our empirical work on the financial analysis of Pošta Slovenije, d. o. o., consider what is written earlier.

Jackson (2022) provides a comprehensive review of trends in the financial statement analysis literature. He speaks about the importance of research on the topic of financial analysis, especially about emerging trends. Research on the topic of financial analysis or financial statement analysis generally deals with two key issues—improving fundamental analysis and identifying market inefficiencies based on financial statement information (Yohn, 2020). Improving the fundamental analysis is important to improve profitability forecasts and more accurately estimate the value of a company. The identification of market inefficiencies is generally the domain of equity and fund analysts, who use certain characteristics of companies or stocks to select hedging portfolios with the aim of beating the market.

If, within the framework of financial analysis, we touch upon the analysis of the company's performance, based on the examination of the literature (mainly foreign), then we find a breakdown of return on equity (ROE) into the so-called operational and financing activities. This is a breakdown of ROE into return on net operating assets (RNOA), net borrowing cost (NBC), and financial leverage (LEV). Under this approach, ROE is equal to RNOA plus the difference between RNOA and NBC multiplied by LEV:

$$ROE = RNOA + ((RNOA - NBC) \times LEV)$$

Esplin et al. (2014) use two different approaches to estimate such a breakdown. First, they estimate a basic model, which they call the aggregate model, as a simple pooled model for calculating ROE. They then use a disaggregated approach, they call the OPFIN model, allowing the RNOA, NBC, and LEV parameters to vary based on their implications for future profitability. Finally, they take the OPFIN model, which assesses the persistence of each component on its own and use sample forecasts of RNOA, NBC, and LEV to predict year-ahead ROE. The results of Esplin et al. (2014) show that the OPFIN model is significantly worse at predicting future returns than the baseline model. However, with separate forecasting of individual components and their subsequent combination into a profitability forecast, the so-called component OPFIN model outperforms the aggregate approach. Another breakdown, which is usually used more often, is the breakdown of RNOA into assets turnover (ATO) and profit margins (PM), where the combination of ATO and PM is useful for understanding the company's strategy. For example, a company following a cost leadership strategy is expected to have low margins but high turnover, while a company with high PM and low ATO is likely to use a superior service or product differentiation strategy.

Fairfield and Yohn (2001) examined whether considering a combination of PM and ATO is useful for predicting business profitability. They examined three types of models: (1) an aggregate model in which the year-ahead change in RNOA is a function of current RNOA, net operating asset growth, and current RNOA change; (2) a model that decomposes current RNOA into current ATO and PM; and (3) a model that decomposes RNOA change into ATO and PM changes.

Soliman (2008), using DuPont's analysis, as shown in Figure 12, extends the findings of Fairfield and Yohn (2001), who argue that the change in the asset turnover ratio, ΔATO, but not the change in the PM, ΔPM, is useful for predicting profitability. Soliman (2008) examines whether the information contained in ΔATO also captures predictions of future abnormal stock returns. If the market incorporates this information into ΔATO, then ΔATO should be unrelated to future stock returns. Soliman (2008) finds a significant positive relationship between ΔATO, and one-year-ahead abnormal stock returns and finds no significant relationship between ΔPM and one-year-ahead abnormal stock returns. These findings suggest that the market misjudges the implications of ΔATO for future profitability and firm value.

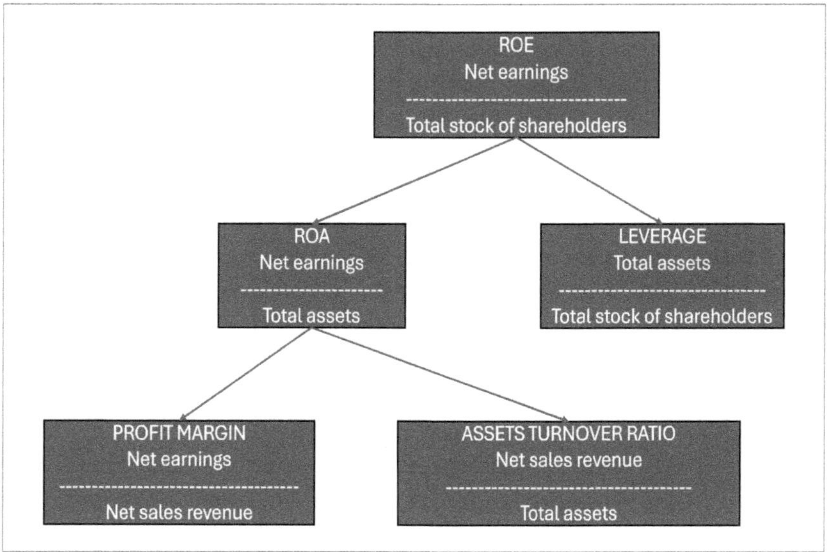

Figure 12. Structure of the DuPont analysis.
Source: Adjusted after Soliman (2008).

One of the latest innovations in the literature in the financial analysis field, which deals with forecasting the performance of a company, is the breakdown of profitability into components related to market information, industry-specific sources, and the so-called idiosyncratic information. This approach is also consistent with many textbooks on financial statement analysis, which advocate starting the fundamental analysis process with a prior understanding of the economy, industry, and strategy of the company being analyzed. Jackson et al. (2018) follow this logic and propose methods that attempt to quantify firm profitability attributable to market information, industry information, and the idiosyncratic component of the firm. With such a breakdown, they then start predicting the profitability of the company in the future period.

Another approach to identifying market inefficiencies through financial statement analysis, as opposed to predicting a company's future performance, is to use financial statement ratios. Mohanram (2005) combines traditional indicators such as profits and cash flows with measures adapted for growing companies such as earnings stability, growth stability, and increased investment in research and development and advertising. The author believes that the traditional analysis is suitable for companies with a high share of book values in the market, while the fundamental analysis, oriented toward growth, is suitable for a low share of book values in the market. Li and Mohanram (2019) extend these results by combining quality-based fundamental analysis strategies with value strategies such as value-to-price ratio and PEG ratio. Obviously, combining quality-based and value-based approaches significantly improves the effectiveness of fundamental analysis.

4.3. Research Questions and Setting of Research Theses, Methodology, and Limitations

We formulate research questions with the aim of focusing on key aspects of the company's financial condition and performance. We are, therefore, interested in (1) the financial situation of Pošta Slovenije, d. o. o., in the 2018–2022 period, (2) the key factors that influenced the company's profitability and stability during this period, (3) the success with which the company managed its financial resources, (4) how Pošta Slovenije, d. o. o., compares with other postal operators in terms of business performance, (5) the adequacy of the financial models and selected financial indicators used to assess the financial health of Pošta Slovenije, d. o. o., and (6) the impact of sustainable operations and the provision of public services on the company's financial performance.

Based on these research questions, we set the following research theses:

1. Pošta Slovenije, d. o. o., successfully maintained financial stability and profitability in the 2018–2022 period, despite rising labor and depreciation costs.
2. The use of Altman's *z*-score enables a good assessment of the company's financial health.
3. Pošta Slovenije, d. o. o., effectively manages its financial resources, which is reflected in the selected financial indicators.
4. Pošta Slovenije, d. o. o., is financially stable and competitive compared to some postal operators abroad.
5. Sustainable operations and compliance with legal obligations in providing universal postal service are important non-financial indicators of the success of Pošta Slovenije, d. o. o.

6. The company's financial success enables sustainable business, which ensures the company provides quality services at competitive prices.

Methodologically, the research was carried out through four phases, i.e., collecting data and information, analyzing the company's operations with the help of selected indicators, analyzing the performance of Pošta Slovenije, d. o. o., operations with some comparable postal operators abroad, and explaining (discussing) the calculated results. In the theoretical part of the research, we used the scientific method of description, as well as the scientific methods of classification, comparison, analysis, and synthesis. In the empirical part of the research, we used formulas to calculate individual financial indicators and Altman's *z*-score to assess the company's financial risk.

For the research, we used secondary data from the annual reports of Pošta Slovenije, d. o. o., and foreign postal operators for the 2018–2022 period.

At this point, we should also mention the limitations we encountered during the research. These relate mainly to the empirical part and arise from the nature of the data and methodology used. These limitations highlight the need for further research to better understand the complex dynamics of business operations. One of the limitations of the analysis is the availability and timeliness of the data, as we relied only on publicly available financial and accounting data that were available for the studied period. Financial transactions and major events that occurred after this period were not included in financial analysis. In addition, the analysis mostly focuses on internal operations and does not address external factors such as macroeconomic conditions, political changes, and the market environment that can significantly affect company's operations. The quantitative nature of the analysis also does not include qualitative aspects such as customer satisfaction, corporate culture, or innovation. Comparison with competitors was included but could have been more in-depth. The research could cover a longer period, say a 10-year period.

4.4. Financial Analysis of Pošta Slovenije, d. o. o.

4.4.1. Assessment of the Company's Business Performance Based on Selected Financial Indicators

With the help of financial indicators, we analyzed various aspects of the company's operations, such as profitability, liquidity, financing, investing, and asset management efficiency. With the help of these indicators, companies can gain insight into their financial structure, discover potential risks and opportunities, and assess whether they are able to safely take advantage of business opportunities on the market without jeopardizing their business. Financial indicators help companies make strategic decisions. In this section, we show the performance of Pošta Slovenije, d. o. o., based on the calculation of various financial indicators, which we classified as they are considered by financial and accounting theory.

4.4.1.1. Financial Leverage

Financial leverage is an indicator that measures how a change in the operating profit [earnings before interest and taxes (EBIT)] affects change in the company's net profit. It shows by what percentage a company's net profit will increase if EBIT increases by 1 percent. High leverage means that the company's profits are highly sensitive to changes in revenue, which can yield greater profits in favorable conditions, but also pose greater risk in the event of revenue fluctuations. We calculate degree of financial leverage (DFL) by using the following formula:

$$DFL = EBIT / (EBIT - \text{Financing costs})$$

In Table 5, we show the calculation of the DFL for our studied company for the 2018–2022 period, and in Graph 1, we present these degrees graphically.

Table 5. Display of elements and DFL for Pošta Slovenije, d. o. o., for the 2018–2022 period

Item/Year in 000s €	2018	2019	2020	2021	2022
EBIT	8,838	4,008	944	9,405	2,363
Financing cost (interests)	247	503	812	920	764
EBIT – Financing cost	8,591	3,505	132	8,485	1,599
DFL	1.03	1.14	7.15	1.11	1.48

Source: Income statements of Pošta Slovenije, d. o. o., for the 2018–2022 period.

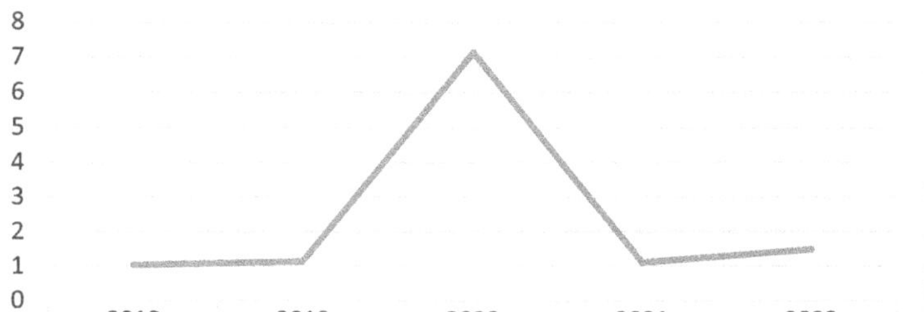

	2018	2019	2020	2021	2022
DFL	1.03	1.14	7.15	1.11	1.48

Graph 1. Movement of DFL for Pošta Slovenije, d. o. o., in the 2018–2022 period.
Source: Table 5.

In the 2018–2022 period, the financial leverage for Pošta Slovenije, d. o. o., changed due to fluctuations in operating profit (EBIT) and financing costs, which also reflected the impacts of the pandemic and increased costs. In 2018, DFL amounted to 1.03, which indicates stable management of liabilities with low borrowing.

In 2019, DFL rose to 1.14, as higher labor costs and depreciation along with increased financing costs slightly increased the company's sensitivity. In 2020, DFL increased sharply to 7.15 due to a significant drop in EBIT caused by the decline in revenue and increased costs due to COVID-19. As a result, the company felt a higher financial risk.

In 2021, DFL fell to 1.11 as higher service revenue and EBIT growth reduced the company's liability sensitivity, despite a slight increase in financing costs. In 2022, DFL rose to 1.48 due to higher labor and energy costs, but the company managed debt by partially repaying loans.

In general, the movement of DFL reflects the impact of changes in EBIT and financing costs. The company experienced greater financial risk during periods of greater challenge but maintained stability by controlling borrowing.

4.4.1.2. EBIT and EBITDA

Earnings before interest and taxes (EBIT) and earnings before interest, taxes, depreciation, and amortization (EBITDA) are types of business results that are not specifically defined by accounting standards, but they have become quite established in practice (Bergant, 2018). When we analyze them, we must start with the purpose and the user's analysis in their definition and adjust both their calculation and their explanation accordingly. We use the following formulas:

$$\text{EBIT} = \text{Sales revenue} - \text{Regular operating expenses}$$
$$\text{EBITDA} = \text{EBIT} + \text{Depreciation} + \text{Amortization}$$
$$\text{EBT} = \text{EBIT} + \text{Other income} - \text{Financing costs}$$
$$\text{E} = \text{EBT} - \text{Taxes}$$

In Table 6, we give the values of individual categories for our studied company in the 2018–2022 period, and in Graph 2, we also present these values graphically.

Table 6. Overview of EBIT, EBITDA, EBT, and net profit indicators for Pošta Slovenije, d. o. o., for the 2018–2022 period

Item/Year *in 000s €*	**2018**	**2019**	**2020**	**2021**	**2022**
Gross sales revenue	234,154	237,142	249,766	269,228	274,354
EBIT	8,838	4,008	944	9,405	2,363
EBIT + DA	22,415	20,856	21,948	28,405	24,523
Financing cost	1,162	435	2,975	0	0
Other	0	−213	−814	0	128
EBT	10,000	4,230	3,106	9,841	4,175
Taxes	10	73	−25	446	117
E (net earnings)	9,990	4,157	3,190	9,395	4,058

Source: Own.

Between 2018 and 2022, the EBIT and EBITDA trends for Pošta Slovenije, d. o. o., were characterized by key cost factors and investments. In 2018, extensive investments in logistics modernization increased depreciation costs, which reduced EBIT, while EBITDA remained stable due to cash flow management.

In 2019, integration costs upon the acquisition of the company Intereuropa, d. d., and higher labor costs further reduced EBIT. Stable EBITDA reflects successful cost optimization despite growing operational liabilities.

The pandemic in 2020 resulted in the lowest EBIT of the period due to higher costs of security measures, but EBITDA was maintained by reducing

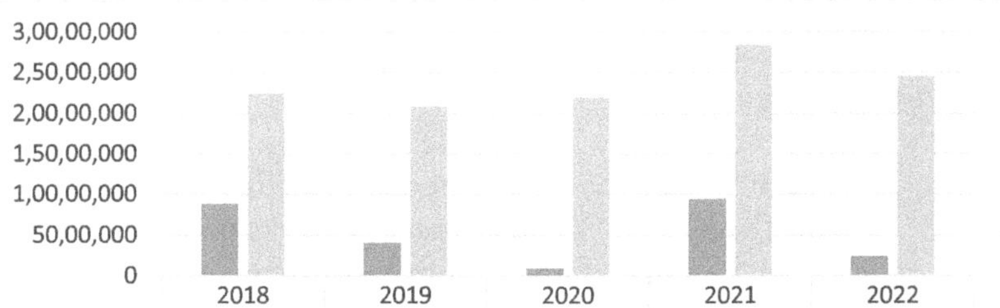

	2018	2019	2020	2021	2022
EBIT	88,38,055	40,08,165	9,44,215	94,04,764	23,62,944
EBIT + DA	2,24,14,866	2,08,56,055	2,19,47,539	2,84,04,480	2,45,23,442

Graph 2. Movement of EBIT and EBITDA values for Pošta Slovenije, d. o. o., in the 2018–2022 period.
Source: Table 6.

other costs and better inventory management. In 2021, EBIT recovered due to an increase in demand for logistics services, while high EBITDA indicated the effective use of digitalization investments.

In 2022, inflation and higher energy costs reduced EBIT, but energy efficiency measures enabled stable EBITDA, despite adverse external conditions.

4.4.1.3. Fundamental Financing Indicators

Although in business economics financing is one of the phases of the business process, financing has a different nature than procurement, production or sales. Pučko (2006) says that financing synthesizes and reflects the entirety of the company's operations in a certain way. For the purposes of our financial analysis, we select the following fundamental financing indicators:

Ownership rate of financing = Equity / Liabilities
Debt-financing ratio = Debts / Liabilities
Level of long-term financing = (Equity, long-term liabilities, provisions and long-term accruals) / Liabilities

In Table 7, we show the values of some balance sheet data and calculated financial indicators for our studied company in the 2018–2022 period, and in Graph 3, we also present these values graphically.

Table 7. Fundamental financing indicators for Pošta Slovenije, d. o. o., in the 2018–2022 period

Item / Year *in 000s €*	**2018**	**2019**	**2020**	**2021**	**2022**
Equity	217,582	216,529	218,677	228,624	229,537
Liabilities	292,721	326,469	363,130	352,835	349,680
Ownership rate of financing	*0.74*	*0.66*	*0.60*	*0.65*	*0.66*
Long-term liabilities	14,085	43,485	62,493	54,878	44,729
Current liabilities	33,021	39,097	48,656	40,271	50,763
Total	47,106	82,581	111,149	95,150	95,492
Debt-financing ratio	*0.16*	*0.25*	*0.31*	*0.27*	*0.27*
Provisions and long-term accruals	15,870	17,603	19,074	18,451	15,403
Total	247,537	277,616	300,244	301,953	289,669
Level of long-term financing	*0.85*	*0.85*	*0.83*	*0.86*	*0.83*

Source: Balance Sheet of Pošta Slovenije, d. o. o., for the period 2018–2022; own.

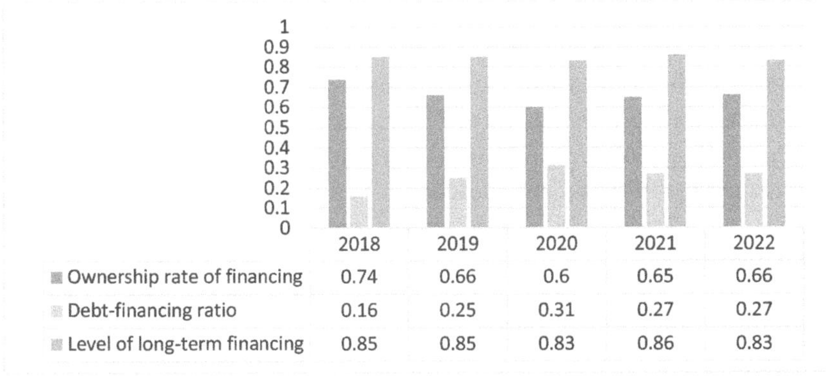

Graph 3. Movement in the value of the fundamental financing indicators for Pošta Slovenije, d. o. o., in the 2018–2022 period.

Source: Table 7.

In the 2018–2022 period, the fundamental financing indicators for Pošta Slovenije, d. o. o., changed due to large-scale investments and strategic decisions. *The ownership level of financing* decreased in 2019 and 2020 due to increased indebtedness, as additional investments were needed to expand logistics capacities and purchase a majority stake in Intereuropa, d. d. This acquisition enabled access to the southeastern markets, but at the same time increased the company's debt obligations and reduced the share of capital in the financing structure.

After 2020, the company focused on deleveraging, which stabilized the ownership level of financing. The level of debt financing initially increased due to short-term business financing and additional investments, but after 2020 it moderated due to the strategy of gradually reducing loans and optimizing financial liabilities.

The level of long-term financing remained high and stable throughout the entire period, which indicates a balanced use of long-term financing sources and, consequently, lower exposure to short-term risks. A slight decrease in the indicator in 2022 is the result of a decrease in long-term liabilities and provisions, but the company continued to maintain a solid financing structure based on long-term resources.

The COVID-19 pandemic in 2020 increased the demand for logistics services, which required additional investment, while costs increased significantly in 2021 and 2022 due to inflation and energy price increases. This encouraged the company to carefully manage its finances, which made it possible to maintain the stability of financing.

The entire period is characterized by the efficient interweaving of investments for growth with debt reduction and financing optimization, which enables Pošta Slovenije, d. o. o., to achieve long-term financial resilience and competitiveness.

4.4.1.4. Fundamental Investment Indicators

In relation to the investment of financial resources, two questions are particularly important: the question of the efficiency of the investment and the question of the riskiness of the investment. In this context, we are also interested in the company's investment ability. Bukvič (2020) defines it as an ability that refers to all types of knowledge that are necessary before the investment itself and for its implementation. Below, let's look at how investment by Pošta Slovenije, d. o. o., reflected in the following investment indicators:

Investment Basic Rate = (Fixed Assets) / Total Assets
Level of long-term investment = (Fixed Assets + Financial Investments + Long-term Business Receivables) / Total Assets
Share of fixed assets in total assets = Fixed Assets / Total Assets
Investment turnover rate = Current Assets / Total Assets

In Table 8, we show the values of some balance sheet data and calculated financial indicators for our studied company in the 2018–2022 period, and in Graph 4, we also present these values graphically.

Table 8. Fundamental investment indicators for Pošta Slovenije, d. o. o., in the 2018–2022 period

Item / Year in 000s €	**2018**	**2019**	**2020**	**2021**	**2022**
Tangible fixed assets	165,088	177,126	174,894	165,798	163,434
Intangible fixed assets	395	1,001	1,819	4,939	5,146
ASSETS	292,721	326,469	363,130	352,835	349,680
Investment basic rate	0.57	0.55	0.49	0.48	0.48
Intangible fixed assets and long-term accruals	395	1,001	1,819	4,939	5,146
Long-term financial investment	16,003	44,749	51,457	58,273	56,957
Long-term business accounts receivables	877	366	264	165	83
FIXED ASSETS	182,363	223,242	228,434	229,174	225,620
Level of long-term investment	0.62	0.68	0.63	0.65	0.65
Share of fixed assets in total assets	0.62	0.68	0.63	0.65	0.65
CURRENT ASSETS	87,989	84,346	113,279	97,851	98,885
SHORT-TERM ACCRUALS	12,256	8,214	11,471	10,242	11,315
Short-term financial investment	-	-	7,300	5,084	5,128
CURRENT ASSETS	101,122	92,926	132,314	113,342	115,410
Investment turnover rate	0.35	0.28	0.36	0.32	0.33

Source: Balance Sheet for Pošta Slovenije, d. o. o., for the period 2018–2022; own.

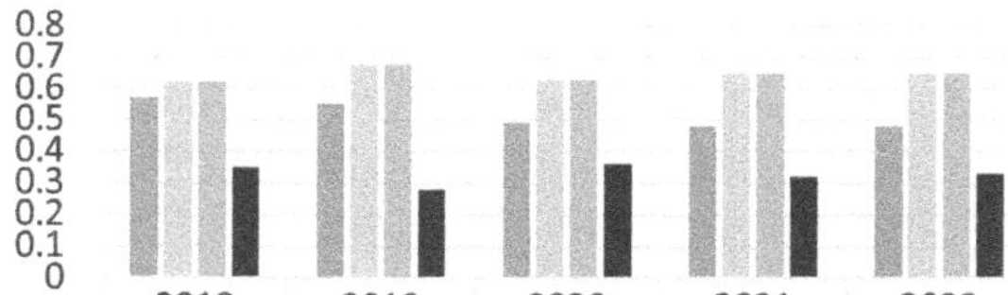

	2018	2019	2020	2021	2022
Investment basic rate	0.57	0.55	0.49	0.48	0.48
Level of long-term investment	0.62	0.68	0.63	0.65	0.65
Share of fixed assets in total assets	62%	68%	63%	65%	65%
Investment turnover rate	0.35	0.28	0.36	0.32	0.33

Graph 4. Movement in the value of fundamental investment indicators for Pošta Slovenije, d. o. o., in the 2018–2022 period.
Source: Table 8.

In the 2018–2022 period, Pošta Slovenije, d. o. o., decided to change the investment policy, which affected the fundamental investment indicators. *The basic rate of investment* decreased in 2018 and 2019 due to the redirection of funds to digital infrastructure and information technology. In 2019, larger investments in the renovation of the business information system (ERP) supported the digital transformation, which reduced the available funds for investments in tangible fixed assets.

In 2019, the *long-term investment rate* increased to 0.68 due to the acquisition of Intereuropa, d. d., which strengthened the company's position on the logistics market in the region. This acquisition contributed to the stability of the company's investment structure in the long term as well.

In 2020, the share of current assets in the assets structure increased due to increased liquidity, which was key to coping with changes in demand for services. This allowed the company to adapt to market uncertainty and to better manage operational risks. Accordingly, the *investment turnover rate* stabilized, which indicates a greater focus on liquidity to manage short-term liabilities and operational needs.

In 2021 and 2022, the indicators stabilized, as the company continued with more careful cash management and adaptation to the new economic conditions. The share of long-term assets in assets remained stable, which confirms the long-term focus on sustainable growth, including investments in e-mobility, electric vehicles, and energy efficiency.

The changes in the investment structure reflect the strategic goals of Pošta Slovenije, d. o. o.: strengthening the presence in logistics, accelerating digital transformation, maintaining liquidity, and pursuing sustainable goals. With this, the company successfully reconciles long-term growth goals with short-term stability and competitiveness.

4.4.1.5. Fundamental Solvency Indicators

The liquidity or solvency of the company can be determined from the sub-balance sheet of short-term assets and sources of funds. Liquidity means the ability to pay obligations that are due at a given point in time. A company that becomes insolvent exposes itself to a serious risk of going bankrupt, highlighting the importance of monitoring and assessing liquidity. When analyzing the financial stability of Pošta Slovenije, d. o. o., we rely on the following indicators:

$$\text{Capital adequacy ratio} = (\text{Equity} + \text{Inventories} - \text{Working capital}) / \text{Current Liabilities}$$

$$\text{Permanent current asset auto financing rate} = \text{Accounts Payable} / (\text{Fixed Assets} + \text{Inventories} + \text{Accounts Receivable})$$

$$\text{Rate of short-term financing of permanent working capital} = (\text{Accounts Receivable} + \text{Inventories} + \text{Working Capital}) / (\text{Inventories} + \text{Accounts Receivable})$$

$$\text{Long-term coverage of fixed assets and inventories} = (\text{Equity} + \text{Long-term Provisions} + \text{Long-term Liabilities}) / (\text{Fixed Assets} + \text{Inventories})$$

In Table 9, we show the values of some balance sheet data and calculated financial indicators for our studied company in the 2018–2022 period, and in Graph 5, we also present these values graphically.

Table 9. Presentation of fundamental solvency indicators for Pošta Slovenije, d. o. o., in the 2018–2022 period

Item / Year in 000s €	2018	2019	2020	2021	2022
Accounts receivable	39,846	43,8767	42,522	47,074	55,136
Inventories	1,291	1,394	1,617	2,005	2,165

(Continued)

Table 9. *(Continued)*

Item / Year in 000s €	**2018**	**2019**	**2020**	**2021**	**2022**
Accounts payable	30,766	31,513	36,022	29,652	37,356
Current assets	100,245	92,560	124,749	108,094	110,200
Current liabilities	45,184	48,853	62,886	50,882	60,011
Net working capital	55,061	43,707	61,863	57,212	50,189
Capital adequacy ratio	5.71	5.91	4.40	5.44	4.54
Permanent current asset auto financing rate	0.75	0.70	0.82	0.60	0.65
Rate of short-term financing of permanent working capital	-0.34	0.03	-0.40	-0.17	0.12
Equity	229,537	228,624	218,678	216,529	217,582
Long-term provisions	15,100	18,220	18,774	17,290	15,557
Long-term liabilities	44,729	54,878	62,493	434,852	14,085
Nominator total	289,366	301,722	299,944	277,304	247,223
Fixed assets	239,480	244,741	238,381	233,909	192,476
Inventories	2,165	2,005	1,617	1,394	1,291
Denominator total	241,645	246,747	239,998	235,303	193,767
Long-term coverage of fixed assets and inventories	1.28	1.18	1.25	1.22	1.2

Source: Annual reports of Pošta Slovenije, d. o. o., for the period 2018–2022; own calculations.

Between 2018 and 2022, the fundamental solvency indicators for Pošta Slovenije, d. o. o., showed the company's transition to a more stable financing structure. *The long-term asset coverage ratio* was high in 2018 (1.28), which indicated sufficient long-term financing necessary for stability in larger investments. In 2019, the ratio decreased to 1.18 due to the acquisition of Intereuropa, d. d., but remained sufficient to cover long-term assets. In 2020, the indicator increased to 1.25, as the company refinanced debts and invested in digitization. In 2021 and 2022, the indicator stabilized around 1.2, which reflects the gradual reduction of debts and the maintenance of long-term stability.

In 2018, *the capital adequacy ratio* was 5.71, which indicates a significant shortfall in working capital and a higher liquidity risk for the company.

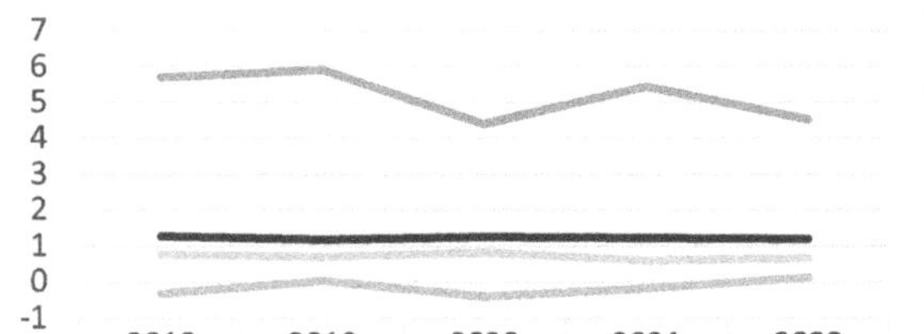

	2018	2019	2020	2021	2022
Capital adequacy ratio	5.71	5.91	4.4	5.44	4.54
Permanent current asset auto financing rate	0.75	0.7	0.82	0.6	0.65
Rate of short-term financing of permanent working capital	-0.34	0.03	-0.4	-0.17	0.12
Long-term coverage of fixed assets and inventories	1.28	1.18	1.25	1.22	1.2

Graph 5. Graphic display of fundamental solvency indicators for Pošta Slovenije, d. o. o., in the 2018–2022 period.
Source: Table 9.

In 2019, the indicator slightly increased to 5.91, which maintained a high level of risk due to the net working capital (NWC) deficit. In 2020, the ratio decreased to 4.40, which indicates a slight improvement in capital adequacy. In 2021, the value of the indicator increased to 5.44, but in 2022, it decreased again to 4.54, which indicates the company's gradual efforts to reduce liquidity risk, although the values were still high and required further adjustments to improve capital stability.

The rate of automatic financing of permanent working capital was 0.75 in 2018, which indicates dependence on short-term sources. In 2019, the ratio dropped to 0.70 due to a higher proportion of long-term financing related to the acquisition of Intereuropa, d. d., but in 2020, it increased to 0.82 due to additional short-term borrowing. It stabilized at 0.65 in 2021 and 2022, reflecting a balanced relationship between short-term and long-term resources.

The rate of short-term financing of permanent working capital in 2018 indicates a partial coverage of working capital with long-term resources (–0.34), which reduced liquidity risk. In 2019, the indicator improved to 0.03 due to greater use of short-term resources. It dropped to –0.40 in 2020 and then reached a positive value of 0.12 by 2022, which indicates the company's flexibility in managing liquidity risks.

Indicators for the 2018–2022 period show that the company is moving toward more long-term stability. Reducing dependence on short-term resources and increasing equity and long-term liabilities contribute to greater resistance to changes in the business environment.

4.4.1.6. Fundamental Indicators of the Financial Intermediary Position

According to Bergant and Manohin (2018), the financial intermediation position shows only one aspect of a company's indebtedness, namely its impact on solvency. It expresses the financial ratio of a company. Every company demands something from the environment on the one hand and owes something to the environment on the other hand. This relationship defines the financial intermediary position of a company, which for Pošta Slovenije, d. o. o., is determined by the following indicator:

$$\text{Capital deployment rate} = \text{Net receivables} / (\text{Equity} + \text{Provisions} + \text{Long-term accruals})$$

In Table 10, we show the values of some balance sheet data and the calculated financial indicator for our studied company in the 2018–2022 period, and in Graph 6, we also present this value graphically.

Table 10. Presentation of the fundamental indicator of financial intermediary position for Pošta Slovenije, d. o. o., in the 2018–2022 period

Item / Year in 000s €	**2018**	**2019**	**2020**	**2021**	**2022**
Productive investment	174,217	186,858	183,971	180,732	176,899
Equity	217,582	216,529	218,678	228,624	229,537
Provisions and long-term accruals	15,870	17,603	19,074	18,451	15,403
Equity + Provisions + Long-term accruals	233,453	234,131	237,751	247,075	244,940
Net accounts receivable	59,236	47,274	53,781	66,343	68,040
Capital deployment rate (in %)	*25.37*	*20.19*	*22.62*	*26.85*	*27.78*

Source: Annual reports of Pošta Slovenije, d. o. o., for the period 2018–2022; own calculations.

Graph 6. Graphic display of the indicator of the capital deployment rate for Pošta Slovenije, d. o. o., in the 2018–2022 period.
Source: Table 10.

The capital deployment rate, which measures the share of equity, provisions and long-term accruals in net receivables, reflects the long-term strategy of Pošta Slovenije, d. o. o., to reduce dependence on external financing and increase financial stability. In the 2018–2022 period, the indicator pointed to a prudent financial policy of the company, which strived to invest capital in net receivables, thereby reducing the need for additional borrowing.

In 2018, *the capital deployment rate* was 25.37%, which indicated a relatively high level of capital placement in net receivables. In 2019, the ratio decreased to 20.19%, reflecting the increase in permanent capital in connection with the acquisition of Intereuropa, d. d., which increased the company's financial stability despite increased capital needs. In 2021 and 2022, the indicator reached a value of 27.78%, which indicates a successful strategy of investing capital in receivables and a reduced need for additional borrowing.

According to the results of the capital deployment rate, the financial intermediary position of Pošta Slovenije, d. o. o., shows a decrease in dependence on external resources of financing and a greater financial resilience, which enables the company to be more flexible and stable in the long term.

4.4.1.7. Fundamental Profitability Indicators

The fundamental purpose of a company's existence and operations is to create business success. According to Pučko (2006), the dilemma arises as soon as we want to concretize this business success. Does business success show the generated profit? There is a difference between the company's economic success of a business and the success traditionally determined by accounting.

For the owners, the difference between the final value of own capital and the initial invested value of this capital is important. Any criterion of a company's profitability that does not take into account the entire cost of capital and does not include all important information for strategic decision-making can be misleading (Bukvič, 2016a). According to Bergant (2018), profitability shows the efficiency of business, measured by profit, compared to output. In this chapter, the authors select only three traditional financial indicators, which are used to analyze the performance of Pošta Slovenije, d. o. o.:

Return on equity (ROE) = Net profit in the financial year / Equity
Return on assets (ROA) = EBIT / Average assets
Productivity of Assets = Total Revenues / Average assets

In Table 11, we show the values of some balance sheet data and calculated financial indicators for our studied company in the 2018–2022 period, and in Graphs 7 and 8, we also present these values graphically.

Table 11. Fundamental profitability indicators for Pošta Slovenije, d. o. o., in the 2018–2022 period

Item / Year in 000s €	2018	2019	2020	2021	2022
Net income in the period	9,990	4,157	3,130	9,395	4,058
Equity	211,020	212,060	215,525	222,086	224,383
ROE (in %)	*4.73*	*1.96*	*1.45*	*4.23*	*1.81*
Average assets	281,589	309,595	344,800	357,983	351,257
ROA (in %)	*3.55*	*1.34*	*0.91*	*2.62*	*1.16*
Total revenues	235,850	238,907	254,948	272,444	279,272
Productivity of assets	*0.84*	*0.77*	*0.74*	*0.76*	*0.8*

Source: Financial statements of Pošta Slovenije, d. o. o., for the period 2018–2022; own.

Fundamental profitability indicators, such as ROE, return on assets (ROA) and productivity of assets, measure the efficiency of Pošta Slovenije, d. o. o., in the use of capital and assets to achieve profit. In the 2018–2022 period, the company's operations changed under the influence of investments, rising costs, and the pandemic, which is also reflected in the movement of these indicators.

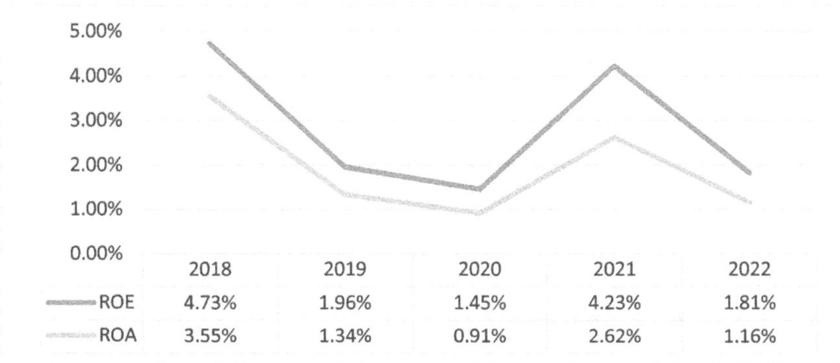

Graph 7. Movement of fundamental profitability indicators for Pošta Slovenije, d. o. o., in the 2018–2022 period.

Source: Table 11.

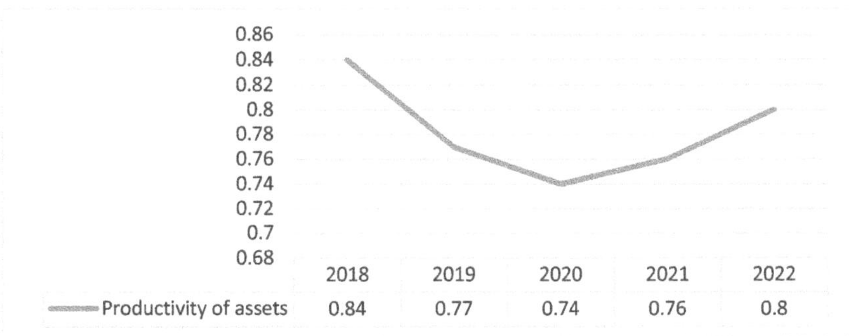

Graph 8. Movement of the indicator productivity of assets for Pošta Slovenije, d. o. o., in the 2018–2022 period.

Source: Table 11.

In 2018, the company achieved relatively high profitability, mainly due to increased demand for package services and effective cost management. Investments in logistics have improved the productivity of the assets.

In 2019, ROE and ROA decreased due to higher labor and depreciation costs related to investments in infrastructure and digitization, although revenues continued to grow.

The year 2020 was marked by the COVID-19 pandemic, which increased the costs of security measures and reorganization, negatively impacting both these ratios. Despite the increase in revenues due to the growth of the internet trade, the costs exceeded the effects of the growth in demand.

In 2021, indicators improved with revenue growth and the introduction of new digital solutions, which improved cost control and asset productivity. Despite rising costs, the company remained competitive.

The year 2022 brought further challenges with the increase of energy and transport costs, which decreased ROE and ROA. Despite this, the company-maintained asset productivity through further strategic investments in logistics.

The 2018–2022 period shows that Pošta Slovenije, d. o. o., maintained competitiveness in a demanding economic environment. Future improvements in profitability will require further efforts to optimize costs and manage assets more efficiently.

4.4.2. NWC Analysis

According to Bergant (2018), NWC is a category that is not found in the balance sheet, as it is a category derived from various balance sheet items. NWC is the part of long-term resources that finances short-term investments. Surplus NWC illustrates a certain financial stability of a company and, at the same time, its investment ability. This is also related to the company's financial flexibility, which encompasses more than just liquidity, as it allows the company to take advantage of market opportunities (conquest of new markets, acquisition of a new subsidiary, development of a new product, etc.) and engage additional cash resources, additional long-term financial resources (Bukvič, 2016b). NWC is a fundamental category in the analysis of financial balance and long-term solvency, and that is exactly what we regard as particularly interesting in the financial analysis of Pošta Slovenije, d. o. o. To analyze net working capital, we use the following formulas:

$$\text{Net working capital (NWC)} = \text{Current assets} - \text{Current liabilities}$$

$$\text{Required working capital (RWC)} = \text{Accounts receivable} + \text{Average inventory} - \text{Accounts payable}$$

$$\text{OK} = \text{RWC} / \text{Optimal working capital}$$

$$\text{Inventory conversion period} = \text{Average inventory} / \text{Cost of goods, materials, and services} \times 365$$

$$\text{Receivables collection period} = \text{Accounts receivable} / \text{Net sales revenue} \times 365$$

$$\text{Payables deferral period} = \text{Payables} / \text{Costs of goods sold} \times 365$$

$$\text{Cash conversion cycle (CCC)} = \text{Inventory conversion period} + \text{Receivables collection period} - \text{Payables deferral period}$$

Table 12 shows data and calculations of individual indicators by year in the 2018–2022 period.

Table 12. Data and calculated indicators of working capital for Pošta Slovenije, d. o. o., by years in the 2018–2022 period

Item / Year in 000s €	2018	2019	2020	2021	2022
Average inventories	1,220	1,342	1,505	1,811	2,085
Cost of goods sold	73,427	72,744	72,443	81,023	84,508
Accounts receivable	39,846	43,877	42,522	47,074	55,136
Accounts payable	30,766	31,513	36,022	29,652	37,356
Net sales revenue	230,154	236,016	240,603	264,722	271,639
Average current assets	87,989	84,346	113,279	97,851	98,885
Average short-term liabilities	33,021	39,097	48,656	40,271	50,763
Net working capital (NWC)	54,968	45,249	64,623	57,580	48,123
Inventory conversion period (days)	6	7	8	8	9
Receivables collection period (days)	63	68	65	65	74
Payables deferral period (days)	153	158	181	134	161
Cash conversion cycle (CCC) (days)	−84	−83	−108	−61	−78
Required working capital (RWC)	10,371	13,757	8,118	19,427	19,945

Source: Financial statements of Pošta Slovenije, d. o. o., for the period 2018–2022; own.

Graphs 9 and 10 provide a graphic representation of the values of the individual categories shown in Table 12.

In the 2018–2022 period, Pošta Slovenije, d. o. o., adjusted its NWC according to strategic needs, which was reflected in the company's financial stability. NWC, defined as the difference between current assets and current liabilities, is not derived directly from current categories, but from changes in equity, provisions, and long-term accruals on one side, and net

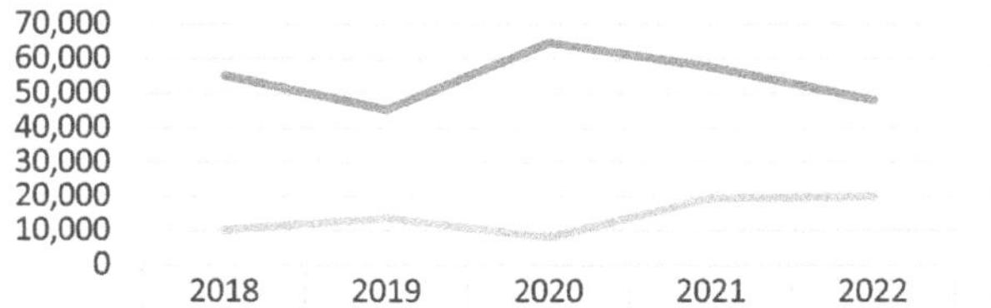

	2018	2019	2020	2021	2022
Net working capital (NWC)	54,968	45,249	64,623	57,580	48,123
Required working capital (RWC)	10,371	13,757	8,118	19,427	19,945

Graph 9. Movement of NWC and required working capital values for Pošta Slovenije, d. o. o., in the 2018–2022 period.

Source: Table 12; own.

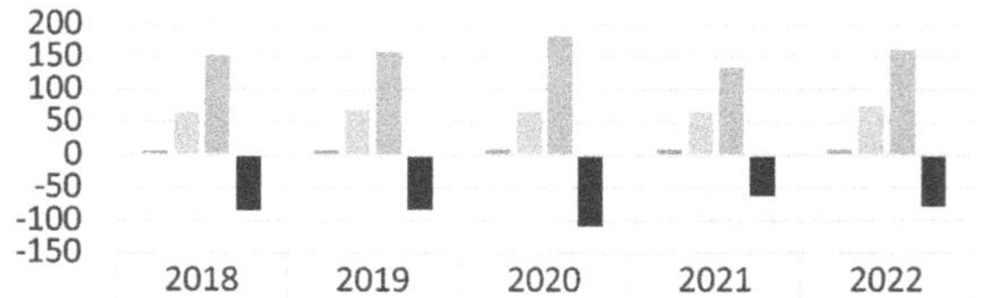

	2018	2019	2020	2021	2022
Inventory conversion period (days)	6	7	8	8	9
Receivables collection period (days)	63	68	65	65	74
Payables deferral period (days)	153	158	181	134	161
Cash conversion cycle (CCC) (days)	-84	-83	-108	-61	-78

Graph 10. Movement within inventory conversion period, receivables collection period, payables deferral period, and cash conversion cycle (CCC) for Pošta Slovenije, d. o. o., in the 2018–2022 period.

Source: Table 12; own.

long-term debt and fixed assets on the other side. The movement of NWC thus represents the company's adjustments to wider changes in the capital structure.

In 2019, the decrease in NWC reflected an increase in equity, provisions, and long-term accruals. In 2020, NWC increased due to a better adjustment of the capital structure, which reduced the need for additional short-term financing. In 2021 and 2022, a further drop in NWC showed the company's adjustments to new market conditions, which required additional long-term financing in order to maintain liquidity.

The inventory conversion period (days tied up in inventory) increased from six days in 2018 to nine days in 2022, indicating more tied-up cash in inventories due to increased demand for logistics services. The receivables collection period has also been extended, which also means a greater need for long-term resources of financing. The payable deferral period peaked in 2020 with 181 days, which shows that Pošta Slovenije, d. o. o., extended payment terms to suppliers as a strategy to maintain liquidity.

Negative cash conversion cycle (CCC) days throughout the period indicate efficient supplier financing. The lowest CCC in 2020 reflects high efficiency in working capital management, as the company successfully financed operations with funds made possible by extended payment terms to suppliers.

In the future, Pošta Slovenije, d. o. o., will have to continue with the optimization of the required working capital (RWC). This will reduce the company's need for additional financing and increase its operational flexibility.

4.4.3. Assessment of the Credit Risk and Probability of Bankruptcy of Pošta Slovenije, d. o. o., According to Altman's z-score

Altman's *z*-score is a recognized tool for assessing financial risk and is widely used in financial analysis, risk assessment and corporate finance to predict a company's financial distress. It should be emphasized that no model is perfect and reliable. Thus, in parallel with Altman's model, we assessed the financial strength of Pošta Slovenije, d. o. o., with Weinrich's model and came to similar conclusions.

For our studied company, which is engaged in service activity, we adapted Altman's *z*-score for private service companies. We did this by adjusting or omitting some of the original variables to better fit the nature and available financial accounting data of the private service sector. Altman's original model includes the following ratios as X variables:

$X1$: Current assets / Total assets
$X2$: Retained earnings / Total assets
$X3$: EBIT / Total assets
$X4$: Market value of equity / Total liabilities
$X5$: Net sales revenue / Total assets

When adjusting for a private service company, the market value of equity ($X4$) is substituted for the book value of equity, since private companies do not have publicly traded shares and consequently the market value of equity cannot be directly determined and net sales revenue ($X5$) is often omitted, because in private companies this information is not made public or does not reflect the company's performance in the same way as in public companies.

The adapted model (z-score formula) for a private service company therefore uses the following variables:

$$z = 6.56\,X1 + 3.26\,X2 + 6.72\,X3 + 1.05\,X4$$

This adjustment allows the model to be used to assess the financial condition and bankruptcy risk of private companies that do not publish all the financial accounting data available from public companies. The corresponding values for the variables Xi are obtained from the company's balance sheet and profit and loss account.

It should be noted that despite the adjustments, the model is still not perfect and has its limitations. When assessing financial risk, it is also advisable to consider qualitative factors, market conditions, and other external influences that may affect the financial health of the company.

Table 13 shows the results of Altman's z-score adapted for Pošta Slovenije, d. o. o., as a service company.

Table 13. Altman's z-score for Pošta Slovenije, d. o. o., in the 2018–2022 period

Item / Year in 000s €	2018	2019	2020	2021	2022
Total assets	292,721	326,469	363,130	352,835	349,680

Table 13. *(Continued)*

Item / Year in 000s €	**2018**	**2019**	**2020**	**2021**	**2022**
Current assets	100,245	92,560	124,750	108,094	110,200
Retained earnings	7,142	12,573	16,392	17,531	21,386
EBIT	8,838	4,008	944	9,405	2,363
Market value of shares – equity	233,453	234,131	237,751	247,075	244,940
Total liabilities	59,269	92,338	125,379	105,760	104,740
Net sales revenue	230,154	236,016	240,603	264,722	271,639
T1 – Current assets / Total assets	2.23	1.84	2.23	2.01	2.07
T2 – Retained earnings / Total assets	0.08	0.13	0.15	0.16	0.20
T3 – EBIT / Total assets	0.20	0.08	0.02	0.18	0.05
T4 – Equity / Total liabilities	4.14	2.66	1.99	2.45	2.46
z-score	6.64	4.71	4.39	4.80	4.77

Source: Own.

Criteria by Altman's *z*-score:
Altman's model for private service companies:
Financially strong companies = *z* value >2.90
Companies in serious trouble = *z* value <1.23
Companies that can go both ways = *z* value between 1.23 and 2.90

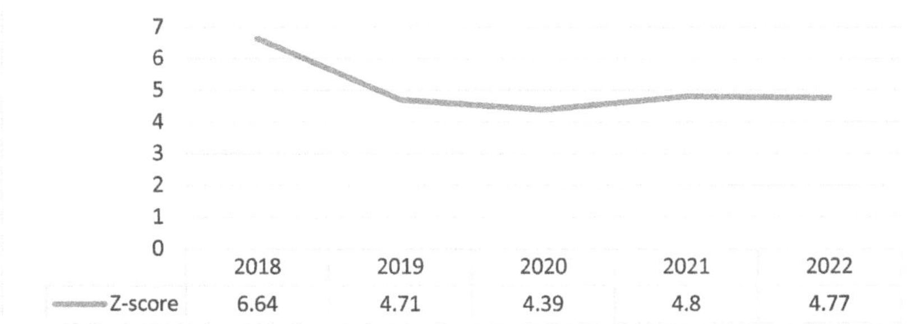

Graph 11. Graphic presentation of Altman's *z*-score for Pošta Slovenije, d. o. o., in the 2018–2022 period.

Source: Table 13.

Altman's z-score, adapted for private service companies, makes it possible to assess the financial stability of Pošta Slovenije, d. o. o., in the 2018–2022 period. z-values greater than 4.00 place the company among financially strong companies with a low risk of bankruptcy, which indicates the ability to manage financial liabilities and long-term business sustainability.

The value of total assets increased until 2020, mainly due to higher short-term assets, which were needed to finance inventories in the face of increased demand for logistics services. In 2021 and 2022, current assets decreased slightly due to the implementation of digital systems for inventory optimization and better receivables management, which contributed to better liquidity.

The growth of *retained earnings* throughout the period indicates prudent financial management and rationalization of costs, which increased the company's equity and reduced dependence on external sources. In 2020, operating profit declined due to costs related to managing the pandemic. Nevertheless, adaptations, such as digitization, contributed to improving business efficiency in 2021. In 2022, due to inflation and higher costs of energy products, business results deteriorated again, which required additional cost control.

The increase in liabilities in 2020 was related to borrowings for emergency investments due to the pandemic. However, in 2021 and 2022, the company managed to reduce debts by taking advantage of favorable interest rates and rationalizing borrowing, which strengthened the long-term financial stability.

The growth in net sales revenue is due to the expansion of services, including digital solutions and logistics improvements. Despite pressure from rising costs, the company managed to maintain revenue growth, which further contributes to financial stability.

z-values greater than 4.00 confirm that Pošta Slovenije, d. o. o., according to Altman's model, belongs to financially strong companies. In order to maintain competitiveness and financial stability, further control of costs and adaptation to market conditions will be key measures for the company.

4.5. Comparative Analysis of the Business Performance of Pošta Slovenije, d. o. o., with Some Comparable Companies Abroad

In this section, we analyze the business performance of the Pošta Slovenije Group in comparison with other similar postal companies abroad. The analysis will be based on a series of key financial indicators, which include quick ratios, debt-to-equity ratios, ROA and equity, and other indicators of business efficiency and stability. By comparing these indicators, we gain insight into the performance of the Pošta Slovenije Group and identify areas where improvement is possible. In this way, we can identify good practices that the Pošta Slovenije Group could use to improve its operations and obtain important findings for further strategic directions.

4.5.1. Selection of Comparable Companies

To conduct a comparative analysis, we selected several postal companies from different countries that operate in a similar business environment to the one of the Pošta Slovenije Group. The criteria for the selection of companies included the size of the company, the type of services offered, the market share, and the availability of financial and accounting data for the period from 2018 to 2022. The aim of the selection was to provide a representative group of companies that enables a relevant and meaningful comparison.

The selected companies represent national postal operators facing similar challenges, such as digitization, the decline of traditional postal services, and competitiveness in the logistics market. We included the following companies in the analysis:

1. *Czech Post*: The national operator in the Czech Republic, offering a wide range of postal and logistics services. The Czech Post is facing challenges, such as digitization and competitiveness in the logistics market.
2. *Hrvatska pošta*: The main provider of postal services in Croatia with an extensive range of logistics and financial services.
3. *Irish Post*: The national operator in Ireland, focused on innovation and sustainable development, which makes for an interesting comparison with the Pošta Slovenije Group.
4. *CTT Correios de Portugal*: The main provider of postal and logistics services in Portugal, which has made a number of strategic changes in recent years, including digitization.
5. *PostNord*: A joint venture between PostNord Denmark and PostNord Sweden that provides postal and logistics services and faces challenges similar to other European postal operators.

The data on these companies enabled us to make an accurate comparison between the Pošta Slovenije Group and selected companies abroad and offered insight into the performance of operations over the past five years.

4.5.2. Comparative Analysis of the Financial Indicators of the Pošta Slovenije Group and Foreign Postal Operators

We focused on analyzing key financial ratios such as Quick liquidity ratio (Acid-test ratio), Debt to Equity Ratio, ROA, ROE, Net Profit Margin, EBITDA Margin, and CAPEX as a percentage of revenue. These indicators showed the financial health and operational efficiency of the Pošta Slovenije Group compared to competitors,

4.5.2.1. Quick Liquidity Ratio

$$\text{Quick liquidity ratio (acid-test ratio)} = (\text{Current assets} - \text{Inventories}) / \text{Current liabilities}$$

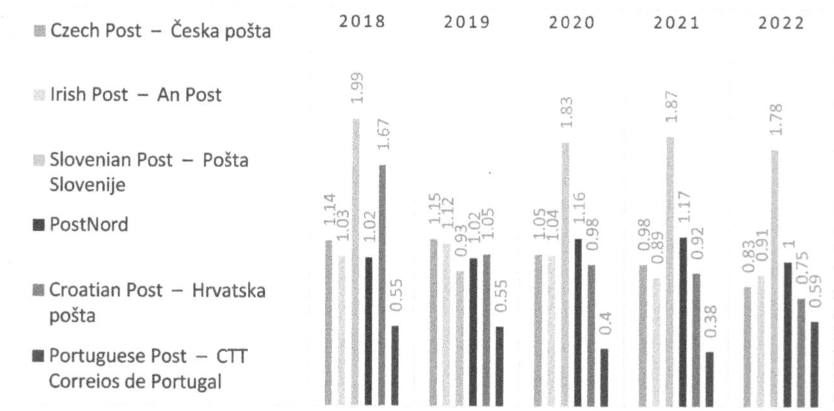

Graph 12. Quick liquidity ratio for some comparable European postal operators in the 2018–2022 period.

Source: Own.

In the 2018–2022 period, the Pošta Slovenije Group showed considerable liquidity stability, although after the acquisition of Intereuropa, d. d., in 2019, the quick liquidity ratio dropped to 0.93. The company later stabilized liquidity through better management of short-term assets, which in 2020–2022 maintained its quick liquidity ratio at a level of around 1.8, which indicates effective management of receivables and liabilities.

Compared to other postal operators, the *Czech Post* gradually worsened its acceleration coefficient, mainly due to the inefficient implementation of restructuring. The *Croatian Post* was under liquidity pressure due to expansion and modernization, which was not sufficiently supported by liquid assets. The *Irish Post* has maintained stable liquidity, but liabilities have increased due to adjustments to market conditions, resulting in a slight reduction in the quick liquidity ratio toward the end of the period. The *Portuguese Post*, on the other hand, faced the lowest quick liquidity ratio due to high short-term liabilities, which increased its risk. By consistently managing receivables, *PostNord* maintained a stable quick liquidity ratio.

Overall, the Pošta Slovenije Group ranks as one of the more stable ones compared to most postal operators that are struggling with liquidity challenges.

4.5.2.2 Debt to Equity Ratio

Debt to equity ratio = Total debt / Equity

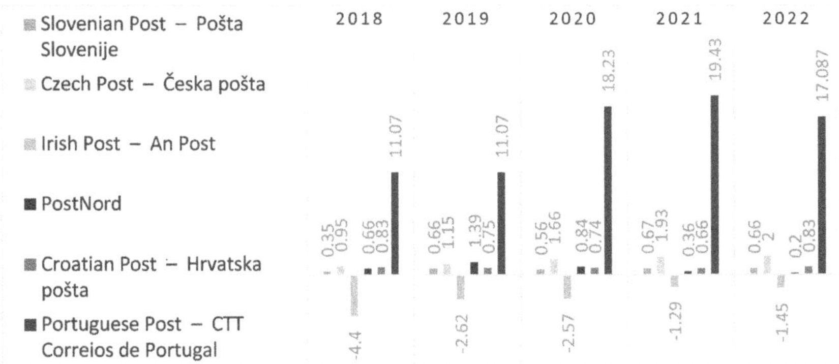

Graph 13. Debt to equity ratio for some comparable European postal operators in the 2018–2022 period.
Source: Own.

The debt-to-equity ratio of the Pošta Slovenije Group increased to 0.66 in 2019 after the acquisition of Intereuropa, d. d., which reflects the larger debt, which the company effectively stabilized with moderate borrowing in the following years. This reflects the company's prudent financial policy. A ratio of value close to 1 indicates that equity and debt are balanced. A value greater than 1 means that there is more debt than equity, while a value less than 1 indicates an excess of equity over debt (Mayr, 2017: 151).

Compared to the *Czech Post*, which significantly increased its debt to 2.00 due to restructuring problems, the *Pošta Slovenije Group* maintains a stable debt. The *Croatian Post* shows low indebtedness, which reflects a conservative financial strategy. The *Irish Post* shows a negative value of the ratio, indicating negative equity. This means that debts are higher than the value of equity, which can lead to greater financial risk and indicate insufficient equity financing. On the other hand, the *Portuguese Post* shows high indebtedness due to short-term obligations related to the provision of banking services. However, *PostNord* managed to reduce debt to 0.20, which ensures better financial stability.

The *Pošta Slovenije Group* thus maintains stable indebtedness compared to the *Czech Post* and the *Portuguese Post*, which have high debt burdens.

4.5.2.3. ROA

$$\text{ROA} = \text{Net income} / \text{Total assets} \times 100$$

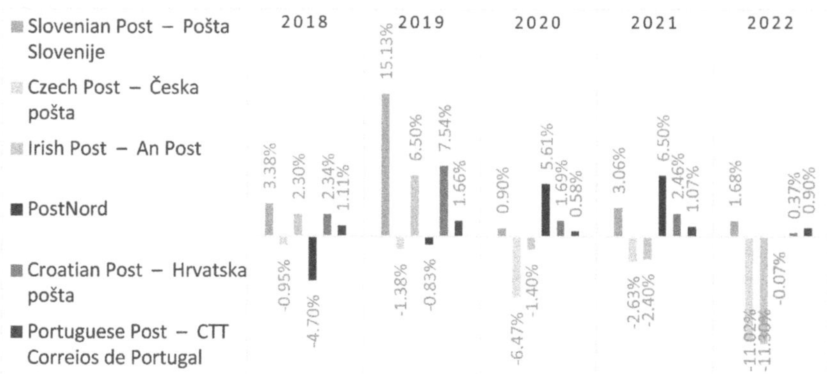

Graph 14. ROA for some comparable European postal operators in the 2018–2022 period.

Source: Own.

In 2019, the *Pošta Slovenije Group* achieved a high ROA due to the one-time effect of the acquisition of Intereuropa, d. d., which increased revenue and profit. The following years showed difficulties in maintaining this level, as the company adapted operational processes and faced challenges in integrating acquired assets.

The *Czech Post* had a negative ROA due to structural problems and excessive costs, while the *Croatian Post* achieved higher profitability in 2019, but later had problems maintaining efficiency. The *Irish Post* showed a negative return due to poor asset utilization. The *Portuguese Post* maintained a low, but stable ROA, indicating relatively successful cost management, while *PostNord* improved operational efficiency in 2020–2021, but still lacked sustainable growth.

In general, the ROA of the *Pošta Slovenije Group* was significantly affected by the specific circumstances of the takeover, while other operators face long-term challenges in using their resources.

4.5.2.4. ROE

$$ROE = \text{Net income} / \text{Equity} \times 100$$

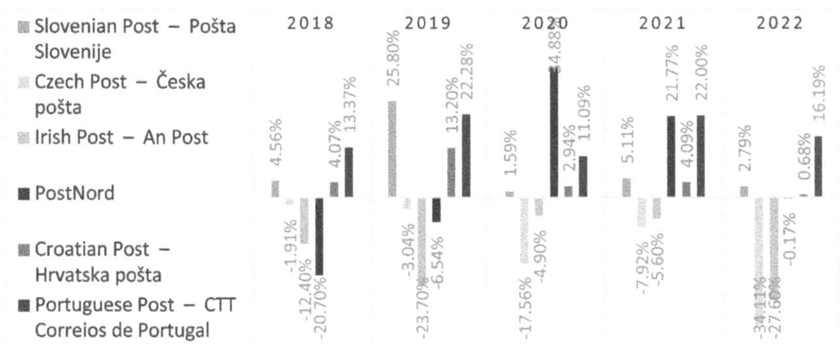

Graph 15. ROE for some comparable European postal operators in the 2018–2022 period.
Source: Own.

ROE of the *Pošta Slovenije Group* was high in 2019 due to one-off factors related to business changes, which increased revenues and temporarily improved efficiency. However, the years after that show problems with the long-term efficiency of the use of capital.

The *Czech Post* showed a persistently negative ROE due to inefficient resource management, while the *Croatian Post* showed a high return on capital in 2019, but later faced cost challenges. The *Irish Post* showed a persistently negative ROE, indicating a need for restructuring and more efficient capital management. The *Portuguese Post* maintained a high return on equity, but faced efficiency requirements, while *PostNord* showed volatility.

Overall, the *Pošta Slovenije Group* stands out with a one-time peak in return on equity, but most comparable companies have problems with long-term return on equity.

4.5.2.5. Net Profit Margin

$$\text{Net profit margin} = \text{Net income} / \text{Net sales revenue} \times 100$$

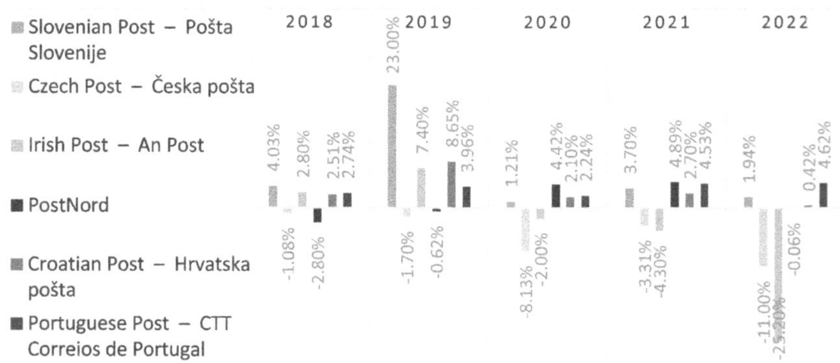

Graph 16. Net profit margin for some comparable European postal operators in the 2018–2022 period.

Source: Own.

In 2019, the *Pošta Slovenije Group* achieved a high *net profit margin* due to the acquisition, but in the following years it faced a decrease due to difficulties in maintaining cost efficiency.

The *Czech Post* had a chronically negative net profit margin due to optimization problems, while the *Croatian Post* achieved high efficiency in 2019, but faced difficulties in maintaining profitability. The *Irish Post* was also facing a negative net profit margin, indicating a need to optimize costs. The *Portuguese Post* shows stable and positive net profit margin, while *PostNord* shows successful cost management with improved net profit margin in 2020 and 2021.

Thus, the *Pošta Slovenije Group* ranks among the most successful in terms of the exceptional result from 2019, but the challenge of cost pressures for sustainable success remains.

4.5.2.5. EBITDA Margin

EBITDA margin = EBITDA / Net sales revenue × 100

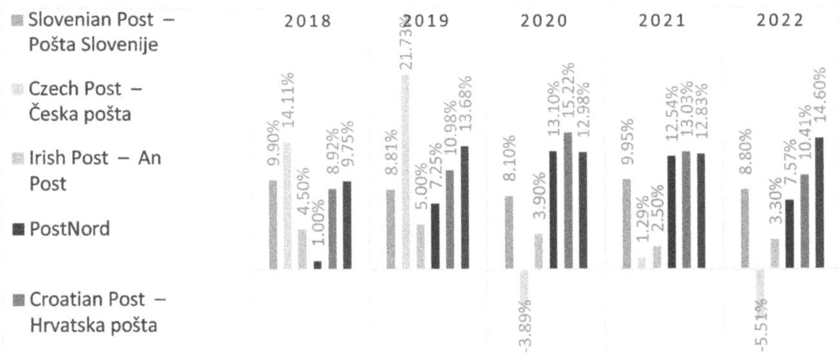

Graph 17. EBITDA margin for some comparable European postal operators in the 2018–2022 period.
Source: Own.

The *EBITDA margin* of the *Pošta Slovenije Group* remained between 8.10% and 9.95% in the 2018–2022 period. It reached its highest value in 2021 due to effective cost management. Despite the challenges of the pandemic and the adaptation of business processes to the new circumstances, the company maintained stable operational efficiency.

The *Czech Post* initially showed a high EBITDA margin, but subsequent operational challenges led to a sharp decline, including negative values. The *Croatian Post* improved its margin in 2020 but faced rising costs. The *Irish Post* had low EBITDA margins due to high reorganization costs. The *Portuguese Post* maintained a stable and high margin, while *PostNord* experienced fluctuations due to cost adjustments.

4.5.2.6. *CAPEX*

CAPEX as a percentage of revenue = CAPEX / Net sales revenue × 100

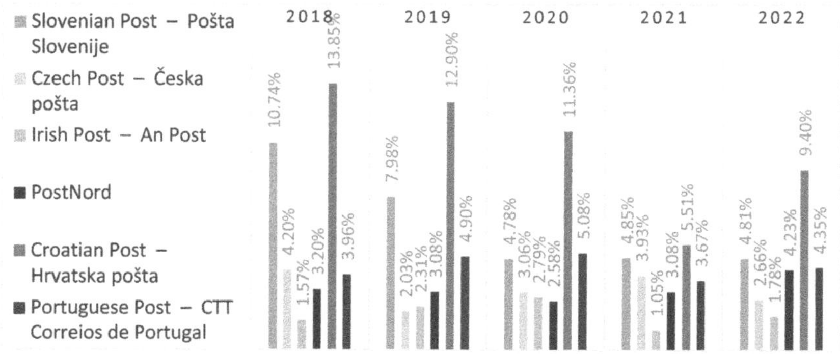

Graph 18. CAPEX as a percentage of revenue for some comparable European postal operators in the 2018–2022 period.
Source: Own.

In the 2018–2022 period, the *Pošta Slovenije Group* showed different CAPEX values, the highest in 2018 and 2019, when it modernized the infrastructure. Subsequently, CAPEX as a percentage of net sales revenue stabilized at around 4.8%, reflecting a moderate but sustainable investment strategy.

The *Czech Post* had low CAPEX values due to limited investments, while the *Croatian Post* stood out with high percentages in the first years due to an aggressive modernization strategy. The *Irish Post* maintained very low CAPEX, indicating a cautious investment approach. The *Portuguese Post* maintained a stable, moderate CAPEX, while *PostNord* gradually increased investments in better operational efficiency.

4.6. Conclusion

After the financial analysis of Pošta Slovenije, d. o. o., for the 2018–2022 period, we can conclude that the company managed to maintain relative financial stability and competitiveness in the market despite many challenges, such as rising costs of labor, depreciation, energy, and unstable economic conditions.

The company successfully fulfills its mission of providing a universal postal service, which is confirmed by high indicators of customer satisfaction and quality services, which are above the average of comparable companies in the region. Pošta Slovenije, d. o. o., maintained a high standard of postal and logistics services in the 2018–2022 period, which indicates the successful fulfillment of its role as a public company.

The analysis of financial indicators, such as indicators of financing, investment, solvency, horizontal financial structure, asset turnover, and profitability, showed that Pošta Slovenije, d. o. o., maintained a stable capital structure in the 2018–2022 period. Despite the increase in indebtedness in 2019 and 2020, mainly due to the purchase of Intereuropa, d. d., and other investments, the company managed to reduce its debt burden in 2021 and 2022. ROA and ROE maintained a positive trend despite fluctuations, which indicates the efficiency of the use of assets and capital.

The key factors that influenced the company's operations were effective management of working capital, optimization of costs, and active management of liabilities. Despite the negative impacts of the COVID-19 pandemic and other external factors, the company managed to maintain a stable EBITDA, which indicates good management of business challenges. EBIT was subject to fluctuations, which reflects the impact on revenues and costs, but Pošta Slovenije, d. o. o., demonstrated flexibility in meeting these challenges.

Altman's *z*-score always showed values greater than 4, which confirms that the company is in good financial shape with a low risk of bankruptcy. Among other things, this means reliability in risk management in an unstable business environment.

In a comparative analysis with other postal operators, the Pošta Slovenije Group demonstrated competitiveness in areas such as liquidity, ROA and cost management efficiency. Although there are some lags in the field of sustainable development, the company has taken important steps in recent years by introducing sustainable practices, which can further strengthen its competitive position.

Based on the analysis, we recommend that Pošta Slovenije, d. o. o., continues to optimize operating costs, increase investments in digitization and technology, and strengthen efforts for sustainable development. Further investments in energy efficiency and the green transition can bring the company additional competitive advantages and long-term business sustainability.

We can answer the research questions: Pošta Slovenije, d. o. o., managed its financial resources effectively during the period under review, maintained financial stability, and achieved profitability despite economic challenges. Sustainable practices have had a positive impact on the long-term stability of the company, but it is necessary to continue investing in environmentally friendly technologies and sustainable practices to strengthen the competitive advantage. Thus, the company maintains its key role as a leading provider of postal and logistics services in Slovenia.

For a more comprehensive understanding of the operations of Pošta Slovenije, d. o. o., and the elimination of the aforementioned limitations, we suggest further research in several directions. One of them is an in-depth analysis of external factors such as macroeconomic trends, regulatory changes, and the competitive environment to better understand how these factors affect the company's operations. Qualitative studies, such as interviews with key stakeholders and surveys among employees and customers, would also offer insight into satisfaction and reveal perceptions and expectations that can affect the performance of Pošta Slovenije, d. o. o., in the future.

A more detailed comparative analysis with key competitors would also help better understand the competitive position of Pošta Slovenije, d. o. o., and identify areas where the company could improve its offer and differentiate itself on the market. Further research could also be aimed at evaluating existing strategies and studying new business models that would stimulate growth and innovation. In addition, it would be reasonable to investigate how digitization, automation, and new technologies affect the operational efficiency, cost structure, and, finally, the exploitation of the company's market opportunities.

Bibliography

Bergant, Ž. (2013). *Analiza poslovanja od teorije do prakse: računovodski in finančni vidiki*. Ljubljana: Inštitut za poslovodno računovodstvo.

Bergant, Ž., & Manohin, I. (2018). *Priročnik za analiziranje poslovanja: zgledi in vaje*. Ljubljana: Inštitut za poslovodno računovodstvo.

Bergant, Ž. (2023). *Kritična presoja sodobnega računovodstva*. Ljubljana: Inštitut za poslovodno računovodstvo.

Bukvič, V. (2016a). Value-based management with some practical examples in Slovenian industries. In T. Vranešević (Ed.), *M-Sphere: Book of Papers* (pp. 222–233). Zagreb: Accent.

Bukvič, V. (2016b). Financial flexibility as one of the key factors that influence firm investment ability. In A. Fošner (Ed.), *Conference Proceedings*. Ljubljana: Gea College—Faculty of Entrepreneurship.

Bukvič, V. (2020). Investicijska sposobnost kot vir konkurenčne prednosti podjetja, temelječa na človeških in finančnih virih – teoretični oris = Investment ability as a source of the company's competitive advantage based on human and financial resources – theoretical outline. *Poslovodno računovodstvo*, *16*(2–3), 4–57.

Bukvič, V. (2023). *Osnove analize poslovanja: teoretični okviri z računskimi nalogami in študijami primerov*. Ljubljana: GEA College—Fakulteta za podjetništvo.

Esplin, A. M., Hewitt, M. R., Plumlee, M. A., & Yohn, T. L. (2014). Disaggregating operating and financial activities: Implications for forecasts of profitability. *Review of Accounting Studies*, *19*(1), 328–362.

Fairfield, P. M., Sweeney, R. J., & Yohn, T. L. (1996). Accounting classification and the predictive content of earnings. *The Accounting Review*, *71*(3), 337–355.

Fairfield, P. M., & Yohn, T. L. (2001). Using asset turnover and profit margin to forecast changes in profitability. *Review of Accounting Studies*, *6*(4), 371–385.

Helfert, E. A. (2001). *Financial Analysis: Tools and Techniques: A Guide for Managers*. New York, NY: McGraw-Hill Education.

Jackson, A. B., Plumlee, M. A., & Rountree, B. R. (2018). Decomposing the market, industry, and firm components of profitability: Implications for forecasts of profitability. *Review of Accounting Studies*, *23*(3), 1071–1095.

Jackson, A. B. (2022). Financial statements analysis: A review and current issues. *China Finance Review International*, *12*(1), 1–19.

Kodeks PFN. (1996). *Kodeks poslovnofinančnih načel*. Ljubljana: Slovenski inštitut za revizijo. Retrieved from <http://www.si-revizija.si/financniki/dokumenti/kodeks_pofin_nacel-celotno.pdf>

Kodeks, KNNP. (2015). *Kodeks načel notranjega poročanja*. Ljubljana: Inštitut za poslovodno računovodstvo pri VŠR in Zveza ekonomistov Slovenije. Retrieved from <https://www.zdruzenje-ns.si/library/1838>

Annual reports of the Czech Post (Česká pošta) (2018–2022). Retrieved from <https://www.postovnimuzeum.cz/en/web/ceskaposta/o-ceske-poste/profil/vyrocni-zpravy>

Annual reports of the Croatian Post (Hrvatska pošta, d. d.) (2018–2022). Retrieved from <https://hrvatska.posta.hr/en/about-us/investors/financials-statements>

Annual reports of the Irish Post (An Post) (2018–2022). Retrieved from <https://www.anpost.com/About/Reports>

Annual reports of the Portuguese Post (CTT – Correios de Portugal) (2018–2022). Retrieved from <https://www.ctt.pt/grupo-ctt/investidores/informacao-financeira/contas-consolidadas?language_id=1>

Annual reports of PostNord (2018–2022). Retrieved from <https://group.postnord.com/financials/financial-reporting/?page=1&topic=annual+and+sustainability+reports>

Annual reports of Pošta Slovenije, d. o. o. (2018–2022). Retrieved from <https://www.posta.si/o-nas/predstavitev/osnovne-informacije/letna-porocila>

Li, K., & Mohanram, P. (2019). Fundamental analysis: Combining the search for quality with the search for value. *Contemporary Accounting Research*, *36*(3), 1263–1298.

Mayr, B. (2017). *Osnove računovodstva*. Ljubljana: Visoka šola za računovodstvo in finance.

Mohanram, P. S. (2005). Separating winners from losers among low book-to-market stocks using financial statement analysis. *Review of Accounting Studies*, *10*(2–3), 133–170.

Price Waterhouse. (1997). *CFO: Architect of the Corporation's Future*. New York, NY: John Wiley & Sons.

Pučko, D. (2006). *Analiza poslovanja*. Ljubljana: Ekonomska fakulteta Univerze v Ljubljani.

Soliman, M. T. (2008). The use of DuPont analysis by market participants. *The Accounting Review*, *83*(3), 823–853.

Subramanyam, K. R., & Wild, J. J. (2012). *Financial Statement Analysis* (11th ed.). New York, NY: McGraw-Hill/Irwin.

Yohn, T. L. (2020). Research on the use of financial statement information for forecasting profitability. *Accounting and Finance*, *60*(3), 3163–3181.

Forecasting and Evaluating Economized Government Procurements Based on an Econometric Model

Zokir Mamadiyarov, Sarvar Turabov, Samariddin Makhmudov, Nargizaxon Shamshiyeva, Bobur Mirzayev, Umida Salikhodjaeva and Alima Tleubergenova

5.1. Introduction

The fact that technical problems associated with the widespread introduction of digital technologies in the effective organization of public procurement negatively affect the competitive environment among business entities requires the need to improve this system. By ensuring transparency, efficiency, and correct and fair distribution of budget funds in public procurement, the country's budget can be used effectively. Ensuring transparency and expanding the competitive environment in the field of public procurement, proper organization of procurement procedures reduces unnecessary costs and strengthens public confidence in the state. The need to optimize public procurement arises due to several main factors. First, inefficient procurement processes can lead to government overspending, misallocation of resources, and lack of accountability. By implementing modern procurement strategies, governments can reduce the risk of corruption, reduce financial losses, and ensure the targeted use of budget funds. In addition, an effective procurement system enhances fair competition among suppliers, which leads to improved quality of goods and services at lower prices. In addition, there is an opportunity to support and strengthen the activities of private businesses and enterprises from a global perspective by improving public procurement. By implementing the main tasks of the public procurement system, it is possible to increase the volume of exported products by improving the competitive environment, encouraging local enterprises to produce quality products and services under international standards. To effectively manage this process, it is necessary to implement comprehensive reforms, which should not be limited to the creation of institutions responsible for developing the state procurement system standards and making their activities transparent, but rather to improving mutual relations. This will make co-operation between organizations possible, and power will be distributed equally.

In particular, in order to prevent and combat corruption in public procurement, it is necessary to combat corruption in our country. If there is no corruption in public procurement, competition will be strengthened and this will lead to the development of public procurement. Legislation based on legal norms and standards for managing the public procurement system in our country has been taking shape since 2017 year. As we all know, any economic process in a country is important for the social life of the population, because the legal outcome of these processes affects the country's population, state policy, and the structures within it. The public procurement system is a complex mechanism of relations between economic entities, and the proper organization of the system's activities and the promotion of effective management contribute to the development of the country's economy. This is the best development of laws and legal systems aimed at improving public procurement, preventing violations of the principles and standards established by law.

In order to effectively organize public procurement in Uzbekistan, it is necessary to ensure budget discipline and modernize the economy. Implementing approaches based on econometric models allows for accurate forecasting and assessment of the volume of economized procurement. In addition, it is possible to achieve savings in public procurement by predicting future trends and developing optimal procurement strategies.

Thus, the effective organization of public procurement has a positive impact on the financial stability of the state, ensuring fair competition and economic growth. The introduction of modern procurement methods stimulates the effective management of public resources and economic development.

5.2. Literature Review and Development Hypothesis

Forecasting and assessing the efficiency of state procurement through econometric methods is of great importance for the effective organization of procurement processes. Forecasting based on statistical methods and econometric models allows assessing the future dynamics and trends of state procurement, which is of great importance for improving the state's procurement strategy.

According to Chapela et al. (2019) "a large procurement function allows for greater savings. According to them, achieving economies of scale leads to a reduction in costs per unit of procurement." According to Jean-Jacques Laffont et al. (2020) "evaluative auctions take into account the bid and the quality of the bidder. The optimal score rule may not be linear, and the model is used to determine the best procurement strategies under different conditions." According to the authors' research, the characteristics of the econometric model include the consumer benefit function, the distribution of costs among participants, and potential savings in public funds.

According to Brianzoni et al. (2012) "the relationship between corruption in public procurement and economic growth, depending on tax revenues in the payment system, has a strong effect on the discrete time interval, determining the level of monitoring of the public interest production process and state corruption." According to the authors' results, the econometric model shows a significant relationship between the salaries of bureaucrats, the amount of tax revenues used for monitoring, corruption, and the level of economic growth, with a significant impact on the level of statistical significance. According to Hafsa et al. (2021) "public procurement is an important tool for promoting sustainability goals in the state's purchase of goods and services." The authors' research has shown that the government, being the largest consumer in the economy, has a significant impact on the market through sustainable procurement. According to the study, public procurement at all levels of government ranged from 19% to 24%, 13% to 56%, 3% to 10%, and 12% to 38% of GDP in the United States, UK, Italy, and the Netherlands, respectively.

Muniswamy and Palanisamy (2024) argue that "public procurement is a critical part of supply chain management and can be subject to a number of unique constraints that can lead to the failure of a major project". According to the research results, improving public procurement, especially in this sector, will allow managers to plan their activities more effectively. Gavurova et al. (2019) state that "the use of European funds is an important parameter affecting the final value of public procurement contracts in higher education".

According to the authors, these factors contribute to the variation of costs and affect the efficiency of procurement practices. According to Fowles and Tandberg (2017) "geographical connectivity affects public higher education spending in neighboring countries, in particular, needs-based provision and spending decisions on higher education". According to the authors' research, based on econometric models, spatial connectivity shows a strong correlation with procurement strategies and financial planning in higher education institutions. Gurayah (2024) states that "the challenges in public procurement in higher education institutions are mainly related to the quality of personnel, processes and technology". Addressing these challenges is essential to improve procurement efficiency.

Analyses and forecasts have been conducted using various econometric models on energy policy, energy risk, environmental conditions, the impact of environmental factors on the digital economy, and factors affecting agricultural efficiency (Akhmetshin et al., 2025, Cahyani et al., 2025; Caporin et al., 2024; Kuchkarov et al., 2025; Kuziboev et al., 2025; Litamahuputty et al., 2025; Nazirjon et al., 2023; Sharipov et al., 2025; Yin et al., 2024).

According to Yadav (2024, January), "The ARIMA model involves estimating parameters for the autoregressive (AR) and moving average (MA) components, which help to obtain the main results from the procurement data." The analysis and estimation of these components in the Autoregressive Integrated Moving Average (ARIMA) model is of great importance in providing statistically reliable forecasts by the model. A group of local economists has effectively utilized econometric models in research on the impact of inflation and credit interest rates on investment, factors influencing the reduction of state shares in commercial banks, digitalization of banks, risks in digital services, and the development of retail banking services (Makhmudov et al., 2024; Mamadiyarov et al., 2024; PANJAITAN et al., 2025; Samariddin et al., 2025; Zhang et al., 2025 Zokir, 2021: Zokir et al., 2021).

According to Zhuravka et al. (2019) "The ARIMA model has been successfully applied to forecasting government debt, which is closely related to procurement activity." In particular, the authors used the ARIMA model in their econometric research to forecast the state debt of the Ukrainian state, which showed its applicability in financial forecasting in the public sector.

According to the author's research, the ARIMA model has been identified as an optimal model for planning and budgeting financing practices by forecasting trends in state military spending.

5.3. Research Methodology

We have developed forecast indicators for the national economy for the coming 2025–2029 based on the ARIMA model. In econometric research, the ARIMA model is considered an effective model for forecasting time series data and is an optimal statistical method for assessing the impact of economic processes.

5.3.1. Data Collection

The research team obtained its data from the official website of the "Uzbekistan Republican Commodity Exchange" JSC (<https://xarid.uzex.uz>). Statistical data from the "Uzbekistan Republican Commodity Exchange" JSC were used, consisting of 32 quarterly observations from 2015 to 2024 and economic indicators. The outcome variable for the econometric forecast was "Volume of government procurement saved at auction" – *gov_proc*.

5.3.2. Methods

According to Valipour et al. (2013) "The ARIMA model formula contains three components, defined as ARIMA (*p*, *d*, *q*)", where:

p is the number of lagged observations in the model (AR part)
d is the number of times the observations are differencing (integrated part).
q is the size of the MA window (MA part).

The general form of the ARIMA (*p*, *d*, *q*) model is given below.

$$y_t = \alpha_0 + \alpha_1 c_1 + \alpha_2 c_2 + \ldots + \alpha_k c_k + \epsilon \quad (1)$$

where, y_t is the value of the time series at time t (after being differentiated d times), c is the constant term, α_t (for $i = 1, 2, \ldots, k$) is the coefficients of the AR part, δ_q = (for $j = 1, 2, \ldots, q$) is the coefficients of the MA part.

ϵ_t – t is the error term at time t (white noise).

5.3.2.1. Explanation of Components

1. According to Khan and Gupta (2020) "Autoregressive (AR) part in ARIMA model". The terms $\alpha_1 y_{t-1}, \alpha_2 y_{t-2}, \ldots, \alpha_p y_{t-k}$ describe the AR part, in which the current value of the series is regressed on its past values.
2. According to Patel et al. (2020) "Integrated (I) Part in ARIMA Model". The parameter d represents the order of differentiation used to realize the stationary state of the series. The differentiation operation is written as:

$$y_t' = y_t - y_{t-1} \ (agar\ d = 1) \tag{2}$$

However, higher order differentiation is used in developing forecast indicators for research. According to Singh et al., (2020) "Moving Average (MA) Part in ARIMA Model".

The terms $\delta_1 \epsilon_{t-1}, \delta_2 \epsilon_{t-2}, \ldots, \delta_q \epsilon_{t-q}$ represent the MA part. In ARIMA model, it is effective in modeling time series data over a wide range by appropriately evolving the parameters p, d, and q.

5.4. Analysis and Results

Figure 13 shows the volume of government procurement saved in Auxinon – gov_proc (outcome variable). An analytical graphical representation of the outcome variable over time at the initial stage of the econometric forecast is presented as in what follows.

Figure 13 shows that the volume of public procurement saved through exchange auctions showed a sharp growth trend in the first half of 2017, and this growth dynamics reached a maximum in the first quarter of 2021. This sharp growth trend was the result of the reforms carried out by the government in exchange operations, which increased confidence in exchange auctions for public procurement.

Following the econometric forecast, the stationarity level of the volume of public procurement saved through national exchange auctions was assessed and the Unit-Root test was used to determine it (Table 14).

According to Table 14, the value of the state procurement volume saved at the national stock exchange auctions is –5.293, which indicates how important

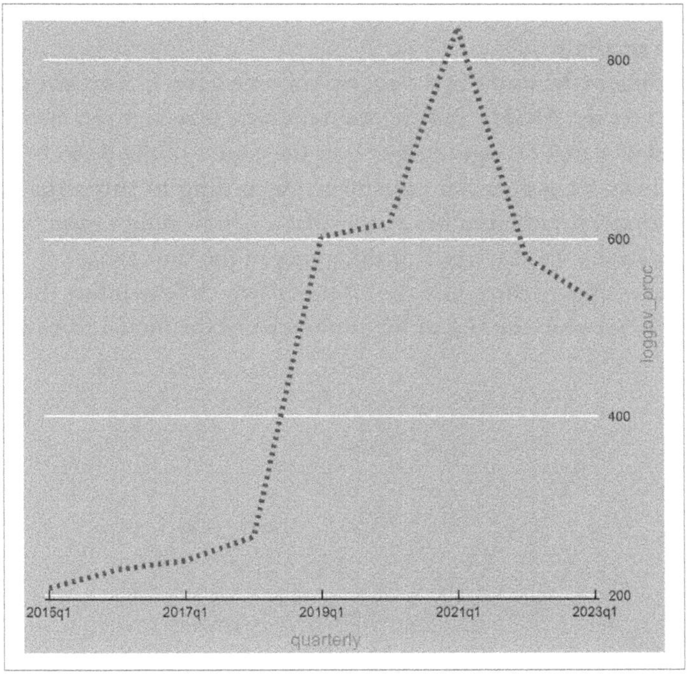

Figure 13. Analytical graphic diagram of the periodic status of the volume of state purchases saved at national stock exchange auctions.

Source: It was developed by the authors based on Stata software.

the stable growth of state procurement in stock exchange operations is in the context of a consistent, clearly cyclical, seasonal periodic stock exchange trading operations. According to it, it can be seen that the statistical value is below the 1%, 5%, and 10% thresholds of significance. In addition, the McKinnon value is minimal with $Z(t) = 0.0000$, which indicates the presence

Table 14. Unit-Root test of the amount of government procurement saved in stock auctions

gov_proc	*Test Statistic*	*1% Critical Value*	*5% Critical Value*	*10% Critical Value*	*p-Value for Z(t)*
	−5.293	−3.716	−2.952	−2.624	0.0000

Source: It was developed by the authors based on Stata software.

of a stationary state of the state procurement volume saved at the stock exchange auctions.

According to the study, in the analysis of time series in forecasting indicators based on the ARIMA model, the stationary sequence retained a significant level of statistical significance over the course of the periodic process, which allows for a positive assessment. According to this sequence, the ARIMA model parameter d has a value of $d = 1$, indicating a good fit and has reached stationarity after the first difference of the time series.

The next step is to introduce the value of p, which determines the indirect correlation between the lags of the time series of the model (Figure 14).

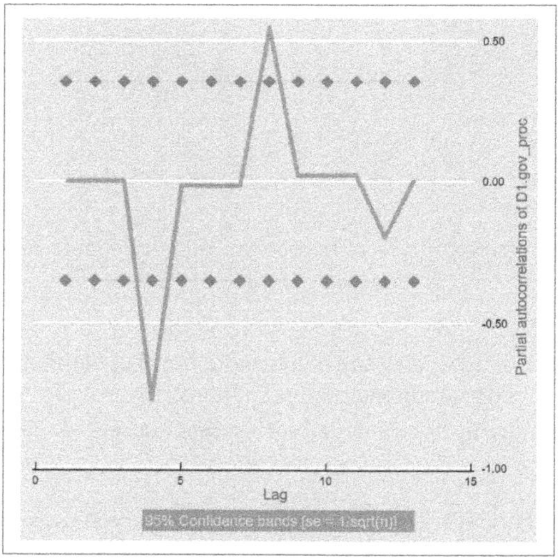

Figure 14. Indirect correlation graph between the lags of the econometric model of the volume of government procurement saved at stock auctions.
Source: It was developed by the authors based on Stata software.

As shown in Figure 14 above, all lags except for two lags have confidence intervals in the indirect correlation analysis. This means that most lags are statistically significant and lie within the confidence interval. The strong positive partial autocorrelation in the model indicates a long-run relationship. The increases in certain lags indicate that there may be seasonal and cyclical components. It is appropriate to use a p-value of 1 or 2 from the data in Figure 14.

The next step in the ARIMA model is to determine the value of *q*, which describes the direct correlation between the lags of the model (Figure 15).

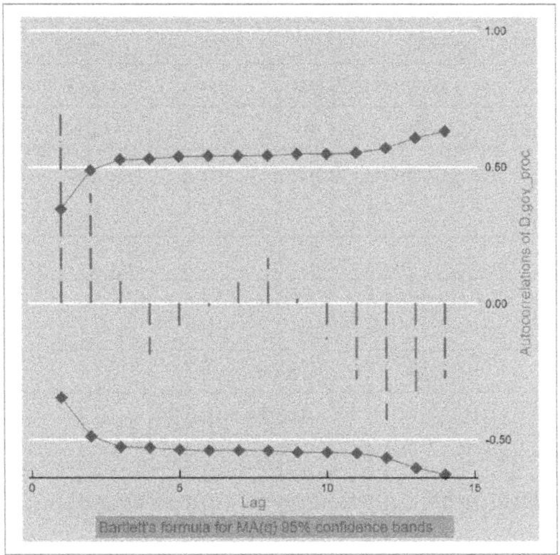

Figure 15. Direct correlation graph between the lags of the econometric model of the volume of government procurement saved at stock auctions.
Source: It was developed by the authors based on Stata software.

Based on the data in Figure 15, all lags except one lag exhibit the specified confidence interval, indicating a strong correlation between lags in the ARIMA model. The observed fluctuations in lags according to the econometric model show some seasonal dynamic behavior. This suggests that potential seasonal adjustments in the model provide promising positive forecast performance based on the ARIMA model. In the ARIMA model, the MA refers to the choice of a value for the parameter q. Since the observed data in the study are consistent with values between 0 and 1 and are located within the confidence intervals, it is recommended to choose a value of q in this range.

When selecting the optimal ARIMA invariant models for forecasting the model, models of the form ARIMA(1,1,1), ARIMA(1,1,2), ARIMA(2,1,1), ARIMA(1,0,2), ARIMA(2,0,1), and ARIMA(2,1,2) were used. Among these models, the ARIMA(2,1,1) model with the best results was selected (Table 15).

Table 15. Econometric equation indicators of the ARIMA(2,1,1) model on the volume of government purchases saved at stock auctions

D.gov_proc	*Coef.*	*St.Err.*	*t-value*	*p-value*	*[95% Conf*	*Interval]*	*Sig*
Constant	14.365	7.627	1.88	0.06	−0.584	29.313	*
L	1.642	0.15	10.94	0	1.348	1.937	***
L2	−0.726	0.169	−4.30	0	−1.057	-.0395	***
L	−0 0.91	0.276	−3.62	0	−1.541	-.0459	***
Constant	27.182	.	.	.	.	.	
Mean dependent var		10.076	*SD dependent var*			41.963	
Number of obs		32	*Chi-square*			498.342	
Prob > chi²		.	*Akaike crit. (AIC)*			312.699	
*** *p<.01,* ** *p<.05,* * *p<.1*							

Source: It was developed by the authors based on Stata software.

Based on the ARIMA model regression result, the econometric equation for the model is given below.

$$y_t = \mu + \phi_1 y_{t-1} + \phi_2 y_{t-2} + \ldots + \theta_1 \varepsilon_{t-1} + \theta_2 \varepsilon_{t-2} + \varepsilon_t \quad (3)$$

According to Table 15, the ARIMA(2,1,1) model looks like this:

$$\Delta gov\_proct = 14.36 + 1.64\Delta gov\_proc_{t-1} - 0.72\Delta gov\_proc_{t-2} - 0.91\varepsilon_{t-1} + \varepsilon_t \quad (4)$$

In the next step, the ARIMA(2,1,1) model was developed to analyze the mean values of the outcome variable and the graphical representation of the residuals (Figures 15 and 16).

Based on Table 16 above, Figure 16, the ARIMA(2,1,1) model has reached stochastic equilibrium, as evidenced by the visual representation of the residuals at the specified time intervals. This representation shows the fit of the ARIMA model to the data and the main stochastic relationships in the data set.

The next step involves checking the stationarity of the residuals of the ARIMA(2,1,1) model and estimating the AR and MA residuals of the national

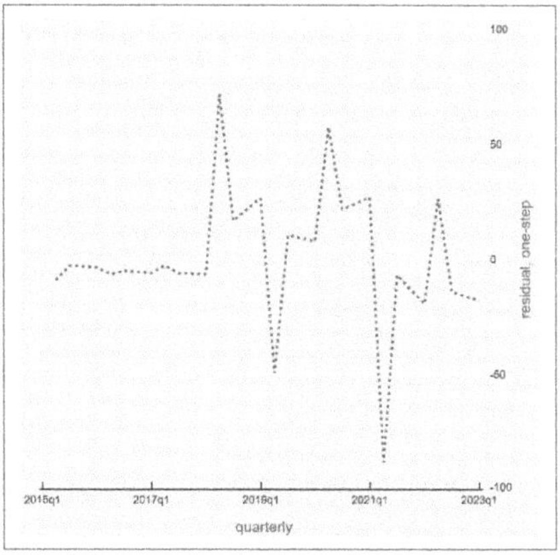

Figure 16. Graph of residual values of the ARIMA(2,1,1) model on the volume of government purchases saved at stock exchange auctions.

Source: It was developed by the authors based on Stata software.

Table 16. ARIMA(2,1,1) model residual values of the resulting factor

Variable factor	*Number of observations*	*Average value*	*Standard deviation*	*Minimum value*	*Maximum value*
Residual value	32	0.7963228	28.20453	−89.33058	71.12888

Source: It was developed by the authors based on Stata software.

stock exchange auctions. The convergence of the ARIMA model to the unit range in forecasting was also checked (Figure 17).

Using the Stata program, a forecast indicator was developed for the volume of state purchases saved at national stock exchange auctions from 2025 to 2029, excluding random factors, using the ARIMA(2,1,1) model (Table 17).

5.5. Findings and Discussion

According to the research, the volume of state purchases saved at exchange auctions provided by the "Uzbekistan Republican Commodity Exchange" JSC for 2015–2024 and the forecast indicator for 2025–2029 is explained below.

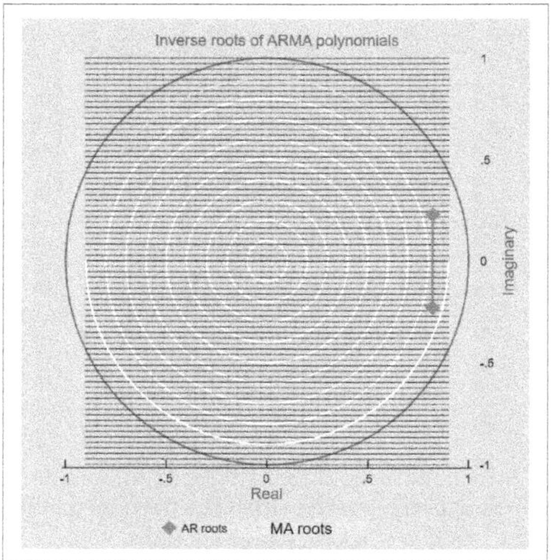

Figure 17. The range of values of the volume of government purchases saved at stock auctions according to the ARIMA(2,1,1) model.

Source: It was developed by the authors based on Stata software.

Table 17. Forecast indicators of the volume of state purchases saved at stock exchange auctions in 2025–2029 (in billion soums)

Years	Pessimistic forecast	Optimistic forecast	Forecast
2025	795.05	878.7	837.01
2026	870.86	954.78	912.82
2027	912.97	996.89	954.93
2028	963.51	1047.43	1005.47
2029	1021.83	1105.75	1063.79

Source: It was developed by the authors based on Stata software.

According to the research results, the volume of state purchases saved at the National Exchange auctions based on the ARIMA(2,1,1) model in 2025–2025, excluding random exogenous and endogenous factors, is projected to reach 837.01 billion soums in 2025, 912.82 billion soums in 2026, 954.03 billion soums in 2027, 1005.47 billion soums in 2028 and 1,063.79 billion soums in 2029, respectively.

5.6. Conclusion

5.6.1. Assessment of the Growth Trend According to the Econometric Model

The growth trend of state purchases financed at the National Exchange auctions according to the ARIMA(2,1,1) model presented a positive forecast. According to the forecast indicators, from 2025 to 2029, stable and positive growth dynamics were formed, indicating optimistic forecast indicators.

5.6.2. Assessment of Quantitative Concepts of Forecast Indicators According to the ARIMA model

According to the ARIMA model, the forecast indicators, which increased from 837.01 billion soums in 2025 to 1063.79 billion soums in 2029, indicate significant economic development. This growth reflects improved fiscal management, increased auction activity, and the effectiveness of economic mechanisms in the process of state procurement.

5.6.3. Econometric Model Assessment of Forecast Performance

An advanced approach to econometric forecasting is presented using the ARIMA(2,1,1) model. The model, excluding random exogenous and endogenous factors, isolates internal trends and ensures that the forecast is based on the main trend.

5.6.4. Econometric Forecast Assessment of Economic Consequences

The steady growth of state procurement, as measured by forecast indicators, indicates an increase in the openness and transparency of auction processes in exchange practices, which, in turn, is an important factor in ensuring reliable economic stability and public finance management.

5.6.5. Econometric Study of Stakeholder Incentives

These results provide an opportunity to assess the positive economic situation of all stakeholders of state procurement, in particular investors and suppliers, and through forecast indicators, indicate a more competitive market.

5.7. Recommendations

Having econometrically assessed the trends in the growth of state procurement and the amount of saved funds, we formulated the following scientific proposals.

5.7.1. Increasing the Accuracy of Forecasting State Procurement

To further increase the accuracy of the forecast, it is necessary to introduce machine learning algorithms working together with the ARIMA(2,1,1) model. As a result, the hybrid ARIMA model increases the accuracy of forecasting and can further improve the processes.

5.7.2. Analyzing the Effectiveness of Tax and Budgetary Policy Based on Econometric Models

Forecasting the volume of state procurement is necessary for rational budget policy. In addition, it is important for the government to optimize public spending and develop procurement strategies that correspond to the forecast results in order to stabilize fiscal policy.

5.7.3. Developing Competitive and Transparent Procurement Markets in the Country

The steady growth of the volume of state procurement requires further transparency in the auction processes in the country. In this regard, the application of blockchain technology to procurement processes will ensure data security, eliminate corruption, and promote fair competition.

Of course, these scientific proposals will serve to increase the efficiency, transparency, and sustainability of the public procurement system in the country, as well as to enhance long-term economic stability and fiscal responsibility.

Bibliography

Akhmetshin, E., Abdullayev, I., Makhmudov, S., Dakhkilgova, K., Korotaeva, I. and Yanovskaya, G. (2025). APPLICATION OF TANH–COTH METHOD FOR COMBINED AND DOUBLE COMBINED SINH–COSH–GORDON EQUATIONS ARISING CHEMICAL REACTIONS TO WATER SURFACE GRAVITY WAVES.

Computational Methods for Differential Equations, (), -. doi: 10.22034/cmde.2025.67655.3234

Brianzoni, S., Raffaella Coppier, and Elisabetta Michetti. "A Growth Model with Corruption in Public Procurement: Equilibria and Policy Implications, Quaderno del Dipartimento di Economia e Diritto n. 68, Submitted." (2012): 1–21. Cahyani, I., Buriev, K., Ngongo, M., Mamadiyarov, Z., Ino, L., Herman, H., Saputra, N., & Baxtishodovich, S. (2025). Exploring the Use of TikTok Application in Enhancing the Skill of Pronunciation: A Case on Students' Perception. Studies in Media and Communication, 13(2), 150–158. doi:http://dx.doi.org/10.11114/smc.v13i2.7553

Caporin, M., Shahbaz, M., Kuziboev, B., Masharipova, M., Allaberganov, S., & Makhmudov, S. (2024). Environmental Kuznets Curve for extended brics economies: do women governance and water stress matter?. International Journal of Energy Economics and Policy, 14(6), 174–183.

Chapela, J. G., Labeaga, J. M., & Medrano, L. A. (2019). Further econometric evidence on the extent and sources of cost savings in competitively tendered contracts. *Empirical Economics*, *56*, 679–701.

Fowles, J. T., & Tandberg, D. A. (2017). State higher education spending: A spatial econometric perspective. *American Behavioral Scientist*, *61*(14), 1773–1798.

Gavurova, B., Tuček, D., & Kováč, V. (2019). Economic aspects of public procurement parameters in tertiary education sector. *Administratie si Management Public*, *32*, 42–62.

Hafsa, F., Darnall, N., & Bretschneider, S. (2021). Estimating the true size of public procurement to assess sustainability impact. *Sustainability*, *13*(3), 1448.

Hussain, A., Khan, M., Rakhmonov, D. A., Mamadiyarov, Z. T., Kurbonbekova, M. T., & Mahmudova, M. Q. K. (2023). Nexus of Training and Development, Organizational Learning Capability, and Organizational Performance in the Service Sector. Sustainability, 15(4), 3246. https://doi.org/10.3390/su15043246

Jayrusha, R., Ramasamy, G., & Gurayah, T. (2024). Public procurement system challenges at selected higher education institutions in KwaZulu-Natal, South Africa.. doi: 10.29086/10413/23042

Khan, F. M., & Gupta, R. (2020). ARIMA and NAR based prediction model for time series analysis of COVID-19 cases in India. *Journal of Safety Science and Resilience*, *1*(1), 12–18.

Kuchkarov, T., Mamadiyarov, Z., Khakimov, Z., Sabirova, O., Matmurodov, K., Raimboyeva, M., & Umarova, S. (2025). Energy-Related Uncertainty and Crypto-Currency Environmental Attention: Time-Varying Perspective. International Journal of Energy Economics and Policy, 15(5), 614–626. https://doi.org/10.32479/ijeep.20784

Kuziboev, B., Khodjaniyazov, E., Ozturk, I., Sabirov, K., Makhmudov, S., & Utegenova, S. (2025). Does oil dependence cause energy risk?. Energy Nexus, 17, 100393.

Laffont, J. J., Perrigne, I., Simioni, M., & Vuong, Q. (2020). Econometrics of scoring auctions. In *Essays in honor of Cheng Hsiao* (Vol. 41, pp. 287–322). Emerald Publishing Limited.

Litamahuputty, J. V., Amiruddin, E. G., Rahim, R., Rahman, A., & Mamadiyarov, Z. (2025). Cryptocurrency Risk Management through Decision Engineering: Evaluating XRPUSD and ADAUSD Portfolio Performance. Journal of Applied Science, Engineering, Technology, and Education, 7(1), 69–81. https://doi.org/10.35877/454RI.asci3871

Mamadiyarov, Z., Hakimov, H., & Askarov, S. (2024). DEVELOPMENT OF RETAIL BANKING SERVICES IN THE CONTEXT OF DIGITAL TRANSFORMATION. Financial and Credit Activity Problems of Theory and Practice, 1(54), 51–67. https://doi.org/10.55643/fcaptp.1.54.2024.4288

Mamadiyarov, Z. Makhmudov, S. Utanov, B. Kasimova, D. Bekmurodova, G. Hakimov, Z. (2025). Fusion of Economic and Financial Factors Affecting Household Deposits in Banks: An Econometric Analysis. Fusion: Practice and Applications, (), 82–91. DOI: https://doi.org/10.54216/FPA.190206

Muniswamy, N., & Palanisamy, P. (2024). Intelligent procurement scheduling system for items involving public procurement. *Applied System Innovation*, 7(5), 81.

Nazirjon, R., Kurbonov, K., Jakhongir, S., Ibodullo, K., Marguba, A., & Gulshoda, Q. (2023, December). Econometric analysis of economic and ecological aspects of sustainable development of regions in terms of digital economy. In *International Conference on Next Generation Wired/Wireless Networking* (pp. 152–165). Cham: Springer Nature Switzerland.

PANJAITAN, M. B., HAMDANAH, H., SIRAIT, J., SUTIKNO, S., FATMAWATI, E., HERMAN, H., & MAMADIYAROV, Z. (2025). THE ROLE OF EMOTIONAL REGULATION IN SHAPING STUDENTS' PERCEPTION OF PHYSICS PROBLEMSOLVING TASKS. TPM – Testing, Psychometrics, Methodology in Applied Psychology, 32(S2(2025): Posted 09 June), 1–10. Retrieved from https://tpmap.org/submission/index.php/tpm/article/view/139

Patel, N., Patel, M., & Patel, R.B. (2020). Electrical energy demand forecasting using time series approach. *International Journal of Technology and Globalisation*, *29*(3s), 594–604.

Samariddin Makhmudov, Kudratillo Tukhsanov, Saifulla Arslanbekov, Akram Amanov, Orifali Tursunov, Umarbek Jabbarov and Muyassarxon Mirzakarimova. 2024. Optimizing Supply Chain Financing Development Prospects of Digital Ecosystems in the European Logistics Industry. In The 8th International Conference on Future Networks & Distributed Systems (ICFNDS '24), December 11–12, 2024, Marakech, Morocco. ACM, New York, NY, USA, 12 Pages. https://doi.org/10.1145/3726122.3726200

Sharipov, K., Abdullayev, I., Kuziboev, B., Makhmudov, S., Kalandarov, F., Khaytboeva, N., & Ilkhamova, Z. (2025). The Effect of Energy Policy Risk on Renewable Energy. International Journal of Energy Economics and Policy, *15*(2), 566.

Singh, S., Parmar, K. S., Kumar, J., & Makkhan, S. J. S. (2020). Development of new hybrid model of discrete wavelet decomposition and autoregressive integrated moving average (ARIMA) models in application to one month forecast the casualty's cases of COVID-19. *Chaos, Solitons & Fractals*, *135*, 109866.

Valipour, M., Banihabib, M. E., & Behbahani, S. M. R. (2013). Comparison of the ARMA, ARIMA, and the autoregressive artificial neural network models in forecasting the monthly inflow of Dez dam reservoir. *Journal of Hydrology*, *476*, 433–441.

Yadav, D.K., Soumya, K., & Goswami, L. (2024, January). Autoregressive integrated moving average model for time series analysis. In *2024 International Conference on Optimization Computing and Wireless Communication (ICOCWC)* (pp. 1–6). IEEE.

Yin, Y., Gulzar, F., Mamadiyarov, Z., Aizhan, A., Yadav, R. S., & Chen, C. (2024). An analysis of the rebound impact of energy consumption and the factors that influence it in China's agricultural productivity. Energy Strategy Reviews, 56, 101585.

Zhang, L., Zhao, Z., Qamri, G. M., & Makhmudov, S. (2025). Unleashing the critical role of renewable energy through global value chains and digitalization: A path towards environmental sustainability. Journal of Environmental Management, 392, 126688.

Zhuravka, F. O., Filatova, H. P., & Aiyedogbon, J. O. (2019). Government debt forecasting based on the ARIMA model. *Public and Municipal Finance*, 8(1), 120–127. <https://doi.org/10.21511/pmf. 08(1).2019.11>

Zokir Toshtemirovich Mamadiyarov. 2022. Risk Management in the Remote Provision of Banking Services in the Conditions of Digital Transformation of Banks. In Proceedings of the 5th International Conference on Future Networks and Distributed Systems (ICFNDS '21). Association for Computing Machinery, New York, NY, USA, 311–317. https://doi.org/10.1145/3508072.3508119

Zokir Toshtemirovich Mamadiyarov, Samandarboy Adhambek ugli Sulaymanov, Sarvar Anvar ugli Askarov, and Durdona Bakhtiyor kizi Uktamova. 2022. Impact of Covid-19 Pandemic on Accelerating the Digitization and Transformation of Banks. In Proceedings of the 5th International Conference on Future Networks and Distributed Systems (ICFNDS '21). Association for Computing Machinery, New York, NY, USA, 706–712. https://doi.org/10.1145/3508072.3508211

Forecasting and Evaluating Public Procurement through Auctions and Electronic Bidding in Budget Organizations Based on an Econometric Model

Mansur Eshov, Jamshid Pardaev, Zokir Mamadiyarov, Raya Karlibaeva, Samariddin Makhmudov, Shahnoza Sunatullayeva, and Nozila Toxtayeva

6.1. Introduction

In recent years, the reforms implemented in the budget and tax system in Uzbekistan have become one of the most important issues at the state policy level, in particular, the establishment and strengthening of strict control over the targeted spending of budget funds, ensuring the openness and transparency of this process. In particular, it is necessary to prevent various illegal actions that occur in the process of using budget funds, in turn, "... it is necessary to further improve the system of effective use of budget funds, any program or project for which funds are allocated from the budget should have result-oriented indicators consisting of qualitative and quantitative indicators." Improving the process of state and corporate procurement in accordance with today's requirements remains one of the urgent issues. Today, state and corporate procurement serves as an important factor in the socio-economic development of the country, by providing recipients of funds from state organizations, the state budget, and state trust funds with necessary and affordable goods and services in a timely manner. Because the sphere of public procurement is of great importance in the development of the economy of each state. These issues determine the relevance and scientific and practical significance of the chosen topic.

Innovative development of the country's economy and socio-economic reforms are the demands of the present day. A number of measures are being implemented in our country to improve the sphere of public procurement and adapt it to the requirements of the present, including the adoption of the Law of the Republic of Uzbekistan "On Public Procurement" on April 9, 2018. The main purpose of the Law "On Public Procurement" is to regulate relations in the sphere of public procurement. As is known, the role of the public sector in ensuring the socio-economic development of our country is of great importance. For its continuous and effective operation, it is necessary to provide it with the relevant goods, services, and works in a timely manner. Public procurement serves as an important factor for this purpose. The electronic form of public procurement can include procurement methods implemented using information and communication technologies through a software and technical complex of a special information portal, such as an electronic store and an auction held to reduce the initial price.

In world practice, many studies are being conducted on public procurement, and in the studies, special attention is paid to public procurement in developing countries, as in developed countries. The research serves to ensure a properly and effectively organized public procurement and a competitive market for local manufacturers. The ongoing research focuses on analyzing the regulatory and legal framework regulating the procurement process in the medical sector. The relevance of the research work is determined by the issues of further reforming the public procurement system through auctions and electronic bidding in budgetary organizations, increasing the efficiency of procurement through the introduction of innovative technologies and advanced foreign experience.

6.2. Literature Review and Development Hypothesis

The ARIMA model is considered one of the most effective forecasting models for forecasting and evaluating public procurement through auctions and electronic auctions in budget organizations. The ARIMA model helps to forecast taking into account the dynamics of changes in tender processes and the role of electronic systems in increasing competition and procurement efficiency. The integration of this econometric analysis with the processes of organizing auctions and electronic auctions is of great importance in optimizing the procurement strategy of budget organizations.

In the econometric models used in Turkey on the application of econometric models in public procurement, it was found that the number of participants has a significant impact on procurement prices. A large number of participants in the auction usually leads to a reduction in procurement costs, which creates a more competitive environment (Onur et al., 2012; Tas, 2014).

Such econometric analyses are important in forecasting future procurement, determining optimal procurement prices for bidders for different types of products, and conducting various scientific studies.

Cost savings can be achieved by using electronic reverse auctions (e-RA) and electronic procurement systems to increase efficiency, transparency, and speed in electronic bidding and auctions. However, the success of e-RA is more related to factors such as competition among suppliers and the complexity of the procurement process than to the number of bidders (Shalev & Asbjornsen, 2010). This suggests that electronic systems can improve the competitive environment and increase the efficiency of procurement. Studies in Slovakia and the Czech Republic show that by increasing the number of bids submitted in electronic auctions, price reductions can be achieved, which in turn increases competition (Pavel & Kubík, 2011; Pavel & Sičáková-Beblavá, 2013). Cost reductions will certainly encourage more bidders, which is a matter of transparency and accessibility of electronic platforms.

The use of game theory models in public procurement, particularly through auctions and electronic bidding within budget organizations, examines how bidders behave during the bidding process. The purpose is to determine bid prices while factoring in expected profits and transaction costs (Schmidt, 2016). These models offer valuable insights into auction dynamics, enabling procurement processes to be structured more efficiently.

To improve public procurement through auctions and e-commerce in government organizations, it is necessary to focus on increasing the efficiency of public procurement, ensuring transparency, and improving the competitive environment:

First, to improve public procurement through auctions and e-commerce in government organizations, it is necessary to introduce electronic market mechanisms into the sector. Gupta et al. (2017) conducted studies on the acceptance of electronic market mechanisms by users in their research and created the Continuous Combinatorial Auctions (CoCoA) project. This project created an interconnected trading system environment and achieved an increase in the number of users by providing customized systems to users. As a result, providing customized systems to users increased the level of acceptance of even complex mechanisms.

Second, it is necessary to create a high-speed auction market project. As Gupta et al. (2016) mentioned in their study, the project "Designing a New

Generation of High-Speed Auction Markets" focuses on creating modern IT tools to improve fast decision-making in fast and information-rich B2B auction markets. They worked with flower auctions in the Netherlands to develop a decision support system that allowed them to optimize auction parameters in real-time. This system helped auctioneers make more money in different market conditions and better secure transactions.

Third, it is necessary to increase user activity in electronic auction markets. Bapna et al. (2019) studied user activity in electronic auction markets and examined how different user behaviors affect market design. Their research is very important in segmenting users and optimizing them with market mechanisms (Abdullah et al., 2025; Bapna et al., 2019; Matyakubova et al., 2025; Muhammad et al., 2025; Romero et al., 2025; Zhao et al., 2025).

Fourth, it is shown that to increase the efficiency of public procurement, it is possible to increase transparency, strengthen competition, and ensure the effective use of budget funds by introducing electronic trading in public procurement. For example, in developed European countries, public procurement accounts for 15–20 percent of GDP, which allows for achieving significant savings through electronic trading.

Analyses and forecasts have been conducted using various econometric models on energy policy, energy risk, environmental conditions, the impact of environmental factors on the digital economy, factors affecting agricultural efficiency, and the stability of the U.S. credit market (Akhmetshin et al., 2025; Cahyani et al., 2025; Inglesi-Lotz et al., 2024; Kuchkarov et al., 2025; Kuziboev et al., 2025; Sharipov et al., 2025).

A group of local economists has effectively utilized econometric models in research on the impact of inflation and credit interest rates on investment, factors influencing the reduction of state shares in commercial banks, digitalization of banks, risks in digital services, and the development of retail banking services (Litamahuputty et al., 2025; Mamadiyarov et al., 2024; PANJAITAN et al., Samariddin et al., 2024; 2025; Zhang et al., 2025; Zokir, 2021; Zokir et al., 2021).

According to Gallego et al. (2021) "With the widespread adoption of e-procurement systems in public institutions, anti-corruption agencies and monitoring organizations have access to valuable information sources that can help identify potentially problematic practices." The authors' research findings suggest that transparency has become essential in curbing negative outcomes in public procurement, such as irregularities, breach of contract, and general inefficiency. Web-based platforms for recording and reporting public transactions have become popular in both developed and developing countries, allowing anti-corruption agencies, monitoring organizations, and citizens to closely monitor the processes and decisions to purchase goods and services.

Nikolopoulos et al. (2021) "explore the urgent and extraordinary nature of the projected increase in public procurement during the COVID-19 pandemic and model short-term supply chain disruptions." The authors conclude that forecasting based on econometric models is essential for many important decisions by governments during emergency medical care, both for supply chain and prevention strategies. Also, since forecasting is an important part of many decision-making processes, research based on econometric equations using this type of statistical method is important (Jahrir et al., 2025; Lin et al., 2025; Mamani et al., 2025; Nikolopoulos et al., 2021; Pradhan et al., 2025).

Astolf et al. (2012) "As the continuous increase in costs puts pressure on government budget allocation, health care delivery, and patients' finances, governments have begun to implement projects using forecasting, especially statistical methods, to support budget planning."

6.3. Research Methodology

The econometric forecast developed forecast indicators for public procurement through auctions and electronic bidding in budget organizations for 2025–2029 based on the ARIMA model.

6.3.1. Developing Forecast Indicators

In developing forecast indicators according to the econometric model, the number of contracts concluded through public procurement auctions and electronic stores, consisting of 33 observations from the quarterly data of the "Uzbekistan Republican Commodity and Raw Materials Exchange" JSC (<https://xarid.uzex.uz>) for 2015–2024, was used. The resulting variable according to the econometric forecast is shown below. The dependent variable in the model is the number of contracts concluded through public procurement auctions and electronic stores—*auc_elect_contr.*

6.3.2. Methods

The general form of the selected ARIMA (*p*, *d*, *q*) model is as follows:

$$y_t = \mathrm{a} + \beta_1 y_{t-1} + \beta_2 y_{t-2} + \ldots + \beta_p y_{t-l} + \mu_1 \epsilon_{t-1} + \mu_2 \epsilon_{t-2} + \ldots + \mu_q \epsilon_{t-l} + \epsilon_t \qquad (1)$$

According to the above formula,

y_t where t is the value of the time series at time t (after being differentiated d times),
a represents the constant term,
β_t = (for $t = 1, 2, \ldots, l$) represents the coefficients of the autoregressive part,
μ_q = (for p=1, 2, …, q) represents the coefficients of the moving average part.
ϵ_t, where t represents the error term (white noise) at time t.

6.4. Analysis and Results

The dependent variable in the model is the number of contracts concluded through public procurement auctions and electronic stores—*auc_elect_contr.* At the initial stage of forecasting according to the econometric model, an analytical graphical plot of the dependent variable is presented (Figure 18).

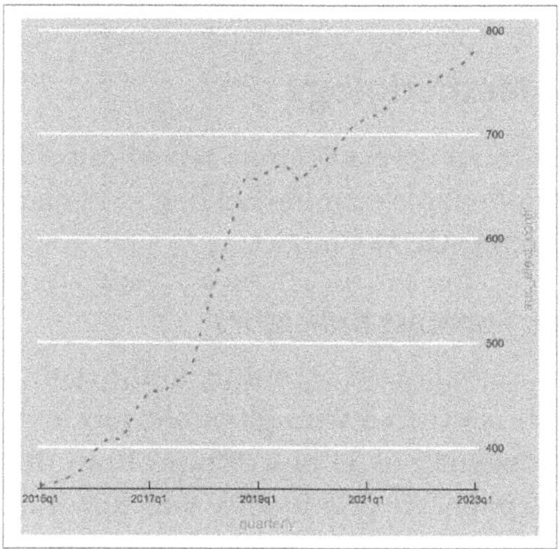

Figure 18. Graphical representation of the number of contracts concluded through public procurement auctions and electronic stores over time.

Source: It was developed by the authors based on Stata software.

Figure 18 shows that the volume of public procurements financed through auctions has been growing steadily since 2018, and this growth rate continues to this day. This trend is due to the recent legal framework developed by the government for public procurements financed through auctions.

In the next stage of the econometric model, the stationarity level of the number of contracts concluded through auctions and e-shops was assessed, and the Unit-Root test was used to determine it (Table 18).

Table 18. Unit-Root test of the number of contracts concluded through public procurement auctions and electronic stores

auc_ elect_ contr	*Test Statistic*	*1% Critical Value*	*5% Critical Value*	*10% Critical Value*	*p-value for Z(t)*
	-7.273	-3.716	-2.986	-2.624	0.0000

Source: It was developed by the authors based on Stata software.

According to Table 18, the test statistical value of the resulting factor is –7.273, which indicates a significant indicator in the stable growth of the number of contracts concluded in exchange practices through public procurement auctions and electronic stores in periodic cyclical, seasonal exchange trading practices. According to it, it can be seen that the statistical value is significant and is below the limits of 1%, 5%, and 10%. In addition, the McKinnon value is minimal with $Z(t) = 0.0000$, which indicates that the number of contracts concluded in exchange practices through public procurement auctions and electronic stores is stationary.

According to the econometric model, it can be seen that the parameter d of the ARIMA model has a value of $d = 1$ and the time series has reached stationarity after one differentiation.

The next step is to calculate the value of p, which determines the indirect correlation between the lags of the time series of the resulting variable according to the econometric equation (Figure 19).

As shown in Figure 19 earlier, all lags except for two lags have confidence intervals in the indirect correlation analysis. Also, most lags are statistically significant and form confidence intervals. The clear positive autocorrelation observed in the model suggests medium-term relationships. Increases in certain lags suggest the potential for seasonal and

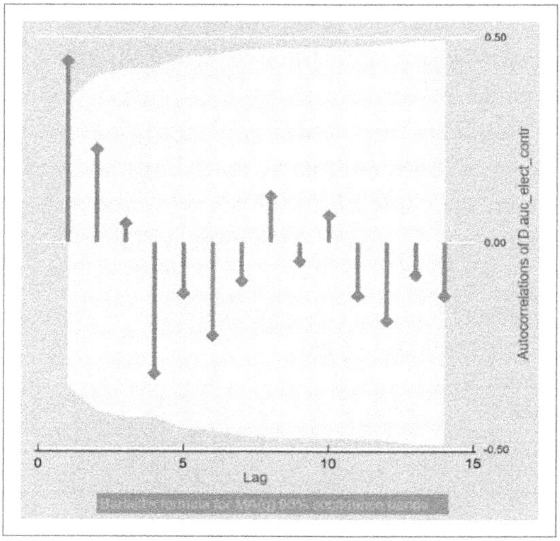

Figure 19. Indirect correlation graph between the lags of the number of contracts concluded through public procurement auctions and electronic stores.
Source: It was developed by the authors based on Stata software.

cyclical components. It is appropriate to use data with a *p*-value of 1 or 2, as shown in Figure 19.

The next step in the ARIMA model is to determine the value of *q*, which describes the direct correlation between the lags of the model (Figure 20). According to the data in Figure 20, all lags, except for one lag, which formed a strong correlation between the lags in the ARIMA model, are within the specified confidence interval. Potential seasonal adjustments in the econometric model provide promising positive forecast indicators based on the ARIMA model.

In accordance with the purpose of choosing a value for the moving average parameter *q* in the ARIMA model. Since the observed data in the study are suitable for values from 0 to 1 and record confidence intervals, it is recommended to choose a value of "*q*" in this range.

In the next step, the ARIMA model is used to estimate the spectral density of the resulting variable, which is reflected in the periodogram graph (Figure 21).

Figure 21 shows a graphically well-defined spectral density function of the outcome variable, which facilitates the identification of the most important

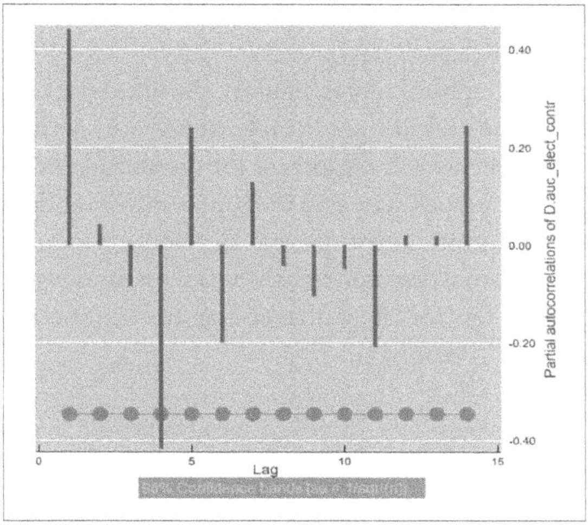

Figure 20. Direct correlation graph between the lags of the number of contracts concluded through public procurement auctions and electronic stores.

Source: It was developed by the authors based on Stata software.

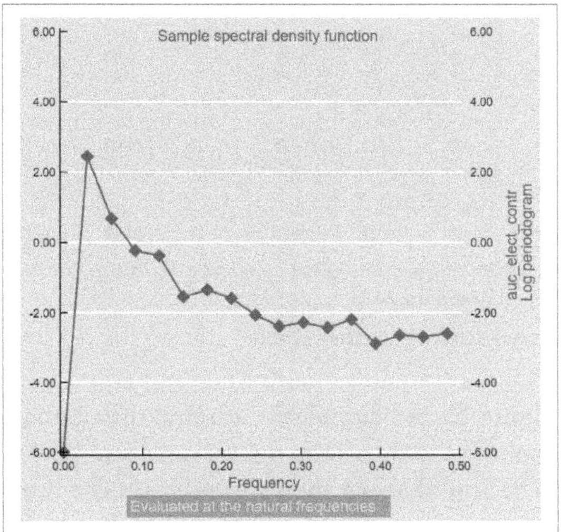

Figure 21. Periodogram graph for estimating the spectral density of the resulting variable.

Source: It was developed by the authors based on Stata software.

frequencies. This accuracy demonstrates reliable conclusions about the periodic and systematic behavior of the data.

According to the graphical representation, the time series are concentrated at low frequencies and exhibit predictable trends and periodic recurrence. Stability at high frequencies is important for the analysis and forecasting of these series, creating a shock state and the limitation of random fluctuations. In the next step, the cumulative spectral distribution periodogram of the outcome variable in the estimation of time series for econometric forecasting and the white noise test for the constant and average variance of the time series were evaluated (Figure 22).

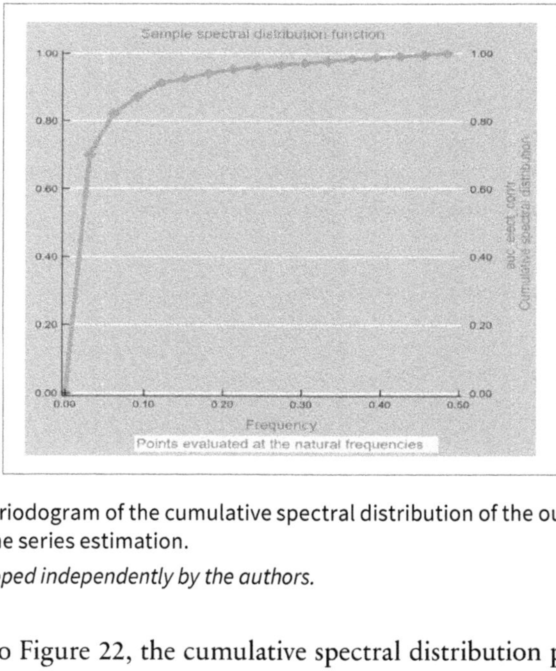

Figure 22. Periodogram of the cumulative spectral distribution of the outcome variable in time series estimation.

Source: Developed independently by the authors.

According to Figure 22, the cumulative spectral distribution periodogram is a graphical tool used to distribute the variance and power of time series by frequency. The initial sharp increase indicates the dominance of the low-frequency components of the time series according to the econometric model. This shows that it provides a diagnostic tool for the model and an important forecast for refining econometric models, while ensuring that the spectral characteristics of the positive factor are consistent.

When selecting the optimal invariant ARIMA models for forecasting the model, the ARIMA(0,1,1), ARIMA(1,1,1), ARIMA(1,1,2), ARIMA(1,0,2), ARIMA(2,0,1), and ARIMA(2,1,1) models were analyzed. Among them, the ARIMA(2,1,1) model with the best results was selected (Table 19). Based on the ARIMA model regression result, the econometric equation for the model is given below.

$$y_t = \beta + \delta_1 y_{t-1} + \delta_2 y_{t-2} + \dots + \mu_1 \varepsilon_{t-1} + \mu_2 \varepsilon_{t-2} + \varepsilon_t \quad (3)$$

Table 19. Econometric equation indicators of the ARIMA(2,1,1) model by the number of contracts concluded through public procurement auctions and electronic stores

D.auc_elect_ contr	Coef.	St. Err.	t-value	p-value	[95% Conf	Interval]	Sig
Constant	13.854	2.604	5.32	0	8.751	18.958	***
L	1.368	.114	12.01	0	1.145	1.592	***
L2	-.486	.134	-3.62	0	-.75	-.223	***
L	-1	.329	-3.04	.002	-1.645	-.355	***
Constant	12.455	.	.	.	.	.	
Mean dependent var	13.056	SD dependent var				151.011	
Number of obs.	32	Chi-square				251.829	
Prob > chi²	.	Akaike crit. (AIC)				262.055	

*** *p*<0.01, ** *p*<0.05, * *p*<0.1

Source: It was developed by the authors based on Stata software.

According to Table 19, the ARIMA(2,1,1) model has the following form.

$$D.auc\_elect\_contr = 13.85 + 1.36auc\_elect\_contr_{t-1} - 0.4836auc\_elect\_contr_{t-2} - 0.96\varepsilon_{t-1} + \varepsilon_t \quad (4)$$

In the next step, the ARIMA(2,1,1) model was developed to analyze the mean values of the outcome variable and the graphical representation of the residuals. According to the ARIMA(2,1,1) model has reached stochastic equilibrium. The ARIMA model was applied to the data to identify the main stochastic relationships in the data set.

Using the Stata program, a forecast indicator was developed for the number of contracts concluded through public procurement auctions and electronic stores from 2025 to 2029, excluding random factors, using the ARIMA(2,1,1) model (Table 20).

Table 20. Number of contracts concluded through public procurement auctions and electronic stores, 2025–2029

Years	Pessimistic forecast	Optimistic forecast	Forecast
2025	945,929	976,529	961,229
2026	1,001,795	1,032,395	1,017,095
2027	1,057,180	1,087,780	1,072,480
2028	1,157,560	1,188,160	1,172,860
2029	945,929	1,198,567	1,183,267

Source: It was developed by the authors based on Stata software.

The study presents a graphical representation of the forecast indicator of the number of contracts concluded through public procurement auctions and electronic stores for 2015–2024 and 2025–2029, provided by the "Uzbekistan Republican Commodity Exchange."

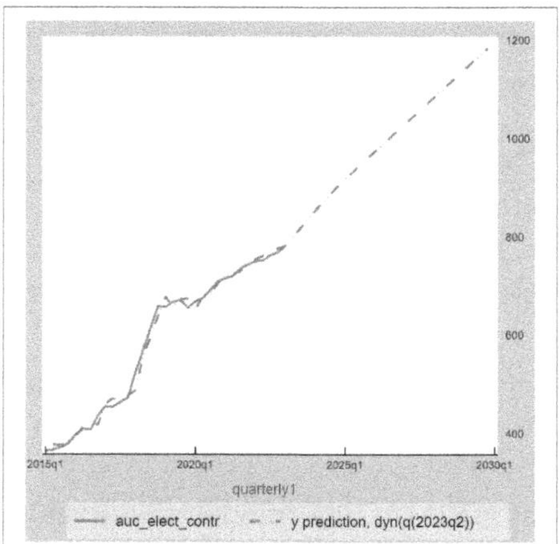

Figure 23. Graph of the dependent variable for 2015–2024 and the forecast for 2025–2029.

Source: It was developed by the authors based on Stata software.

Figure 23 shows the number of contracts concluded through public procurement auctions and electronic stores for the years 2015–2024 and 2025–2029, as well as the forecast graphs. According to it, the direction graph indicates the reliability of the forecast indicators for the coming years, excluding random factors, since the two lines are located almost side by side.

6.5. Findings and Discussion

The study analyzed the forecast indicators for the number of contracts concluded through public procurement auctions and electronic stores for 2015–2024 and for 2025–2029 as follows. The study showed that the forecast results based on the ARIMA(2,1,1) model showed positive and optimistic forecast indicators in the public procurement system for 2025–2029.

According to the results of the study, based on the ARIMA(2,1,1) model, the number of contracts concluded through public procurement auctions and electronic stores in 2025–2029, excluding random exogenous and endogenous factors, was projected to be 961,229 in 2025, 1,017,095 in 2026, 1,072,480 in 2027, 1,172,860 in 2028, and 1,183,267 in 2029, respectively.

6.6. Conclusion

6.6.1. The Emergence of a Steady Growth Trend in the Procurement System

The increase in the number of contracts from 961,229 in 2025 to 1,183,267 in 2029 indicates a steady growth in the public procurement system. This positive trend is of great importance in the implementation of efficient and transparent transactions after contracts through auctions and electronic stores in the procurement practice.

6.6.2. Trends in the Development of Convenience and Acceptance Processes in the Procurement Practice

A significant increase in the number of contracts indicates the increasing popularity of electronic procurement platforms and their widespread use by participants. This practice represents a positive step towards the transformation of digital mobility, reliability, and success in the procurement practice.

6.6.3. Assessment of the Reliability of the Forecasted Econometric Model

The clear and highly dynamic trajectory of the number of contracts of the ARIMA(2,1,1) model demonstrates the reliability of this model as a forecasting tool. This is of great importance for the government in planning public expenditures and in decision-making by stakeholders.

6.6.4. Increasing the Importance of a Strong Institutional Legal Framework

The strong growth reflects the strength and stability of public procurement practices, which allows for an expansion of the number of contracts and at the same time serves to ensure fair competition, transparency and openness.

6.6.5. Success of Reforms Being Undertaken by the Government

The increasing number of contracts in the procurement system demonstrates the government's successful work in this area, as well as reforms aimed at optimizing the sector, promoting electronic platforms, and minimizing barriers to participation in digital transactions.

6.6.6. Assessment of Future Opportunities for Optimization

With the forecast indicating stable growth in the economic system, further improving the e-procurement system, improving the user experience and expanding the range of goods and services offered through these platforms will further increase the opportunity.

6.7. Recommendations

The authors formulated the following scientific proposals for the economically efficient organization and forecasting of public procurement through auctions and electronic trading:

6.7.1. Using Machine Learning and Artificial Intelligence (AI) Approaches

In future studies, it is necessary to use Neural Networks (Artificial Neural Networks) in-depth analysis and forecasting processes of large volumes of procurement data to accurately forecast future trends in procurement using

Random Forest and Gradient Boosting models. In particular, it is considered very effective in identifying corruption risks in public procurement through clustering and anomaly detection methods.

6.7.2. Developing Indicators to Improve the Efficiency of Public Procurement

To increase the transparency and efficiency of public procurement processes, it is necessary to develop performance-based procurement metrics, and to conduct research on the widespread use of Cost–Benefit Analysis and Economic Impact Analysis methods to measure the impact of the procurement system.

6.7.3. Introducing Blockchain Technology to Public Procurement

To reduce illegal transactions in the procurement process and increase transparency, it is necessary to widely use blockchain-based contract automation and smart contracts. Using Distributed Ledger Technology to monitor public procurement processes in real time, and maintaining procurement history using blockchain technology to improve auditing and monitoring of the procurement system, will be effective.

Bibliography

Abdullah, M. A., Han, X., Amjad, M. A., & Makhmudov, S. (2025). Revisit the role of financial development on economic growth, human development, and sustainable development in higher-income countries. *Journal of Environmental Management*, *392*, 126874.

Akhmetshin, E., Abdullayev, I., Makhmudov, S., Dakhkilgova, K., Korotaeva, I. and Yanovskaya, G. (2025). APPLICATION OF TANH–COTH METHOD FOR COMBINED AND DOUBLE COMBINED SINH–COSH–GORDON EQUATIONS ARISING CHEMICAL REACTIONS TO WATER SURFACE GRAVITY WAVES. Computational Methods for Differential Equations, (), -. doi: 10.22034/cmde.2025.67655.3234

Astolfi, R., Lorenzoni, L., & Oderkirk, J. (2012). Informing policy makers about future health spending: a comparative analysis of forecasting methods in OECD countries. *Health Policy*, *107*(1), 1–10.

Bapna, R., Goes, P., & Gupta, A. (2019). User heterogeneity and its impact on electronic auction markets. *MIS Quarterly*, *43*(2), 345–372.

Cahyani, I., Buriev, K., Ngongo, M., Mamadiyarov, Z., Ino, L., Herman, H., Saputra, N., & Baxtishodovich, S. (2025). Exploring the Use of TikTok Application in Enhancing the Skill of Pronunciation: A Case on Students' Perception. Studies in Media and Communication, 13(2), 150–158. doi:http://dx.doi.org/10.11114/smc.v13i2.7553

Gallego, J., Rivero, G., & Martínez, J. (2021). Preventing rather than punishing: An early warning model of malfeasance in public procurement. *International Journal of Forecasting*, *37*(1), 360–377.

Gupta, A., Stahl, F., & Weinhardt, C. (2016). CoCoA: A combinatorial auction framework for electronic procurement. *Decision Support Systems*, *89*, 1–11.

Gupta, A., Weinhardt, C., & Bichler, M. (2017). Next-generation high-speed auction markets: Design and decision support. *European Journal of Operational Research*, *257*(3), 839–853.

Inglesi-Lotz, R., Oosthuizen, A. M., Jumaniyazova, S., Kuziboev, B., & Liu, J. (2024). Exploring the impact of women governance on CO2 emissions in the European Union and Central Asia. *International Journal of Energy Economics and Policy*, *14*(3), 639–646.

Hussain, A., Khan, M., Rakhmonov, D. A., Mamadiyarov, Z. T., Kurbonbekova, M. T., & Mahmudova, M. Q. K. (2023). Nexus of Training and Development, Organizational Learning Capability, and Organizational Performance in the Service Sector. Sustainability, 15(4), 3246. https://doi.org/10.3390/su15043246

Jahrir, A., Gultom, Y., Herman, H., Zabadi, F., Ngongo, M., Mamadiyarov, Z., Fatmawati, E., & Saputra, N. (2025). Investigating the Elements of Short Commercial Mineral Water Advertisement: A Case on Discourse Analysis. Studies in Media and Communication, 13(4), 94–104. doi:http://dx.doi.org/10.11114/smc.v13i4.7813

Kuchkarov, T., Mamadiyarov, Z., Khakimov, Z., Sabirova, O., Matmurodov, K., Raimboyeva, M., & Umarova, S. (2025). Energy-Related Uncertainty and Crypto-Currency Environmental Attention: Time-Varying Perspective. International Journal of Energy Economics and Policy, 15(5), 614–626. https://doi.org/10.32479/ijeep.20784

Kurbonov, K. (2025). Quantitative easing and its long-term effects on US credit market sustainability: A neutrosophic science perspective. *International Journal of Neutrosophic Science (IJNS)*, *25*(3).

Kuziboev, B., Khodjaniyazov, E., Ozturk, I., Sabirov, K., Makhmudov, S., & Utegenova, S. (2025). Does oil dependence cause energy risk?. Energy Nexus, 17, 100393.

Lin, M.H., Matchanova, B., Nurmatovich, H.A. *et al.* Optimal Operation of the Multi-Carrier Energy System Considering Energy Markets and Renewable Energies Participation. *Int. J. Appl. Comput. Math* **11**, 170 (2025). https://doi.org/10.1007/s40819-025-02002-9

Litamahuputty, J. V., Amiruddin, E. G., Rahim, R., Rahman, A., & Mamadiyarov, Z. (2025). Cryptocurrency Risk Management through Decision Engineering: Evaluating XRPUSD and ADAUSD Portfolio Performance. Journal of Applied Science, Engineering, Technology, and Education, 7(1), 69–81. https://doi.org/10.35877/454RI.asci3871

Mamadiyarov, Z., Hakimov, H., & Askarov, S. (2024). DEVELOPMENT OF RETAIL BANKING SERVICES IN THE CONTEXT OF DIGITAL TRANSFORMATION. Financial and Credit Activity Problems of Theory and Practice, 1(54), 51–67. https://doi.org/10.55643/fcaptp.1.54.2024.4288

Mamadiyarov, Z. Makhmudov, S. Utanov, B. Kasimova, D. Bekmurodova, G. Hakimov, Z. (2025). Fusion of Economic and Financial Factors Affecting Household Deposits in Banks: An Econometric Analysis. Fusion: Practice and Applications, (), 82–91. DOI: https://doi.org/10.54216/FPA.190206

Mamani, J.C.M., Miri, M., Vorobev, Y. et al. Optimal Operation of Energy Microgrid Considering Economic and Emission Indices. Oper. Res. Forum 6, 122 (2025). https://doi.org/10.1007/s43069-025-00523-z

Matyakubova, A., Makhmudov, S., Ozturk, I., Kurbonov, K., Ismailov, F., Yokubboeva, S., & Urozov, A. (2025). Responses of Economic Policy Uncertainty, Financial Stress and Energy-Related Uncertainty to the Shocks in US-China Tension in US. *International Journal of Energy Economics and Policy*, *15*(4), 701–708. https://doi.org/10.32479/ijeep.20369

Muhammad Zubair, Irfanud Din, Nadeem Sarwar et al. Revolutionizing Sepsis Diagnosis Using Machine Learning and Deep Learning Models: A Systematic Literature Review, 10 June 2025, PREPRINT (Version 1) available at Research Square [https://doi.org/10.21203/rs.3.rs-6731418/v1]

Nikolopoulos, K., Punia, S., Schäfers, A., Tsinopoulos, C., & Vasilakis, C. (2021). Forecasting and planning during a pandemic: COVID-19 growth rates, supply chain disruptions, and governmental decisions. *European Journal of Operational Research*, *290*(1), 99–115.

PANJAITAN, M. B., HAMDANAH, H., SIRAIT, J., SUTIKNO, S., FATMAWATI, E., HERMAN, H., & MAMADIYAROV, Z. (2025). THE ROLE OF EMOTIONAL REGULATION IN SHAPING STUDENTS' PERCEPTION OF PHYSICS PROBLEMSOLVING TASKS. TPM – Testing, Psychometrics, Methodology in Applied Psychology, 32(S2(2025) : Posted 09 June), 1–10. Retrieved from https://tpmap.org/submission/index.php/tpm/article/view/139

Onur, I., Ozcan, R., & Onur Tas, B. K. (2012). Public procurement auctions and competition in Turkey. *Review of Industrial Organization*, *40*(3), 207–223. <https://doi.org/10.1007/S11151-011-9299-3>

Pavel, J., & Kubík, R. (2011). Impact of e-auctions on public procurement effectiveness. In Proceedings of the 2nd International Conference on Innovation, Management and Service, Singapore, 16–18 September 2011.

Pavel, J., & Sičáková-Beblavá, E. (2013). Do e-auctions really improve the efficiency of public procurement? The case of the Slovak municipalities. Prague Economic Papers, 22(1), 111–124.

Pradhan, R., Hajiyev, E., Shichiyakh, R. *et al.* Optimal Techno-Economic Feasibility of an Off-Grid Microgrid System Using Load Flow Energy Management Strategies. *Oper. Res. Forum* **6**, 120 (2025). https://doi.org/10.1007/s43069-025-00524-y

Romero, R. M., Zelinskaya, M., Makhmudov, S., Sapaev, S., & Rustambekovich, J. U. (2025, September). Modelling and Optimal Utilisation of the Renewable Energy Systems in Microgrid with Improving Reliability and Energy Efficiency. In Operations Research Forum (Vol. 6, No. 3, pp. 1–20). Springer International Publishing.

Schmidt, M. (2016). Stanovení nabídkových cen ve veřejných zakázkách: simulace. *Politicka Ekonomie*, *64*(5), 541–558. <https://doi.org/10.18267/J.POLEK.1087>

Shalev, M. E., & Asbjornsen, S. (2010). Electronic reverse auctions and the public sector: factors of success. *Social Science Research Network*. <https://papers.ssrn.com/sol3/papers.cfm?abstract_id=1727409>

Sharipov, K., Abdullayev, I., Kuziboev, B., Makhmudov, S., Kalandarov, F., Khaytboeva, N., & Ilkhamova, Z. (2025). The Effect of Energy Policy

Risk on Renewable Energy. International Journal of Energy Economics and Policy, 15(2), 566.

Samariddin Makhmudov, Kudratillo Tukhsanov, Saifulla Arslanbekov, Akram Amanov, Orifali Tursunov, Umarbek Jabbarov and Muyassarxon Mirzakarimova. 2024. Optimizing Supply Chain Financing Development Prospects of Digital Ecosystems in the European Logistics Industry. In The 8th International Conference on Future Networks & Distributed Systems (ICFNDS '24), December 11–12, 2024, Marakech, Morocco. ACM, New York, NY, USA, 12 Pages. https://doi.org/10.1145/3726122.3726200

Su, R., Xiao, Y., Hamza, F., Mamadiyarov, Z., & Wahab, A. (2025). Scaling up green hydrogen in China: Economic opportunities and challenges. *International Journal of Hydrogen Energy*, *131*, 60–69.

Tas, B. K. O. (2014). How to achieve efficiency in public procurement auctions. *Research Papers in Economics*. <https://ecomod.net/system/files/PPA_N_Efficiency.pdf>

Zhang, L., Zhao, Z., Qamri, G. M., & Makhmudov, S. (2025). Unleashing the critical role of renewable energy through global value chains and digitalization: A path towards environmental sustainability. Journal of Environmental Management, 392, 126688.

Zhao, Q., Pervaiz, A., Makhmudov, S., & Fatima, A. (2025). Do environmental stringent policies enhance the impact of renewable energy on CO_2 reduction? Evidence from BRICS-T economies. Journal of Environmental Management, 391, 126464.

Zokir Toshtemirovich Mamadiyarov. 2022. Risk Management in the Remote Provision of Banking Services in the Conditions of Digital Transformation of Banks. In Proceedings of the 5th International Conference on Future Networks and Distributed Systems (ICFNDS '21). Association for Computing Machinery, New York, NY, USA, 311–317. https://doi.org/10.1145/3508072.3508119

Zokir Toshtemirovich Mamadiyarov, Samandarboy Adhambek ugli Sulaymanov, Sarvar Anvar ugli Askarov, and Durdona Bakhtiyor kizi Uktamova. 2022. Impact of Covid-19 Pandemic on Accelerating the Digitization and Transformation of Banks. In Proceedings of the 5th International Conference on Future Networks and Distributed Systems (ICFNDS '21). Association for Computing Machinery, New York, NY, USA, 706–712. https://doi.org/10.1145/3508072.3508211

Wallet or Won't It? Helping Merchants Discover the Value of M-Payments

Sabrina Leo and Ida Claudia Panetta

7.1. Merchants' Role in the Mobile Wallet Ecosystem

In the M-wallet ecosystem, consumers and merchants are the two groups that need to be "convinced" to use this service. Both are important to demand in a two-sided market, but they have partially different but complementary preferences when it comes to the payment system (Panetta & Leo, 2017, 2022).

On the merchant's side, general expectations can be identified regarding the transaction's speed, certainty, and low cost, as well as, indirectly, customer satisfaction (in terms of process speed, simplicity, and transparency, as well as safety). Merchants are willing to accept this payment method if it is commonly used among consumers, as they would not invest in adding in-store technology unless there is a significant demand for it (Leo & Panetta, 2019).

In the context of the M-wallet ecosystem, users and merchants establish a different relationship with the supply-side operators. Within this sector, roles are not always clearly defined and uniquely identifiable. In particular, the merchant can play several roles, including:

- wallet acceptor, an entity that accepts payments from an M-wallet;
- wallet issuer or service provider, an entity that provides payment from an M-wallet;
- Technology providers, such as some M-device manufacturers, fall into this category.

The merchant, therefore, is one of the leading players in the M-wallet ecosystem: the "weight" the merchant can take is the result of a complex evaluation process. Depending on the choices made, the merchant can either simply meet the demand for payment services (wallet acceptor) or actively help package the offer of M-wallets (i.e., wallet issuer). This means that the merchant can either accept payments through wallets offered by others or give users their own wallet. The attributes of the rival proposal and technological advancement must be prominent to favor one solution over the other, among other factors. Wallet offerings evolve swiftly across different contexts; at times, merchants may need to implement multiple solutions concurrently based on the geographical location of their customers. Moreover, mobile technologies are distinguished by a significant rate of innovation and may necessitate ongoing updates, which can be costly.

7.2. Factors Influencing Merchants' Decisions: A Review of Literature

Although there are various studies from the customer standpoint (Cruz-Cárdenas et al., 2021; Hassan & Wood, 2020; Liébana-Cabanillas et al., 2014; Liu et al., 2019; Panetta et al., 2021, 2025), most articles that assume an ecosystem perception focus on M-payment providers, such as Mobile Network Operators (MNOs) or banks (Gaur & Ondrus, 2012), while not much attention is paid to the role of merchants in the M-payment ecosystem. The current literature on the "merchant point of view" can be categorized into three primary strands: the first addresses the merchants' behavioral intentions regarding the adoption of new technology; the second examines factors influencing merchant attitudes towards mobile payments; and the final strand concentrates on the benefits and value enhancements resulting from the utilization of mobile wallet services. In the sections that follow, we explore these three main strands.

7.2.1. Behavioral Intention

Most existing M-wallet structures combine old and new technologies, marked by the interaction of hardware and software. To these two components, the element "communication" must be added. The basis of mobile technologies is the connection between wireless devices, which can only be achieved if there is a shared language and structure for data and information transfers.

The extent of development and dissemination of individual technologies across different markets, including geographic factors, as well as the financial and digital literacy of users and merchants, significantly influences behavioral intentions regarding the adoption of new technology. As demonstrated by Plouffe et al. (2001), merchants who use QR codes, cloud technology, and quick response codes and who have been disappointed with card service processes are more inclined to M-wallet technologies.

Studies on merchants' behavioral intention for adopting a new technology began in 2007–2009 (Brown & Dant, 2008a; 2008b; Grewal & Levy, 2007; Grewal et al., 2009). These studies provide valuable insights into technology adoption behavior, showing that globally, 20 percent increased their investment in mobile payments and M-wallets, and only for payment transactions in restaurants, fast food, or service stations (Mallat & Tuunainen, 2008). Grewal et al. (2009) discovered that the widespread adoption and acceptance of M-payment were sluggish and did not rise as anticipated, attributed to the critical nature of the M-payment process and inadequate infrastructure support. The issues of intention and acceptance regarding new mobile payment technology have been extensively studied (Li, 2018; Liébana Cabanillas et al., 2016, 2018; Mallat & Tuunainen, 2008) utilizing various frameworks and conceptual models, including the Technology Acceptance Model (TAM), Innovation Diffusion Theory (IDT), Theory of Planned Behavior, Unified Theory of Acceptance and Use of Technology (UTAUT), and social cognitive theory (Dahlberg et al., 2008; Ondrus et al., 2009; Venkatesh et al., 2012). These conceptual models found that compatibility and ease of use are the most influential variables, followed by perceived trust and risk (Dahlberg et al., 2015). The application of the models highlights the gap in identifying merchants' expectations of technology and factors contributing to technology acceptance and usage (Duarte et al., 2018). The variables that explain merchants' adoption of technology, as discussed in the literature, are presented in Table 21.

7.2.2. Merchants' Adoption of M-Payment

In the last decades, only a few papers have focused on adopting M-payment from the merchant's point of view. The papers examined the initial successful implementation of M-payment systems (Van der Heijden, 2002), the analysis of factors influencing merchant adoption of M-payment (Mallat & Tuunainen, 2005, 2008; Teo et al., 2005), and a comprehensive overview of the fundamental concepts elucidating retail merchant adoption (Lai & Chuah, 2010). Most of these papers used qualitative methods due to the newness of the issue and the lack of previous research based on IDT theory (Rogers, 1995). Table 22 presents a summary of the studies on merchants' adoption of M-payment.

Table 21. Behavioral intention to use new technology: Evidence from the literature

Variables	Literature
Usefulness	Ondrus and Pigneur (2006); Chen and Chen (2010); Liébana-Cabanillas et al. (2016); Liébana-Cabanillas et al. (2017); Możdżyński (2018
User/Merchant knowledge	Mallat and Tuunainen (2018); Liébana-Cabanillas et al. (2016); Liébana-Cabanillas et a1. (2017)
Trust	Hayashi and Bradford (2014); Liébana-Cabanillas et al. (2016); Liébana-Cabanillas et al. (2017)
Security	Liébana-Cabanillas et a1. (2017); Li (2018)
Technological/Infrastructural drivers and barriers	Mallat and Tuunainen (2008); Hayashi and Bradford (2014); Liébana Cabanillas et al. (2016); Liébana-Cabanillas et al. (2017); Li (2018)
Performance expectancy	Liébana-Cabanillas et al. (2017); Możdżyński (2018)
Costs	Mallat and Tuunainen (2008); Ondnis and Pigneur (2009); Chen and Chen (2010); Hayashi and Bradford (2014); Li (2018)
Value-added/Convenience	Mallat and Tuunainen (2008); Ondrus and Pigneur (2009); Chen and Chen (2010); Hayashi and Bradford (2014); Liébana-Cabanillas et al. (2017); Możdżyński (2018); Li (2018)
Social influence	Li (2018); Możdżyński (2018)
Others: effort expectancy, gender, age, the voluntariness of use	Możdżyński (2018)

7.2.3. Benefits and Value Addition Associated with M-Wallet Services

Studies that have delved into M-wallet adoption are mainly focused on:

Table 22. Merchants' adoption of M-payment: Evidence from the literature

Variables	Literature
Easy to use	Van der Heijden (2002); Teo et al. (2005)
Perceived risk	Van der Heijden (2002); Lai and Chuah (2010)
Trust	Mallat and Tuunainen (2005, 2008)
Potential increase in impulse purchase	Teo et al. (2005); Mallat and Tuunainen (2008)
Security	Van der Heijden (2002); Mallat and Tuunainen (2005); Teo et al. (2005); Lai and Chuah (2010)
User experience	Van der Heijden (2002); Mallat and Tuunainen (2008); Lai and Chuah (2010)
Costs	Van der Heijden (2002); Mallat and Tuunainen (2005, 2008); Teo et al. (2005)
Relative advantages	Mallat and Tuunainen (2005, 2008); Lai and Chuah (2010)
Compatibility	Mallat and Tuunainen (2005, 2008); Lai and Chuah (2010)
Standardizations	Mallat and Tuunainen (2005, 2008); Lai and Chuah (2010)
Complexity	Mallat and Tuunainen (2005, 2008); Teo et al. (2005); Lai and Chuah (2010)
Monopoly	Teo et al. (2005)
Managerial willingness	Lai and Chuah (2010)
Technology maturity	Mallat and Tuunainen (2008)
Network externality	Van der Heijden (2002)
Organisational enablers	Lai and Chuah (2010)
Competitive forces	Lai and Chuah (2010)

- contingency changes, i.e., regulatory/government, technological/infrastructural, social/cultural, and commercial changes (Ondrus & Pigneur, 2006);
- competitive factors linked to users, merchants, networks, and payment providers (Hayashi, 2012; Liébana Cabanillas et al., 2016, 2017).

The studies mentioned earlier have identified that these features may build up barriers to adopting technology and affect the trust of interested merchants (Liébana Cabanillas et al., 2016, 2017). Another crucial factor is merchants' perceived benefit and value addition of M-wallet services. For merchants, accepting payments via M-wallets means an opportunity to offer customers faster and more suitable services, thus increasing their satisfaction. Varki and Mark (2001) define value addition as customer satisfaction based on emotional, physical, and social responses and the rating given to the service or retailer. Li (2018) recognizes the significant impact of facilitating conditions, accessibility, perceived benefits, and mobile usefulness on merchants' plans to use M-wallet services. The study shows that merchants, before offering M-wallets, need to be knowledgeable about all the components (practice, functionalities, competencies) of this payment technology.

Cost and trust directly impact the merchants' willingness to adopt M-wallets. Carlos and Taylor (2008) reported that merchants find M-wallets more cost-effective than traditional near-field communication (NFC) payment cards (Liébana Cabanillas et al., 2016). Similarly, Możdżyński (2018), after studying behavioral intentions behind merchants' acceptance of M-payments, acknowledged the significant influence of perceived cost, perceived trust, and experience. In light of the above, then, the most significant variables that affect M-wallet adoption by the merchant are identified as:

- perceived cost, perceived trust, and facilitating conditions (Hu et al., 2008; Liébana Cabanillas et al., 2016; Możdżyński, 2018);
- technical and functional aspects of technology or services (Li, 2018 Liébana Cabanillas et al., 2016, 2017).

Table 23 summarizes the key studies that explain merchants' adoption of M-wallets.

Evidence from the existing literature emphasizes the necessity for merchants to have a comprehensive understanding of the intricate phenomenon of M-wallets. This would help alleviate the primary fears and skepticism regarding new payment technologies that ultimately enhance customer experience. Deepening the knowledge of the main characteristics

Table 23. M-wallet benefits and value addition for merchants: Evidence from the literature

Variables	Literature
Contingency changes	Ondrus and Pigneur (2009)
Competitive factors	Hayashi (2012); Liébana-Cabanillas et al. (2016, 2017)
Value addition	Varki and Mark (2001); Liébana-Cabanillas et al. (2016, 2017)
Knowledge	Liébana-Cabanillas et al. (2016, 2017); Li (2018)
Costs	Carlos and Taylor (2008); Hu et al. (2008); Liébana-Cabanillas et a1. (2016); Li (2018); Możdżyński (2018)
Test	Carlos and Taylor (2008); Hu et al. (2008); Liébana-Cabanillas et al. (2016); Li (2018); Możdżyński (2018)

and improving awareness of M-wallet payment would help to increase its adoption.

7.3. A Simplified Roadmap for the Aware Merchant

In the increasingly digitalized economy, merchants are finding new ways to meet changing consumer expectations for commerce. To better fit the new demand-side requests, merchants evaluate different payment options, trying to make the best of retailer payment acceptance strategies and plans. So, they should carefully evaluate each M-wallet solution, considering not only its functions and services, but also their concerns:

- the consumer experience and services included in the M-wallet;
- the data management and acceptance terms concerns;
- the profitability.

We propose reflections on each item as in what follows.

7.3.1. Consumer Experience and Services Included in the M-Wallet

Consumers significantly influence merchants' decisions regarding M-wallet structures. The rise in customer "mobility," influenced by changing purchasing behaviors and elevated demands for mobile capabilities, poses both challenges and opportunities. Studies (Dahlberg et al., 2008; De Kerviler et al., 2016; Marriott & Mclean, 2019) indicate that M-wallet adoption hinges on enhancing the shopping experience. Key engagement factors include service customization, loyalty rewards, and accessible transaction information (e.g., grocery lists, receipts, and warranties), as well as user-friendly payment options. Both Issuers introducing new M-wallets and merchants adopting them must anticipate consumer needs, refining features accordingly.

Some merchants, particularly smaller retailers, may only seek to provide basic M-wallet payment services without additional engagement features. Conversely, large-scale retailers often opt for proprietary solutions that strengthen customer relationships and offset costs. Closed-loop M-wallets restrict consumer purchases to a single merchant but offer extensive complementary services, whereas open-loop solutions, more practical for smaller merchants, provide fundamental payment functionalities while ceding customer engagement to Issuers.

Key considerations for merchants include the M-wallet's usage channel—whether remote, proximity-based, mobile, or in-app—as this influences service perception. Additionally, device compatibility is crucial. While wearable payments enhance convenience, they may also serve as status symbols or novelty features that appeal to specific consumers.

M-wallet services should align with the merchant's strategic objectives. The choice between offering core payment functions or incorporating additional non-financial services is vital. Expanding M-wallet use benefits merchants by maximizing consumer data and enhancing customer experience, often necessitating supplementary service offerings. However, not all M-wallets seamlessly integrate loyalty programs, requiring merchants to assess flexibility and suitability.

Another important factor is segment-specific functionalities. For instance, P2P payments, particularly relevant to millennials, facilitate cost-sharing among multiple users. If this demographic represents a substantial customer base, a split-payment feature could be a competitive advantage.

Merchants should also evaluate M-wallet features that streamline customer interactions. Some solutions consolidate loyalty rewards and payment processing into a single scan, enhancing shopping convenience. The cost–benefit analysis of these features is critical in decision-making. Finally, one must examine the supported payment methods. Some third-party applications only accept credit or debit cards, which may not align with a merchant's needs if they rely on alternative payment methods such as CCTV gift cards, Automated Clearing House (ACH), or private-label options. Careful selection ensures the M-wallet complements existing payment strategies.

7.3.2. Data Management and Acceptance Terms Concerns

Data management is a critical aspect of the consumer–merchant relationship, closely linked to security concerns. Consumers may express apprehension regarding the protection of their sensitive data, necessitating merchants to effectively address data security risks. This not only safeguards merchants from reputational damage or financial loss but also prevents fraudulent account provisioning and ensures the security of payees' data.

Within these inherently sensitive dynamic, multiple stakeholders may legally engage in the exchange of customer data, including payment credentials and transaction details. Consequently, meticulous attention must be paid to the type and volume of data processed within each proposed or adopted M-payment solution. Merchants must navigate data security challenges to mitigate potential risks, including reputational damage and financial losses, such as customer attrition.

Accordingly, a thorough understanding of how individual mobile wallets collect, utilize, and store payment information is essential. The following key factors require careful assessment:

- The storage site of cardholder payment data and the compliance of data transmission with established security standards.
- The provision of tokenization and encryption solutions to protect the Primary Account Number (PAN) and additional personal information.
- The implications of technological choices, including:
    - implementation of in-app wallets;
    - cardholder verification methods (CVM), encompassing biometric and on-device CVM;
    - rooting configurations;

  - authentication techniques and authorization rejections.

- Whether payment data is stored solely within the mobile application or extends to loyalty program information.

In various geographical contexts, regulatory frameworks establish guidelines that affect data management practices, necessitating a comprehensive analysis of these variables. Furthermore, the contractual terms binding merchants to payment networks necessitate thorough legal scrutiny to prevent substantial financial implications. Beyond direct costs, the risk of reputational damage associated with specific payment solutions has to be considered. Key evaluation criteria include:

- the range of accepted mobile payment solutions;
- the timeframe for ensuring the certainty of monetary transfers;
- potential challenges related to currency conversion; and
- failure and error management systems.

For NFC or contactless payments, further considerations are required. Once transactions are accepted via a Point of Sale (POS) system, merchants may not have direct contractual relationships with individual wallet issuers. Moreover, they may lack the ability to differentiate, select, or reject specific transactions. If transaction sources cannot be automatically distinguished, merchant customer service and promotional activities may be adversely affected.

7.3.3. Financial Point of Attention

Entrepreneurs must assess the financial implications of adopting an M-wallet solution, including its benefits and costs. Key cost components include:

- start-up costs: development, implementation, staff training, and promotional expenses;
- recurring costs: maintenance, hosting, licensing, and transaction fees; and
- one-off costs: initial setup expenditures.

Merchants must also account for costs related to payment terminals, such as POS systems, and the impact of commissions on Card-Not-Present (CNP) transactions, which can be higher than standard card fees.

Security investments are crucial, as merchants bear responsibility for fraud in CNP transactions, leading to reputational and financial risks. Costs may arise from fraud management and staff training.

A partial mitigation strategy is 3DS authentication, which shifts fraud liability to wallet issuers but may impact customer experience. Emerging technologies like device ID, geolocation, and biometrics can further enhance security while refining authentication strategies and risk management.

Merchants aiming to control acceptance costs should balance debit and credit card options while considering alternative payment methods such as ACH, closed-loop, or private label cards. Higher transaction fees should be weighed against the need for payment compatibility.

However, M-wallet adoption can also reduce costs by eliminating paper-based processes, such as receipts and promotional materials, while enabling targeted marketing campaigns. By leveraging digital solutions, merchants can enhance profitability through cost savings and revenue generation from new customer segments.

7.4. Conclusion and Lesson Learned

In the current economic landscape, merchants have to adjust their operations to evolving consumer behavior and increasing global competition, facilitated by smartphone accessibility. While M-commerce offers significant opportunities, merchants still perceive M-wallet transactions as challenging, favoring traditional cash and digital payment methods.

Despite its potential, M-wallet adoption remains limited, preventing its widespread acceptance (Lee & Shin, 2018). The market is ready for expansion, but success depends on enhancing consumer experience and merchant willingness. Educating both groups about M-wallet technologies, costs, structures, and value propositions is key. Providing small retailers with foundational knowledge can help them navigate available options, assess risks, and make informed decisions.

This chapter aims to simplify M-wallet components, guiding merchants in strategic choices. Literature indicates that most studies focus on merchant intent, attitude towards M-payment, and perceived benefits. A common barrier is limited financial and digital literacy regarding M-wallets. Thus, a comprehensive understanding of M-wallet complexities is essential. This exploratory study examines key M-wallet technologies and structures from the merchant's perspective.

To align with evolving consumer expectations, merchants must evaluate various payment options to refine payment acceptance strategies. This involves assessing:

- consumer experience and included M-wallet services;
- data management and acceptance terms; and
- profitability.

Accepting M-wallet payments enhances accounting and administrative efficiency. Digital transactions improve tracking, reduce errors, and simplify financial reconciliation, lowering cash management costs. Additionally, M-wallets provide valuable customer data, enabling personalized marketing strategies and improving promotional campaign effectiveness. Security is a crucial factor in M-wallet adoption. Advanced encryption and authentication technologies reduce fraud risks, safeguarding merchants and consumers from unauthorized transactions. Enhanced security boosts merchant reputation and strengthens customer trust.

The decision-making process affects both existing and prospective customers. Merchants and stakeholders involved in M-wallet development must consider all these factors to optimize adoption and maximize benefits.

Bibliography

Brown, J. R., Dant, R. P., & Rajiv P. (2008a). Scientific method and retailing research: a retrospective. *Journal of Retailing*, *84*(April), 1–13.

Brown, J. R., Dant, R. P., & Rajiv P. (2008b). On what makes a significant contribution to the retailing literature. *Journal of Retailing*, *84*(June), 131–135.

Carlos, A., & Taylor, V. (2008). Merchant acceptance, costs, and perceptions of retail payments: A Canadian survey. *Discussion Paper. Bank of Canada* (No. 2008–2012).

Chen, C. F., & Chen, F. S. (2010). Experience quality, perceived value, satisfaction and behavioral intentions for heritage tourists. *Tourism Management, 31*, 29–35.

Cruz-Cárdenas, J., Zabelina, E., Guadalupe-Lanas, J., Palacio-Fierro, A., & Ramos-Galarza, C. (2021). COVID-19, consumer behavior, technology, and society: A literature review and bibliometric analysis. *Technological Forecasting and Social Change, 173*, 121179. <https://doi.org/10.1016/j.techfore.2021.121179>.

Dahlberg, T., Guo, J., & Ondrus, J. (2015). A critical review of mobile payment research. Electron. *Commerce Research and Applications, 14*, 265–284.

Dahlberg, T., Mallat, N., Ondrus, J., & Zmijewska, A. (2008). Past, present and future of mobile payments research: A literature review. *Electronic Commerce Research and Application*s, 7(2), 165–181.

De Kerviler, G., Demoulin, N. T., & Zidda, P. (2016). Adoption of in-store mobile payment: Are perceived risk and convenience the only drivers? *Journal of Retailing and Consumer Services, 31*, 334–344.

Duarte, P., Silva, S. C., & Ferreira, M. B. (2018). How convenient is it? Delivering online shopping convenience to enhance customer satisfaction and encourage e-WOM. *Journal of Retailing and Consumer Service, 44*, 161–169.

Gaur, A., & Ondrus, J. (2012). The role of banks in the mobile payment ecosystem: a strategic asset perspective. In *Proceedings of the 14th Annual International Conference on Electronic Commerce* (pp. 171–177).

Grewal, D., & Levy, M. (2007). Passing the baton journal of retailing 2001–2007. *Journal of Retailing, 83*(December), 371–373.

Grewal, D., Levy, M., & Kumar, V. (2009). Customer experience management in retailing: an organizing framework. *Journal of Retailing, 85*, 1–14.

Hassan, H., & Wood, V. (2020). Does country culture influence consumers' perceptions toward mobile banking? A comparison between Egypt and the United States. *Telematics Informatics, 46*. <https://doi.org/10.1016/j.tele.2019.101312>.

Hayashi, F. (2012). The new debit card regulations: initial effects on networks and banks. Federal Reserve Bank of Kansas City. *Economic Review*, 97(4), 79–115.

Hayashi, F., & Bradford, T. (2014). Mobile payments: Merchants' perspectives. *Economic Review, 99*, 5–30.

Hu, X., Li, W., & Hu, Q. (2008). Are mobile payment and banking the killer apps for mobile commerce? In *Proceedings of the 41st Hawaii International Conference on System Sciences*, 7–10 January, Waikoloa, Big Island, HI, USA. Washington.

Lai, P. M., & Chuah, K. B. (2010). Developing an analytical framework for M-payments adoption in retailing: A supply-side perspective. In *Proceedings of 2010 IEEE Fourth International Conference on Management of e-commerce and e-government* (ICMeCG) (pp. 356–361).

Lee, I., & Shin, Y. J. (2018). Fintech: ecosystem, business models, investment decisions, and challenges. *Business Horizonz, 61*(1), 35–46.

Leo, S., Delle Foglie, A. & Panetta, I. C. (2025). Mobile payments: Chatting with literature to spot what is left to reveal. *International Journal of Financial Innovation in Banking*, in press.

Leo, S., & Panetta, I.,C. (2019). *Mobile wallet: aspetti teorici ed evidenze empiriche a stelle e strisce*. UniversItalia.

Li, Y. (2018). The strategic decision on mobile payment: a study on Merchants adoption. In *Proceedings of the Conference Adoption and Diffusion of Information Technology* (SIGADIT), AMCIS 2018, USA.

Liébana Cabanillas, F., Slade, E., & Dwivedi, Y. (2016). Time for a different perspective: A preliminary investigation of barriers of merchants' adoption of mobile payments. In *Proceedings of the 22nd Americas Conference on Information Systems*. San Diego.

Liébana-Cabanillas, F., Leiva, F. M., & Fernández, J. S. (2017). Examining merchants' refusal to adopt mobile payment systems in Spain. Published in book in smartphones from an applied research perspective. *IntechOpen* <https://doi.org/10.5772/intechopen>.

Liébana-Cabanillas, F., Sánchez-Fernández, J., & Muñoz-Leiva, F. (2014). Antecedents of the adoption of the new mobile payment systems: the moderating effect of age. *Computers in Human Behavior, 35*(2), 464–478.

Liébana-Cabanillas, F. L., Marinkovic, V., Luna, I. R., & Kalinic, Z. (2018). Predicting the determinants of mobile payment acceptance: a hybrid SEM-neural network approach. *Technological Forecasting and Social Change, 129*, 117–130.

Liu, Z., Ben, S., & Zhang, R. (2019). Factors affecting consumers' mobile payment behavior: A meta-analysis. *Electronic Commerce Research, 19*, 575–601. <https://doi.org/10.1007/s10660-019-09349-4>.

Mallat, N. & Tuunainen, V. K. (2005). Merchant adoption of m-payment systems. In *Proceedings of the IEEE International Conference on Mobile Business* (ICMB 2005) (pp. 347–353).

Mallat, N., & Tuunainen, V. K. (2008). Exploring merchant adoption of mobile payment systems: An empirical study. *e-Service Journal*, *6*(2), 24–57.

Marriott, H., & McLean, G. (2019, May). Developing the mUTAUT model—A mobile shopping perspective. In *2019 Academy of Marketing Science Annual Conference*.

Możdżyński, D. (2018). Acceptance of payment systems from the perspective of merchants. *Information Systems Management*, *7*.

Ondrus, J., & Pigneur, Y. (2006). Towards a holistic analysis of mobile payments: A multiple perspectives approach. *Electronic Commerce Research and Applications*, *5*(3), 246–257.

Ondrus, J., Lyytinen, K., & Pigneur, Y. (2009). Why mobile payments fail? Towards a dynamic and multi-perspective explanation. In *2009 42nd Hawaii International Conference on System Sciences* (pp. 1–10). IEEE.

Panetta, I. C., & Leo, S. (2017). *Mobile payment industry: Caratteristiche operative e modelli di business*. F. Angeli.

Panetta, I. C., & Leo, S. (2022). Why are M-payment platforms so attractive? M-payment as the entry level to the digital financial era. In *Social and Economic Studies within the Framework of Emerging Global Developments*, Volume 1 (pp. 43–58). Peter Lang GmbH.

Panetta, I. C., Leo, S., & Delle Foglie, A. (2023). The development of digital payments–past, present, and future–from the literature. *Research in International Business and Finance*, *64*, 101855.

Plouffe, C. R., Hulland, J. S., & Vandenbosch, M. (2001). Research report: Richness versus parsimony in modeling technology adoption decisions—Understanding merchant adoption of a smart card-based payment system. *Information Systems Research*, *12*(2), 208–222. <https://10.1287/isre.12.2.208.9697>

Rogers, E. M. (1995). *Diffusion of innovations* (4th ed.). New York: Free Press.

Teo, E., Fraunholz, B., & Unnithan, C. (2005, July). Inhibitors and facilitators for mobile payment adoption in Australia: A preliminary study. In International Conference on Mobile Business (ICMB'05) (pp. 663–666). IEEE.

Van der Heijden, H. (2002). Factors affecting the successful introduction of mobile payment systems. In *Proceedings of the 15th Bled Electronic Commerce Conference*, Bled, Slovenia.

Varki, S. & Mark, C. (2001). The role of price perceptions in an integrated model of behavioral intentions. *Journal of Service Research*, *3*(3), 232–240.

Venkatesh, V., Thong, J., & Xu, X. (2012). Consumer acceptance and use of information technology: Extending the unified theory of acceptance and use of technology. *MIS Quarterly*, *36*(1), 157–178.

Increasing the Capacity of Digital Payment Systems by Investing in Digital Infrastructure (as an Example of OECD Countries)

Samariddin Makhmudov, Khayrilla Kurbonov, Zokir Mamadiyarov, Akbar Jumayev, Mirzabek Jonuzokov, Bakhtiyor Klichev, and Shakhzoda Farxadova

8.1. Introduction

Financial digitalization has been an essential component of the modern financial world (Kasri et al.). In this sense, digital technologies, which have fundamentally transformed financial operations, have enabled the delivery of financial services in more cost-efficient and effective ways (Niu et al, 2022). Modern mobile payment platforms, in particular, have become an essential component of contemporary people's financial practices. With digital payment services, mobile banking, and social payment platforms now part of the interface that customers use to manage their finances, new mobile financial applications are acting as middlemen between customers and traditional financial institutions (Westermeier, 2020). These recent developments in digital infrastructure have not only made it possible for traditional brick-and-mortar financial institutions to revitalize their operations, but also contributed to the modern, individualized approach to each client. In other words, the services offered by the banking industry have seen a substantial transformation due to advancements in technology including e-wallets, mobile payments, electronic money, internet banking, and electronic payments (Berger, 2003; Hollanders, 2008). To improve positioning in the international market, banks invest in cutting-edge technologies including digital payment systems, online banking platforms, and cybersecurity measures that ultimately enhance operational efficiency and customer experience. These developments may increase the effectiveness of banks, boost their general performance, and eventually lead to increased banking stability (Hasan et al., 2012). While such concerns have not slowed down the dissemination of digital payment systems, as more people use mobile phones and the internet, mobile payments have become increasingly prevalent. Having replaced traditional methods, it has boosted the effectiveness of electronic payment services and decreased human error (Hanseth & Lyytinen, 2010). The banking sector is considered the most important actor in the financial system. Today, the banking sector determines the volume and depth of financial transactions, performs the function of financial intermediation, and contributes to the creation of welfare (Senel, 2022).

This study investigates whether the proposed advantages of making investments in digital infrastructure to raise the efficiency of digital payment systems in OECD nations. There are two main objectives: an extensive literature review to assess the impact of digital infrastructure investments on the efficacy and capacity of digital payment systems and digital transformation. Next, Fixed Effects Estimator (FEE) and Random Effects Estimator (REE) models were implemented to assess the factors contributing to digital transformation. Overall, our findings highlight the significance of strategic and ongoing investments in digital infrastructure in the financial sector to promote economic growth and facilitate enterprises' competitive advantage in expediting their digital transformation in OECD countries.

8.2. Literature Review

It is claimed that technological evolution and innovation are key components of the development and advancement of human society. (Coccia, 2021). Coupled with digital infrastructure elements that constitutes online platforms, mobile connectivity, and high-speed internet access, it can boost market accessibility, the dissemination of information, and simplify and popularize financial transactions even in remote locations (Jiang & Jin, 2024; Singh et al., 2023). In this way, these technologies complement one another to encourage wider engagement in the digital economy and bridge the gap between developed and underdeveloped areas leading to improvement in the user efficiency and accessibility of financial services. So, digital infrastructure is characterized as an open, dynamic, and unbounded sociotechnical system that includes systems, networks, and both human and technological elements (Hanseth & Lyytinen, 2010). This indicates that it is strongly related to digital payment systems, which enable safe and effective financial transactions by integrating different platforms, technologies, and user interactions. Therefore, information and communication technology applications and the associated infrastructure are collectively referred to as digital infrastructure (Autio et al., 2018). Digital infrastructures are fundamentally generative systems, allowing user communities to access a variety of heterogeneous systems, supporting long-term growth and evolution (Osmundsen & Bygstad, 2022). In this regard, the evolution of digital infrastructures is a constant sociotechnical dynamic in which systems, stakeholders, and norms evolve to achieve specific goals and adjust the systems to fit those objectives (Cordella, 2011). Especially in open systems like the internet and other platforms, where user growth has been thoroughly studied, this generation of digital infrastructures is characterized by slow expansions in both functionality and users (Ambagahawita, 2022). According to statistical results, trust is a significant factor in determining intentions and opinions of the consumers regarding the value of mobile internet because of their biased inner emotional and external social judgment. In other words, consumers are more inclined to view technology favorably when their beliefs relate to its trustworthiness, helpfulness, and competency (Alalwan et al., 2018; Lin et al., 2025; Pradhan et al., 2025; Su et al., 2025). Interaction with technology is established when consumers have confidence in their choice of technology, particularly when they trust the usefulness, usability, and overall convenience of digital payment options.

Another group of local economists, who examined various aspects of investment in digital infrastructure and digital payment systems, has successfully used econometric models in their research on the impact of inflation and credit interest rates on investment, factors affecting the reduction of the state's share in commercial banks, the digitalization of banks, risks in digital services, and the development of retail payment services (Cahyani et al., 2025; Kuchkarov et al., 2025; Litamahuputty et al., 2025; Mamadiyarov et al., 2024; PANJAITAN et al., 2025).

However, most companies that employ mobile internet services to offer better value and benefits raise the perceived utility of these services, which in turn increases brand loyalty (Cyr et al., 2006). Mobile service providers could additionally improve their instant messaging platforms to promote positive network externalities and guarantee a positive user experience, as the results show that perceived usefulness and satisfaction—two factors that are crucial for user loyalty—are greatly influenced by network externalities and flow experience (Abdullah et al., 2025; Matyakubova et al., 2025; Muhammad et al., 2025; Romero et al., 2025; Zhou & Lu, 2011). In general, necessary investments in digital infrastructure can enhance the accessibility and user confidence in digital payment systems, which in turn can lead to a rise in customers and increased utility. As such, customer confidence is critical to the successful implementation and expansion of digital payment systems.

Analyses and forecasts have been conducted using various econometric models on factors affecting remittances, energy intensity and economic development, energy policy, energy risk, environmental status and the impact of environmental aspects on the digital economy, agricultural productivity, and the stability of the US credit market (Akhmetshin et al., 2025; Caporin et al., 2024; Jakhongir et al., 2024; Kuziboev et al., 2024; Samariddin et al., 2024; Sharipov et al., 2025; Zhang et al., 2025; Zokir et al., 2021;).

Our research attempts to fill the gap through the provision of an in-depth econometric analysis into the relations between components of digital infrastructure and the adoption of digital services among enterprises in OECD countries. We used the REE model to estimate the contribution of access to high-speed internet, investment in digital infrastructure, and mobile network coverage individually to the level of adoption of digital services by firms. The research emphasizes all these factors that interact with each other and cause digital transformation, market extension, and access to better financial services.

8.3. Research Methodology and Development Hypothesis

The methodology section of a research article describes the process to answer the research questions and test the hypotheses. It includes the overall research design, data collection, and analytical techniques, ensuring replicability of the research.

The sample data was obtained from OECD nations (<https://www.oecd.org>) and the World Bank (<https://data.worldbank.org/>). The econometric equations for the quarterly results of 22 OECD countries from 2018 to 2022 were developed using FEE and REE models based on the panel's data on increasing the potential of digital payment systems by investing in digital infrastructure. A total of 440 indicators were observed using those data sources. The study employed descriptive statistical analytical techniques, visual drawings, correlation matrices, and graphic descriptions to evaluate the relationship between the independent and dependent variables. The Hausman test between the FEE and REE models was used to assess the test indicators in order to determine which model best fits the econometric equation (Amini et al., 2012). A confidence interval test was implemented to ascertain the multicollinearity of the dependent and independent variables.

Considering a fixed effect model in economic research, the FEE is a famous econometric model for taking into account the unobserved variability of panel data (Brüderl & Ludwig, 2015). Because individual-specific intercepts are permitted, the fixed-effects model is a useful model for taking unobserved heterogeneity into account.

The FEE model is shown below (Bai, 2009).

$$Y_{it} = \beta_i + \gamma z_{it} + u_{it} \tag{1}$$

where,

Y_{it} symbolizes object i's dependent variable at time t;
z_{it} for item i at time t, stands for the vector of independent variables;
β is an individual (fixed) effect that indicates continuity over time; and
γ denotes the independent variable's vector of coefficients.
u_{it} is an error term unrelated to z_{it} that is believed to have zero mean.

In econometric analysis, the REE is known to be a useful tool for identifying variability across dimensions and modeling data with internal correlations (Baltagi, 2008; Jahrir et al., 2025; Mamani et al., 2025). This makes it possible for researchers to take into consideration both random and continuous variation over time or between data. Panel data analysis and hierarchical data structures are just two of the many applications for it.

The REE gives the following expression for the model:

$$Y_{it} = \beta + x_{it}\mu + \eta_i + \varepsilon_{it} \tag{2}$$

Here,

Y_{it} is the variable that depends on object i at time t.
x_{it}, vector of independent factors that explain item i at time t.

β represents a common cross section that is constant for all objects.

μ, independent variables' vector of coefficients, which shows how they affect the dependent variable.

η_i is the random effect on an individual basis (also known as random intercept). Although it varies among entities, it remains consistent for every entity over time.

ε_{it} is an error term that varies across objects and over time.

The dependent and independent variables to increase the capabilities of digital payment systems through digital infrastructure investments are displayed as in what follows. Every element is logarithmized naturally.

Number of companies using the digital service—*Logdig_serv_comp* (dependent variable), amount of investments in digital infrastructures—*lndig_paym_plat* (independent variable), internet access level—*logacc_internet* (independent variable), mobile network coverage - *logmob_net_cov* (independent variable).

The econometric model was constructed with the following hypotheses in consideration:

H_0: In OECD nations, there is no statistically significant relationship between variables like the number of companies utilizing digital services, the volume of investments in digital infrastructure, and the coverage of mobile networks and Internet access.

Ha: In OECD nations, there is statistically significant relationship between variables like the number of companies utilizing digital services, the volume of investments in digital infrastructure, and the coverage of mobile networks and internet access.

8.4. Analysis and Results

At the preliminary stage of the research, the dependent and independent variables' descriptive statistics were as follows (Table 24).

From Table 24, which presents descriptive summary data for the four variables, it can be inferred that investments in digital infrastructure and mobile network coverage exhibits significant skewness and kurtosis, providing summary statistics for these four variables and indicating the presence of extreme values. According to it, even though the competition for digital

Table 24. Descriptive statistics on dependent and independent variables

	logdig_serv_ comp	*logInvest_ dig_infr*	*logacc_ internet*	*logmob_net_ cov*
Mean	7.735778	4.006837	3.705982	3.269466
Maximum	8.935904	4.305416	4.204693	3.718438
Minimum	5.828946	3.367296	2.809403	2.282382
Std. Dev	0.7646141	0.1869699	0.2932952	0.2647465
Skewness	0.5846348	-1.677502	-0.6414587	-1.560363
Kurtosis	-0.4789596	4.939509	3.01307	5.846373
Observation	440	440	440	440

Source: It was developed by the authors based on Stata software.

services and high internet penetration remains constant across the observations, there are significant differences for investment in digital infrastructure and mobile network coverage.

The number of companies utilizing the digital service and the variables influencing it were shown in Figure 24.

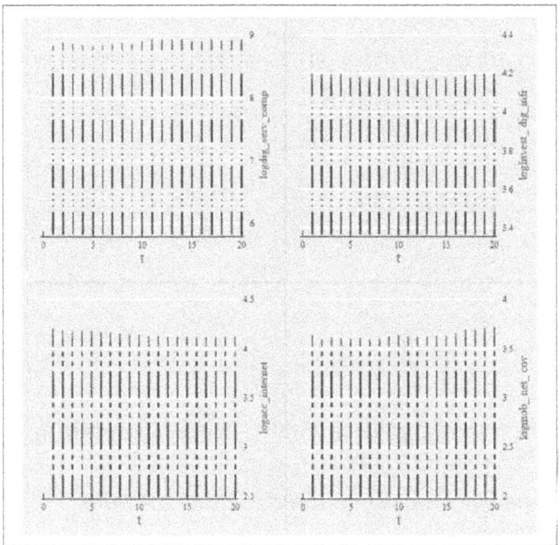

Figure 24. Analytical graphic representation of the number of companies using the digital service and the factors affecting it over time.

Source: It was developed by the authors based on Stata software.

The factors have produced a stochastic state, as seen in Figure 24. Owing to the influence of independent variables, positive trend in the use of digital services is represented by companies in their adoption of digital infrastructures as well as the projected increase of companies that utilize digital services in the future.

The dependent and independent variables (rconnected) are illustrated graphically at the subsequent step of the research analysis (Figure 25).

Figure 25 shows that all variable density images correspond to the overall statistics analyzed in Table 24. The peaks and steep flactuations indicate major tendencies in digital infrastructure investment and mobile network coverage.

Despite natural fluctuations, there is consistency in acceptance of digital tools, which may explain the reasons companies switching to employing non-traditional financing methods of digital parameters over time.

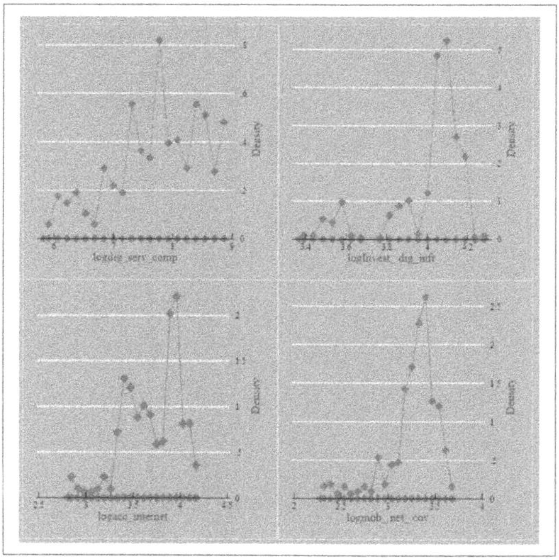

Figure 25. A histogram showing the amount of companies utilizing a digital service and the variables influencing it.

Source: It was developed by the authors based on Stata software.

As per the study, a scatter plot of dependent and independent variables as well as an analytical graphic matrix were developed (Figure 26). Based on econometric analysis and results of Figure 26, there is a high correlation and density cluster between the variables. Therefore, it demonstrates the efficiency of sustainable development among the economic factors that impact the companies operating digital technologies.

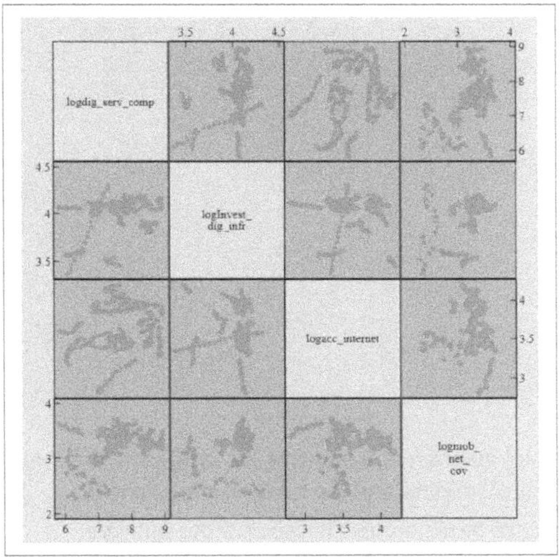

Figure 26. A graphic matrix of the relationship between the number of companies using digital services and the factors affecting it.
Source: It was developed by the authors based on Stata software.

According to Figure 27, competition for digital services and Internet access is quite widespread, with some concentrations being invisible at medium and high levels, indicating a positive shift in these factors. A highly concentrated distribution of investments in digital infrastructure and mobile network coverage provides a more positive outlook for regionally balanced investments and mobile network coverage.

Following that, we developed a correlation matrix for each dependent and independent variable (Table 25).

According to Table 25, the results of the test conducted based on the Stata program showed the existence of a significant, strong, and inverse correlation between the number of companies using digital services and its influencing factors. Additionally, the correlation matrix showed that there is no multicollinearity between the dependent and independent variables. Following that,

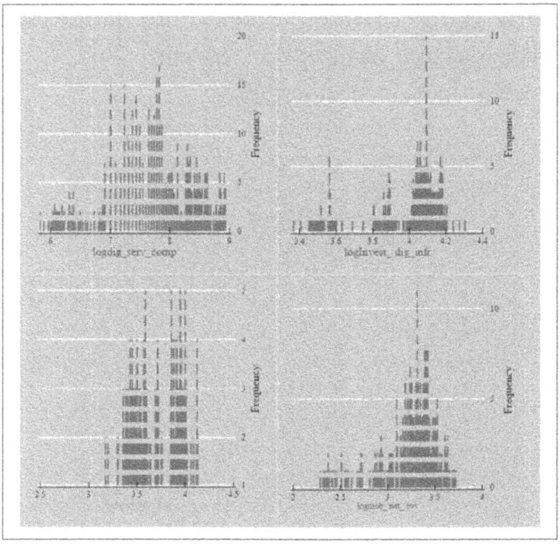

Figure 27. A spike plot diagram representing the incidence and value of the number of companies using digital services and the factors influencing it.

Source: It was developed by the authors based on Stata software.

Table 25. Intercorrelation matrix of the number of companies using the digital service and the factors affecting it

Variables	(1)	(2)	(3)	(4)
logdig_serv_comp	1.000			
logInvest_dig_infr	0.5657	1.000		
	(0.0000)			***
logacc_internet	0.4729	-0.4843	1.000	
	(0.0000)	(0.0090)		***
logmob_net_cov	0.7023	0.4504	-0.2481	1.000
	(0.0000)	(0.0000)	(0.0929)	***

Source: It was developed by the authors based on Stata software.

the parameters of econometric equations were used to develop the FEE and REE models (from Tables 26 and 27). Also, the FEE and REE of the model indicators were checked to evaluate the model consistency and efficiency through the Hausman test, which is the standard test for determining the difference in fixed and random effects in panel data models (Hausman, 1978).

8.4.1. REE Model Analysis

The indicators of the econometric equation according to the REE model of the study are presented in Table 26.

Table 26. Random effects estimator (REE) model indicators

logdig_serv_comp	Coef.	St. Err.	*t*-value	*p*-value	[95% Conf	Interval]	Sig
logInvest_dig_infr	0.614	0.114	5.38	0	0.391	0.838	***
logacc_internet	1.374	0.121	11.37	0	1.137	1.611	***
logmob_net_cov	0.435	0.116	3.77	0	0.209	0.662	***
Constant	−1.243	0.706	−1.76	0.078	−2.625	0.14	*
Mean dependent var		7.736	SD dependent var.			0.765	
Overall *r*-squared		0.137	Number of obs			440	
Chi-square		193.413	Prob > chi^2			0.000	
R-squared within		0.616	*R*-squared between			0.127	

*** $p < 0.01$, ** $p < 0.05$; * $p < 0.1$

Source: It was developed by the authors based on Stata software.

The model (REE) developed for the research is the following:

$$logdig\_serv\_comp = -1.24 + 0.61 logInvest\_dig\_infr + 1.37\, logacc\_internet + + 0.43 logmob\_net\_cov \quad (3)$$

Based on the REE)model, the chi-square statistic determined a value of 193.41, indicating a positive correlation between the actual and expected values. This, in turn, is the continual positive prediction of the independent variable to the dependent variable in the model.

As a result, the *R*-squared value of 0.61, accounting for 61% of the changes, shows the significant predictive influence of the independent components on the dependent variable and indicates how best the equation fits.

A 1% increase in digital infrastructure investment among OECD countries engenders to a 0.61% rise in the number of companies using digital services. While, a 1% increase in high-speed internet penetration results in a 1.37% increase in the number of companies using digital services in OECD countries. At the same time, when it comes to mobile network coverage, its 1% increase leads to a 0.43% increase in the number of companies using digital services in these regions.

The Hausman test statistic for econometric research was 0.29 according to the REE econometric model. In essence, if the level of statistical significance is greater than 0.05 between $H_0: y = 0$ and $H_1: y \neq 0$, the null hypothesis (H_0) is considered statistically significant owing to results of the test.

Thus, it is preferable to accept the null hypothesis and use the fixed effects and REE models. In addition, the observed *p*-value >0.05 met the requirements of the Hausman test, confirming the validity of the results and the appropriate application of the test to the data set.

8.4.2. FEE Model Analysis

The indicators of the econometric equation according to the FEE model of the study are presented in Table 27.

Table 27. Fixed effects estimator (FEE) model indicators

logdig_serv_comp	Coef.	St. Err.	*t*-value	*p*-value	[95% Conf	Interval]	Sig
logInvest_dig_infr	0.596	0.115	5.18	0	0.37	0.822	***
logacc_internet	1.422	0.124	11.47	0	1.179	1.666	***
logmob_net_cov	0.42	0.118	3.58	0	0.189	0.651	***
Constant	−1.299	0.701	−1.85	0.065	−2.676	0.079	*
Mean dependent var	7.736		SD dependent var		0.765		
R-squared	0.516		Number of obs		440		
F-test	64.002		Prob > *F*		0.000		
Akaike crit. (AIC)	−350.298		Bayesian crit. (BIC)		−333.951		
*** *p*<.01, ** *p*<.05, * *p*<.1							

Source: It was developed by the authors based on Stata software.

The FEE model developed for this study has the following form:

$$logdig\_serv\_comp = -1.24 + 0.59logInvest\_dig\_infr + 1.42logacc\_internet + 0.42logmob\_net\_cov \quad (4)$$

As shown in Table 27, the observed value was 64.02, and the *R*-squared coefficient was 0.51, indicating positive values.

As a result, a 1% increase in investment in digital infrastructure leads to a 0.59% increase in the number of companies using digital services in OECD countries. In contrast, a 1% increase in high-speed internet access results in a 1.42% increase in the number of companies utilizing digital services in these regions. Simultaneously, a 1% increase in mobile network coverage causes a 0.42% increase in the number of companies using digital services in OECD countries.

8.5. Conclusion

Based on the analysis and conclusions of the study regarding the interaction of variables such as the number of companies using digital services, the number of investments in digital infrastructure, the level of high-speed internet access, and mobile network coverage, we determined, when comparing the REE model with the FEE model, that the REE model is the best choice. The Hausman test yielded a *p*-value of 0.29, suggesting that the REE is superior to the FEE in this case.

8.5.1. REE Model

$$logdig\_serv\_comp = -1.24 + 0.61logInvest\_dig\_infr + 1.37\ logacc\_internet + 0.43logmob\_net\_cov \quad (5)$$

according to which:

1. A 1% increase in high-speed internet access leads to a 1.37% increase in the number of companies implementing digital services. This would tend to indicate that superior internet connectivity forms the bedrock of the assimilation of digital practices into the enterprise sector; therefore, encouraging investment in the infrastructure for high-speed internet will be one possible way for business enterprises to implement digital technologies.

2. A 1% rise of investments in digital infrastructure engenders in a 0.61% increase in the number of companies using digital services. It means digital transformation fosters continuous investments in digital infrastructure which ultimately adopt new and efficient digital solutions leading to increased productivity and competitiveness.
3. A 1% increase in mobile network coverage results in a 0.43% increase in the number of companies using digital services. This finding not only underlines the increasingly crucial role of mobile connectivity in digital adoption for business that is dependent on mobile networks for remote work, digital transactions, and mobile apps but also indicates that much more has to be done in this regard. Secondly, an expanded mobile network will have the added advantage of increasingly expanding the use of digital services in the region while reducing the digital divide in OECD countries.
4. Some aspects of digital infrastructure—such as general infrastructure, mobile networks, and internet access—have a positive effect on the adoption of digital technologies among enterprises. Moreover, achieving digital transformation in a company demands a holistic strategy starting from investments in digital infrastructure, mobile network expansion, and ending with improvements in high-speed internet access. It is supported by the findings of the econometric analysis suggesting that every additional investment in digital infrastructure and network coverage can potentially lead to even greater economic prosperity and technological progress among OECD countries.

In summary, increased investment in digital infrastructure in OECD countries enhances the capacity of digital payment systems, while enhancing digital services promotes international business transactions. This, in turn creates more employment opportunities and expand financial markets, demonstrating the ultimate synergy between digital infrastructure and business digitalization.

Bibliography

Abdullah, M. A., Han, X., Amjad, M. A., & Makhmudov, S. (2025). Revisit the role of financial development on economic growth, human development, and sustainable development in higher-income countries. *Journal of Environmental Management*, *392*, 126874.

Akhmetshin, E., Abdullayev, I., Makhmudov, S., Dakhkilgova, K., Korotaeva, I. and Yanovskaya, G. (2025). APPLICATION OF TANH–COTH METHOD FOR COMBINED AND DOUBLE COMBINED SINH–COSH–GORDON EQUATIONS ARISING CHEMICAL REACTIONS TO WATER SURFACE GRAVITY WAVES. Computational Methods for Differential Equations, (), -. doi: 10.22034/cmde.2025.67655.3234

Alalwan, A. A., Baabdullah, A. M., Rana, N. P., Tamilmani, K., & Dwivedi, Y. K. (2018). Examining adoption of mobile internet in Saudi Arabia: Extending TAM with perceived enjoyment, innovativeness, and trust. *Technology in Society*, *55*, 100–110.

Al-Okaily, M., Lutfi, A., Alsaad, A., Taamneh, A., & Alsyouf, A. (2020). The determinants of digital payment systems' acceptance under cultural orientation differences: The case of uncertainty avoidance. *Technology in Society*, *63*, 101367.

Ambagahawita, K. (2022). *Accessing regulated digital infrastructures: A case study of the UK's retail payment infrastructure* [Doctoral dissertation, London School of Economics and Political Science].

Amini, S., Delgado, M. S., Henderson, D. J., & Parmeter, C. F. (2012). Fixed vs random: The Hausman test four decades later. In *Essays in Honor of Jerry Hausman* (Vol. 29, pp. 479–513). Emerald Group Publishing Limited.

Autio, E., Nambisan, S., Thomas, L. D., & Wright, M. (2018). Digital affordances, spatial affordances, and the genesis of entrepreneurial ecosystems. *Strategic Entrepreneurship Journal*, *12*(1), 72–95.

Bai, J. (2009). Panel data models with interactive fixed effects. *Econometrica*, *77*(4), 1229–1279.

Baltagi, B. H. (2008). *Econometric analysis of panel data* (Vol. 4, pp. 135–145). Chichester: Wiley.

Berger, A. N. (2003). The economic effects of technological progress: Evidence from the banking industry. *Journal of Money, Credit and Banking*, 141–176.

Brüderl, J., & Ludwig, V. (2015). Fixed-effects panel regression. In *The Sage Handbook of Regression Analysis and Causal Inference* (p. 357). Sage Publications.

Cahyani, I., Buriev, K., Ngongo, M., Mamadiyarov, Z., Ino, L., Herman, H., Saputra, N., & Baxtishodovich, S. (2025). Exploring the Use of TikTok

Application in Enhancing the Skill of Pronunciation: A Case on Students' Perception. Studies in Media and Communication, 13(2), 150–158. doi:http://dx.doi.org/10.11114/smc.v13i2.7553

Caporin, M., Shahbaz, M., Kuziboev, B., Masharipova, M., Allaberganov, S., & Makhmudov, S. (2024). Environmental Kuznets Curve for extended brics economies: do women governance and water stress matter?. International Journal of Energy Economics and Policy, 14(6), 174–183.

Coccia, M. (2021). Technological innovation. *Innovations*, *11*, I12.

Cordella, A. (2011). Emerging standardization. *International Journal of Actor-Network Theory and Technological Innovation*, *3*, 49–64.

Cyr, D., Head, M., & Ivanov, A. (2006). Design aesthetics leading to m-loyalty in mobile commerce. *Information & Management*, *43*(8), 950–963.

Ferrari, M. V. (2022). The platformisation of digital payments: The fabrication of consumer interest in the EU FinTech agenda. *Computer Law & Security Review*, *45*, 105687.

Hanseth, O., & Lyytinen, K. (2010). Design theory for dynamic complexity in information infrastructures: The case of building internet. *Journal of Information Technology*, *25*, 1–19.

Hasan, I., Schmiedel, H., & Song, L. (2012). Returns to retail banking and payments. *Journal of Financial Services Research*, *41*, 163–195.

Hausman, J. A. (1978). Specification tests in econometrics. *Econometrica*, *46*, 1251–1270.

Hollanders, M. (2008, August). Innovations in retail payments and the BIS statistics on payment and settlement systems. In *Proceedings of the IFC Conference* (Vol. 31, pp. 431–438). Basel.

Hussain, A., Khan, M., Rakhmonov, D. A., Mamadiyarov, Z. T., Kurbonbekova, M. T., & Mahmudova, M. Q. K. (2023). Nexus of Training and Development, Organizational Learning Capability, and Organizational Performance in the Service Sector. Sustainability, 15(4), 3246. https://doi.org/10.3390/su15043246

Jahrir, A., Gultom, Y., Herman, H., Zabadi, F., Ngongo, M., Mamadiyarov, Z., Fatmawati, E., & Saputra, N. (2025). Investigating the Elements of Short Commercial Mineral Water Advertisement: A Case on Discourse

Analysis. Studies in Media and Communication, 13(4), 94–104. doi:http://dx.doi.org/10.11114/smc.v13i4.7813

Jakhongir, S., Muhabbat, H., Khayrilla, K., Kholmuratov, S., Nazirjon, R., Nilufar, F., & Farxod, T. (2024). Crafting a neutrosophic-driven tool to probe turnover propensities in manufacturing entities. *International Journal of Neutrosophic Science (IJNS)*, *23*(2).

Jiang, C., & Jin, B. (2024). Does the development of digital economy infrastructure reduce the urban-rural income gap? Theoretical experience and empirical data from China. *Kybernetes*, *53*(2), 600–619.

Kasri, R. A., Indrastomo, B. S., Hendranastiti, N. D., & Prasetyo, M. B. (2022). Digital payment and banking stability in emerging economy with dual banking system. *Heliyon*, *8*(11).

Kuchkarov, T., Mamadiyarov, Z., Khakimov, Z., Sabirova, O., Matmurodov, K., Raimboyeva, M., & Umarova, S. (2025). Energy-Related Uncertainty and Crypto-Currency Environmental Attention: Time-Varying Perspective. International Journal of Energy Economics and Policy, 15(5), 614–626. https://doi.org/10.32479/ijeep.20784

Kuziboev, B., Khodjaniyazov, E., Ozturk, I., Sabirov, K., Makhmudov, S., & Utegenova, S. (2025). Does oil dependence cause energy risk?. Energy Nexus, 17, 100393.

Kuziboev, B., Saidmamatov, O., Khodjaniyazov, E., Ibragimov, J., Marty, P., Ruzmetov, D., ..., & Ibadullaev, D. (2024). CO2 emissions, remittances, energy intensity and economic development: The evidence from Central Asia. *Economies*, *12*(4), 95.

Lin, M.H., Matchanova, B., Nurmatovich, H.A. *et al.* Optimal Operation of the Multi-Carrier Energy System Considering Energy Markets and Renewable Energies Participation. *Int. J. Appl. Comput. Math* **11**, 170 (2025). https://doi.org/10.1007/s40819-025-02002-9

Litamahuputty, J. V., Amiruddin, E. G., Rahim, R., Rahman, A., & Mamadiyarov, Z. (2025). Cryptocurrency Risk Management through Decision Engineering: Evaluating XRPUSD and ADAUSD Portfolio Performance. *Journal of Applied Science, Engineering, Technology, and Education*, 7(1), 69–81. https://doi.org/10.35877/454RI.asci3871

Mamadiyarov, Z., Hakimov, H., & Askarov, S. (2024). DEVELOPMENT OF RETAIL BANKING SERVICES IN THE CONTEXT OF DIGITAL TRANSFORMATION. Financial and Credit Activity Problems of Theory and Practice, 1(54), 51–67. https://doi.org/10.55643/fcaptp.1.54.2024.4288

Mamadiyarov, Z. Makhmudov, S. Utanov, B. Kasimova, D. Bekmurodova, G. Hakimov, Z. (2025). Fusion of Economic and Financial Factors Affecting Household Deposits in Banks: An Econometric Analysis. Fusion: Practice and Applications, (), 82–91. DOI: https://doi.org/10.54216/FPA.190206

Mamani, J.C.M., Miri, M., Vorobev, Y. et al. Optimal Operation of Energy Microgrid Considering Economic and Emission Indices. Oper. Res. Forum 6, 122 (2025). https://doi.org/10.1007/s43069-025-00523-z

Matyakubova, A., Makhmudov, S., Ozturk, I., Kurbonov, K., Ismailov, F., Yokubboeva, S., & Urozov, A. (2025). Responses of Economic Policy Uncertainty, Financial Stress and Energy-Related Uncertainty to the Shocks in US-China Tension in US. *International Journal of Energy Economics and Policy, 15*(4), 701–708. https://doi.org/10.32479/ijeep.20369

Muhammad Zubair, Irfanud Din, Nadeem Sarwar et al. Revolutionizing Sepsis Diagnosis Using Machine Learning and Deep Learning Models: A Systematic Literature Review, 10 June 2025, PREPRINT (Version 1) available at Research Square [https://doi.org/10.21203/rs.3.rs-6731418/v1]

Niu, G., Jin, X., Wang, Q., & Zhou, Y. (2022). Broadband infrastructure and digital financial inclusion in rural China. *China Economic Review, 76*, 101853.

Osmundsen, K., & Bygstad, B. (2022). Making sense of continuous development of digital infrastructures. *Journal of Information Technology, 37*, 144–164.

PANJAITAN, M. B., HAMDANAH, H., SIRAIT, J., SUTIKNO, S., FATMAWATI, E., HERMAN, H., & MAMADIYAROV, Z. (2025). THE ROLE OF EMOTIONAL REGULATION IN SHAPING STUDENTS' PERCEPTION OF PHYSICS PROBLEMSOLVING TASKS. TPM – Testing, Psychometrics, Methodology in Applied Psychology, 32(S2(2025) : Posted 09 June), 1–10. Retrieved from https://tpmap.org/submission/index.php/tpm/article/view/139

Pradhan, R., Hajiyev, E., Shichiyakh, R. *et al.* Optimal Techno-Economic Feasibility of an Off-Grid Microgrid System Using Load Flow Energy Management Strategies. *Oper. Res. Forum* **6**, 120 (2025). https://doi.org/10.1007/s43069-025-00524-y

Romero, R. M., Zelinskaya, M., Makhmudov, S., Sapaev, S., & Rustambekovich, J. U. (2025, September). Modelling and Optimal Utilisation of the Renewable Energy Systems in Microgrid with Improving Reliability and Energy Efficiency. In Operations Research Forum (Vol. 6, No. 3, pp. 1–20). Springer International Publishing.

Samariddin Makhmudov, Kudratillo Tukhsanov, Saifulla Arslanbekov, Akram Amanov, Orifali Tursunov, Umarbek Jabbarov and Muyassarxon Mirzakarimova. 2024. Optimizing Supply Chain Financing Development Prospects of Digital Ecosystems in the European Logistics Industry. In The 8th International Conference on Future Networks & Distributed Systems (ICFNDS '24), December 11–12, 2024, Marakech, Morocco. ACM, New York, NY, USA, 12 Pages. https://doi.org/10.1145/3726122.3726200

Sharipov, K., Abdullayev, I., Kuziboev, B., Makhmudov, S., Kalandarov, F., Khaytboeva, N., & Ilkhamova, Z. (2025). The Effect of Energy Policy Risk on Renewable Energy. International Journal of Energy Economics and Policy, *15*(2), 566.

Senel, C. (2022). Mevduat bankalarinin hisse senedi getirilerine etki eden finansal faktörler [Financial factors affecting the stock returns of deposit banks]. *İşletme Araştırmaları Dergisi [Journal of Business Studies]*, *14*(3), 1880–1889.

Singh, N., Kumar, A., & Dey, K. (2023). Unlocking the potential of knowledge economy for rural resilience: The role of digital platforms. *Journal of Rural Studies*, *104*, 103164.

Su, R., Xiao, Y., Hamza, F., Mamadiyarov, Z., & Wahab, A. (2025). Scaling up green hydrogen in China: Economic opportunities and challenges. *International Journal of Hydrogen Energy*, *131*, 60–69.

Westermeier, C. (2020). Money is data—The platformization of financial transactions. *Information, Communication & Society*, *23*(14), 2047–2063.

Zhang, L., Zhao, Z., Qamri, G. M., & Makhmudov, S. (2025). Unleashing the critical role of renewable energy through global value chains and digitalization: A path towards environmental sustainability. Journal of Environmental Management, 392, 126688.

Zhou, T., & Lu, Y. (2011). Examining mobile instant messaging user loyalty from the perspectives of network externalities and flow experience. *Computers in Human Behavior*, *27*(2), 883–889.

Zokir Toshtemirovich Mamadiyarov, Samandarboy Adhambek ugli Sulaymanov, Sarvar Anvar ugli Askarov, and Durdona Bakhtiyor kizi Uktamova. 2022. Impact of Covid-19 Pandemic on Accelerating the Digitization and Transformation of Banks. In Proceedings of the 5th International Conference on Future Networks and Distributed Systems (ICFNDS '21). Association for Computing Machinery, New York, NY, USA, 706–712. https://doi.org/10.1145/3508072.3508211

Econometric Evaluation of Payment System Modernization Amid Digital Transformation: Insights from Uzbekistan's Central Bank

Zokir Mamadiyarov, Samariddin Makhmudov, Siddik Sayfullayev, Aziza Azlarova, Gulshat Karlibaeva, Boburbek Giyosidinov, and Mirzabek Jonuzokov

9.1. Introduction

Many more countries in the world face the pressure of rapidly digitalizing global economy that lead to modernize their payment infrastructures. To get against such backdrop Uzbekistan has placed digital transformation at the epicenter of recent strategical and economic reforms occurring in the country. In doing so, it is expected to stabilize the national financial system as well as encourage inclusive and efficient transactions on digital platforms. In this sense, the Central Bank of Uzbekistan plays a major role to lead and encourage the projects aimed at updating and expanding the country's payment infrastructure on digital landscape on fast pace. The efforts of the Central Bank initiatives to make the financial system more reliable, accessible, and efficient demonstrates the strategic goal of withstanding to global economic downturns and establishing higher economic stability in financial sector of the country on global scale.

Our research, in turn, tries to examine the results of modernization applying econometric methodologies to assess the performance and responses of the Central Bank's payment system in given period. In addition, the study examines whether a range of digital financial technologies impact important economic factors such as processing speed, transaction prices, and overall operational efficiency of the banking sector. To be more precise, this study intends to provide a better and broader understanding of the technological and regulatory hurdles that the Central Bank of Uzbekistan must face and overcome to be on the same foot with international financial trends while also taking into account the specifics of the domestic market developments. The findings from this research are intended to be used as assessment point for providing insights into the key determinants of resilient and efficient financial infrastructure and digitalization practices. The findings can also be applied to plan and develop policy recommendations for a country to advance the digitalization agenda in the banking sector of Uzbekistan.

9.2. Literature Review

Recent wage of technological developments especially the rise of artificial intelligence has changed the orthodox practices in financial landscape. In this sense, digitalization is a game-changer in global financial systems which is putting the central banks under a burden to consider Central bank digital currencies (CBDC) as a tool for developing and modernizing national payment infrastructures. This study represents a critical review of the current literature on CBDC in the context of improving the payment systems and efforts to digitalize the financial sector. The main objective is to assess the effects of CBDC on monetary policy, financial inclusion, and regional stability, taking into account the larger digital transformation process in Uzbekistan.

The central banks tend to improve monetary control and digitalize payment systems, mentioning interest in CBDCs has increased around the world. In addition, the study of Prodan et al. (2024) demonstrates how CBDCs have become a safer and more efficient substitute for real currency when regarding making payments. The Republic of Uzbekistan, a country that is actively pursuing digital transformation to improve the efficiency of its payment infrastructure, is particularly interested and actively implementing strategies of diversification through digitalization. Another study analyzed the state of CBDCs in Latin America and the Caribbean countries which revealed that financial exclusion and instability are perennial features (Alfonso et al., 2024).

Digital payment systems have significantly increased customer satisfaction by making transactions faster, more secure, and more convenient. In particular, internet banking, mobile applications, and credit/debit cards have improved the customer experience and increased loyalty to banks that offer advanced digital services (Saunders & Scholnick, 2006). In particular, innovations introduced into the mobile payment system are having a significant impact on banking, while traditional payment methods are becoming obsolete (Tran, 2021).

Payment banks have been operating in India as a competitor to commercial banks. They are valued for their convenience, security, and speed and for performing specialized transactions (Mani & Agarwal, 2022). Although not all banking transactions have been digitized yet, the payments banking model is accelerating the transition to a digital economy (Kesavan, 2023). The improvement of retail banking services in the context of digital transformation has accelerated, especially during the COVID-19 pandemic. However, special attention must be paid to the risks involved in managing digital banking services (Akhmetshin et al., 2025; Jahrir et al., 2025; Kuchkarov et al., 2025; Mamadiyarov et al., 2024; Mamani et al., 2025; Samariddin et al., 2024; Zokir et al., 2021).

Further research illustrates the CBDCs capability for direct access to central bank money that shows to help in furthering financial inclusion (Fernández-Villaverde et al., 2021). In this sense, especially in Uzbekistan, the country is pushing to improve financial services for previously underserved parts of the population. Additionally, CBDCs are believed to contribute to enhanced financial stability according to Gaipov et al. (2024) and He et al. (2024). Another research indicates that CBDCs could contribute to regional economic stability increasing the transparency and robustness of monetary systems (International Review of Economics & Finance, 2024). As to Uzbekistan, this framework could have given insights into economic benefits which could be drawn by the introduction of CBDCs into the banking system (Cahyani et al., 2025; Fayzieva et al., 2024; Hussain et al., 2023; Kalandarov et al., 2025; Litamahuputty et al., 2025; Khayrilla et al., 2025; Kurbonov et al., 2024; Mamadiyarov et al., 2024; Mamadiyarov et al., 2025; Muhammad et al., 2025; PANJAITAN et al., 2025; Zhang et al., 2025). According to the study conducted by Özüdoğru and Sönmez (2023), the use of data analytics and machine learning solutions for the insurance industry is expected to increase.

Another study examined the importance of CBDCs in improving the effectiveness of monetary policy in controlling inflation through bank liquidity management (Davoodaalhosseini, 2022). Mamadiyorov et al. (2025) conducted research on the digitalization of the financing system of banks in Uzbekistan, in particular, financing. To be precise, the report highlighted that financial services have now become more accessible in many remote areas. Econometric models have been built to study whether the impact of digitization on the Central Bank of Uzbekistan has been significant through refinancing rate and revealed that digital transformation have strongly affected central bank policies, particularly in terms of interest rates and monetary control (Lin et al., 2025; Litamahuputty et al., 2025; Mamadiyarov et al., 2025; Pradhan et al., 2025; Su et al., 2025). Banna et al. (2022) examined how fintech can be used to reduce risk for widespread access to financial services. A non-traditional approach (Savelli et al., 2024) explored the application of CBDC to the energy sector, suggesting that CBDCs can reduce risk and increase efficiency in payments and transactions. Overall, these studies provide evidences for promoting and using digitalization and CBDCs that could improve financial inclusion, improve monetary policy, and expand economic opportunities.

While, most of the existing studies have focused either on advanced economies or large emerging markets, little attention is being paid to those specific economic and institutional features that might apply to smaller or developing countries like Uzbekistan, with very unique structural and economic challenges. The paper seeks to fill these gaps by providing a more context-sensitive, localized analysis of CBDCs within the financial ecosystem in Uzbekistan. Our objective is not only trying to find out the possible economic benefits but also discuss in practical ways the challenges arising during the implementation of CBDCs within the fast-evolving financial sector of Uzbekistan. Coupled with econometric methodologies with data for Uzbekistan, our study seeks to deepen the understanding of the extent CBDCs interact with broader economic and financial goals of the country, especially in monetary policy, financial inclusion, and regional stability. In this sense, our study contributes to the better comprehension of CBDC adoption policies in emerging economies by central banks and is further oriented toward providing useful insights for policymakers and financial stakeholders across this transformational challenges.

9.3. Research Methodology and Development Hypothesis

Structural equation modeling (SEM) and regression equations for multivariate linear regression (LS) were implemented as main tool of analysis. The data of 49 monthly observations from the Central Bank of the Republic of Uzbekistan were studied and examined in the period from 2020 to 2023. In addition to it, diagnostic tests such as the Gauss–Markov, Durbin–Watson, Shapiro–Wilk, and Breusch–Pagan tests were implemented to verify statistical significance and further advance the reliability of the research model. The statistical significance of the SEM regression model was evaluated through tests based on the chi-square test, Comparative Fit Index (CFI), Root Mean Square Error of Approximation (RMSEA), and Standardized Root Mean Square Residual (SRMR) respectively, while multicollinearity and constructing a correlation matrix were also examined in accordance with regression model.

To develop the econometric model of the Central Bank's effective payment system in the national economy, we used a multivariate LS model and non-linear SEM due to the fact that the collected data is multivariate time series.

Additionally, based on the data from the Central Bank of the Republic of Uzbekistan (<https://www.cbu.uz/>), a total of 49 monthly observations from 2020 to 2023 were utilized in our research. Also, statistical significance in the multivariate LS model was calculated with diagnostic tests such as the Gauss–Markov, Durbin–Watson, Shapiro–Wilk, and Breusch–Pagan tests. The statistical significance of the SEM regression model was, meanwhile, evaluated through diagnostic tests based on the chi-square test, CFI, RMSEA, and SRMR.

To make econometric models for the study, visual representations and statistical tables were developed in order to study the variables. Additionally, multicollinearity assessed the relationships between dependent and independent variables, while also a correlation matrix was constructed and explained. Both the multivariate regression (LS) model and the SEM regression equations were developed and evaluated.

9.3.1. Variables

In the econometric study, dependent and independent variables were defined as follows:
Dependent variable is:

lnpaym_non_cash—The share of non-cash transactions in the total payment volume within the banking system.

Independent variables are the followings:

lnvol_mob_bank—The volume of mobile banking operations within the banking system.

lnelect_paym_platf—The number of electronic payment platforms in the banking system.

lnremote_bank_syst—The number of users utilizing remote banking services in the banking system.

9.3.2. Hypotheses

The following hypotheses were tested in the study:

H_0 (Null Hypothesis): The volume of mobile banking operations, the number of electronic payment platforms, and the number of users of remote banking systems do not significantly affect the share of non-cash transactions in the banking system.

$$\text{Mathematically, } H_0: \beta_1 = 0, \beta_2 = 0, \beta_3 = 0,$$

where β_1, β_2, and β_3 represent the coefficients for all independent variables.

H_1 (Alternative Hypothesis): The volume of mobile banking operations, the number of electronic payment platforms, and the number of users of remote banking systems have a significant positive impact on the share of non-cash transactions in the banking system.

$$\text{Mathematically, } H_1: \beta_1 \neq 0, \beta_2 \neq 0, \beta_3 \neq 0.$$

Additional alternative hypotheses: Separate alternative hypotheses are proposed for the individual effects of each independent variable:

H_1a: The volume of mobile banking operations positively affects the share of non-cash transactions in the banking system.

H_1b: The number of electronic payment platforms positively affects the share of non-cash transactions in the banking system.

H_1c: The number of users of remote banking systems positively affects the share of non-cash transactions in the banking system.

9.4. Analysis and Results

The study presents an analytical graph of the share of non-cash transactions in the total payment volume within the banking system and the time-based analysis of the factors influencing these indicators (Figure 28).

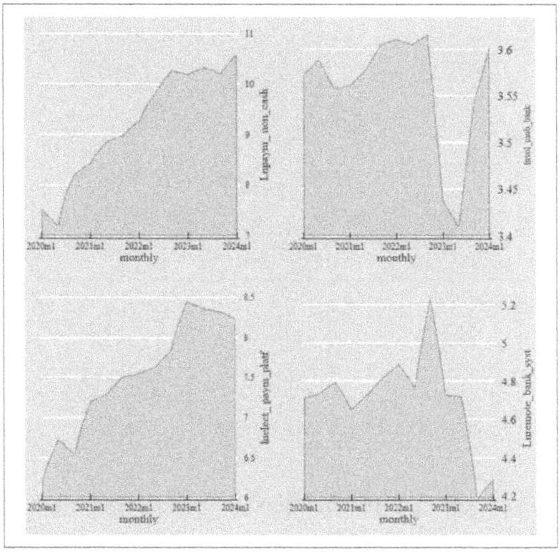

Figure 28. Analytical graphic drawing of indicators of dependent variable and influencing factors over time.

Source: It was developed by the authors based on Stata software.

According to Figure 28, the time-based analytical graph of dependent and independent variables indicates an overall upward trend during the analyzed period. Based on the graphical representation, the share of non-cash transactions in the banking system and the number of electronic payment platforms within the system have demonstrated a consistent growth trend. This outcome is largely the result of reforms implemented by the government within the banking system.

Additionally, the volume of mobile banking operations and the number of users of remote banking services saw a sharp decline in the early months of 2023. Despite this temporary dip, the graph shows a positive growth forecast for the variables in the future. In the next stage of the study, the analytical correlation (reconnected) graph of the dependent and independent variables' indicators is presented in Figure 29.

According to Figure 29, the graphical representation of the dependent and independent variables shows that the increase in the share of non-cash transactions in the total payment volume within the banking system expands the coverage of digital services in banks. This, in turn, provides a forecast for the growth of financial profitability indicators in commercial banks.

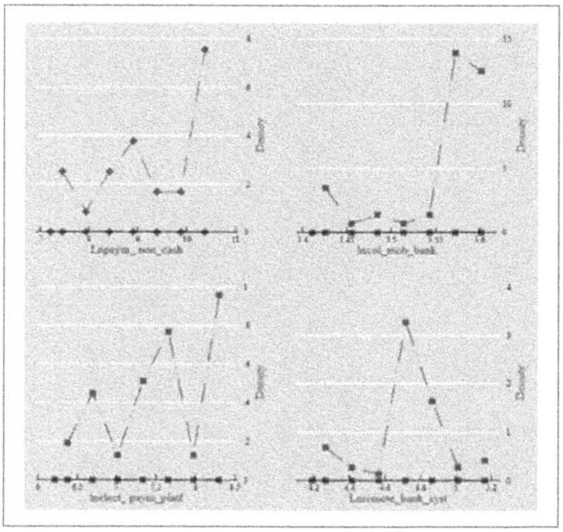

Figure 29. The share of non-cash transactions in the total payment volume in the banking system and the analytical dependence (rconnected) graph of the factors affecting them.

Source: It was developed by the authors based on Stata software.

As the total volume of non-cash transactions increases, it contributes to the development of digital operations within the banking system and supports the advancement of an effective payment system.

In the next stage, the graphical matrix and scatter plot of the dependent and independent variables are presented (Figures 30 and 31).

According to Figures 30 and 31, the visual representations from the graphical matrix and scatter plots indicate a strong correlation between the dependent and independent variables, showing a clear concentration of density effects. These density schemes highlight the concentration of relationships, demonstrating the tendency of data points for all variables to cluster in specific regions on the graph.

In the next stage of the study, a standardized normal probability plot was applied to estimate the probable distributions of the dependent and independent variables (Figure 32).

According to Figure 32, the standardized normal probability plot for the dependent and independent variables shows a significant forecast of the estimated probability of the linear data points along the diagonal. Additionally, the consistent adherence of the variables to the diagonal trajectory indicates strengthened confidence in the normal probability plot. In the next stage,

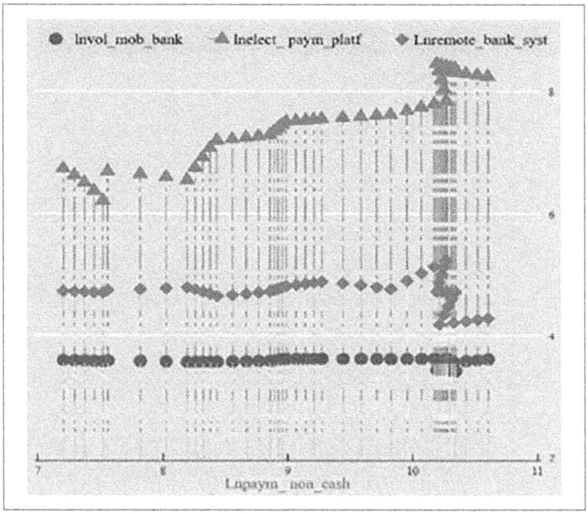

Figure 30. Graphical matrix of the relationship between dependent and independent variables.

Source: It was developed by the authors based on Stata software.

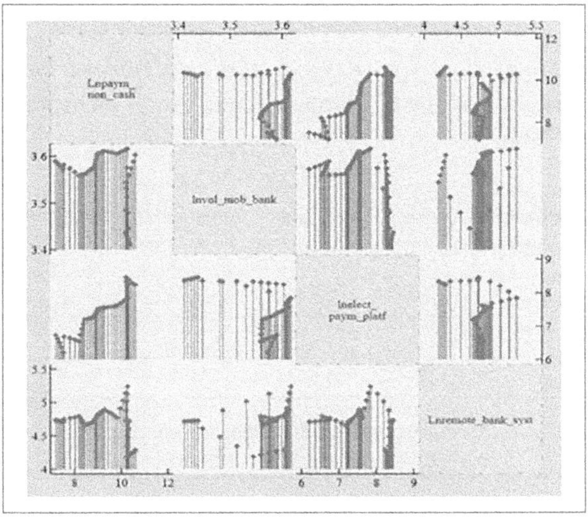

Figure 31. Scatter plot matrix of the relationship between dependent and independent variables.

Source: It was developed by the authors based on Stata software.

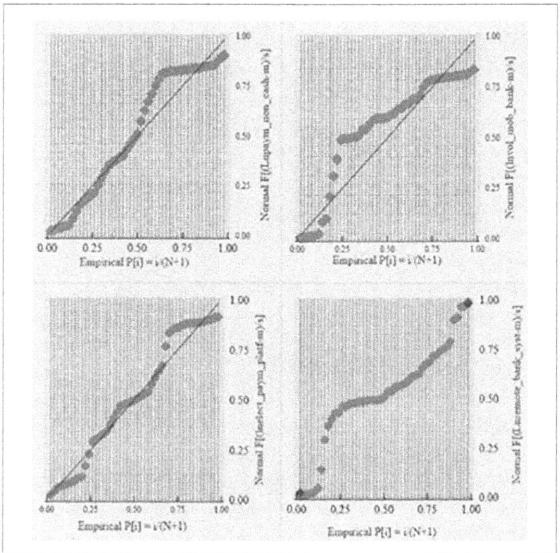

Figure 32. A standardized normal probability plot of the dependent variable and its influencing factors.

Source: It was developed by the authors based on Stata software.

the correlation matrix of the share of non-cash transactions in the total payment volume within the banking system and the factors affecting it was examined (see Table 28).

Table 28. The correlation matrix of the share of non-cash transactions in the total payment volume within the banking system and the factors influencing it

Variables	(1)	(2)	(3)	(4)	Significant
Lnpaym_non~h	1.000				
lnvol_mob_~k	−0. 5511	1.000			
	(0.034)				***
lnelect_pa~f	0.6976	−0.4962	1.000		
	(0.0000)	(0.0003)			***
Lnremote_b~t	0.5384	0.2230	−0.2376	1.000	
	(0.0012)	***(0.1023)***	***(0.0000)***		***

Source: It was developed by the authors based on Stata software.

According to the results in Table 28, there is a strong, statistically significant, and inverse correlation between the dependent and independent variables. The correlation matrix indicates that there is no multicollinearity among the influencing factors. Additionally, the reliability coefficient between the share of non-cash transactions in the total payment volume within the banking system and the factors influencing it stands at 65.84%, demonstrating a positive relationship between the constructed econometric equations and the quality indicators.

An econometric model was developed for the study using a multivariate LS analysis. The multivariate LS model used in the study involves the natural logarithms of the dependent and independent variables.

The econometric model formula derived from the multivariate LS approach is as follows:

$$Lnpaym\_non\_cash = \beta_0 + \beta_1 lnvol\_mob\_bank + \beta_2 lnelect\_paym\_platf + \beta_3 Lnremote\_bank\_syst \quad (1)$$

where:

- β_0 represents the intercept (constant term);
- β_1, β_2, and β_3 represent the coefficients for the independent variables in the model.

The multivariate LS model results for the study are presented in Table 29.

According to the regression results, the coefficients are expressed in the following formula:

$$ln(paym\_non\_cash) = -14.91 + 2.77 \cdot ln(vol\_mob\_bank) + 1.66 ln(elect\_paym\_platf) + 0.361 \cdot ln(remote\_bank\_syst) \quad (2)$$

Statistical significance of the regression equation: All coefficients are statistically significant at a 0.05 level, as all *p*-values are <0.05.

Model fit of the econometric model:

R-squared (0.943): This indicates that approximately 94.3% of the variance in the share of non-cash transactions in the total payment volume is explained by the model.

Table 29. Multifactor linear regression (LS) model indicators of the share of non-cash operations in the total payment volume in the banking system and factors affecting it

Lnpaym_non_cash	Coef.	St. Err.	*t*-value	*p*-value	[95% Conf	Interval]	Sig
lnvol_mob_bank	2.77	0.609	4.55	0	1.543	3.997	***
lnelect_paym_platf	1.667	0.087	19.16	0	1.492	1.842	***
Lnremote_bank_syst	0.362	0.117	3.09	0.003	0.126	0.598	***
Constant	−14.92	02.813	−5.30	0	−20.586	−9.254	***

Mean dependent var	9.251	SD dependent var	1.043
R-squared	0.943	Number of obs	49
Adj *R*-squared	0. 939	Root MSE	0.256
F-test	177.893	Prob > F	0.000
Akaike crit. (AIC)	9.600	Bayesian crit. (BIC)	17.167
*** $p < 0.01$, ** $p < 0.05$, * $p < 0.1$			

Source: It was developed by the authors based on Stata software.

Adjusted *R*-squared (0.939): Reflects the *R*-squared value adjusted for the number of predictors in the model.

F-statistic value: 177.89 ($p = 0.0000$), indicating that the model is statistically significant overall.

9.5. Results and Discussions

A 1% increase in mobile banking operations volume results in a 2.77% increase in the share of non-cash transactions in the total payment volume.

A 1% increase in the number of electronic payment platforms leads to a 1.66% increase in the share of non-cash transactions.

A 1% increase in the number of users of remote banking systems results in a 0.36% increase in the share of non-cash transactions.

The Gauss–Markov conditions were tested through diagnostic tests for the econometric equations. Applying the Durbin–Watson test to the multivariate LS model produced a coefficient of 0.43. Additionally, the analysis revealed a Shapiro–Wilk W-test statistic of 0.78. The null hypothesis H_0: $y = 0$ and the corresponding alternative hypothesis H1: $y \neq 0$ were evaluated with $p > 0.05$. Since the p-value exceeded 0.05, the null hypothesis was confirmed.

The econometric analysis showed that the key conditions of the Gauss–Markov theorem were met. The VIF test was used to assess multicollinearity, and the VIF value of 1.26 indicated no multicollinearity in the model. This demonstrated a relationship between the share of non-cash transactions and the influencing factors in the banking system.

Furthermore, the analysis of the multivariate LS model showed statistical significance at $p < 0.10$, leading to the rejection of the alternative hypothesis. The VIF test results were within the acceptable range (between 1 and 10).

Additionally, during the study, the SEM regression model's diagram and test results appeared as shown in Figure 33.

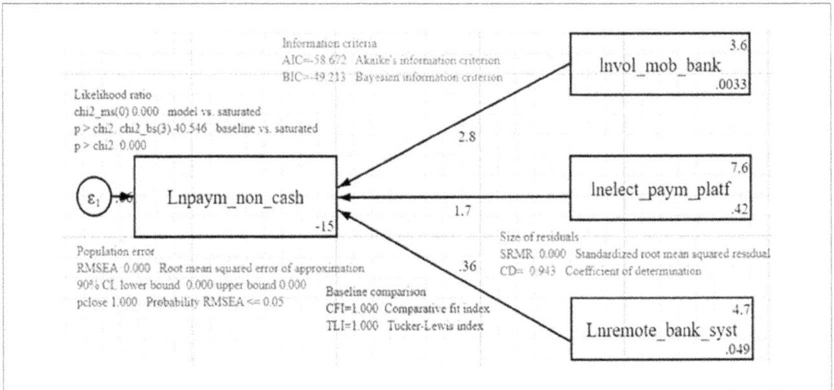

Figure 33. Schematic view of the SEM regression model between the share of non-cash transactions in the total payment volume and the factors affecting it in the banking system.

Source: It was developed by the authors based on Stata software.

According to Figure 33, the SEM diagram confirms a robust positive relationship between dependent and independent variables. It is clear that the coefficients reveal that mobile banking and electronic payment platforms have the largest impact on non-cash payments, while remote banking systems, despite generating a smaller coefficient, still hold statistical significance in the model. The fit indices (AIC, BIC, RMSEA, SRMR, CFI, TLI) collectively indicate that the econometric model is rather successful, demonstrating high explanatory power and minimal error.

9.6. Conclusion

The econometric analysis shows the factors that impact the share of non-cash transactions in the banking system like mobile banking operations, the number of electronic payment platforms, and the number of users of remote banking systems, and ultimately leads to the following conclusions:

1. The coefficient of mobile banking operations is 2.77, indicating a 1% increase in mobile banking volume results in a 2.77% increase in the share of non-cash transactions. This highlights that digital transformation in the banking sector, particularly mobile banking, provides essential services in modern banks as driver for the transition to non-cash transactions.
2. It is also revealed that mobile banking transactions increase engender to more users opt for non-cash methods in financial operations. In this sense, improving mobile banking services can have a multiplicative effect that aims to promote the adoption of non-cash payment systems and enhancing the financial efficiency of the banking system.
3. Having found the coefficient for electronic payment platforms is 1.66, it indicates that a 1% increase in the number of electronic payment platforms leads to a 1.66% rise in the share of non-cash transactions. This, in particular, demonstrates that the expansion of electronic payment platforms (such as online gateways and mobile wallets) directly improves and contributes to the transition of non-cash transactions.
4. Aforementioned digital platforms, in this regard, offer greater accessibility and convenience to users, which lead to reduction of physical cash. In this matter, strong correlations of digital platforms providing greater accessibility and convenience indicate that robust digital payment infrastructure can support digital economies and incentivize non-cash payments in the whole economy.

Overall, the results of the econometric model demonstrate that digitalization of banking services, particularly through mobile banking and electronic payment platforms, has a significant positive impact on the share of non-cash transactions and popularization of digital practices. As more banks and financial institutions continue to transform to digitization of services, the share of non-cash transactions will increase further in the coming future, which ultimately would lead to better efficient and innovative banking system.

Bibliography

Abdullah, M. A., Han, X., Amjad, M. A., & Makhmudov, S. (2025). Revisit the role of financial development on economic growth, human development, and sustainable development in higher-income countries. *Journal of Environmental Management*, *392*, 126874.

Akhmetshin, E., Abdullayev, I., Makhmudov, S., Dakhkilgova, K., Korotaeva, I. and Yanovskaya, G. (2025). APPLICATION OF TANH–COTH METHOD FOR COMBINED AND DOUBLE COMBINED SINH–COSH–GORDON EQUATIONS ARISING CHEMICAL REACTIONS TO WATER SURFACE GRAVITY WAVES. Computational Methods for Differential Equations, (), -. doi: 10.22034/cmde.2025.67655.3234

Alfonso, C. V., Kamin, S., & Zampolli, F. (2024). Central bank digital currencies (CBDCs) in Latin America and the Caribbean. *Latin American Journal of Central Banking*, *2024*, 100140. <https://doi.org/10.1016/j.latcb.2024.100140>

Banna, H., Mia, M. A., Nourani, M., & Yarovaya, L. (2022). Fintech-based financial inclusion and risk-taking of microfinance institutions (MFIs): Evidence from Sub-Saharan Africa. *Finance Research Letters*, *45*, 102149. <https://doi.org/10.1016/j.frl.2021.102149>

Cahyani, I., Buriev, K., Ngongo, M., Mamadiyarov, Z., Ino, L., Herman, H., Saputra, N., & Baxtishodovich, S. (2025). Exploring the Use of TikTok Application in Enhancing the Skill of Pronunciation: A Case on Students' Perception. Studies in Media and Communication, 13(2), 150–158. doi:http://dx.doi.org/10.11114/smc.v13i2.7553

Central bank digital currency, financial technology level, and regional financial stability. (2024). *International Review of Economics & Finance*, *96*, 103598. <https://doi.org/10.1016/j.iref.2024.103598>

Davoodalhosseini, S. M. (2022). Central bank digital currency and monetary policy. *Journal of Economic Dynamics and Control*, *142*, 104150. <https://doi.org/10.1016/j.jedc.2021.104150>

Fernández-Villaverde, J., Sanches, D., Schilling, L., & Uhlig, H. (2021). Central bank digital currency: Central banking for all? *Review of Economic Dynamics*, *41*, 225–242. <https://doi.org/10.1016/j.red.2020.12.004>

Hussain, A., Khan, M., Rakhmonov, D. A., Mamadiyarov, Z. T., Kurbonbekova, M. T., & Mahmudova, M. Q. K. (2023). Nexus of Training and Development, Organizational Learning Capability, and Organizational Performance in the Service Sector. *Sustainability*, *15*(4), 3246. https://doi.org/10.3390/su15043246

Jahrir, A., Gultom, Y., Herman, H., Zabadi, F., Ngongo, M., Mamadiyarov, Z., Fatmawati, E., & Saputra, N. (2025). Investigating the Elements of Short Commercial Mineral Water Advertisement: A Case on Discourse Analysis. Studies in Media and Communication, 13(4), 94–104. doi:http://dx.doi.org/10.11114/smc.v13i4.7813

Kalandarov, F., Makhmudov, S., Ibadullaev, D., Matniyozov, M., Nasretdinova, F., Sabirov, K., & Bahodirov, N. M. (2025). Low-Carbon Energy Risk and Renewable Energy Development: Insigths from Method of Moments Quantile Regression. International Journal of Energy Economics and Policy, *15*(3), 524–536.

Kesavan, V. (2023). Present state and future directions of digital payments system: A historical and bibliographic examination. *International Journal of Professional Business Review*, *8*(6), e02317. <https://doi.org/10.26668/businessreview/2023.v8i6.2317>

Kuchkarov, T., Mamadiyarov, Z., Khakimov, Z., Sabirova, O., Matmurodov, K., Raimboyeva, M., & Umarova, S. (2025). Energy-Related Uncertainty and Crypto-Currency Environmental Attention: Time-Varying Perspective. International Journal of Energy Economics and Policy, 15(5), 614–626. https://doi.org/10.32479/ijeep.20784

Kurbonov, K. (2025). Quantitative easing and its long-term effects on US credit market sustainability: A neutrosophic science perspective. International Journal of Neutrosophic Science (IJNS), 25(3).

Khayrilla Kurbonov, Samariddin Makhmudov, Shakhzod Erkinov, Umidjon Dadabaev, Gulnora Bekimbetova, Rukhiddin Zayniddinov, and Mirzabek Jonuzokov. 2025. Evaluating the Impact of Marketing Practices Digitalization and Investment on Labor Market Efficiency and Commercial Bank Performance Using Econometric Models. In Proceedings of the 8th International Conference on Future Networks & Distributed Systems (ICFNDS '24). Association for Computing Machinery, New York, NY, USA, 786–796. https://doi.org/10.1145/3726122.3726237

Lin, M.H., Matchanova, B., Nurmatovich, H.A. *et al.* Optimal Operation of the Multi-Carrier Energy System Considering Energy Markets and Renewable Energies Participation. *Int. J. Appl. Comput. Math* **11**, 170 (2025). https://doi.org/10.1007/s40819-025-02002-9

Litamahuputty, J. V., Amiruddin, E. G., Rahim, R., Rahman, A., & Mamadiyarov, Z. (2025). Cryptocurrency Risk Management through Decision Engineering: Evaluating XRPUSD and ADAUSD Portfolio Performance. Journal of Applied Science, Engineering, Technology, and Education, 7(1), 69–81. https://doi.org/10.35877/454RI.asci3871

Mamadiyarov, Z., Hakimov, H., & Askarov, S. (2024). DEVELOPMENT OF RETAIL BANKING SERVICES IN THE CONTEXT OF DIGITAL TRANSFORMATION. *Financial and Credit Activity Problems of Theory and Practice*, *1*(54), 51–67. https://doi.org/10.55643/fcaptp.1.54.2024.4288

Mamadiyarov, Z., Eshov, M., Otakhonova, D., Utegenova, S., Sabirov, K., Marks, A., & Bahodirov, N. (2025). Does Energy Policy Risk Threaten Energy Sources Diversification?. *International Journal of Energy Economics and Policy*, *15*(5), 730–740. https://doi.org/10.32479/ijeep.21140

Mamadiyarov, Z. Makhmudov, S. Utanov, B. Kasimova, D. Bekmurodova, G. Hakimov, Z. (2025). Fusion of Economic and Financial Factors Affecting Household Deposits in Banks: An Econometric Analysis. *Fusion: Practice and Applications*, (), 82–91. DOI: https://doi.org/10.54216/FPA.190206

Mamani, J.C.M., Miri, M., Vorobev, Y. et al. Optimal Operation of Energy Microgrid Considering Economic and Emission Indices. Oper. Res. Forum 6, 122 (2025). https://doi.org/10.1007/s43069-025-00523-z

Mani, M., & Agarwal, R. K. (2022). Payment banks in India: Insights from the customers' perception. *International Journal of Asian Business and Information Management*, *13*(1), 1–15. <https://doi.org/10.4018/ijabim.297851>

Matyakubova, A., Makhmudov, S., Ozturk, I., Kurbonov, K., Ismailov, F., Yokubboeva, S., & Urozov, A. (2025). Responses of Economic Policy Uncertainty, Financial Stress and Energy-Related Uncertainty to the Shocks in US-China Tension in US. *International Journal of Energy Economics and Policy, 15*(4), 701–708. https://doi.org/10.32479/ijeep.20369

Muhammad Zubair, Irfanud Din, Nadeem Sarwar et al. Revolutionizing Sepsis Diagnosis Using Machine Learning and Deep Learning Models: A Systematic Literature Review, 10 June 2025, PREPRINT (Version 1) available at Research Square [https://doi.org/10.21203/rs.3.rs-6731418/v1]

PANJAITAN, M. B., HAMDANAH, H., SIRAIT, J., SUTIKNO, S., FATMAWATI, E., HERMAN, H., & MAMADIYAROV, Z. (2025). THE ROLE OF EMOTIONAL REGULATION IN SHAPING STUDENTS' PERCEPTION OF PHYSICS PROBLEMSOLVING TASKS. TPM – Testing, Psychometrics, Methodology in Applied Psychology, 32(S2(2025) : Posted 09 June), 1–10. Retrieved from https://tpmap.org/submission/index.php/tpm/article/view/139

Özüdoğru, H. & Sönmez, S. S. (2024). The impact of artificial intelligence and machine learning on the insurance industry. *Journal of Banking and Financial Research, 11*(1), 45–53.

Pradhan, R., Hajiyev, E., Shichiyakh, R. *et al.* Optimal Techno-Economic Feasibility of an Off-Grid Microgrid System Using Load Flow Energy Management Strategies. *Oper. Res. Forum* **6**, 120 (2025). https://doi.org/10.1007/s43069-025-00524-y

Prodan, I., Konhäusner, P., Dabija, D.-C., Lazaroiu, G., & Marincean, L. (2024). The rise in popularity of central bank digital currencies: A systematic review. *Heliyon, 10*(9), e30561. <https://doi.org/10.1016/j.heliyon.2024.e30561>

Romero, R. M., Zelinskaya, M., Makhmudov, S., Sapaev, S., & Rustambekovich, J. U. (2025, September). Modelling and Optimal Utilisation of the Renewable Energy Systems in Microgrid with Improving Reliability and Energy Efficiency. In Operations Research Forum (Vol. 6, No. 3, pp. 1–20). Springer International Publishing.

Samariddin Makhmudov, Kudratillo Tukhsanov, Saifulla Arslanbekov, Akram Amanov, Orifali Tursunov, Umarbek Jabbarov and Muyassarxon Mirzakarimova. 2024. Optimizing Supply Chain Financing Development Prospects of Digital Ecosystems in the European

Logistics Industry. In The 8th International Conference on Future Networks & Distributed Systems (ICFNDS '24), December 11–12, 2024, Marakech, Morocco. ACM, New York, NY, USA, 12 Pages. https://doi.org/10.1145/3726122.3726200

Savelli, I., Hepburn, C., & Morstyn, T. (2024). A blueprint for energy systems in the era of central bank digital currencies. *Technological Forecasting and Social Change*, *207*, 123637. <https://doi.org/10.1016/j.techfore.2024.123637>

Saunders, A., & Scholnick, B. (2006). Frontiers in payment and settlement systems: Introduction. *Journal of Banking and Finance*, *30*(6), 1605–1612. <https://doi.org/10.1016/J.JBANKFIN.2005.09.007>

Sharipov, K., Abdullayev, I., Kuziboev, B., Makhmudov, S., Kalandarov, F., Khaytboeva, N., & Ilkhamova, Z. (2025). The Effect of Energy Policy Risk on Renewable Energy. International Journal of Energy Economics and Policy, *15*(2), 566.

Su, R., Xiao, Y., Hamza, F., Mamadiyarov, Z., & Wahab, A. (2025). Scaling up green hydrogen in China: Economic opportunities and challenges. *International Journal of Hydrogen Energy*, *131*, 60–69.

Tran, M. H. (2021). Payment system and bank performance: Evidence from Vietnam. *The Journal of Contemporary Issues in Business and Government*, *27*(2), 91–94. <https://doi.org/10.47750/CIBG.2021.27.02.012>

Zhang, L., Zhao, Z., Qamri, G. M., & Makhmudov, S. (2025). Unleashing the critical role of renewable energy through global value chains and digitalization: A path towards environmental sustainability. Journal of Environmental Management, 392, 126688.

Zokir Toshtemirovich Mamadiyarov, Samandarboy Adhambek ugli Sulaymanov, Sarvar Anvar ugli Askarov, and Durdona Bakhtiyor kizi Uktamova. 2022. Impact of Covid-19 Pandemic on Accelerating the Digitization and Transformation of Banks. In Proceedings of the 5th International Conference on Future Networks and Distributed Systems (ICFNDS '21). Association for Computing Machinery, New York, NY, USA, 706–712. https://doi.org/10.1145/3508072.3508211

Mapping Renewable Energy Insurance Using Bibliometric Visualization

Valentina Ninova and Nikolay Ninov

10.1. Introduction

Humanity faces serious challenges related to environmental protection and climate change. This, in turn, has been a catalyst for identifying and implementing methods and mechanisms to minimize and eventually neutralize the key issues involved (Costantini & Martini, 2010). To effectively address these significant and pressing challenges, which by their very nature extend beyond public policies and legal norms, targeted actions and adequate tools are being implemented, including the use of renewable energy sources (RES). "We need a lot of green electricity to meet our climate goals" (Petersen, 2022).

An alternative to fossil fuels is the various sources of renewable energy (e.g., wind energy, solar energy, geothermal energy, biomass, biofuels, etc.). They contribute to minimizing and limiting greenhouse gas emissions, reducing energy supply and dependence on fossil fuels, mainly oil and natural gas. Recapitulating the current situation on a global scale and from a technological point of view, the share of renewable wind energy is found to be the largest and most significant. Starting from the idea of mankind's need for more green energy, the promotion, investment, and exploitation of RES are fully in line with the commitment to sustainable development, which represents a kind of symbiosis between the environment, economic development, and social progress (ICF International, 2022). On the other hand, energy efficiency, or the peculiar development of RES, has two benefits for humanity: increasing energy security and mitigating climate change. To achieve these objectives, it is necessary to accelerate the processes related to the deployment and exploitation of RES and to use them on an industrial scale. There is also a need for shorter and simpler procedures for obtaining authorization for their commissioning. This provokes the need for extended and detail-focused research in this critically important area for modern society.

10.2. Literature Review

There are several publications in the world literature focusing on the impact of using renewable energy (Abbasi & Abbasi, 2000; Kumar, 2020; Prakash & Bhat, 2009; Sheikh et al., 2016). The finding is that wind is predominantly used as a RES on an industrial scale. Since the goal is to provide clean and green energy on a large scale, other alternatives are also being explored—e.g., tidal power, large solar installations, and the use of algae for biofuels (European Parliament, 2022). This, in turn, is a "starting point" for increasing RES operation, improving energy efficiency, and achieving significant emission reductions in the energy sector (Barton et al., 2004).

The implementation of this objective follows a certain algorithm, essential elements of which are securing sufficient financial resources for investment, project development, and management. Developing renewable energy projects requires the expenditure of significant financial resources, which are necessary at every stage. The need to make these substantial investments is the reason why specific research on renewable energy investments is found in global databases (Scopus, Web of Science, Google Scholar, etc.) (Abba et al., 2022; Bergmann et al., 2006; Strantzali & Aravossis, 2016).

It is logical that if the process of investing in projects related to RES is accompanied by the management of significant financial resources, then there is a significant risk of adverse events occurring, the consequences of which may be negative for investors and business organizations. In this line of thought, a key role is assigned to insurance activity (Ninova & Ninov, 2023). The risks inherent in RES investment are numerous and can be briefly classified as construction and project start-up risks, fire and natural disaster risks, market risks, and other operational risks. All of these give rise to the need to apply insurance as an economic activity aimed at minimizing and/or neutralizing the negative consequences associated with the investment and operation of RES. The inclusion of insurance activity as part of the processes accompanying sustainable development (through the application of insurance coverage aimed at RES) gives rise, in turn, to the need for the insurance industry to have sufficient and comprehensive information on all the risks mentioned. The aim is to have sufficient empirical data based on which the indicators—frequency and severity of damage—can be calculated. The scientific publications on the measurement and analysis of these indicators are Beaumont (2007), Bromiley et al. (2015), Froot et al. (1993), Jastrzębska et al. (2014), McShane et al. (2011), and Ward (2001).

Along with the thematic areas mentioned so far, the topic of publications dedicated to the insurance market renewable energy deserves a significant place and serious attention (Joof et al., 2023; Mills, 2003; Pata & Samour, 2023). Moreover, scientific developments in renewable energy insurance are also of significant interest from the point of view of insurance science. The same research is closely focused on renewable energy options for insurance loss reduction (Mills, 2003; Vine, 1998; Vine et al., 2000).

10.3. Methodology

The application of bibliometric analysis aims to objectively and reliably analyze existing bibliographic arrays (databases) on a given topic or scientific field based on quantitative characteristics for evaluation and classification according to different categories: geographical, chronological, by author, language, accepted classification system, and so on (Ellili et al., 2023). By applying a specific tool for this purpose, it is possible to study the dynamics of development, publication activity, and trends of documents on a specific topic.

The present study is aimed at carrying out a bibliometric analysis on the topic "Renewable energy insurance", and within it, information from the Scopus database is extracted and analyzed. For the period 1981–2024, as of 02 April 2024, Scopus is one of the largest bibliographic and referencing databases containing abstracts and citations, as well as a tool for tracking the citability of research published in specialized journals. In this study, we use Scopus as a data source, asking (TITLE-ABS-KEY (insurance) AND TITLE-ABS-KEY (renewable AND energy)) search within (Article title, Abstract, Keywords).

As a result of the set criteria and the search, 246 documents were generated. To correctly and comprehensively analyze the state of development and hot topics in the field of Renewableenergy insurance and to develop visualizations for them, this study investigated—the state of the documents and hot spot trends using VOSviewer (Nees Jan van Eck and Ludo Waltman; Version 1.6.20) (Jan van Eck & Waltman, n.d.). In this study, the tool used is to create bibliographic maps of co-authorship, co-occurrence, and co-citation. When applying the mentioned software tool, the lines on the map illustrate objectively the existing relationships between important items (Ninova, 2024). The coloring of the circles illustrates the correspondence in the clusters to which the items belong (Ninova, 2024). The detailed steps in conducting the study are visualized in Figure 34.

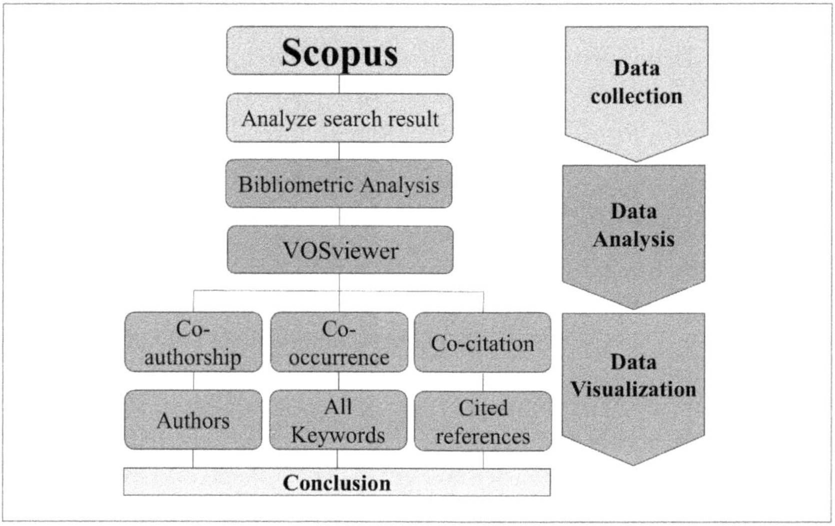

Figure 34. Bibliometric analysis and the recommended workflow for scientific mapping. Renewable Energy Insurance; Scopus.
Source: Authors' design based on Xie et al. (2021).

10.4. Results

Before presenting the visualized maps from the conducted type analysis, based on the information retrieved from the Scopus database, Figure 35 presents the results of documents by year, for the period 1981–2024, on the topic of "Renewable Energy Insurance."

For the period 1981–2024, 246 documents on the subject were identified in the Scopus bibliographic arrays. The largest proportion of research was conducted, published, and indexed by Scopus in 2023, in which the number reached 31. The second and third places were occupied by 2022 and 2012, in which 21 and 18 documents on the topic were indexed, respectively.

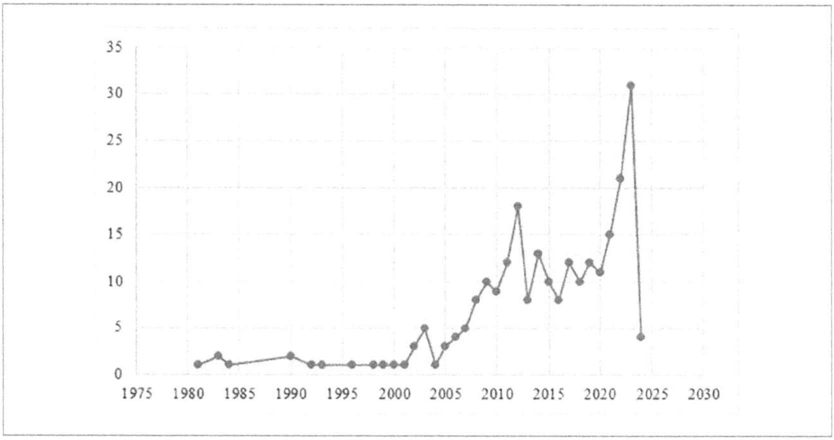

Figure 35. Documents by year.
Source: Author's design based on Elsevier BV (1981–2024).

Figure 36 visualizes the first type of analysis—co-authorship analysis, according to authors, with weights based on documents. The identified cluster represents the extent to which authors are co-authors, and the width of the lines demonstrates the intensity of co-author interactions.

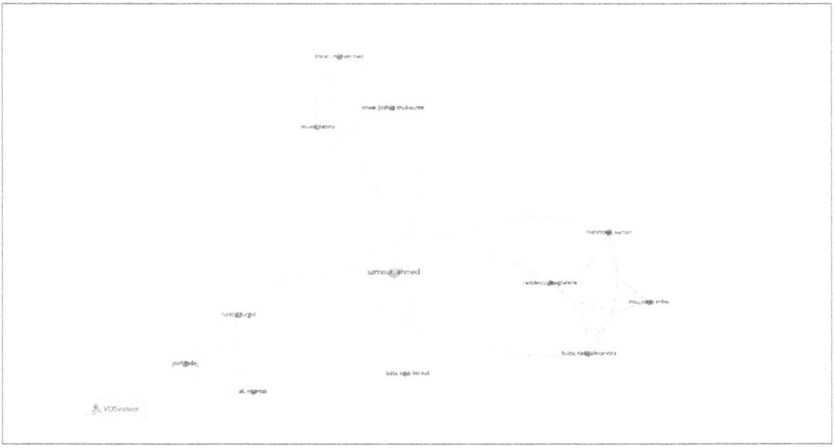

Figure 36. Bibliographic data map: Co-authorship analysis: Authors.
Source: Visualization map from VOSviewer based on the Scopus database.

Using the VOSviewer software application, with information from the Scopus database, the resulting bibliographic data map consists of 12 items, 4 clusters, and 23 links. The figure shows the largest set, which includes 12 of the 668 authors.

In the scope of the present study on the topic "Renewable energy insurance," Figure 37 presents an analysis of co-occurrence, based on all keywords and a visualized bibliographic data map (weight is based on occurrence). Minimum number of occurrences of keyword—5.

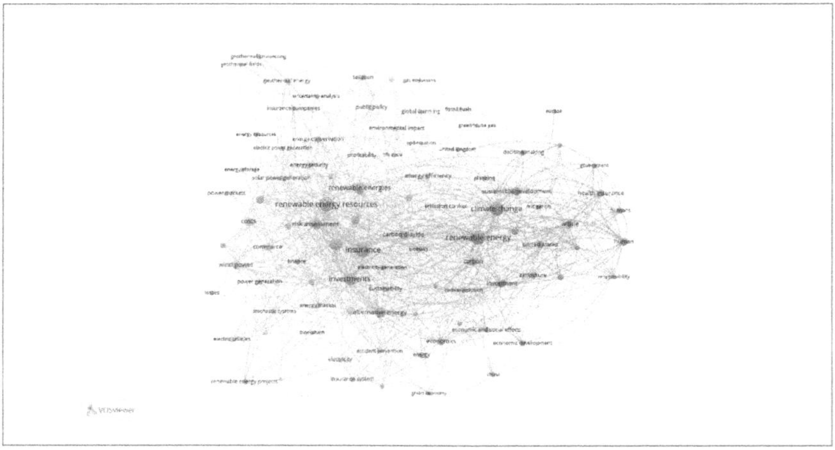

Figure 37. Bibliographic data map: Co-occurrence: All keywords.
Source: Visualization map from VOSviewer based on Scopus database.

In this regard, 94 items were found, and the values of the attributes clusters, links, and total link strength were 7, 1813, and 3650, respectively.

Next, we present the top ten most frequent keywords in renewable energy insurance publications and co-occurrences in Scopus. The results of the survey are presented in Table 30.

From the information presented in Table 30, we find that within Cluster 5, most of the top 5 keywords are present—"Insurance," "Renewable energy resources," "Energy policy," "Renewable energies," and "Risk assessment." In terms of the Total Links Strength attribute, the leading ones are "Insurance," "Renewable energy resources," and "Renewable energy," and in terms of occurrences, the same have values of 58, 48, and 50, respectively.

Table 30. The top ten most frequent keywords in renewable energy insurance publications and co-occurrences in Scopus

Keyword	Cluster	Total Links Strength	Occurrences
Insurance	5	366	58
Renewable energy resources	5	306	48
Renewable energy	1	291	50
Climate change	1	270	42
Investments	3	260	37
Energy policy	5	235	39
Renewable energies	5	179	33
Risk assessment	5	155	25
Alternative energy	3	140	26
Costs	6	132	19

Source: Author's design-based result from research with VOSviewer.

The last analysis, whose results are visualized, is co-citation analysis based on cited references and a bibliographic data map and is presented in Figure 38.

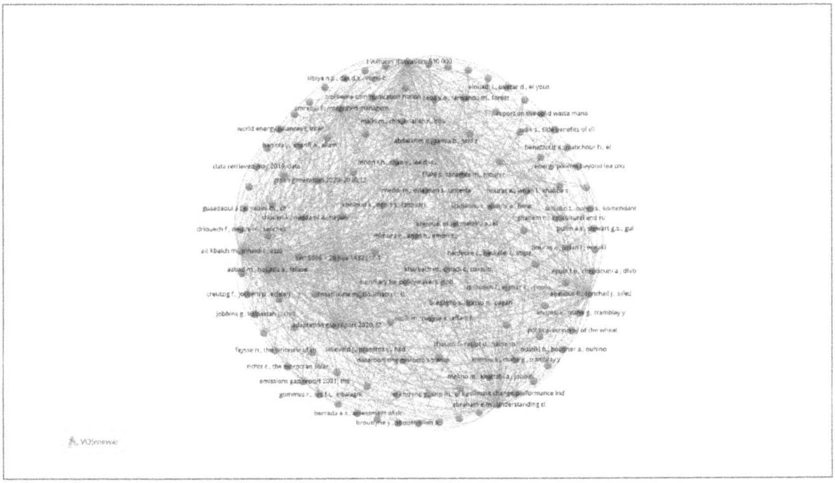

Figure 38. Bibliographic data map: Co-citation: Cited references.
Source: Visualization map from VOSviewer based on Scopus database.

The visualized map highlights the results of a co-citation analysis based on cited references, having established 7361 that meet the threshold. On a full counting, 196 items, 1 cluster, and 19,110 links are reported.

In addition to the analyses, we also present information on the distribution of the 246 documents found on the topic of Renewable energy insurance, broken down by country or territory.

Figure 39. Documents by country or territory.
Source: Author's design based on Elsevier BV (1981–2024).

The results of Figure 39 outline indisputably the following factology: the largest number of scientific publications on the topic from the Scopus database is produced in the United States (46 documents), followed by China and the United Kingdom (22 documents for each country).

10.5. Conclusion

In the context of the set objective defined as the identification of the trends in the scientific literature on the topic of "Renewable energy insurance," we should generalize the following achieved results of the conducted research:

(i) Over the period 1981–2024, the number of scientific publications on the topic, worldwide, has shown a steady upward trend, entirely in line with the increase in public attention and political commitment to the green energy concept and economy, of which RES are an integral part.
(ii) The number of publications on RES, and in particular, renewable energy insurance, is multiplying as a result of both the multidisciplinary scientific quest to reduce emissions and help combat climate change and the promotion of the exploitation of RES. They are the subject of a large number of studies published within the last decade—marked by global socioeconomic and geo-political events.
(iii) Authors from the world's leading economies, such as those of the United States, China, the United Kingdom, India, Canada, and Germany, appear to be the most active about the production of RES research on technological advances, sectoral regulations, regulatory framework, cost-effectiveness, and insurance.
(iv) Large-scale investments in RES extraction and commissioning capacity projects are associated with a high degree of risk and uncertainty for business investors and investment funds, a reason why the insurance industry has an important place in this ecosystem. Evidence for this finding is the significant number of publications in the field of "Renewable energy insurance"—the subject of the present bibliometric analysis of 246 documents.
(v) Using the specialized software for performing bibliometric analysis VOSviewer, the following conclusions were reached: the main keywords that occupy a leading position on the subject under consideration are "insurance," "renewable energy resources," "renewable energy," "climate change," and "investments"; 668 authors with publications on the subject under consideration were identified; a map representing the largest set consisting of 12 authors was visualized (co-authorship analysis).

Bibliography

Abba, Z. Y., Balta-Ozkan, N., & Hart, P. (2022). A holistic risk management framework for renewable energy investments. *Renewable and Sustainable Energy Reviews*, *160*, 112305. <https://doi.org/10.1016/j.rser.2022.112305>

Abbasi, S. A., & Abbasi, N. (2000). The likely adverse environmental impacts of renewable energy sources. *Applied Energy, 65*(1–4), 121–144. <https://doi.org/10.1016/S0306-2619(99)00077-X>

Barton, B., Redgwell, C., Ronne, A., & Zillman, D. (2004). *Managing risk in a dynamic legal and regulatory environment, energy security.* New York, NY, USA: Oxford University Press.

Beaumont, V. (2007). Zen and 5 steps to ERM. *Risk Management*, 36–40.

Bergmann, A., Hanley, N., & Wright, R. (2006). Valuing the attributes of renewable energy investments. *Energy Policy*, *34*(9), 1004–1014. <https://doi.org/10.1016/j.enpol.2004.08.035>

Bromiley, P., McShane, M., Nair, E., & Rustambekov, E. (2015). Enterprise risk management: review, critique, and research directions. *Long Range Plan*, 265–276.

Costantini, V., & Martini, C. (2010). The causality between energy consumption and economic growth: A multi-sectoral analysis using non-stationary cointegrated panel data. *Energy Economics*, 591–603.

Ellili, N., Nobanee, H., Alodat, A., Dilshad, M. N., & Nuzhat, S. (2023). Mapping marine insurance: A bibliometric review: A taxonomical study using bibliometric visualization and systematic analysis. *Journal of Financial Services Marketing* <https://doi.org/10.1057/s41264-023-00232-w>

Elsevier BV (1981–2024). *Analyze search results: (TITLE-ABS-KEY (insurance) AND TITLE-ABS-KEY (renewable AND energy))*. Изтеглено на 2 April 2024 г. от Elsevier BV: <https://www.scopus.com/term/analyzer.uri?sort=plf-f&src=s&sid=8b283db09183bfbb7b3e8168f83b528e&sot=a&sdt=a&sl=66&s=%28TITLE-ABS-KEY%28insurance%29+AND+TITLE-ABS-KEY%28renewable+AND+energy%29%29&origin=resultslist&count=10&analyzeResults=Analyze+results>

European Parliament. (22.4.2022 r.). <https://www.europarl.europa.eu/news/en/headlines/economy/20210930STO13911/eu-measures-to-guarantee-safe-and-green-energy>. Извлечено от <https://www.europarl.europa.eu/portal/bg>: <https://www.europarl.europa.eu/news/en/headlines/economy/20210930STO13911/eu-measures-to-guarantee-safe-and-green-energy>

Froot, K., Scharfstein, D., & Stein, J. (1993). Risk management: Coordinating corporate investment and financing policies. *The Journal of Finance*, *48*(5), 1629–1658. <https://doi.org/10.1111/j.1540-6261.1993.tb05123.x>

ICF International. (22.4.2022 r.). *<https://www.icf.com/work/program-implementation/economic-financial-analysis>*. Извлечено от <https://www.icf.com/>: <https://www.icf.com/work/program-implementation/economic-financial-analysis>

Jan van Eck, N., & Waltman, L. (n.d.). *Documentation/Manual_VOSviewer_1.6.20.* Retrieved from VOSviewer: <https://www.vosviewer.com/documentation/Manual_VOSviewer_1.6.20.pdf>

Jastrzębska, M., Janowicz-Lomott, M., & Łyskawa, K. (2014). *Zarządzanie Ryzykiem w Działalności Jednostek Samorządu Terytorialnego ze Szczególnym Uwzględnieniem Ryzyka Katastroficznego*. Warszawa, Poland: Wolters Kluwer Polska.

Joof, F., Samour, A., Tursoy, T., & Ali, M. (2023). Climate change, insurance market, renewable energy, and biodiversity: Double-materiality concept from BRICS countries. *Environmental Science and Pollution Research, 30*(11), 28676–28689. <https://doi.org/10.1007/s11356-022-24068-4>

Kumar, M. (2020). Social, economic, and environmental impacts of renewable energy resources. In K. Okedu, A. Tahour, & A. G. Aissaoui (Eds.), *Wind solar hybrid renewable energy system.1* (Vol. 1, pp. 227–237). London, United Kingdom: IntechOpen. <https://doi.org/DOI: 10.5772/intechopen.89494>

McShane, M., Nair, A., & Rustambekov, E. (2011). Does enterprise risk management increase firm value? *Journal of Accounting, Auditing & Finance, 26*(4), 641–658. <https://doi.org/10.1177/0148558X11409160>

Mills, E. (2003). The insurance and risk management industries: new players in the delivery of energy-efficient and renewable energy products and services. *Energy Policy, 31*(12), 1257–1272. <https://doi.org/10.1016/S0301-4215(02)00186-6>

Ninova, V. (2024). Artificial intelligence and insurance: A bibliometric analysis. In *Current Dynamics in Business and Economics: Theoretical Approaches and Empirical Discoveries* (pp. 115–141). Peter Lang AG. Retrieved from <https://www.scopus.com/record/display.uri?eid=2-s2.0-85214605042&origin=recordpage>

Ninova, V., & Ninov, N. (2023). The effect of the COVID-19 pandemic on the health insurance market in Bulgaria: Empirical analysis of market concentration. *Optimizing Energy Efficiency During a Global Energy Crisis*, 165–177. <https://doi.org/10.4018/979-8-3693-0400-6.ch011>

Pata, U. K., & Samour, A. (2023). Assessing the role of the insurance market and renewable energy in the load capacity factor of OECD countries. *Environmental Science and Pollution Research*, *30*(16), 48604–48616. <https://doi.org/10.1007/s11356-023-25747-6>

Petersen, M. (22.4.2022 г.). *<https://www.europarl.europa.eu/https://www.europarl.europa.eu/news/en/press-room/20220210IPR23015/boost-offshore-renewable-energy-sources-to-meet-climate-targets>*. Извлечено от <https://www.europarl.europa.eu/portal/en>: <https://www.europarl.europa.eu/news/en/press-room/20220210IPR23015/boost-offshore-renewable-energy-sources-to-meet-climate-targets>

Prakash, R., & Bhat, I. K. (2009). Energy, economics and environmental impacts of renewable energy systems. *Renewable and Sustainable Energy Reviews*, *13*(9), 2716–2721. <https://doi.org/10.1016/j.rser.2009.05.007>

Sheikh, N. J., Kocaoglu, D. F., & Lutzenhiser, L. (2016). Social and political impacts of renewable energy: Literature review. *Technological Forecasting and Social Change*, *108*, 102–110. <https://doi.org/10.1016/j.techfore.2016.04.022>

Strantzali, E., & Aravossis, K. (2016). Decision making in renewable energy investments: A review. *Renewable and Sustainable Energy Reviews*, *55*, 885–898. <https://doi.org/10.1016/j.rser.2015.11.021>

Vine, E. (1998). Energy efficiency and renewable energy options for risk management and insurance loss reduction: An inventory of technologies, research capabilities, and research facilities at the US Department of Energy's National Laboratories. Retrieved from <https://escholarship.org/content/qt3s93d6wb/qt3s93d6wb.pdf>

Vine, E., Mills, E., & Chen, A. (2000). Energy-efficiency and renewable energy options for risk management and insurance loss reduction. *Energy*, *25*(2), 131–147. <https://doi.org/10.1016/S0360-5442(99)00068-7>

Ward, S. (2001). Exploring the role of the corporate risk manager. *Risk Management*, 3(1), 7–25.

Xie, H., Wen, Y., Choi, Y., & Zhang, X. (2021). Global trends on food security research: A bibliometric analysis. *Land*, *10*(2), 119. <https://doi.org/10.3390/land10020119>

Assessment of the Impact of Advanced Digital Technologies on Industrial Economic Structures in Uzbekistan

Samariddin Makhmudov, Zokir Mamadiyarov, Alisher Ruziyev, Saodat Yuldasheva, Mirzabek Jonuzokov, Feruza Bekbayeva, and Gulnaz Aymurzaeva

11.1. Introduction

Globalization and technological advances are the star drivers of the sustained growth in the economy that modern society is experiencing (He et al., 2024). These days, scientific and technological developments in information technology, biotechnology, and electronics are driving changes in the economy and industry (Smirnova & Ponomareva, 2022). This is most prominent in the high-tech industries, which produce significant added value by taking advantage of the newest technologies and production processes (Gaipov et al., 2023). It is also true for industrial constructions that adapt to the requirement of the new tech-oriented world where the digitalization of the processes are the first to be implemented. For the purpose of promoting effective co-operation in the economic sector, it is imperative to identify and analyze the primary characteristics of inter-regional collaboration in the production of high-tech products, because this is fundamental to the growth and advancement of industrial sectors.

At its core, the process of digitalization took place in the field of microelectronics from 1960s which helped to decrease the cost, consumption of power, and size of hardware required to operate (Oloyede et al., 2023). The successful integration of the digital economy into the industrial system depends on a comprehensive approach involving public policy, strategic planning, and continuous monitoring of digital transformation (Fernández-Portillo et al., 2020). While digital technologies can be broadly beneficial to developing countries, their impact varies significantly at the regional level. Capital, skilled labor, and other production factors tend to flow toward regions with high levels of digital technology development, transforming these areas into hubs of economic activity and innovation. By contrast, regions with lower levels of digital technology development often struggle to keep pace, retaining outdated production capacities and facing challenges in modernization. Given the centrality of individual absorptive capacity to innovation and change within organizations, it is a critical issue to what extent individual absorptive capacity affects organizational outcomes (Unluonen & Boylu, 2020).

Analyses and forecasts have been conducted using various econometric models on factors affecting remittances, energy intensity and economic development, energy policy, energy risk, environmental status and the impact of environmental aspects on the digital economy, agricultural productivity, and the stability of the US credit market (Akhmetshin et al., 2025; Jakhongir et al., 2024; Kuziboev et al., 2024, 2025; Sharipov et al., 2025). Notwithstanding the various nuances of digital transformation within industrial sectors, it generally has a positive impact on the overall economy (Mamadiyorov et al., 2024).

The present study has three primary objectives. First, to assess the impact of advanced digital technologies on industrial economic structures; second, to examine how different sectors of the economy adapt to and integrate these technologies; and third, to analyze the challenges and opportunities posed by the digital transformation of industries in Uzbekistan. The study takes Uzbekistan's industrial sector as its focus. First, we review the literature on digital technologies and their impact on economic structures to develop a conceptual framework. Second, by collecting data from various industrial sectors in Uzbekistan, we provide empirical evidence on the transformative effects of digital technologies. Finally, we offer policy recommendations for fostering digital innovation and improving the competitiveness of Uzbekistan's industrial economy.

11.2. Literature Review

With the deep integration of intelligent technologies in the manufacturing industry, digital transformation has significantly altered traditional production and operations management methods (Neuhofer et al., 2015). It has been studied that the application of big data and analytics is closely interlinked, enabling manufacturing firms to make better decisions (Wamba et al., 2015). Specifically, digital technologies such as big data and predictive analytics leverage advanced information technology tools and architectures to collect, store, extract, and analyze large volumes of data for decision-making processes (Gunasekaran et al., 2017). Furthermore, big data and predictive analytics can enhance supply chain performance through improved visibility and decision-making (Ben-Daya et al., 2019). Additionally, the Internet of Things facilitates the remote co-ordination and management of supply chain operations (Urunov et al., 2024; Mamadiyarov et al., 2025). This integration of data-driven insights into industrial structures not only optimizes processes but also fosters greater adaptability and quick communication within the manufacturing sector, ultimately contributing to more efficient and resilient industrial systems (Govindan et al., 2018). Additionally, advanced technologies are establishing a digitally driven network within the supply chain and to support communication within and across organizational boundaries (Frank et al., 2019).

Another group of local economists, who examined various aspects of investment in digital infrastructure and digital payment systems, has successfully used econometric models in their research on the impact of inflation and credit interest rates on investment, factors affecting the reduction of the state's share in commercial banks, the digitalization of banks, risks in digital services, and the development of retail payment services (Cahyani et al., 2025; Hussain et al., 2023; Litamahuputty et al., 2025; Mamadiyarov et al., 2024, 2025; Mamani, et al., 2025; PANJAITAN et al., 2025; Zokir et al., 2021). Determining the lending behavior of banks, especially under unfavorable economic conditions, is important for economic growth, the financial health of banks, and public sector economic planning and policy development (Lin et al., 2025; Mamadiyarov et al., 2025; Pradhan et al., 2025; Samariddin et al., 2024; Senel & Aslan, 2018; Su et al., 2025).

There is a growing interest in researching the adoption of digital technologies in manufacturing firms at the supply chain level. However, this adoption does not always succeed (Rai, 2000). Many manufacturing firms invest heavily in digital transformation but often fail to realize the expected business value (Correani et al., 2020). This failure is frequently due to a disconnect between strategy formulation and implementation (Frank et al., 2019). In a survey of 92 manufacturing companies, it was found that companies that are advanced in adopting digital manufacturing technologies tend to use digital platforms for connecting with supply chain partners at a high level (Addo-Tenkorang & Helo, 2016). It is also clearly noted that operations management and environmental management are one of highly information-intensive activities (Kiel et al., 2017) that helps to achieve strong economic and environmental performance within industrial systems relying on having sufficient information and effective information processing capabilities. While it is true that the adoption of digital technology is influenced by various factors—including technological, organizational, and environmental aspects (Jahrir et al., 2025; Yang et al., 2021, Zhang et al., 2025), it is essential for firms in the industrial sector to clarify the reasons and motivations behind their choices. In this situation, improperly adopting digital technologies can cause disruptive changes, leading to significant risks and uncertainties during the transformation process (Kuchkarov et al., 2025; Kuziboev et al., 2025). According to the study conducted by Özüdoğru and Sönmez (2023), the use of data analytics and machine learning solutions for the insurance industry is expected to increase.

The integration of digital technologies into the industrial economic sector is inherently complex and demands careful attention to multiple factors (Makhmudov et al., 2024). This complexity stems from the necessity to align technological advancements with current organizational structures, workforce skills, and market needs (Abdullah et al., 2025; Martins et al., 2021; Muhammad et al., 2025; Romero et al., 2025). In developing countries like Uzbekistan, these challenges can be even more significant due to limited resources, varying levels of technological preparedness, and different regulatory frameworks. To navigate these issues effectively, further research is crucial to understand how digital technologies can be successfully integrated into the industrial sectors of Uzbekistan.

11.3. Research Methodology and Development Hypothesis

The development of econometric model was done using the World Bank (<https://data.worldbank.org/>), the Ministry of Digital Technologies of the Republic of Uzbekistan (<https://gov.uz/>), and Uzbekistan Economic and Digital Indicators—of which there are 22—which comprise quarterly data from 2018 to 2023 from the Statistical Agency (<https://stat.uz/uz/>) to evaluating the effects of digital technologies on industrial economic structures.

The Autoregressive Distributed Lag (ARDL) model is a valuable econometric method for examining dynamic relationships between variables across short and long time periods. More versatility in empirical research across areas is made possible by its particular utility in scenarios where data series are integrated in diverse orders, such $i(0)$ and $i(1)$.

Below formulation of the ARDL model is given:

$$y_t = \beta + \beta 1_{y\text{-}1} + \beta 2_{y\text{-}2} + \ldots + \beta k_{yt\text{-}k} + \delta 1_{x\text{-}1} + \delta 2_{xt\text{-}2} + \ldots + \delta m_{xm} + \tau 1_{lt\text{-}1} + \tau 2_{lt\text{-}2} + \ldots + lr_{kt\text{-}f} + \varepsilon t \quad (1)$$

Here, y_t represents represents the dependent variable at time t.

$y_{t-1}, y_{t-2}, \ldots, y_{t-k}$ denotes the lagged values of the dependent variable.

$x_{t-k}, x_{t-k-1}, \ldots, x_{t-k-m}$ denotes the lagged values of the independent variable. $l_{t-1}, l_{t-2}, \ldots, l_{t-f}$ represents the lagged values of other factors influencing the dependent variables.

$\beta_1, \beta_2, \ldots, \beta_k, \delta_1, \delta_2, \delta_q, \tau_1, \tau_2, \ldots, \tau_r$ denotes the estimated coefficients represent values

ε_t represents error in time t.

According to the econometric model, all variables are natural logarithmized.

Below are all the variables of the econometric model.

The variables are as follows:

Added value of products produced in industry—***Lnpp_ind (dependent variable)***,

The degree of automation of industrial enterprises—***Lnaut_ind_entp (independent variable)***,

The share of skilled professionals in digital technologies in industrial enterprises—***Lnprof_ind_ent (independent variable)***,

Volume of financial and technological investments for digital infrastructures—***Lnfin_tech_dig (independent variable)***.

The following hypotheses were formulated during econometric research.

Null hypothesis (H_0): The added value of products produced in the industrial sector, the level of automation in industrial enterprises, the share of qualified specialists in digital technologies, and the volume of financial and technological investments in digital infrastructure do not have a statistically significant effect on the national economy.

Alternative hypothesis (H_1): The added value of products produced in the industrial sector, the level of automation in industrial enterprises, the share of qualified specialists in digital technologies, and the volume of financial and technological investments in digital infrastructure have a statistically significant effect on the national economy.

11.4. Analysis and Results

In the first stage of the study, the descriptive statistics for the dependent and independent variables were as follows (Table 31). It can be seen from Table 31 that the descriptive statistics of the model fall within the confidence interval, with positive values for each variable. This indicates that the values of the variables are clustered around the mean.

Table 31. Descriptive statistics on dependent and independent variables

	Lnpp_ind	*Lnaut_ind_entp*	*Lnprof_ind_ent*	*Lnfin_tech_dig*
Mean	4.668278	4.566017	4.621949	4.625838
Maximum	7.664668	5.20849	6.719558	5.524916
Minimum	0.2847197	3.282372	3.282372	2.763266
Std. Dev	1.739048	0.434971	0.434971	0.984128
Std. Err.	0.1707662	0.0927361	0.2109009	0.2098168
Skewness	-0.8442687	-1.011111	-0.8109757	0.9685079
Kurtosis	3.327404	4.733323	5.176913	-0.9105948
Observation	22	22	22	22

Source: It was developed by the authors based on Stata software.

According to the study, the analytical graphical representation of the added value of products produced in the industrial sector and the factors influencing it over time is presented in Figure 40.

Figure 40 indicates that, throughout the period under analysis, each variable exhibited a stochastic increase. The visual representation also shows a growth forecast for the future based on the selected criteria.

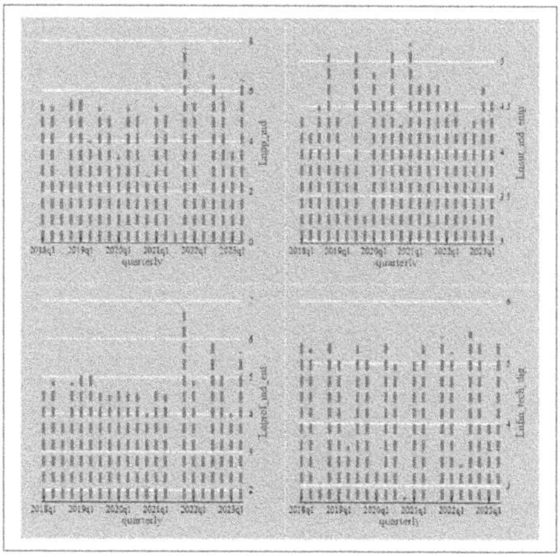

Figure 40. Analytical graphical representation of the intercorrelation matrix of dependent and independent variables over time.

Source: It was developed by the authors based on Stata software.

At the next stage, the graphic matrix and scatter plot of dependent and independent variables are presented (Figure 41).

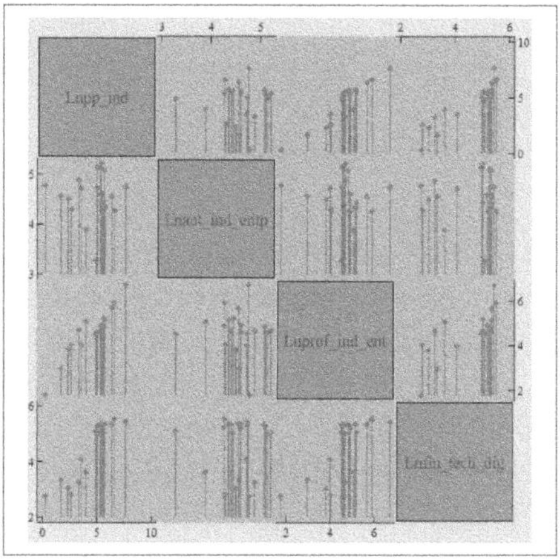

Figure 41. Graphical matrix representation of dependent and independent variables.

Source: It was developed by the authors based on Stata software.

Indicating a distinct density effect in the dataset, Figure 42 demonstrate a substantial association between the outcomes and the prominent factors. The density-based cluster analysis of the visual variable data points revealed significant effects.

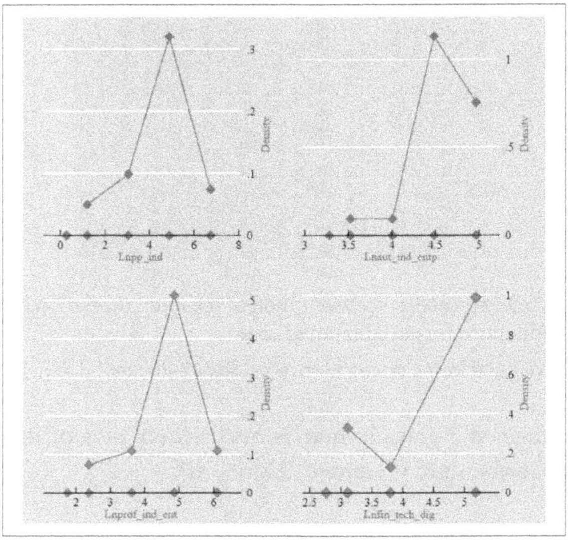

Figure 42. Analytical connection (rconnected) graphical representation of dependent and independent variables.

Source: It was developed by the authors based on Stata software.

Based on Figure 42, a relatively homogenous dynamic distribution was observed between the added value of items produced in the industrial industry and the percentage of competent specialists in digital technologies. According to the graphic distribution, growth dynamics were produced by the level of automation of industrial companies and the amount of money and technology invested in digital infrastructures. As the industrial sector moves toward digital platforms, the research indicates that the added value of the products produced in this sector will rise along with their prospects of breaking into local, national, and global markets.

In order to analyze the dependent and independent variables across the study, we created a cross-correlation matrix (Table 32).

Table 32. Intercorrelation matrix of dependent and independent variables

Variables	(1)	(2)	(3)	(4)
Lnpp_ind	1.000			
Lnaut_ind_entp	0.746	1.000		
	(0.016)			***
Lnprof_ind_ent	0.721	0.690	1.000	
	(0.000)	(0.090)		***
Lnfin_tech_dig	0.615	0.751	0.421	1.000
	(0.000)	(0.051)	(0.000)	***

*** *p<.01,* ** *p<.05,* * *p<.1*

Source: It was developed by the authors based on Stata software.

The factors influencing the added value of the products produced in the industrial sector and their correlation with it are highly significant, stable, and correlated, as indicated in Table 32.

Additionally, considering that the table's *p*-value for the correlation coefficient <0.05, it indicates the correlation coefficient's significance level. To ascertain if the dependent and independent variables were stationar, the Unit-Root test was performed in the following stage (Table 33).

Table 33. Unit-Root test scores for dependent and independent variables

Variables	Test Statistic	1% Critical Value	5% Critical Value	10% Critical Value	*p*-value for *Z*(*t*)
Lnexp_high_tech (Dependent variable)	-6.991	-3.750	-3.000	-2.630	0.0000
Lndig_trad_pl (Independent variable)	-6.494	-3.750	-3.000	-2.630	0.0000
Lntransact_dig~l (Independent variable)	-6.568	-3.750	-3.000	-2.630	0.0000
Lnnondig_trad_pl (Independent variable)	-7.084	-3.750	-3.000	-2.630	0.0000

Source: It was developed by the authors based on Stata software.

Table 33 shows that the Unit-Root test results for the dependent variable were –6.991, while the results for the independent variables were –6.494, –6.568, and –7.084. These values indicate that the influencing factors and the added value of goods produced in the industrial sector have achieved stationarity. McKinnon's critical values of $Z(t)$ at 0.0000 support this conclusion.

Additionally, after the initial integration of the independent and dependent variables, the unit root test results confirmed stationarity. This suggests that both independent and dependent variables have maintained their statistical properties throughout time, and that time series analysis offers a crucial prediction for modeling.

At the next stage of the research, a regression equation was developed using the ARDL model. Below are econometric equations for long-term (LR) and short-term (SR) dynamic relationships based on the ARDL model.

According to long-term (LR):

$$lnpp\_ind_t = \beta_1 \cdot lnaut\_ind\_entp_t + \beta_2 \cdot lnprof\_ind\_ent_t + \beta_3 \cdot lnfin\_tech\_dig_t \quad (2)$$

According to the short-term dynamic (SR):

$$\begin{gathered} \Delta lnpp\_ind_t = \gamma_1 \Delta lnpp\_ind_{t-1} + \gamma_2 \Delta lnaut\_ind\_entp_t + \\ \gamma_3 \Delta lnprof\_ind\_ent_t + \gamma_4 \Delta lnfin\_tech\_dig_t \end{gathered} \quad (3)$$

The indicators of the econometric equation of the ARDL model are presented in Table 34.

The coefficient indicators of the econometric equation based on the **ARDL(2,2,2,2)** model are presented below.

$$\begin{gathered} \Delta lnpp\_ind_t = -7.45 - 1.66 lnpp\_ind_{t-1} - 0.22 lnaut\_ind\_entp_t + \\ 0.89 lnprof\_ind\_ent_t + 0.84 lnfin\_tech\_dig_t + 0.79 \Delta lnpp\_ind_{t-1} - \\ 0.26 \Delta lnaut\_ind\_entp_t - 0.13 \Delta lnaut\_ind\_entp_{t-1} - 0.59 \Delta lnprof\_ind\_ent_t - \\ 0.70 \Delta lnprof\_ind\_ent_{t-1} - 0.54 \cdot \Delta lnfin\_tech\_dig_t - 0.77 \Delta lnfin\_tech\_dig_{t-1} \end{gathered} \quad (4)$$

11.4.1. An overview of the ARDL(2,2,2,2) model

With an R-squared of 0.9597, the model accounts for approximately 95.97% of the variation in the value added of produced goods. Positive model significance to the observed data is shown by a high R-squared value.

Table 34. ARDL(2,2,2,2) model regression equation indicators

ARDL(2,2,2,2) regression | Number of obs = 22

Sample: 2018q3 – 2023q2 | *R*-squared = 0.9597

Log likelihood = 32.365857 | Adj *R*-squared = 0.9549

Root MSE = 0.0758

D.Lnpp_ind	**Coef.**	**Std. Err.**	***t***	***P > t***	**[95%Conf.**	**Interv] Sig**
ADJ						
Lnpp_ind						
L1.	-1.669	0.284	-5.870	0.000	-2.325	-1.013 ***
LR						
Lnaut_ind_entp	0.228	0.070	3.280	0.011	0.067	0.388 ***
Lnprof_ind_ent	0.899	0.073	12.290	0.000	0.730	1.068 ***
Lnfin_tech_dig	0.850	0.113	7.520	0.000	0.589	1.110 ***
SR						
Lnpp_ind						
LD.	0.799	0.189	4.220	0.003	0.362	1.235 ***
Lnaut_ind_entp						
D1.	−0.268	0.112	−2.390	0.044	−0.527	−0.009 ***
LD.	−0.138	0.061	−2.250	0.054	−0.280	0.003 **
Lnprof_ind_ent						
D1.	−0.598	0.319	−1.870	0.098	−1.334	0.138 *
LD.	−0.708	0.189	−3.740	0.006	−1.144	−0.272 ***
Lnfin_tech_dig						
D1.	−0.548	0.218	−2.510	0.036	−1.051	−0.045 ***
LD.	−0.774	0.183	−4.230	0.003	−1.196	−0.352 ***
_cons	-7.452	1.556	-4.790	0.001	-11.041	-3.862 ***

Source: It was developed by the authors based on Stata software.

Adjusted for the number of predictors in the econometric model, the adj *R*-squared value is 0.9549, meaning that, considering the model's complexity, 95.49% of the variation is explained.

The log likelihood value of 32.365 indicates a favorable fit of the econometric equation.

The root mean square error (RMSE), which represents the average value of the prediction error for the dependent variable, is 0.0758. This small RMSE value suggests that the model's forecasting capability is reliable.

After the study's ARDL(2,2,2,2) model test, the null hypothesis was rejected in this instance based on the *F*- and *t*-statistics obtained at a statistical significance level of 0.05. The alternative hypothesis (H_1) was thus approved.

The study's ARDL(2,2,2,2) bound test looked at the model's cointegration level (Tables 35 and 36).

Table 35. Bound *F*-test for cointegration

									F = 13.661
	[I_0]	[I_1]	[I_0]	[I_1]	[I_0]	[I_1]	[I_0]	[I_1]	
	L_1	L_1	L_05	L_05	L_025	L_025	L_01	L_01	
K_3	2.72	3.77	3.23	4.35	3.69	4.89	4.29	5.61	

Source: It was developed by the authors based on Stata software.

According to Table 35, the value of *F*-statistic is 13.661 and it is greater than the critical limits for all intervals and it shows the presence of cointegration. According to him, the Bound test indicates a positive result for the *F*-statistic value.

Table 36. Bound *t*-test for cointegration

									F = –5.866
	[I_0]	[I_1]	[I_0]	[I_1]	[I_0]	[I_1]	[I_0]	[I_1]	
	L_1	L_1	L_05	L_05	L_025	L_025	L_01	L_01	
K_3	−2.57	−3.46	−2.86	−3.78	−3.13	−4.05	−3.43	−4.37	

Source: It was developed by the authors based on Stata software.

The *t*-statistic result in Table 36 is –5.866, indicating the presence of cointegration and being greater than the critical limits for all intervals. He claimed that the *t*-statistic value was positively determined by the Bound test.

According to the ARDL(2,2,2,2) model, the added value of goods produced in the industrial sector will increase by 0.22% in long-term relationships for every 1% increase in the automation of industrial firms within the national economy. Additionally, a 1% increase in the proportion of skilled specialists in digital technologies in industrial businesses will result in a 0.89% rise in the added value of manufactured goods. Furthermore, a 1% increase in financial and technological investments in the region's digital infrastructure will lead to a 0.85% increase in the added value of the industrial output.

In the next step of the research, the CUSUM diagnostic test was examined for the ARDL(2,2,2,2) model (Figures 43 and 44).

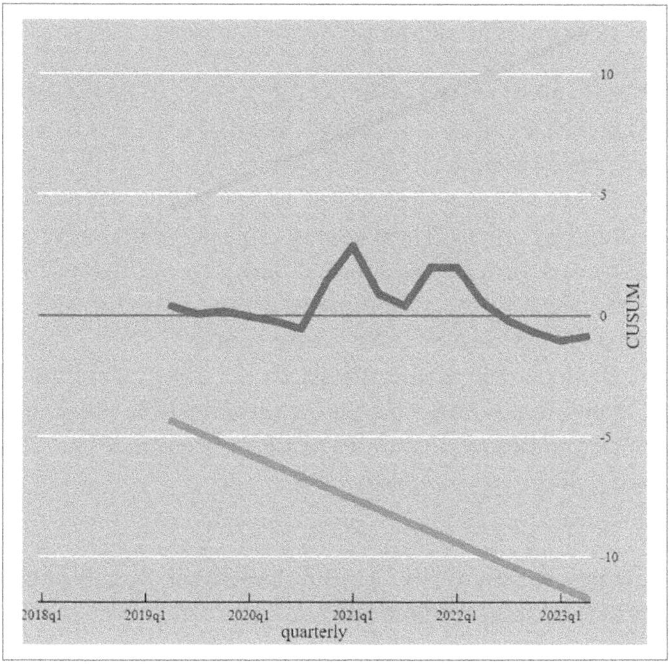

Figure 43. CUSUM diagnostic test chart.

Source: It was developed by the authors based on Stata software.

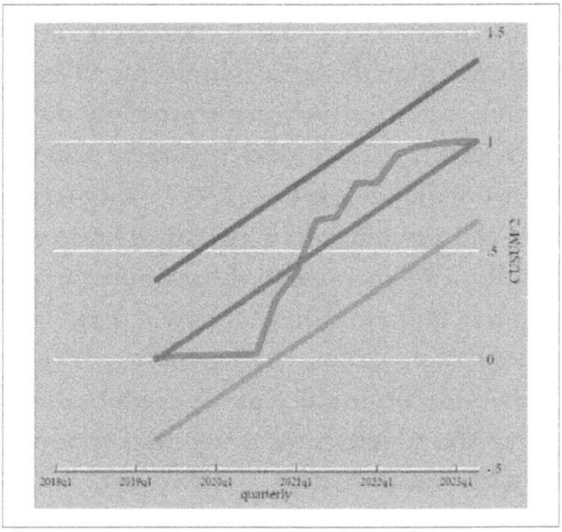

Figure 44. CUSUM diagnostic test chart.
Source: It was developed by the authors based on Stata software.

The CUSUM diagnostic test used in the ARDL(2,2,2,2) model included the following hypotheses when assessing the stability of the parameters in the regression model over time:

1. H_0—Null Hypothesis: The model is stable over time (there are no systematic changes in the parameters). The residuals follow a stationary process, indicating that the estimated parameters of the ARDL(2,2,2,2) model do not change over the sample period.
2. H_1—Alternative Hypothesis: The ARDL(2,2,2,2) model is unstable over time (there are systematic changes in the parameters). The residuals show instability, indicating that the model parameters may have changed at certain points in the sample period.

11.4.2. Interpretation of the CUSUM Diagnostic Result According to the ARDL(2,2,2,2) Model

Since the CUSUM test was successful, the null hypothesis (H_0) was not rejected, meaning that the ARDL(2,2,2,2) model was not stable over the analyzed period. According to it, according to the ARDL(2,2,2,2) model, it represents that the relations between the added value of the products produced in the industrial industry and the factors affecting it are consistently maintained without any systematic breaks and parameters instability.

11.4.2.1. Explanation of the Graphical Representation of the CUSUM Test

In the CUSUM test, the sum of the recursive residuals is plotted against time with the upper and lower limits representing the critical limits and the diagnostic test statistics remained within the significant limits and no significant deviations were observed during the analyzed period.

11.5. Conclusion

According to the ARDL(2,2,2,2) regression model, the added value of the products manufactured in the industrial sector, the degree of automation of industrial enterprises, the proportion of qualified digital specialists in industrial enterprises, and the state of digital infrastructures are significant factors influencing the national economy. Based on the analysis and findings of the study on the relationship between the volume of financial and technological investments, the following suggestions and proposals were made.

According to the ARDL(2,2,2,2) model,

1. The development of automated processes as a driver of efficiency and productivity in the industrial sector.The added value of industrial products increased by 0.22% as a result of a 1% increase in the automation level of industrial companies, indicating a significant increase in automated procedures. Automated procedures increase productivity, reduce the human factor and optimize production processes—all of which support long-term growth. This positive effect contributes to the competitiveness of the industrial sector in the domestic and international markets.
2. Digital parameters significantly increase innovation and competitiveness in the manufacturing industry. The importance of human capital in the growth of industrial companies is underlined by the 1% increase in the share of skilled digital specialists and the 0.89% increase in the added value of goods in the industrial sector. When it comes to implementing production technologies, creative solutions and making

the best use of digital technologies, skilled specialists play a decisive role. This stimulates production and also makes it easier for industrial companies to adapt to rapidly changing technological processes.

3. Investments in digital infrastructure contribute to the growth of the industrial sector. The 0.85% increase in the added value of manufactured goods in the industrial sector as a result of a 1% increase in financial and technological investments in digital infrastructure underlines the importance of continuing investments in new technologies. This will enable digital infrastructure, such as modern ICT systems, automation equipment, and communication networks, to increase productivity, operational efficiency, and product quality.

Bibliography

Abdullah, M. A., Han, X., Amjad, M. A., & Makhmudov, S. (2025). Revisit the role of financial development on economic growth, human development, and sustainable development in higher-income countries. *Journal of Environmental Management*, *392*, 126874.

Addo-Tenkorang, R. and Helo, P. T., 2016. Big data applications in operations/supply-chain management: A literature review. *Computers & Industrial Engineering*, *101*, 528–543.

Akhmetshin, E., Abdullayev, I., Makhmudov, S., Dakhkilgova, K., Korotaeva, I. and Yanovskaya, G. (2025). APPLICATION OF TANH–COTH METHOD FOR COMBINED AND DOUBLE COMBINED SINH–COSH–GORDON EQUATIONS ARISING CHEMICAL REACTIONS TO WATER SURFACE GRAVITY WAVES. Computational Methods for Differential Equations, (), -. doi: 10.22034/cmde.2025.67655.3234

Ben-Daya, M., Hassini, E. and Bahroun, Z. (2019). Internet of things and supply chain management: A literature review. *International Journal of Production Research*, 57(15–16), 4719–4742.

Cahyani, I., Buriev, K., Ngongo, M., Mamadiyarov, Z., Ino, L., Herman, H., Saputra, N., & Baxtishodovich, S. (2025). Exploring the Use of TikTok Application in Enhancing the Skill of Pronunciation: A Case on Students' Perception. Studies in Media and Communication, 13(2), 150–158. doi:http://dx.doi.org/10.11114/smc.v13i2.7553

Correani, A., De Massis, A., Frattini, F., Petruzzelli, A. M. and Natalicchio, A. (2020). Implementing a digital strategy: Learning from the experience of three digital transformation projects. *California Management Review*, *62*(4), 37–56.

Fernández-Portillo, A., Almodóvar-González, M., & Hernández-Mogollón, R. (2020). Impact of ICT development on economic growth. A study of OECD European union countries. *Technology in Society*, *63*, 101420.

Frank, A. G., Dalenogare, L. S., & Ayala, N. F. (2019). Industry 4.0 technologies: Implementation patterns in manufacturing companies. *International Journal of Production Economics*, *210*, 15–26.

Gaipov, J., Fayzieva, M., Makhmudov, S., Urinov, B., & Xodjayeva, J. (2023, December). The influencing factors of high-technology industries in the global market. In *Proceedings of the 7th International Conference on Future Networks and Distributed Systems* (pp. 58–64).

Govindan, K., Cheng, T. E., Mishra, N., & Shukla, N. (2018). Big data analytics and application for logistics and supply chain management. *Transportation Research Part E: Logistics and Transportation Review*, *114*, 343–349.

Gunasekaran, A., Papadopoulos, T., Dubey, R., Wamba, S. F., Childe, S. J., Hazen, B., & Akter, S., 2017. Big data and predictive analytics for supply chain and organizational performance. *Journal of Business Research*, *70*, 308–317.

He, B., Jie, W., He, H., Alsubih, M., Arnone, G., & Makhmudov, S. (2024). From resources to resilience: How green innovation, fintech and natural resources shape sustainability in OECD countries. *Resources Policy*, *91*, 104856.

Hussain, A., Khan, M., Rakhmonov, D. A., Mamadiyarov, Z. T., Kurbonbekova, M. T., & Mahmudova, M. Q. K. (2023). Nexus of Training and Development, Organizational Learning Capability, and Organizational Performance in the Service Sector. Sustainability, 15(4), 3246. https://doi.org/10.3390/su15043246

Jahrir, A., Gultom, Y., Herman, H., Zabadi, F., Ngongo, M., Mamadiyarov, Z., Fatmawati, E., & Saputra, N. (2025). Investigating the Elements of Short Commercial Mineral Water Advertisement: A Case on Discourse Analysis. Studies in Media and Communication, 13(4), 94–104. doi:http://dx.doi.org/10.11114/smc.v13i4.7813

Jakhongir, S., Muhabbat, H., Khayrilla, K., Kholmuratov, S., Nazirjon, R., Nilufar, F., & Farxod, T. (2024). Crafting a neutrosophic-driven tool to probe turnover propensities in manufacturing entities. *International Journal of Neutrosophic Science (IJNS)*, *23*(2).

Kiel, D., Müller, J. M., Arnold, C., & Voigt, K. I. (2017). Sustainable industrial value creation: Benefits and challenges of industry 4.0. *International Journal of Innovation Management*, *21*(08), 1740015.

Kuchkarov, T., Mamadiyarov, Z., Khakimov, Z., Sabirova, O., Matmurodov, K., Raimboyeva, M., & Umarova, S. (2025). Energy-Related Uncertainty and Crypto-Currency Environmental Attention: Time-Varying Perspective. International Journal of Energy Economics and Policy, 15(5), 614–626. https://doi.org/10.32479/ijeep.20784

Kuziboev, B., Ozturk, I., Kalandarov, F., Samandarov, O., Bekjanov, D., & Makhmudov, S. (2025). PROMOTING ENERGY SOURCES DIVERSIFICATION THROUGH ESG PERFORMANCE. Energy, 136009.

Kuziboev, B., Khodjaniyazov, E., Ozturk, I., Sabirov, K., Makhmudov, S., & Utegenova, S. (2025). Does oil dependence cause energy risk?. Energy Nexus, 17, 100393.

Kuziboev, B., Saidmamatov, O., Khodjaniyazov, E., Ibragimov, J., Marty, P., Ruzmetov, D., ..., & Ibadullaev, D. (2024). CO2 emissions, remittances, energy intensity and economic development: The evidence from Central Asia. *Economies*, *12*(4), 95.

Lin, M.H., Matchanova, B., Nurmatovich, H.A. *et al.* Optimal Operation of the Multi-Carrier Energy System Considering Energy Markets and Renewable Energies Participation. *Int. J. Appl. Comput. Math* **11**, 170 (2025). https://doi.org/10.1007/s40819-025-02002-9

Litamahuputty, J. V., Amiruddin, E. G., Rahim, R., Rahman, A., & Mamadiyarov, Z. (2025). Cryptocurrency Risk Management through Decision Engineering: Evaluating XRPUSD and ADAUSD Portfolio Performance. Journal of Applied Science, Engineering, Technology, and Education, 7(1), 69–81. https://doi.org/10.35877/454RI.asci3871

Mamadiyarov, Z., Hakimov, H., & Askarov, S. (2024). DEVELOPMENT OF RETAIL BANKING SERVICES IN THE CONTEXT OF DIGITAL TRANSFORMATION. Financial and Credit Activity Problems of Theory and Practice, 1(54), 51–67. https://doi.org/10.55643/fcaptp.1.54.2024.4288

Mamadiyarov, Z. Makhmudov, S. Utanov, B. Kasimova, D. Bekmurodova, G. Hakimov, Z. (2025). Fusion of Economic and Financial Factors Affecting Household Deposits in Banks: An Econometric Analysis. Fusion: Practice and Applications, (), 82–91. DOI: https://doi.org/10.54216/FPA.190206

Mamadiyarov, Z., Eshov, M., Otakhonova, D., Utegenova, S., Sabirov, K., Marks, A., & Bahodirov, N. (2025). Does Energy Policy Risk Threaten Energy Sources Diversification?. International Journal of Energy Economics and Policy, 15(5), 730–740. https://doi.org/10.32479/ijeep.21140

Mamani, J.C.M., Miri, M., Vorobev, Y. et al. Optimal Operation of Energy Microgrid Considering Economic and Emission Indices. Oper. Res. Forum 6, 122 (2025). https://doi.org/10.1007/s43069-025-00523-z

Martins, L. O. S., Amorim, I. R., de Araújo Mendes, V., Silva, M. S., Freires, F. G. M., Teles, E. O., & Torres, E. A. (2021). Price and income elasticities of residential electricity demand in Brazil and policy implications. *Utilities Policy*, *71*, 101250.

Muhammad Zubair, Irfanud Din, Nadeem Sarwar et al. Revolutionizing Sepsis Diagnosis Using Machine Learning and Deep Learning Models: A Systematic Literature Review, 10 June 2025, PREPRINT (Version 1) available at Research Square [https://doi.org/10.21203/rs.3.rs-6731418/v1]

Neuhofer, B., Buhalis, D., and Ladkin, A., 2015. Smart technologies for personalized experiences: A case study in the hospitality domain. *Electronic Markets*, *25*, 243–254.

Oloyede, A. A., Faruk, N., Noma, N., Tebepah, E., & Nwaulune, A. K. (2023). Measuring the impact of the digital economy in developing countries: A systematic review and meta-analysis. *Heliyon*, *9*(7).

Özüdoğru, H., & Sönmez, S. S. (2024). The impact of artificial intelligence and machine learning on the insurance industry. *Journal of Banking and Financial Research*, *11*(1), 45–53.

PANJAITAN, M. B., HAMDANAH, H., SIRAIT, J., SUTIKNO, S., FATMAWATI, E., HERMAN, H., & MAMADIYAROV, Z. (2025). THE ROLE OF EMOTIONAL REGULATION IN SHAPING STUDENTS' PERCEPTION OF PHYSICS PROBLEMSOLVING TASKS.

TPM – Testing, Psychometrics, Methodology in Applied Psychology, 32(S2(2025) : Posted 09 June), 1–10. Retrieved from https://tpmap.org/submission/index.php/tpm/article/view/139

Pradhan, R., Hajiyev, E., Shichiyakh, R. *et al.* Optimal Techno-Economic Feasibility of an Off-Grid Microgrid System Using Load Flow Energy Management Strategies. *Oper. Res. Forum* **6**, 120 (2025). https://doi.org/10.1007/s43069-025-00524-y

Rai, A. (2000). Editorial preface: Developing sense-and-respond capabilities for the digital economy. *Information Resources Management Journal*, *13*(4), 3.

Romero, R. M., Zelinskaya, M., Makhmudov, S., Sapaev, S., & Rustambekovich, J. U. (2025, September). Modelling and Optimal Utilisation of the Renewable Energy Systems in Microgrid with Improving Reliability and Energy Efficiency. In Operations Research Forum (Vol. 6, No. 3, pp. 1–20). Springer International Publishing.

Samariddin Makhmudov, Kudratillo Tukhsanov, Saifulla Arslanbekov, Akram Amanov, Orifali Tursunov, Umarbek Jabbarov and Muyassarxon Mirzakarimova. 2024. Optimizing Supply Chain Financing Development Prospects of Digital Ecosystems in the European Logistics Industry. In The 8th International Conference on Future Networks & Distributed Systems (ICFNDS '24), December 11–12, 2024, Marakech, Morocco. ACM, New York, NY, USA, 12 Pages. https://doi.org/10.1145/3726122.3726200

Senel, C., & Arslan, M. (2018). Olumsuz Ekonomik Dönemlerde Bankaların Kredilendirme Davranışlarının Analizi: 2008–2016 Dönemi Türk Bankacılık Sisteminde Bir Uygulama [Analysis of Banks' Lending Behavior in Unfavorable Economic Periods: An Application in the Turkish Banking System for the 2008–2016 Period]. *İşletme Araştırmaları Dergisi [Journal of Business Studies]*, *10/2*(2018), 720–739.

Sharipov, K., Abdullayev, I., Kuziboev, B., Makhmudov, S., Kalandarov, F., Khaytboeva, N., & Ilkhamova, Z. (2025). The Effect of Energy Policy Risk on Renewable Energy. International Journal of Energy Economics and Policy, *15*(2), 566.

Smirnova, O., & Ponomareva, A. (2022). Structural effects of the introduction of cross-industrial advanced manufacturing technologies: experience of the European Union. In *Digital Transformation in Industry:*

Digital Twins and New Business Models (pp. 149–161). Cham: Springer International Publishing.

Su, R., Xiao, Y., Hamza, F., Mamadiyarov, Z., & Wahab, A. (2025). Scaling up green hydrogen in China: Economic opportunities and challenges. *International Journal of Hydrogen Energy*, *131*, 60–69.

Sturgeon, T. J. (2021). Upgrading strategies for the digital economy. *Global Strategy Journal*, *11*(1), 34–57.

Unluonen, M. B., & Boylu, Y. (2020). Özümseme Kapasitesi Literatürüne Yönelik Bir Değerlendirme. *Third Sector Social Economic Review*, *55*(4), 2399–2419.

Wamba, S. F., Akter, S., Edwards, A., Chopin, G., & Gnanzou, D. (2015). How 'big data'can make big impact: Findings from a systematic review and a longitudinal case study. *International Journal of Production Economics*, *165*, 234–246.

Yang, M., Fu, M., & Zhang, Z. (2021). The adoption of digital technologies in supply chains: Drivers, process and impact. *Technological Forecasting and Social Change*, *169*, 120795.

Zhang, L., Zhao, Z., Qamri, G. M., & Makhmudov, S. (2025). Unleashing the critical role of renewable energy through global value chains and digitalization: A path towards environmental sustainability. Journal of Environmental Management, 392, 126688.

Zokir Toshtemirovich Mamadiyarov, Samandarboy Adhambek ugli Sulaymanov, Sarvar Anvar ugli Askarov, and Durdona Bakhtiyor kizi Uktamova. 2022. Impact of Covid-19 Pandemic on Accelerating the Digitization and Transformation of Banks. In Proceedings of the 5th International Conference on Future Networks and Distributed Systems (ICFNDS '21). Association for Computing Machinery, New York, NY, USA, 706–712. https://doi.org/10.1145/3508072.3508211

Econometric Analysis of the Process of Fiscal and Monetary Policy Co-ordination in the Economy of Uzbekistan based on Multivariate Linear (LS) and ARDL Models

Samariddin Makhmudov, Hakimjon A. Hakimov, Zokir Mamadiyarov, Dilnoza Azlarova, Isroilova Muhabbat, Gulchekhra Nigmatullayeva, and Mirzabek Jonuzokov

12.1. Introduction

The balance between monetary and fiscal policy is a key aspect of macroeconomic management, particularly in emerging economies like Uzbekistan. Fiscal policy, which is driven primarily by government expenditure and taxation, is linked to monetary policy that impacts supply of money in economy, interest rates, and inflationary pressures. Co-ordination in these policies is necessity which is needed to attain macroeconomic stability, foster sustainable economic growth, and minimize the risk of inflation (Fischer, 1993).

In recent years, Uzbekistan has undergone deep economic reforms. The state has implemented policies to liberalize the markets, aimed to enhance the effectiveness of monetary policy, and attract foreign investment (IMF, 2023; World Bank, 2022). As such, in the majority of developing economies, imbalance in policy co-ordination is likely to lead to inflation volatility and suboptimal growth performance (Mishkin, 2007; Romero et al., 2025).

The research employs ARDL and multivariate linear (LS) models in investigating relationships between government growth, inflation, household consumption, government spending, and monetary growth in Uzbekistan. Household spending has been determined to be one of the prominent causes of economic growth, while monetary growth is to fuel inflation if gone unregulated (Bernanke & Gertler, 1995). By analyzing these interactions, this study provides valuable information on the economic policy climate of Uzbekistan, while showing evidence-based recommendations for optimizing and adapting fiscal and monetary policies. These findings are intended to contribute in the broader discussion of economic policy co-ordination in transition economies and studies on the importance of policy harmonization for long-term economic stability.

12.2. Literature Review and Development Hypothesis

For many years, monetary and fiscal policy co-ordination has been the subject of extensive research in the economics literature, with important contributions emphasizing their impact on macroeconomic stability and growth. Keynesian economics believes that the use of fiscal policy is crucial for economic growth, particularly in times of recession, whereas monetarist schools emphasize money supply control for inflation and business cycle control (Friedman, 1968). The extent of the success of such policies in emerging economies, and particularly in transition economies like Uzbekistan, is currently the subject of ongoing research.

Monetary and fiscal policy effectiveness in developing countries is often affected by structural factors such as weak financial institutions, weak access to capital, and widespread informal economic activity (Ghura & Pattillo, 2012). Fiscal expansionary policy is also prevalent in emerging markets to spur growth, but it leads to high inflation and debt instability when there is excess government spending with no revenue mobilization (Adam & Bevan, 2005). Equally, emerging economies' monetary policy is often constrained by under developed financial markets and exchange rate uncertainty, making inflation targeting and interest rate management difficult (Abdullah et al., 2025; Mishra et al., 2012; Muhammad et al., 2025).

Another group of economists has successfully used econometric models such as Fixed Effects Estimator (FEE), Random Effects Estimator (REE), LS, and ARDL in their research on investment in digital infrastructure, various aspects of digital payment systems, the impact of inflation and credit interest rates on investment, factors affecting the reduction of the state's share in commercial banks, the digitalization of banks, risks in digital services, and the development of retail payment services (Cahyani et al., 2025; Caporin et al., 2024; Kuchkarov et al., 2025; Litamahuputty et al., 2025; Mamadiyarov et al., 2024, Mamani et al., 2025; 2025; PANJAITAN et al., 2025; Samariddin et al., 2024; Zhang et al., 2025; Zokir et al., 2021).

Earlier research on Uzbekistan's economic policy has a tendency to focus on a particular policy instrument relative to others. Khan and Sokolov (2020) examine the effect of fiscal stimulus on the growth of the economy, whereas Karimov and Lee (2021) examine monetary tightening and its influence on inflation control. Even though such works are extremely informative, they fail to provide a general assessment of the combined effect of fiscal and monetary policy on macroeconomic performance (Karimov and Lee, 2021; Lin et al., 2025; Mamadiyarov et al., 2025; Pradhan et al., 2025; Su et al., 2025).

Analyses and forecasts have been conducted using LS, ARDL, ARIMA, and other various econometric models on factors affecting remittances, energy intensity and economic development, energy policy, energy risk, environmental status and the impact of environmental aspects on the digital economy, agricultural productivity, and the stability of the US credit market (Akhmetshin et al., 2025; Inglesi-Lotz et al., 2024; Jahrir et al., 2025; Kuziboev et al., 2025; Sharipov et al., 2025).

This study will bridge this gap by employing a mixed econometric approach with LS and ARDL models to investigate the Uzbekistan monetary and fiscal policy co-ordination. In contrast to existing literature that provides single-policy effects, our study provides an integrated analysis with dynamic interactions between private consumption, government spending, inflation, money supply, and exchange rate stability.

12.3. Research Methodology

In developing econometric models, we used 47 economic indicators, consisting of quarterly data from the World Bank (<https://data.worldbank.org/>), the Central Bank of the Republic of Uzbekistan (<https://cbu.uz/oz/>), and the Statistical Agency (<https://stat.uz/uz/>) for the first econometric model from 2011 to 2023, to assess the impact of the fiscal and monetary policy co-ordination process on the national economy.

The formula for the ARDL model is given below.

$$Y_t = \alpha + \sum_{i=1}^{p} \beta_i Y_{t-i} + \sum_{k=1}^{n} \sum_{j=0}^{qk} \gamma_{k,j} X_{k,t-j} + \varepsilon_t \qquad (1)$$

Here, Y_t represents the dependent variable at time t.

Y_{t-1}, $Y_{t-2}, \ldots, Y_{t-k}$ are the lagged values of the dependent variable, X_t is the independent variable at time t, α is a constant, β_i Y is the coefficient of the dependent variable Y for the i-th lag. (where i is from 1 to p), γ_i X

is the coefficient of the j-th lag of the independent variable X (where j is from 0 to q), ε_t is the error term or the error at time t, n is the number of independent variables, $\gamma_{k,j}$ are the coefficients of the lagged values of the k-independent variables X_k, q_k is the lag length for each independent variable X_k.

All variables in the econometric model are natural logarithmic. Below are all variables in the econometric model.

Variables:

Gross domestic product of the country—*logGDP (dependent variable)*;
Final consumption expenditure of households—*logcons_expend (independent variable)*;
Final consumption expenditure of state administration bodies—*log pub_admin (independent variable)*;
Final consumption expenditure of non-profit organizations serving households—*lognon-prod_org (independent variable)*;
Export volume of goods and services—*logexport (independent variable)*.

The following hypotheses were reflected in the development of the econometric study.

Null hypothesis (H_0): There is no statistically significant effect of household final consumption expenditure, household final consumption expenditure, government final consumption expenditure, exports of goods and services, and gross domestic product (GDP) on the national economy.

Alternative hypothesis (H_1): There is a statistically significant effect of household final consumption expenditure, household final consumption expenditure, government final consumption expenditure, exports of goods and services, and GDP on the national economy.

12.4. Analysis and Results

Descriptive statistics were developed for the dependent and independent variables in the econometric study (Table 37).

As can be seen from Table 37, the descriptive statistics of the model have produced a statistically significant level of significance, with positive indicators for each variable. Also, the indicators of the variables correspond to the average value.

Table 37. Descriptive statistics for dependent and independent variables

	logGDP	logcons_ expend	log pub_admin	lognon-prod_org	logexport
Mean	7.82811	7.363812	5.831822	2.935575	6.229707
Maximum	8.962288	8.48837	7.145247	3.877411	7.68607
Minimum	6.624832	6.166171	4.549121	1.807107	5.252147
Std. Dev	0.6832673	0.6655858	0.7608778	0.6250061	0.798347
Std. Err.	0.0996648	0.0970857	0.1109854	0.0911665	0.1164509
Skewness	0.0112822	0.4430045	0.1143202	−0.1137315	0.5250809
Kurtosis	1.870849	−0.0602291	1.91516	1.726531	1.633083
Observation	47	47	47	47	47

Source: It was developed by the authors based on Stata software.

We have developed a correlation matrix between GDP and its influencing factors based on the econometric model (Table 38).

According to the results of Table 38, a strong, stable relationship was presented between GDP and the factors affecting it. Taking into account the p-value of <0.05 according to the table, it was presented as a significance level for the correlation coefficient. Also, there is no multicollinearity between all variables.

Table 38. Correlation matrix of dependent and independent variables

Variables	*(1)*	*(2)*	*(3)*	*(4)*	*(5)*	*(6)*
logGDP	1.000					
logcons_ expend	0.7290	1.000				
	(0.0000)					***
log pub_admin	0.6781	0.6961	1.000			
	(0.0000)	(0.0000)				***
lognon-prod_org	0.6726	0.6696	0.6639	1.000		
	(0.0000)	(0.0000)	(0.0000)			***
logexport	0.7553	0.6449	0.6552	0.7203	1.000	
	(0.0000)	(0.0000)	(0.0000)	(0.0000)		***

Source: It was developed by the authors based on Stata software.

In the next step, a Unit-Root test was conducted to determine the stationarity of the dependent and independent variables (Table 39).

Table 39. Unit-Root test results for dependent and independent variables

Variables	*Test Statistic*	*1% Critical Value*	*5% Critical Value*	*10% Critical Value*	*p-value for Z(t)*
logGDP (dependent variable)	-6.491	-3.607	-2.941	-2.605	0.0000
logcons_ expend (independent variable)	-5.471	-3.607	-2.941	-2.605	0.0000
log pub_admin (independent variable)	-4.468	-3.607	-2.941	-2.605	0.0000
lognon-prod_org (independent variable)	-5.084	-3.607	-2.941	-2.605	0.0000
logexport (independent variable)	-4.264	-3.607	-2.941	-2.605	0.0000

Source: It was developed by the authors based on Stata software.

According to Table 39, the results of the Unit-Root test were –6.491 for the dependent variable, and –5.471, –4.468, –5.084, and –4.264 for the independent variables. According to this, these values showed that the GDP and the factors affecting it reached stationarity.

The indicators of the econometric equation of the ARDL model are presented in Table 40.

Below are econometric equations for long-run (LR) and short-run (SR) dynamic relationships based on the ARDL model.

In the LR dynamics:

$$logGDP_t = \alpha + \beta_1 logcons\_expend_t + \beta_2 logpub\_admin_t + \beta_3 lognonprod\_org_t + \beta_4 logexport + \epsilon_t \quad (2)$$

Error Correction Period:

$$ECT_{t-1} = -0.22 \cdot logGDP_{t-1} \quad (3)$$

According to the short-term dynamics (SR):

$$DlogGDP_t = \gamma_0 + \gamma_1 \cdot DlogGDP_{t-1} + \gamma_2 Dlogcons\_expend_t + \gamma_3 Dlogcons\_expend_{t-1} + \gamma_4 Dlognonprod\_org_t + \gamma_5 Dlognonprod\_org_{t-1} + ECT_{t-1} + \nu_t \quad (4)$$

The coefficients of the econometric equation based on the ARDL(2,2,0,2,0) model are given below.

Table 40. ARDL(2,2,0,2,0) model regression equation indicators

ARDL(2,2,0,2,2) regression — Number of obs = 45

Sample: 2012q1–2023q1 — *R*-squared = 0.9602

Log likelihood = 208.46137 — Adj *R*-squared = 0.9484

Root MSE = 0.0027

D.logGDP	**Coef.**	**Std. Err.**	**t**	***P > t***	**[95%Conf.**	**Interval]**
ADJ logGDP						
L1.	−0.222	0.052	−4.240	0.000	−0.328	−0.116 ***
LR						
logcons_expend	0.648	0.043	14.990	0.000	0.560	0.736 ***
logpub_admin	0.147	0.058	2.520	0.016	0.029	0.265 ***
lognonprod_org	0.098	0.021	4.750	0.000	0.056	0.141 ***
logexport	0.098	0.023	4.310	0.000	0.052	0.145 ***
SR logGDP						
LD.	0.570	0.126	4.520	0.000	0.033	0.826 ***
logcons_expend						
D1.	0.605	0.074	8.190	0.000	0.045	0.755 ***
LD.	−0.532	0.108	−4.920	0.000	−0.072	−0.312 ***
lognonprod_org						
D1.	0.101	0.024	4.270	0.000	0.053	0.149 ***
LD.	−0.116	0.028	−4.200	0.000	−0.172	−0.060 ***
_cons	0.297	0.074	4.040	0.000	0.147	0.446 ***

Source: It was developed by the authors based on Stata software.

According to the econometric equation ARDL(2,2,0,2,0) for the LR dynamics:

$$logGDP_t = 0.64logcons\_expend_t + 0.14logpub\_admin_t + 0.09lognonprod\_org_t + 0.09logexport_t - 0.22logGDP_{t-1} \quad (5)$$

According to the econometric equation ARDL(2,2,0,2,0) for the SR dynamics:

$$DlogGDP_t = 0.29 + 0.56DlogGDP_{t-1} + 0.60Dlogcon\_expend_t - 0.53Dlogcon\_expend_{t-1} + 0.10Dlognonprod\_org_t - 0.11Dlognonprod\_org_{t-1} + ECT_{t-1} \quad (6)$$

12.4.1. General Description of the ARDL(2,2,0,2,0) Model

R-squared value: 0.9602, indicating that approximately 96.02% of the variation in the value added of products produced in the industry is explained by the model. A high *R*-squared value indicates a positive significance level of the model to the observed data.

Log likelihood: 208.4613, which is explained by a positive assessment of the fit of the econometric equation.

Root MSE: 0.0027, which indicates the average value of the error in forecasting the dependent variable. Considering that this value is small, it indicates the reliability of the forecasting performance of the model.

The ARDL(2,2,0,2,0) model was tested in the study, and the results showed that the *F*-statistic and *t*-statistic had a statistical significance level of 0.05, in which case the null hypothesis was rejected. As a result, the alternative hypothesis (H_1) was accepted. The model was tested for cointegration using the ARDL(2,2,0,2,0) Bound test (Tables 41 and 42).

Table 41. Bound *F*-test for cointegration

									F = 6.747
	[I_0]	[I_1]	[I_0]	[I_1]	[I_0]	[I_1]	[I_0]	[I_1]	
	L_1	L_1	L_05	L_05	L_025	L_025	L_01	L_01	
K_4	2.45	3.52	2.86	4.01	3.25	4.49	3.74	5.06	

Source: It was developed by the authors based on Stata software.

According to Table 41, the F-statistic value is 6.747, which is greater than the critical limits for all intervals and indicates the presence of cointegration. Accordingly, the Bound test indicates a positive result for the F-statistic value.

Table 42. Bound *t*-test for cointegration

									***F*=-4.241**
	[I_0]	[I_1]	[I_0]	[I_1]	[I_0]	[I_1]	[I_0]	[I_1]	
	L_1	L_1	L_05	L_05	L_025	L_025	L_01	L_01	
K_4	-2.57	-3.66	-2.86	-3.99	-3.13	-4.26	-3.43	-4.60	

Source: It was developed by the authors based on Stata software.

12.4.1.1. Result

Applying the ARDL(2,2,0,2,0) model, a 1% rise in the final consumption expenditure of household units means an increase of 0.64% in the long run of the country's GDP. A 1% rise in the final consumption expenditure of government institutions in the national economy means an increase of 0.14% in the country's GDP.

According to Table 42, the t-statistic value is –5.866, which is greater than the critical limits for all intervals and indicates the presence of cointegration.

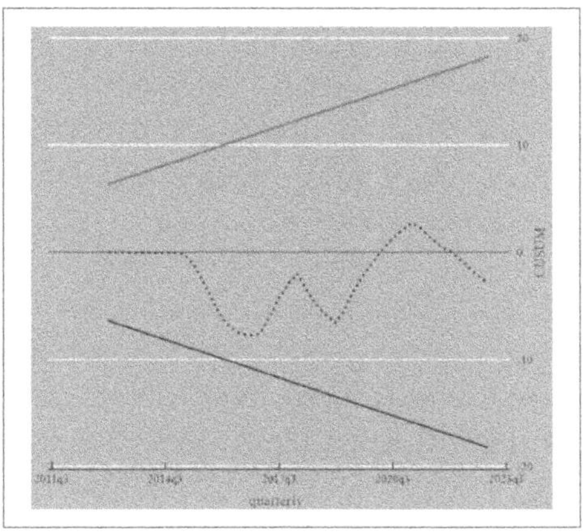

Figure 45. CUSUM diagnostic test chart.
Source: It was developed by the authors based on Stata software.

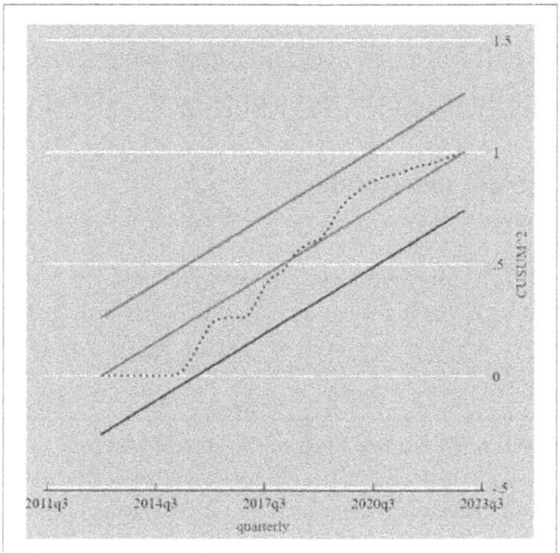

Figure 46. CUSUM diagnostic test chart.
Source: It was developed by the authors based on Stata software.

Accordingly, the Bound test provided a positive result for the *t*-statistic value. A 1% increase in the terminal consumption spending of non-profit institutions serving households of the national economy leads to the increase of the country's GDP by 0.09%.

In the second stage of the research, the CUSUM diagnostic test was conducted on the basis of the ARDL(2,2,0,2,0) model.

CUSUM (Cumulative Sum) test on the ARDL(2,2,0,2,0) model obtains the following hypothesis during the determination of parameter stability with time for regression equations:

1. *Null hypothesis* (H_0*—Baseline hypothesis*): The model does not change over time (there is no systematic change in the parameters). The residuals follow a stable process, which indicates that the probable parameters of the ARDL(2,2,0,2,0) model are not distinct over the sample period.
2. *Alternative hypothesis* (H_1*—Alternative hypothesis*): The ARDL(2,2,2,2) model is not stable over time (there is a systematic change in the parameters). The residuals are unstable, which implies that the model parameters changed at some points in the sample period.

Interpretation of the CUSUM diagnostic result for the ARDL(2,2,0,2,0) model: Since the CUSUM test was passed, the null hypothesis (H_0) of the ARDL(2,2,0,2,0) model could not be rejected, i.e., the ARDL(2,2,0,2,0) model was stable during the period of review. Correspondingly, according to the ARDL(2,2,0,2,0) model, the relationship between GDP and the determinants of GDP is generally constant without systematic breaks and parameter instability.

12.4.1.2. Explanation to the CUSUM Test Graphic

For the CUSUM test, the graph of the sum of the recursive residuals plotted against time is constructed with upper and lower limits as the critical limits, and the diagnostic test statistics fall within the critical limits over the entire period under consideration and no significant deviations are observed.

To build the second econometric model of the research, 83 economic indicators, in the form of monthly indicators of the World Bank (<https://data.worldbank.org/>), the Central Bank of the Republic of Uzbekistan (<https://cbu.uz/oz/>), and the Statistical Agency (<https://stat.uz/uz/>), were used from 2016 to 2023 in order to quantify the impact of the process of co-ordination of the fiscal and monetary policy on the national economy.

The formula for a LS model is as follows.

$$y_t = \alpha_0 + \alpha_1 c_1 + \alpha_2 c_2 + \cdots + \alpha_m c_m + \epsilon \tag{7}$$

Here, y_t represents the dependent variable; c_1, c_2, c_3 represent the independent variables; α_0 represents the intercept; α_1, α_2, α_m represents the coefficient of the independent variables; and ϵ represents the error term.

The econometric model evaluates the interaction of money supply, exchange rate, GDP, and export and import volumes as factors affecting the level of inflation in the national economy.

All the variables of the econometric equation were transformed into natural logarithms.

The resultant variable and the determinants of the same in the econometric model are given as in what follows.

Inflation rate of the national economy is *lninflation_rate* (dependent variable), money supply is *lnmoney_of* (independent variable), exchange rate is *lnexchange_rat*e (independent variable), volume of GDP is *lnGDP_vol* (independent variable), volume of export is *lnexport_vol* (independent variable), and volume of import is *lnimport_vol* (independent variable).

While constructing the econometric model, the null hypothesis (H_0) and alternative hypothesis (H_1) were formulated:

Null hypothesis (H_0): Exchange rate, GDP volume, and exports and imports are not at all determinants of the inflation rate in the national economy.
Alternative hypothesis (H_1): Money supply, exchange rate, GDP, and exports and imports are determinants of the inflation rate in the national economy.

During the beginning stage of research, descriptive measures of statistics were measured for the dependent and independent variables (Table 43).

Table 43. Descriptive statistics of dependent and independent variables according to the econometric model

	Lninflation_ rate	lnmoney_ of	lnexchange_ rate	lnGDP_ vol	lnexport_ vol	lnimport_ vol
Mean	2.526908	11.36464	8.905313	13.02086	9.658333	9.968046
Maximum	3.00072	12.09947	9.341387	13.56741	10.04945	10.49951
Minimum	2.04122	10.65228	7.948558	12.35292	9.400514	9.404063
Std. Dev	0.2362538	0.3882271	0.4783304	0.4008807	0.1712043	0.30075
Std. Err.	0.0259322	0.0426135	0.0525036	0.0440024	0.0187921	0.0330116
Skewness	0.0559849	−0.1373413	−1.093071	−0.235133	0.2360544	−0.3345576
Kurtosis	2.335739	2.216944	2.511774	1.630357	2.385729	2.248337
Observation	83	83	83	83	83	83

Source: It was developed by the authors based on Stata software.

As Table 37 shows, the descriptive statistical measures of the model recorded positive average values of the independent and dependent variables in the confidence intervals. The implication is the possibility of developing meaningful conditions for the next stages of the econometric model.

From the diagram, the graphical presentation of the frequency distribution of inflation rate and its determinants illustrates the stability of the clustered frequency distribution in the economic context under study according to econometric studies. According to the research, the dynamics of changing the inflation rate, money supply, exchange rates, gross domestic product,

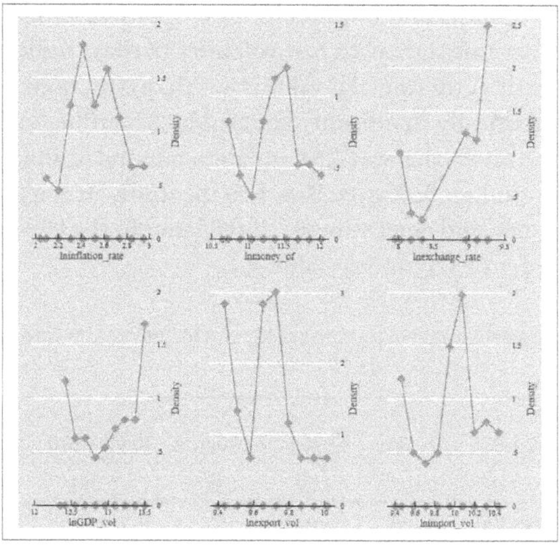

Figure 47. Graphical representation of the analytical relationship (rconnected) of the variables affecting the inflation rate.

Source: It was developed by the authors based on Stata software.

Table 44. Cross-correlation matrix of inflation rate and factors influencing it

Variables	*(1)*	*(2)*	*(3)*	*(4)*	*(5)*	*(6)*	*(7)*
Lninflation_rate	1.000						
lnmoney_of	0.4907	1.000					
	(0.0032)						***
lnexchange_rate	0.4947	0.7075	1.000				
	(0.0002)	(0.0000)					***
lnGDP_vol	0.7906	0.7690	0.7015	1.000			
	(0.0000)	(0.0000)	(0.0000)				***
lnexport_vol	0.4723	0.7540	0.7341	0.9120	1.000		
	(0.0982)	(0.0000)	(0.0000)	(0.0000)			*
lnimport_vol	0.4032	0.7852	0.7200	0.7507	0.7779	1.000	
	(0.0654)	(0.0000)	(0.0000)	(0.0000)	(0.0000)		*

Source: It was developed by the authors based on Stata software.

and volumes of exports and imports into the specified ranges demonstrate equilibrium economic state with low volatility of these indicators.

According to this criterion, if *p*-value is less than 0.05, then the correlation coefficient is statistically significant and reliable. According to the econometric study, VIf indicator value was 2.63. Inflation rate and its influencing factors do not have any multicollinearity. Based on the study, an econometric model of the inflation rate and determinants of the latter in the local economy was developed based on a LS model (Table 45).

Table 45. Regression equation indicators for the inflation rate and factors affecting it

lninflation_ rate	Coef.	St. Err.	*t*-value	*p*-value	[95% Conf	Interval]	Sig
lnmoney_of	0.325	0.195	1.67	0.099	−0.063	0.713	*
lnexchange_ rate	0.533	0.106	5.04	0	0.322	0.744	***
lnGDP_vol	−1.476	0.124	−11.88	0	−1.724	−1.229	***
lnexport_vol	−2.231	0.562	−3.97	0	−3.351	−1.112	***
lnimport_vol	2.081	0.502	4.15	0	1.082	3.08	***
Constant	14.115	1.951	7.24	0	10.23	17.999	***
Mean dependent var	2.527			**SD dependent var**	0.236		
R-squared	0.805			**Number of obs**	83		
F-test	63.636			**Prob > F**	0.000		
Akaike crit. (AIC)	−128.724			**Bayesian crit. (BIC)**	−114.211		
*** $p < 0.01$, ** $p < 0.05$, * $p < 0.1$							

Source: It was developed by the authors based on Stata software.

The fixed effects depend on the variables included and the structure of the econometric equation used.

$$lninflation\_rate = 14.11 + 0.32lnmoney\_of + 0.53lnexchange\_rate - 1.47lnGDP\_vol - 2.23lnexport\_vol + 2.08lnimport\_vol + \epsilon \quad (8)$$

12.4.2. Statistical Significance

All the independent variables also have *p*-values <0.05, indicating that they are significant predictors of the inflation rate at the 5% level of significance.

R-squared (0.80): This indicates that the inflation rate explains 80.5% of the variables, indicating a positive relationship in terms of the quality of the econometric equation.

12.4.2.1. Result

An increase in the money supply in the national economy by 1% increases the inflation rate by 0.32%. A depreciation of the exchange rate in the national economy by 1% increases the inflation rate by 0.52%. An increase in the GDP in the national economy by 1% decreases the inflation rate by 1.47%. A 1% point increase in the export size in the nation's economy causes deflation in the inflation rate by 2.23%. Furthermore, an increase in the import size by a 1% point in the domestic economy leads to inflation of the inflation rate by 2.08%.

Gauss–Markov assumptions were addressed in the study. The Durbin–Watson test of the regression line was 0.43. Further, Shapiro–Wilk W test was 0.17 and Breusch–Pagan test was 0.59. The primary hypotheses $H_0: y = 0$ and $H_1: y \neq 0$, $p > 0.05$ significance level were verified.

With respect to outcomes gained through conducting the Durbin–Watson and Shapiro–Wilk tests on econometric research, null was taken to be so. Since the limiting value of significance levels at which null can hold was $p > 0.05$, Gauss–Markov's condition that distinguishes a deficiency of relationship between error terms and the independent variables does hold as far as our analysis formulation goes. Our analysis formulation conforms to the major requirement conditions of Gauss–Markov's assumption in econometric analysis.

12.5. Findings and Discussion

The study, following the findings and conclusion of the econometric analysis of the process of co-ordination of fiscal and monetary policy in the national economy under LS and ARDL models, has led to the development of the following proposals and recommendations.

According to the ARDL(2,2,0,2,0) model of GDP and its influencing factors:

1. *Assessment of household consumption expenditure's effect on GDP*: An increase in household final consumption expenditure by 1% leads to an increase in GDP by 0.64%. This discovery indicates that consumption by households plays a major role in economic development. Expenditure by households on goods and services, as a result of increased demand within the economy, attracts companies to production and investment, therefore leading to GDP growth.
2. *Quantifying the impact of money supply on inflation*: When money supply rises by 1% in the economy as a whole, it increases the inflation rate by 0.32%. This is consistent with economic theory, which is that more money supply leads to more inflation because of its impact of raising the money supply to spend, which also raises the demand for goods and services.
3. *Impulse effect of depreciation of currency on domestic economy inflation*: A 1% depreciation of the currency raises the inflation rate by 0.52%. Currency depreciation raises the price of imports, and, therefore, a higher amount of local currency is required to buy foreign goods and services. Such an increase in import costs leads to higher inflation, since businesses pass on greater import costs to consumers. The comparatively high elasticity (0.52%) indicates that the economy is sensitive to exchange rate variations, which also means that exchange rate stability is crucial in controlling inflation.
4. *The economic significance of the impact of GDP growth on inflation*: A 1% growth in GDP lowers the inflation rate by 1.47%. This is a negative relationship, which shows that with economic growth, inflation will decrease, and this is due to an increase in potential efficiency and an increase in the supply of goods and services. High GDP growth raises economic efficiency higher, fulfills the demand of consumers, and reduces inflation pressures.
5. *Assessing the role of export quantity in contributing to inflation*: A 1% increase in export quantity brings the inflation rate down by 2.23%. This high, negative effect can be concluded that exports are acting as an inflation stabilizer. Increased exports stimulate production, bring

about a growth in the economy, and can reduce the inflation rate with an increase in the quantity of production.

6. *Estimation of the impact of import volume on inflation*: A 1% increase in import volume leads to a 2.08% increase in inflation. This is a desirable effect because higher imports can increase demand for foreign currency, which can create pressure for the devaluation of the home currency, thereby increasing the cost of imported goods and services. Conversely, if the economy is import-oriented, an increase in import demand will be a cause of inflationary pressure, especially for consumer goods, since they are most immediately affected by the increase in import prices.

Bibliography

Abdullah, M. A., Han, X., Amjad, M. A., & Makhmudov, S. (2025). Revisit the role of financial development on economic growth, human development, and sustainable development in higher-income countries. *Journal of Environmental Management*, *392*, 126874.

Adam, C., & Bevan, D. (2005). Fiscal deficits and growth in developing countries. *Journal of Public Economics*, *89*(4), 571–597.

Akhmetshin, E., Abdullayev, I., Makhmudov, S., Dakhkilgova, K., Korotaeva, I. and Yanovskaya, G. (2025). APPLICATION OF TANH–COTH METHOD FOR COMBINED AND DOUBLE COMBINED SINH–COSH–GORDON EQUATIONS ARISING CHEMICAL REACTIONS TO WATER SURFACE GRAVITY WAVES. Computational Methods for Differential Equations, (), -. doi: 10.22034/cmde.2025.67655.3234

Bernanke, B. S., & Gertler, M. (1995). Inside the black box: The credit channel of monetary policy transmission. *Journal of Economic Perspectives*, 9(4), 27–48. <https://doi.org/10.1257/jep.9.4.27>

Cahyani, I., Buriev, K., Ngongo, M., Mamadiyarov, Z., Ino, L., Herman, H., Saputra, N., & Baxtishodovich, S. (2025). Exploring the Use of TikTok Application in Enhancing the Skill of Pronunciation: A Case on Students' Perception. Studies in Media and Communication, 13(2), 150–158. doi:http://dx.doi.org/10.11114/smc.v13i2.7553

Caporin, M., Shahbaz, M., Kuziboev, B., Masharipova, M., Allaberganov, S., & Makhmudov, S. (2024). Environmental Kuznets Curve for extended brics economies: do women governance and water stress matter?. International Journal of Energy Economics and Policy, *14*(6), 174–183.

Fischer, S. (1993). The role of macroeconomic factors in growth. *Journal of Monetary Economics*, *32*(3), 485–512. <https://doi.org/10.1016/0304-3932(93)90027-D>

Friedman, M. (1968). The role of monetary policy. *American Economic Review*, *58*(1), 1–17.

Ghura, D., & Pattillo, C. (2012). Macroeconomic challenges for low-income countries. *IMF Staff Papers*, *59*(2), 1–25.

Inglesi-Lotz, R., Oosthuizen, A. M., Jumaniyazova, S., Kuziboev, B., & Liu, J. (2024). Exploring the impact of women governance on CO2 emissions in the European Union and Central Asia. *International Journal of Energy Economics and Policy*, *14*(3), 639–646.

International Monetary Fund (IMF) (2023). *Uzbekistan economic outlook: Policy reforms and macroeconomic performance*. IMF Report. Retrieved from [<https://www.imf.org/en/Publications>] (Accessed 10/02/2023)

Hussain, A., Khan, M., Rakhmonov, D. A., Mamadiyarov, Z. T., Kurbonbekova, M. T., & Mahmudova, M. Q. K. (2023). Nexus of Training and Development, Organizational Learning Capability, and Organizational Performance in the Service Sector. *Sustainability*, *15*(4), 3246. https://doi.org/10.3390/su15043246

Jahrir, A., Gultom, Y., Herman, H., Zabadi, F., Ngongo, M., Mamadiyarov, Z., Fatmawati, E., & Saputra, N. (2025). Investigating the Elements of Short Commercial Mineral Water Advertisement: A Case on Discourse Analysis. Studies in Media and Communication, *13*(4), 94–104. doi:http://dx.doi.org/10.11114/smc.v13i4.7813

Karimov, B., & Lee, C. (2021). Monetary policy effectiveness in Uzbekistan: An empirical study. *Emerging Markets Review*, *30*, 101–115.

Khan, R., & Sokolov, D. (2020). Fiscal policy and economic growth: Evidence from transition economies. *Journal of Economic Policy Research*, *14*(2), 45–62.

Kurbonov, K. (2025). Quantitative easing and its long-term effects on us credit market sustainability: A neutrosophic science perspective. *International Journal of Neutrosophic Science (IJNS)*, *25*(3).

Kuchkarov, T., Mamadiyarov, Z., Khakimov, Z., Sabirova, O., Matmurodov, K., Raimboyeva, M., & Umarova, S. (2025). Energy-Related Uncertainty and Crypto-Currency Environmental Attention: Time-Varying Perspective. International Journal of Energy Economics and Policy, 15(5), 614–626. https://doi.org/10.32479/ijeep.20784

Khodjaniyazov, N., Mirkhoshimova, M., Kalandarov, F., Matyokubova, D., Utegenova, S., Makhmudov, S., & Khudayberganov, M. (2025). Time-Varying Impacts of Financial Stress on Energy-Related Uncertainty. International Journal of Energy Economics and Policy, 15(3), 689–698.

Kuziboev, B., Ozturk, I., Kalandarov, F., Samandarov, O., Bekjanov, D., & Makhmudov, S. (2025). PROMOTING ENERGY SOURCES DIVERSIFICATION THROUGH ESG PERFORMANCE. Energy, 136009.

Lin, M.H., Matchanova, B., Nurmatovich, H.A. *et al.* Optimal Operation of the Multi-Carrier Energy System Considering Energy Markets and Renewable Energies Participation. *Int. J. Appl. Comput. Math* **11**, 170 (2025). https://doi.org/10.1007/s40819-025-02002-9

Litamahuputty, J. V., Amiruddin, E. G., Rahim, R., Rahman, A., & Mamadiyarov, Z. (2025). Cryptocurrency Risk Management through Decision Engineering: Evaluating XRPUSD and ADAUSD Portfolio Performance. Journal of Applied Science, Engineering, Technology, and Education, 7(1), 69–81. https://doi.org/10.35877/454RI.asci3871

Mamadiyarov, Z., Hakimov, H., & Askarov, S. (2024). DEVELOPMENT OF RETAIL BANKING SERVICES IN THE CONTEXT OF DIGITAL TRANSFORMATION. *Financial and Credit Activity Problems of Theory and Practice*, *1*(54), 51–67. https://doi.org/10.55643/fcaptp.1.54.2024.4288

Mamadiyarov, Z. Makhmudov, S. Utanov, B. Kasimova, D. Bekmurodova, G. Hakimov, Z. (2025). Fusion of Economic and Financial Factors Affecting Household Deposits in Banks: An Econometric Analysis. *Fusion: Practice and Applications*, (), 82–91. DOI: https://doi.org/10.54216/FPA.190206

Mamani, J.C.M., Miri, M., Vorobev, Y. et al. Optimal Operation of Energy Microgrid Considering Economic and Emission Indices. Oper. Res. Forum 6, 122 (2025). https://doi.org/10.1007/s43069-025-00523-z

Mishkin, F. S. (2007). *Monetary policy strategy*. Cambridge, MA: MIT Press.

Mishra, P., Montiel, P., & Spilimbergo, A. (2012). Monetary transmission in low-income countries. *IMF Economic Review*, *60*(2), 270–302.

Muhammad Zubair, Irfanud Din, Nadeem Sarwar et al. Revolutionizing Sepsis Diagnosis Using Machine Learning and Deep Learning Models: A Systematic Literature Review, 10 June 2025, PREPRINT (Version 1) available at Research Square [https://doi.org/10.21203/rs.3.rs-6731418/v1]

PANJAITAN, M. B., HAMDANAH, H., SIRAIT, J., SUTIKNO, S., FATMAWATI, E., HERMAN, H., & MAMADIYAROV, Z. (2025). THE ROLE OF EMOTIONAL REGULATION IN SHAPING STUDENTS' PERCEPTION OF PHYSICS PROBLEMSOLVING TASKS. TPM – Testing, Psychometrics, Methodology in Applied Psychology, 32(S2(2025): Posted 09 June), 1–10. Retrieved from https://tpmap.org/submission/index.php/tpm/article/view/139

Pradhan, R., Hajiyev, E., Shichiyakh, R. *et al.* Optimal Techno-Economic Feasibility of an Off-Grid Microgrid System Using Load Flow Energy Management Strategies. *Oper. Res. Forum* **6**, 120 (2025). https://doi.org/10.1007/s43069-025-00524-y

Romero, R. M., Zelinskaya, M., Makhmudov, S., Sapaev, S., & Rustambekovich, J. U. (2025, September). Modelling and Optimal Utilisation of the Renewable Energy Systems in Microgrid with Improving Reliability and Energy Efficiency. In Operations Research Forum (Vol. 6, No. 3, pp. 1–20). Springer International Publishing.

Roztocki, N., Soja, P., & Weistroffer, H. R. (2017). Enterprise systems in transition economies: Research landscape and framework for socioeconomic development. *Information Technology for Development*. <https://doi.org/10.1080/02681102.2017.1377148>.

Samariddin Makhmudov, Kudratillo Tukhsanov, Saifulla Arslanbekov, Akram Amanov, Orifali Tursunov, Umarbek Jabbarov and Muyassarxon Mirzakarimova. 2024. Optimizing Supply Chain Financing Development Prospects of Digital Ecosystems in the European Logistics Industry. In The 8th International Conference on Future Networks & Distributed Systems (ICFNDS '24), December 11–12, 2024, Marakech, Morocco. ACM, New York, NY, USA, 12 Pages. https://doi.org/10.1145/3726122.3726200

Sharipov, K., Abdullayev, I., Kuziboev, B., Makhmudov, S., Kalandarov, F., Khaytboeva, N., & Ilkhamova, Z. (2025). The Effect of Energy Policy Risk on Renewable Energy. International Journal of Energy Economics and Policy, *15*(2), 566.

Su, R., Xiao, Y., Hamza, F., Mamadiyarov, Z., & Wahab, A. (2025). Scaling up green hydrogen in China: Economic opportunities and challenges. *International Journal of Hydrogen Energy, 131*, 60–69.

Zhang, L., Zhao, Z., Qamri, G. M., & Makhmudov, S. (2025). Unleashing the critical role of renewable energy through global value chains and digitalization: A path towards environmental sustainability. Journal of Environmental Management, 392, 126688.

Zokir Toshtemirovich Mamadiyarov, Samandarboy Adhambek ugli Sulaymanov, Sarvar Anvar ugli Askarov, and Durdona Bakhtiyor kizi Uktamova. 2022. Impact of Covid-19 Pandemic on Accelerating the Digitization and Transformation of Banks. In Proceedings of the 5th International Conference on Future Networks and Distributed Systems (ICFNDS '21). Association for Computing Machinery, New York, NY, USA, 706–712. https://doi.org/10.1145/3508072.3508211

Econometric Analysis of the Impact of Numerical Parameters and Deposit Rates on Increasing Liquidity Dynamics in the Process of Transforming the Banking system

Zokir Mamadiyarov, Samariddin Makhmudov, Sultanov Makhmud, Malika Umarova, Gafurov Ubaydullo, Zaripa Akbarova, and Mirzabek Jonuzokov

13.1. Introduction

The banking system reform is an inevitable process of enhancing financial efficiency, resource allocation optimization, and adaptation to the demands of a rapidly changing digital world. The application of digital technologies, including remote banking services, complex transaction systems, and data-based financial policies, has become an integral part of commercial banks' financial efficiency enhancement and liquidity. Such variations enable banks to deliver better services, make customers happier, and enhance their overall financial position. As it stands, it is necessary that the impacts of key variables, i.e., remote users, transaction volumes, and deposit rate, on commercial banks' liquidity trends are ascertained in a bid to inform future financial planning.

This study investigates the relationship between these variables and the size of highly liquid assets in commercial banks over the years 2020–2024. For this purpose, an econometric method, i.e., multivariate linear regression (MLR), is applied. The MLR model is a strong statistical model that enables the estimation of the relationship between a single dependent variable (in our case, highly liquid assets) and a number of independent variables (such as far users, transaction level, and deposit rates).With the help of this model, the study attempts to quantify the effect of mobility in these variables on commercial bank efficiency and liquidity and comprehend drivers of financial performance.

The econometric model used here posits that the dependent variable (liquid assets) is a linear function of the independent variables. The model has error terms in order to take into account the unobserved variables influencing the relationship. The validity and reliability of the model are checked by statistical tests such as the Durbin–Watson test, Shapiro–Wilk test, and Breusch–Pagan test. The result of this analysis will be used in determining the strength and direction of the relationship among the variables, in the achievement of an enhanced understanding of how financial practice and digitalization shape the liquidity behavior of commercial banks.

13.2. Literature Review

Technological revolution, economic performance, and bank policy have been the greatest determinants of commercial banks' profitability. These factors have been the focus of research in recent years with scholars still investigating to what extent bank profitability and efficiency are determined by various different internal and external determinants, primarily as it relates to evolving market conditions and technology.

The trend of digitalization has revolutionized the banking sector by making financial services more efficient and accessible. In a study paper, Lihua Zuo et al. (2020) analyzed the impact of digital transformation on the efficiency of Chinese commercial banks. According to the authors, while big banks will surely benefit from digital technology, small and medium-sized banks find it difficult to gain similar benefits. This suggests that organizational readiness and digital uptake are influential determinants for the level of efficiency within the banks. Similarly, Furst et al. (2002) study also pointed out that information technology (IT) infrastructure deployment directly correlates with increased operating efficiency improvement, customer satisfaction, and profitability at banks.

Technologies such as cloud computing, mobile banking applications, and data analytics are key drivers to enhance the efficiency of the banking operations and services, as can be seen from the work of Rizwan et al. (2020). Such technologies enhance the satisfaction of the customers, reduce the operational cost, and increase the number of transactions, hence profitability. The interaction between bank performance and macroeconomic variables has been the core area of focus in econometric analysis. It has been tested on numerous occasions as far as the impact of macroeconomic variables such as Gross Domestic Product (GDP), inflation, and interest rates on banks' profitability and efficiency is concerned. Mollah et al. (2020), for instance, investigated the effect of macroeconomic indicators on the profitability of Bangladeshi commercial banks. Their findings indicated that the levels of GDP and inflation had a significant impact on profitability in banks, whereas interest rates had a mixed impact depending on the size and capital of the bank. On the contrary, a study report by Mahajan and Rani (2020) held that higher interest rates led to lower profitability for commercial banks of India, especially when the banks had a high percentage of NPLs.

Multivariate linear regression (LS), ARDL, ARIMA, and various other econometric models were used to forecast and estimate variables determining energy intensity and economic growth, energy policy, energy risk, environmental condition, and the influence of environmental variables on the digital economy, agricultural production, remittances, and stability of the U.S. credit market (Akhmetshin et al., 2025; Caporin et al., 2024; Jahrir et al., 2025; Litamahuputty et al., 2025; Kuchkarov et al., 2025; Kuziboev et al., 2024, 2025; Sharipov et al., 2025). Inflation impact studies have also produced conflicting findings. Sufian and Habibullah (2009) concluded that inflation had a negative effect on Malaysian commercial bank profitability as a result of its reliance on rising operating costs and lowering asset quality. Kozak et al. (2020) also conducted other studies indicating that inflation at a moderate rate will boost economic growth, and growth in economic activity in turn will increase the demand for credit and banking services and enhance bank performance.

Deposits and volume of transactions are central drivers of bank liquidity and profitability. Possibly, according to a study conducted by Ali et al. (2020), commercial bank financial stability is most directly linked with deposit mobilization to a great extent. Commercial banks with large volumes of transactions have stable levels of liquidity, which allows for increased loan extension and higher profitability. Similarly, the deposit interest rate is also a central driver of bank liquidity. The rate of deposit is well known to have an effect on the behavior of depositors and borrowers and, as a result, impact financial performance and levels of liquidity, as suggested by Ranjbar et al. (2019). Deposit structures in banks control bank liquidity. The findings in Davydenko et al. (2020) are that the higher the proportion of short-term deposits a bank has, the riskier the bank's liquidity than banks that hold a larger proportion of longer-term deposits. Conversely, banks with a diversified funding base that includes demand deposits and term deposits will have more stable levels of liquidity.

Econometric methods, particularly regression analysis, are used to a large extent to examine the determinants of bank performance. Gwahula Raphael (2014) used panel data and multivariate regression models to analyze the macroeconomic determinants of Tanzanian banking performance. The study proved that GDP growth rate and inflation positively influenced bank efficiency, while the interest rate and exchange rate influenced a combined effect.

Bozkurt and Kaya (2023), investigates the foremost firm-specific factors having an impact on financial distress and bankruptcy in the acute stage of the Covid-19 crisis based on data from approximately 9,000 enterprises in 25 countries. According to the study conducted by Özüdoğru and Sönmez (2023), the use of data analytics and machine learning solutions for the insurance industry is expected to increase.

Concurrently, in the Indian banking industry, Soni and Goyal (2019) applied multiple regression analysis to examine the drivers of financial performance. In its conclusion, the study identified that profitability drivers were influenced by the capital adequacy, asset quality, and operational efficiency. The study also examined the macroeconomic stability driver of commercial bank performance.

Further, econometric models have also been applied to measure the impact of digital transformation on bank profitability. Kohli and Shankar (2021) utilized panel data regression to analyze the relationship between IT spending and financial performance of Indian commercial banks. The results showed that IT spending was positively and significantly related to profitability, and the banks with higher levels of digital usage performed better compared to the others (Abdullah et al., 2025; Kohli and Shankar, 2021; Matyakubova et al., 2025; Romero et al., 2025).

Some economists have successfully used econometric models such as Fixed Effects Estimator (FEE), Random Effects Estimator (REE), multivariate linear (LS), and ARDL in analyzing investment in digital infrastructure, various components of digital payment systems, impacts of inflation and credit interest rates on investment, determinants of the decreasing state share in commercial banks, digital banking, risks in digital services, and retail payment service development (Cahyani et al., 2025; Makhmudov et al., 2024; Mamadiyarov et al., 2024, Mamani et al., 2025; Muhammad et al., 2025;

PANJAITAN et al., 2025; Samariddin et al., 2024; Zhang et al., 2025; Zokir et al., 2021). Similarly, in a cross-country analysis of the banking sector of European Union countries, Demirguc-Kunt and Levine (2001) found that the regulatory framework and financial system development were critical factors in shaping the performance of banks. Countries with stronger regulatory frameworks and more developed financial systems had improved efficiency and profitability in their banking sectors.

13.3. Research Methodology and Development Hypothesis

Since data for the study were built on the basis of multivariate time series foundations, a multivariate linear regression (LS) model was used to estimate econometric equations.

In building econometric models, the Central Bank of the Republic of Uzbekistan (<https://cbu.uz>) with the number of observations for the period 2020–2024 was used in attempting to determine the variables that affect the increase in financial efficiency. The Gauss–Markov assumptions of multivariate regression (LS) model were taken into account and the statistical significance level was calculated using Durbin–Watson, Shapiro–Wilk, and Breusch–Pagan confidence tests.

Plot charts and summary tables of statistics were constructed to measure the trends for each of the variables based on the econometric model. Concurrently, the correlation matrix was constructed to check the interaction between independent variables and dependent variable, as well as to check for multicollinearity.

MLR is a helpful statistical method of estimating the influence, relationship, and predictive ability of multiple independent variables and one dependent variable by statistical analysis of econometric equations. The formula for the MLR model is given below.

$$y_t = \lambda_0 + \lambda_1 m_1 + \lambda_2 m_2 + \ldots + \lambda_{nmn} + \epsilon \quad (1)$$

Here, y_t represents the dependent variable, m_1, m_2, m_3 represent independent variables, λ_0 represents the intercept, $\lambda_1 \lambda_2$, λ_n represent the coefficients of the independent variables, and ϵ represents the error term.

The econometric relationship quantifies the interaction between distant users, commercial bank transactions volume, and weighted average deposit rate for a maximum of one year as determinants of highly liquid assets. All the variables used in the econometric analysis were natural logarithmized and are presented below.

All variables in the econometric model are presented below.

> Commercial banks' high liquid assets index—*loghigh_liquid_asset* (dependent variable), Commercial banks' number of remote users—*logremote_serv* (independent variable), commercial banks' transaction volume—*logvol_transac* (independent variable), weighted average deposit rate up to one year—*logweighted_depos_1* (independent variable);

The hypotheses for the econometric model were formulated as follows:

Null hypothesis (H_0): The number of remote users, the volume of commercial bank transactions, and the weighted average deposit rate for up to one year do not significantly affect highly liquid assets.

Alternative hypotheses (H_1): The number of remote users, the volume of commercial bank transactions, and the weighted average deposit rate for up to one year have a significant relationship with highly liquid assets.

13.4. Analysis and Results

In the first stage of the study, the descriptive statistical indicators for the dependent and independent variables are presented in Table 46.

According to Table 46, the descriptive statistical indicators of the model recorded confidence intervals with positive average values of the dependent and independent variables. This indicates the prospects for the development of important conditions in the next stages of the econometric model.

According to the study, the graphical plot of the dependent and independent variables over time is shown in Figure 48.

According to Figure 48, in the time span under study, highly liquid assets and variables determining them in Uzbekistan's banking sector followed a robust growth trend. According to it, future estimation of these variables suggested a trend of growth. The impact of variables such as the number of remote users and the volume of commercial bank transactions on the evolution of highly liquid assets can be seen from the graphs. The weighted

Table 46. Descriptive statistics of dependent and independent variables according to the econometric model

	loghigh_ liquid_asset	logremote_ serv	logvol_transac	logweghted_ depos_1
Mean	11.05538	8.172237	3.339986	2.830421
Maximum	11.63459	9.101255	3.722302	2.96255
Minimum	10.37343	6.580084	3.049529	2.668837
Std. Dev	0.4042323	0.5222613	0.1964556	0.0839263
Std. Err.	0.0616449	0.0796441	0.0299592	0.0127986
Skewness	-0.325776	-0.6633678	0.4507193	-0.3385685
Kurtosis	1.87969	3.564386	1.956889	1.922506
Observation	43	43	43	43

Source: It was developed by the authors based on Stata software.

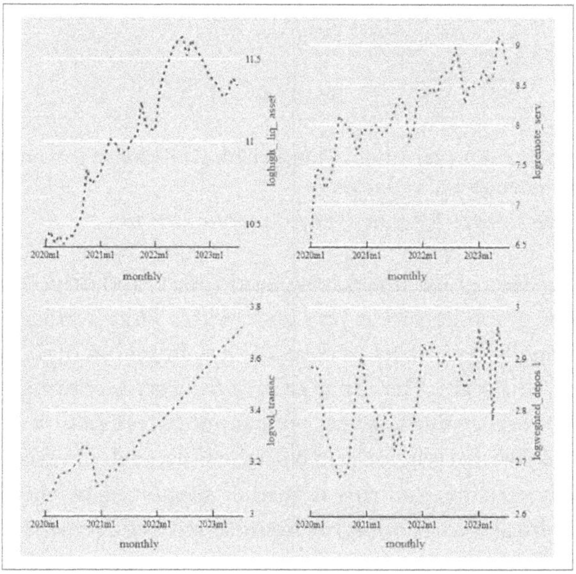

Figure 48. Analytical graphical representation of dependent and independent variables over time.

Source: It was developed by the authors based on Stata software.

average deposit rate for one year or less went through a stationary state during the period in question. This is an indication of a positive correlation effect in the next stage.

In the next stage, the analytical relationship (rconnected) between the volume of highly liquid assets and factors affecting it is presented in Figure 49.

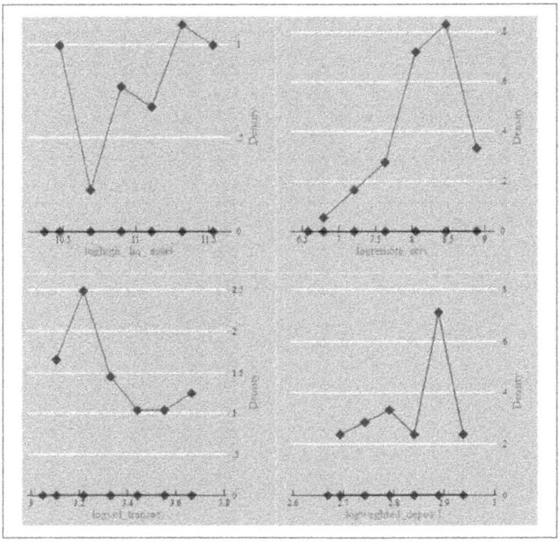

Figure 49. Graphical representation of the analytical relationship (rconnected) of the dependent and independent variables.

Source: It was developed by the authors based on Stata software.

Figure 49 provides a graph illustrating liquid assets and drivers of them. The peak shown by graph density is very wide with a large average span. Liquid assets undoubtedly have their peak at 7.5–8.0, implying high value congregation within this scale. The range of far-out users according to the graph implies high influence due to a very wide range of transaction activities. The graph depicts a positive relationship with the independent variables affecting the dependent variable, and this is further supported by the econometric model. A graphical matrix of highly liquid assets and factors affecting them are presented in Figure 50.

Also, the trend in the scatter plot was positive, indicating that the weighted average deposit rate and the number of transactions are related positively.

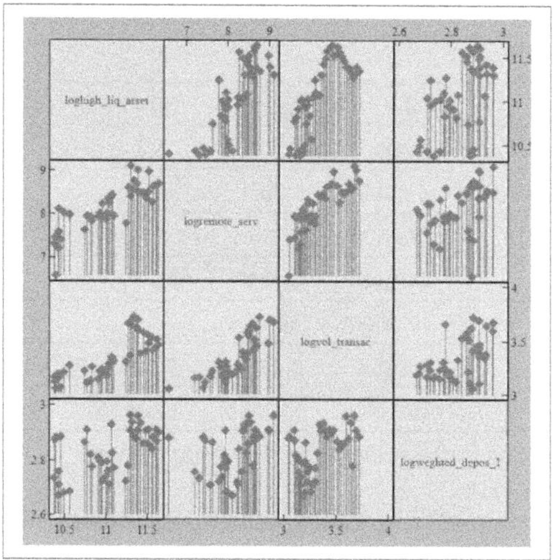

Figure 50. Graphical matrix of highly liquid assets of commercial banks and variables affecting them.

Source: It was developed by the authors based on Stata software.

The graphical matrix and scatter plot provide a visual understanding of the progression of the regression equation to the next step.

13.5. Findings and Discussion

In the next stage of the study, a cross-correlation matrix was developed for each of the highly liquid assets of commercial banks and the influencing variables (Table 47).

Table 47 presents the results of the strong and significant correlation between the variables. In addition, the correlation matrix in Table 46 showed that there is multicollinearity between the dependent and independent variables. Considering that the p-value <0.05, it can be seen that the correlation coefficient is reliable and statistically significant.

According to the study, an econometric equation of highly liquid assets of commercial banks and the factors affecting it was developed using a multivariate linear regression (LS) model (Table 48).

Table 47. Cross-correlation matrix of highly liquid assets of commercial banks and factors affecting them

Variables	**(1)**	**(2)**	**(3)**	**(4)**	**(5)**
loghigh_liquid_asset	1.000				
logremote_serv ginfl_rate	0.8252	1.000			
	(0.0000)				***
logvol_transac	0.7945	0.8298	1.000		
	(0.0000)	(0.0000)			***
logweghted_depos_1	0.5565	0.4357	0.5042	1.000	
	(0.0000)	(0.0035)	(0.0006)		***

Source: It was developed by the authors based on Stata software.

Table 48. Regression equation indicators for highly liquid assets of commercial banks and factors affecting them

loghigh_liq_ asset	**Coef.**	**St. Err.**	**t-value**	**p-value**	**[95% Conf**	**Interval]**	**Sig**
logremote_serv	0.404	0.111	3.62	0.001	0.178	0.629	***
logvol_transac	0.54	0.309	1.75	0.088	−0.085	1.165	*
logweghted_ depos1	0.948	0.448	2.12	0.041	0.042	1.855	**
Constant	3.268	1.097	2.98	0.005	1.05	5.486	***
Mean dependent var	11.055			SD dependent var		0.404	
R-squared	0.748			Number of obs		43	
F-test	38.686			Prob > F		0.000	
Akaike crit. (AIC)	−8.229			Bayesian crit. (BIC)		−1.185	
*** $p < 0.01$, ** $p < 0.05$, * $p < 0.1$							

Source: It was developed by the authors based on Stata software.

$$loghigh\_liq\_asset = 3.26 + 0.40 logremote\_serv + 0.54 logvol\_transac + 0.94 logweghted\_depos1 \quad (2)$$

The p-value of all independent variables is less than 0.05, indicating that the high liquid assets of commercial banks are statistically significant predictors at the 5% significance level.

R-squared (0.771): According to it, the high liquid assets of commercial banks explain 77.10% of the probability of the variables, indicating a positive relationship in terms of the quality of the econometric equation.

Based on the hypothesis testing of the regression model, it is clear that the null hypothesis ($H_0: y = 0$) is rejected when $F < 0.05$ and $t < 0.05$, indicating that the main hypothesis ($H_0: y = 0$) is statistically insignificant. Consequently, the main hypothesis is rejected in favor of accepting the alternative hypothesis ($H_1: y \neq 0$), which is statistically significant.

Result: A 1% increase in the number of remote users of commercial banks leads to an increase in the indicator of highly liquid assets of commercial banks by 0.40%. A 1% increase in the volume of transactions in commercial banks leads to an increase in the indicator of highly liquid assets of commercial banks by 0.54%. Also, a 1% increase in the weighted average deposit rate for commercial banks up to one year leads to an increase in the indicator of highly liquid assets of commercial banks by 0.94%.

The study considered Gauss–Markov conditions.

The Durbin–Watson test for the regression equation yielded a value of 0.94. Also, the Shapiro–Wilk W-test yielded a value of 0.95, and the Breusch–Pagan test yielded a value of 0.69. The primary hypothesis $H_0: y = 0$ and $H_1: y \neq 0$, $p > 0.05$, were tested at a significance level.

Based on the results of the Durbin–Watson and Shapiro–Wilk tests for econometric research, the null hypothesis was accepted. At the $p > 0.05$ threshold, the Gauss–Markov assumption, which confirms that there is no relationship between the error terms and the independent variables, is valid within the framework of our analysis. The main conditions of the Gauss–Markov assumption for the econometric model are met

13.6. Conclusion

The findings reveal the clear positive nexus between investment in digital technology and the growth of the service sector. The preferred REE model, as confirmed by the Hausman test *p*-value of 0.62, suggests that the development of digital infrastructure—i.e., increasing the number of personal computers, internet-connected computers, and skilled ICT workers—can lead to measurable improvements in the size and productivity of the service sector.

These results exhibit the strong impact of ICT-related determinants on the service sector of the national economy. As much as personal computers are relevant, internet-connected computers and an ICT-skilled labor force have a more positive and direct impact on the growth and development of services within the economy.

13.7. Recommendations

According to the econometric model, the following proposals and recommendations were developed as a result of the analysis and conclusions on the interaction between the number of remote users of commercial banks, the volume of commercial bank transactions, the weighted average deposit rate for up to one year, and the volume of highly liquid assets.

The following conclusions were drawn based on the results of the multivariate linear (LS) model on the volume of highly liquid assets of commercial banks and the factors affecting it.

1. *The significance of the impact of remote users on highly liquid assets of commercial banks*: A 1% increase in the number of remote users of commercial banks leads to an increase in highly liquid assets by 0.40%. According to this result, there is a positive relationship between the introduction of remote banking services and the increase in the liquidity and efficiency indicators of commercial banks. According to him, as a result of the increase in the use of online and remote banking services by customers in commercial banks, the liquid assets of banks will further increase.

2. *Volume of transactions to have an influence on highly liquid commercial bank assets*: The financial performance is obtained by 0.54% more than highly liquid commercial bank assets due to the increase by 1% of the volume of transactions at commercial banks. It shows significant causality from the volume of transactions to performance measures. As a result of the increase in the number of transactions, commercial banks will be holding more liquid assets, thereby enabling commercial banks to wipe out existing liabilities as a result of increased operating income through financial funds' increase.

3. *Evaluation of the effect of deposit rates on highly liquid assets*: A rise in the weighted average deposit rate on deposits with a maturity of up to one year by 1% results in an increase in highly liquid assets by 0.94%. Based on this finding, deposit rates, including through the attraction of financial resources on short-term deposits, contribute to the growth of the liquidity indicators of commercial banks. Providing competitive deposit rates encourages the mobility of deposits and enhances the level of liquid funds available.
4. Based on the econometric analysis results, all the variables influencing the dependent variable are highly correlated and reflect a positive impact. This increases the financial effectiveness of commercial banks in the processes of transformation.

Bibliography

Abdullah, M. A., Han, X., Amjad, M. A., & Makhmudov, S. (2025). Revisit the role of financial development on economic growth, human development, and sustainable development in higher-income countries. *Journal of Environmental Management*, *392*, 126874.

Akhmetshin, E., Abdullayev, I., Makhmudov, S., Dakhkilgova, K., Korotaeva, I. and Yanovskaya, G. (2025). APPLICATION OF TANH–COTH METHOD FOR COMBINED AND DOUBLE COMBINED SINH–COSH–GORDON EQUATIONS ARISING CHEMICAL REACTIONS TO WATER SURFACE GRAVITY WAVES. Computational Methods for Differential Equations, (), -. doi: 10.22034/cmde.2025.67655.3234

Ali, M., Abbas, S. M., & Riaz, S. (2020). Deposit mobilization and bank liquidity in emerging markets. *Journal of Banking and Finance*, *44*(1), 49–67.

Bozkurt, İ. & Kaya, M. V. (2023). Foremost features affecting financial distress and bankruptcy in the acute stage of COVID-19 crisis. *Applied Economics Letters*, *30*(8), 1112–1123.

Cahyani, I., Buriev, K., Ngongo, M., Mamadiyarov, Z., Ino, L., Herman, H., Saputra, N., & Baxtishodovich, S. (2025). Exploring the Use of TikTok Application in Enhancing the Skill of Pronunciation: A Case on

Students' Perception. Studies in Media and Communication, *13*(2), 150–158. doi:http://dx.doi.org/10.11114/smc.v13i2.7553

Caporin, M., Shahbaz, M., Kuziboev, B., Masharipova, M., Allaberganov, S., & Makhmudov, S. (2024). Environmental Kuznets Curve for extended brics economies: do women governance and water stress matter?. International Journal of Energy Economics and Policy, *14*(6), 174–183.

Davydenko, O., Starchenko, S., & Makarov, A. (2020). Liquidity management in commercial banks: A cross-country analysis. *European Financial Management*, *26*(4), 1203–1236.

Demirguc-Kunt, A., & Levine, R. (2001). Banking and finance in the European Union. *European Economic Review*, *45*(3), 421–444.

Furst, K., Weller, C. E., & McNamara, T. (2002). The role of technology in bank performance: Evidence from U.S. banks. *Journal of Financial Services Research*, *21*(2–3), 155–168.

Gwahula, R. (2014). Macroeconomic determinants of bank performance: Evidence from Tanzania. *African Journal of Business Management*, *8*(9), 246–259.

Hussain, A., Khan, M., Rakhmonov, D. A., Mamadiyarov, Z. T., Kurbonbekova, M. T., & Mahmudova, M. Q. K. (2023). Nexus of Training and Development, Organizational Learning Capability, and Organizational Performance in the Service Sector. Sustainability, *15*(4), 3246. https://doi.org/10.3390/su15043246

Jahrir, A., Gultom, Y., Herman, H., Zabadi, F., Ngongo, M., Mamadiyarov, Z., Fatmawati, E., & Saputra, N. (2025). Investigating the Elements of Short Commercial Mineral Water Advertisement: A Case on Discourse Analysis. Studies in Media and Communication, *13*(4), 94–104. doi:http://dx.doi.org/10.11114/smc.v13i4.7813

Khayrilla Kurbonov, Samariddin Makhmudov, Shakhzod Erkinov, Umidjon Dadabaev, Gulnora Bekimbetova, Rukhiddin Zayniddinov, and Mirzabek Jonuzokov. 2025. Evaluating the Impact of Marketing Practices Digitalization and Investment on Labor Market Efficiency and Commercial Bank Performance Using Econometric Models. In Proceedings of the 8th International Conference on Future Networks & Distributed Systems (ICFNDS '24). Association for Computing Machinery, New York, NY, USA, 786–796. https://doi.org/10.1145/3726122.3726237

Kohli, P., & Shankar, R. (2021). Impact of IT investments on bank profitability: Evidence from India. *International Journal of Bank Marketing*, *39*(1), 110–130.

Kozak, K., Martin, C., & Ross, T. (2020). Inflation, economic growth, and bank performance: Evidence from central and Eastern Europe. *Journal of International Financial Markets*, *35*(5), 254–267.

Kurbonov, K. (2025). Quantitative easing and its long-term effects on US credit market sustainability: A neutrosophic science perspective. *International Journal of Neutrosophic Science (IJNS)*, *25*(3).

Kuchkarov, T., Mamadiyarov, Z., Khakimov, Z., Sabirova, O., Matmurodov, K., Raimboyeva, M., & Umarova, S. (2025). Energy-Related Uncertainty and Crypto-Currency Environmental Attention: Time-Varying Perspective. International Journal of Energy Economics and Policy, *15*(5), 614–626. https://doi.org/10.32479/ijeep.20784

Kuziboev, B., Ozturk, I., Kalandarov, F., Samandarov, O., Bekjanov, D., & Makhmudov, S. (2025). PROMOTING ENERGY SOURCES DIVERSIFICATION THROUGH ESG PERFORMANCE. Energy, 136009.

Kuziboev, B., Saidmamatov, O., Khodjaniyazov, E., Ibragimov, J., Marty, P., Ruzmetov, D., ..., & Ibadullaev, D. (2024). CO2 emissions, remittances, energy intensity and economic development: The evidence from Central Asia. *Economies*, *12*(4), 95.

Lihua, Z., Zhiqiang, L., & Wei, H. (2020). Digital transformation and banking efficiency: Evidence from China. *Financial Innovation*, *6*(12), 15–30.

Lin, M.H., Matchanova, B., Nurmatovich, H.A. *et al.* Optimal Operation of the Multi-Carrier Energy System Considering Energy Markets and Renewable Energies Participation. *Int. J. Appl. Comput. Math* **11**, 170 (2025). https://doi.org/10.1007/s40819-025-02002-9

Litamahuputty, J. V., Amiruddin, E. G., Rahim, R., Rahman, A., & Mamadiyarov, Z. (2025). Cryptocurrency Risk Management through Decision Engineering: Evaluating XRPUSD and ADAUSD Portfolio Performance. Journal of Applied Science, Engineering, Technology, and Education, 7(1), 69–81. https://doi.org/10.35877/454RI.asci3871

Mahajan, A., & Rani, R. (2020). Effect of interest rates on bank profitability: Evidence from India. *Asian Economic Policy Review*, *15*(4), 789–803.

Makridakis, S., Spiliotis, E., & Assimakopoulos, V. (2022). M5 accuracy competition: Results, findings, and conclusions. *International Journal of Forecasting*, *38*(4), 1346–1364.

Mamadiyarov, Z., Hakimov, H., & Askarov, S. (2024). DEVELOPMENT OF RETAIL BANKING SERVICES IN THE CONTEXT OF DIGITAL TRANSFORMATION. *Financial and Credit Activity Problems of Theory and Practice*, *1*(54), 51–67. https://doi.org/10.55643/fcaptp.1.54.2024.4288

Mamadiyarov, Z. Makhmudov, S. Utanov, B. Kasimova, D. Bekmurodova, G. Hakimov, Z. (2025). Fusion of Economic and Financial Factors Affecting Household Deposits in Banks: An Econometric Analysis. *Fusion: Practice and Applications*, (), 82–91. DOI: https://doi.org/10.54216/FPA.190206

Mamani, J.C.M., Miri, M., Vorobev, Y. et al. Optimal Operation of Energy Microgrid Considering Economic and Emission Indices. Oper. Res. Forum 6, 122 (2025). https://doi.org/10.1007/s43069-025-00523-z

Matyakubova, A., Makhmudov, S., Ozturk, I., Kurbonov, K., Ismailov, F., Yokubboeva, S., & Urozov, A. (2025). Responses of Economic Policy Uncertainty, Financial Stress and Energy-Related Uncertainty to the Shocks in US-China Tension in US. *International Journal of Energy Economics and Policy*, *15*(4), 701–708. https://doi.org/10.32479/ijeep.20369

Mollah, M. D., & Hoque, M. M. (2020). Macroeconomic determinants of bank profitability: Evidence from Bangladesh. *The International Journal of Finance & Economics*, *25*(3), 489–502.

Muhammad Zubair, Irfanud Din, Nadeem Sarwar et al. Revolutionizing Sepsis Diagnosis Using Machine Learning and Deep Learning Models: A Systematic Literature Review, 10 June 2025, PREPRINT (Version 1) available at Research Square [https://doi.org/10.21203/rs.3.rs-6731418/v1]

PANJAITAN, M. B., HAMDANAH, H., SIRAIT, J., SUTIKNO, S., FATMAWATI, E., HERMAN, H., & MAMADIYAROV, Z. (2025). THE ROLE OF EMOTIONAL REGULATION IN SHAPING STUDENTS' PERCEPTION OF PHYSICS PROBLEMSOLVING TASKS. TPM – Testing, Psychometrics, Methodology in Applied Psychology, 32(S2(2025): Posted 09 June), 1–10. Retrieved from https://tpmap.org/submission/index.php/tpm/article/view/139

Özüdoğru, H. & Sönmez, S. S. (2024). The impact of artificial intelligence and machine learning on the insurance industry. *Journal of Banking and Financial Research*, *11*(1), 45–53.

Pradhan, R., Hajiyev, E., Shichiyakh, R. *et al.* Optimal Techno-Economic Feasibility of an Off-Grid Microgrid System Using Load Flow Energy Management Strategies. *Oper. Res. Forum* **6**, 120 (2025). https://doi.org/10.1007/s43069-025-00524-y

Ranjbar, F., & Amiri, R. (2019). The effect of deposit rates on bank liquidity. *Journal of Financial Intermediation*, *14*(1), 45–60.

Rizwan, M., & Asim, M. (2020). Digital banking and operational efficiency: Evidence from Pakistan. *Journal of Banking and Financial Technology*, *4*(1), 21–34.

Romero, R. M., Zelinskaya, M., Makhmudov, S., Sapaev, S., & Rustambekovich, J. U. (2025, September). Modelling and Optimal Utilisation of the Renewable Energy Systems in Microgrid with Improving Reliability and Energy Efficiency. In Operations Research Forum (Vol. 6, No. 3, pp. 1–20). Springer International Publishing.

Samariddin Makhmudov, Malika Umarova, Khayrilla Kurbonov, Laylo Akbarova, Durdona Davletova, Nilufar Shanazarova, and Toshmurod Kulmanov. 2025. Evaluating the forecast indicators of the volume of highly liquid assets of commercial banks in the process of digital transformation. In Proceedings of the 8th International Conference on Future Networks & Distributed Systems (ICFNDS '24). Association for Computing Machinery, New York, NY, USA, 698–704. https://doi.org/10.1145/3726122.3726222

Samariddin Makhmudov, Kudratillo Tukhsanov, Saifulla Arslanbekov, Akram Amanov, Orifali Tursunov, Umarbek Jabbarov and Muyassarxon Mirzakarimova. 2024. Optimizing Supply Chain Financing Development Prospects of Digital Ecosystems in the European Logistics Industry. In The 8th International Conference on Future Networks & Distributed Systems (ICFNDS '24), December 11–12, 2024, Marakech, Morocco. ACM, New York, NY, USA, 12 Pages. https://doi.org/10.1145/3726122.3726200

Sharipov, K., Abdullayev, I., Kuziboev, B., Makhmudov, S., Kalandarov, F., Khaytboeva, N., & Ilkhamova, Z. (2025). The Effect of Energy Policy Risk on Renewable Energy. International Journal of Energy Economics and Policy, *15*(2), 566.

Soni, S., & Goyal, S. (2019). Determinants of financial performance of commercial banks in India: A regression approach. *Global Business Review*, *20*(3), 577–594.

Su, R., Xiao, Y., Hamza, F., Mamadiyarov, Z., & Wahab, A. (2025). Scaling up green hydrogen in China: Economic opportunities and challenges. *International Journal of Hydrogen Energy, 131*, 60–69.

Sufian, F., & Habibullah, M. (2009). Determinants of bank profitability: Evidence from Malaysia. *Asian Academy of Management Journal of Accounting and Finance*, *5*(2), 65–87.

Zhang, L., Zhao, Z., Qamri, G. M., & Makhmudov, S. (2025). Unleashing the critical role of renewable energy through global value chains and digitalization: A path towards environmental sustainability. Journal of Environmental Management, 392, 126688.

Zokir Toshtemirovich Mamadiyarov, Samandarboy Adhambek ugli Sulaymanov, Sarvar Anvar ugli Askarov, and Durdona Bakhtiyor kizi Uktamova. 2022. Impact of Covid-19 Pandemic on Accelerating the Digitization and Transformation of Banks. In Proceedings of the 5th International Conference on Future Networks and Distributed Systems (ICFNDS '21). Association for Computing Machinery, New York, NY, USA, 706–712. https://doi.org/10.1145/3508072.3508211

Forecasting and Planning the Process of Co-ordinating Fiscal and Monetary Policy in the National Economy Based on the ARIMA Model

Hakimjon A. Hakimov, Zokir Mamadiyarov, Samariddin Makhmudov, Odil Norboev, Feruza Daniarova, Matluba Abdurakhmanova, and Mirjalol Eshboev

14.1. Introduction

The process of co-ordinating fiscal and monetary policy in the national economy involves a complex economic mechanism that includes strategic co-operation between the government and central bank authorities to achieve macroeconomic stability. This co-ordination plays a crucial role in managing inflation, economic growth, and employment levels. Various macroeconomic factors, including the economic environment, policy regimes, and the specific objectives of each economic operation, influence this process.

In the context of modern economic development, the co-ordination of fiscal and monetary policies in the national economy is one of the pressing issues. In a market economy, the fiscal policy of the state (tax and budget policy) and the monetary policy conducted by the central bank play an important role in ensuring economic stability. The co-ordinated implementation of these policies serves to ensure stable growth of macroeconomic indicators, control the inflation rate, and increase investment activity.

In the process of forecasting and planning, it is necessary to widely use statistical and economic modeling methods. In this regard, the ARIMA (Autoregressive Integrated Moving Average) model based on time series analysis is considered one of the most effective tools. This model allows you to predict future trends based on the values of variables in past periods in time series. The ARIMA model serves as an effective tool for analyzing the dynamics of fiscal and monetary policy indicators and determining the relationship between them.

The relevance of the study is that making wrong decisions in the process of co-ordinating fiscal and monetary policy can lead to economic instability, high inflation, sharp fluctuations in the exchange rate, and a deterioration in the investment climate. Therefore, planning public policy using scientifically based forecasting methods is of great importance.

This study forecasts the process of co-ordinating fiscal and monetary policy based on the ARIMA model and assesses its impact on the national economy. Based on the results of the study, practical recommendations for effective policymaking are developed.

14.2. Literature Review and Development Hypothesis

Especially Augustin Ndarihoranye et al. (2020) "quantify the co-ordination between monetary and fiscal policies in Rwanda from 2008 to 2018. The authors use Granger causality testing and vector autoregressive (VAR) to develop their forecasting models to identify the interaction and co-ordination between monetary and fiscal policies in Rwanda. The results show that a positive shock to government spending leads to an increase in broad money supply, which in turn leads to an increase in liquidity in the economy."

Analyses and forecasts have been conducted using multivariate linear regression (LS), ARDL, ARIMA, and other various econometric models on factors affecting remittances, energy intensity and economic development, energy policy, energy risk, environmental status and the impact of environmental aspects on the digital economy, agricultural productivity, and the stability of the U.S. credit market (Akhmetshin et al., 2025; Inglesi-Lotz et al., 2024; Kurbonov, 2025; K

uziboev et al., 2025; Samariddin et al., 2024; Sharipov et al., 2025).

Kazeem et al. (2023) "examine the interaction between fiscal and monetary policies in achieving macroeconomic objectives, especially their complementarity. The authors estimate the interaction between fiscal and monetary policies in Nigeria and South Africa using a dynamic stochastic general equilibrium (DSGE) model" (Abdullah et al., 2025; Kazeem et al., 2023; Matyakubova et al., 2025; Muhammad et al., 2025; Romero et al., 2025).

The results show that fiscal and monetary policy variables interact in both economies. Inflation responds to fiscal policy shocks such as government spending, income, and borrowing shocks. Monetary policy decisions such as interest rates and inflation also affect fiscal policy variables.

According to Sharma et al. (2022), "High levels of public debt make it difficult to co-ordinate fiscal and monetary policies. In these scenarios, strict inflation targeting by monetary authorities is counterproductive, requiring unconventional monetary policies."

Another group of economists has successfully used econometric models such as Fixed Effects Estimator (FEE), Random Effects Estimator (REE), multivariate linear (LS), and ARDL in their research on investment in digital infrastructure, various aspects of digital payment systems, the impact of inflation and credit interest rates on investment, factors affecting the reduction of the state's share in commercial banks, non-performing loans in commercial banks, the digitalization of banks, risks in digital services, and the development of retail payment services (Cahyani et al., 2025; Kuchkarov et al., 2025; Litamahuputty et al., 2025; Mamadiyarov et al., 2024, Mamani, et al., 2025; PANJAITAN et al., 2025; Zhang et al., 2025; Zokir et al., 2021).

According to Rugea Felicia Elisabeta et al. (2018) "The degree of co-ordination between fiscal and monetary policy in Romania during 2004–2016 used the Set Theoretic Approach (STA) model to determine the relationship between the two policies, GDP, inflation, money supply and budget deficit." The study suggests that solutions to optimize co-ordination stem from a sound economic vision and responsible economic governance. Quantitative analysis also shows that macroeconomic variables such as budget deficit (as a share of GDP), money supply (as a share of GDP), annual inflation rate, and annual GDP are strongly correlated. Elisabeth Brielin Sinu et al. (2024) in their research states, "The ARIMA model has been used to forecast GDP in various countries, including Indonesia and Moldova. These studies demonstrate the effectiveness of the model in forecasting economic growth, which is important for planning fiscal policy and assessing the impact of fiscal measures on the economy."

14.3. Research Methodology

For the next six years we have developed forecast indicators based on the ARIMA model for the process of co-ordinating fiscal and monetary policy in the national economy.

The World Bank (<https://data.worldbank.org/>), the Central Bank of the Republic of Uzbekistan (<https://cbu.uz/oz/>), and the Statistical Agency under the President of the Republic of Uzbekistan (<https://stat.uz/uz/>) provided the data used in developing econometric models to assess the impact of fiscal and monetary policy co-ordination on the national economy. The number of observations consisting of quarterly data from 2011 to 2023 on gross domestic product (GDP) ***volume*** is 47. For ***inflation***, the macroeconomic data consists of 83 observations indicators, covering the period ***from*** 2016 to 2023.

In the development of forecast indicators based on the econometric model, the components ***(p, d, q) of the ARIMA model*** were determined.

The time series data for the outcome variables of the econometric model were analyzed using periodic graphical representation analysis. In addition, the stationarity of the variables was assessed using the Unit-Root test, and the direct and indirect relationships between the lags of the time series were identified.

In the process of analyzing the forecast indicators, autoregressive (AR) and moving average (MA) residuals were considered, while checking the stationarity of the residuals. Also, based on the forecast results, optimal regression equations for the ARIMA model were developed.

Forecasting fiscal and monetary policy using the ARIMA model is a time-based approach to forecasting future economic performance. The use of time series data is becoming increasingly important, which allows government decisions to be made. The ARIMA model is widely used in economic processes due to its flexibility and efficiency in processing various types of time series data.

According to Uswatun Hasanah (2023), "The ARIMA model has been effectively used to forecast interest rates, such as the BI rate in Indonesia, which is important for controlling inflation and managing monetary policy". The author's research showed a downward trend in the BI rate using the ARIMA(1,1,0) model, which allowed for adjustments in monetary policy to stabilize the economy. According to Lui (2022), "The ARIMA model was also used to estimate the impact of quantitative easing on the U.S. stock market during the COVID-19 pandemic. The findings showed that expansionary monetary policy had a positive impact on stock market activity, demonstrating the model's ability to estimate the impact of policy on financial markets".

The results showed that the effect of aggressive expansionary monetary policy on stock market activity through the growth of money supply in financial assets was confirmed by using ARIMA models. As Qingjie Liu et al.

(2015) point out, "The ARIMA model plays an important role in forecasting state budget revenues and preparing financial budgets, allowing us to determine the long-term equilibrium relationship between revenues and expenditures, which serves to more accurately plan the budget and formulate fiscal policy."

The general form of the ARIMA(p, d, q) model is expressed as follows.

$$y_t = b + \gamma_1 y_{t-1} + \gamma_2 y_{t-2} + \dots + \gamma_p y_{t-pe} t + \mu_{1-1} + \mu_2 e_{t-2} + \dots + \mu_{qq} e_{t-q} + e_t \quad (1)$$

where y_t is the value of the time series at time t *(after differencing d times)*, b is a constant term, γ_i *(for* $i = 1, 2, \dots, p$) represents the coefficients of the AR part, μ_j *(for* $j = 1, 2, \dots, q$) represents the coefficients of the MA part. ϵ_t *is the error term at time t* (white noise).

14.3.1. Explanation of Components

1. *Autoregressive (AR) part*: $\gamma_1, y_{t-1}, \gamma_2, y_{t-2}, \dots, \gamma_p, y_{t-p}$ terms represent the AR part, in which the current value of the series is regressed on its past values.
2. *Integrated (I) part*: The parameter d represents the differentiation procedure used to make the series stationary. The differentiation operation can be written as:

$$y_t' = y_t - y_{t-1} \ (if\ d = 1) \quad (2)$$

3. *Moving average (MA) part*: $\mu_1 \epsilon_{t-1}, \mu_2 \epsilon_{t-2}, \dots, \mu_q \epsilon_{t-1}$. The terms refers to a MA, where the current value is affected by past error terms. The ARIMA model describes a flexible tool used to analyze various types of time series data by adjusting the parameters p, d, and q accordingly.

The resulting factors predicted by the econometric study are expressed as follows.

The size of GDP in the national economy is GDP_vol (result variable).

The inflation rate in the national economy is Infl_rate (result variable).

14.4. Analysis and Results

An analytical graphical representation of the dependent variables at the initial stage of econometric forecasting is presented in Figures 51 and 52.

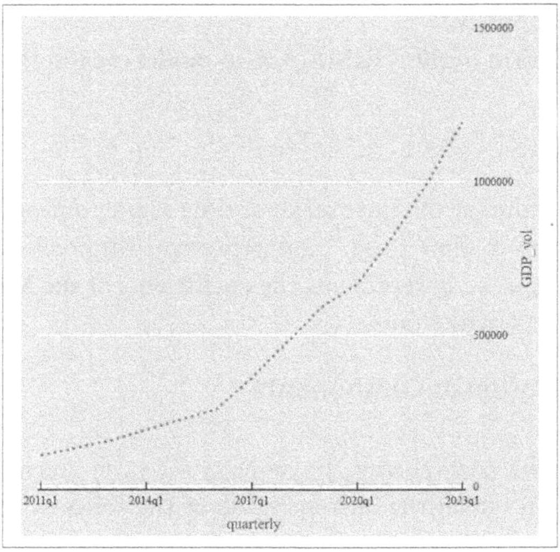

Figure 51. Analytical graphical representation of GDP volume over time in the national economy.

Source: It was developed by the authors based on Stata software.

Figure 51 shows that while the GDP volume in the national economy has shown a sharp growth dynamics during the analyzed period, the inflation rate has shown a downward trend after a sharp increase in 2018. This indicates that a balanced situation in macroeconomic indicators in the national economy has emerged and that economic reforms in the country are changing in a positive direction.

In the next stage of the study, the stationarity of the dependent variables was checked and the Unit-Root test was used to determine it (Table 49).

According to Table 49, in the national economy the values of GDP and inflation rate (**–6.954 and –7.365**), respectively, indicate the importance of the fluctuations in macroeconomic indicators. This result shows that the statistical value is below the 1%, 5%, and 10% thresholds of significance.

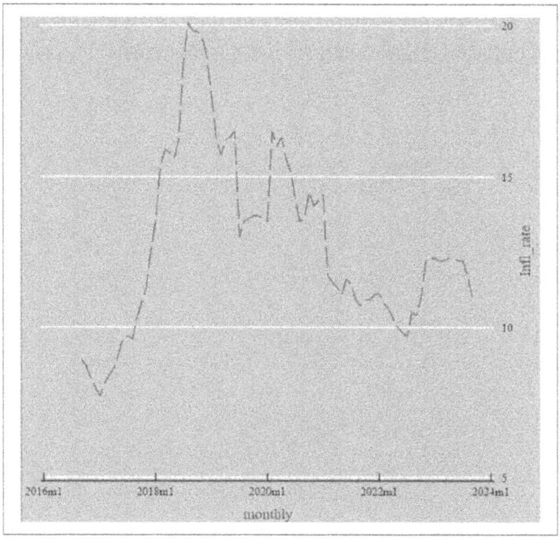

Figure 52. Analytical graphical representation of the inflation rate in the national economy over time.

Source: It was developed by the authors based on Stata software.

Table 49. Unit-Root test of GDP volume and inflation rate in the national economy

Dependent variables	*Test Statistics*	*1% Critical Value*	*5% Critical Value*	*10% Critical Value*	*p-value for Z(t)*
GDP_vol	-6.954	-3.607	-2.941	-2.596	0.0 000
Inflation rate	-7.365	-3.534	-2.904	-2.587	0.0 000

Source: It was developed by the authors based on Stata software.

In the analysis of time series in econometric research based on the ARIMA model, the stationary series retained important statistical properties over the course of the periodic process, which made it possible to draw reliable forecasts and conclusions. The results of the Unit-Root test and the MacKinnon value confirmed the stationarity of the data, indicating that the GDP volume and the inflation rate are statistically significant in the co-ordination of monetary and fiscal policies. According to Table 49, the parameter d of the ARIMA model was set to the value of $d = 1$, indicating a good fit, and achieved stationarity after the first difference of the time series.

The next step is to present the value of *p*, which determines the indirect correlation between the time series lags of the model variables (Figures 53 and 54).

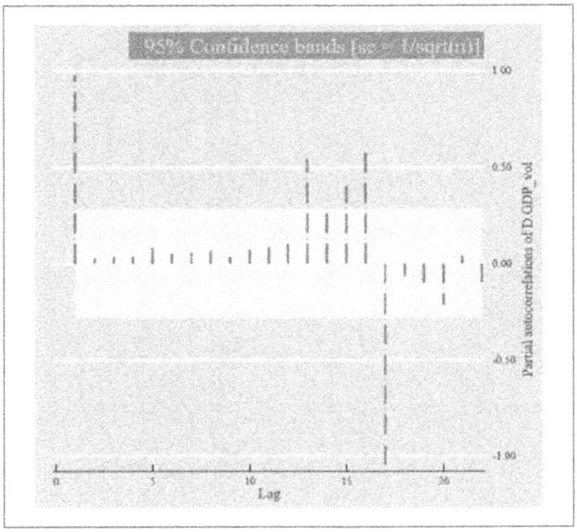

Figure 53. Indirect correlation graph between lags in GDP size in the national economy.

Source: It was developed by the authors based on Stata software.

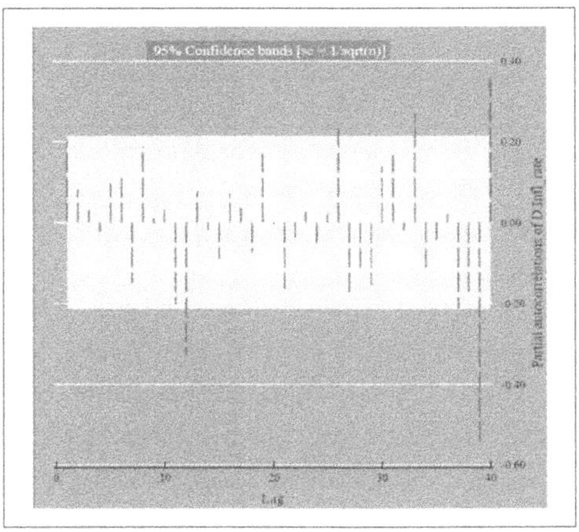

Figure 54. Indirect correlation graph between lags in the inflation rate in the national economy.

Source: It was developed by the authors based on Stata software.

In Figures 53 and 54, the outcome variables, except for lags two, three, and four, all other lags are within the confidence interval in the indirect correlation analysis. This indicates that most lags are statistically significant and lie within the confidence interval. In the ARIMA model, it is important to select appropriate lag values while considering confidence intervals. In this case, it is appropriate to use a *p*-value of 2, 3, or 4. Most lags are consistent, and all lags are within the confidence interval, and the correlation analysis shows a significant *p*-value of 2, 3, and 4. Also, the final decision is appropriate to take into account a complete understanding of the data, model diagnostics, and other relevant criteria.

In the next step of the ARIMA model, the value of *q*, which describes the direct correlation between the lags of the dependent variables, is determined (Figures 55 and 56). As shown in Figures 55 and 56, the ARIMA model exhibits a strong correlation between lags, with all lag values falling within the specified confidence interval. This indicates that the lag values are statistically significant and suitable for econometric forecasting.

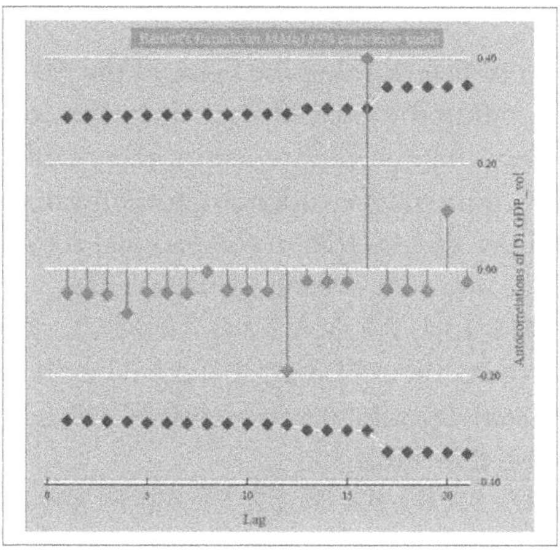

Figure 55. Graph of direct correlation between GDP volume lags in the national economy.
Source: It was developed by the authors based on Stata software.

However, since all lag values lie within the confidence interval, this indicates that they are reliable for inclusion in the model. Choosing one of these

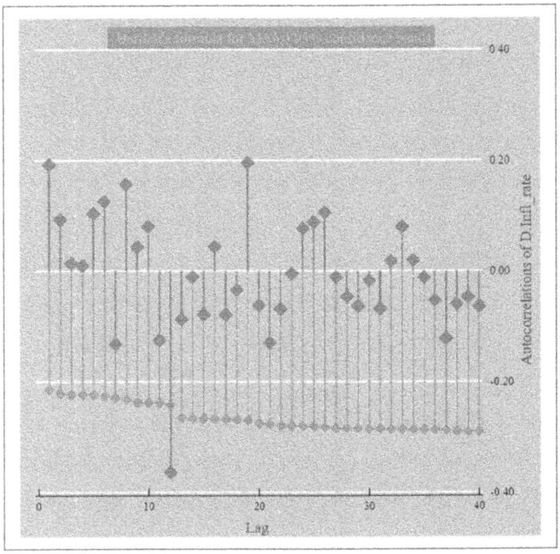

Figure 56. Direct correlation graph between lags of inflation rate in the national economy.

Source: It was developed by the authors based on Stata software.

values is the process of determining the value of the MA parameter q in an ARIMA model for optimal model fitting. Since the observed data of the outcome variables for econometric forecasting are suitable and lie within the confidence intervals, it is recommended to choose a value of q in this range.

We have studied the size of GDP in the national economy. When selecting optimal ARIMA invariant models for forecasting, models of the form ARIMA(1,2,1), ARIMA(2,1,1), ARIMA(2,2,1), ARIMA(1,1,2), and ARIMA(1,1,1) were used. Among these, the ARIMA(2,2,1) model with the best results was selected. The regression equation parameters for GDP, according to ARIMA (2,2,1) model, are listed in Table 50.

According to Table 50, the ARIMA(2,2,1) model looks like this.

$$\Delta_2 GDP\_vol_t = 965.80 + 0.82\Delta^2 GDP\_vol_{t-1} - 0.076\Delta_2 GDP\_vol_{t-2} - 1.01\varepsilon_{t-1} + \varepsilon_t \qquad (2)$$

Also, when selecting optimal ARIMA invariant models for forecasting the inflation rate in our national economy, we used models of the form

Table 50. GDP size according to regression equation parameters of the ARIMA(2,2,1) model

D2.GDP_vol	*Coef.*	*St. Err.*	*t-value*	*p-value*	*[95% Conf*	*Interval]*	*Sig*
Constant	965,802	219,434	4.40	0	535,719	1395.885	***
L	0.824	0.338	2.44	0.015	0.161	1.486	**
L_2	−0.076	0.342	−0.22	0.082	−0.746	0.594	*
L	−1.01	0.187	−5.34	0	−1.367	−0.633	***
Constant	3987.929	.	.	.	.	.	
Mean dependent variable		916,127	SD dependent var		40313.356		
Number of observations		47	Chi-square		31,891		
Prob > Chi²			Akaike crit. (AIC)		922,867		
*** $p < 0.01$, ** $p < 0.05$, * $p < 0.1$							

Source: It was developed by the authors based on Stata software.

ARIMA(0,1,1), ARIMA(2,1,1), ARIMA(2,2,1), ARIMA(2,1,0), ARIMA(1,1,2), and ARIMA(1,1,1). Among these, the ARIMA(2,2,1) model with the best results was selected (Table 50).

Table 51. Inflation level according to regression equation parameters of the ARIMA(1,1,2) model

D.Infl_rate	**Coef.**	**St. Err.**	***t*-value**	***p*-value**	**[95% Conf**	**Interval]**	**Sig**
Constant	0.023	0.124	0.18	0.085	−0.221	0.266	*
L	−0.903	0.342	−2.64	0.008	−1.574	−0.232	***
L	1.091	0.353	3.09	0.002	0.399	1.782	***
L_2	0.21	0.126	1.67	0.095	−0.037	0.457	*
Constant	0.814	0.034	23.70	0	0.747	0.882	***
Mean dependent variable		0.025	SD dependent var		0.839		
Number of observations		84	Chi-square		18,313		
Prob > Chi²		.	Akaike crit. (AIC)		213,972		
*** $p < 0.01$, ** $p < 0.05$, * $p < 0.1$							

Source: It was developed by the authors based on Stata software.

According to Table 51, the ARIMA(1,1,2) model looks like this:

$$\Delta Infl\_rate_t = 0.02 - 0.90\Delta Infl\_rate_t - 1 + 1.09\epsilon_t - 1 + 0.21\epsilon t - 2 + \epsilon t \quad (3)$$

In the next step, an analysis of the average values of the resulting variable according to the ARIMA model was developed using a graphical representation of the residuals (Figures 57 and 58).

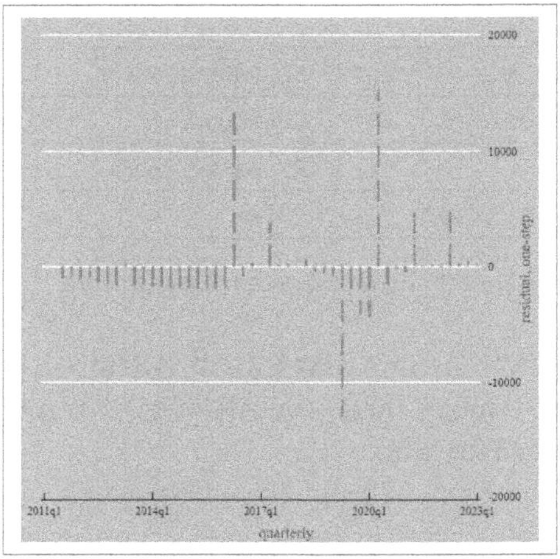

Figure 57. ARIMA(2,2,1) model residuals graph by GDP volume.
Source: It was developed by the authors based on Stata software.

In Figures 57 and 58, the ARIMA(2,2,1) model for GDP and the ARIMA(1,1,2) model for inflation have achieved stochastic equilibrium by visually displaying the residuals over a given time period. This plot demonstrates the model's fit to the data and its ability to correctly capture the underlying stochastic patterns in the data set. The closeness of the residuals to zero, their random distribution, indicates that the model effectively accounts for the underlying autocorrelation structure in the data.

In the next step, the validity of the ARIMA(2,2,1) model for GDP and the ARIMA(1,1,2) model for inflation was assessed using specific criteria. This included testing the stationarity of the residuals and estimating the AR and MA components of the residuals. In addition, the convergence of the model to unity was checked (Figures 59 and 60).

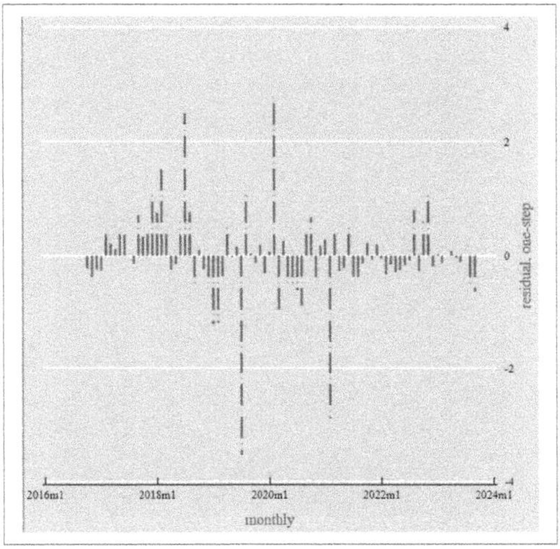

Figure 58. ARIMA(1,1,2) model inflation rate residual values graph.
Source: It was developed by the authors based on Stata software.

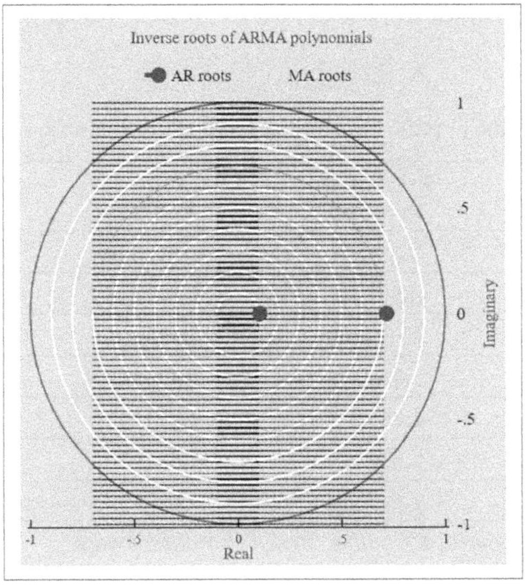

Figure 59. The area of AR and MA values by GDP size.
Source: It was developed by the authors based on Stata software.

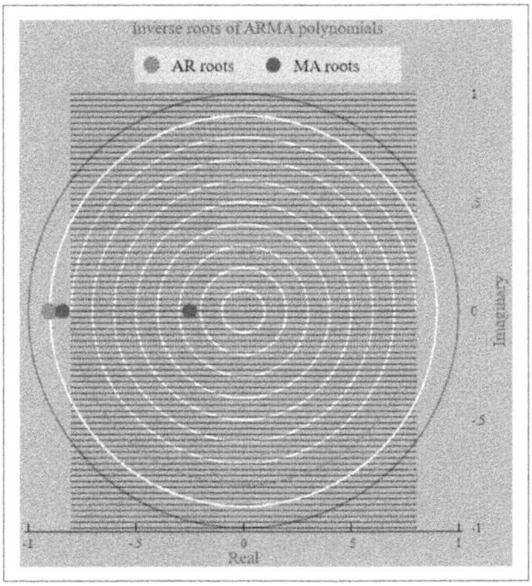

Figure 60. The range of AR and MA values by inflation rate.
Source: It was developed by the authors based on Stata software.

According to the research, a forecast for GDP volume was developed using the ARIMA(2,2,1) model for the period 2025–2030, excluding random factors (Table 52).

Table 52. GDP volume in 2025–2030 forecast indicators (billion in soums)

Years	Pessimistic forecast	Optimistic forecast	Forecast
2024	1,351,178	1,431,804	1,391,491
2025	1,561,419	1,642,045	1,601,732
2026	1,785,909	1,866,535	1,826,222
2027	2,025,535	2,106,161	2,065,848
2028	2,280,529	2,361,155	2,320,842
2029	2,550,954	2,631,580	2,591,267
2030	2,836,826	2,917,452	2,877,139

Source: It was developed by the authors based on Stata software.

In the national economy, under the co-ordination of fiscal and monetary policy, the GDP volume was ***forecasted to be*** 1,391,491 billion soums in 2024,

1,601,732 billion soums in 2025, 1,826,222 billion soums in 2026, 2,065,848 billion soums in 2027, 2,320,842 billion soums in 2028, 2,591,267 billion soums in 2029, and 2,877,139 billion soums in 2030, respectively, according to the ARIMA(2,2,1) model, excluding random factors. The forecast results also showed a positive result, reflecting the growth trend of the resulting factor.

According to the research, a forecast for the inflation rate was developed using the ARIMA (1,1,2) model for the period 2024–2030, without considering the random factors (Table 53).

Table 53. Forecast indicators of the inflation rate for 2025–2030 (%)

Years	Pessimistic forecast	Optimistic forecast	Forecast
2024	10.94	11.77	10.94
2025	11.21	12.04	11.21
2026	11.49	12.32	11.49
2027	11.76	12.59	11.76
2028	12.03	12.86	12.03
2029	12.31	13,14	12.31
2030	12.58	13.41	12.58

Source: It was developed by the authors based on Stata software.

In the national economy, under the co-ordination of fiscal and monetary policy, the inflation rate, excluding random factors, was projected **to be 10.94%** in 2024, 11.21% in 2025, 11.49% in 2026, 11.76% in 2027, 12.03% in 2028, 12.31% in 2029, and 12.58% in 2030, respectively, according to the ARIMA(1,1,2) model.

14.5. Conclusion

The initial stage of econometric forecasting shows a balanced situation in macroeconomic indicators in the national economy, with a downward trend in the inflation rate after a sharp increase in 2018. The stationarity of the dependent variables was checked using the Unit-Root test, and the employment rate in the labor market was found to be stationary. The ARIMA model was used to analyze time series, retaining important statistical properties over the periodic process, allowing for reliable forecasts and conclusions. The results of the Unit-Root test and MacKinnon value confirmed the stationarity of the data, indicating that GDP volume and inflation rate are statistically significant in the co-ordination of monetary and fiscal policies.

The ARIMA model is a statistical tool used for predicting economic outcomes. It uses the MA parameter q to determine the correlation between dependent variables' lags. The model exhibits a strong correlation between lags, with all values falling within the specified confidence interval. This indicates that the lag values are statistically significant and suitable for econometric forecasting.

The study examined the size of GDP in the national economy and selected optimal ARIMA invariant models for forecasting. The ARIMA(2,2,1) model was chosen due to its best results. The regression equation parameters for GDP size and inflation rate were also analyzed. In co-ordinating monetary and fiscal policy in the national economy, the GDP volume forecast indicators ARIMA(2,2,1) model, while the inflation rate forecast indicators are based on the ARIMA(1,1,2) model. The interest rate forecasts for the years 2025–2030 are explained as in what follows.

14.5.1. Research Results: Forecast Indicators of GDP Volume According to the ARIMA(2,2,1) Model

1. *Impact of strong economic growth*: GDP forecasts show a stable and significant growth trend, i.e., from 1,391,491 billion soums in 2024 to 2,877,139 billion soums in 2030. The nearly doubling of GDP over seven years reflects a solid trajectory, indicating the effectiveness of fiscal and monetary policy co-ordination in stimulating economic development.
2. *The significance of the average annual growth rate*: The annual growth rate from 2024 to 2030 is approximately 13.5%. This high growth rate indicates that the economy is on a path of rapid expansion without external disruptions or random shocks.
3. *Effectiveness of government-led economic reforms*: The projected growth reflects well-coordinated fiscal and monetary policies that ensure macroeconomic stability and encourage long-term investment. Fiscal policy plays a key role in stimulating demand, while monetary policy ensures the availability of liquidity and credit for economic activity.

4. *Importance of fiscal policy*: To ensure sustainable and inclusive growth, it is appropriate to focus on effective investments in infrastructure, education, and technology.
5. *Importance of monetary policy*: A balanced approach is needed to prevent the economy from overheating and to manage inflationary pressures arising from rapid growth. The government should continue to support sectors with high multiplier effects, such as technology, logistics, and industrial production.
6. *Importance of using projections in strategic planning*: The ARIMA(2,2,1) model offers a valuable framework for national economic planning, enabling policymakers to set realistic targets for fiscal revenues, government expenditures, and debt management. These forecasts can guide long-term strategies for infrastructure development, industrial modernization, and technological progress.

14.5.2. Research Results: Forecast Indicators of Inflation Rate According to the ARIMA(1,1,2) Model

1. *Inflation trend of stable and forecast indicators*: Forecast indicators start at 10.94% in 2024 and gradually increase to 12.58% in 2030, reflecting the controlled inflationary pressure that can be managed in a growing economy.
2. *Expression of the degree of coherence with economic growth*: The simultaneous growth of GDP and inflation indicates that the co-ordination of fiscal and monetary policies is providing a healthy balance between economic expansion and price stability. Inflation rates in the 10–13% range are not uncommon in emerging economies experiencing rapid growth, suggesting that the economy is dynamically adjusting to higher levels of output and consumption.

Bibliography

Abdullah, M. A., Han, X., Amjad, M. A., & Makhmudov, S. (2025). Revisit the role of financial development on economic growth, human development, and sustainable development in higher-income countries. *Journal of Environmental Management*, *392*, 126874.

Akhmetshin, E., Abdullayev, I., Makhmudov, S., Dakhkilgova, K., Korotaeva, I. and Yanovskaya, G. (2025). APPLICATION OF TANH–COTH METHOD FOR COMBINED AND DOUBLE COMBINED SINH–COSH–GORDON EQUATIONS ARISING CHEMICAL REACTIONS TO WATER SURFACE GRAVITY WAVES. Computational Methods for Differential Equations, (), -. doi: 10.22034/cmde.2025.67655.3234

Augustin, N., Gedion, A., Omwono, O. (2020). *Fiscal and Monetary Policies Coordination Rwandan Experience*, *1*(2), 193–203. <https://doi.org/10.47175/RISSJ.V1I2.44>

Cahyani, I., Buriev, K., Ngongo, M., Mamadiyarov, Z., Ino, L., Herman, H., Saputra, N., & Baxtishodovich, S. (2025). Exploring the Use of TikTok Application in Enhancing the Skill of Pronunciation: A Case on Students' Perception. Studies in Media and Communication, *13*(2), 150–158. doi:http://dx.doi.org/10.11114/smc.v13i2.7553

Caporin, M., Shahbaz, M., Kuziboev, B., Masharipova, M., Allaberganov, S., & Makhmudov, S. (2024). Environmental Kuznets Curve for extended brics economies: do women governance and water stress matter?. International Journal of Energy Economics and Policy, *14*(6), 174–183

Inglesi-Lotz, R., Oosthuizen, A. M., Jumaniyazova, S., Kuziboev, B., & Liu, J. (2024). Exploring the impact of women governance on CO2 emissions in the European Union and Central Asia. *International Journal of Energy Economics and Policy*, *14*(3), *639–646*.

Jahrir, A., Gultom, Y., Herman, H., Zabadi, F., Ngongo, M., Mamadiyarov, Z., Fatmawati, E., & Saputra, N. (2025). Investigating the Elements of Short Commercial Mineral Water Advertisement: A Case on Discourse Analysis. *Studies in Media and Communication, 13*(4), 94–104. doi:http://dx.doi.org/10.11114/smc.v13i4.7813

Hussain, A., Khan, M., Rakhmonov, D. A., Mamadiyarov, Z. T., Kurbonbekova, M. T., & Mahmudova, M. Q. K. (2023). Nexus of Training and Development, Organizational Learning Capability, and Organizational Performance in the Service Sector. Sustainability, *15*(4), 3246. https://doi.org/10.3390/su15043246

Kurbonov, K. (2025). Quantitative easing and its long-term effects on US credit market sustainability: A neutrosophic science perspective. *International Journal of Neutrosophic Science (IJNS)*, *25*(3).

Kuchkarov, T., Mamadiyarov, Z., Khakimov, Z., Sabirova, O., Matmurodov, K., Raimboyeva, M., & Umarova, S. (2025). Energy-Related Uncertainty and Crypto-Currency Environmental Attention: Time-Varying Perspective. International Journal of Energy Economics and Policy, *15*(5), 614–626. https://doi.org/10.32479/ijeep.20784

Kuziboev, B., Khodjaniyazov, E., Ozturk, I., Sabirov, K., Makhmudov, S., & Utegenova, S. (2025). Does oil dependence cause energy risk?. Energy Nexus, 17, 100393.

Lin, M.H., Matchanova, B., Nurmatovich, H.A. *et al.* Optimal Operation of the Multi-Carrier Energy System Considering Energy Markets and Renewable Energies Participation. *Int. J. Appl. Comput. Math* **11**, 170 (2025). https://doi.org/10.1007/s40819-025-02002-9

Litamahuputty, J. V., Amiruddin, E. G., Rahim, R., Rahman, A., & Mamadiyarov, Z. (2025). Cryptocurrency Risk Management through Decision Engineering: Evaluating XRPUSD and ADAUSD Portfolio Performance. Journal of Applied Science, Engineering, Technology, and Education, 7(1), 69–81. https://doi.org/10.35877/454RI.asci387

Mamadiyarov, Z., Hakimov, H., & Askarov, S. (2024). DEVELOPMENT OF RETAIL BANKING SERVICES IN THE CONTEXT OF DIGITAL TRANSFORMATION. Financial and Credit Activity Problems of Theory and Practice, *1*(54), 51–67. https://doi.org/10.55643/fcaptp.1.54.2024.4288

Mamadiyarov, Z. Makhmudov, S. Utanov, B. Kasimova, D. Bekmurodova, G. Hakimov, Z. (2025). Fusion of Economic and Financial Factors Affecting Household Deposits in Banks: An Econometric Analysis. Fusion: Practice and Applications, (), 82–91. DOI: https://doi.org/10.54216/FPA.190206

Mamani, J.C.M., Miri, M., Vorobev, Y. et al. Optimal Operation of Energy Microgrid Considering Economic and Emission Indices. Oper. Res. Forum 6, 122 (2025). https://doi.org/10.1007/s43069-025-00523-z

Matyakubova, A., Makhmudov, S., Ozturk, I., Kurbonov, K., Ismailov, F., Yokubboeva, S., & Urozov, A. (2025). Responses of Economic Policy Uncertainty, Financial Stress and Energy-Related Uncertainty to the Shocks in US-China Tension in US. *International Journal of Energy Economics and Policy, 15*(4), 701–708. https://doi.org/10.32479/ijeep.20369

Muhammad Zubair, Irfanud Din, Nadeem Sarwar et al. Revolutionizing Sepsis Diagnosis Using Machine Learning and Deep Learning Models: A Systematic Literature Review, 10 June 2025, PREPRINT (Version 1) available at Research Square [https://doi.org/10.21203/rs.3.rs-6731418/v1]

PANJAITAN, M. B., HAMDANAH, H., SIRAIT, J., SUTIKNO, S., FATMAWATI, E., HERMAN, H., & MAMADIYAROV, Z. (2025). THE ROLE OF EMOTIONAL REGULATION IN SHAPING STUDENTS' PERCEPTION OF PHYSICS PROBLEMSOLVING TASKS. TPM – Testing, Psychometrics, Methodology in Applied Psychology, 32(S2(2025): Posted 09 June), 1–10. Retrieved from https://tpmap.org/submission/index.php/tpm/article/view/139

Pradhan, R., Hajiyev, E., Shichiyakh, R. *et al.* Optimal Techno-Economic Feasibility of an Off-Grid Microgrid System Using Load Flow Energy Management Strategies. *Oper. Res. Forum* **6**, 120 (2025). https://doi.org/10.1007/s43069-025-00524-y

Qingjie, Liu., & Huachun, Wang (2015). Research on the forecast and development of China's public fiscal revenue based on ARIMA model. *Theoretical Economics Letters*, *05*(4), 482–493. <https://doi.org/10.4236/TEL.2015.54057>

Romero, R. M., Zelinskaya, M., Makhmudov, S., Sapaev, S., & Rustambekovich, J. U. (2025, September). Modelling and Optimal Utilisation of the Renewable Energy Systems in Microgrid with Improving Reliability and Energy Efficiency. In Operations Research Forum (Vol. 6, No. 3, pp. 1–20). Springer International Publishing.

Rugea, F. E. (2018). The coordination of fiscal and monetary policies in developing countries: The case of Romania. *Annals of Faculty of Economics*, *28*(1), 227–236.

Samariddin Makhmudov, Kudratillo Tukhsanov, Saifulla Arslanbekov, Akram Amanov, Orifali Tursunov, Umarbek Jabbarov and Muyassarxon Mirzakarimova. 2024. Optimizing Supply Chain Financing Development Prospects of Digital Ecosystems in the European Logistics Industry. In The 8th International Conference on Future Networks & Distributed Systems (ICFNDS '24), December 11–12, 2024, Marakech, Morocco. ACM, New York, NY, USA, 12 Pages. https://doi.org/10.1145/3726122.3726200

Sanusi, K. A., & Dickason-Koekemoer, Z. (2023). Fiscal and monetary policies interactions in Nigeria and South Africa: Dynamic stochastic general equilibrium approach. *International Journal of Economics and Financial Issues*, <https://doi.org/10.32479/ijefi.14551>

Sharipov, K., Abdullayev, I., Kuziboev, B., Makhmudov, S., Kalandarov, F., Khaytboeva, N., & Ilkhamova, Z. (2025). The Effect of Energy Policy

Risk on Renewable Energy. International Journal of Energy Economics and Policy, *15*(2), 566.

Sharma., S., Padhi, I., & Dhal, S. (2022). Monetary-fiscal coordination: When, why and how? *Social Science Research Network*. <https://doi.org/10.2139/ssrn.4181076>

Sinu, E. B., Kleden, M. A., & Atty, A. (2024). Application of ARIMA model for forecasting national economic growth: A focus on gross domestic product data. *Barekeng*, *18*(2), 1261–1272. <https://doi.org/10.30598/barekengvol18iss2pp1261-1272

Su, R., Xiao, Y., Hamza, F., Mamadiyarov, Z., & Wahab, A. (2025). Scaling up green hydrogen in China: Economic opportunities and challenges. *International Journal of Hydrogen Energy*, *131*, 60–69.

Uswatun, H. (2023). Peramalan BI rate di Indonesia dengan metode time series model ARIMA. doi: <10.32505/ ihtiyath.v 7i2.7318>

Zhang, L., Zhao, Z., Qamri, G. M., & Makhmudov, S. (2025). Unleashing the critical role of renewable energy through global value chains and digitalization: A path towards environmental sustainability. Journal of Environmental Management, 392, 126688

Zhao, Q., Pervaiz, A., Makhmudov, S., & Fatima, A. (2025). Do environmental stringent policies enhance the impact of renewable energy on CO2 reduction? Evidence from BRICS-T economies. Journal of Environmental Management, 391, 126464

Zheheng, Liu (2022). Prediction of quantitative easing policy effect on the US stock market using ARIMA model. *BCP Business & Management*, *34*, 1242–1249. https://doi.org/10.54691/ bcpbm.v 34i.3165

Zokir Toshtemirovich Mamadiyarov, Samandarboy Adhambek ugli Sulaymanov, Sarvar Anvar ugli Askarov, and Durdona Bakhtiyor kizi Uktamova. 2022. Impact of Covid-19 Pandemic on Accelerating the Digitization and Transformation of Banks. In Proceedings of the 5th International Conference on Future Networks and Distributed Systems (ICFNDS '21). Association for Computing Machinery, New York, NY, USA, 706–712. https://doi.org/10.1145/3508072.3508211

<https://data.worldbank.org/indicator/NY.GDP.MKTP.CD?view=chart>

<https://cbu.uz/oz/monetary-policy/annual-inflation/indicators/>

<https://stat.uz/uz/rasmiy-statistika/national-accounts-2>

National in the Economy Customs Office Evaluating the Forecasting of the Amount of Payments Based on an Econometric Model

Samariddin Makhmudov, Tulkin Pardayev, Zokir Mamadiyarov, Khaitmurat Khujakulov, Mukaddas Elbaeva, Tolib Nutfulloyev, and Mirjalol Eshboev

15.1. Introduction

Forecasting the amount of customs payments is of great importance for economic planning and the development of stability in the national economy in order to further increase budget revenues. Accurate forecasts of customs revenues provide the government with the opportunity to effectively manage public finances, ensure liquidity, and further support infrastructure development. Various methods, including statistical methods and econometric models, are widely used to increase the accuracy of these forecasts.

Customs policy plays an important role in ensuring the sustainable development of the national economy. Customs payments are one of the important sources of income of the state budget, serve to regulate the country's foreign trade policy and ensure economic security. Therefore, accurate forecasting and effective planning of the volume of customs payments is an urgent issue for public administration. The use of modern economic modeling and econometric methods in the process of forecasting the volume of customs payments is of great importance. In particular, through econometric models, it is possible to determine the relationship between customs payments and their shaping factors and assess future trends. This study considers the issues of forecasting and assessing the volume of customs payments based on econometric models.

The relevance of the study is that incorrect forecasting of the volume of customs payments can lead to errors in planning state budget revenues. Therefore, determining and forecasting the volume of payments using scientifically based econometric models serves to increase the effectiveness of public policy.

Effective implementation of customs policy contributes to increasing the country's foreign trade potential, improving the business environment and stabilizing economic growth rates. From this point of view, the process of forecasting customs payments is not limited only to determining state budget revenues, but it also serves as an important factor in forming future plans of participants in foreign economic activity.

The aim of this study is to analyze the future dynamics of customs payments based on an econometric model, identify the main economic factors affecting it, and form a scientific basis for the forecasting process. In this process, trends in customs payments are analyzed based on historical data, with their variability and causes examined in depth.

Various econometric models are used in the process of forecasting customs payments, including time series analysis and panel data models. These models are used to assess the impact of factors shaping customs revenues, including import volumes, export composition, tariff rates, economic activity levels, and other indicators. As a result, scientifically based recommendations are developed that serve as the basis for state policy.

Within the framework of the study, in order to increase the accuracy and reliability of the customs payment forecasting methodology, the following stages are carried out: collecting a statistical database, cleaning and adjusting data, selecting a model, and evaluating its results. Also, recommendations are developed based on checking the compliance of the model results with real economic conditions and analyzing them.

The results of this study are useful for state bodies, business entities, and economic analysts, who can use them in the process of planning and implementing customs policy. Based on the results of the study, practical recommendations are developed to improve the efficiency of the customs system in the national economy and further improve foreign trade processes.

The results of the analysis show that when forecasting the amount of customs duties, it is necessary to analyze not only historical data, but also global economic trends and factors influencing the development of the national economy. From this point of view, the development of accurate and reliable forecasting methods based on econometric models is of strategic importance for state policy.

The practical significance of this study is that by forecasting customs duties, it will be possible to develop measures aimed at effective management of state budget revenues, optimization of export–import operations, and sustainable development of the national economy. This, in turn, will serve to improve economic policy and increase the country's investment attractiveness.

15.2. Literature Review and Development Hypothesis

Many foreign scientists have conducted *theoretical and econometric studies on forecasting the amount of* customs payments.

According to Jordan Simonov et al. (2021) "the importance of accurate forecasts of customs revenues in planning the state budget and ensuring liquidity is that they allow for optimizing revenue collection and controlling expenditures".

According to Hafizh Adam Muslim (2022) "customs revenue is an important source of financing for infrastructure projects. Reliable forecast indicators allow for the efficient allocation of resources to projects that support economic growth". The authors' econometric study using the ARIMA (AutoRegressive Integrated Moving Average) model in forecasting showed a positive significance in estimating the ARIMA model, with a root mean square percentage error (RMSPE) value of <10%. According to Inna Kiyanchuk (2017) "customs payments play an important role in solving economic stability problems and ensuring the financial security of the country, contributing to the country's economic security by ensuring a stable revenue stream." The authors noted that, according to the results of the analysis, in 2017, a clear trend was observed in increasing revenues to the state budget, including from customs duties, according to which the total amount of customs duties amounted to 277.27 billion Ukrainian hryvnias, which is an increase of 57.24 billion compared to the previous year (220.03 billion Ukrainian hryvnias).

According to Zhang Da-bin (2009), "dynamic models are used in customs revenue forecasting, and these models are used as an effective statistical method to forecast export values taking into account various economic factors". The authors noted that the export value of Hubei Province, China, will increase during the forecast period. The forecast indicators are based on historical data analysis using the GM(1,1) model, which ensures high forecast accuracy.

According to Ekaterina Zavyalova, "accurate forecasts of customs payments allow the government to change tariffs and duties to optimize revenues without harming economic activity." According to the author's scientific results, she identified the main reasons for the negative shortcomings in the collection of customs payments and made proposals for improving the control activities of customs authorities over the completeness and timeliness of customs payments.

According to Liepa Mikulevichi, "the ARIMA model is a robust statistical method for nonlinear data sets and external factors affecting customs revenues." The author's research results showed that the forecast indicators according to the NNAR(1,3) model indicate a potential decrease in customs revenues, suggesting the need to implement significant measures to increase revenues in the country's economy in the near future.

Analyses and forecasts have been conducted using multivariate linear regression (LS), ARDL, ARIMA, and other various econometric models on factors affecting remittances, energy intensity and economic development, energy policy, energy risk, environmental status and the impact of environmental aspects on the digital economy, agricultural productivity, and the stability of the U.S. credit market (Akhmetshin et al., 2025; Jahrir et al., 2025; Jakhongir et al., 2024; Kuchkarov et al., 2025; Kuziboev et al., 2025; Litamahuputty et al., 2025; Mamani et al., 2025; PANJAITAN et al., 2025; Samariddin et al., 2024; Sharipov et al., 2025; Zhang et al., 2025).

According to Le Thi Anh Tuyet (2020), "In predicting the relationship between tariff reduction and customs revenue changes in Vietnam, it is important to consider the impact of various factors on customs revenue." The author's research results showed that reducing customs tariffs does not have a negative impact on customs revenue. In addition, reducing customs tariffs increases import turnover, improves tax compliance by import–export enterprises, and leads to a decrease in smuggling and trade fraud. According to Yana Bugrimova (2018), "customs-related data provide specific indicators that offer a clear understanding of the economic dimensions and interpretations of data." Using an econometric model developed based on the research results, the impact of macroeconomic indicators on future trends in export and import activity increases (Abdullah et al., 2025; Romero et al., 2025; Yana, 2018).

Bozkurt and Kaya (2023) investigates the foremost firm-specific factors having an impact on financial distress and bankruptcy in the acute stage of the Covid-19 crisis based on data from approximately 9,000 enterprises in 25 countries.

Another group of economists has successfully used econometric models such as Fixed Effects Estimator, Random Effects Estimator, multivariate linear (LS), and ARDL in their research on investment in digital infrastructure, various aspects of digital payment systems, the impact of inflation and credit interest rates on investment, factors affecting the reduction of the state's share in commercial banks, non-performing loans in commercial banks, the digitalization of banks, risks in digital services, and the development of retail payment services (Cahyani et al., 2025; Caporin et al., 2024; Kalandarov et al., 2025; Kuziboev et al., 2025; Mamadiyarov et al., 2025, Muhammad et al., 2025; Singagerda et al., 2025; Su et al., 2025; Zokir et al., 2021). Gunnar Bårdsen and others (2005) argue that "the rapid growth of online shopping and the movement of goods between different countries means that governments are making a significant contribution to maintaining each country's economy."

15.3. Research Methodology

We have developed forecast indicators for the amount of customs duties in the national economy for the next four years based on *the ARIMA model.*

In forecasting economic processes, the ARIMA model has been widely used as an important statistical method due to its effective modeling of time series data and its predictive ability.

One of the strengths of the ARIMA model is its simplicity, flexibility, and ability to handle a wide variety of data patterns, including trends and seasonality, which makes it an effective tool for forecasting future economic dynamics. According to Dinesh Kumar Yadav (2024), "The ARIMA model effectively captures the underlying dynamics of economic data, such as trends and seasonality, which are important for accurate forecasting." According to Elisabeth Brielin Sinu (2024), "the ARIMA model has been successfully used in forecasting national economic growth, particularly GDP forecasting." According to her, in Indonesia, the ARIMA(0,1,0)(0,0,1) model was found to be effective in forecasting quarterly GDP, which aids in strategic economic planning.

According to Deepan (2024), "in the volatile sector of the stock market, ARIMA models are widely used due to their ability to provide short-term forecasts." The author's research results provide short-term performance in forecasting stock prices in stock markets, including the Chinese stock market. According to Dihan Zhang (2023), “the ARIMA model has proven to be robust in forecasting unemployment rates even during severe economic downturns such as the global financial crisis and the COVID-19 pandemic.” The author concludes that the model is effective in understanding labor market dynamics and enabling potential formation.

“While ARIMA models are powerful, they have limitations in long-term forecasting, particularly in producing linear forecasts.” Zhang says that this can be simplified by integrating the model, which is important for capturing information and improving forecast accuracy. According to John Levendis, “The ARIMA model’s reliance on historical data requires careful consideration of data stationarity and parameter estimation to provide accurate forecasts”. The ARIMA model is a popular econometric model used for forecasting time series. It incorporates an autoregressive (AR) component and a moving average (MA) component, and includes the difference in making the time series stationary.

The ARIMA model formula contains three components and is denoted as ARIMA*(p, d, q)*, where:

p represents the number of lagged observations in the model (AR part);
d indicates how many times the raw observations differ (the integrated part); and
q represents the size of the MA window (MA section).

The general form of the ARIMA(p, d, q) model can be expressed as follows:

$$y_t = a + \beta_1 y_{t-1} + b_2 y_{t-2} + \ldots + b_p y_{t-p} + \vartheta_1 e_{t-1} + \vartheta_2 \epsilon_{t-2} + \ldots + \vartheta_{q\epsilon t-q} + \epsilon_t \quad (1)$$

where y_t represents the value of the time series at time t (*after differencing d times*), a represents a constant term, β_t = (for i = 1, 2, …, p) represents the coefficients of the AR part, ϑ_q = (for j = 1, 2, …, q) represents the coefficients of the MA part and ϵ_t is the error term at time t (white noise).

15.3.1. Explanation of Components

1. *Autoregressive (AR) part*: $\boldsymbol{b_1 y_{t-1}}$, $\boldsymbol{b_2 y_{t-2}}$, …, $b_p y_{t-p}$ terms describe the AR part, in which the current value of the series is regressed on its past values.

2. *Integrated (I) part*: The parameter d represents the differentiation procedure used to realize the stationary state of the series. The differentiation operation is written as follows:

$$y_t' = y_t - y_{t-1} \text{ (if } d = 1) \tag{2}$$

At the same time, a high level of differentiation is used in developing forecast indicators for research.

3. *Moving average (MA) part*: $\vartheta_1 e_{t-1}, \vartheta_2 e_{t-2}, \ldots, \vartheta_q e_{t-q}$. These terms represent the MA component and the dependence of the error terms on the current value. The ARIMA model is a multivariate model that is used to model a wide range of time series data by appropriately evolving the parameters p, δ, and κ.

15.4. Analysis and Results

The econometric study included 40 quarterly observations of the amount of customs payments in the national economy in 2010–2023, using data sources from the Customs Committee under the Ministry of Economy and Finance of the Republic of Uzbekistan (<https://customs.uz>).

The resulting factor according to the econometric forecast is expressed as follows.

customs_fees—amount of customs fees (*Dependent variable*).

An analytical graphical representation of the dependent variable at the initial stage of econometric forecasting is presented in Figure 61.

According to Figure 61, an analytical graphic representation of the amount of customs payments in the national economy for the period from the first quarter of 2013 to the first quarter of 2023 is presented. As shown, customs duties have increased significantly during the analyzed period, and this economic process is reflected in the increase in foreign trade activity and the reforms carried out by our government in customs practice.

The sharp acceleration in growth rates since 2018 was due to the optimization of the customs policy applied to import operations.

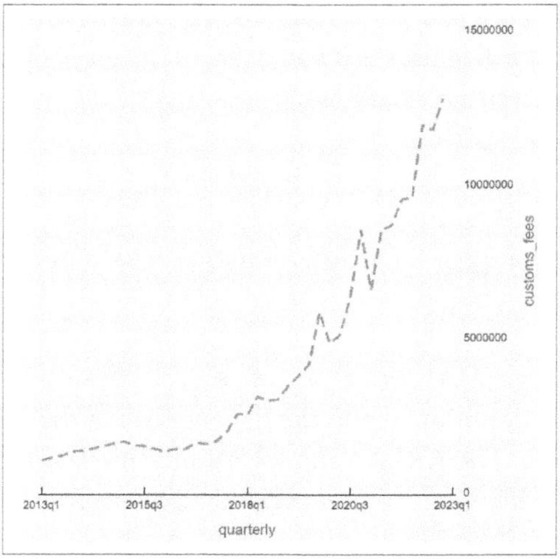

Figure 61. Analytical graphic representation of the amount of customs duties in the national economy over time.

Source: It was developed by the authors based on Stata software.

The COVID-19 pandemic, which affected global trade in the third quarter of 2020, also caused some fluctuations due to economic disruptions. The growth situation in the period after 2020 reflected the recovery process from global disruptions against the background of the development of foreign trade activity. Following the econometric forecast, the stationarity level of the amount of customs duties in the national economy was assessed and the Unit-Root test was used to determine it.

Table 54. Unit-Root of the amount of customs duties in the national economy test

customs_ fees	**Test Statistics**	**1% Critical Value**	**5% Critical Value**	**10% Critical Value**	***p*-value for *Z*(*t*)**
	-9.229	-3.634	-2.952	-2.610	0.0000

Source: It was developed by the authors based on Stata software.

The information from Table 54 shows that the amount of customs payments in the national economy is **–9.229,** indicating its significance in external trade and customs practice. The statistical value is below the **1%, 5%, and 10% thresholds** of significance.

Furthermore, the McKinnon value is minimal with $Z(t)=0.0000$, which indicates that the amount of customs duties in the national economy is stationary. In the econometric research forecasting based on the ARIMA model, the stationary series in the analysis of time series retained important statistical properties over the course of the periodic process, which made it possible to draw reliable forecasts and conclusions. The results of the Unit-Root test and the MacKinnon value showed that they were statistically significant, confirming the stationarity of the data. According to Table 54, the ARIMA model parameter $d = 1$, indicating that it is suitable and achieved stationarity after the first differentiation of the time series.

The next step is to present the value of p, which determines the indirect correlation between the lags of the time series of the model (Figure 62).

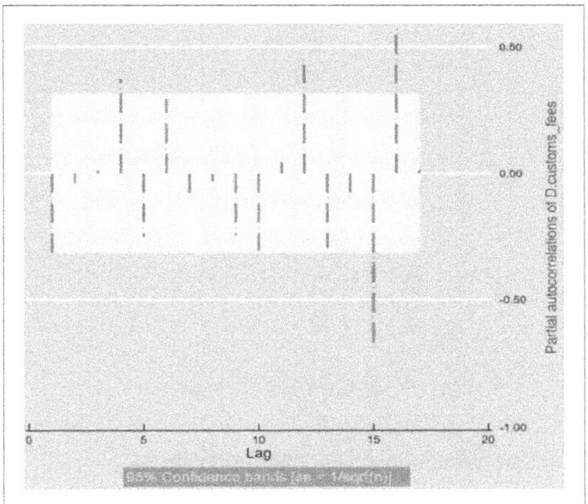

Figure 62. Indirect correlation graph between the lags of the model.
Source: It was developed by the authors based on Stata software.

According to Figure 62, except for lags two and three, all other lags are within the confidence interval in the indirect correlation analysis. Also, most of the lags are statistically significant and lie within the confidence interval. It is appropriate to use the data in Figure 62, with a p-value of 0.1 or 2. Most lags fit within the confidence interval.

In the next step of the ARIMA model, the value of q, which describes the direct correlation between the lags of the model, was determined (Figure 63).

Based on the data in Figure 63, we can see that the ARIMA model exhibits a strong correlation between the lags, with all lag values falling within the specified confidence interval. This means that the lag values are statistically significant and provide promising forecast indicators.

Also, since all lags are within the confidence interval, this indicates that they are reliable for use in the model. The decision to choose one of these values refers to the choice of a value for the MA parameter q in the ARIMA model. Since the observed data from the study are consistent with values between 0 and 1 and lie within the confidence intervals, it is recommended to choose a value of q in this range.

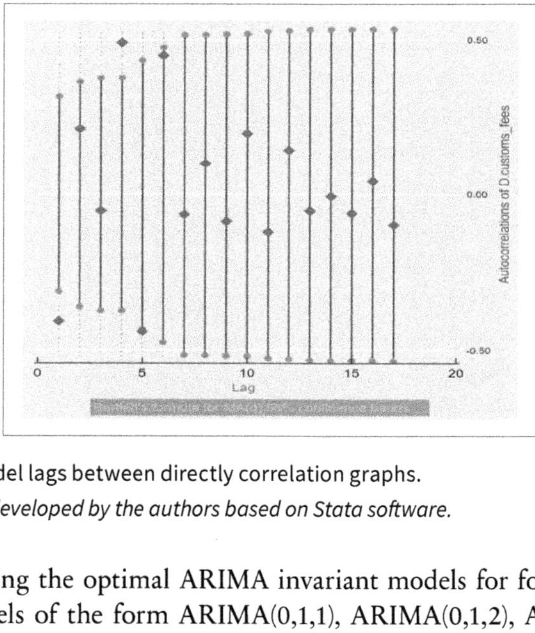

Figure 63. Model lags between directly correlation graphs.
Source: It was developed by the authors based on Stata software.

When selecting the optimal ARIMA invariant models for forecasting the model, models of the form ARIMA(0,1,1), ARIMA(0,1,2), ARIMA(1,1,1), ARIMA(1,1,0) ARIMA(2,0,1), and ARIMA(1,1,2) were used. Among these models, the ARIMA(1,1,2) model with the best results was selected (Table 55).

Based on the results of the ARIMA model regression, the econometric equation of the model is presented in what follows.

$$D.customs\_fees_t = b_0 + \varphi_1 \, D.customs\_fees_{t-1} + e_t + \theta_1 \, e_{t-1} + \theta_2 \, e_{t-2} \qquad (2)$$

Table 55. The amount of customs duties in the national economy according to ARIMA(1,1,2) model econometric equation indicators

D.customs_ fees	*Coef.*	*St. Err.*	*t-value*	*p-value*	*[95% Conf*	*Interval]*	*Sig*
Constant	4254.3	457172.22	0.91	.365	−481786.78	1310295.4	
L	.954	.104	9.16	0	.75	1.158	***
L	−1.662	.086	−19.30	0	−1.831	−1.494	***
L2	.836	.073	11.50	0	.693	.978	***
Constant	2595.31	56095.659	10.21	0	2649.84	2540.78	***
Mean dependent variable		2015.187	SD dependent var		6838.052		
Number of observations		39	Chi-square		382,161		
Prob > chi²		.	Akaike crit. (AIC)		1157,782		
*** p <0.01, ** p < 0.05, * p < 0.1							

Source: It was developed by the authors based on Stata software.

According to Table 55, the ARIMA(1,1,2) model looks like this:

$$D.custom\_fees_{t} = 4254.3 + 0.95D.customs\_fees_{t-1} + e_t - 1.66\, e_{t-1} + 0.83\, e_{t-2} \quad (3)$$

In the next step, the ARIMA(2,1,0) model was developed to analyze the mean values and residuals of the resulting variable graphically (Figure 64).

Based on Figure 64, the ARIMA(1,1,2) model has reached stochastic equilibrium, as evidenced by the visual representation of the residuals at the specified time intervals. This representation provides an indication of the ARIMA model's fit to the data and its ability to effectively capture the underlying stochastic relationship in the data set.

In the next stage, the validity of the ARIMA(1,1,2) model of customs payments in the national economy was assessed based on certain criteria. This included checking the stationarity of the residuals and estimating the AR and MA residuals. The convergence of the ARIMA model to the unit range in forecasting was also checked (Figure 65).

Using the Stata program, a forecast indicator of the amount of customs payments in the national economy from 2024 to 2028, excluding random

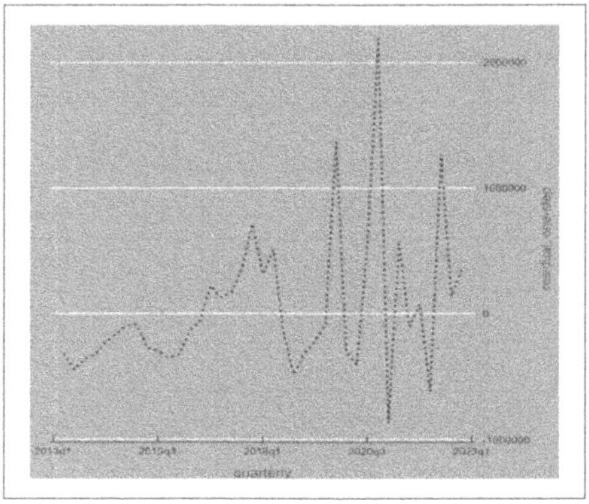

Figure 64. Graph of residual values of the ARIMA(1,1,2) model on the amount of customs duties in the national economy.

Source: It was developed by the authors based on Stata software.

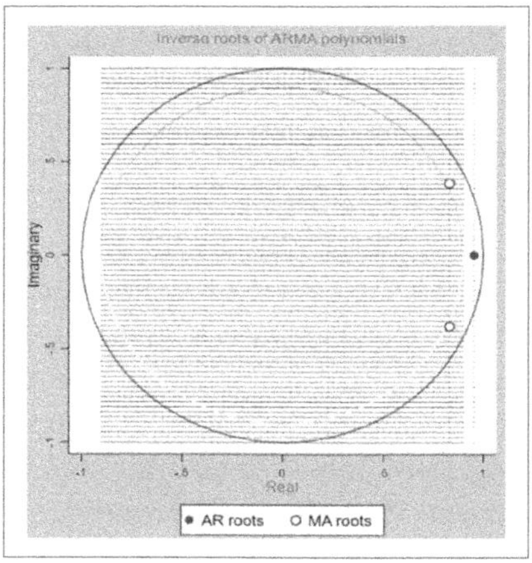

Figure 65. The range of values of the amount of customs duties in the national economy according to the ARIMA(1,1,2) model.

Source: It was developed by the authors based on Stata software.

factors, was developed using the ARIMA(1,1,2) model to further develop foreign trade practices and increase budget revenues (Table 56).

The study, presented by the Customs Committee under the Ministry of Economy and Finance of the Republic of Uzbekistan, presents the volume of

Table 56. Forecast indicators of the amount of customs payments in the national economy for 2024–2028 (in billion soums)

Years	Pessimistic forecast	Optimistic forecast	Forecast
2024	62,534,339	79,353,479	68,336,443
2025	67,740,327	83,328,767	74,421,767
2026	75,912,274	86,370,819	79,491,819
2027	81,415,263	91,678,541	86,526,541

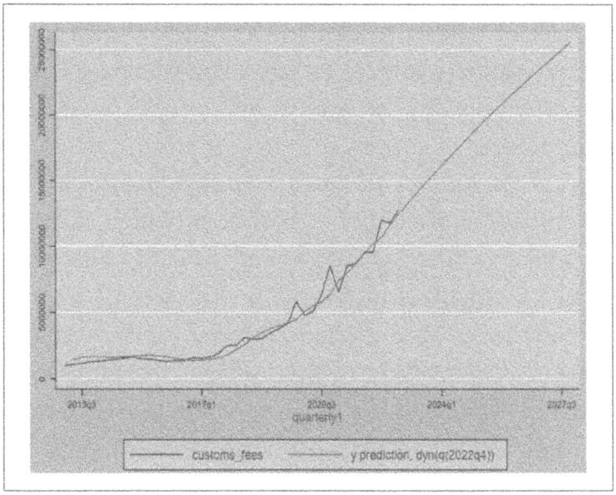

Figure 66. Graph of the dependent variable for 2010–2023 and the forecast for 2024–2028.

Source: It was developed by the authors based on Stata software.

customs payments in the national economy for 2010–2023 and 2024–2028, as well as the forecast graphs (Figure 66).

15.5. Conclusion

The econometric forecast for the amount of customs duties in the national economy in 2024–2028 based on the ARIMA(1,1,2) model, presented by the Customs Committee under the Ministry of Economy and Finance of the Republic of Uzbekistan, is as follows.

According to the results of the study, based on the ARIMA(1,1,2) model, the amount of customs payments in the national economy in 2024–2028, ***excluding random exogenous and endogenous factors,*** will be 68,336,443 billion soums in 2024, 74,421,767 billion soums in 2025, and 79,491,819 billion soums in 2026 and is projected to reach 86,526,541 billion soums in 2027.

1. ***Steady growth in customs revenues—The impact assessment:*** The results of the econometric forecast show a consistent increase in the amount of customs duties from 68,336,443 billion soums in 2024 to 86,526,541 billion soums in 2027. Against the backdrop of steady trade growth, customs duties are showing a positive trajectory in the volume and value of imports subject to payment. Steady growth in customs revenues contributes to the overall fiscal policy of the economy with stable trade flows.
2. ***Assessment of the impact on national budget revenues:*** This result suggests that additional fiscal policy will be provided through investment in public services, infrastructure, and development projects. Higher customs revenues will allow financing of strategic sectors such as transport, digital infrastructure, and industrial modernization.
3. ***The volume of customs duties is an indicator of economic development.*** The expansion of trade, including imports of raw materials, machinery, and consumer goods, indicates growing economic activity and integration into world markets. The growth of customs duties leads to foreign investment and business expansion, as well as growth in trade-oriented economic sectors.
4. ***Stability, regardless of exogenous factors, clearly excludes the forecast indicators from random external shocks.*** Even under normal conditions, the economy shows strong growth in customs revenues. If a favorable legal framework and market conditions are introduced, customs revenues will significantly exceed forecasts.
5. The projected increase in customs duties reflects the positive prospects for trade-economic development in the national economy. This implies increased trade volumes, fiscal stability, and opportunities for future policy and infrastructure improvements. These trends will not only support sustainable economic growth, but also position the economy to benefit from globalization and the digitalization of trade processes.

Bibliography

Abdullah, M. A., Han, X., Amjad, M. A., & Makhmudov, S. (2025). Revisit the role of financial development on economic growth, human development, and sustainable development in higher-income countries. *Journal of Environmental Management, 392*, 126874.

Again, B., & Again, B. (2018). Economic indicators as basis in the assessment of efficiency of activity of customs authorities. *Mathematics in Economics*. <https://doi.org/10.26526/CONFERENCEARTICLE_5C24B1D1636AD1.45614102>.

Akhmetshin, E., Abdullayev, I., Makhmudov, S., Dakhkilgova, K., Korotaeva, I. and Yanovskaya, G. (2025). APPLICATION OF TANH–COTH METHOD FOR COMBINED AND DOUBLE COMBINED SINH–COSH–GORDON EQUATIONS ARISING CHEMICAL REACTIONS TO WATER SURFACE GRAVITY WAVES. Computational Methods for Differential Equations, (), -. doi: 10.22034/cmde.2025.67655.3234

Bozkurt, İ., & Kaya, M. V. (2023). Foremost features affecting financial distress and bankruptcy in the acute stage of COVID-19 crisis. *Applied Economics Letters, 30*(8), 1112–1123.

Cahyani, I., Buriev, K., Ngongo, M., Mamadiyarov, Z., Ino, L., Herman, H., Saputra, N., & Baxtishodovich, S. (2025). Exploring the Use of TikTok Application in Enhancing the Skill of Pronunciation: A Case on Students' Perception. Studies in Media and Communication, 13(2), 150–158. doi:http://dx.doi.org/10.11114/smc.v13i2.7553

Caporin, M., Shahbaz, M., Kuziboev, B., Masharipova, M., Allaberganov, S., & Makhmudov, S. (2024). Environmental Kuznets Curve for extended brics economies: do women governance and water stress matter?. International Journal of Energy Economics and Policy, 14(6), 174–183.

Deepan, S., Reddy, P. S., Muluka, V., Kacham, T., Bollikonda, A., & Parne, N. (2024). Prediction and analysis of stock markets using ARIMA models, 268–271. <https://doi.org/10.1109/iccmso61761.2024.00061>

Dihan, Z. (2023). Forecasting USA unemployment rate base on ARIMA model. *Advances in Economics, Management and Political Sciences*. <https://doi.org/10.54254/2754-1169/49/20230486>

Dinesh Kumar, Y., & Laxmi, G. (2024). Autoregressive integrated moving average model for time series analysis, 1–6. doi: <https://doi.org/10.1109/icocwc60930.2024.10470488>

Elisabeth, B. S., Kleden, M. A., & Atty, A. (2024). Application of ARIMA model for forecasting national economic growth: A focus on gross domestic product data. *Barekeng*, *18*(2), 1261–1272. <https:///doi.org/10.30598/barekengvol18iss2pp1261-1272>

Bårdsen, G., Eitrheim, Ø., Jansen, E. S., & Nymoen, R. (2005). Forecasting using econometric models, 245–280. <https://doi.org/10.1093/oso/9780199246496.003.0011>

Hafiz, A. M. (2022). Time series analysis for customs revenue prediction using ARIMA model in Python. *Journal of Information Technology and Its Utilization*. <https://doi.org/10.56873/jitu.5.2.4927>

Hussain, A., Khan, M., Rakhmonov, D. A., Mamadiyarov, Z. T., Kurbonbekova, M. T., & Mahmudova, M. Q. K. (2023). Nexus of Training and Development, Organizational Learning Capability, and Organizational Performance in the Service Sector. *Sustainability*, *15*(4), 3246. https://doi.org/10.3390/su15043246

Inna, K. (2017). Influence of customs payments on the economic security of the country, problems and ways of overcoming. *Baltic Journal of Economic Studies*, *3*(3), 32–37. <https://doi.org/10.30525/2256-0742/2017-3-3-32-37>

Jahrir, A., Gultom, Y., Herman, H., Zabadi, F., Ngongo, M., Mamadiyarov, Z., Fatmawati, E., & Saputra, N. (2025). Investigating the Elements of Short Commercial Mineral Water Advertisement: A Case on Discourse Analysis. Studies in Media and Communication, 13(4), 94–104. doi:http://dx.doi.org/10.11114/smc.v13i4.7813

Jakhongir, S., Muhabbat, H., Khayrilla, K., Kholmuratov, S., Nazirjon, R., Nilufar, F., & Farxod, T. (2024). Crafting a neutrosophic-driven tool to probe turnover propensities in manufacturing entities. *International Journal of Neutrosophic Science (IJNS)*, *23*(2).

John, L. (2023). ARMA(p, q) processes. Springer texts in business and economics, 11–48. <https://doi.org/10.1007/978-3-031-37310-7_2>

Jordan, S., & Zoran, G. (2021). Customs revenues prediction using ensemble methods (statistical modeling vs machine learning). *World Customs Journal*, <https://doi.org/10.55596/001c.116452>

Kuchkarov, T., Mamadiyarov, Z., Khakimov, Z., Sabirova, O., Matmurodov, K., Raimboyeva, M., & Umarova, S. (2025). Energy-Related Uncertainty and Crypto-Currency Environmental Attention:

Time-Varying Perspective. International Journal of Energy Economics and Policy, 15(5), 614–626. https://doi.org/10.32479/ijeep.20784

Kuziboev, B., Khodjaniyazov, E., Ozturk, I., Sabirov, K., Makhmudov, S., & Utegenova, S. (2025). Does oil dependence cause energy risk? *Energy Nexus*, 100393.

Kuziboev, B., Ozturk, I., Kalandarov, F., Samandarov, O., Bekjanov, D., & Makhmudov, S. (2025). PROMOTING ENERGY SOURCES DIVERSIFICATION THROUGH ESG PERFORMANCE. Energy, 136009.

Le, Thi, & Anh, Tuyet (2020). Applying the LASSO method to predict the impact of tariff reductions on customs revenues in Vietnam. *Economics of Development*, *19*(3), 19–31. <https://doi.org/10.21511/ED.19(3).2020.03>

Liepa, M. (2022). Modeling customs revenue in ghana using novel time series methods. *Applied Computational Intelligence and Soft Computing*, *2022*, 1–8. <https://doi.org/10.1155/2022/2111587>

Litamahuputty, J. V., Amiruddin, E. G., Rahim, R., Rahman, A., & Mamadiyarov, Z. (2025). Cryptocurrency Risk Management through Decision Engineering: Evaluating XRPUSD and ADAUSD Portfolio Performance. Journal of Applied Science, Engineering, Technology, and Education, 7(1), 69–81. https://doi.org/10.35877/454RI.asci3871

Mamadiyarov, Z., Hakimov, H., & Askarov, S. (2024). DEVELOPMENT OF RETAIL BANKING SERVICES IN THE CONTEXT OF DIGITAL TRANSFORMATION. Financial and Credit Activity Problems of Theory and Practice, 1(54), 51–67. https://doi.org/10.55643/fcaptp.1.54.2024.4288

Mamadiyarov, Z. Makhmudov, S. Utanov, B. Kasimova, D. Bekmurodova, G. Hakimov, Z. (2025). Fusion of Economic and Financial Factors Affecting Household Deposits in Banks: An Econometric Analysis. *Fusion: Practice and Applications*, (), 82–91. DOI: https://doi.org/10.54216/FPA.190206

Mamadiyarov, Z., Saidov, O., Abdurazakova, N., Makhmudov, S., Nazarov, M., Rajabova, N., … Ruzmetova, I. (2025). Energy-Related Uncertainty and Tourism Stock Markets: New Insights from Time-Varying Relationship with TVP- VAR Approach. *International Journal of Energy Economics and Policy*, *15*(4), 730–737. https://doi.org/10.32479/ijeep.20480

Mamani, J.C.M., Miri, M., Vorobev, Y. et al. Optimal Operation of Energy Microgrid Considering Economic and Emission Indices. Oper. Res. Forum 6, 122 (2025). https://doi.org/10.1007/s43069-025-00523-z

Muhammad Zubair, Irfanud Din, Nadeem Sarwar et al. Revolutionizing Sepsis Diagnosis Using Machine Learning and Deep Learning Models: A Systematic Literature Review, 10 June 2025, PREPRINT (Version 1) available at Research Square [https://doi.org/10.21203/rs.3.rs-6731418/v1]

PANJAITAN, M. B., HAMDANAH, H., SIRAIT, J., SUTIKNO, S., FATMAWATI, E., HERMAN, H., & MAMADIYAROV, Z. (2025). THE ROLE OF EMOTIONAL REGULATION IN SHAPING STUDENTS' PERCEPTION OF PHYSICS PROBLEMSOLVING TASKS. *TPM – Testing, Psychometrics, Methodology in Applied Psychology*, *32*(S2(2025): Posted 09 June), 1–10. Retrieved from https://tpmap.org/submission/index.php/tpm/article/view/139

Romero, R. M., Zelinskaya, M., Makhmudov, S., Sapaev, S., & Rustambekovich, J. U. (2025, September). Modelling and Optimal Utilisation of the Renewable Energy Systems in Microgrid with Improving Reliability and Energy Efficiency. In Operations Research Forum (Vol. 6, No. 3, pp. 1–20). Springer International Publishing.

Samariddin Makhmudov, Kudratillo Tukhsanov, Saifulla Arslanbekov, Akram Amanov, Orifali Tursunov, Umarbek Jabbarov and Muyassarxon Mirzakarimova. 2024. Optimizing Supply Chain Financing Development Prospects of Digital Ecosystems in the European Logistics Industry. In The 8th International Conference on Future Networks & Distributed Systems (ICFNDS '24), December 11–12, 2024, Marakech, Morocco. ACM, New York, NY, USA, 12 Pages. https://doi.org/10.1145/3726122.3726200

Sharipov, K., Abdullayev, I., Kuziboev, B., Makhmudov, S., Kalandarov, F., Khaytboeva, N., & Ilkhamova, Z. (2025). The Effect of Energy Policy Risk on Renewable Energy. International Journal of Energy Economics and Policy, *15*(2), 566.

Singagerda, F. S., Pratama, M. R., Alfairus, M. Q., Iskandar, A., & Mamadiyarov, Z. (2025). A Decision-Centric Approach to Risk Management in Aviation Stock Investments Using Value at Risk and Portfolio Optimization. *Journal of Applied Science, Engineering, Technology, and Education*, 7(1), 114–125. https://doi.org/10.35877/454RI.asci3870

Su, R., Xiao, Y., Hamza, F., Mamadiyarov, Z., & Wahab, A. (2025). Scaling up green hydrogen in China: Economic opportunities and challenges. *International Journal of Hydrogen Energy*, *131*, 60–69.

Zhang, Da-bin, Zhu, Hou, Zhang, Jing-guang (2009). Forecasting of customs export based on gray theory, 630–633. <https://doi.org/10.1109/BIFE.2009.148>

Zhang, L., Zhao, Z., Qamri, G. M., & Makhmudov, S. (2025). Unleashing the critical role of renewable energy through global value chains and digitalization: A path towards environmental sustainability. Journal of Environmental Management, 392, 126688.

Zokir Toshtemirovich Mamadiyarov, Samandarboy Adhambek ugli Sulaymanov, Sarvar Anvar ugli Askarov, and Durdona Bakhtiyor kizi Uktamova. 2022. Impact of Covid-19 Pandemic on Accelerating the Digitization and Transformation of Banks. In Proceedings of the 5th International Conference on Future Networks and Distributed Systems (ICFNDS '21). Association for Computing Machinery, New York, NY, USA, 706–712. https://doi.org/10.1145/3508072.3508211

High Education Institutions State Purchases done in Increasing Financial of Practices Econometric Models Based on the Impact Assessment

Sarvar Turabov, Samariddin Makhmudov, Zokir Mamadiyarov, Ma'mura Abdujaborova, Nurguzal Kabulova, Mohigul Murodova, and Mirjalol Eshboev

16.1. Introduction

In assessing the impact of public procurement practices in higher education institutions, issues of transparency, accountability, efficiency, and sustainability are of great importance. According to them, the impact of procurement processes, especially public procurement, on the operating income and financial performance of higher education institutions is significantly visible. Problems related to financial relations in public procurement processes vary from region to region.

The effective functioning of higher education institutions largely depends on their financial management, in particular, on the process of implementing public procurement. Public procurement directly affects the operating income of universities, financial performance, and the efficiency of resource allocation. Therefore, transparency, accountability, efficiency, and sustainability of this process are among the pressing issues.

Econometric models are an important tool in assessing the financial practices and public procurement processes of higher education institutions. These models allow for statistical analysis of procurement efficiency, financial effectiveness, targeted spending of public funds, and the level of transparency. In addition, the economic efficiency of public procurement, the openness of tender processes, and the role of electronic procurement systems in reducing transaction costs are also assessed based on econometric models.

This study uses econometric models to assess the impact of financial practices in public procurement in higher education institutions. The study analyzes factors related to the transparency, efficiency, and sustainability of public procurement and determines how they affect the financial performance of higher education institutions. The results of the study will serve to develop practical recommendations for further optimizing public procurement, effectively allocating resources, and improving financial management.

16.2. Literature Review and Development Hypothesis

In particular, Akhmetshin et al., 2025; in his scientific work noted that "public procurement in higher education institutions in Ethiopia has suffered from negative practices characterized by corruption, insufficient transparency and low accountability." According to the author's research, the problems listed earlier have led to inefficiency and mismanagement of funds and the misuse of public procurement guidelines.

According to Muhammad, et al. (2025), "Inadequate procurement practices in Ghana lead to waste and fraud of public resources, which highlights the need for ethical behavior training and strict adherence to rules to mitigate irregularities in procurement." According to Jin Xue et al. (2024), "with the increasing focus on sustainability in public procurement financial practices, universities in China and Brazil have encountered difficulties in implementing sustainable procurement due to limited training and emphasized the importance of integrating it into procurement practices." The authors argue that by optimizing sustainable procurement policies, universities can achieve more efficient resource allocation and reduce unnecessary resource consumption.

According to Belgica Pacheco-Blanconi (2016), "GPP initiatives in HEIs are a way to promote sustainable consumption and production, highlighting the important role of financial practices in supporting universities' sustainability goals and adopting green procurement practices to enhance their environmental impact." The author's research results showed that 21.5% of Spanish universities have implemented significant green procurement activities, with 72.5% of these universities having a department dedicated to environmental issues, demonstrating a systematic approach to sustainability. Many econometric studies have been conducted by foreign researchers on the impact of financial practices on public procurement in higher education institutions.

According to Winnie Dlamini (2012), "The introduction of best practices in procurement in HEIs emphasizes the use of preferential scoring systems of 80/20 and 90/10 systems in evaluating public procurement tenders." According to the author's research, procurement practices have demonstrated their importance in promoting competition and ensuring value for money in procurement processes. John Mutiso Munyaoni (2018) stated that "the practice of e-procurement in public universities has reduced transaction costs in procurement and expedited the procurement process, and has recommended that government institutions adopt the least used electronic resources such as e-RFX and e-contracts." Since the adoption of electronic payment practices, such as internet payments and e-cards, is not widely used in the public sector, there is a need to adopt and implement these electronic payment practices on a larger scale.

According to Rukhiddin, et al. (2025), "as the cost of higher education increases and competition for students increases, the use of tuition discounts as a means of managing tuition will also increase." The author's research results showed that for public institutions, during the period under review, the discount rate offered to students, total tuition and fees charged to students, enrollment diversification, and the percentage of students receiving federal financial aid presented a statistically significant correlation. According to Litamahuputty et al. (2025), "higher education is one of the key elements in stimulating a country's development in terms of economic growth, social status, and the well-being of its citizens." According to the authors' research, factors such as knowledge, skills, and talent are increasingly important in effectively coordinating the financial management of higher education in order to meet the rapid demands of competitive educational trends. Saridogan and Kaya (2019) analyzed the impact of the knowledge economy on economic performance by examining selected economics components of seven main topics in the World Bank KAM methodology Custom Scorecards.

According to Bao Wei (2011), "The debt behavior of universities is affected by government policies." The author's research suggests that investment lending practices between financial institutions and universities through the choice of borrowing affect the growth of inequalities and the financial sustainability and academic goals of different universities. According to Ursula Kelly et al. (2004), "optimizing public procurement in universities is a priority in increasing the country's economic competitiveness and ensuring a high-quality higher education workforce." According to the authors, higher education, as well as the social and cultural environment, has a broad impact on educational activities as a result of independent purchasing practices and institutional spending by higher education institutions.

16.3. Research Methodology

In this article, 24 quarterly economic indicators from the quarterly reports of the Central Bank of the Republic of Uzbekistan (<https://cbu.uz/>), the Statistical Agency under the President of the Republic of Uzbekistan (<https://stat.uz/uz/>), and the Uzbekistan Commodity Exchange (<http://xaruz2018>) for the period from 2018 to 2024 were used to develop the econometric equation.

When constructing the econometric equation, we used the ARDL (Autoregressive Distributed Lag) model to estimate the long-term relationships between variables, given that the data are based on multivariate time series (Usman et al., 2022). In analyzing the stationarity of dependent and independent variables according to the econometric equation, a Unit-Root test (Sun & Xu, 2017) for unit root and a regression equation of the ARDL model were developed. At the same time, the Bound test and Cusum diagnostic test (Ghulam et al., 2021; Jahrir et al., 2025; Lin et al., 2025; Su et al., 2025) for cointegration were examined in assessing the short- and long-run dependence relationships according to the ARDL model. According to the econometric equation, the ARDL model was evaluated based on the expression of the extent to which all variables will have an impact in the following years.

Another group of economists has successfully used econometric models such as Fixed Effects Estimator (FEE), Random Effects Estimator (REE), multivariate linear (LS), and ARDL in their research on investment in digital infrastructure, various aspects of digital payment systems, the impact of inflation and credit interest rates on investment, factors affecting the reduction of the state's share in commercial banks, non-performing loans in commercial banks, the digitalization of banks, risks in digital services, and the development of retail payment services (Cahyani et al., 2025; Hussain et al., 2023; Kuchkarov et al., 2025; Litamahuputty et al., 2025; Pradhan, et al., 2025; Samariddin et al., 2025; Zokir et al., 2021).

Also, during the study, analytical statistical plots, scatter and graphic matrix distribution schematic plots, normal distribution plots, correlation matrix, analytical graphs of time series, and dependence diagrams of dependent and independent variables were developed. At the same time, multicollinearity tests were examined in econometric research.

In econometric research, the ARDL model is an important statistical method for assessing the short-term and long-term dynamic relationship between dependent and independent variables. Analyses and forecasts have been conducted using multivariate linear regression (LS), ARDL, ARIMA, and other various econometric models on factors affecting remittances, energy intensity and economic development, energy policy, energy risk, environmental status and the impact of environmental aspects on the digital economy, agricultural productivity, and the stability of the U.S. credit market (Abdullah, et al., 2025; Caporin et al., 2024; Jakhongir et al., 2024; Kuziboev et al., 2025; Mamani, et al., 2025; Sharipov et al., 2025; Yin et al., 2024 Zhang et al., 2025).

According to Kleanthis Natsiopoulos et al., "The tests used by the ARDL model to assess the existence of long-run relationships between variables include the order of the test indicators." These diagnostic tests strengthen the integrative order of the variables and make it a powerful econometric tool for empirical analysis.

The ARDL model formulation is given below.

$$Y_t = \beta_0 + \sum_{i=1}^{m} \delta_i y_{t-i} + \sum_{j=1}^{r} \mu_j z_{t-j} + \varepsilon_t \quad (1)$$

where Y_t represents dependent variable at time t; z_t represents independent variable(s) at time t; β_0 represents intercept term; δ_i represents coefficients of lagged dependent variables (autoregressive terms); μ_j represents coefficients capturing the current and lagged effects of factors (distributed lag terms); m represents number of lags for the dependent variable; r represents number of lags for the independent variables; *and* ε_t represents the error term.

According to the econometric model all the variables are natural logarithmic. Below are the variables expressed according to the econometric model.

Variables:

Economy done state purchases size—***loggov_proc*** (result variable),
Electronic purchases—***logelect_purch*** (independent variable),
Currency your chair change—***logexchange_rate*** (independent variable),
Inflation rate—***loginfl_rate*** (independent variable).
Online purchase contracts number—***logonline_purch*** (independent variable).
In the econometric analysis, the null hypothesis (H0) and the alternative hypothesis (H1) were tested, and the results were found to be contrary to expectations.

Combined model hypothesis structure:

Null hypothesis (H0): Electronic purchases, national currency fluctuations, the inflation rate, and the number of online purchase contracts do not have a significant impact on the size of state purchases in the economy, nor do they exhibit signs of dependency.
Alternative hypothesis (H1): Electronic purchases, national currency fluctuations, the inflation rate, and the number of online purchase contracts have a significant impact on the size of state purchases in the national economy, showing a strong correlation.

16.4. Analysis and Results

In the initial phase of the econometric research, the size of state purchases and the influencing variables are presented according to their descriptive statistical values (Table 57).

Table 57. Dependent and independent variables according to descriptive statistic indicators

	loggov_ proc	*logelect_ purch*	*logexchange_ rate*	*loginfl_rate*	*logonline_ purch*
Mean	4.664772	4.662926	4.690077	4.844658	4.844658
Maximum	4.946739	4.768919	5.526095	5.178526	5.057892
Minimum	4.460179	4.017148	4.012655	4.367763	3.823904
Std. Dev	0.129159	0.1440128	0.2699918	0.1727838	0.2597819
Std. Err.	0.0263645	0.0293965	0.0551118	0.0352694	0.0530278
Skewness	0.2570735	0.2570735	0.8855496	-0.2665274	-0.7833746
Kurtosis	2.262825	18.38294	0.6513004	4.136715	4.643552
Observation	24	24	24	24	24

Source: It was developed by the authors based on Stata software.

According to Table 57, the descriptive statistics of the model formed a confidence interval with positive average values for the volume of economized public procurement and the factors affecting it. All variables had a complete set of 24 observations, providing positive conclusions for the analysis at the next stage in the data set.

This shows the prospects for developing further terms of the econometric equation. All variables are centered in a similar range, which suggests a comparable magnitude across the data set. The table data shows that the standard errors of the variables are small, indicating that the model means correspond to reliable values.

According to the study, a graphical representation of the volume of economized public procurement and the variables affecting it over time was developed (Figure 67).

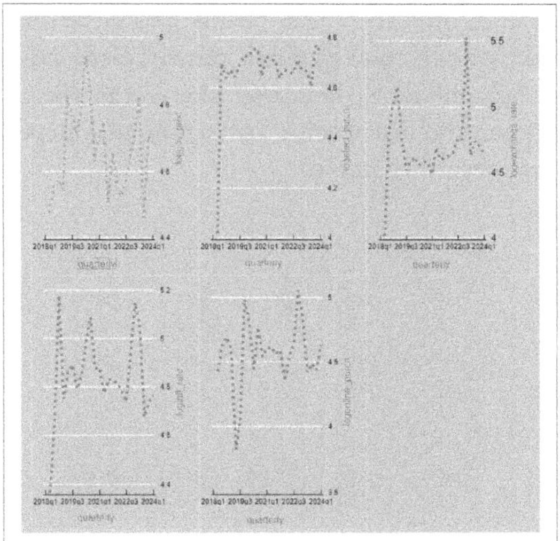

Figure 67. Analytical graphical representation of the volume of saved public procurement and the factors affecting it over time.

Source: It was developed by the authors based on Stata software.

According to Figure 67, all variables presented a stochastic trend. This figure allows us to draw positive conclusions about the ARDL model and demonstrate a positive trend in the prospective forecast indicators for all variables in the model. During the analyzed period, especially between 2018 and 2024, the average dynamic value of the state procurement practices in the national economy was formed. This means that the state procurement practices, along with other factors, showed a strong correlation with the inflation rate and online purchases.

From the data of Figure 67, it can be seen that the fluctuations in electronic sales and exchange rate changes in purchases formed a proportional growth dynamics. Also, the stochastic values according to the figure are considered an important process in fulfilling the stationarity condition of the ARDL model. In the next stage of the econometric study, a graphical matrix of the dependent and independent variables were created (Figure 68).

This indicates that the variables are systematically linked and allows for effective modeling in econometric research. The graph indicates a potential positive relationship, indicating that online and electronic procurement activities will lead to an increase in public procurement in higher education institutions. At the same time, the scatter plot reveals the variability in the relationship between the distribution pattern of all independent variables with respect to the resulting factor.

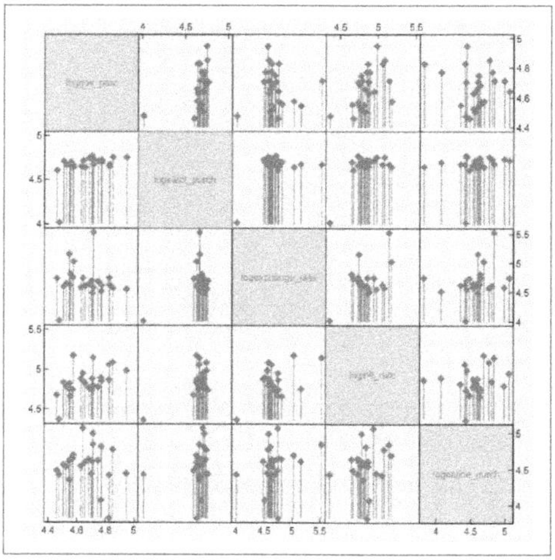

Figure 68. Economy done state purchases size and to him/her effect provider of factors graphic matrix image.

Source: It was developed by the authors based on Stata software.

The study developed a correlation matrix between the volume of public procurement and the factors affecting it (Table 58).

Based on the results of Table 58, a strong, robust, and inverse correlation relationship between the volume of public procurement saved and

Table 58. The cross-correlation matrix of factors affecting the volume of public procurement saved

Variables	*(1)*	*(2)*	*(3)*	*(4)*	*(5)*	*Significant*
loggov_proc	1.000					
logelect_purch	0.4392	1.000				
	(0.0318)					***
logexchange_rate	0.5201	0.4313	1.000			
	(0.0025)	(0.0354)				***
loginfl_rate	0.5402	0.5647	0.5152	1.000		
	(0.0064)	(0.0040)	(0.0100)			***
logonline_purch	0.5511	0.3762	0.4321	0.4015	1.000	
	(0.0080)	(0.0092)	(0.0070)	(0.0794)		***

Source: It was developed by the authors based on Stata software.

the factors affecting it is presented. The significant positive correlation between e-procurement and online sales indicates that public procurement is benefiting from digital platforms. The moderate positive relationship between the inflation rate and public procurement saved reflects the potential price pressure. Although this may indicate economic activity, it also emphasizes the need for careful planning of procurement to avoid the effects of inflation.

Also, considering that the p-value according to the table is <0.05, the condition of statistical significance for the correlation coefficient is met.

In the next step, a Unit-Root test was conducted to determine the stationarity of the volume of public procurement saved and the factors affecting it (Table 59).

According to Table 59, the Unit-Root test value of the dependent variable is −6.923, and the test results of the independent variables are −14.964, −6.804, −5.271, and −4.915, respectively. These values indicate the statistical significance and coherence of the volume of government procurement and the factors affecting it.

From the table data, the McKinnon's value of 0.0000 indicates the statistical significance of the critical values of $Z(t)$. Also, the results of the Unit-Root test indicate the stationarity of the volume of government procurement and the factors affecting it after the initial integration.

Table 59. Unit-Root test results for the indicator of the volume of public procurement saved and the factors affecting it

Variables	*Test Statistics*	*1% Critical Value*	*5% Critical Value*	*10% Critical Value*	*p-value for Z(t)*
loggov_proc (dependency changeable)	-6.923	-3.750	-3.000	-2.630	0.0000
logelect_purch (independent variable)	-14.964	-3.750	-3.000	-2.630	0.0000
logexchange_rate (independent variable)	-6.804	-3.750	-3.000	-2.630	0.0000
loginfl_rate (independent variable)	-5.271	-3.750	-3.000	-2.630	0.0000
logonline_purch (independent variable)	-4.915	-3.750	-3.000	-2.630	0.0000

Source: It was developed by the authors based on Stata software.

In the next stage of the econometric study, a regression equation was developed using the ARDL model (Table 60).

ARDL model formula indicators below cited.

Based on the ARDL(2,2,2,1,2) model, the long-term relationship is represented by the econometric equation given below:

$$loggov\_proc = 1.69 logelect\_purch - 0.11 logexchange\_rate + 0.85 loginfl\_rate - 0.16 logonline\_purch \quad (2)$$

16.4.1. ARDL(2,2,2,1,2) Model General Description

R-squared value: The *R*-squared value is 0.9516, which indicates that approximately 95.16% of the variation in the size of state purchases in the economy is explained by the influencing factors. The high *R*-squared value demonstrates the strong explanatory power of the model.

Log likelihood: The log-likelihood value is 43.775445, which indicates a positive evaluation of the econometric model's compatibility.

Table 60. Regression equation indicators based on the ARDL(2,2,2,1,2) model of the volume of saved government purchases and the factors affecting it

ARDL(2,2,2,1,2) regression **Sample: 2018q4 thru 2024q1** **Log likelihood = 43.775445**					**Number of obs = 22** **R-squared=0.9516** **Adj R-squar=0.8729** **Root MSE=0.0549**	
D.loggov_proc	Coefficient	Std. err.	t	P>t	[95% conf.	interval]
ADJ loggov_proc						
L1.	-2.289	0.344	-6.650	0.000	-3.083	-1.496
LR						
logelect_purch	1.694	0.247	6.850	0.000	1.124	2.265
logexchange_rate	-0.114	0.057	-2.000	0.081	-0.245	0.017
logonline_purch	0.855	0.081	10.570	0.000	0.669	1.042
loginfl_rate	-0.163	0.052	-3.160	0.013	-0.282	-0.044
SR						
loggov_proc						
LD.	0.200	0.144	1.390	0.202	-0.132	0.533
logelect_purch						
D1.	-0.974	0.458	-2.130	0.066	-2.031	0.083
LD.	0.264	0.167	1.580	0.153	-0.122	0.650
logexchange_rate						
D1.	-0.198	0.100	-1.970	0.085	-0.429	0.034
LD.	-0.446	0.099	-4.510	0.002	-0.674	-0.218
loginfl_rate						
D1.	-0.828	0.236	-3.510	0.008	-1.372	-0.284
logonline_purch						
D1.	0.060	0.087	0.690	0.511	-0.141	0.260
LD.	0.264	0.077	3.450	0.009	0.088	0.441
_cons	-14.099	2.738	-5.150	0.001	-20.413	-7.786

Source: It was developed by the authors based on Stata software.

Root MSE: The root mean square error (RMSE) is 0.0549, reflecting the average forecast error of the dependent variable. The low value indicates that the model provides reliable forecasts.

According to the ARDL(2,2,2,1,2) econometric model, the tests were conducted, and the results showed that the *F*-statistics and *t*-statistics are statistically significant at the 0.05 level. Based on these results, the null hypothesis (H0) was rejected, and the alternative hypothesis (H1) was accepted.

Cointegration in the research was tested using the ARDL(2,2,2,1,2) model through the bounds testing approach. The *F*-statistics and *t*-statistics were examined (Tables 61 and 62).

Table 61. Bound *F*-test for cointegration

					***F* = 12.481**
	[I_0] [I_1]	[I_0] [I_1]	[I_0] [I_1]	[I_0] [I_1]	
	L_1 L_1	L_05 L_05	L_025 L_025	L_01 L_01	
K_4	2.45 3.52	2.86 4.01	3.25 4.49	3.74 5.06	

Source: It was developed by the authors based on Stata software.

Based on Table 61, the model indicates the existence of cointegration, as evidenced by an *F*-statistic value of 12.481. This value exceeds the critical upper bound at the 1% significance level, confirming the positive result of the Bound test.

Table 62. Bound *t*-test for cointegration

					***F* = -6.661**
	[I_0] [I_1]	[I_0] [I_1]	[I_0] [I_1]	[I_0] [I_1]	
	L_1 L_1	L_05 L_05	L_025 L_025	L_01 L_01	
K_3	-2.57 -3.66	-2.86 -3.99	-3.13 -4.26	-3.43 -4.60	

Source: It was developed by the authors based on Stata software.

According to Table 62, the *t*-statistic value of –8.889 exceeds the critical bounds at all confidence levels, providing evidence of cointegration. This confirms a positive result for the Bound *t*-test.

According to the ARDL(2,2,2,1,2) model, in the long term, a 1% increase in electronic purchases leads to a 1.69% increase in the volume of state purchases in the economy. Conversely, a 1% depreciation of the national currency results in a 0.11% decrease in the volume of state purchases. Additionally, a 1% increase in the number of online purchase contracts contributes to a 0.85% increase in the volume of state purchases.

Additionally, a 1% increase in the national inflation rate results in a 0.16% decrease in the volume of state purchases in the economy.

In the next step of the research, the ARDL(2,2,2,1,2) model was evaluated using the CUSUM diagnostic test (Figures 69 and 70).

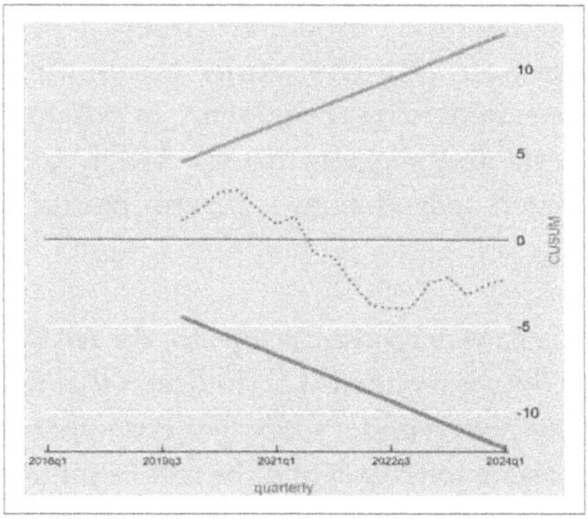

Figure 69. CUSUM diagnostic test chart.

Source: It was developed by the authors based on Stata software.

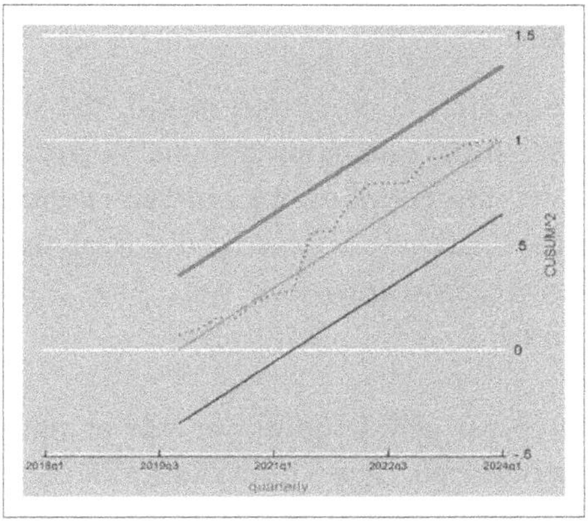

Figure 70. CUSUM diagnostic test chart.

Source: It was developed by the authors based on Stata software.

In the ARDL(2,2,2,1,2) model, the CUSUM (Cumulative Sum) diagnostic test was used to evaluate the stability of the econometric equation parameters over time, based on the following hypotheses:

1. *Null hypothesis* (*H0—Main hypothesis*): The model is stable over time, with no systematic changes in its parameters. This means that the ARDL(2,2,2,1,2) model's estimated parameters remain approximately constant throughout the period under study.
2. *Alternative hypothesis* (*H1—Alternative hypothesis*): The model is not stable over time, indicating the presence of systematic changes in the parameters. Instability suggests that the ARDL(2,2,2,1,2) model's estimated parameters may change at certain points during the period under study.

According to the CUSUM diagnostic results for the ARDL(2,2,2,1,2) model, the null hypothesis (H0) is retained. This indicates that the model remained stable throughout the period under study. The econometric equation, which examines the size of state purchases and the factors influencing it, shows no systematic changes or parameter instability. Additionally, the diagnostic test statistics remain within the critical bounds during the entire period, and no significant deviations were observed.

16.5. Conclusion

Based on the ARDL(2,2,2,1,2) regression model, the study examined the mutual impact of electronic purchases, national currency fluctuations, the inflation rate, and the number of online purchase contracts on the size of state purchases in the economy. Following this analysis, conclusions were drawn, and relevant recommendations were provided according to the ARDL(2,2,2,1,2) model.

1. Electronic purchases play a significant role in state purchases. A 1% increase in electronic purchases leads to a 1.69% increase in the volume of state purchases, highlighting the transformative effect of digitization. This result indicates that promoting and expanding electronic purchases

can improve the efficiency of state purchase processes, increase transparency, and create opportunities for cost savings.

2. *Assessment of the Impact of Currency Fluctuations on State Purchases*: A 1% depreciation of the national currency leads to a 0.11% decrease in the volume of state purchases. This demonstrates how currency fluctuations affect macroeconomic relationships. Consequently, minimizing the negative impact of exchange rate variability on state purchases highlights the need for reasonable economic reforms by the government.
3. *Assessment of the Impact of Online Purchase Contracts on State Purchases:* A 1% increase in the number of online purchase contracts leads to a 0.85% increase in the volume of state purchases. This demonstrates the importance of digital platforms in optimizing purchase operations, enhancing transparency, promoting competition, and improving economic efficiency in current online procurement mechanisms.
4. *Assessment of the Impact of Inflation on State Purchases:* A 1% increase in the inflation rate leads to a 0.16% decrease in the volume of state purchases. Although the impact is relatively small, it demonstrates that inflationary pressures can affect the management of state purchase funds. This finding highlights the importance of controlling inflationary expectations and implementing strategies to protect the efficiency of state procurement processes.
5. The results of the econometric research indicate that the use of digital tools and platforms plays an important role in improving the state procurement system and enhancing the efficiency of state expenditures. Investments in digital infrastructure for state purchases can help stabilize key macroeconomic indicators, such as inflation and currency fluctuations, highlighting the importance of government attention and professional management in these areas.

Bibliography

Abdullah, M. A., Han, X., Amjad, M. A., & Makhmudov, S. (2025). Revisit the role of financial development on economic growth, human development, and sustainable development in higher-income countries. Journal of Environmental Management, 392, 126874.

Akhmetshin, E., Abdullayev, I., Makhmudov, S., Dakhkilgova, K., Korotaeva, I. and Yanovskaya, G. (2025). APPLICATION OF TANH–COTH METHOD FOR COMBINED AND DOUBLE COMBINED SINH–COSH–GORDON EQUATIONS ARISING CHEMICAL REACTIONS TO WATER SURFACE GRAVITY WAVES. Computational Methods for Differential Equations, (), -. doi: 10.22034/cmde.2025.67655.3234

Bao, Wei. (2011). An empirical analysis of the financial characteristics and borrowing behavior of universities in China after rapid expansion. *Peking University Education Review*, *9*(1), 33–52.

Bélgica, P.-B., & Bastante-Ceca, M. J. (2016). 10. Green public procurement as an initiative for sustainable consumption. An exploratory study of Spanish public universities. *Journal of Cleaner Production*, <https://doi.org/10.1016/J.JCLEPRO.2016.05.056>

Cahyani, I., Buriev, K., Ngongo, M., Mamadiyarov, Z., Ino, L., Herman, H., Saputra, N., & Baxtishodovich, S. (2025). Exploring the Use of TikTok Application in Enhancing the Skill of Pronunciation: A Case on Students' Perception. Studies in Media and Communication, *13*(2), 150–158. doi:http://dx.doi.org/10.11114/smc.v13i2.7553

Caporin, M., Shahbaz, M., Kuziboev, B., Masharipova, M., Allaberganov, S., & Makhmudov, S. (2024). Environmental Kuznets Curve for extended brics economies: do women governance and water stress matter?. International Journal of Energy Economics and Policy, *14*(6), 174–183.

Natsiopoulos, K., & Tzeremes, N. G. (2022). ARDL: An R package for the analysis of level relationships. *The Journal of Open Source Software*, *7*(79), 3496–3496. <https://doi.org/10.21105/joss.03496>

Fuinhas, J. A., & Marques, A. C. (2012). Energy consumption and economic growth nexus in Portugal, Italy, Greece, Spain and Turkey: An ARDL bounds test approach (1965–2009). *Energy Economics*, *34*(2), 511–517.

Hussain, A., Khan, M., Rakhmonov, D. A., Mamadiyarov, Z. T., Kurbonbekova, M. T., & Mahmudova, M. Q. K. (2023). Nexus of Training and Development, Organizational Learning Capability, and Organizational Performance in the Service Sector. Sustainability, *15*(4), 3246. https://doi.org/10.3390/su15043246

Jahrir, A., Gultom, Y., Herman, H., Zabadi, F., Ngongo, M., Mamadiyarov, Z., Fatmawati, E., & Saputra, N. (2025). Investigating the Elements of Short Commercial Mineral Water Advertisement: A Case on Discourse Analysis. *Studies in Media and Communication, 13*(4), 94–104. doi:http://dx.doi.org/10.11114/smc.v13i4.7813

Jakhongir, S., Muhabbat, H., Khayrilla, K., Kholmuratov, S., Nazirjon, R., Nilufar, F., & Farxod, T. (2024). Crafting a neutrosophic-driven tool to probe turnover propensities in manufacturing entities. *International Journal of Neutrosophic Science (IJNS), 23*(2).

Jin, Xue, S. M., Ferdous, A., & Jacquline, T. (2024). Challenges of sustainable public procurement in Chinese higher education institutions: A Delphi study. *Journal of Public Procurement*. <https://doi.org/10.1108/jopp-05-2024-0051>

Kuchkarov, T., Mamadiyarov, Z., Khakimov, Z., Sabirova, O., Matmurodov, K., Raimboyeva, M., & Umarova, S. (2025). Energy-Related Uncertainty and Crypto-Currency Environmental Attention: Time-Varying Perspective. International Journal of Energy Economics and Policy, 15(5), 614–626. https://doi.org/10.32479/ijeep.20784

Kelly., U., McNicoll, I., & McLellan, D. (2004). The economic impact of UK higher education institutions.

Kuziboev, B., Khodjaniyazov, E., Ozturk, I., Sabirov, K., Makhmudov, S., & Utegenova, S. (2025). Does oil dependence cause energy risk?. Energy Nexus, 17, 100393.

Lin, M.H., Matchanova, B., Nurmatovich, H.A. *et al.* Optimal Operation of the Multi-Carrier Energy System Considering Energy Markets and Renewable Energies Participation. *Int. J. Appl. Comput. Math* **11**, 170 (2025). https://doi.org/10.1007/s40819-025-02002-9

Litamahuputty, J. V., Amiruddin, E. G., Rahim, R., Rahman, A., & Mamadiyarov, Z. (2025). Cryptocurrency Risk Management through Decision Engineering: Evaluating XRPUSD and ADAUSD Portfolio Performance. Journal of Applied Science, Engineering, Technology, and Education, 7(1), 69–81. https://doi.org/10.35877/454RI.asci3871

Mamani, J.C.M., Miri, M., Vorobev, Y. et al. Optimal Operation of Energy Microgrid Considering Economic and Emission Indices. Oper. Res. Forum 6, 122 (2025). https://doi.org/10.1007/s43069-025-00523-z

Mamadiyarov, Z., Hakimov, H., & Askarov, S. (2024). DEVELOPMENT OF RETAIL BANKING SERVICES IN THE CONTEXT OF DIGITAL TRANSFORMATION. Financial and Credit Activity Problems of Theory and Practice, 1(54), 51–67. https://doi.org/10.55643/fcaptp.1.54.2024.4288

Mamadiyarov, Z. Makhmudov, S. Utanov, B. Kasimova, D. Bekmurodova, G. Hakimov, Z. (2025). Fusion of Economic and Financial Factors Affecting Household Deposits in Banks: An Econometric Analysis. Fusion: Practice and Applications, (), 82–91. DOI: https://doi.org/10.54216/FPA.190206

Muhammad Zubair, Irfanud Din, Nadeem Sarwar et al. Revolutionizing Sepsis Diagnosis Using Machine Learning and Deep Learning Models: A Systematic Literature Review, 10 June 2025, PREPRINT (Version 1) available at Research Square [https://doi.org/10.21203/rs.3.rs-6731418/v1]

Munyao, J. M. (2018). Influence of e-procurement practices on the performance of procurement in public universities in Kenya. *Strategic Journal of Business & Change Management*, *5*(2).

PANJAITAN, M. B., HAMDANAH, H., SIRAIT, J., SUTIKNO, S., FATMAWATI, E., HERMAN, H., & MAMADIYAROV, Z. (2025). THE ROLE OF EMOTIONAL REGULATION IN SHAPING STUDENTS' PERCEPTION OF PHYSICS PROBLEMSOLVING TASKS. TPM – Testing, Psychometrics, Methodology in Applied Psychology, 32(S2(2025): Posted 09 June), 1–10. Retrieved from https://tpmap.org/submission/index.php/tpm/article/view/139

Pradhan, R., Hajiyev, E., Shichiyakh, R. et al. Optimal Techno-Economic Feasibility of an Off-Grid Microgrid System Using Load Flow Energy Management Strategies. Oper. Res. Forum 6, 120 (2025). https://doi.org/10.1007/s43069-025-00524-y

Romero, R. M., Zelinskaya, M., Makhmudov, S., Sapaev, S., & Rustambekovich, J. U. (2025, September). Modelling and Optimal Utilisation of the Renewable Energy Systems in Microgrid with Improving Reliability and Energy Efficiency. In Operations Research Forum (Vol. 6, No. 3, pp. 1–20). Springer International Publishing.

Rukhiddin Zayniddinov, Nodir Jumaev, Gulbakhor Irgasheva, Alam Asadov, Nosir Makhmudov, Sirojiddin Abrorov, and Samariddin Makhmudov. 2025. The Influence of the Digital Economy on Economic

Development Evidence from Uzbekistan. In Proceedings of the 8th International Conference on Future Networks & Distributed Systems (ICFNDS '24). Association for Computing Machinery, New York, NY, USA, 831–839. https://doi.org/10.1145/3726122.3726242

Samariddin Makhmudov, Kudratillo Tukhsanov, Saifulla Arslanbekov, Akram Amanov, Orifali Tursunov, Umarbek Jabbarov and Muyassarxon Mirzakarimova. 2024. Optimizing Supply Chain Financing Development Prospects of Digital Ecosystems in the European Logistics Industry. In The 8th International Conference on Future Networks & Distributed Systems (ICFNDS '24), December 11–12, 2024, Marakech, Morocco. ACM, New York, NY, USA, 12 Pages. https://doi.org/10.1145/3726122.3726200

Sarıdoğan, H. Ö. & Kaya, M. V. (2019). Knowledge economy and economic performance: A comparison between Turkey and the European Union. *Mehmet Akif Ersoy University Journal of Economics and Administrative Sciences*, 6(3), 916–935.

Sharipov, K., Abdullayev, I., Kuziboev, B., Makhmudov, S., Kalandarov, F., Khaytboeva, N., & Ilkhamova, Z. (2025). The Effect of Energy Policy Risk on Renewable Energy. International Journal of Energy Economics and Policy, 15(2), 566.

Su, R., Xiao, Y., Hamza, F., Mamadiyarov, Z., & Wahab, A. (2025). Scaling up green hydrogen in China: Economic opportunities and challenges. *International Journal of Hydrogen Energy*, *131*, 60–69.

Sun, C., Zhang, F., & Xu, M. (2017). Investigation of pollution haven hypothesis for China: An ARDL approach with breakpoint unit root tests. *Journal of Cleaner Production*, *161*, 153–164.

Usman, A., et al. (2022). Revealing the nexus between nuclear energy and ecological footprint in STIRPAT model of advanced economies: Fresh evidence from novel CS-ARDL model. *Progress in Nuclear Energy*, T. 148.–S. 104220.

Winnie, D., & Intaher, M. A. (2012). 11. The influence of public procurement policies on the implementation of procurement best practices in South African universities. *Journal of Transport and Supply Chain Management*. <https://doi.org/10.4102/JTSCM.V6I1.65>

Zhang, L., Zhao, Z., Qamri, G. M., & Makhmudov, S. (2025). Unleashing the critical role of renewable energy through global value chains and digitalization: A path towards environmental sustainability. Journal of Environmental Management, 392, 126688.

Zhao, Q., Pervaiz, A., Makhmudov, S., & Fatima, A. (2025). Do environmental stringent policies enhance the impact of renewable energy on CO2 reduction? Evidence from BRICS-T economies. Journal of Environmental Management, 391, 126464.

Zokir Toshtemirovich Mamadiyarov, Samandarboy Adhambek ugli Sulaymanov, Sarvar Anvar ugli Askarov, and Durdona Bakhtiyor kizi Uktamova. 2022. Impact of Covid-19 Pandemic on Accelerating the Digitization and Transformation of Banks. In Proceedings of the 5th International Conference on Future Networks and Distributed Systems (ICFNDS '21). Association for Computing Machinery, New York, NY, USA, 706–712. https://doi.org/10.1145/3508072.3508211

Forecasting and Planning the Proportion of Enterprises Not Using Digital Technologies Based on the ARIMA Model

Zokir Mamadiyarov, Makhmudov Samariddin, Nuriddin Javliev, Nargiza Talapova, Nigora Khayitova, Mirjalol Eshboev, and Gulzar Jumatova

17.1. Introduction

In the modern economy, the use of sustainable technologies in entrepreneurship or similar production enterprises is becoming the basis of business success. Also, sustainable technologies significantly increase innovation, efficiency, and similar indicators. However, despite the increasing trend towards digital transformation, many enterprises, especially small businesses in developing countries, continue to operate without using sustainable technologies or without fully understanding them. In this regard, small businesses in Uzbekistan are lagging behind such changes. Therefore, the digital transformation in the country is not being put in place. This leads to the fact that enterprises are losing efficiency in the globalization that is taking shape due to digital progress and are not serving to sustainably maintain the country's economic growth, and similar factors.

This study will help determine the number of enterprises in the country that are operating without using digital technologies in the future, both for the country and for small businesses, to develop the necessary reforms and attract investments to fill this gap. The scope of this study will allow the government, financial institutions, and small businesses to make the necessary decisions on investments, technological integration, and economic reforms.

This study uses the ARIMA (Autoregressive Integrated Moving Average) econometric model to provide a comprehensive forecast of the number of enterprises operating without using digital technologies in Uzbekistan from 2025 to 2029. Using data from the Statistics Agency of the Republic of Uzbekistan, this study offers a clear and forward-looking analysis of data-driven trends. The conclusions drawn from the study will enable the country's economic reforms to promote and encourage the use of sustainable technologies in its business activities, optimize resource allocation, and mitigate the risk of economic exclusion faced by non-digital enterprises. This forecast is intended not only to inform immediate policy decisions, but also to serve as a basis for developing strategies for the country's economic reforms in the short and long term, ensuring that the business landscape of the Republic of Uzbekistan develops in line with the requirements of the digital economy.

17.2. Literature Review and Development Hypothesis

In the currently developing field of financial forecasting, various econometric models have been developed to predict financial distress and analyze the performance of enterprises that do not use sustainable technologies or do not involve digital technologies in production. The relevance of the research can be seen by analyzing several studies in the literatures as in what follows. Ran (2023) proposed a completely new approach to predict financial distress using the method of relative weighted neutrosophic value distances. This econometric model showed its effectiveness with great accuracy in assessing the performance of a microfinance group. It is worth mentioning that in the study by Erfina Dukalang et al. (2024), researchers presented several econometric models to forecast financial distress. Of the presented econometric models, the CA-Score model was considered the most reliable. This is because the model had an accuracy of 97.14% and a type II error of 2.86%. We can see that it outperforms established models such as Altman, Zavgren, and Ohlson by the above accuracy index.

Dong Mei (2022) employed a logistic regression model to predict financial distress in digital economy enterprises, focusing on financial indicators from China's A-share companies during 2017–2021. This study underlined the significance of integrating enterprise-specific characteristics for precise predictions. Similarly, Dr. Jyoti Nair et al. (2022) modeled financial distress for Indian manufacturing companies using eighteen financial ratios, showcasing the reliability of logistic regression for industry-specific distress prediction.

Chavez et al. (2023) analyzed corporate bankruptcies using asymmetric information flows, examining 905 corporations over a decade. The study revealed that 651 companies experienced financial distress, highlighting the effectiveness of long-term data for forecasting (Jahrir et al., 2025; Lin et al., 2025; Pradhan et al., 2025; Su et al., 2025). Meanwhile, Aidas Malakauskas (2021) applied machine learning techniques, including logistic regression, artificial neural networks, and random forests, to predict distress in small and medium enterprises. This comprehensive study emphasized financial obligations over bankruptcy likelihood as key distress indicators.

Inggar Nur Arini (2021) conducted a comparative analysis of four models—Altman, Springate, Taffler, and Grover—using data from global retail companies. The results indicated the Grover model's superior accuracy (76.67%) for financial distress predictions. Similarly, Feng Shen et al. (2020) developed a dynamic forecasting model to handle unbalanced data environments. The study demonstrated the ANS-REA model's capacity to address conceptual changes in asymmetric data flow, marking a significant advancement in prediction methodologies.

The ARIMA model has been widely recognized for its robust time-series forecasting capabilities. It has been used to predict cash flows, financial needs, and investment trends, making it particularly effective for analyzing fixed capital investments and stock markets (Matyakubova et al., 2025; Romero et al., 2025; Zhang et al., 2025). However, its reliance on historical data necessitates hybrid approaches to address market volatility. For instance, the ARIMA-SVR hybrid model integrates ARIMA's statistical strength with the adaptability of support vector regression to forecast volatile financial data, as demonstrated by Zhangong Huang and Huwei Li (2024).

Analyses and forecasts have been conducted using multivariate linear regression (LS), ARDL, ARIMA, and other various econometric models on factors affecting remittances, energy intensity and economic development, energy policy, energy risk, environmental status and the impact of environmental aspects on the digital economy, agricultural productivity, and the stability of the U.S. credit market (Abdullah, et al., 2025 Caporin et al., 2024; Hussain et al., 2023; Jakhongir et al., 2024; Kuziboev et al., 2025; Sharipov et al., 2025; Yin et al., 2024).

Case studies, such as those conducted by Dutch company Lady, illustrate the practical benefits of ARIMA models in optimizing financial management. The model's application in predicting non-digital firm shares for 2025–2029 further underscores its versatility in business and economic contexts (Khyrina et al., 2024; Samariddin et al., 2024; Zhao et al., 2025.

Another group of economists has successfully used econometric models such as Fixed Effects Estimator (FEE), Random Effects Estimator (REE), multivariate linear (LS), and ARDL in their research on investment in digital infrastructure, various aspects of digital payment systems, the impact of inflation and credit interest rates on investment, factors affecting the reduction of the state's share in commercial banks, non-performing loans in commercial banks, the digitalization of banks, risks in digital services, and the development of retail payment services (Cahyani et al., 2025; Kuchkarov et al., 2025; Litamahuputty et al., 2025; Mamadiyarov et al., 2024a, 2024b; Mamani, et al., 2025; PANJAITAN et al., 2025; Zokir et al., 2021).

These studies collectively highlight the growing relevance of econometric models in predicting financial distress and ensuring sustainable enterprise growth. The integration of advanced statistical methods, machine learning, and hybrid models like ARIMA-SVR offers a comprehensive toolkit for stakeholders to navigate financial uncertainties effectively.

17.3. Research Methodology

The econometric equation of the ARIMA model is as follows.

The ARIMA model is a statistical method that has been successfully used to forecast future values in time series data. It includes an autoregressive (AR) part, a moving average (MA) part, and takes into account non-stationary data by differencing to stabilize the series.

The ARIMA model formula contains three components, denoted as ARIMA(p, d, q), where:

p represents the number of lagged observations in the model (AR part);
d, the number of times the raw observations are differed (integrated part); and
q, the size of the MA window (MA part).

The general form of the ARIMA(p, d, q) model can be expressed as:

$$y_t = c + \mu_1{}^{*}y_{t-1} + \mu_1{}^{*}y_{t-2} + \dots + \mu_p{}^{*}y_{t-p} + \tau_1{}^{*}\epsilon_{t-1} + \tau_2{}^{*}\epsilon_{t-2} + \dots + \tau_q{}^{*}\epsilon_{t-q} + \epsilon_t \quad (1)$$

where y_t represents the value of the differenced time series at time t (after differencing (d) times), c is a constant term, $\mu_i = (for\ i = 1, 2, \dots, p)$ denotes the coefficients of the AR part, and $\tau_j = (for\, j = 1, 2, \ldots, q)$ represents the coefficients of the MA part, and ϵ_t **represents the error tem at** time t (white noise).

17.3.1. Explanation of Components

1. *Autoregressive (AR) part*: The terms $\mu_1{}^*y_{t-1}$, $\mu_2{}^*y_{t-2}$, …, $\mu_p{}^*y_{t-p}$ represent the AR part, where the current value of the series is regressed on its past values.
2. *Integrated (I) part*: The parameter d refers to the differencing process used to make the series stationary. The differencing operation can be written as:

$$y_t' = y_t - y_{t-1} \text{ (if } d = 1) \tag{2}$$

At the same time, a high level of differentiation can be used in developing forecast indicators for research.

3. *Moving Average (MA) part*: The terms $\tau_1\epsilon_{t-1}$, $\tau_2\epsilon_{t-2}$, …, $\tau_q\epsilon_{t-q}$ represent the MA part, where the current value is influenced by past error terms.

The econometric study was developed using data from the Statistical Agency under the President of the Republic of Uzbekistan (<https://stat.uz/uz/>), which included 37 quarterly observations of the number of non-operating enterprises and organizations by economic sector for 2014–2023.

The resulting factor for the econometric forecast is expressed as follows:

Number of companies not using digital technologies—*non_operat_company* (dependent variable).

17.4. Analysis and Results

An analytical graphical representation of the dependent variable at the initial stage of econometric forecasting is presented in Figure 71.

According to Figure 71, the number of enterprises that did not use digital technologies showed a sharp increase in the last quarter of 2019. This indicates that this type of enterprises fell into the period of the COVID-2019

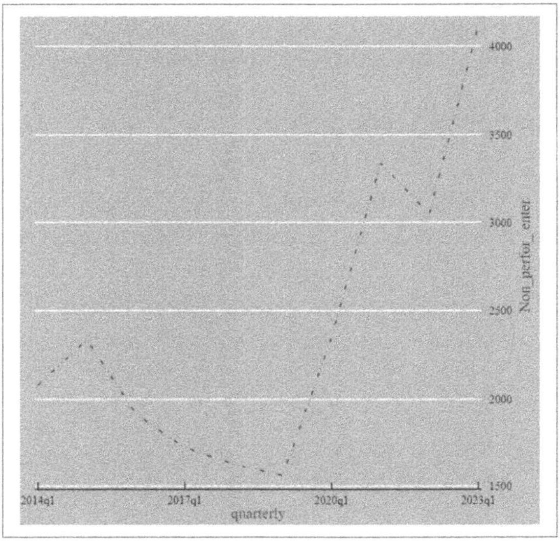

Figure 71. Analytical graph of the number of companies not using digital technologies over time.

Source: It was developed by the authors based on Stata software.

pandemic. This trend continues to some extent in the post-pandemic period and is forecast to grow further in the future.

In the next stage of the study, the stationarity of the resulting factor was checked and the Unit-Root test was used to determine it (Table 63).

Table 63. Unit-Root test indicator of the number of enterprises not using digital technologies

non_operat_ company	*Test Statistic*	*1% Critical Value*	*5% Critical Value*	*10% Critical Value*	*p-value for Z(t)*
	−5.680	−3.689	−2.975	−2.619	0.0000

Source: It was developed by the authors based on Stata software.

According to Table 63, the number of companies that do not use digital technologies produced a value of –5,680. It can be seen that this result is below the 1%, 5%, and 10% thresholds for statistical significance. In addition, the MacKinnon value is minimal with $Z(t) = 0.0000$, which indicates that the number of enterprises and organizations that do not operate in the sector of the economy is stationary.

The results of the Unit-Root test and the MacKinnon value show how statistically significant the number of enterprises that do not use digital technologies is to the gross income of the national economy, confirming the stationarity of the data.

According to Table 63, the parameter δ of the ARIMA model yielded a value of $d = 2$, which provides a positive fit, indicating that the time series has reached stationarity after being differencing twice.

The next step is to find the value of π, which determines the indirect correlation between the lags of the time series of the model (Figure 72). Also, in the next step, the p-value was determined, which indicates the indirect relationship between the lags of the time series in the model (Figure 72).

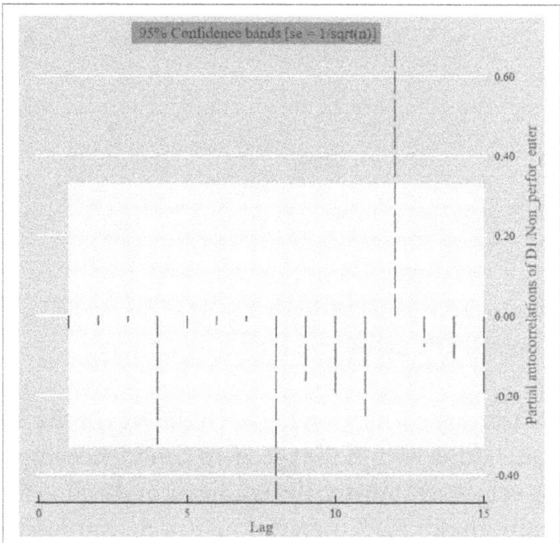

Figure 72. Indirect correlation graph between the lags of the model.
Source: It was developed by the authors based on Stata software.

According to Figure 72, except for two lags, all other lags provided confidence intervals in the autocorrelation analysis. According to this, most of the lags are statistically significant and lie within the confidence limits. According to the ARIMA model, ensuring that the lags fit the confidence interval is important for the correct fitting of the model. In this case, it is appropriate to use a *p*-value of 0.1 or 2.

In the next step of the ARIMA model, the value of *q* was determined, which describes the direct correlation between the lags of the model (Figure 73).

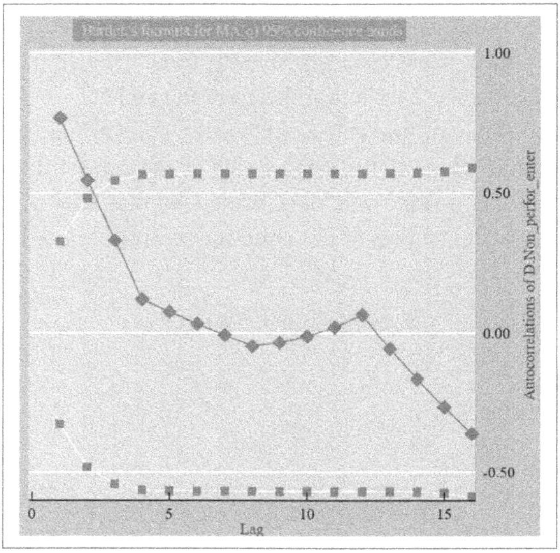

Figure 73. Direct correlation graph between the lags of the model.
Source: It was developed by the authors based on Stata software.

Figure 73 shows a strong correlation between the lags in the ARIMA model, with all lag values falling within the specified confidence interval. This indicates that the lag values are statistically significant and a good fit for the model

Choosing one of these values corresponds to determining the value of the MA parameter *q* in the ARIMA model.

Since the observed data for the study are suitable and lie within the confidence interval from 0 to 2, it is recommended to choose a *q* value in this range.

When selecting the optimal ARIMA invariant models for forecasting the model, the models of the form ARIMA(0,1,1), ARIMA(0,1,2), ARIMA(1,1,1), ARIMA(1,1,0), ARIMA(1,1,2), and ARIMA(2,0,1) were used. Among these, the ARIMA(1,1,2) model with the best result was selected (see Table 64).

The ARIMA(1,1,2) regression equation is given below.

According to Table 64, the ARIMA(1,1,2) model looks like this:

$$\Delta Y_t = 60.13 + 0.54Y_{t-1} - 0.07\varepsilon_{t-1} + 0.65\varepsilon_{t-2} + \varepsilon_t \quad (2)$$

Table 64. Econometric equation indicators of the ARIMA(1,1,2) model

D.Non_ perfor_enter	Coeff.	St. Err.	*t*-value	*p*-value	[95% Conf	Interval]	Sig
Constant	60.134	59.767	1.01	0.0414	-57.007	177.274	*
L	0.547	0.237	2.30	0.021	0.082	1.012	**
L	0.078	0.279	0.28	0.078	−0.469	0.625	*
L2	0.658	0.117	5.63	0	0.429	0.888	***
Constant	82.569	9.539	8.66	0	63.874	101.264	***
Mean dependent var	56.556		SD dependent var		137.827		
Number of obs	36		Chi-square		46.249		
Prob > chi²	.		Akaike crit. (AIC)		431.868		
*** $p < 0.01$, ** $p < 0.05$, * $p < 0.1$.							

Source: It was developed by the authors based on Stata software.

In the next step, the ARIMA(1,1,2) model was developed to analyze the mean values of the resulting variable and the graphical representation of the residuals (Figure 74 and Table 65).

The residuals exhibit significant fluctuations, with particularly large spikes around 2020, which may indicate model misfitting during specific periods, possibly due to external shocks or structural breaks in the data. These irregularities could be a sign that the model struggles to accurately predict during these times, potentially due to factors not captured in the model, such as sudden economic disruptions, like the COVID-19 pandemic.

Additionally, the presence of large positive and negative residuals suggests that the model might not fully account for the underlying dynamics of the data during certain periods, requiring further refinement or the inclusion of additional explanatory variables.

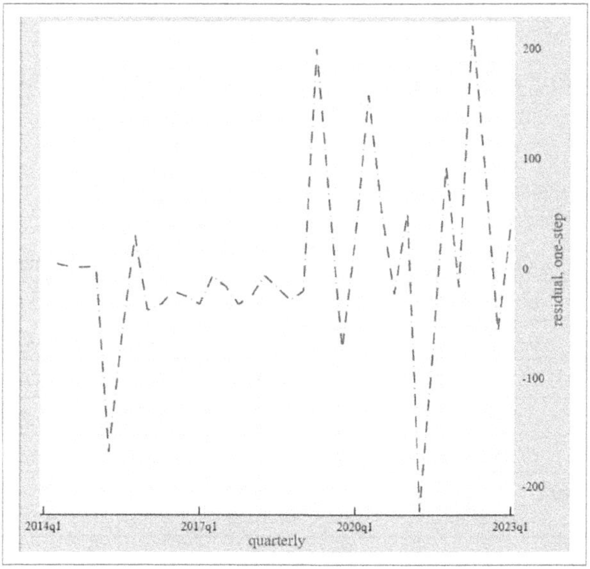

Figure 74. ARIMA(1,1,2) model residuals plot by outcome variable.
Source: It was developed by the authors based on Stata software.

Table 65. ARIMA(1,1,2) model residual values of the resulting factor

Variable	Number of observations	Mean value	Standard deviation	Minimum value	Maximum value
Residual value	36	0.5935287	84.21365	−223.0585	220.9507

Source: It was developed by the authors based on Stata software.

Based on Table 65 and Figure 74, the ARIMA(1,1,2) model has reached stochastic equilibrium, as shown by the visual representation of the residuals at the given time intervals. The closeness of the residuals to zero and their random distribution indicate that the model adequately accounts for the autocorrelation structure in the data.

In the next step, the validity of the ARIMA(1,1,2) model was assessed based on certain criteria. This included checking the stationarity of the residuals and evaluating the AR and MA residuals. In addition, the convergence of the model to unity was also checked (Figure 75).

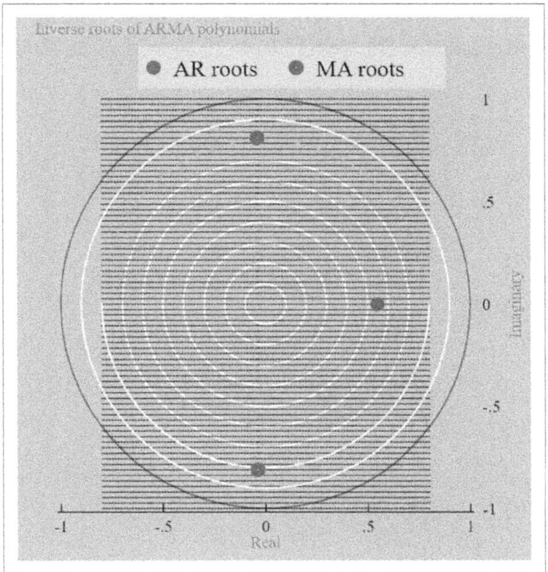

Figure 75. Domain of MA values according to the AR(2,1,0) model.
Source: It was developed by the authors based on Stata software.

Using the Stata program, forecast indicators for the number of non-operating enterprises and organizations by economic sector were developed using the ARIMA(1,1,2) model, excluding random (exogenous and endogenous) factors from 2025 to 2029 (Table 66).

Table 66. Forecast indicators of the number of enterprises not using digital technologies in 2025–2029

Years	Pessimistic forecast	Optimistic forecast	Forecast
2025	4,691	4,965	4,828
2026	4,934	5,208	5,071
2027	5,174	5,448	5,311
2028	5,415	5,689	5,552
2029	5,655	5,929	5,792

Source: It was developed by the authors based on Stata software

The results of the study are presented in the form of graphs showing the organization's forecast for the years 2014–2024 and 2025–2029 (Figure 75).

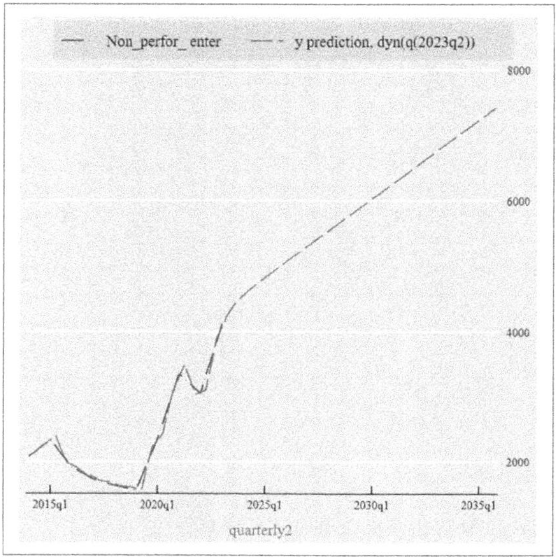

Figure 76. Graph of the dependent variable for 2014–2024 and the forecast for 2025–2029.

Source: It was developed by the authors based on Stata software.

Figure 76 shows the number of enterprises not using digital technologies in 2014–2024 and 2025–2029, as well as the forecast graphs. According to it, the direction graph indicates the reliability of the forecast indicators for the coming years, excluding random factors, since the two lines are located almost side by side.

17.5. Conclusion

To calculate the number of enterprises that have not adopted digital technologies in Uzbekistan, the authors selected the ARIMA(1,1,2) model and, according to it, calculated the econometric forecast of the number of enterprises that have not adopted digital technologies in 2024–2029. Based on the results obtained, we offer the following conclusions:

1. According to the econometric forecast, the number of enterprises that do not use digital technologies is projected to reach 4,828 in 2025, 5,071 in 2026, 5,311 in 2027, 5,552 in 2028, and 792 in 2029 (excluding random factors).
2. *Forecast growth rate*: The number of enterprises that do not use digital technologies is projected to grow steadily during 2025–2029. This gradual increase indicates that structural changes have occurred in economic sectors.
3. The ARIMA model effectively captures the main trends and random factors and provides a reliable forecast for decision-makers. This forecast is of great importance in developing a strategy aimed at reducing the number of inactive enterprises and improving overall economic activity.
4. *Assessment of strategic planning*: The expected increase from 4,828 in 2025 to 5,792 in 2029 provides stakeholders with a clear picture when developing strategic plans. Taking into account the forecast indicators, the government and business entities need to create targeted state programs to improve efficiency and re-engage inactive enterprises.
5. *Allocation of financial resources*: Understanding these future trends will allow for more efficient allocation of resources. Failure to develop the sector financially, technologically, and innovatively increases the risk of business failure.
6. The results obtained show that the sector needs economic and financial reforms. Early implementation of strategies for early and targeted implementation of measures can promote economic stability and growth and reduce risks.

Bibliography

Abdullah, M. A., Han, X., Amjad, M. A., & Makhmudov, S. (2025). Revisit the role of financial development on economic growth, human development, and sustainable development in higher-income countries. Journal of Environmental Management, 392, 126874.

Akhmetshin, E., Abdullayev, I., Makhmudov, S., Dakhkilgova, K., Korotaeva, I. and Yanovskaya, G. (2025). APPLICATION OF TANH–COTH METHOD FOR COMBINED AND DOUBLE COMBINED SINH–COSH–GORDON EQUATIONS ARISING

CHEMICAL REACTIONS TO WATER SURFACE GRAVITY WAVES. Computational Methods for Differential Equations, (), -. doi: 10.22034/cmde.2025.67655.3234

Arini, I. N. (2021). Analisis Akurasi Model-Model Prediksi Financial Distress. *Jurnal Ilmu Manajemen*, *9*(3), 1196–1204. <https://doi.org/10.26740/JIM.V9N3.P%P>

Cahyani, I., Buriev, K., Ngongo, M., Mamadiyarov, Z., Ino, L., Herman, H., Saputra, N., & Baxtishodovich, S. (2025). Exploring the Use of TikTok Application in Enhancing the Skill of Pronunciation: A Case on Students' Perception. Studies in Media and Communication, *13*(2), 150–158. doi:http://dx.doi.org/10.11114/smc.v13i2.7553

Caporin, M., Shahbaz, M., Kuziboev, B., Masharipova, M., Allaberganov, S., & Makhmudov, S. (2024). Environmental Kuznets Curve for extended brics economies: do women governance and water stress matter?. International Journal of Energy Economics and Policy, *14*(6), 174–183.

Chaves, R., Rossi, L. E., & García, L. E. (2023). Financial distress prediction in an imbalanced data stream environment. *Lecture Notes in Computer Science*, 168–179. <https://doi.org/10.1007/978-3-031-40725-3_15>

Dong, M., Li, K., Xu, Y., Daisy, L., Jiang, Y., Tang, M., Lu, C., & Mo, G. (2022). Financial distress prediction for digital economy firms: Based on PCA-logistic. *Journal of Risk Analysis and Crisis Response*, *12*(1). <https://doi.org/10.54560/jracr.v12i1.319>

Erfina, D., Irfan, Z., & Zulkifli, Abu (2024). Analysis of financial distress predictions using Altman, Zavgren, Fulmer, Ohlson, Taffler, and CA-score models as early warning systems in manufacturing companies. *Nominal Barometer Riset Akuntansi dan Manajemen Indonesia*, *13*(1), 81–97. <https://doi.org/10.21831/nominal.v13i1.65081>

Huang, Z., & Li, H. (2024). ARIMA-SVR-based risk aggregation modeling in financial behavior. *Kybernetes*. <https://doi.org/10.1108/k-01-2024-0249>

Hussain, A., Khan, M., Rakhmonov, D. A., Mamadiyarov, Z. T., Kurbonbekova, M. T., & Mahmudova, M. Q. K. (2023). Nexus of Training and Development, Organizational Learning Capability, and Organizational Performance in the Service Sector. Sustainability, *15*(4), 3246. https://doi.org/10.3390/su15043246

Jahrir, A., Gultom, Y., Herman, H., Zabadi, F., Ngongo, M., Mamadiyarov, Z., Fatmawati, E., & Saputra, N. (2025). Investigating the Elements of Short Commercial Mineral Water Advertisement: A Case on Discourse Analysis. *Studies in Media and Communication, 13*(4), 94–104. doi:http://dx.doi.org/10.11114/smc.v13i4.7813

Jakhongir, S., Muhabbat, H., Khayrilla, K., Kholmuratov, S., Nazirjon, R., Nilufar, F., & Farxod, T. (2024). Crafting a neutrosophic-driven tool to probe turnover propensities in manufacturing entities. *International Journal of Neutrosophic Science (IJNS), 23*(2).

Khyrina, A., Abu Samah, F., Mohd Khalid, N. A., Jasmis, J., Deraman, L. S. R., & Othman, Z. (2024). Autoregressive Integrated Moving Average (ARIMA) algorithm adaptation for business financial forecasting. *Journal of Advanced Research in Applied Sciences and Engineering Technology, 38*(1), 37–47. <https://doi.org/10.37934/araset.38.1.3747>

Kuchkarov, T., Mamadiyarov, Z., Khakimov, Z., Sabirova, O., Matmurodov, K., Raimboyeva, M., & Umarova, S. (2025). Energy-Related Uncertainty and Crypto-Currency Environmental Attention: Time-Varying Perspective. International Journal of Energy Economics and Policy, *15*(5), 614–626. https://doi.org/10.32479/ijeep.20784

Kuziboev, B., Khodjaniyazov, E., Ozturk, I., Sabirov, K., Makhmudov, S., & Utegenova, S. (2025). Does oil dependence cause energy risk?. Energy Nexus, 17, 100393.

Litamahuputty, J. V., Amiruddin, E. G., Rahim, R., Rahman, A., & Mamadiyarov, Z. (2025). Cryptocurrency Risk Management through Decision Engineering: Evaluating XRPUSD and ADAUSD Portfolio Performance. Journal of Applied Science, Engineering, Technology, and Education, 7(1), 69–81. https://doi.org/10.35877/454RI.asci3871

Lin, M.H., Matchanova, B., Nurmatovich, H.A. *et al.* Optimal Operation of the Multi-Carrier Energy System Considering Energy Markets and Renewable Energies Participation. *Int. J. Appl. Comput. Math* **11**, 170 (2025). https://doi.org/10.1007/s40819-025-02002-9

Malakauskas, A., & Lakštutienė, A. (2021). Financial distress prediction for small and medium enterprises using machine learning techniques. *Engineering Economics, 32*(1), 4–14. <https://doi.org/10.5755/J01.EE.32.1.27382>

Mamadiyarov, Z., Hakimov, H., & Askarov, S. (2024). DEVELOPMENT OF RETAIL BANKING SERVICES IN THE CONTEXT OF DIGITAL TRANSFORMATION. Financial and Credit Activity Problems of Theory and Practice, *1*(54), 51–67. https://doi.org/10.55643/fcaptp.1.54.2024.4288

Mamadiyarov, Z. Makhmudov, S. Utanov, B. Kasimova, D. Bekmurodova, G. Hakimov, Z. (2025). Fusion of Economic and Financial Factors Affecting Household Deposits in Banks: An Econometric Analysis. Fusion: Practice and Applications, (), 82–91. DOI: https://doi.org/10.54216/FPA.190206

Mamani, J.C.M., Miri, M., Vorobev, Y. et al. Optimal Operation of Energy Microgrid Considering Economic and Emission Indices. Oper. Res. Forum 6, 122 (2025). https://doi.org/10.1007/s43069-025-00523-z

Matenda, F. R., Sibanda, M., Chikodza, E., & Gumbo, V. (2020). Corporate default risk modeling under distressed economic and financial conditions in a developing economy. *Journal of Credit Risk*. <https://doi.org/10.21314/JCR.2020.267>

Matyakubova, A., Makhmudov, S., Ozturk, I., Kurbonov, K., Ismailov, F., Yokubboeva, S., & Urozov, A. (2025). Responses of Economic Policy Uncertainty, Financial Stress and Energy-Related Uncertainty to the Shocks in US-China Tension in US. *International Journal of Energy Economics and Policy*, *15*(4), 701–708. https://doi.org/10.32479/ijeep.20369

Nair, J., & Sachdeva, J. K. (2022). Predictive modelling for financial distress amongst manufacturing companies in India. *Journal of Global Economy*, *18*(4), 261–276. <https://doi.org/10.1956/jge.v18i4.665>

PANJAITAN, M. B., HAMDANAH, H., SIRAIT, J., SUTIKNO, S., FATMAWATI, E., HERMAN, H., & MAMADIYAROV, Z. (2025). THE ROLE OF EMOTIONAL REGULATION IN SHAPING STUDENTS' PERCEPTION OF PHYSICS PROBLEMSOLVING TASKS. TPM – Testing, Psychometrics, Methodology in Applied Psychology, 32(S2(2025): Posted 09 June), 1–10. Retrieved from https://tpmap.org/submission/index.php/tpm/article/view/139

Petrova, A. Y., & Deyneka, M. (2022). ARIMA-models: Modeling and forecasting prices of stocks. *Internauka*. <https://doi.org/10.25313/2520-2294-2022-2-7921>

Pradhan, R., Hajiyev, E., Shichiyakh, R. *et al.* Optimal Techno-Economic Feasibility of an Off-Grid Microgrid System Using Load Flow Energy

Management Strategies. *Oper. Res. Forum* **6**, 120 (2025). https://doi.org/10.1007/s43069-025-00524-y

Ran, H. (2023). MABAC method for multiple attribute group decision-making under single-valued neutrosophic sets and applications to performance evaluation of sustainable microfinance group lending. *PLOS ONE*, *18*(1), e0280239.

Romero, R. M., Zelinskaya, M., Makhmudov, S., Sapaev, S., & Rustambekovich, J. U. (2025, September). Modelling and Optimal Utilisation of the Renewable Energy Systems in Microgrid with Improving Reliability and Energy Efficiency. In Operations Research Forum (Vol. 6, No. 3, pp. 1–20). Springer International Publishing.

Samariddin Makhmudov, Malika Umarova, Khayrilla Kurbonov, Laylo Akbarova, Durdona Davletova, Nilufar Shanazarova, and Toshmurod Kulmanov. 2025. Evaluating the forecast indicators of the volume of highly liquid assets of commercial banks in the process of digital transformation. In Proceedings of the 8th International Conference on Future Networks & Distributed Systems (ICFNDS '24). Association for Computing Machinery, New York, NY, USA, 698–704. https://doi.org/10.1145/3726122.3726222

Sharipov, K., Abdullayev, I., Kuziboev, B., Makhmudov, S., Kalandarov, F., Khaytboeva, N., & Ilkhamova, Z. (2025). The Effect of Energy Policy Risk on Renewable Energy. International Journal of Energy Economics and Policy, *15*(2), 566.

Shen, F., Liu, Y., Wang, R., & Zhou, W. (2020). A dynamic financial distress forecast model with multiple forecast results under unbalanced data environment. *Knowledge-Based Systems*, *192*, 105365. <https://doi.org/10.1016/J.KNOSYS.2019.105365>

Su, R., Xiao, Y., Hamza, F., Mamadiyarov, Z., & Wahab, A. (2025). Scaling up green hydrogen in China: Economic opportunities and challenges. *International Journal of Hydrogen Energy*, *131*, 60–69.

Zhang, L., Zhao, Z., Qamri, G. M., & Makhmudov, S. (2025). Unleashing the critical role of renewable energy through global value chains and digitalization: A path towards environmental sustainability. Journal of Environmental Management, 392, 126688.

Zhao, Q., Pervaiz, A., Makhmudov, S., & Fatima, A. (2025). Do environmental stringent policies enhance the impact of renewable energy on CO2 reduction? Evidence from BRICS-T economies. Journal of Environmental Management, 391, 126464.

Zokir Toshtemirovich Mamadiyarov, Samandarboy Adhambek ugli Sulaymanov, Sarvar Anvar ugli Askarov, and Durdona Bakhtiyor kizi Uktamova. 2022. Impact of Covid-19 Pandemic on Accelerating the Digitization and Transformation of Banks. In Proceedings of the 5th International Conference on Future Networks and Distributed Systems (ICFNDS '21). Association for Computing Machinery, New York, NY, USA, 706–712. https://doi.org/10.1145/3508072.3508211

Evaluating the Impact of Human Capital Investment on Economic Processes

Zokir Mamadiyarov, Olmos Ochilov, Samariddin Makhmudov, Khayrilla Kurbonov, Askarjon Samadov, Rasul Salayev, and Saidov Mashal

18.1. Introduction

In their desires to ensure economic growth, the government is focusing on investing in physical capital—magnificent legs, new roads, modern airports, and other infrastructure.

In general, we are not interested in investing in human capital, including the health, knowledge, technology, experience, and lifestyle of the population. This is a big mistake because ignoring investment in human capital can rapidly reduce the country's competitiveness. After all, in order for the state to develop economically, we must train talented people. Investment in human capital is justified only if the profitability and the recovery period of investment are sufficiently high. Thus, when there is an investment policy related to investment in human capital, this is an urgent problem in analyzing risks and evaluating the economic efficiency of investment. Regarding the development of science, technology, and artificial intelligence, human capital is a factor for determining the future of the country. Human capital investment is an investment in the development and enhancement of human abilities and technology, with the ultimate goal of improving productivity. It also represents a strategy that includes time, effort, and financial resources that people study, improve knowledge, restore health, and improve health. This concept recognizes the innate value of an individual and recognizes the long-term benefits related to the investment in socioeconomic growth and people's welfare at the home and social level. Investment in human capital is greatly dependent on the joint efforts of the government, corporations, organizations, and individuals. In this regard, the government develops special programs, allocates funds for education and health care, and creates a favorable environment for education. Companies invest in employees' education and development. You can also invest in yourself for independent management, continuous education, and active personal and professional development. The development of the company and the national economy depends on investment distribution in a timely manner for the number of funds allocated for the development of human capital.

Foreign research shows that today's major sectors in the economic sectors are to increase the effects of investment in human capital, stimulate the economic process, increase labor productivity, and ensure sustainable development strategies. This is considered a key element of people's socioeconomic development, including their knowledge and the formation of technology. Investment in human capital increases not only personal efficiency, but also competitiveness and innovation, which has a significant impact on the size of the national macro economy.

18.2. Literature Review and Development Hypothesis

In assessing the impact of increasing the efficiency of investments in human capital, scientific theoretical studies have been conducted by reputable foreign scientists, and hypotheses developed on the basis of econometric models have been confirmed.

In particular, Tsiklashvili et al. (2023) state that "Investments in human capital are directly related to economic growth." According to the authors' research results, improving the skills and knowledge of the workforce helps to increase the productivity indicators of their knowledge and skills in the regions and increases the need for a strong workforce capable of education and training. According to Khodjaniyazov et al., 2025 "separate sectors such as agriculture and tourism can significantly benefit from targeted human capital investments." According to the authors' research results, effective investment practices in human capital lead to cross-border co-operation in agriculture and the adaptation of the vocational education sector to modern requirements (Khodjaniyazov et al., 2025; Lin et al., 2025; Mamadiyarov et al., 2024; Pradhan et al., 2025; Su et al., 2025).

According to E.M. Sumual et al. (2024), "investments in human capital in the digital era are crucial to adapt to technological changes." According to the authors, education and training programs focused on digital skills will help meet the needs of developing technological processes. According to V.B. Salakhova (2024), "one of the main problems in investing in human capital is the lack of standardized criteria for assessing the effectiveness of investments." The authors' results show that this makes it difficult to assess the profitability of investments and optimize resource allocation.

Evgeny Kotov and Arkady Nikolaevich Silenko in their scientific work noted that "investments in human capital are fraught with risks such as potential mismatches between acquired skills and market requirements." According to the authors, this requires strategic approaches to aligning curricula in the education system with industry needs (Kotov & Silenko, 2024). According to R.E. Janshanlo et al., "investments in higher education significantly increase the quality and relevance of the education provided in the formation of human capital." The authors' research results showed that as a result of investing in education, it helps to develop the intellectual potential of regions and ensure strategic competitive advantage in an innovative economy (Janshanlo et al., 2024).

According to econometric models by Hummerly Dhobha and Elvis Madondo, "Despite large investments in education and health, South Africa has remained economically disadvantaged, with socioeconomic factors hindering the effectiveness of human capital investments (Dhobha et al., 2024)." Also, public spending on human capital health has a positive impact on economic performance, reflecting a positive relationship between increased health spending and GDP growth. Conversely, secondary school enrollment has an inverse relationship with economic growth. Saridogan and Kaya (2019) analyzed the impact of the knowledge economy on economic performance by examining selected economics components of seven main topics in the World Bank KAM methodology Custom Scorecards.

Another group of economists has successfully used econometric models such as Fixed Effects Estimator (FEE), Random Effects Estimator (REE), multivariate linear (LS), and ARDL in their research on investment in digital infrastructure, various aspects of digital payment systems, the impact of inflation and credit interest rates on investment, factors affecting the reduction of the state's share in commercial banks, non-performing loans in commercial banks, the digitalization of banks, risks in digital services, and the development of retail payment services (Cahyani et al., 2025; Kuchkarov et al., 2025; Mamadiyarov, et al., 2025; Litamahuputty et al., 2025; Mamani, et al., 2025; PANJAITAN et al., 2025; Zokir et al., 2021).

In their study, Shaodong Shi and Xinbo Wang "used Bayesian quantum regression models to better understand the dynamic impact of human capital on economic growth." The authors found that, according to the results of the econometric model, the contribution of human capital to GDP growth during the high-speed growth phase was 16.2 ± 3.1%, and during the period of adjustment of the structure of industrial sectors, it increased to 23.8 ± 3.4% (Shi & Wang, 2024). According to the scientific work of T. Tsetsiarynets, "Econometric models made it possible to assess the effectiveness of investments in human capital in Belarus, taking into account the processes of formation, accumulation and capitalization of human capital in the state (Tsetsiarynets, 2023)." According to the author's research, it is noted that despite the increase in the volume of social and environmental financing for the development of human capital from 2015 to 2021, a significant decrease in the rural population was observed. In a world of growing competition and rapid change, the importance of strategic human resource practices become more essential each day. One of these is the orientation training, which plays an important function in the life of the company by helping employees to become acquainted with the culture of the company, the business environment, and functions as rapidly as possible (Unluonen & Boylu, 2016).

Analyses and forecasts have been conducted using multivariate linear regression (LS), ARDL, ARIMA, and other various econometric models on factors affecting remittances, energy intensity and economic development, energy policy, energy risk, environmental status and the impact of environmental aspects on the digital economy, agricultural productivity, and the stability of the U.S. credit market (Abdullah, et al., 2025; Caporin et al., 2024; Hussain et al., 2023; Jahrir et al., 2025; Kuziboev et al., 2025; Mamadiyarov et al., 2025; Samariddin et al., 2024; Sharipov et al., 2025; Yin et al., 2024 Zhao et al., 2025). According to Sadik Aden Dirir et al., "formulate hypotheses on the potential of human capital investment in contributing to economic growth in Eastern and Southern African countries, using the (ARDL) model and Granger causality tests". The authors found that the education level of the population, public spending on education, and the labor force had a positive impact on economic growth in the region in the long and short run, based on data from 2001 to 2020 (Dirir, 2023; Romero et al., 2025; Rukhiddin et al., 2025).

18.3. Research Methodology

In this study, econometric equations were developed based on the Pooled Ordinary Least Squares (POLS) estimator, FEE, and REE models based on panel data of eight enterprises operating in Uzbekistan, using data sources covering a five-year period from 2020 to 2024, to increase the efficiency of investments in human capital, consisting of a total number of observations of 40 indicators. In the study, a correlation matrix, graphic and visual plots, and descriptive statistical analyses were developed to assess the relationship between the outcome variable and the independent variables affecting it.

Also, during the study, test indicators were evaluated using the Hausman test between the FEE and REE models to determine the optimal econometric model. The VIF test was used to determine the multicollinearity of the outcome variable and the independent variables affecting it. The panel effect model is a comprehensive statistical method for modeling and formulating economic processes in panel data. Pooled effects model in panel data is a comprehensive statistical method for modeling and modeling economic processes.

The POLS estimator model looks like this.

$$y_{it} = \delta_0 + \delta_1 x_{it1} + \beta_2 x_{it2} + \ldots + \delta_k x_{itl} + \varepsilon_{it} \quad (1)$$

$i = 1, \ldots, n$; $t = 1, \ldots, t$, and *it* represents the number of observations.

Here, y_{it} is the resultant factor for the cross-sectional unit *i* at time *t*; x_{it1}, $x_{it2}, \ldots, x_{itl}$ are the independent variables for the cross-sectional unit *i* at time *t*; δ_0 is the intercept term, $\delta_1, \ldots, \delta_k$ are the coefficients of the independent variables; ε_{it} is the error term, which is the deviation of the actual *yit* from the value predicted by the model.

The FEE model is expressed as follows:

$$(Y_{it} - Y_i^-) = \beta(x_{it} - x_i^-) + (\epsilon_{it} - \epsilon_i^-) \quad (2)$$

The REE model is a versatile statistical tool in econometric research and is effective in analyzing data with internal correlation and identifying variability along different dimensions.

The REE model is expressed as:

$$y_{it} = \alpha + x_{it}\beta + \eta_i + \varepsilon_{it} \quad (3)$$

18.4. Analysis and Results

According to the study, the dependent and independent variables *Ln_AT_ratio* on the impact of increasing the efficiency of investments in human capital were expressed as follows. All factors were natural logarithmized.

LnROIHC—Return on investment in human capital (dependent variable),
Ln_AT_ratio—Return on assets coefficient (independent variable),
Ln_ROA—Return on assets (independent variable).
Ln_ROE—Return on equity (independent variable).

The following hypotheses were reflected in the construction of the econometric model for the study.

Null hypothesis (H0): There is no statistically significant relationship between variables such as return on assets coefficient, return on equity, and return on investment in human capital of enterprises in the national economy.

Alternative Hypothesis (Ha): In the national economy, enterprises have a statistically significant relationship between variables such as return on assets, return on equity, and return on investment in human capital. At the initial stage of the study, descriptive statistical indicators on return on investment in human capital and the variables affecting it were as follows (Table 67).

Table 67. Descriptive statistics on return on investment in human capital and the variables affecting it

	LnROIHC	*Ln_AT_ratio*	*Ln_ROA*	*Ln_ROE*
Mean	3.747618	4.105642	1.114196	1.84746
Maximum	6.833608	6.042299	6.042299	4.175333
Minimum	−0.2725926	1.154664	-3.48209	-1.886216
Std. Dev	1.59061	1.247027	1.844993	1.532305*x*
Std. err.	0.0265106	0.0214765	0.0307488	0.0255384
Skewness	−0.492929	−0.5314837	−0.5267428	−0.3977949
Kurtosis	2.964368	2.533043	2.535376	2.341619
Observation	39	39	39	39

Source: It was developed by the authors based on Stata software.

The data in Table 67 show that the return on investment in human capital in enterprises is positive. The average value of the resulting variable indicates that enterprises are receiving positive and significant returns from investments in capital. The average standard deviation of positive values indicates that the observations are concentrated around the average with several extreme values. The asset turnover ratio has an average value of 4.1056, which indicates that enterprises use assets effectively to generate income. Accordingly, the relatively low standard deviation (1.2470) indicates the financial consistency of the turnover of enterprise assets according to the observations, which in this case directly affects the investments in human capital by enterprises.

The return on equity (Ln_ROE) in the table data is 1.8475 on average, indicating a healthy return on equity and is important in strengthening the sustainability of investments in human capital. The dependent and independent variables show standard deviations, which indicate changes in the average level of enterprises, and the standard errors are relatively small, indicating reliable model forecasts.

In the next stage of the study, an analytical graphical representation of the return on investment in human capital and the factors affecting it over time was presented (Figure 77).

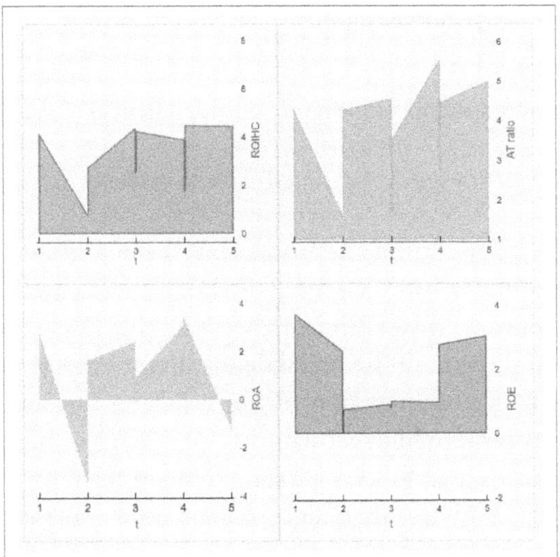

Figure 77. Analytical graphical representation of the return on investment in human capital and the factors affecting it over time.

Source: It was developed by the authors based on Stata software.

In the data of Figure 77, the resulting variable shows fluctuations, reflecting the dynamics of growth and shows the progressive return on investment in human capital of enterprises. Also, the periodic decrease of this variable suggests strategic reinvestments and changes in external conditions over a certain period, which indicates the stability of the forecast in the future.

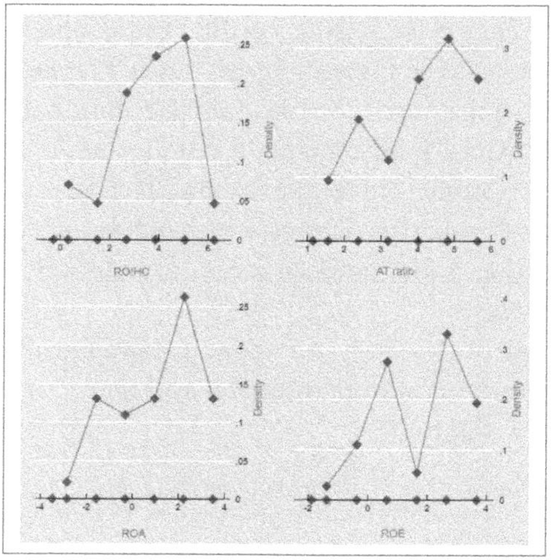

Figure 78. A connected picture of the return on investment in human capital and the factors affecting it.

Source: It was developed by the authors based on Stata software.

At the next stage of the study, the histogram of the normal probability distribution of dependent and independent variables was analyzed. Figure 78 shows the distribution and relationship between the return on investment in human capital and the main financial determinants affecting it: the density graph. A significant concentration of the resulting variable indicates that many enterprises achieve high returns on investment in human capital.

The ROA density graph follows a strong trend in the return on investment in human capital, showing that high returns on these assets lead to high efficiency in labor investment. In this case, it emphasizes the importance of asset management based on profitability in improving labor efficiency. One of the important aspects of this correlation graph is that the distribution of the ROE indicator peaks at high values, indicating that high returns can be obtained for enterprises with strong shareholder returns. This serves to ensure the long-term financial sustainability of investments in human capital.

According to the study, an analytical graphical matrix and scatter plot of the dependent and independent variables were developed. Figures 79 and 80 indicate a strong correlation and density between all variables. The dependent variable presents a consistent positive relationship between the return on investment in human capital and the factors affecting it.

According to the analytical images, it shows a promising forecast for enterprises that strategically manage the efficiency, profitability, and capital gains of their assets. By improving the indicators of these factors, enterprises have the opportunity to maximize their profits through traditional and alternative financing of the workforce, which creates the basis for the formation of sustainable growth and improved financial indicators in enterprises.

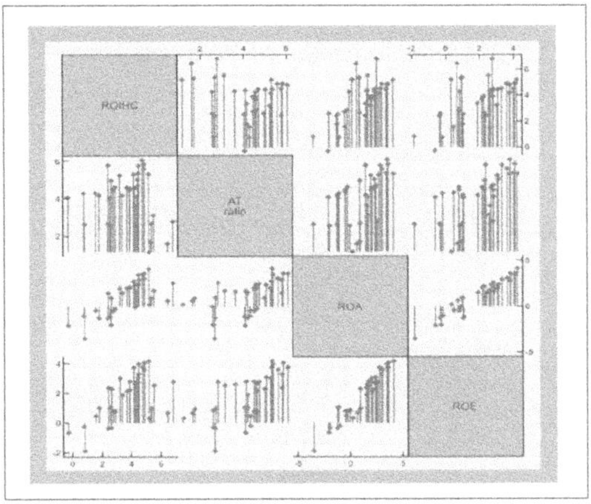

Figure 79. Graphical matrix of the relationship between return on investment in human capital and the factors affecting it.

Source: It was developed by the authors based on Stata software.

At the next stage of the study, a correlation matrix was developed for each of the factors affecting the return on investment in human capital. Table 68 shows that the results showed a significant, strong, and inverse correlation between the dependent variable and its influencing factors. The correlation matrix also showed that there was no multicollinearity between the dependent and independent variables.

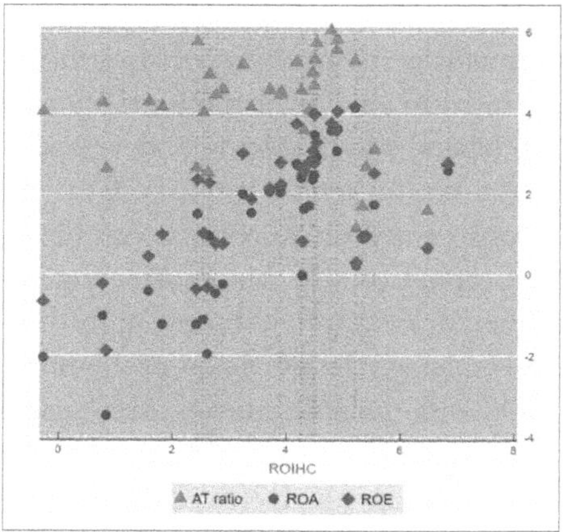

Figure 80. Scatter plot of the relationship between return on investment in human capital and factors influencing it.

Source: It was developed by the authors based on Stata software.

Table 68. Correlation matrix of dependent and independent variables

Variables	(1)	(2)	(3)	(4)
LnROIHC	1.000			
Ln_AT_ratio	−0.4139	1.000		
	(0.0405)			**
Ln_ROA	0.7872	0.5463	1.000	
	(0.0000)	(0.0000)		***
Ln_ROE	0.5875	0.6706	0.8564	1.000
	(0.0002)	(0.0000)	(0.0000)	***

Source: It was developed by the authors based on Stata software.

In the next step of the study, the parameters of the econometric equations, POLSE, FEE, and REE models were developed (Tables 69–71).

At the same time, the Hausman test was used to assess the adequacy of the model indicators for the FEE and REE.

The POLSE model developed for the study was as follows.

$$LnROIHC = 6.46 - 1.03LnAT\_\text{ratio} + 0.66LnROA + 0.42LnROE + \varepsilon \quad (4)$$

The study tested the hypotheses using the POLSE model. The dependent variable (y) is equal to zero according to the null hypothesis (H0), but it is different from zero according to the alternative hypothesis (H1).

Table 69. Pooled OLS estimator (POLSE) model parameters

LnROIHC	*Coef.*	*St.Err.*	*t-value*	*p-value*	*[95% Conf*	*Interval]*	*Sig*
LnAT_ratio	−1.035	0.101	−10.25	0	−1.241	−0.829	***
LnROA	0.663	0.179	3.70	0.001	0.298	1.028	***
LnROE	0.43	0.244	1.77	0.087	−0.066	0.926	*
Constant	6.464	0.312	20.70	0	5.828	7.1	***
Mean dependent var		3.748	SD dependent var			1.591	
R-squared		0.905	Number of obs			36	
F-test		101.631	Prob > *F*			0.000	
Akaike crit. (AIC)		57.821	Bayesian crit. (BIC)			64.155	

*** $p < 0.01$, ** $p < 0.05$, * $p < 0.1$

Source: It was developed by the authors based on Stata software.

The test results show that the t-statistic and F-statistic showed a significance level of less than 0.05, which indicates the acceptance of the alternative hypothesis and the rejection of the null hypothesis. The POLS model also shows a high R-square of 0.90, indicating a good model quality.

Result: A 1% increase in the ROA of the analyzed enterprises in the national economy leads to a 1.03% decrease in the return on investment in human capital in these enterprises. A 1% increase in the ROA coefficient of the analyzed enterprises in the national economy leads to a 0.66% increase in the return on investment in human capital in these enterprises. Also, a 1% increase in the ROE coefficient of the analyzed enterprises in the national economy leads to a 0.43% increase in the return on investment in human capital in these enterprises.

1. *REE model analysis*. The econometric equation indicators for the REE model for the study are presented in Table 70.

Table 70. Random effects estimator (REE) model parameters

LnROIHC	Coef.	St.Err.	*t*-value	*p*-value	[95% Conf	Interval]	Sig
LnAT_ratio	−0.861	0.143	−6.02	0	−1.142	−0.581	***
LnROA	0.745	0.16	4.65	0	0.431	1.059	***
LnROE	0.342	0.201	1.71	0.088	−0.051	0.735	*
Constant	5.799	0.584	9.93	0	4.654	6.943	***
Mean dependent var		3.748	SD dependent var		1.591		
Overall R-squared		0.886	Number of obs		36		
Chi-square		287.548	Prob > chi²		0.000		
R-squared within		0.902	R-squared between		0.891		
*** $p < 0.01$, ** $p < 0.05$, * $p < 0.1$.							

Source: It was developed by the authors based on Stata software.

The REE model developed for the study was as follows.

$$LnROIHC_{it} = 5.79 - 0.86LnAT\_ratio_{it} + 0.74LnROA_{it} + 0.34LnROE_{it} + u_i + \varepsilon_{it} \quad (6)$$

The chi-square statistic according to the REE model was 287.54, indicating a good fit between the actual and expected values. This indicates that the model fits the data and confirms the positive prediction of the outcome variable by the independent variables.

According to the econometric model, a model with an R-square value of 0.90 explains 90% of the variability. This indicates the suitability of the model during the data collection process and indicates the significant predictive effect of the influencing factors on the outcome variable. For the study, the REE model was designed as follows.

Result: A 1% increase in the ROA of the analyzed enterprises in the national economy leads to a decrease in the return on investment in human capital in these enterprises by 0.86%. A 1% increase in the ROA coefficient of the analyzed enterprises in the national economy leads to an increase in the return on investment in human capital in these enterprises by 0.74%. Also, a 1% increase in the ROE coefficient of the analyzed enterprises in the national economy leads to an increase in the return on investment in human capital in these enterprises by 0.34%.

2. *FEE model analysis*. The econometric equation indicators for the FEE model for the study are presented in Table 71. The FEE model developed in the study was as follows.

$$LnROIHC_{it} = 4.84 - 0.62LnAT\_ratio_{it} + 0.72ROA_{it} + 0.34LnROE_{it} + u_i + \varepsilon_{it} \quad (7)$$

As shown in Table 18.5, the observed value was 57.92. The *R*-squared coefficient was also 0.58, which produced positive values.

Table 71. Fixed effects estimator (FEE) model parameters

LnROIHC	*Coef.*	*St.Err.*	*t-value*	*p-value*	*[95% Conf*	*Interval]*	*Sig*
LnAT_ratio	−0.62	0.206	−3.02	0.006	−1.044	−0.197	***
LnROA	0.721	0.171	4.20	0	0.368	1.074	***
LnROE	0.348	0.209	1.67	0.098	−0.082	0.778	*
Constant	4.849	0.819	5.92	0	3.162	6.536	***
Mean dependent var		3.748	SD dependent var			1.591	
R-squared		0.907	Number of obs			36	
F-test		81.550	Prob > F			0.000	
Akaike crit. (AIC)		14.849	Bayesian crit. (BIC)			21.184	
*** $p < 0.01$, ** $p < 0.05$, * $p < 0.1$							

Source: It was developed by the authors based on Stata software.

Result: A 1% increase in the ROA coefficient of the analyzed enterprises in the national economy causes a 0.62% decrease in the return on investment in human capital in these enterprises. A 1% increase in the ROA coefficient of the analyzed enterprises in the national economy leads to an increase in the return on investment in human capital in these enterprises by 0.72%. Also, a 1% increase in the ROE coefficient of the analyzed enterprises in the national economy results in a 0.34% increase in the return on investment in human capital in these enterprises.

18.5. Conclusion

As a result of the analysis and conclusions of the study on the interaction of variables such as ROA, return on equity, and return on investment in human capital of unselected enterprises in the national economy, the following proposals and recommendations were developed.

1. Based on the panel data, the three models mentioned earlier were used to analyze the factors affecting the return on investment in national human capital. In addition, according to the results of comparing the REE model and the FEE models, we concluded that the REE model is suitable for their analysis. This conclusion is based on the fact that the *p*-value of the Hausman test is $p = 0.38$, and the REE model was selected as the optimal model over the FEE model.
2. Assessment of the impact of ROA as a key factor of growth. An increase in ROA by 1% leads to an increase in the return on investment in human capital by 0.74%, which indicates that companies that use their assets effectively generate higher returns on investments in human capital. According to this result, it is possible to significantly increase the efficiency of human capital and value creation by optimizing asset productivity.
3. Assessment of ROE as a key factor in ensuring the growth of human capital. According to the econometric model, a 1% increase in ROE leads to a 0.34% increase in return on human capital investment. According to this result, enterprises that generate high returns to shareholders also create high value for human capital, emphasizing the importance of profitability and financial stability in developing human capital.

Bibliography

Abdullah, M. A., Han, X., Amjad, M. A., & Makhmudov, S. (2025). Revisit the role of financial development on economic growth, human development, and sustainable development in higher-income countries. Journal of Environmental Management, 392, 126874.

Cahyani, I., Buriev, K., Ngongo, M., Mamadiyarov, Z., Ino, L., Herman, H., Saputra, N., & Baxtishodovich, S. (2025). Exploring the Use of TikTok Application in Enhancing the Skill of Pronunciation: A Case on Students' Perception. Studies in Media and Communication, *13*(2), 150–158. doi:http://dx.doi.org/10.11114/smc.v13i2.7553

Caporin, M., Shahbaz, M., Kuziboev, B., Masharipova, M., Allaberganov, S., & Makhmudov, S. (2024). Environmental Kuznets Curve for extended brics economies: do women governance and water stress matter?. International Journal of Energy Economics and Policy, *14*(6), 174–183.

Dhobha, H., & Madondo, E. (2024). The role of human capital investment in economic growth: a study of South Africa. *International Journal of Business Ecosystem & Strategy (2687–2293)*, *6*(5), 138–145.

Dirir, S. A. (2023). The potential of human capital investment in contributing to economic growth: ARDL approach in the context of eastern and southern Africa. *Eurasian Journal of Economic and Business Studies*, *67*(1), 52–69.

Hussain, A., Khan, M., Rakhmonov, D. A., Mamadiyarov, Z. T., Kurbonbekova, M. T., & Mahmudova, M. Q. K. (2023). Nexus of Training and Development, Organizational Learning Capability, and Organizational Performance in the Service Sector. Sustainability, *15*(4), 3246. https://doi.org/10.3390/su15043246

Jahrir, A., Gultom, Y., Herman, H., Zabadi, F., Ngongo, M., Mamadiyarov, Z., Fatmawati, E., & Saputra, N. (2025). Investigating the Elements of Short Commercial Mineral Water Advertisement: A Case on Discourse Analysis. Studies in Media and Communication, *13*(4), 94–104. doi:http://dx.doi.org/10.11114/smc.v13i4.7813

Janshanlo, R. E., Kogut, O. Y., Aktureeva, E. A., & Kupenova, Z. K. (2024). Evaluation of the effectiveness of investments into human capital at the macro level. *Journal of Economic Research & Business Administration*, *2*(148), 84–95.

Khodjaniyazov, N., Mirkhoshimova, M., Kalandarov, F., Matyokubova, D., Utegenova, S., Makhmudov, S., & Khudayberganov, M. (2025). Time-Varying Impacts of Financial Stress on Energy-Related Uncertainty. International Journal of Energy Economics and Policy, *15*(3), 689–698.

Kotov, E., & Silenko, A. N. (2024). Human capital development technologies as resource base for industrial development. *Vestnik Kemerovskogo Gosudarstvennogo Universiteta*, 253–262. <https://doi.org/10.21603/2500-3372-2024-9-2-253-262>

Kuchkarov, T., Mamadiyarov, Z., Khakimov, Z., Sabirova, O., Matmurodov, K., Raimboyeva, M., & Umarova, S. (2025). Energy-Related Uncertainty and Crypto-Currency Environmental Attention: Time-Varying Perspective. International Journal of Energy Economics and Policy, *15*(5), 614–626. https://doi.org/10.32479/ijeep.20784

Kuziboev, B., Khodjaniyazov, E., Ozturk, I., Sabirov, K., Makhmudov, S., & Utegenova, S. (2025). Does oil dependence cause energy risk?. Energy Nexus, *17*, 100393.

Lin, M.H., Matchanova, B., Nurmatovich, H.A. *et al.* Optimal Operation of the Multi-Carrier Energy System Considering Energy Markets and Renewable Energies Participation. *Int. J. Appl. Comput. Math* **11**, 170 (2025). https://doi.org/10.1007/s40819-025-02002-9

Litamahuputty, J. V., Amiruddin, E. G., Rahim, R., Rahman, A., & Mamadiyarov, Z. (2025). Cryptocurrency Risk Management through Decision Engineering: Evaluating XRPUSD and ADAUSD Portfolio Performance. Journal of Applied Science, Engineering, Technology, and Education, *7*(1), 69–81. https://doi.org/10.35877/454RI.asci3871

Mamani, J.C.M., Miri, M., Vorobev, Y. et al. Optimal Operation of Energy Microgrid Considering Economic and Emission Indices. Oper. Res. Forum 6, 122 (2025). https://doi.org/10.1007/s43069-025-00523-z

Mamadiyarov, Z., Eshov, M., Otakhonova, D., Utegenova, S., Sabirov, K., Marks, A., & Bahodirov, N. (2025). Does Energy Policy Risk Threaten Energy Sources Diversification?. International Journal of Energy Economics and Policy, *15*(5), 730–740. https://doi.org/10.32479/ijeep.21140

Mamadiyarov, Z., Hakimov, H., & Askarov, S. (2024). DEVELOPMENT OF RETAIL BANKING SERVICES IN THE CONTEXT OF DIGITAL TRANSFORMATION. *Financial and Credit Activity Problems of Theory and Practice*, *1*(54), 51–67. https://doi.org/10.55643/fcaptp.1.54.2024.4288

Mamadiyarov, Z. Makhmudov, S. Utanov, B. Kasimova, D. Bekmurodova, G. Hakimov, Z. (2025). Fusion of Economic and Financial Factors Affecting Household Deposits in Banks: An Econometric Analysis.

Fusion: Practice and Applications, (), 82–91. DOI: https://doi.org/10.54216/FPA.190206

Matyakubova, A., Makhmudov, S., Ozturk, I., Kurbonov, K., Ismailov, F., Yokubboeva, S., & Urozov, A. (2025). Responses of Economic Policy Uncertainty, Financial Stress and Energy-Related Uncertainty to the Shocks in US-China Tension in US. *International Journal of Energy Economics and Policy*, *15*(4), 701–708. https://doi.org/10.32479/ijeep.20369

Muhammad Zubair, Irfanud Din, Nadeem Sarwar et al. Revolutionizing Sepsis Diagnosis Using Machine Learning and Deep Learning Models: A Systematic Literature Review, 10 June 2025, PREPRINT (Version 1) available at Research Square [https://doi.org/10.21203/rs.3.rs-6731418/v1]

PANJAITAN, M. B., HAMDANAH, H., SIRAIT, J., SUTIKNO, S., FATMAWATI, E., HERMAN, H., & MAMADIYAROV, Z. (2025). THE ROLE OF EMOTIONAL REGULATION IN SHAPING STUDENTS' PERCEPTION OF PHYSICS PROBLEMSOLVING TASKS. TPM – Testing, Psychometrics, Methodology in Applied Psychology, 32(S2(2025): Posted 09 June), 1–10. Retrieved from https://tpmap.org/submission/index.php/tpm/article/view/139

Pradhan, R., Hajiyev, E., Shichiyakh, R. *et al.* Optimal Techno-Economic Feasibility of an Off-Grid Microgrid System Using Load Flow Energy Management Strategies. *Oper. Res. Forum* **6**, 120 (2025). https://doi.org/10.1007/s43069-025-00524-y

Romero, R. M., Zelinskaya, M., Makhmudov, S., Sapaev, S., & Rustambekovich, J. U. (2025, September). Modelling and Optimal Utilisation of the Renewable Energy Systems in Microgrid with Improving Reliability and Energy Efficiency. In Operations Research Forum (Vol. 6, No. 3, pp. 1–20). Springer International Publishing.

Rukhiddin Zayniddinov, Nodir Jumaev, Gulbakhor Irgasheva, Alam Asadov, Nosir Makhmudov, Sirojiddin Abrorov, and Samariddin Makhmudov. 2025. The Influence of the Digital Economy on Economic Development Evidence from Uzbekistan. In Proceedings of the 8th International Conference on Future Networks & Distributed Systems (ICFNDS '24). Association for Computing Machinery, New York, NY, USA, 831–839. https://doi.org/10.1145/3726122.3726242

Sarıdoğan, H. Ö. & Kaya, M. V. (2019). Knowledge economy and economic performance: A comparison between Turkey and the

European Union. *Mehmet Akif Ersoy University Journal of Economics and Administrative Sciences*, *6*(3), 916–935.

Salakhova, V. B. (2024). Investments in human potential and human capital as a leading factor of economic development. *Obŝestvo: Politika, Èkonomika, Pravo*. <https://doi.org/10.24158/pep.2024.1.12>

Samariddin Makhmudov, Malika Umarova, Khayrilla Kurbonov, Laylo Akbarova, Durdona Davletova, Nilufar Shanazarova, and Toshmurod Kulmanov. 2025. Evaluating the forecast indicators of the volume of highly liquid assets of commercial banks in the process of digital transformation. In Proceedings of the 8th International Conference on Future Networks & Distributed Systems (ICFNDS '24). Association for Computing Machinery, New York, NY, USA, 698–704. https://doi.org/10.1145/3726122.3726222

Sharipov, K., Abdullayev, I., Kuziboev, B., Makhmudov, S., Kalandarov, F., Khaytboeva, N., & Ilkhamova, Z. (2025). The Effect of Energy Policy Risk on Renewable Energy. International Journal of Energy Economics and Policy, *15*(2), 566.

Shi, S., & Wang, X. (2024). Analysis of human capital effects introducing Bayesian quantile regression in the process of industrial structural upgrading. *PLOS One*, *19*(7), e0304730.

Su, R., Xiao, Y., Hamza, F., Mamadiyarov, Z., & Wahab, A. (2025). Scaling up green hydrogen in China: Economic opportunities and challenges. *International Journal of Hydrogen Energy*, *131*, 60–69.

Sumual, T., Lumapow, H., & Rotty, V. (2024). The role of human capital investment in improving the quality of human resources (HR) in education in the digital era. *Asian Journal of Engineering, Social and Health*, *3*(11), 2520–2528.

Tsetsiarynets, T. (2023). Investments in human capital development: analysis and evaluation of efficiency of use. *Agrarian Economics*, (1), 38–49.

Tsiklashvili, N., Jabnidze, N., Beridze, T., & Turmanidze, T. (2023, January). Investments in human capital and its effectiveness. In *Economic Science for Rural Development Conference Proceedings* (No. 57).

Unluonen, M. B., & Boylu, Y. (2016). İşe Alıştırma eğitimlerinin iş tatmini üzerindeki etkisi: Otel işletmelerinde bir araştırma. *Journal of Business Research—Turk*, *8*(2), 407–426.

Zhao, Q., Pervaiz, A., Makhmudov, S., & Fatima, A. (2025). Do environmental stringent policies enhance the impact of renewable energy on CO2 reduction? Evidence from BRICS-T economies. Journal of Environmental Management, 391, 126464.

Zokir Toshtemirovich Mamadiyarov, Samandarboy Adhambek ugli Sulaymanov, Sarvar Anvar ugli Askarov, and Durdona Bakhtiyor kizi Uktamova. 2022. Impact of Covid-19 Pandemic on Accelerating the Digitization and Transformation of Banks. In Proceedings of the 5th International Conference on Future Networks and Distributed Systems (ICFNDS '21). Association for Computing Machinery, New York, NY, USA, 706–712. https://doi.org/10.1145/3508072.3508211

Forecasting of Grain Crops Productivity Based on Brown and Hold Models

Gulizahro Turayeva, Shoh-Jakhon Rakhmat ogli Khamdamov, Fakhriddin Ikromovich Isayev, Komil Rabbimovich Khotamov, Nurbek Kadirovich Rizaev, and Nafisa Mukhammadiyeva

19.1. Introduction

Ensuring food security and sustainable agriculture is a pressing global challenge, especially in regions that rely heavily on crop production. In Uzbekistan, agriculture plays a key role in the economy, with grain crops accounting for a significant portion of the country's agricultural output. The Syrdarya region, known for its favorable agro-climatic conditions, is a key supplier of grain to Uzbekistan. However, yield fluctuations due to climate variability, soil degradation, and inconsistent farming practices pose challenges to maintaining stable productivity.

In New Uzbekistan, crop development in the food industry is being advanced through modern processing methods to ensure stable production of its products, market supply, clusters, and co-operatives in the production–consumption chain. Comprehensive measures are being implemented in areas such as the optimization of integration processes and improvement of organizational and economic mechanisms by means of communications (Decision PD-22 of the President of the Republic of Uzbekistan, 2023).

19.2. Literature Review

Accurate forecasting of grain crop productivity is a multifaceted challenge influenced by a variety of factors. These factors range from meteorological conditions and soil properties to technological advancements in data analysis and machine learning (Kurbonov et al., 2023; Turayeva, 2023a). The integration of these elements into predictive models is crucial for enhancing the accuracy of yield forecasts, which are vital for agricultural planning and resource management.

Population growth and CO_2 emissions are significant socio-economic factors influencing cereal production predictions. These factors are crucial in developing countries where agricultural practices are closely tied to demographic changes (Makhmudov et al., 2023; Salimov et al., 2023; Turayeva et al., 2022).

Long-term forecasting models that incorporate historical yield data and environmental factors, such as climate change and sanctions, can reduce prediction errors over extended periods (Mamadiyorov et al., 2023; Turayeva, 2023b).

Many scientific research works have been conducted on creating econometric models of the processes of growing agricultural products in the regions and forecasting their prospects in economic sectors to ensure food security for the population.

Among the economists contributing to this field are C. G'ulomov, D. S. Allamatova, and B. E. The works of Mamarakhimov and others can be cited. In the studies of country's scientists Gulomov and Allamatova (2016), the issues of the development of the agricultural sector in the regions were comprehensively studied, in which the state's policy on ensuring food security and the role of innovations in the development of the agrarian sector in the regions were shown. Mamarakhimov (2016) has also studied the issues of development of the agricultural sector, and in his opinion, ensuring food security in the region is mainly carried out at the expense of the development of its own agricultural production and domestic sales markets, and partly at the expense of importing food products from abroad. The expediency is shown. Foreign scientists Lekhilovsky et al. (2012) paid special attention in their research to the issues of promoting the agricultural sector to ensure food security in the regions. However, in the studies of the aforementioned scientists, at the regional level, in particular, in the case of the Syrdarya region, the cultivation of the main types of agricultural products, forecasting, and the study of socio-economic problems in this area have not been sufficiently studied. From this point of view, the issues of modeling the processes of agricultural production, regional development, state support, and future forecasting remain relevant today.

This research work is devoted to the issues of exponential smoothing of the yield dynamics of agricultural products, optimization of adaptation parameters of Brown and Holt models (Holt et al., 2008). Also, multi-variant forecast indicators of grain product yield until 2026 have been developed in Syrdarya region.

19.3. Results and Discussions

According to the Resolution No. 546 of the Cabinet of Ministers of the Republic of Uzbekistan (2020), the measures for the cultivation of spiked grain in 2021 were developed to ensure stable prices for grain and bread products in the domestic market. The quantity of grain at free prices based on futures, forward contracts, or through stock exchanges shopping is marked. This had an important impact on solving the problems of ensuring the stability of grain production and strengthening social stability. Also, grain cultivation in agriculture and grain industry play an important role in ensuring food security in the world, satisfying the population's material needs and requirements for bread and bakery products to a certain extent. According to the Food and Agriculture Organization of the United Nations (FAO) and the World Health Organization, more than 840 million people in the world do not have enough to eat—not even a single piece of bread, let alone other products in the consumer basket. This is almost one in eight of the world's population. In addition, more than 30 percent of the population of the planet is experiencing the problem of malnutrition, lack of the most basic microelements and vitamins (Bobakulov et al., 2024; Bobamuratova et al., 2019). Accordingly, in our research work, regulatory models were planned and values of economic indicators were calculated to ensure sustainable grain cultivation.

There is a quantitative economic and mathematical model of sustainable grain production, which can be divided into descriptive and normative types. All these are the past period or base period and the future periods, depending on the quantitative data entered into the model.

Table 72. Determination of period intervals, basis methods, and sliding averages in determining the dynamics of grain products grown in Syrdarya region

Years	2021	2022	2023
Grain production output (thousand tons)	493,345	478,384	513,234

Source: Based on the author's development.

The descriptive method of economic and mathematical model of periods of sustainable grain cultivation is the time reflection method, which is divided into statistical and dynamic methods.

As an example, when determining the dynamics of grain products grown in the Syrdarya region, we can consider the relationship between periods, basic methods, and moving averages as follows. 493,345 thousand tons in 2021, 478,384 thousand tons in 2022, and contributed by producing 513,234 thousand tons of grain in 2023 (Table 72). By determining the absolute change of this gross yield in the basic method, we can determine the gross yield in the difference of years by the analytical indicators of the dynamic series. (See Table 73) The absolute change of the gross yield is determined using the following formula.

$$DY_{\beta} = Y_i - Y_0 \quad (1)$$

Table 73. Determination of period intervals, basis methods, and sliding averages in determining the dynamics of grain products grown in Syrdarya region

Absolutely Change	Sometimes Method	Dynamic of the Line Analytical Indicator
$DY_{\beta} = Y_1 - Y_0$	478,384–493,345	–14,961
$DY_{\beta} = Y_2 - Y_1$	513,234–478,384	34,850

Source: Based on the author's development.

Based on the information in Table 73, the index of dynamic line of accounted results in 2022 differs with the amount of –14,961 thousand tons compared to 2021, while in 2023 this trend differs from 2022 with the amount of 34,850 thousand tons. The power of influence of dynamic average annual total crop of produced wheat increases in comparison to initial period of current term, and it simplifies the economic and statistic analysis and conclusive benefit (Gafurov et al., 2022; Mamatkulov, 2023). The expansion of periodic intervals was determined by comparing dynamic average productivity using the formula as in what follows.

$$D_{\gamma} = DY_t / n \quad (2)$$

Table 74. Expansion of period ranges and moving average of productivity

Years	Cultivate d Grain Product	3 Years Old According to K E NGAIT Periods	Average (thousand tons)	A Slip Average Count	Slippery Average Value (Thousand Tons)
2021	493,345	(493345+ 478384 + 513234) : 3	494,988	-	-
2022	478,384			(493,345 + 478,384 + 513,234) : 3	494988
2023	513,234			(478,384 + 513,234) : 2	495809

Source: Based on the author's development.

The data in Table 74 shows that the average value of the rolling average for 3 years is 493,345 thousand tons in 2021, 494,988 thousand tons in 2022, and 495,809 thousand tons in 2023, and the volume of grain produced in the Syrdarya region is steadily increasing over the period in which the rolling averages are calculated. In our research work, we considered methods of ensuring sustainable grain production using the time reflection method, specifically economic and mathematical models such as statistical and dynamic methods. It is also necessary to consider other classifications of economic and mathematical models in dynamic models for ensuring sustainable yield.

One of the most important methods for determining the trend in dynamic series in statistical and dynamic models for ensuring sustainable grain production is analytical smoothing.

In statistical models for ensuring sustainable grain production, the characteristics of the object under study are characterized at a single time, most often in one year. In dynamic models, the characteristics of the studied object are presented in several periods.

There are other classifications of economic and mathematical models, but the main ones given earlier are sufficient to solve the economic and mathematical problem of ensuring the sustainability of grain production.

The smoothed value of the series observation S_t relative to the time point t is determined by the following formula:

$$S_t = \alpha g_t + (1 - \alpha) S_{t-1} \tag{3}$$

where α is the smoothing parameter describing the weight of the observation being smoothed, which satisfies the condition $0 < \alpha < 1$. Using the exponential average in short-term forecasting requires the following expression as a series model:

$$y_t = a_{1,t} + \varepsilon_t \tag{4}$$

where $a_{1,t}$ is the average level of the variable series over time; ε_t is an uncorrelated random deviation with zero mathematical expectation and variance σ^2. By $\bar{y}_t(t)$ we denote the value of the forecast made one time unit (step) ahead at time t. The concept of exponential averaging can be generalized to the case of a slightly higher order of exponential averaging.

After the exponential averages S_t are calculated according to the formula, they themselves form a new time series. We define their limits by $S_t^{(1)}$. A superscript indicates that the string is the result of the first alignment. This series can be smoothed again by the following expression similar to formula:

$$S_t^{(2)} = aS_t^{(1)} + bS^{(2)}_{t-1} \tag{5}$$

The resulting smoothed $S_t^{(2)}$ series is double-smoothed with respect to the original series, and is therfore called a second-order exponential average. The second-order exponential mean is found by the following expression:

$$S_t^{(k)} = aS_t^{(k-1)} + bS^{(k)}_{t-1} \tag{6}$$

If the investigated process trend is described by a p-degree polynomial, the t-step forward forecast is carried out using the following formula:

$$\bar{y}_t = \bar{a}_1 + \bar{a}_2\, t + \bar{a}_3\, t^2 + \ldots + \bar{a}_{p+1} + t^p \tag{7}$$

where $\bar{a}_1 + \bar{a}_2 + \bar{a}_3 + \ldots + \bar{a}_{p+1}$ represents the parameter estimate.

According to the basic theorem of the exponential smoothing and forecasting method by R. Brown and R. Maers, the unknown coefficients of p-order polynomial (i.e., $p+1$ coefficients) can be represented by a linear combination of exponential averages. As a result, this forecast method can be applied with orders rangin from 1 to $(p+1)$. The variable e represents the required number of exponential averages, while their linear combination through polynomial coefficients is determined. Using this approach, forecasting by means of the polynomial becomes possible (Bobamuratov et al., 2020; Daminova et al., 2022; Eliseeva et al., 2023). R. Browning's adaptive polynomial models apply this method, with the main formulas given in Table 75.

Table 75. H-fertility forecasting for adaptive polynomial models main formulas

Model Order	**Primary A Must**	**e, Exponential Average**
$n = 1$	$S_0^{(1)} = \bar{a}_{1,0} - b/a \cdot \bar{a}_{2,0}$;	$S_t^{(1)} = a y_t + b \cdot S^{(1)}_{t-1}$
	$S_t^{(2)} = \bar{a}_{1,0} - 2b/a \cdot \bar{a}_{2,0}$;	$S_t^{(2)} = a \cdot S_t + b \cdot S^{(2)}_{t-1}$
$n = 2$	$S_0^{(1)} = \bar{a}_{1,0} - b/a \cdot_{2,0} + (\beta(2-\alpha))/2 \cdot \alpha^2 \cdot \bar{a}_{3,0}$;	$S_t^{(1)} = a y_t + b \cdot S^{(1)}_{t-1}$
	$S_0^{(2)} = \bar{a}_{1,0} - b/a \cdot \bar{a}_{2,0} + (\beta \cdot (3 - 2 \cdot \alpha))/2 \cdot \alpha^2 \cdot \bar{a}_{3,0}$;	$S_t^{(2)} = a \cdot S_t^{(1)} + b\, S^{(2)}_{t-1}$
	$S_0^{(3)} = \bar{a}_{1,0} - 3 \cdot b/a \cdot \bar{a}_{2,0} + (3 \cdot b \cdot (4 - 3 \cdot \alpha))/2 \cdot \alpha^2 \cdot \bar{a}_{3,0}$;	$S_t^{(3)} = a \cdot S_t^{(2)} + b\, S^{(3)}_{t-1}$
Model Order	Coefficients evaluation	Prognosis model
$n = 1$	$\bar{a}_{1,t} = 2 \cdot S_t^{(1)} - S_t^{(2)}$	$\bar{y}_t(t) = \bar{a}_{1,t} + \tau \bar{a}_{2,t}$
	$\bar{a}_{2,t} = a/b \cdot [S_t^{(1)} - S_t^{(2)}]$	
$n = 2$	$\bar{a}_{1,t} = 3 \cdot (S_t^{(1)} - S_t^{(2)}) + S_t^{(3)}$	$\bar{y}_t(t) = \bar{a}_{1,t} + \tau \cdot \bar{a}_{2,t} + \bar{a}_{3,t} \tfrac{1}{2} \cdot \tau^2_{3,t}$
	$\bar{a}_{2,t} = a/b \cdot [(6 - 5 \cdot \alpha)\, S_t^{(1)} - 2 - (5 - 4 \cdot \alpha)\, S_t^{(2)} + (4 - 3 \cdot \alpha)\, S^{(3)}_t]$	
	$\bar{a}_{3,t} = a^2/b^2 \cdot [S_t^{(1)} - 2 \cdot S_t^{(2)} + S_t^{(3)}]$	

Source: Based on the author's development.

The two parameterized Holt model is the first improved version of the Brownian model for the polynomial order forecasting. According to the Holt model, the t-step forward forecast with the following formula is represented by:

$$\bar{y}_t(t) = (\bar{a}_{1,t} + \tau \cdot \bar{a}_{2,t}) \tag{8}$$

Coefficients update as follows done is increased:

$$\bar{a}_{1,t} = a_1 y_1 + (1 - a_1)(\bar{a}_{1,t-1} + \bar{a}_{2,t-1}) \tag{9}$$

$$\bar{a}_{2,t} = \bar{a}_2 + (a_{1,t-1} + \bar{a}_{1,t-1}) + (1 + a_1)\bar{a}_{2,t-1} \tag{10}$$

where a_1, a_2 are adaptation parameters, $0 < a_1, a_2 < 1$; $\bar{a}_{1,t}$ and $\bar{a}_{2,t}$ are the development trend characteristics. The adaptation parameter lies within the interval [0, 1]; the closer its value is to 1, the more weight is given to recent observations in the forecast.

In this model, the forecast values depend on both past and current trend components, as well as on the initial coefficient values $\bar{a}_1$,0, $\bar{a}_2$,0, and $\bar{a}_3$,0, together with the adaptation parameters a, a_1, and a_2.

In the Brown and Holt models, the error e is calculated as the sum of squared errors (SSE). When the total squared error does not increase at 0.5, the adaptation parameters α, α_1, and α_2 tend to shift in the positive direction. Conversely, when the total squared error increases at 0.5, these

Table 76. Results of adaptive polynomial models of agricultural yield indicators, optimal values of adaptation parameters, and model error calculations

Product Name	First According To The Ordered Brownian Model			Second According To The Ordered Brownian Model			According To The Holt Model			
	Model equation	Adaptation parameter optimal value (a)	Model Error SSE (a)	Model equation	Adaptation parameter optimal value (a)	Model Error SSE(a)	Model equation	Adaptation parameter optimal value (a) a_1	Adaptation parameter optimal value (a) a_2	Model Error SSE(a)
Cereals (bread and bakery products)	$\bar{y}_t(t)$=5 13, 33 − 0.5635t	0.761	4.397	$\bar{y}_t(t)$= 5 13.058 + 0.927t − 0.146t^2	0.486	2.607	$\bar{y}_t(t)$= 5 13, 325− 0.497t	0.473	0.803	3.484

Source: Based on the author's development.

adaptation parameters tend to shift in the negative direction (Holt et al., 2005; Khamdamov et al., 2024).

This resulted in a decrease in the forecast error in one of the models considered when calculating the forecast values of the yield of agricultural products in the Syrdarya region.

Table 76 presents the results of adaptive polynomial models of agricultural yield indicators, optimal values of adaptation parameters, and model error calculations.

The analysis of the adequacy and accuracy characteristics of the models presented in Table 76 shows that there is a very strong relationship between the coefficients of determination in all three models. From the data of Table 76, we can see that the average absolute error of the second-order Brown model in the wheat yield indicator is less than the other two models.

Table 77. Syrdarya adaptation of productivity indicators in the cultivation of grain products in the agriculture of region *q* polynomial models 2024–2026 for forecast options

	First Brown Model			Second Brownian Model			According to the Holt Model		
Product Name	2024 years	2025 years	2026 years	2024 years	2025 years	2026 years	2024 years	2025 years	2026 years
Wheat	511.7	511.9	512.1	513.3	513.8	514.5	512.3	512.8	513.2

According to Table 19.6, the productivity indicators of village economies in the Syrdarya region for grain cultivation were determined using forecast values obtained from adaptive polynomial models.

19.4. Conclusion

In conclusion, we can say that the results of the analysis show that the obtained forecast values of grain production and productivity indicators in agriculture in the Syrdarya region indicate that positive trends in the level of providing the population of the region with this product relative to the physiological norm will not be maintained in 2024–2026. Based on the aforementioned data, we can conclude that the following measures can be implemented to further increase the productivity indicators in grain production in agriculture in the Syrdarya region:

- restoration of the productive forces of agricultural lands;
- implementation of land reclamation measures;
- scientific optimization of the use of mineral fertilizers and various additives will ensure the achievement of high yields.

Bibliography

Bobakulov, T., Alimardonov, I., Ishnazarov, A., Salikhodjaeva, U., & Kurbonova, N. N. (2024). Strategies for macroeconomic stability: Financial insights from Uzbekistan's economic policies. *Innovations and Contemporary Trends in Business & Economics*, 377–390.

Bobamuratova, D. T., Boymuradov, S. A., Polvanov, R. B., Ibragimov, D. D., & Kayumov, I. N. (2019). A complex approach to the health improvement of patients with jaw fractures, with introduction of adequate nutrition, therapeutic physical exercise and comprehensive oral hygiene. *International Journal of Pharmaceutical Research*, *11*(3), 1224–1237.

Bobomuratov, T. A., Rasulov, S. K., Dzhurayeva, Z. A., Samadov, A. A., & Kuliyev, O. A. (2020). Nutritional support with products of fruit origin in prevention of micronutrients deficiency in the "mother-child" system. *International Journal of Pharmaceutical Research*, *12*(4), 450–456.

Daminova, K. M., Gafforova, S., & Sayfutdinova, N. (2022). Evaluation of prodromal stage biomarkers in Parkinson's disease and their role in disease progression using modern digital technologies. In *Proceedings of the 6th International Conference on Future Networks & Distributed Systems* (pp. 408–411).

Decision PD-22 of the President of the Republic of Uzbekistan. (2023). Measures for the establishment of the International Institute of Food Technology and Engineering, dated January 26, 2023.

Eliseeva, I. I., Kurysheva, S. V., & Kosteeva, T. V. (2013). *Econometrics.* Moscow: Finance and Statistics

Gafurov, U., Juzbaev, A. O., & Akbarov, N. G. (2022, December). Improving the mechanism for financing activities of small businesses in the digital economy: In case of the Republic of Karakalpakstan. In *Proceedings of the 6th International Conference on Future Networks & Distributed Systems* (pp. 223–230).

Gulomov, S. S., & Allamatova, D. S. (2016). The role of innovation in regional food security. In *Materials of the Republican Scientific-Practical Conference on the Problems of Modernization and Development of Innovative Management Activities in the Branches of the Agro-Industrial Complex of the Republic of Uzbekistan* (Part 1) (pp. 24–26). Tashkent: TDAU.

Holt, J. W., Brown, G. E., Kuo, T. T. S., Holt, J. D., & Machleidt, R. (2008). Shell model description of the C 14 dating β decay with Brown-Rho-Scaled NN interactions. *Physical Review Letters*, 100(6), 062501.

Holt, R. D., Keitt, T. H., Lewis, M. A., Maurer, B. A., & Taper, M. L. (2005). Theoretical models of species' borders: single species approaches. *Oikos*, *108*(1), 18–27.

Khamdamov, S.-J. R., Usmanov, A. S., Sayfullayev, S. N., Xamitova, M. S., & Adkhamjonov, S. B. (2024). The influence of the main rate of the central bank on GDP growth in Uzbekistan and the transition to international financial reporting. *Advanced Series in Management*, 33A, 107–112.

Kurbonov, K., Makhmudov, S., Mamadiyorov, Z., Samadov, A., & Djalilov, F. (2023). The impact of digital technologies on economic growth in the example of Central Asian and European countries. *ACM International Conference Proceeding Series*, 403–409.

Leshchilovsky, P. V., Gusakov, V. G., & Kiveysha, E. I. (2012). *Economy of enterprises and industries in the agro-industrial complex: Textbook*. Minsk: BGEU.

Makhmudov, S., Khamdamov, S.-J., Karlibaeva, R., Khujamurodov, A., & Imomov, K. (2023). The impact of digital technologies on the labor market of Uzbekistan. *ACM International Conference Proceeding Series*, 260–267.

Mamadiyorov, Z., Sultanova, N., Makhmudov, S., Mirpulatova, L., & Jumayev, A. (2023). The impact of digitalization on microfinance services in Uzbekistan. *ACM International Conference Proceeding Series*, 453–463.

Mamarakhimov, B. E. (2016). Ensuring food safety and developing industry in Uzbekistan. *Economy and Innovative Technologies*, *5*(September–October), 4–6.

Mamatkulov, B., Khamdamov, S.-J., Togayniyazov, S., Quldoshev, Q., & Qarshiev, D. (2023). Predicting future living standards in Uzbekistan: Utilizing econometric analysis. *ACM International Conference Proceeding Series*, 425–431.

Resolution No. 546 of the Cabinet of Ministers of the Republic of Uzbekistan. (2020). Dated September 8, 2020.

Salimov, B., Kholikova, R., Khamdamov, S.-J., Nosirova, N., & Akhmedova, D. (2023). Strategies for integrating digitalization in leveraging regional economic and scientific expertise for the innovative growth of small and medium enterprises. *ACM International Conference Proceeding Series*, 483–490.

Turayeva, G. (2023a). The significance of sustainability of grain production in the consumer basket. *E3S Web of Conferences*, *420*, 01019.

Turayeva, G. (2023b). The significance of sustainability of grain production in the consumer basket. *E3S Web of Conferences*, *420*, 01019.

Turayeva, G., Mukhametov, A., Abduvohidov, A., & Berdiyev, G. (2022). Opportunities to use financial services – "1 C PROGRAM." In *Proceedings of the 6th International Conference on Future Networks & Distributed Systems* (pp. 556–561).

Fiscal Sustainability in the European Union: A Heterogeneous Macro-Panel Approach

Olgica Glavaški and Emilija Beker Pucar

20.1. Introduction

Maintaining fiscal sustainability is essential for macroeconomic stability, enabling positive effects on real economy. However, public debt growth in the European Union (EU) economies during recent pandemic crisis and current geo-political crisis have become substantial. The question of fiscal sustainability depends on the specific relationship between primary balances and differential of interest rate on debt and growth rate. However, fiscal adjustments differ in the EU due to: (1) the lack of common fiscal policy, (2) the phase of the business cycle (recession/expansion), and (3) composition and size of government revenues/expenditure/debt. The complexity of achieving fiscal sustainability is the focus of the revised EU rules with the intention to strengthen fiscal sustainability through improvement of primary balance and debt positions.

In the circumstances when questions related to fiscal sustainability are renewed, the empirical analysis of fiscal adjustments and its effects on the real economy becomes crucial. Therefore, this chapter assesses fiscal sustainability through long-run cointegration relationship between government expenditure, government revenues, and government debt in the EU-27 in the period 2010q1–2024q2 using econometric framework of non-stationary, heterogeneous, cross-sectional dependent panels. In order to cover the lack of unique fiscal policy, Pooled Mean Group (PMG) method is used, allowing homogeneous long-run equilibrium relationship and heterogeneous adjustment coefficients for each EU economy. Different phases of business cycle are covered by defining subsamples as Sovereign debt crisis (2010q1–2014q4), Stabilization phase (2015q1–2019q4), Pandemic and Geo-political crisis (2020q1–2024q2), while specificities due to composition and size of fiscal variables are analyzed by separation of economies into those with higher/lower than 60% of GDP average government debt. The main empirical questions are whether fiscal sustainability is achieved in the EU economies in the period 2010q1–2024q2 and how fiscal adjustments provided fiscal sustainability in crisis/stabilization periods and in the economies high/low debt.

The remainder of this paper is organized as follows. Section 2 briefly reviews existing empirical literature of fiscal sustainability. Section 3 presents trend in fiscal variables. Section 4 elaborates used methodology and research hypothesis. Section 5 covers empirical results and discussion, while Section 6 presents conclusions and policy recommendations.

20.2. Literature Review

Numerous literature deals with the question of fiscal sustainability, using comparative analysis of different groups of economies, periods, and different econometric techniques for estimation. Marín-Rodríguez et al. (2023) provided comprehensive review of scientific literature from Scopus and Web of Science database of fiscal sustainability, trend topics, influential studies, and key contributors. From the wide group of papers addressing fiscal sustainability, key topics can be distinguished as: (1) specifies of the EU fiscal policy, (2) fiscal adjustments during the business cycle or in high/low-debt economies, (3) causality nexus, and (4) econometric technique.

1. Fiscal policy framework in the EU is based on Maastricht Treaty (1992), Stability and Growth Pact (1997), "Six-pack" (2011), Fiscal Compact (2012), and independent fiscal institutions such as European Fiscal Board. Recent efforts are related to the definition of "new generation" fiscal rules (Medium-Term Fiscal Structural Plans) which will be able to combine fiscal sustainability and flexibility. However, new fiscal rules exhibit both weaknesses and strengths, while Darvas et al. (2023) showed that the new fiscal rules would require significant structural primary surpluses in high indebted economies such as Belgium and Italy.
2. In the last two decades, global crisis triggered the need for fiscal adjustments in the majority of the EU economies and opened the question fiscal adjustments adequacy according to the phase of business cycle. Majority of the EU economies in the post-crisis period undertook fiscal consolidation (Alesina et al. 2015), due to the opinion that fiscal

adjustments must not be undertaken early in the recession phase and should be introduced gradually to secure economic recovery (Corsetti et al. 2010). On the other hand, Balassone et al. (2010) and Cronin and McQuinn (2021) highlighted the issue of pro-cyclical effects of government expenditure policies, which could be asymmetric or opposite to the EU fiscal rules. Cross-country differences are also emphasized by Krogstrup (2002) and Kostin et al. (2021), showing that differences in public debts are found to lead to asymmetries in taxes and primary expenditures across the EU countries.

3. Question of causality nexus in relation to government expenditure—government revenue has often been addressed (Afonso & Rault, 2009; Darrat, 2002). Fiscal sustainability has often been tested under the assumption of "*spend and tax*" hypothesis, namely, that government expenditure determines revenues (Afonso & Rault, 2015; Campo-Robledo & Melo-Velandia, 2015). On the other hand, determination of government expenditure by government revenues ("*tax and spend*" hypothesis) are implemented in paper by Bravo and Silvestre (2002), Kollias and Makrydakis (2010), and Glavaški et al. (2022). Vamvoukas (2011) and Afonso and Jalles (2012, 2015) present two-way results, that is, for the case when government expenditure causes government revenue and *vice versa*, referring to "*fiscal synchronization*" hypothesis. The identification of direction of causality nexus is of great importance, because it provides useful insights into how each economy and the EU as a whole could manage their finance (Richter & Dimitrios, 2013).
4. The traditional approach of fiscal sustainability is based on cointegration analysis (Hakkio & Rush 1991; Quintos 1995). Recent studies are directed towards heterogeneous effects across economies implying the use of panel models with heterogeneous parameters (Bertarelli et al. 2014; Ferreiro et al. 2012; Feld et al. 2020; Glavaški & Beker Pucar 2021; Josifidis et al. 2018; Polat & Polat 2021).

The contribution of this paper to the existing empirical literature is to fill the gap related to heterogeneity of fiscal adjustments in different phases of business cycles and between economies with different levels of indebtedness in the EU in the framework of heterogeneous macro-panel approach.

20.3. Trends in Fiscal Policy

Specifies of the economic policy of the EU is related to the two main macroeconomic policy instruments, namely, monetary and fiscal policy. Since that eurozone create common monetary policy for majority of the EU economies (20 economies), trying to implement "one-size-fits-all" monetary policy, fiscal policy is under attack, namely, adjustments mechanisms are mostly on the side of fiscal policy, which is becoming heterogeneous especially in the period of crisis. Figure 81 shows key fiscal variables, government debt (primary axis), government revenues, and government expenditure (secondary axis) in the period 2010–2023, indicating obvious fiscal adjustments. The analyzed period could be separated in three subperiods. First subperiod, related to the period of Sovereign debt crisis, 2010–2014, characterized by rapid growth of government debt and fiscal contraction in context of government revenues growth and government expenditure restrictions. These adjustments are expected after the global financial crisis outbreak (2008–2010), when all EU economies went into recession. Sovereign debt crisis is therefore the consequence of previous crisis, and it was pronounced

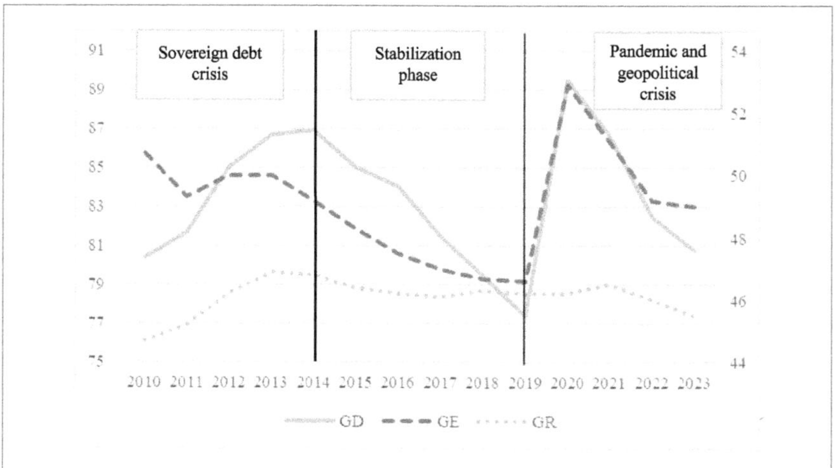

Figure 81. Dynamics of average government debt, revenues, and expenditure in the EU-27.

Source: Author's view based on Eurostat database data.

especially in the EU peripheral economies (PIIGS—Portugal, Italy, Ireland, Greece, Spain). Second subperiod is Stabilization phase, 2015–2019, when fiscal policy has faced a challenge of post-crisis adjustments. Average government debt and government expenditure sharply declined, while the level of government revenues was stable. Third subperiod, Pandemic and Geopolitical crises caused structural break in fiscal variables, with sharp increase of average government debt and expenditure in 2020, and adjustments in following years.

In different EU economies, heterogeneous fiscal adjustments were implemented with different effects in the crisis periods and stabilization period. The greatest divergence was observed related to government debt, with maximum value of 209.4 % of GDP in Greece (2020), and minimum value of 7.6% of GDP in Estonia (2011). Taking into a consideration debt asymmetry (Krogstrup, 2002) the sample is separated into two groups, economies with average debt higher than 60% of GDP,[1] and economies with lower average government debt.[2] Government debt of 60% of GDP is undertaken as limit, according to Maastricht criteria related to preferred level of indebtedness. Figure 82 reveals average position in EU economies with low and high indebtedness for the period 2010–2023, pointing to huge differences in defined groups of economies. First part of the Figure 82 shows moderate average government expenditure between 40% and 45% of GDP, covered by stabile government revenues and average government debt oscillating about 40% of GDP and reaching minimum value of 34.11% at the end of stabilization period (2019) in low indebted EU economies. However, in high indebted economies, average government expenditure between 46% and 51% of GDP is covered by stabile revenues (about 45%) and enormous average government debt between 85% and 105% of GDP in average (secondary axis). Since that similar way of adjustment is detected in fiscal variables in two groups of the EU economies, but with huge differences in magnitude of adjustments, further econometric analysis is needed.

---

1 Austria, Belgium, Croatia, Cyprus, France, Finland, Germany, Greece, Hungary, Ireland, Italy, Portugal, Slovenia, and Spain.

2 Bulgaria, Czechia, Denmark, Estonia, Latvia, Lithuania, Luxembourg, Malta, Netherlands, Poland, Romania, Slovakia, and Sweden.

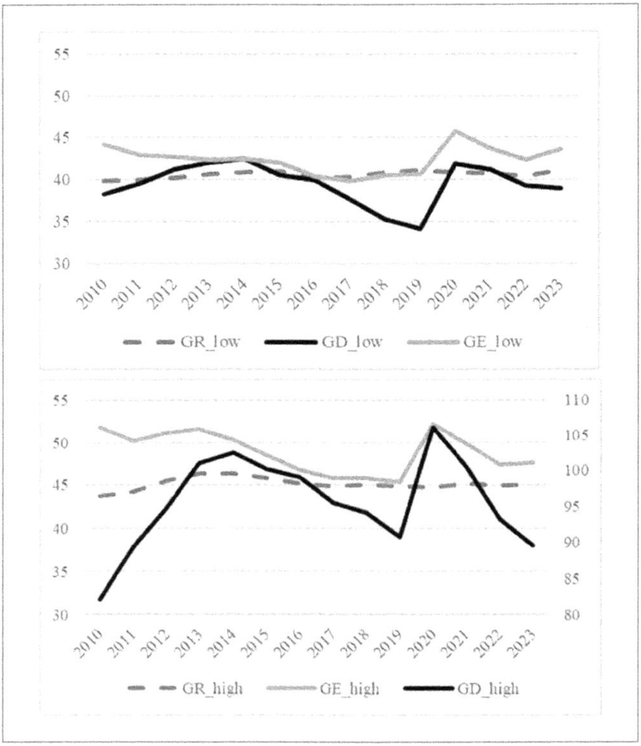

Figure 82. Fiscal variables in the EU economies with high and low level of indebtedness in the period 2010–2023.

Source: Author's view based on Eurostat database data.

20.4. Research Methodology

In the analysis of fiscal sustainability three key variables are used: government consolidated gross debt—*GD*, total general government revenue—*GR*, and total general government expenditure—*GE*[3]. The focus of the paper is whether fiscal sustainability is achieved and what are the fiscal adjustment mechanisms used. It is assumed that the relationship between *GR*, *GD*, and *GE* would be positive and significant; however, crisis period or high

[3] All variables are measured as share in GDP, and the source of data is Eurostat (2025).

indebtedness of economies may lead to a different conclusion. The analysis is based on quarterly data for the period is 2010q1–2024q2 in the EU-27, taking into a consideration three subperiods: Sovereign debt crisis (2010q1–2014q4), Stabilization phase (2015q1–2019q4), and Pandemic and Geopolitical Crisis (2020q1–2024q2), and two subgroups of economies: economies with average government debt > 60% of GDP, and economies with average government debt < 60% of GDP.

Since that time dimension is $T = 58$ in 27 EU economies ($N = 27$), heterogeneous, non-stationary panels with cross-sectional dependence (CSD) are used. Method of estimation used in the paper is PMG estimator (Pesaran et al. 1999) which is based on a combination of pooling and averaging of coefficients, providing homogeneous long-run relationships and heterogeneous short-run coefficients, which is tested using Hausman test. Namely, the Hausman test is applied to distinguish whether the restriction in long-run equilibrium relationship is true in PMG model.

The specification of PMG model is based on error-correction model:

$$\Delta GE_{it} = j_i\left(GE_{i,t-1} - q_{1i}GR_{it} - \theta_{2i}GD_{it}\right) + \sum_{j=1}^{p-1} l_{ij}\Delta GE_{it-1} + \sum_{j=0}^{q-1}\delta_{ij}\Delta GR_{it-j} + \sum_{j=0}^{q-1}\delta_{ij}\Delta GD_{it-j} + m_i + u_{it} \quad (1)$$

where the number of periods is represented by $t = 1, 2, \ldots, T$; the cross-section units by $i = 1, 2, \ldots, N$; dependent variable is GE_{it}, while explanatory variables are GR_{it} and GD_{it}; l_{ij} is coefficient of lagged dependent variable, δ_{ij} is short-run parameters for each panel unit, m_i represents individual effects, and u_{it} stochastic disturbance term. Equation (1) provides two long-run relationships: 1) q_{1i}—long-run cointegration relationship between GE and GR expecting to be positive, and confirming fiscal sustainability in the sample, and 2) and θ_{1i}—long-run cointegration relationship between GE and GD, thought to be positive. Moreover, j_i is error-correction parameter, which is expected to be significant and negative, showing speed of the adjustment to the long-run relationship.

In order to estimate Equation (1) using PMG method, the following empirical steps previously need to be undertaken: (1) causality testing; (2) test of CSD; (3) second generation panel stationarity test; (4) cointegration test; (5) PMG estimation and Hausman test; (6) estimation of homogeneous long-run equilibrium relationships and short-run parameters for all sample, subsamples, and subperiods.

In this research, proposed methodology is considered as appropriate since that long-run relationship is expected to be homogeneous due to common fiscal policy framework; however, some heterogeneity is expected due to different policy actions implemented in crisis period in the EU economies. Therefore, hypotheses in this paper are defined according to theoretical points and possibilities of the heterogeneous macro-panel model approach:

H_1: The long-run equilibrium relationships between *GR*, *GD*, and *GE* are *homogeneous and positive* on a sample of 27 EU economies in the period 2010q1–2024q2, indicating fiscal sustainability.

H_2: The speed of fiscal adjustments and short-run coefficients *differ in crisis vs. stabilization periods* on a sample of 27 EU economies in the period 2010q1–2024q2.

H_3: The speed of fiscal adjustments and short-run coefficients *differ in economies with high vs. low average indebtedness* on a sample of 27 EU economies in the period 2010q1–2024q2.

20.5. Findings and Discussion

The first step in the econometric analysis is to test causality nexus, in order to identify the direction of influence between *GR*, *GE*, and *GD* in the sample of EU-27 for the period 2010q1–2024q2. Using Dumitrescu-Hurlin (2012) and Juodis, Karavias, and Sarafidis tests (Xiao et al. 2021), Granger non-causality is analyzed (Table 78). The null hypothesis refers to the assumption of homogeneous non-causality, as opposed to the alternative hypothesis, meaning that there is causality at least in one panel unit (heterogeneous assumption).

Causality testing showed that directions $GR \rightarrow GE$ and $GD \rightarrow GE$ are valid, referring that "*tax and spend*" hypothesis exists in some of the EU-27 economies (Table 78). Namely, alternative hypothesis meaning that *GR* and *GD* caused *GE* in at least one of the core Eurozone economies has to be accepted. The same conclusion could be drawn for EU economies with high and low *GD*, relying on both tests. This result has two implications: (a) the analysis is continued based on "*tax and spend*" hypothesis; (b) heterogeneous panel techniques are used in estimation of fiscal sustainability.

Table 78. Causality testing

Dumitrescu & Hurlin (2012) Granger non-causality test				
Government revenues → government expenditure Government debt → government expenditure				
	W-stat.	$\overline{Z}$-stat.	W-stat.	$\overline{Z}$-stat.
EU-27	3.64	7.01***	5.45	6.451***
High GD	4.47	9.19***	4.35	4.412***
Low GD	6.21	13.36***	3.56	6.541***
Juodis, Karavias, and Sarafidis (2021)			**Granger non-causality test**	
EU-27	−0.174***		−0.363*** (lag number: 2)	
High GD	−0.212**		−0.439*** (lag number: 1)	
Low GD	−0.156***		0.151*** (lag number: 1)	

* *p-value < 0.1* ** *p-value < 0.5,* *** *p-value < 0.01.*

Source: Authors' calculations.

The second step in the analysis is to test existence and nature of CSD in the sample. The null hypothesis of cross-section independence has to be rejected for all analyzed variables using Pesaran CD test (Table 79), namely, variables *GE*, *GR*, and *GD* are characterized by CSD existence. In order to investigate the nature of CSD—presence of weak or strong CSD—additional CD tests are applied: (1) weighted CD test—CDw by Juodis and Reese (2022), (2) CDw including the power enhancement—CDw+ by Fan et al. (2015), and (3) CD* proposed by Pesaran and Xie (2021). The weighted CD test and CD* test indicated strong CSD for all analyzed variables, while CDw results showed that for variables *GE* and *GR*, the null hypothesis is rejected, indicating the presence of weak CSD. Therefore, it is concluded that CSD exists in the panel, and that the nature of CSD is mostly strong CSD (Table 79). This indicates a high degree of correlation between the standard errors of different observation units. In the case of strong CSD, biased estimates may occur—as this violates the assumption of independent errors. Therefore, in the next econometric steps, methods that could cover CSD have to be implemented. The detected dependence is expected and caused by the strong institutional framework and common policies in the EU economies (Glavaški et al. 2022).

Table 79. Cross-sectional dependence (CSD) tests

Variable	Pesaran CD test	CDw	CDw+	CD*
H_0: Cross-sectional independence; H_1: Cross-sectional dependence		H_0: Weak cross-sectional dependence; H_1: Strong cross-sectional dependence		
GE	61.52***	−0.13	1183.4***	−2.42**
GR	18.35***	0.000	858.8***	2.71***
GD	32.26***	−2.17***	1184.3***	2.79***

** p-value < 0.1 ** p-value < 0.5, *** p-value < 0.01.*

Source: Authors calculations.

In order to test the stationarity of the analyzed variables, Pesaran (2007) Cross-Sectionally Augmented Im, Pesaran, Shin (CIPS) test is used, since that second-generation panel unit root test include CSD. Table 80 represents the results of CIPS test for the whole sample, as well as for the subsamples, both at the levels of the variables and at their first differences. Results indicated the acceptance of the H1 hypothesis, meaning stationarity for the first differences of the analyzed variables in all subsamples, except in the stabilization period 2015q1–2019q4, for which results indicated that variables are stationary in the level. Therefore, we could conclude that in the majority of subsamples, variables *GE*, *GR*, and *GD* are integrated of the first order, which is the basis for the further cointegration relationship.

Table 80. Pesaran (CIPS) panel Unit-Root test

Pesaran CIPS test in the level; H0: I(1); H1: I(0)							
2010q1–2024q2			2010q1–2014q4	2015q1–2019q4	2020q1–2024q2	High GD	Low GD
GE	0	−17.59***	−7.956***	−10.88***	−7.159***	−5.933***	−4.282***
	1	−10.404***	−1.050	−3.077***	−5.051***	−7.117***	−1.422
	2	−4.408**	1.170	−1.282*	0.289	−0.879	1.953
GR	0	−18.575***	−14.31***	−9.299***	−7.048***	−5.509***	−7.639
	1	−14.960***	−11.77***	−10.157***	−8.048***	−2.338	−1.863
	2	−5.817***	−3.65***	−1.221*	−1.203	−0.396	−0.132

Table 80. (*Continued*)

Pesaran CIPS test in the level; H0: I(1); H1: I(0)							
GD	0	1.693	−0.682	−3.573***	−3.666***	−3.056***	−1.717*
	1	3.133	−0.978	−1.821**	0.022	0.831	−1.118
	2	3.728	−1.008	−0.812*	3.131	3.286	0.560
Pesaran (CIPS) test at the first differences; H0: I(1); H1: I(0)							
GE	0		−21.02***		−17.686***	−12.164***	−12.956***
	1	10.404***	−12.98***		−14.033***	−10.530***	−9.224***
	2		−7.152***		−6.664***	−5.706***	−2.498***
GR	0				−16.513***	−10.553***	−15.213***
	1				−12.349***	−10.668***	−9.835***
	2				−6.934***	−3.775***	−3.957***
GD	0	1224.76***	−16.46***		−21.006***	−14.103***	−12.956***
	1	852.243***	−6.985***		−11.251***	−7.683***	−8.278***
		474.372***	−5.047***		−6.003***	−3.642***	−4.078***

** p-value < 0.1; ** p-value < 0.5; *** p-value < 0.01.*

Source: Authors' calculations.

The Westerlund (2007) test is further used to analyze cointegration relationship for variables in the fiscal sustainability model. The test provides four possible statistics: Ga and Gt, which allows for heterogeneous assumptions, and Pa and Pt, which are based on homogeneous assumptions. The results of Westerlund cointegration test undoubtedly show that at least one panel is cointegrated (Table 81). Those results are based on the robust *p*-values since that bootstrapping procedure is undertaken due to CSD existence in the model.

Since that cointegration is detected in the model, the PMG method of estimation is applied (Table 82), which provides homogeneous long-run relationships and heterogeneous short-run coefficients. As expected, the dynamic *GR* and *GD* create significantly positive long-run equilibrium relationships with *GE* in the period 2010q1–2024q2 in the EU-27 economies, confirming research hypothesis H1. Long-run relationship with *GR* indicates fiscal sustainability in the sample, confirming "*tax and spend*" hypothesis. The same direction

Table 81. Westerlund cointegration test

	2010q1–2024q4	2010q1–2014q4	2015q1–2019q4	2020q1–2024q2	Hight GD	Low GD
H0: No cointegration; H1: At least one panel unit is cointegrated						
Gt	−3.386***	−1.672*	−1.576*	−1.635*	−3.397***	−3.374***
Ga	−21.04***	−4.045	−4.317	−4.125	−19.596***	−22.615***
H0: No cointegration; H1: All panel units are cointegrated						
Pt	−18.68***	−9.233***	−11.288***	−6.711*	−14.129***	−11.542***
Pa	−21.86***	−4.920***	−5.994***	−3.954**	−21.622***	−22.629***

Robust p-value < 0.1; ** robust p-value < 0.5; * robust p-value < 0.01.*

Source: Authors' calculations.

of influence is estimated for the short-run. However, the influence of *GD* is with the higher magnitude of influence in the short-run, indicating that *GD* as the source of financing is often used as short-run goal for *GE* financing. Error-correction parameter is negative and between 0 and 1, as it is expected, meaning that 70.8% of the deviation from long-run equilibrium relationship is corrected in one year. The result of the Hausman test indicates that PMG estimator is efficient estimator under the null hypothesis in comparison to

Table 82. Fiscal sustainability estimated by PMG Method in the EU economies for the period 2010q1–2024q2

Dependent variable: *GE*		2010q1–2024q2	2010q1–2014q4	2015q1–2019q4	2020q1–2024q2
Long-run	*GR*	0.517***	0.736***	0.800***	0.385**
Relationship	*GD*	0.053***	**−0.035*****	0.081***	0.168**
Error-correction		−0.708***	−0.810***	−0.827***	−1.03***
Short-run	*GR*	0.253***	−0.037	−0.022	0.214
effects	*GD*	0.619***	**0.564*****	0.129	**0.615*****
	Constant	13.712***	13.88***	2.653***	11.606
Hausman test		3.91	1.90	2.51	0.72

** p-value < 0.1; ** p-value < 0.05; *** p-value < 0.01.*

Source: Authors' calculations.

Mean Group (MG) estimation. Specifically, the restriction on the long-run equilibrium relationship is true, creating homogeneous long-run cointegration relationships with heterogeneous adjustment parameters, which is in line with common framework for fiscal sustainability achievement in the EU, and heterogeneous mechanisms to reach that goal.

Heterogeneous coefficients of error-correction and short-run parameters are given in Appendix, Table 84 for the basic model, which covers period 2010q1–2024q2. According to the results, error-correction coefficients are significant and negative in all economies, indicating the presence of significant fiscal adjustments (with overadjustments in Cyprus, Spain, and Poland). In Table 84, economies are presented individually but within the groups of economies with average public debt higher and lower than 60% of GDP. Short-run parameters in economies with average government debt higher than 60% of GDP had significant effects of government debt in the short-run. This leads to the conclusion that these economies relied to a large extent on public debt to ensure fiscal sustainability.

The interpretation of the results related to sub-samples is similar when the focus is on the long-run relationship (Table 82). During crises and stabilization periods, *GR* and *GD* created significantly positive long-run equilibrium relationship with *GE*, as well as the adjustments are with the similar magnitude of influence. However, short-run parameters are not significant in the stabilization period (2015q1–2019q4), indicating that long-run fiscal sustainability is already achieved. However, short-run parameters in the crisis periods (2010q1–2014q4 and 2020q1–2024q2) indicate an exclusive focus in crisis circumstances on financing through an increase in public debt. This is particularly pronounced during the Sovereign debt crisis (2010q1–2014q4) when reliance on *GD* was at its peak, and the relationship with *GE* became negative, due to overindebtedness (especially in the economies that had implemented bail-out programs, Beljić & Glavaški, 2020). Therefore, it is concluded that the speed of fiscal adjustments and short-run coefficients differ in crisis vs. stabilization periods, confirming research hypothesis, H2.

With the intention to provide more evidence of fiscal sustainability achievements, not only for the different periods—stabilization vs. crisis periods, economies are separated into two groups (Table 83). Economies with average *GD* above and below 60% showed similar long-run tendencies in fiscal sustainability achievements (*GR* and *GD* create significantly positive long-run equilibrium relationship with *GE*, with significant fiscal adjustments). However, substantial differences are identified in relation to short-run parameters in crisis periods. Specifically, economies with average *GD* lower that 60% adjusted *GR* and *GD* in order to influence *GE*. However, in highly indebted economies, the short-run coefficients are significant only for *GD*, meaning that fiscal sustainability is endangered due to orientation toward further debt in order to get out the crisis, which confirms research hypothesis, H3.

Table 83. Fiscal sustainability estimated by PMG method in economies with low vs. high government debt

Dependent variable: *GE*		**2010q1–2024q2**	**2015q1–2019q4**	**2020q1–2024q2**
Economies with average *GD* > 60% GDP				
Long-run	*GR*	0.981***	1.23***	0.870***
relationship	*GD*	−0.051***	0.071***	0.178***
Error-correction		−0.774***	−0.657***	**−1.090*** **
Short-run	*GR*	−0.112	−0.123	−0.078
effects	*GD*	**0.501*** **	−0.043	**0.630*** **
	Constant	9.002***	−10.770***	−9.797***
Hausman test		0.27	1.42	0.50
Economies with average *GD* < 60% GDP				
Long-run	*GR*	0.528***	0.279***	0.280***
relationship	*GD*	−0.86***	0.122***	0.254***
Error-correction		−0.829***	−0.9117***	−0.952***
Short-run	*GR*	0.159**	0.243	0.399***
effects	*GD*	**0.644*** **	0.044	**0.592*** **
	Constant	19.581***	22.21***	20.179***
Hausman test		1.92	2.66	0.33

** p-value < 0.1; ** p-value < 0.05; *** p-value < 0.01.*

Source: Authors' calculations.

20.6. Conclusion

Vulnerability of the EU fiscal sustainability is result of the unique fiscal policy absence, heterogeneity, and real economy divergence of its members and the crisis conditions in the last two decades. The analysis in this paper is based on specific relation between government expenditure, revenues, and debt in the EU economies during the period 2010Q1–2014q2, as well as in the sub-periods covering Sovereign debt crisis, Stabilization period, Pandemic and Geopolitical crisis, and sub-samples of economies with average government debt above or below 60% of GDP.

Econometric framework of non-stationary, heterogeneous, cross-sectional dependent macro-panels, using PMG method of estimation, showed that fiscal sustainability is achieved in the EU economies during the period 2010q1–2024q2, due to significant positive long-run relationship of *GR* and *GD* with *GE*, based on "*tax and spend*" hypothesis. In the short-run, government debt is with the higher magnitude of influence in comparison to government revenue, indicating that debt as the source of financing is often used as short-run goal for government expenditure financing. Moreover, the substantial difference is detected in the speed of fiscal adjustments and short-run coefficients in crisis vs. stabilization periods, and in economies with high- vs. low-average indebtedness. More specifically, in the crisis periods (Sovereign debt crisis, 2010q1–2014q4; Pandemic and Geopolitical crisis, 2020q1–2024q2) short-run parameters indicate an exclusive focus on financing through an increase in government debt. Similarly, in highly indebted economies, the short-run coefficients are significant only for government debt, meaning that fiscal sustainability is endangered due to orientation toward further debt with the aim to get out of the crisis. Those economies reacted during all analyzed period as they are all the time in the crisis conditions. Therefore, recommendation for policy makers is directed toward redirection of fiscal adjustments from government debt to government revenues in the short-run. Improvement of primary balances could directly improve fiscal sustainability achievements and alleviate crises' effects, especially in the overindebted EU economies.

Bibliography

Afonso, A., & Rault, C. (2009). Spend-and-Tax: A panel data investigation for the EU. *Economic Bulletin*, *29*(4), 2542–2548. <https://dx.doi.org/10.2139/ssrn.1433678>

Afonso, A., & Jalles, J. T. (2012). Revisiting fiscal sustainability: Panel cointegration and structural breaks in OECD countries. *European Central Bank Working Paper 1465/August 2012*. ISSN 1725–2806 (online). Available at: https://www.ecb.europa.eu/pub/pdf/scpwps/ecbwp1465.pdf

Afonso, A., & Jalles, J. T. (2015). Fiscal Sustainability: A Panel Assessment for Advanced Economies. *University of Lisbon Working Paper WP/05/2015/DE/UECE*. ISSN 2183-1815. Available at: https://depeco.iseg.ulisboa.pt/wp/wp052015.pdf

Afonso, A., & Rault, C. (2015). Multi-Step analysis of public finances sustainability. *Economic Modelling*, *48*(C), 199–209. <https://doi.org/10.1016/j.econmod.2014.10.011>

Alesina, A., Barbiero, O., Favero, C., Giavazzi, F., & Paradisi, M. (2015). Austerity in 2009–2013. *Economic Policy*, *30*(83), 383–437.

Balassone, F., Maura F., & Zotteri, S. (2010). Cyclical asymmetry in fiscal variables in the EU. *Empirica*, *37*, 381–402.

Beljić, M., & Glavaški, O. (2020). Effectiveness of bail-out mechanisms in the eurozone: Global vs. Pandemic crisis. *Anali Ekonomskog fakulteta u Subotici*, *57*(45), 79–95. <https://doi.org/10.5937/AnEkSub2145079B>

Bertarelli, S., Censolo R., & Colombo, C. (2014), Fiscal convergence in the European Union before crisis. *Contemporary Economic Policy*, *32*, 784–801.

Bravo Santos, A., & Silvestre, A. L. (2002). Intertemporal sustainability of fiscal policies: some tests for European countries. *European Journal of Political Economy*, *18*(2002), 517–528. Doi: <https://doi.org/10.1016/S0176-2680(02)00103-9>

Campo-Robledo, J., & Melo-Velandia, L. (2015). Sustainability of Latin American fiscal deficits: A panel data approach. *Empirical Economics*, *49*(3), 889–907. <https://doi.org/10.1007/s00181-014-0905-8>

Corsetti, G., Kuester, K., Meier, A., & Muller, G. J. (2010). Debt consolidation and fiscal stabilization of deep recessions. *American Economic Review*, 100, 41–45.

Cronin, D., & McQuinn, K. (2021). The (pro-) cyclicality of government consumption in the EU and official expectations of future output growth: New evidence. *International Economics and Economic Policy*, *18*, 331–345.

Darrat, A. (2002). Budget balance through spending cuts or tax adjustments? *Contemporary Economic Policy*, *20*(3), 221–230. <https://doi.org/10.1093/cep/20.3.221>

Darvas, Z., Welslau, L., & Zettelmeyer, J. (2023). A quantitative evaluation of the European commission's fiscal governance proposal. *Working Paper, 16/2023*, Bruegel.

Dumitrescu, I. E., & Hurlin, C. (2012). Testing for granger non-causality in heterogeneous panels. *Economic Modelling*, *29*(4), 1450–1460. <https://doi.org/10.1016/j.econmod.2012.02.014>

Fan, J., Liao, Y., & Yao, J. (2015). Power enhancement in high-dimensional cross-sectional tests. *Econometrica*, *83*(4), 1497–1541. <https://doi.org/10.3982/ECTA12749>

Feld, L. P., Köhler, A. E., & Wolfinger, J. (2020). Modeling fiscal sustainability in dynamic macro-panels with heterogeneous effects: Evidence from German federal states. *International Tax and Public Finance*, *27*, 215–239.

Ferreiro, J., García de Valle, M., & Gómez, C. (2012). Similarities and differences in the composition of public expenditures in the European Union. *Journal of Economic Issues*, *46*, 633–659.

Glavaški, O., & Beker Pucar, E. (2021). Heterogeneity of fiscal adjustments in EU Economies in the pre- and post crisis periods: Common correlated effects approach. *Eurasian Economic Review: Journal in Applied Macroeconomics and Finance*, *11*(1), 191–226. <https://doi.org/10.1007/s40822-020-00164-z>

Glavaški, O., Beker Pucar, E., & Stojkov, S. (2022). Public revenues and public expenditure nexus: Evidence of Eurozone heterogeneity. *The Annals of the Faculty of Economics in Subotica*, *58*(48), 83–99.

Glavaški, O. Beker Pucar, E., Beljić, M., & Stojkov, S. (2022). Coordination vs. competitiveness of effective average tax rates in relation to FDI: The case of emerging EU economies. *Sustainability*, *15*(1), 227. <https://doi.org/10.3390/su15010227>

Hakkio, C. S., & Rush, M. (1991). Is the budget deficit too large? *Economic Inquiry*, 29, 429–445.

Josifidis, K., Dragutinović Mitrović, R., Glavaški, O., & Supić, N. (2018). Public policies influence on fiscal deficit in the EU-28: Common correlated effects approach. *Hacienda Pública Española/Review of Public Economics*, *227*(4). <https://doi.org/10.7866/HPE-RPE.18.4.3>

Juodis, A., & Reese, S. (2022). The incidental parameters problem in testing for remaining cross-section correlation. *Journal of Business Economics and Statistics*, *40*(3).

Kollias, C., & Makrydakis, S. (2010). Tax and spend or spend and tax? Empirical evidence from Greece, Spain, Portugal and Ireland. *Applied Economics*, *32*(5), 533–546. <https://doi.org/10.1080/000368400322444>

Kostin, K. B., Runge, P., & Adams, R. (2021). Investment strategies in pandemic situations: An analysis and comparison of prospective returns between developed and emerging markets. *Strategic Management*, *26*, 034–052.

Krogstrup, S. (2002). Public debt asymmetries: the effect on taxes and spending in the European Union. *European Central Bank Working Paper*, 162. <https://doi.org/10.2139/ssrn.358020>

Marín-Rodríguez, N. J., Gonzalez-Ruiz, J. D., & Botero, S. (2023). Assessing fiscal sustainability in the landscape of economics research. *Economies*, *11*(12), 300. <https://doi.org/10.3390/economies11120300>

Pesaran, H., Shin, Y., & Smith, R. (1999). Pooled mean group estimation of dynamic heterogeneous panels. *Journal of American Statistical Association*, *94*, 621–634.

Pesaran, M. H. (2007). A simple panel unit root test in the presence of cross-section dependence. *Journal of Applied Econometrics*, *22*(2), 265–312.

Pesaran, M. H., & Xie, Y. (2021). A bias-corrected CD test for error cross-sectional dependence in panel data models with latent factors. *Cambridge Working Papers in Economics*, 215.

Polat, G. E., & Polat, O. (2021). Fiscal sustainability analysis in EU Countries: A dynamic macro-panel approach. *Eastern Journal of European Studies*, 12, 219–241.

Quintos, C. E. (1995). Sustainability of deficit process with structural shifts. *Journal of Business and Economic Statistic*, *13*(4), 409–417.

Richter, C., & Dimitrios, P. (2013). Tax and spend, spend and tax, fiscal synchronisation or institutional separation? Examining the case of Greece. *Romanian Journal of Fiscal Policy*, *4*(2), 1–17.

Vamvoukas, G. (2011). Panel data modelling and the tax-spend controversy in the Euro zone. *Applied Economics*, *44*(31), 4073–4085. <https://doi.org/10.1080/00036846.2011.587777>

Westerlund, J., & Prohl, S. (2007). Panel cointegration tests of the sustainability hypothesis in rich OECD countries. *Applied Economics*, *42*(10–12), 1355–1364. <10.1080/00036840701721323>

Xiao, J., Juodis, A., Karavias, Y., & Sarafidis, V. (2021). Improved test for granger non-causality in panel data. *Munich Personal PePEc Archive Paper No. 107180*.

Appendix

Table 84. Heterogeneous coefficients of the PMG method of estimation in the EU economies in the period 2010q1–2024q2

Economies	Error-Correction (ϕ_i)	ΔGR	ΔGD	μ_i
	Economies with average *GD* > 60% GDP			
Austria	−0.602***	0.449***	0.999***	13.246***
Belgium	−0.549***	−0.077***	0.674***	12.341***
Croatia	−0.720***	1.047***	0.857***	14.763***
Cyprus	−1.050***	−0.020	0.502*	18.504***
France	−0.591***	−0.021	0.614***	14.603***
Finland	−0.187**	−0.061	0.575***	4.195
Germany	−0.369***	0.481***	0.225	7.076***
Greece	−0.562***	0.339***	0.481***	10.411***
Hungary	−1.017***	0.411***	0.377*	21.789***
Ireland	−0.496***	0.536***	0.900***	6.696***
Italy	−0.485***	0.277***	0.122**	9.509***
Portugal	−0.862***	0.114	0.283***	15.474***
Slovenia	−0.774***	0.674**	0.778***	16.453***
Spain	−1.496***	−0.557***	1.332***	28.415***
	Economies with average *GD* < 60% GDP			
Bulgaria	−0.118***	0.031	0.894	19.82***
Czechia	−0.672***	0.402**	0.561***	12.947***
Denmark	−0.185***	0.464***	0.178	4.051***
Estonia	−0.747***	0.112	0.655***	14.067***
Latvia	−0.058***	−0.018	0.517	20.346***
Lithuania	−0.654***	0.613***	0.413*	10.778***
Luxembourg	−0.917***	0.356*	0.018	17.319***
Malta	−0.715***	0.257***	1.118***	12.237***
Netherlands	−0.533***	−0.141**	1.112***	10.655***
Poland	−1.019***	−0.206	0.942***	20.439***
Romania	−0.693***	0.579***	1.132***	12.229***
Slovakia	−0.531***	1.068***	0.243*	10.129***
Sweden	−0.519***	−0.269**	0.508***	11.731***

** p-value < 0.1 ** p-value < 0.05, *** p-value < 0.01.*

Source: Authors' calculations.

Bibliometric Analysis Based on Scopus Database: Government Size

Seda Bayrakdar

21.1. Introduction

For centuries, the extent of government involvement in the economy has been a pressing question. This issue spans multiple disciplines, attracting the attention of both economists and political scientists. Recently, efforts in economic literature have sought a mathematical resolution through empirical applications. However, the ideal government size is contingent upon each country's specific conditions and potential. There are two predominant perspectives on government size: the first advocates for minimal government involvement. Proponents of this view emphasize three main points. Firstly, a smaller government results in a reduced tax burden, allowing individuals and businesses to save more for investments, savings, and expenditures. Secondly, a leaner government enhances economic efficiency; with fewer bureaucratic inefficiencies, resources can be allocated more effectively. Lastly, it promotes greater individual freedom, as limited government intervention allows for increased personal autonomy and choice. Conversely, the opposing view argues for greater government involvement in the economy. Supporters of a larger government assert that it is necessary to address market failures, ensure social equality, and provide essential services such as education and healthcare. They maintain that government intervention is crucial in cases of market failures, including monopolies, pollution, and information asymmetry. Furthermore, the state must create a social safety net and offer assistance like unemployment insurance and support for socially vulnerable groups. The government is viewed as vital for delivering public goods such as national defense, infrastructure, and environmental protection, areas where the private sector may fall short.

Of course, the first step in discussing government size is to define what is meant by it. Government size can be measured through different metrics, including taxes and governmental structure. Expenditures, subsidies, or monetary and fiscal policies implemented by the state give us an idea of the size. It is known that various techniques are used to measure the place of the state in the economy: the ratio of government consumption to total consumption; transfer expenditures and subsidies as a percentage of GDP; the ratio of government investments in total investments; tax rates on income and wages; state enterprises and investments can be examined through rates such as top marginal income/wage tax and the number of people employed in government services (Acar, 2010; European Communities, 2004:7; Feldmann, 2006; Mink, 2004). The methods used to measure the size of the government sector have their advantages and disadvantages. For example, measuring the size of the government sector by the number of employees or, in other words, employment, may not give an accurate result. Because the state may choose to substitute capital instead of labor to perform the same job over time. Instead, government expenditures per capita may be more meaningful than total government expenditures. Another method of measuring the size of the state is revenues. Which of these two methods is chosen is especially important in periods when the budget deficit is high. However, measuring government size by taking government expenditures into account is considered a better method than measuring government revenues, and this method is widely used in the literature. Government revenues have higher volatility than government expenditures and can only be controlled by legislators. In addition, incomes are more sensitive to economic conditions. Another reason the expenditures method is preferred in measuring government size is that expenditures and revenues temporarily differ depending on the budget deficit. However, this difference must eventually be brought into balance. Therefore, reducing taxes without cutting spending does not permanently reduce the size of the state. Measuring government size through revenues can give a misleading impression, making the government appear smaller than it is. A certain level of spending requires taxpayers to allocate resources, whether financed by debt or through taxes (Labonte, 2010:17).

Within the scope of the study, answers to the following questions will be sought;

- What is the level of development of studies on "government size" over the years?

- How have the journal, author, subject, citation, country, and university-based analyses of studies on government size developed?
- Which are the most effective studies on government size?

In this study, the bibliometric analysis method, one of the quantitative analysis techniques, was preferred during the data collection and subsequent analysis process. The method was first used by Pritchard in 1969. According to Pritchard (1969), bibliometrics is the application of mathematical and statistical methods to books and other communication tools. Bibliometric analysis is an important method for identifying potentially under-researched areas (Wallin, 2005). In short, bibliometric analysis is a method that examines the field of a subject, that is, the literature, in general terms and presents it systematically (Şekeroğlu, 2021). It provides an in-depth analysis of the intellectual structure related to any concept or discipline, its development over the years, and the relationships between the authors, subjects, and studies by mapping. Performance and scientific mapping analyses are carried out with bibliometric analysis. In the performance analysis, data on publications and citations for authors, institutions, countries, and journals are obtained (Gürler, 2022).

While searching the Scopus database, the fields of mathematics, engineering, computer science, psychology, medicine, Earth and Planetary Sciences, and Biochemistry, Genetics, and Molecular Biology were excluded. In addition, the expression "government size" was searched within the keyword, author, article title, and abstract.

21.2. Findings

In the Scopus database, the keyword, article title, and abstract include "*government size*." As a result of the search, it was determined that 706 studies were published between 1979 and 2025. The first of these publications was the article "Area-Distance, Contact Technology and Administrative Intensity in Societies" written by Nolan, published in 1979 (Nolan, 1979). This article has received 6 citations in total.

Figure 83 shows the course of studies carried out between 1979 and 2025. When the distribution of the studies by years is examined, it is seen that the

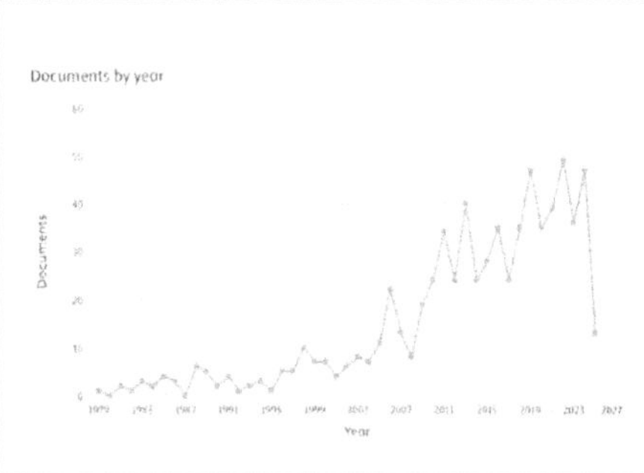

Years	Documents by year	Years	Documents by year
2025	13	**2014**	24
2024	47	**2013**	40
2023	36	**2012**	24
2022	49	**2011**	34
2021	39	**2010**	24
2020	35	**2009**	19
2019	47	**2008**	8
2018	35	**2007**	13
2017	24	**2006**	22
2016	35	**2005**	11
2015	28		

Figure 83. Distribution of articles by years.

popularity of the subject has increased over the years and even the highest number of publications was reached in 2019 and 2024, and 47 studies on the subject were published in these years. It has been determined that 13 studies have been published this year, that is, in 2025, even though it is only the fourth month of the year.

Figure 84 shows the distribution of studies published on the subject by the journal. The journal with the most articles is *Government Choice.* A total of 37 articles were published in this journal, specifically four articles in 1988 and five articles in 2013. The journals with the most publications in total are:

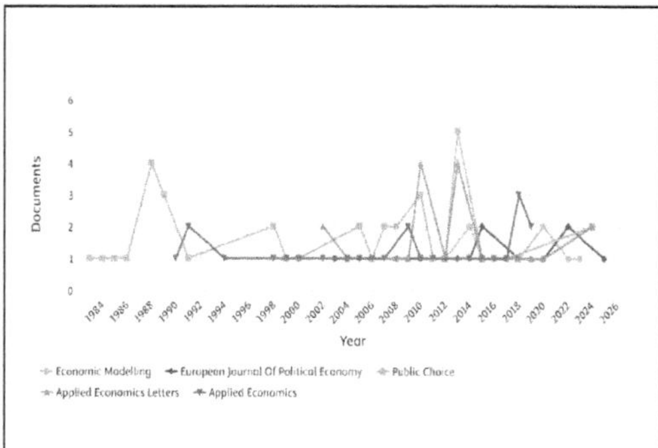

Government Choice	37
Applied Economics	25
Applied Economics Letters	20
European Journal Of Political Economy	16
Economic Modelling	15
Government Finance Review	13
Journal Of Policy Modeling	10
International Tax And Government Finance	8
Economics Letters	7
Economics Bulletin	7

Figure 84. Distribution of the number of articles by year and journals (the top ten most published journals).

Applied Economics 25, Applied Economics Letters 20, European Journal of Political Economy 16, Economic Modelling 15, Government Finance Review 13, Journal of Policy Modeling 10, International Tax and Government Finance 8, Economics Letters 7, Economics Bulletin 7.

Another image belongs to the academics who have published the most on the subject. If Figure 85 is examined, the authors who published the most on the subject can be seen. Goel ranks first with 17 studies, followed by Ferris with 8, Jalles 7, Afonso 6, Bergh 6, Copus 6, Jetter 6, Marlow 6, Mollick 6, and Karras published 5 studies. A noteworthy point is that the authors who have done the most work on the subject differ from the authors who have received the most citations.

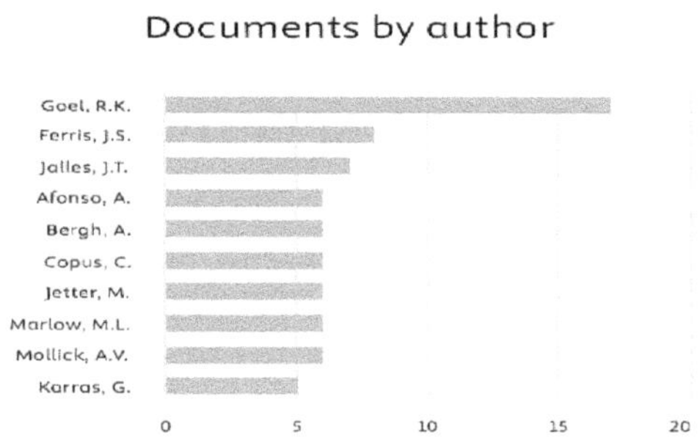

Goel, R.K.	17
Ferris, J.S.	8
Jalles, J.T.	7
Afonso, A.	6
Bergh, A.	6
Copus, C.	6
Jetter, M.	6
Marlow, M.L.	6
Mollick, A.V.	6
Karras, G.	5

Figure 85. Top ten academics who published the most on the subject.

The most cited authors and their works on the subject are listed in Table 85. The most cited author on the subject is Hood. Hood is the first most cited author, with 2,633 citations to his work. Rodrik reached the second-highest number of citations with 1,598 citations. Husted is in third place with 600 citations. It is seen that the authors in the first three rows carried out their studies on the subject as a single author. The other most cited authors carried out their work together with other authors.

Countries where studies within the scope of the analyzed keywords were published: United States, United Kingdom, China, Germany, Spain, Italy, Australia, Turkey, India, and France. The most published studies were in the United States with 202, the United Kingdom with 59, China with 39,

Table 85. Most cited author and citation information on the subject

Author and Government Information	Number of Citations
Hood, C. (1995). The "new government management" in the 1980s: Variations on a theme. *Accounting, Organizations And Society*, *20*(2), 93–109.	2,633
Rodrik, D. (1998). Why do more open economies have bigger governments? *Journal of Political Economy*, *106*(5), 997–1032.	1,598
Husted, B. W. (1999). Wealth, culture, and corruption. *Journal of International Business Studies*, *30*(2), 339–359.	600
Montınola, G. R., & Jackman, R. W. (2002). Sources of corruption: A cross-country study. *British Journal of Political Science*, *32*(1), 147–170.	459
Alesina, A. & Wacziarg, R. (1998). Openness, country size and government. *Journal of Government Economics*, Elsevier, *69*(3), 305–321.	419
Author and Governmentation Information	**Number of Citations**
Fölster, Stefan, & Och Magnus Henrekson (2006). Growth effects of government expenditure and taxation in rich countries. A reply. *European Economic Review*, *50*(1), 219–221.	316
Chowdhury, F., Audretsch, D. B., & Belitski, M. (2019). Institutions and entrepreneurship quality. *Entrepreneurship Theory and Practice*, *43*(1), 51–81.	314
Goel, R. K., & Nelson, M. A. (1998). Corruption and government size: A disaggregated analysis. *Government Choice*, *97*(1/2), 107–120.	261
Bel, G., & Warner, M. E. (2015). Inter-municipal cooperation and costs: Expectations and evidence. *Government Administration (London)*, *93*(1), 52–67.	260
Afonso, A., & Furceri, A. (2008). government size, composition, volatility and economic growth. *Working Papers Department Of Economics 2008/04*, ISEG—Lisbon School of Economics and Management, Department of Economics, University of Lisbon.	238

Germany with 38, Spain with 35, Italy with 33, Australia with 29, Turkey with 29, India with 27, and France with 26 (Figure 86).

When the studies on the research topic are analyzed, out of a total of 706 studies, 659 are articles, 25 are book chapters, 2 are books, 13 are reviews, 3 are conference papers, 2 are letters, 1 is editorial, and 1 is note.

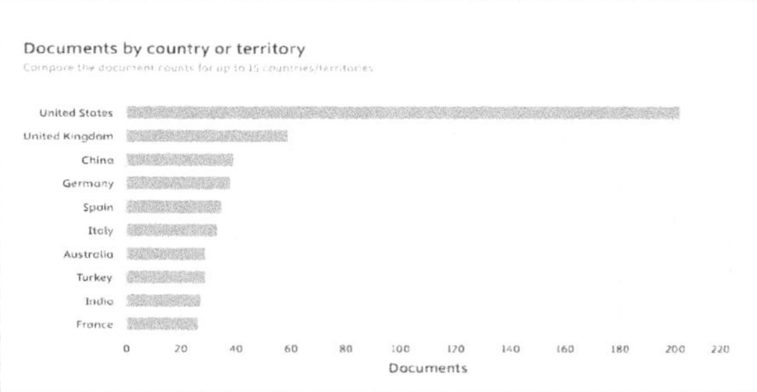

United States	202
United Kingdom	59
China	39
Germany	38
Spain	35
Italy	33
Australia	29
Turkey	29
India	27
France	26

Figure 86. Top ten countries with the most publications on the subject.

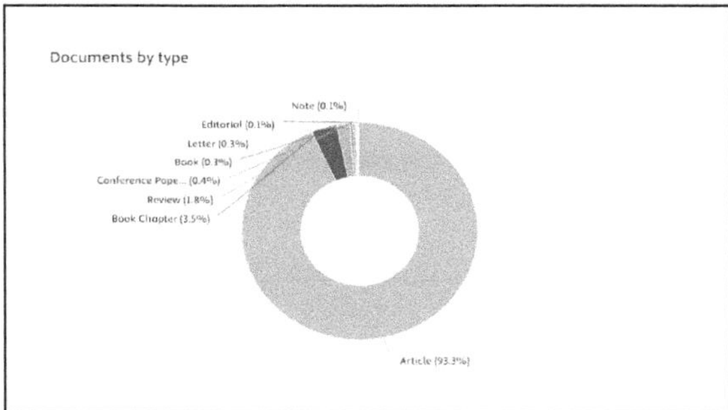

Article	659
Book Chapter	25
Review	13
Conference Paper	3
Book	2
Letter	2
Editorial	1
Note	1

Figure 87. Quality of studies conducted on the subject.

If we analyze the institutions and universities of the authors who conducted studies on the subject presented in Figure 88, Illinois State University ranks first in corporate identity publications, with a total of 22 publications. Following that, Carleton University has 11 publications, ISEG Lisbon School of Economics and Management has 11 publications, University of Economics Ho Chi Minh City has 9 publications, Indiana University Bloomington has 8 publications, the Institute for the World Economy at the University of Kiel has 8 publications, the University of Lisbon has 8 publications, the London School of Economics and Political Science has 7 publications, and the University of Roma Tre and Renmin University of China each have 7 publications.

If the distribution of 706 studies published in Figure 89 by subject areas is examined, 508 publications fall within the scope of Economics, Econometrics, and Finance; 313 publications are in the field of Social Sciences; 150 publications are in Business, Management, and Accounting; 29 are in Environmental

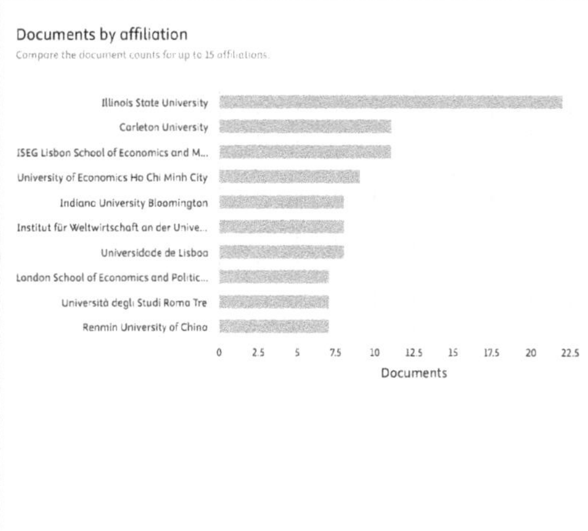

Illinois State University	22
Carleton University	11
ISEG Lisbon School of Economics and Management	11
University of Economics Ho Chi Minh City	9
Indiana University Bloomington	8
Institute for the World Economy at the University of Kiel	8
University of Lisbon	8
London School of Economics and Political Science	7
University of Roma Tre	7
Renmin University of China	7

Figure 88. Institutions and universities affiliated to the authors who produce studies on the subject.

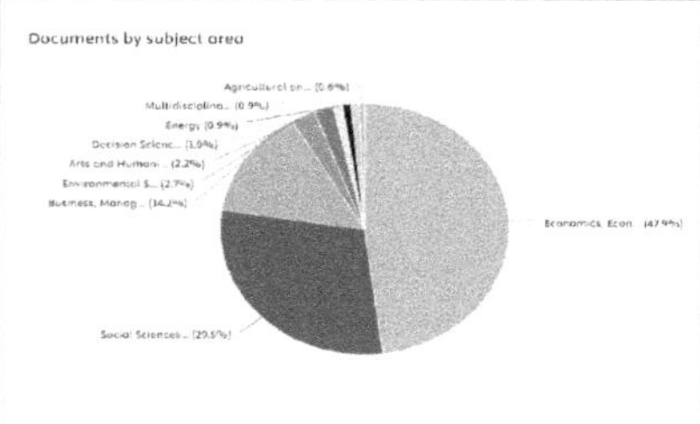

Economics, Econometrics and Finance	508
Social Sciences	313
Business, Management and Accounting	150
Environmental Science	29
Arts and Humanities	23
Decision Sciences	11
Energy	10
Multidisciplinary	10
Agricultural and Biological Sciences	6

Figure 89. Subject areas of published studies.

Science; 23 are in Arts and Humanities; 11 are in Decision Sciences; 10 are in Energy; 10 are Multidisciplinary; and 6 are in Agricultural and Biological Sciences. However, it should not be ignored that some subject areas overlap, indicating that they have intersections.

21.3. Discussion and Conclusion

In this study, the bibliometric analysis method, which is a quantitative analytics approach, was employed to reveal the structure and development of research on "government size." Numerical data were interpreted through visualization in figures and analyzed using statistical methods. The bibliometric approach was chosen because it enables a comprehensive examination of the topic and its progression in the field. Data for the study considered only research from the Scopus database. During the search of the Scopus database, the fields of mathematics, engineering, computer science, psychology, medicine, Earth and Planetary Sciences, as well as Biochemistry, Genetics, and Molecular Biology, were excluded. Additionally, the term "government size" was searched within keywords, author names, article titles, and abstracts.

As a result of scanning the Scopus database with the words "government size" in keywords, article titles, and abstracts, it was determined that 706 studies were published between 1979 and 2025. The first of these publications was the article "Area-Distance, Contact Technology, and Administrative Intensity in Societies," written by Nolan and published in 1979 (Nolan, 1979). This article received six citations in total. The distribution of studies by years shows that the popularity of the subject has increased over the years, and the highest number of publications was reached in 2019 and 2024, and 47 studies on the subject were published in these years. Although it is only in the fourth month of the year, 13 studies have been published. Among the articles, it is the journal with the most publications on the subject (37 publications). *Government Choice* is a journal that has been published in United States since 1966. It is extremely prestigious in its field, scanned in the Web of Science database, and published bimonthly. Rajeev K. Goel, the most published author on the subject, Chicago, United States works at Illinois State University. As a result of the analysis, the country where the subject has been most researched is the United States, and the institution with the highest concentration of studies is Illinois State University. This indicates that the analysis is comparatively validated.

In addition, another point that draws attention as a result of the analysis is the most cited authors. Hood is one of the authors who work on the subject and is not among the top ten, but still receives the most citations for his work. Hood became the most cited author with 2,633 citations to his work. Rodrik reached the second-highest number of citations, with 1,598 citations. Husted is in third place with 600 citations. It is seen that the authors in the first three rows carried out their studies on the subject as a single author. The other most cited authors carried out their work together with other authors.

Approximately 47% of the studies (99 in total) were conducted within the scope of Economics, Econometrics, and Finance; 29.5% were published in Social Sciences, 14.2% in Business, Management, and Accounting, 2.7% in Environmental Science, 2.2% in Arts and Humanities, 1% in Decision Sciences, 0.9% in Energy, 0.9% in Multidisciplinary, and 0.6% in Agricultural and Biological Sciences.

Bibliography

Acar, M. (2010). Free trade, economic freedoms and welfare. *Bilig, 53*, Bahar, 1–28.

Afonso, A. & Furceri, D. (2008). government size, composition, volatility and economic growth. *Working Papers Department of Economics 2008/04*, Iseg—Lisbon School of Economics and Management, Department of Economics, University of Lisbon.

Alesina, A. & Wacziarg, R. (1998). Openness, Country Size and Government. *Journal of Government Economics, 69*(3), 305–321, September. Elsevier.

Chowdhury, F. & Audretsch, D. B., & Belitski, M. (2019). institutions and entrepreneurship quality. *Entrepreneurship Theory and Practice*, *43*(1), 51–81, January.

European Communities (2004). The size of the government sector – How to measure, *24th CEIES Seminar*, Vienna, Luxembourg: Office for Official Publications of the European Communities.

Feldmann, H. (2006). Government size and unemployment: Evidence from industrial countries. *Government Choice*, *127*(3–4), 451–467.

Fölster, S., & Henrekson. O. M. (2006). Growth effects of government expenditure and taxation in rich countries. A reply. *European Economic Review*, *50*(1), 219–221.

Germà, B. & Warner, M. (2015). Inter-municipal cooperation and costs: Expectatıons and evidence. *Government Administration (London)*, *93*(1), 52–67.

Goel, R. K., & Nelson, M. A. (1998). Corruption and government size: A disaggregated analysis. *Government Choice*, *97*(1/2), 107–120.

Öztürk, O. (2022). Bibliyometrik araştırmaların tasarımına ilişkin bir çerçeve. In Oğuzhan Öztürk, & Gökhan Gürler (Eds.), *Bir Literatür İnceleme Aracı Olarak Bibliyometrik Analiz* içinde (pp. 33–52). Ankara: Nobel Yayınevi.

Hood, C. (1995). The "new government management" in the 1980s: variations on a theme. *Accounting, Organizations and Society*, *20*(2), 93–109.

Husted, B. W. (1999). Institute of Technology and Studies. Wealth, culture, and corruption. *Journal of International Business Studies*, *30*(2), 339–359.

Labonte, M. (2010). *The size and role of government: economic issues*, (15.04.2025) <http://www.fas.org/sgp/crs/misc/RL32162.pdf>

Mink, R. (2004). The size of the government sector in the euro area, the US and Japan: How to measure. *24th CEIES Seminar*, Vienna, Luxembourg: Office for Official Publications of The European Communities.

Montınola, G. R., & Jackman, R. W. (2002). Sources of Corruption: A cross-country study. *British Journal of Political Science*, *32*(1), 147–170.

Nolan, P. D. (1979). Area-distance, contact technology and administrative intensity in societies. *Social Forces*, *58*(2), 614–629.

Pritchard, A. (1969). Statistical bibliography or bibliometrics. *Journal of Documentation*, *25*(4), 348–349.

Rodrik, D. (1998). Why do more open economies have bigger governments? *Journal of Political Economy*, *106*(5), 997–1032.

Şekeroğlu, G. (2021). Geçmişten Günümüze Portföy Yönetiminde Neler Değişti? R Programı ile Bibliyometrik Analiz. *Selçuk Üniversitesi Sosyal Ve Teknik Araştırmalar Dergisi*, *19*, 22–33.

Wallin J. A. (2005). Bibliometric methods: pitfalls and possibilities. *Basic & Clinical Pharmacology & Toxicology*, *97*(5), 261–275.

The Impact of Healthcare Accessibility on Community Economic Resilience

Constantinos Challoumis

22.1. Introduction

For communities to thrive, healthcare accessibility stands as a foundational attribute, reflecting not only the physical proximity of medical facilities but also the availability of resources to enable individuals to seek care when necessary. The concept encompasses both geographical and non-geographical barriers, such as financial constraints and societal attitudes toward healthcare. Proximity alone does not suffice; one must also consider how economic factors, including income levels and insurance coverage, play an imperative role in shaping individuals' ability to access healthcare. Thus, healthcare accessibility emerges as a dynamic interplay of various determinants that ultimately influences community welfare and resilience. The presence of accessible healthcare signifies that community members can obtain preventive services, imperative treatments, and emergency care without undue hardship. This accessibility is particularly significant in ensuring that small businesses and individual livelihoods do not falter due to health crises. In systems where healthcare accessibility is optimized, individuals are empowered to maintain their health, which in turn sustains productivity levels and bolsters the local economy. When healthcare is effectively integrated into the fabric of community life, households are better positioned to avoid the detrimental effects of illness on earning potential and savings, thereby contributing to the overall financial ecosystem (Amoah et al., 2021; Döring & Paul, 2010; Islam et al., 2020; Manchadi et al., 2023; Mohamed et al., 2023; Reibling et al., 2019).

An effective healthcare delivery system operates seamlessly within a community, fostering not only improved health outcomes but also economic resilience. The enhancement of healthcare accessibility holds a reciprocal relationship with economic structures, as it influences consumer spending, workforce participation, and the overall vitality of local economies. For instance, in a community characterized by high enforcement savings (ES), the flow of money reinvested in local healthcare can catalyze improvements in systemic health infrastructure, thereby accelerating the money cycle as households experience fewer financial drains from health-related issues. In essence, healthcare accessibility becomes a pivotal determinant in establishing and maintaining a robust economic framework.

22.2. Literature Review

Influencing the discourse on healthcare accessibility are various measurement metrics that seek to quantify how effectively communities can access necessary health services. These measurements can include parameters such as the ratio of healthcare providers to the population, the affordability of services, and the distance individuals must travel to obtain medical care. Moreover, qualitative measures, such as patient satisfaction and perceived barriers, offer insights into the user experience, ultimately shaping the broader understanding of accessibility. It is through this investigative lens that we can advocate for initiatives aimed at enhancing healthcare delivery. The issue of healthcare accessibility requires a comprehensive evaluation of both quantitative and qualitative data. Healthcare becomes not only a measure of community health but also a lens through which we can view economic resilience. By investing in healthcare systems that promote accessibility, communities unlock the potential for a self-reinforcing cycle of economic growth and improved health outcomes. Moreover, the economic conditions prevalent in a community can directly influence public health outcomes. Areas experiencing economic hardships often witness declining healthcare services, increased unemployment, and a rise in mental health issues, which leads to adverse health outcomes (Cerf, 2023; Götmark & Andersson, 2020; Junaidi & Liza, 2023; Kumar, 2023; Li & Tang, 2023; Lo Storto & Goncharuk, 2017; Tegegne & Wubante, 2022; Tu, 2024; Valle, 2016; Zhang & Xu, 2022). Conversely, regions with strong economic foundations tend to have better investment in healthcare facilities, resulting in improved health quality. This cyclical relationship highlights the need for a dual approach that incorporates both health and economic strategies in policy planning; when one sector suffers, the repercussions reverberate throughout the other, highlighting their intertwined fates. Below surface-level health disparities lie geographic barriers, which can substantially affect healthcare accessibility. Rural regions often lack sufficient healthcare facilities, forcing individuals to travel considerable distances to access basic services.

These distances not only exacerbate health issues through delayed treatments but also drain financial resources, as residents may have to rely on costly transport options or miss work to receive care (Challoumis, 2018, 2019, 2021, 2023b, 2023e, 2024a; Challoumis & Eriotis, 2024a). The intricacies of healthcare financing, in conjunction with limited education on available resources, create a formidable obstacle for many community members. Without adequate understanding or trust in the healthcare system, individuals may perceive barriers that do not exist, leading to missed opportunities for preventive care. This overarching issue highlights the need for strategic investment in health literacy programs and supportive initiatives aimed at demonstrating the value of preventative measures, thereby encouraging individuals to utilize local resources effectively.

Many communities thrive when their members have access to comprehensive healthcare services. This access significantly influences physical health outcomes, as it enables individuals to receive timely medical attention and preventive care. For instance, preventive services such as vaccinations, regular check-ups, and screenings can drastically reduce the incidence of chronic diseases. According to studies, populations with better healthcare access exhibit lower rates of preventable conditions like diabetes and cardiovascular diseases. This reduction not only improves individual health but also reduces the economic burden on the local healthcare system, allowing for more efficient allocation of resources and promoting a cycle of ES (Challoumis, 2024c, 2024e; Challoumis & Eriotis, 2024b, 2025). As individuals within these communities maintain better health, their capacity to contribute to the economy increases, resulting in a reinforced cycle of money that elevates the entire community's economic structure. Moreover, healthcare accessibility has a profound impact on overall community resilience. A sound healthcare system allows individuals to recover more quickly from illnesses or injuries, thereby reducing the economic implications of lost productivity. This resilience is an embodiment of the money cycle theory, where both ES and local investments are bolstered. When mental health services are easily accessible, individuals are more likely to seek help early, resulting in better management of their conditions. Importantly, this early intervention can prevent the escalation of issues that might otherwise lead to more severe problems, including substance abuse, homelessness, and increased healthcare costs, which could decimate local economies through escape savings (ESC) (Challoumis, 2022, 2023a, 2023c, 2023d, 2023f, 2024b, 2024d). By addressing mental health proactively, communities can enhance the overall quality of life, leading to increased collective resilience and a more stable economic environment where local businesses can flourish.

All facets of economic stability and progress hinge upon the capabilities of the workforce. Healthcare accessibility is a pivotal determinant of productivity, which ultimately drives labor force participation. When community members have reliable access to healthcare services, they can maintain better physical and mental health, effectively minimizing absenteeism in the workplace. This productive engagement translates into a more robust economy, one where individuals contribute their skills and talents with greater frequency and efficiency. Consequently, industries experience a heightened output, thus fostering an environment where businesses can flourish and innovate. Economic theories such as the Cycle of Money elucidate how increased productivity feeds the system of ES, enhancing the overall economic structure. Moreover, the relationship between healthcare accessibility and labor force participation is further solidified when we consider the long-term effects. Individuals who can access preventive care and treatment are more likely to remain in the workforce longer, delaying retirement and enhancing their lifetime earnings (Challoumis, 2022). Universal healthcare models emerge as vital mechanisms to ensure that all individuals receive the health services, they need without facing financial hardship. Data suggests that communities supported by universal healthcare systems tend to enjoy higher rates of workforce participation and lower rates of morbidity, which ultimately contribute to a more robust local economy. By investing in preventive healthcare and ensuring equitable access to services, universal healthcare models can enhance economic stability and resilience. Accessibility to healthcare remains a systemic challenge, especially in regions where financial barriers inhibit individuals from seeking timely medical attention. A shift toward universal healthcare would necessitate the implementation of progressive tax policies that ensure adequate funding for these services, as delineated in the theory of the cycle of money, which highlights the significance of ES (Grove et al., 2020; Hartz & John, 2009; Margaret, 2021," 2019; Lacombe, 2019; Pablo et al., 2021;Vadalouca). For instance, communities with high ratios of ES tend to reinvest in local health systems, promoting a cycle where money circulates within the economy (Challoumis, 2025). This creates a win–win scenario: community members gain access to necessary healthcare, and the economic structure benefits from the reinvestment of those funds back into the local economy.

22.3. Methodology

The methodology is based on the Quantification of Everything (QE) method on the basis of the theory of Cycle of Money (which is a validation method based on generators). This is not a classic model of the cycle of money. This section presents the formal equations used in modeling the relationship between healthcare accessibility and community economic resilience. Each equation is followed by its economic interpretation, reflecting the structure of the QE method and the Cycle of Money theory (Challoumis, 2024e).

Total Healthcare Accessibility:

$$a = a_s + a_t \tag{1}$$

The total accessibility potential a is the sum of structural accessibility a_s (e.g., number of clinics, hospitals) and technical accessibility a_t (e.g., availability of staff, medical technology).

Accessibility Input Configuration:

$$a_{pki} = a_{p1} + a_{p2} + a_{p3} \tag{2}$$

The i-th combination of healthcare investment is composed of components a_{p1}, a_{p2}, a_{p3}, such as subsidies, mobile units, and preventive programs. These represent alternative strategies tested via the QE method.

Modified Money Input:

$$m_{ki} = m_1 + a_{pki} \tag{3}$$

The modified money flow m_{ki} in the local economy is the baseline monetary input m_1, plus the added investment from the accessibility configuration a_{pki}.

Net Economic Surplus:

$$x_{mki} = m_{ki} - a \tag{4}$$

This measures the net benefit or loss produced by a given healthcare input. It compares the total money introduced to the actual accessibility need.

Cycle Multiplication Coefficient:

$$c_{mk_i} = \frac{x_{mk_i}}{a} \tag{5}$$

This coefficient quantifies how much net benefit is produced per unit of accessibility effort. Higher values indicate more effective amplification of healthcare investments.

Monetary Efficiency Coefficient:

$$c_{\alpha k_i} = \frac{x_{mk_i}}{m_{k_i}} \tag{6}$$

This ratio indicates how efficiently the total money injected is converted into economic surplus. A higher value suggests fewer losses and better local money circulation.

Cycle Yield:

$$c_{yki} = c_{mki} - c_{\alpha ki} \tag{7}$$

Cycle yield is the core measure of economic resilience. It reflects how well the healthcare investment both amplifies economic activity and retains money within the local system. A high c_{yki} implies strong resilience, low ESC, and maximized ES. These equations form the theoretical core of our simulation model and serve as a practical framework for policymakers to assess which healthcare strategies optimize both social outcomes and local economic performance. In alignment with the Cycle of Money theory, the cost function developed in this model reflects the dynamic interaction between two key components:

Enforcement Savings (ES): Money that is reinvested into the community, reinforcing the economic cycle through increased local spending, job creation, and sustainable growth.

Escape Savings (ESC): Money that leaves the local economy, whether through inefficiency, health expenditures outside the region, or systemic leakage, thus weakening the cycle of money and reducing economic resilience.

To simulate the impact of healthcare accessibility on these components, we define the synthetic cost function as:

$$\text{cost}_i = \left(1 - c_{yki}\right) \cdot a_{pki} \tag{8}$$

where c_{yki} is the cycle yield coefficient for the *i*-th healthcare accessibility strategy; a_{pki} is the aggregated healthcare accessibility investment for strategy *i*.

This cost function reflects inefficiency in the allocation of healthcare resources:

When cost_i is low, the corresponding cycle yield is high, indicating that most of the invested money remains within the local economy, thus, ES dominates.

When cost_i is high, the healthcare input fails to generate adequate cycle yield, meaning resources leak from the local system, therefore, ESC increases.

Consequently, this cost function serves as a diagnostic tool for optimizing healthcare investment strategies. It enables policymakers and planners to identify accessibility configurations that maximize ES while minimizing ESC, thereby reinforcing the local economic cycle and enhancing community resilience.

22.4. Findings and Discussion

Based on Equations (1)–(8), the simulated data and results are defined in the next scheme (Challoumis, 2024e):

The simulation results illustrated in the graph provide empirical support for the thesis that healthcare accessibility functions as a critical component of the Cycle of Money, contributing directly to economic resilience. Across most iterations, the synthetic costs for various healthcare investment strategies remain near or above zero, indicating that the majority of configurations produce favorable cycle yields. This suggests that money invested in accessible healthcare services, whether through infrastructure, staffing, or mobile units, is not lost to inefficiency but rather reinvested into the local economy (Al-Habib, 2020; Ćwiklicki et al., 2020; Islam et al., 2020; Jagadeeswari et al., 2018; Li et al., 2020; Li & Tang,

Table 86. Simulation coefficients

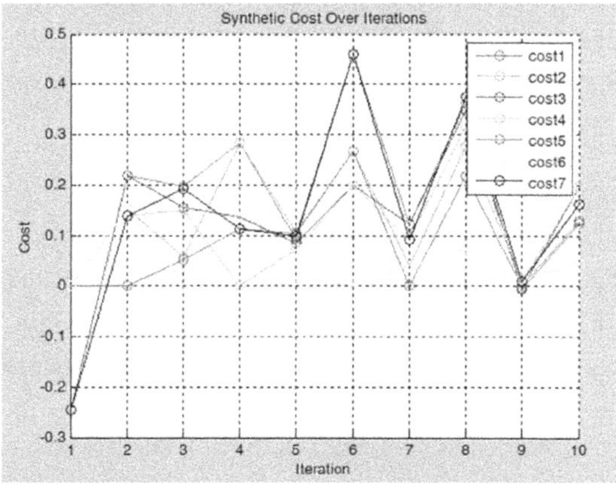

Coefficient	Maximum value (range)
α_s	0.6
α_s	0.7
m_1	0.9
α_{p1}	0.4
α_{p2}	0.3
α_{p3}	0.2

Table 87. Synthetic Cost Compile (see Appendix)

Results						
−0.2445	0	−0.2445	−0.2445	0	0	−0.2445
0.2182	0.1526	0.2182	0.1381	0	0.1526	0.1381
0.1972	0.0572	0.155	0.1495	0.051	0.0064	0.1922
0.2838	0.2838	0.1372	0	0.1133	0.1372	0.1133
0.0916	0.106	0.0844	0.0737	0.1028	0.019	0.0988
0.459	0.2668	0.1997	0.1997	0.2668	0	0.459
0.1219	0.0393	0.1219	0.0929	0	0.0393	0.0929
0.3631	0.276	0.35	0.3154	0.2178	0.0761	0.3745
−0.0066	0.0152	−0.0046	0.011	0.0017	0.0139	0.0095
0.1246	0.162	0.1973	0.1975	0.1294	0.0456	0.1616

2023; Manchadi et al., 2023; Pablo et al., 2021; Shafqat et al., 2020; Wang et al., 2023). As per the Cycle of Money theory, such investments translate into ES, strengthening local economic activity by keeping financial resources circulating within the community. In contrast, very few points fall below zero, which would signify ESC or economic leakage. The relatively stable and positive synthetic cost levels demonstrate that when healthcare accessibility is optimized, it not only improves public health outcomes but also minimizes systemic inefficiencies, reinforcing the local economic structure. This validates the healthcare system's role as a regenerative force in economic cycles, making it not merely a social necessity but a strategic economic engine within the community.

22.5. Conclusion

The intricate relationship between healthcare accessibility and community economic resilience is akin to the delicate balance observed in the cosmos, where every component, however minuscule, contributes to the grandeur of the whole. Communities that enjoy robust healthcare systems are not merely repositories of health; they serve as the bedrock upon which economic activities flourish. A population that is healthy is inherently more productive, better equipped to engage in labor, and less prone to the debilitating effects of chronic illnesses that can thwart both individual aspirations and collective economic progress. As such, the accessibility of healthcare can stimulate a virtuous cycle, where improvements in public health led to enhanced workforce participation, increased local spending, and ultimately, a fortified community economy. It is a self-reinforcing system, demonstrating that the well-being of individuals does not exist in isolation but rather as an interwoven fabric of societal prosperity.

Appendix

The following code is on MATLAB and is based on QE method:

```
Constantinos Challoumis 2025 ©® All Rights Reserved
% Initialize simulation data
t = 0;
tab = [];
cost_tab = [];

while t < 10
   t = t + 1;

   if rand() < 0.9
      as = 0.6 * rand();
   else
      as = 0;
   end
```

```
if rand() < 0.9
   at = 0.7 * rand();
else
   at = 0;
end

if rand() < 0.9
   m1 = 0.9 * rand();
else
   m1 = 0;
end

if rand() < 0.9
   ap1 = 0.4 * rand();
else
   ap1 = 0;
end

if rand() < 0.9
   ap2 = 0.3 * rand();
else
   ap2 = 0;
end

if rand() < 0.9
   ap3 = 0.2 * rand();
else
   ap3 = 0;
end

a = as + at;
apk = [ap1+ap2+ap3, ap2+ap3, ap1+ap3, ap1, ap2, ap3, ap1+ap2];
cyk = zeros(1, 7);
costs = zeros(1, 7);

for i = 1:7
   mk = m1 + apk(i);
   xmk = mk - a;

   if a ~= 0
      cmk = xmk / a;
   else
```

```
            cmk = 0;
        end

        if mk ~= 0
            cak = xmk / mk;
        else
            cak = 0;
        end

        cyk(i) = cmk - cak;
        costs(i) = (1 - cyk(i)) * apk(i);  % Synthetic cost model
    end

    tab = [tab; apk, cyk];
    cost_tab = [cost_tab; costs];
end

% Display synthetic costs
disp('Synthetic Cost Table:');
disp(cost_tab);

% Plot the results
figure;
hold on;
colors = 'rgbcmyk';
for i = 1:7
    plot(1:10, cost_tab(:,i), ['-o' colors(i)], 'DisplayName', ['cost' num2str(i)]);
end
title('Synthetic Cost Over Iterations');
xlabel('Iteration');
ylabel('Cost');
legend show;
grid on;
hold off;
```

Bibliography

Al-Habib, N. (2020). Leadership and organizational performance: Is it essential in healthcare systems improvement? A review of literature. *Saudi Journal of Anaesthesia*. Retrieved from <https://doi.org/10.4103/sja.SJA_288_19>

Amoah, P. A., Nyamekye, K. A., & Owusu-Addo, E. (2021). A multidimensional study of public satisfaction with the healthcare system: a mixed-method inquiry in Ghana. *BMC Health Services Research*, *21*(1). Retrieved from <https://doi.org/10.1186/s12913-021-07288-1>

Byrne, J. D., Wentworth, A. J., Chai, P. R., Huang, H. W., Babaee, S., Li, C., …, Traverso, G. (2020). Injection Molded Autoclavable, Scalable, Conformable (iMASC) system for aerosol-based protection: A prospective single-arm feasibility study. *BMJ Open*, *10*(7). Retrieved from <https://doi.org/10.1136/bmjopen-2020-039120>

Challoumis, C. (2018). Methods of controlled transactions and the behavior of companies according to the public and tax policy. *Economics*, *6*(1), 33–43. Retrieved from <https://doi.org/10.2478/eoik-2018-0003>

Challoumis, C. (2019). The R.B.Q. (Rational, Behavioral and Quantified) Model. *Ekonomika*, *98*(1), 6–18. Retrieved from <https://doi.org/10.15388/ekon.2019.1.1>

Challoumis, C. (2021). Index of the cycle of money—The case of Bulgaria. *Economic Alternatives*, *27*(2), 225–234. Retrieved from <https://www.unwe.bg/doi/eajournal/2021.2/EA.2021.2.04.pdf>

Challoumis, C. (2022). Conditions of the CM (Cycle of Money). In V. Kaya (Ed.), *Social and economic studies within the framework of emerging global developments* (Vol. 1, pp. 13–24). Retrieved from <https://doi.org/10.3726/b19907>

Challoumis, C. (2023a). A comparison of the velocities of minimum escaped savings and financial liquidity. In V. Kaya (Ed.), *Social and economic studies within the framework of emerging global developments* (Vol. 4, pp. 41–56). Retrieved from <https://doi.org/10.3726/b21202>

Challoumis, C. (2023b). From savings to escape and enforcement savings. *Cogito*, *XV*(4), 206–216.

Challoumis, C. (2023c). Impact factor of liability of tax system according to the theory of cycle of money. In V. Kaya (Ed.), *Social and economic studies within the framework of emerging global developments* (Vol. 3, pp. 31–42). Retrieved from <https://doi.org/10.3726/b20968>

Challoumis, C. (2023d). Index of the cycle of money: The case of Costa Rica. *Sapienza*, *4*(3), 1–11. Retrieved from <https://journals.sapienzaeditorial.com/index.php/SIJIS>

Challoumis, C. (2023e). Risk on the tax system of the E.U. from 2016 to 2022. *Economics*, *11*(2), 55–72.

Challoumis, C. (2023f). Utility of cycle of money without the escaping savings (protection of the economy). In V. Kaya (Ed.), *Social and economic studies within the framework of emerging global developments* (Vol. 2, pp. 53–64). Retrieved from <https://doi.org/10.3726/b20509>

Challoumis, C. (2024a). From economics to economic engineering (the cycle of money): The case of Romania. *Cogito*, *XVII*(2), 161–170.

Challoumis, C. (2024b). Impact factor of liability using the sensitivity method. In Bayrakdar, S. & Chodnicka-Jaworska, P.(Ed.), Social and economic studies within the framework of emerging global developments. Berlin, Germany: Peter Lang, 77–86. Retrieved from < 10.3726/b22541>

Challoumis, C. (2024c). Integrating money cycle dynamics and economocracy for optimal resource allocation and economic stability. *Journal of Risk and Financial Management*, *17*(9), 1–25. Retrieved from <https://doi.org/10.3390/jrfm17090422>

Challoumis, C. (2024d). Rewarding taxes on the cycle of money. Social and Economic Studies within the Framework of Emerging Global Developments (Vol. 5).

Challoumis, C. (2024e). The index of the cycle of money: The case of Switzerland. *Journal of Risk and Financial Management*, *17*(4), 1–24. Retrieved from <https://doi.org/https://doi.org/10.3390/jrfm17040135>

Challoumis, C. (2025). The impact factor of tangibles and intangibles of controlled transactions on economic performance. *Economic Alternatives*, *31*(1), 64–76. Retrieved from <https://www.unwe.bg/doi/eajournal/2025.1/EA.2025.1.04.pdf>

Challoumis, C., & Eriotis, N. (2024a). A historical analysis of the banking system and its impact on Greek economy. *Edelweiss Applied Science and Technology*, *8*(6), 1598–1617. Retrieved from <https://learning-gate.com/index.php/2576-8484/article/view/2282/892>

Challoumis, C., & Eriotis, N. (2024b). The historical view of banking system in greece during the financial crisis. *Journal of Ecohumanism*, *5*(8), 991–1011. Retrieved from <https://ecohumanism.co.uk/joe/ecohumanism/article/view/4776>

Challoumis, C., & Eriotis, N. (2025). Management of enterprises in the Greek economy. *Journal of Management World*, *2025*(3), 17–30. Retrieved from <https://www.managementworld.online/index.php/mw/article/view/1039>

Ćwiklicki, M., Klich, J., & Chen, J. (2020). The adaptiveness of the healthcare system to the fourth industrial revolution: A preliminary analysis. *Futures*, 122. Retrieved from <https://doi.org/10.1016/j.futures.2020.102602>

Döring, A., & Paul, F. (2010). The German healthcare system. *EPMA Journal.* Retrieved from <https://doi.org/10.1007/s13167-010-0060-z>

Grove, A., Sanders, T., Salway, S., Goyder, E., & Hampshaw, S. (2020). A qualitative exploration of evidence-based decision making in public health practice and policy: The perceived usefulness of a diabetes economic model for decision makers. *Evidence and Policy*, *15*(4). Retrieved from <https://doi.org/10.1332/174426418X15245020185055>

Hartz, S., & John, J. (2009). Public health policy decisions on medical innovations: What role can early economic evaluation play? *Health Policy*, *89*(2). Retrieved from <https://doi.org/10.1016/j.healthpol.2008.05.011>

Margaret Mary, Hanumanthappa. M., Sangamithra A. (2019). Intelligent predicting learning disabilities in school going children using fuzzy logic K mean clustering in machine learning. *International Journal of Recent Technology and Engineering*, *8*(4). Retrieved from <https://doi.org/10.35940/ijrte.c5620.118419>

Islam, M. M., Rahaman, A., & Islam, M. R. (2020). Development of smart healthcare monitoring system in IoT environment. *SN Computer Science*, *1*(3). Retrieved from <https://doi.org/10.1007/s42979-020-00195-y>

Jagadeeswari, V., Subramaniyaswamy, V., Logesh, R., & Vijayakumar, V. (2018). A study on medical Internet of Things and Big Data in personalized healthcare system. *Health Information Science and Systems*, *6*(1). Retrieved from <https://doi.org/10.1007/s13755-018-0049-x>

Kern, J., & Strnad, M. (2005). [Informatics in the Croatian health care system]. *Acta Medica Croatica*, *59*(3), 161–8.

Lacombe, D. (2019). Data sharing as a continuum to the role of international networks: Beyond clinical research. *Tumori*, 105(2), 50–52.

Li, J., Cai, J., Khan, F., Rehman, A. U., Balasubramaniam, V., Sun, J., & Venu, P. (2020). A secured framework for SDN-based edge computing in IoT-enabled healthcare system. *IEEE Access*, 8. Retrieved from <https://doi.org/10.1109/ACCESS.2020.3011503>

Li, Y., & Tang, M. (2023). Blockchain-powered distributed data auditing scheme for cloud-edge healthcare system. *Cyber Security and Applications*, 1. Retrieved from <https://doi.org/10.1016/j.csa.2023.100017>

Manchadi, O., Ben-Bouazza, F. E., & Jioudi, B. (2023). Predictive maintenance in healthcare system: A survey. *IEEE Access*, 11. Retrieved from <https://doi.org/10.1109/ACCESS.2023.3287490>

Mohamed, N., Al-Jaroodi, J., Jawhar, I., & Kesserwan, N. (2023). Leveraging digital twins for healthcare systems engineering. *IEEE Access*, 11. Retrieved from <https://doi.org/10.1109/ACCESS.2023.3292119>

Pablo, R. G. J., Roberto, D. P., Victor, S. U., Isabel, G. R., Paul, C., & Elizabeth, O. R. (2021). Big data in the healthcare system: A synergy with artificial intelligence and blockchain technology. *Journal of Integrative Bioinformatics*. Retrieved from <https://doi.org/10.1515/jib-2020-0035>

Reibling, N., Ariaans, M., & Wendt, C. (2019). Worlds of healthcare: A healthcare system typology of OECD countries. *Health Policy*. Retrieved from <https://doi.org/10.1016/j.healthpol.2019.05.001>

Shafqat, S., Kishwer, S., Rasool, R. U., Qadir, J., Amjad, T., & Ahmad, H. F. (2020). Big data analytics enhanced healthcare systems: A review. *Journal of Supercomputing*, *76*(3). Retrieved from <https://doi.org/10.1007/s11227-017-2222-4>

Studnicki, J., Berndt, D. J., & Fisher, J. W. (2007). Using information systems for public health administration. *Public Health Administration: Principles for Population-Based Management*, (2).

Vadalouca, A., Rekatsina, M., & Siafaka, I. (2019). ESRA19-0691 neuropathic pain registries: Lessons learned from international, european or national initiatives. Retrieved from <https://doi.org/10.1136/rapm-2019-esraabs2019.51>

Wang, W., Li, X., Qiu, X., Zhang, X., Zhao, J., & Brusic, V. (2023). A privacy preserving framework for federated learning in smart healthcare systems. *Information Processing and Management*, *60*(1). Retrieved from <https://doi.org/10.1016/j.ipm.2022.103167>

The Features of Integration of the Republic of Moldova in European Foreign Exchange Market

Svetlana Biloocaia

23.1. Introduction

The financial market as a system of interrelated and interdependent financial flows is a complex structural formation, determined by the specifics of internal development and by the influence of external factors. The mobilization of capital necessary for large-scale investments, organization of settlements between participants of complex economic chains, minimization of credit and currency risks in the modern economy are impossible without the integration of the national financial system into the global system.

International experience proves that a highly integrated financial system contributes to economic growth and enhances the competitiveness of the country by reducing the cost of capital, minimizing risks, and facilitating a more efficient distribution of financial resources. Financial integration provides an opportunity to direct capital where it can be used with maximum efficiency, contributing to an increase in the volume of attracted investment capital, smoothing consumption, and unifying monetary policy (European Investment Bank, 2022). Free movement of capital is the cornerstone of the European Union (EU) development. Over the past decades, many different initiatives have been implemented to strengthen the processes of financial integration within Europe. Particularly relevant is the task of integrating the national market into the global financial system and the global foreign exchange market for developing countries (Hakkarainen, 2018).

The foreign exchange market is one the most important element of communication between the national and world economies; foreign currency is used in settlements, accumulated in bank deposits, issued to the borrower during credit operations; quotes for securities and financial derivatives are set on international exchanges in foreign currency (Ivanovsky, 2012).

The Republic of Moldova and the EU have lasting and sustainable economic and financial ties. In 2022, based on the application submitted, the European Council granted the Republic of Moldova the status of an EU candidate country, and were officially opened negotiations with Moldova on joining the EU in 2024. The new status of Moldova presumes the implementation of different complex tasks, including the integration of various segments of the national financial market into the EU market.

The purpose of this study is based on modern EU methods for estimating the degree of financial integration, to investigate the level of the Moldovan foreign exchange market integration into the European foreign exchange market, and to analyze how the dynamic of the integration of the national exchange market coincides with main trends characteristic of markets in some EU and non-EU European non-euro countries, and to identify the main factors that influence it.

23.2. Theoretical Framework

Financial integration as a phenomenon has existed for a long time, which has been studied by scientists worldwide. However, despite the wide coverage in scientific literature, both content and quality of existing theoretical investigations on this problem are scarce. There are various definitions of financial integration. Some investigations argue that financial integration is a phenomenon whereby financial markets in global, regional, or neighboring economies are closely linked to each other; for example, through cross-border capital flows, the presence of foreign participants in domestic financial markets, and the existence of information exchange between financial institutions (<https://capital.com/financial-integration-definition>).

According to the European Investment Bank interpretation "international financial integration can be broadly defined as the process of strengthening cross-border links between financial markets" (Hoffman et al., 2019). The European Central Bank (ECB) definition assumes that integration in a given market is achieved if all its participants have identical characteristics: they all face similar rules when dealing with respective financial instruments; they have the same access to these financial instruments; and they are handled the same way when providing activity in the market (Baele et al., 2004).

The extent of financial integration is assessed through various indicators. Several studies investigate the level of integration by analyzing accumulated savings of households and firms, their investment decisions, and cross-border links. The essence of this concept is that in scenarios of perfect integration, the relationship between domestic saving and domestic investment should be insignificant, since domestic investments can be financed by global savings and, in turn, domestic savings can be directed worldwide to maximize profit. Several studies investigate the level of financial integration through the ability of the integrated market to provide risk sharing (Nardo et al., 2020). A number of research papers proposed composite indicators to assess integration; for example, in the European Investment Bank' study, an econometric model and factor-augmented vector autoregression were used, which calculation was based on information about price dynamics (asset price convergence) and quantity series (cross-border asset holdings).

The results obtained in this study revealed that during times of world and sovereign financial crises, the extent of financial integration decreases, but after their finalization, the trend reverses (Hoffman et al., 2019). A significant number of studies evaluating financial integration relies on the *law of one price* (Babecky et al., 2013; Coeurdacier et al., 2019; Hoffmann et al., 2019; Soofi, 2008). According to this law, under conditions of financial integration, in similar conditions, identical assets in different countries should be sold at same price.

The ECB studies the dynamics of eurozone markets' financial integration since 2005. Initially, ECB's research was based on the analysis of price-based indicators, news-based indicators, and quantity-based indicators. To date, the ECB calculates indicators that estimate the integration of various sectors of the Eurozone financial market, infrastructure indicators, risk sharing, and composite indicators, indicators that were previously reflected in the ECB's annual reports on financial structures (ECB, 2022).

Several studies were implemented to assess the financial integration of EU currency and money markets. For example, a study was conducted to evaluate how the launch of a single EU currency (euro) influenced the level of its financial integration (ECB, 2010). Additionally, the degree of integration of Central and Eastern Europe countries was studied, which was accomplished by investigating the evolution of the foreign exchange rate in the region (Hung, 2019). Similar studies to estimate the financial integration based on foreign exchange markets analysis were conducted on the African continent (Boubaker et al., 2019).

23.3. Applied Methods

This study, aimed at evaluating the integration of European exchange markets, applied *price-based* categories of measures, in conditions of the relevance of the *law of one price*, and involves the use of *β-convergence* and *σ-convergence* concepts.

To assess *β-convergence*, regression analysis or the panel estimation method is relevant:

$$\Delta R_{i,t} = \alpha_i + \beta R_{i,t-1} + \sum_{l=1}^{L} \eta_l \Delta R_{i,t-l} + \varepsilon_{i,t} \tag{1.1}$$

where $R_{i,t}$ is the difference between growth rate of the exchange rates of country i and benchmark country at time t, Δ is the difference operator, α_i is an individual intercept for the analyzed country, L is the chosen lag, and $\varepsilon_{t,i}$ is a random term. The size of β-coefficient is a measure of the convergence speed. The closer the calculated β-coefficient to –1, the higher the speed of convergence. If β values vary from –1 to 0, this indicates the presence of monotonous convergence, if the β-coefficient is in the range from –2 to –1, this indicates oscillating convergence.

Estimation of *σ-convergence* is based on computing the standard deviation:

$$\sigma_t = \sqrt{\frac{\sum_{i=1}^{N}\left[\log\left(Y_{i,t}\right) - \log\left(Y_t^B\right)\right]^2}{N}} \tag{1.2}$$

where $Y_{i,t}$ is the growth rate of exchange rate in country i and Y_t^B is the correspondent exchange rate in benchmark-country over time t. As this analysis examines the evolution of σ between two countries, $N = 2$. The smaller the computed the values of σ, the greater the degree of convergence among the markets of the countries studied, full integration is reached when σ is equal to zero (Baele et al., 2004).

The comparative analysis of the levels of financial integration based on the evolution of exchange rates of European countries currencies against the euro covered:

- EU countries which still use own currency (Hungary, Romania);
- non-EU European countries (Belarus, Republic of Moldova, Ukraine).

Analysis of financial integration was conducted for 2017–2024. Since various factors had an impact on the financial systems in this period, it was divided into three periods:

- In 2017–2019, there were no significant negative factors affecting financial markets;
- In 2020–2021, the national financial markets were affected by the COVID-19 pandemic and related consequences;
- In 2022–2024, the economy and financial sectors of the countries studied were affected by various specific for each country factors.

The study is based on a comparative analysis of the dynamics of the exchange rate of the national currency of each of the investigated countries in relation to the euro with the dynamics of the exchange rate of the national currency of the benchmark-country—Sweden, also in relation to the euro. Calculation relied on the average daily data. Data were obtained from the countries' Central Banks' websites.

23.4. Results and Discussions

In recent years, significant progress has been made in Europe in integrating various sectors of the financial market, including foreign exchange markets. The assessment of involved countries' financial integration dynamics made it possible to highlight the features of integration evolution and prospects for further development.

1. *Price-based measures carried out based on concepts of β-convergence.* The results of the implemented estimation of the β-coefficient executed using econometric model 1.1 are reflected in Table 88.

An analysis of the outcomes of the computations of the β-coefficient on exchange markets of investigated European countries, reveals that:

- During all the analyzed periods, the extent of financial integration of all the countries studied, estimated based on the evolution of the exchange

Table 88. Dynamics of β-coefficient, 2017–2024

Country	β-coefficient		
	2017–2019	2020–2021	2022–2024
Hungary	–1.052229	–1.079559	–0.999501
Romania	–1.019142	–1.289446	–0.988839
Belarus	–0.858671	–0.855040	–0.920376
Ukraine	–0.945142	–0.934465	–1.025756
Republic of Moldova	–0.968973	–1.053495	–0.958695

Source: Developed by the author based on the websites: <https://bank.gov.ua/ua/markets/exchangerate-chart?cn%5B%5D=EUR&startDate=01.01. 2015&endDate=13.06.2023>, <https://www.bnm.md/en/content/official-exchange-rates>, <https://www.bnr.ro/Statistics-report-1124.aspx>, <https://www.mnb.hu/en/arfolyam-lekerdezes>, <https://www.nbrb.by/engl/statistics/rates/ratesdaily.asp>, <https://www.riksbank.se/en-gb/statistics/search-interest--exchange-rates/cross-rates/?cpa0 =SEK&cpb0=SEKEURPMI&cpa1=&cpb1=&cpa2=&cpb2=&cpa3=&cpb3=&cpa4=&cpb4=&from=02%2F01%2F2017&to=30%2F06%2F2023&f=Day&s=Comma>.

rates of their national currencies against the euro, demonstrates a fairly high level, with some decrease during the COVID-19 pandemic.

- During the 2017–2019 period, the maximum extent of financial integration and the greater the speed of convergence was registered in Romania. Both Romania and Hungary were characterized by oscillating convergence, while Belarus and Ukraine were characterized by the least degree of financial. For these countries, as well as for the Moldova, monotonous convergence is typical.
- During the 2020–2021 period, the maximum level of financial integration as well as the greater the speed of convergence was registered in the Republic of Moldova, Ukraine, and Hungary, while the least extent of financial integration was observed in Romania. For all countries except Ukraine and Belarus, convergence was characteristically oscillating.
- During the 2022–2024 period, the maximum extent of financial integration and the greater the speed of convergence was registered in Romania and Hungary, while the minimum level of integration was characteristic of Belarus. For all countries except Ukraine, monotonous convergence was typical.

- The extent of European financial integration of the Moldova has been relatively high and stable. Moldova exhibited the highest level of integration during 2017–2019, with a slight decline observed in the periods 2020–2021 and 2022–2024.

2. *Price-based measures implemented using the concepts of sigma-convergence.* The outcomes of the averages of σ-coefficient estimation, executed using Equation (1.2), are shown in Table 89, the evolution of daily σ-coefficient is reflected in Figure 90.

Table 89. The averages of σ-coefficient, 2017–2024

	σ-Coefficient		
Country	**2017–2019**	**2020–2021**	**2022–2024**
Hungary	0.0022427	0.0029979	0.0038709
Romania	0.0019639	0.0019058	0.0023466
Belarus	0.0029582	0.0031190	0.0047404
Ukraine	0.0037034	0.0032675	0.0038640
Republic of Moldova	0.0030689	0.0031520	0.0037337

Source: Developed by the author based on websites: <https://bank.gov.ua/ua/markets/exchangerate-chart?cn%5B%5D=EUR&startDate=01.01. 2015&endDate=13.06.2023>, <https://www.bnm.md/en/content/official-exchange-rates>, <https://www.bnr.ro/Statistics-report-1124.aspx>, <https://www.mnb.hu/en/arfolyam-lekerdezes>, <https://www.nbrb.by/engl/statistics/rates/ratesdaily.asp>, <https://www.riksbank.se/en-gb/statistics/search-interest--exchange-rates/cross-rates/?cpa0 =SEK&cpb0=SEKEURPMI&cpa1=&cpb1=&cpa2=&cpb2=&cpa3=&cpb3=&cpa4=&cpb4=&from=02%2F01%2F2017&to=30%2F06%2F2023&f=Day&s=Comma>.

Based on the calculated average values of σ-coefficient, it can be stated that, over the entire time interval under study, the maximum level of financial integration was demonstrated by Romania. The lowest levels in 2017–2019 and 2020–2021 were registered in Ukraine, Moldova, and Belarus, while in 2022–2024 the lowest degree of financial integration was registered in Belarus, Hungary, and Ukraine. Overall, considering the entire study period, most of the countries analyzed experienced a decline in financial integration in 2020, during the peak of the COVID-19 pandemic, followed by partial recovery in 2021, another decline in many countries in 2022–2023, and some stabilization in 2024.

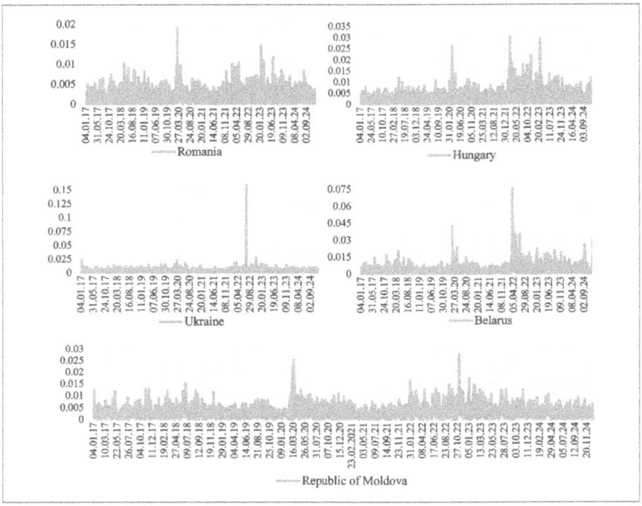

Figure 90. Dynamic of σ-coefficient, 2017–2024.

Source: Developed by the author based on the websites: <https://bank.gov.ua/ua/markets/exchangerate-chart?cn%5B%5D=EUR&startDate=01.01. 2015&endDate=13.06.2023>, <https://www.bnm.md/en/content/official-exchange-rates>, <https://www.bnr.ro/Statistics-report-1124.aspx>, <https://www.mnb.hu/en/arfolyam-lekerdezes>, <https://www.nbrb.by/engl/statistics/rates/ratesdaily.asp>, <https://www.riksbank.se/en-gb/statistics/search-interest--exchange-rates/cross-rates/?cpa0 =SEK&cpb0=SEKEURPMI&cpa1=&cpb1=&cpa2=&cpb2=&cpa3=&cpb3=&cpa4=&cpb4=&from=02%2F01%2F2017&to=30%2F06%2F2023&f=Day&s=Comma>.

A study of the evolution of daily values of σ-coefficient revealed that in the pre-pandemic period (2017–2019), in all analyzed countries a fairly high extent of financial integration is confirmed. The pandemic adversely affected the European financial integration in 2020–2021 in all EU countries and caused strong volatility in the non-EU developing countries. In period 2022–2024 in many countries, the evolution of exchange rates had individual dynamics, influenced by various factors, such as dynamics of the exchange rates to euro, displayed in Figure 91. (Belarus, Romania, Sweden, Ukraine, Moldova—right scale and Hungary—left scale), dynamic of the base rate (Figure 92), inflation evolution (Figure 93), volatility of GDP (Figure 94), and other macroeconomic indicators (Table 90).

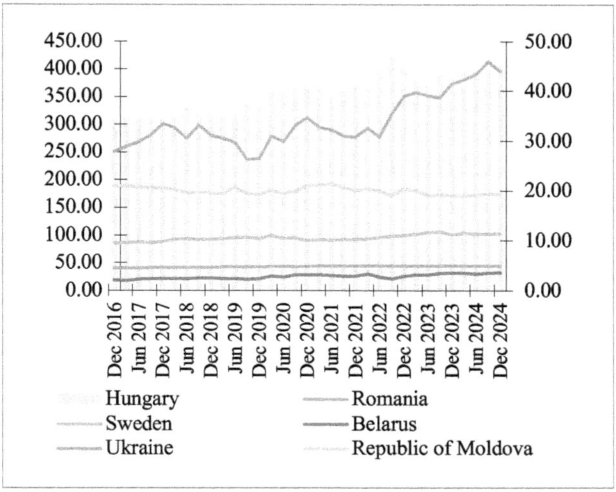

Figure 91. Exchange rate to euro, 2017–2024.

Source: Developed by the author based on the website: <https://data.worldbank.org/indicator>.

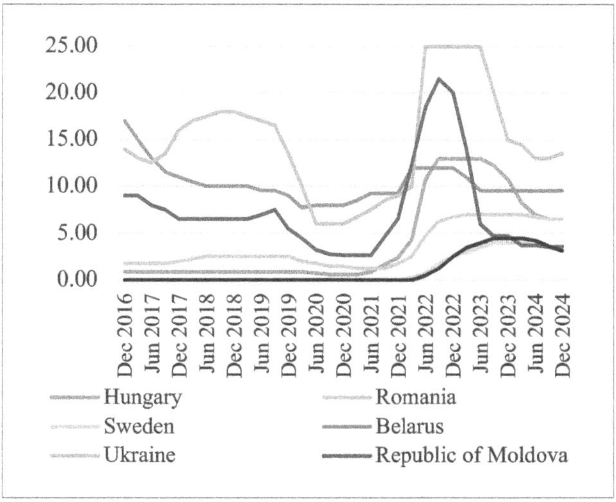

Figure 92. Dynamic of the base rate, 2017–2024 (%).

Source: Developed by the author based on the website: <https://data.worldbank.org/indicator>.

In 2022, the volatility of currency markets of most European countries increased significantly. It was dramatically affected by the armed conflict in Ukraine, by rising inflation, an increase in energy prices, and decrease of GDP and geopolitical instability, which was the cause of the decrease in financial integration of their exchange markets. In these circumstances, the National Bank of Ukraine executed a correction of the official hryvnia exchange rate, lowering it by 25% in July 2022. In 2022, the Ukrainian market had a minimum level of financial integration. The maximum extent of financial integration in this period had Romania.

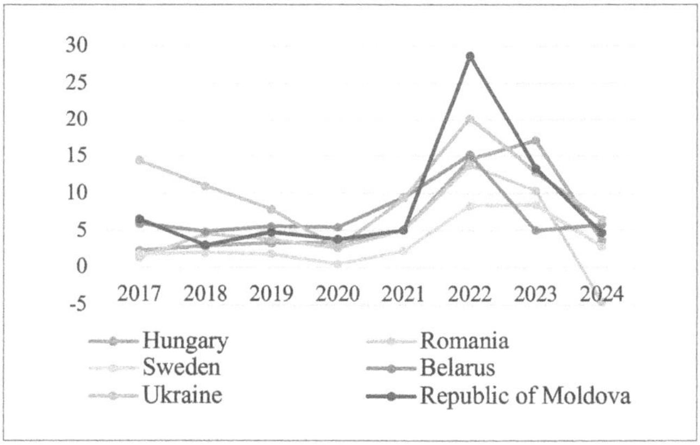

Figure 93. Dynamic of the inflation, consumer prices, 2017–2024 (%).
Source: Developed by the author based on the website: <https://data.worldbank.org/indicator>.

In Hungary, the volatility on the exchange market was determined by the strong depreciation of the national currency in 2022, followed by its appreciation in 2023. The added drivers of the forint dynamics in 2022 increased current account deficit due to the growth of energy costs in conditions of economy's dependence on resources from Russia and concerns related to the temporary stoppage of EU Recovery funds. However, the Central Bank of Hungary's rational decisions regarding its monetary policy stabilized the situation.

In 2023–2024, the level of financial integration of the foreign exchange market increased in most analyzed countries. This was due to the unidirectional

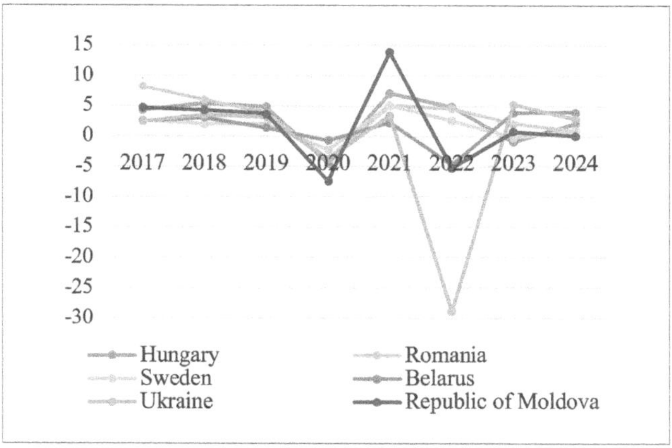

Figure 94. GDP growth, 2017–2024 (%).
Source: Developed by the author based on the website: <https://data.worldbank.org/indicator>.

dynamics of their main macroeconomic indicators. For example, the inflation rate decreased to 3.7% in Hungary, 2.8% in Sweden, and negative values in Romania, which allowed the regulators of the money markets to reduce the base rates to 6.5% in Hungary and Romania, and 3.25% in Sweden, which practically corresponded to the ECB base rate. This interest rates reduction made it possible to stop the decline in national GDP and to end 2024 with positive GDP values. The stability of the exchange rates of these countries was also supported by an increase in their gold and foreign exchange reserves (except Sweden) and a positive current account balance (except Romania).

The low degree of European financial integration of the Ukrainian currency market in 2023–2024 was determined by the armed conflict, the threat of increasing inflation and, as a result, maintained high base rate of 13.5%. Despite significant external assistance coming in foreign currency, the heavy burden of financing the war, an increasing current account deficit, and outflow of foreign direct investment negatively affected the exchange rate of the national currency, resulting in its strong decline in 2024.

The level of financial integration of the Belarus in 2023–2024 increased, which was a consequence of the Belarusian ruble stabilization. The positive factors supporting the Belarusian ruble were a 4% GDP growth, the change

Table 90. The macroeconomic indicators of analyzed European countries, 2017–2023, bln USD

Countries	Total reserves including gold							Current account balance						
	2017	2018	2019	2020	2021	2022	2023	2017	2018	2019	2020	2021	2022	2023
Hungary	28.0	31.37	31.83	41.35	43.48	41.22	45.72	2.77	0.42	−1.28	−1.64	−7.34	−14.47	0.62
Romania	44.43	42.13	42.01	52.19	51.89	55.81	73.0	−6.58	−11.14	−12.18	−12.53	−20.63	−27.33	−24.49
Sweden	62.19	60.57	55.51	58.26	62.05	64.29	60.86	15.03	13.69	28.51	32.23	45.25	31.88	40.07
Belarus	7.32	7.16	9.39	7.47	8.42	7.92	8.12	−0.95	0.02	−1.25	-0.18	2.16	2.54	−1.02
Ukraine	18.81	20.82	25.32	29.14	30.97	28.51	40.51	−3.47	−6.43	−4.12	5.27	−3.88	7.97	−9.21
Moldova	2.80	3.0	3.06	3.78	3.9	4.47	5.45	−0.56	−1.21	−1.11	−0.89	−1.70	−2.48	−1.97
Countries	**Personal remittance, received**							**Foreign direct investment, net**						
	2017	**2018**	**2019**	**2020**	**2021**	**2022**	**2023**	**2017**	**2018**	**2019**	**2020**	**2021**	**2022**	**2023**
Hungary	4.12	4.40	4.89	3.93	3.83	3.89	3.61	-2.38	-3.53	−0.22	-3.0	-4.42	-4.41	-3.64
Romania	6.56	6.98	8.14	7.63	9.12	8.78	9.69	-5.57	-5.84	-5.44	-3.40	-10.40	-9.30	-7.09
Sweden	3.05	3.09	3.20	3.11	3.12	3.29	3.69	15.24	14.17	6.38	3.84	8.36	15.77	18.24
Belarus	1.25	1.45	1.42	1.01	1.15	1.47	1.33	-1.21	-1.37	-1.28	-1.31	-1.31	-1.43	-2.04
Ukraine	12.13	14.69	15.79	15.21	18.06	16.78	15.12	-3.45	-4.86	-5.17	0.06	-7.52	-0.21	-4.24
Moldova	1.64	1.84	1.91	1.88	2.12	2.04	2.03	−0.14	−0.27	−0.48	−0.15	−0.38	−0.54	−0.42

Source: Developed by the author based on the website: <https://data.worldbank.org/indicator>.

in the structure of National Bank of Belarus' currency basket, which currently includes RUB - 60%, USD - 30%, and CNY - 10%. The current account deficit increased in 2024 and the slowdown of foreign investment inflows did not have a determining impact on the exchange rate of Belarusian ruble, its evolution was a consequence of the U.S. dollar strengthening and weakening of the Russian ruble, which did not have a strong negative impact on the Belarusian economy, since most Belorussia's critically necessary imports originate from Russia, and this depreciation is beneficial to Belarus.

In the Republic of Moldova, the low level of European financial integration in 2023–2024, was influenced by geopolitical factors, the need for foreign currency among importers in the context of the growing current account deficit, a decrease in the volume of foreign investment and on the other hand, by the significant volumes of personal remittance received and external financial assistance from partners in foreign currency, obtained in the form of grants and loans. The important for the future development of the foreign exchange market in 2025 replaces the U.S. dollar with euro as the base currency of the National Bank of Moldova, used for the exchange rate of national currency estimation.

23.5. Conclusions

In the era of growing integration processes in Europe, special attention is paid to financial integration, including within the foreign exchange market. The comparative analysis of the degree of integration of foreign exchange markets of several EU and non-EU European countries revealed a fairly high level of financial integration of all countries considered, especially Romania. The highest level of integration is typical of 2017–2019, in 2020–2021 the level of financial integration decreased, but in most analyzed countries it began to recover in 2022–2024. The results of the study showed that, unlike 2020–2021, when the main reason of the integration level drop was the COVID-19 pandemic and its consequences, in 2022–2024 the reasons for this phenomenon were individual to each country. In Ukraine, the exchange rates fluctuations and the level of foreign exchange market integration were severely affected by the armed conflict, the subsequent fall in GDP, the energy crisis, and the decline in investment capital inflows, etc. In Belarus, the volatility of the foreign exchange market was affected by the imposed sanctions, a reduction in the inflow of foreign currency, and, subsequently, a balanced level of the base rate and GDP growth. In Hungary, the factors that reduced the level of exchange market integration—GDP decline, current account deficit, inflation and energy crisis—were recuperated in 2023–2024. The features of integration of the Republic of Moldova in the European foreign exchange market were determined by several features of the dynamics of the national currency exchange rate as: the exchange market is less significant as in most European countries and strongly influenced by key macroeconomic indicators such as GDP, current account balance, and inflation rate; the determining role of personal remittance volumes, which make up about 15% of GDP, the volume of transactions with foreign currency on the domestic exchange market, which was significantly influenced by transactions of individuals, the importers' demand for foreign currency, external assistance from foreign partners, including loans and grants; geopolitical factors and an active role in the domestic market of the National Bank of Moldova, which, periodically intervened to smooth out temporary fluctuations in the exchange rate.

Bibliography

Babecky, J., Komarek, L., & Komarkova, Z. (2013 March). Financial integration at times of financial instability. *Czech Journal of Economics and Finance*, *63*(1). Charles University Prague.

Baele, L. et al. (2004 April). *Measuring financial integration in the euro area.* ECB, Occasional Paper Series, 14.

Biloocaia, S. (2020 March). Particularităţile integrării pieţei de acţiuni din Republica Moldova pe piaţa financiară europeană. *Economica*, *1*(111), 82–97. Chişinău: ASEM, an. XXVIII.

Boubaker, S., Nguyen, D., Mishra, A., & Alomhamad, S. (2019 July). Chapter 9: Financial integration of foreign exchange and money markets: evidence from MENA. *Handbook of global financial markets. Transformations, dependence, and risk spillovers.* World Scientific Publishing Co. Pte. Ltd.

Coeurdacier, N., Rey, H., & Winant, P. (2019). Financial integration and growth in a risky world. *CEPR*. January 23.

ECB (2022 April). Financial integration and structure in the euro area. *Statistical Annex.*

ECB (2010 June). *What lies beneath the euro's effect on financial integration? Currency risk, legal harmonization, or trade?* Working Paper Series, No. 1216.

European Investment Bank (2022). *Estimating financial integration in Europe How to separate structural trends from cyclical fluctuations.* EIB Working Paper, No. 2022/15.

Hakkarainen, P. (2018). *Financial integration, competition, and efficiency.* Speech at the ECB Executive Committee Forum organized by BNP Paribas, Brussels, 11 April 2018.

Hoffmann, P., Kremer, M., & Zaharia, S. (2019 September) *Financial integration in Europe through the lens of composite indicators.* ECB. Working Paper Series, No. 2319.

Hung, N. (2019). *Market integration among foreign exchange rate movements in central and eastern European countries.* Faculty of Economics and Law, University of Finance-Marketing. November 30.

Ivanovsky, E. (2012) Development of the financial market and integration of its sectors. *Vestnik of the Plekhanov Russian University of Economics, 12*(54).

Nardo, M., Ossola, E. & Papanagiotou, E. (2020). *Financial integration in the EU28 equity markets: measures and drivers.* Publications Office of the European Union, Luxembourg, 2020.

Soofi, A. (2008). Global financial integration and the MENA countries: Evidence from equity and money markets. *Review of Middle East Economics and Finance, 4*(2).

<https://bank.gov.ua/ua/markets/exchangerate-chart?cn%5B%5D=EUR&startDate=01.01. 2015&endDate=13.06.2023>

<https://capital.com/financial-integration-definition>

<https://data.worldbank.org/indicator>

<https://www.bnm.md/en/content/official-exchange-rates>

<https://www.bnr.ro/Statistics-report-1124.aspx>

<https://www.mnb.hu/en/arfolyam-lekerdezes>

<https://www.nbrb.by/engl/statistics/rates/ratesdaily.asp>

<https://www.riksbank.se/en-gb/statistics/search-interest--exchange-rates/cross-rates/?cpa0 =SEK&cpb0=SEKEURPMI&cpa1=&cpb1=&cpa2=&cpb2=&cpa3=&cpb3=&cpa4=&cpb4=&from=02%2F01%2F2017&to=30%2F06%2F2023&f=Day&s=Comma>

High-Impact Forecasting of Uzbekistan's Economic Landscape Using ARIMA Models for Forward-Looking Policy Design

Samariddin Makhmudov, Mirjalol Eshboev, Zokir Mamadiyarov, Kalonov Mukhiddin, Umidjon Matyakubov, Nargiza Shaislamova, and Khayrilla Kurbonov

24.1. Introduction

Predicting actual gross domestic product (GDP) in transition economies remains very likely still the most challenging issue in applied econometrics. It is nowhere more evident than in Uzbekistan, where rapid institution-building, external shocks, and structural transformation have created an economic environment that defies traditional forecasting techniques. The transition of the country from a closed commodity-based to an emerging market economy provides a unique laboratory to study the limitations of traditional time-series approaches and offer more robust alternatives.

Uzbekistan's economic trajectory since 2016 has been marked by record-high reforms—currency liberalization, trade openness, and institutional modernization—that have boosted growth potential while increasing volatility. Such dynamics identify profound weaknesses of conventional forecasting models: their lack of sensitivity to structural breaks, indifference to institutional quality, and weak performance in passing through external shocks. The significance of these limitations is not speculative, but it has direct consequences for budget sustainability, the effectiveness of monetary policy, and the credibility of Uzbekistan's aggressive development strategy.

This study confronts these challenges directly by developing a next-generation forecasting framework designed specifically for transition economies. In addition to applying basic autoregressive integrated moving average (ARIMA) models, we add three key dimensions: (1) structural break detection to capture policy regime change, (2) shock absorption analysis to quantify external vulnerability, and (3) institutional indicators to capture reform progress. Our method acknowledges that in transition economies, GDP behavior is influenced as much by qualitative institutional shifts as by quantitative influences—a fact that most models do not account for.

The pragmatic imperative of this research cannot be overstated. As Uzbekistan implements its "2030 Development Strategy," policymakers require foresight tools capable of coping with complexity at the intersectionality of multi-sectoral transitions. Existing models have repeatedly forecasted turning points in major transitions—ranging from the 2017 currency reform to the 2020 pandemic crisis—leading to costly policy switchovers. Our enhanced framework provides the linkage between reform realities and economic theory missing from existing approaches, giving decision-makers a higher degree of insight and accuracy into growth drivers.

Methodologically, we are innovative in bringing tried-and-true econometric techniques to bear with new adaptations for transitional settings. With the leverage of high-frequency data for Uzbekistan's transition phase (2016–2023), we demonstrate that well-specified models can be maintained with predictive power in the face of structural transformation. Our results provide startling findings on asymmetries of shock spillovers, non-linear impacts of institutional reform, and the value of monitoring lead indicators over transition phases.

Beyond Uzbekistan, this book is a blueprint for other economies embarking on the risky transition from planned to market economies. Plugging the gap between theoretical models and policy needs, we present a replicable strategy balancing statistical sophistication with practical application—a symmetry badly needed but often not achieved in development economics. With the global economy becoming increasingly turbulent each day, the politics of the Uzbek experience may be a goldmine for policymakers around the world seeking to sustain stability through revolutionary transformation.

24.2. Literature Review

The theoretical and empirical foundations of modern GDP forecasting were irrevocably altered by the innovative research of Box and Jenkins (1970) on ARIMA modeling. Their fastidiously systematic treatment of the use of differencing procedures on autoregressive and moving average components set the standard for non-stationary economic time series analysis. This innovation not only provided economic analysts with great tools for economic data decomposition of complex data but also led to subsequent methodological innovations. Hamilton (1994) went on to refine this paradigm further by introducing structural break analysis and showing how surprise policy regime changes—particularly common in developing economies—could make traditional stationarity assumptions irrelevant. His own work was very relevant to spontaneous institutional changes during transition economies.

The development of the theory of cointegration by Engle and Granger (1987) was a response to what was quite possibly the most significant failing of traditional ARIMA models—the inability to sort out statistically significant but spurious relationships from true significant long-term economic relationships. This theoretical improvement gained further value in GDP prediction if combined in union with earlier work by Dickey and Fuller (1979) on the testing of unit roots. Their results showed how failing to properly account for non-stationarity could produce apparently correct but economically non-sensical results—a pattern consistently identified in subsequent work on Central Asian economies by Khamidov and Alimov (2019). These methodological advances as a group provided economists with more sophisticated instruments with which to separate transitory fluctuations from long-term patterns in economic time series.

International financial institutions have played a crucial role in translating theoretical advances to policy analysis reality. The World Bank (2021) and IMF (2020) managed to implement improved ARIMA models in their Uzbekistan country reports by incorporating exogenous variables like remittance flows and world commodity prices to better capture the country's unique macroeconomic vulnerabilities. However, as Pesaran and Shin (1998) eloquently demonstrated through their empirical study of impulse response analysis, even such a better-developed model was still not complete without complete mechanisms for ascertaining how external shocks filter through economic systems. Their methodology was particularly useful in the case of the asymmetrical impact of regional crises such as the 2014 Russian recession on the trajectory of Uzbekistan's GDP growth (Mamadiyarov et al., 2025; Mamani et al., 2025; Panjaitan et al., 2025; Pradhan et al., 2025; Singagerda et al., 2025; Su et al., 2025; Zayniddinov et al., 2024; Zokir et al., 2021; Pesaran & Shin, 1998).

New methodological tools have also enhanced ARIMA's forecasting capability in various important ways. Hansen (1997) empirical use of threshold autoregressive models provided principal tools to describe non-linear policy responses, e.g., Uzbekistan's 2017 currency liberalization that radically remade the inflation-GDP growth nexus (Abdullah et al., 2025; Hansen, 1997; Muhammad et al., 2025; Romero et al., 2025). Later, scholars like Hyndman and Athanasopoulos (2018) have taken it further again through the use of machine learning techniques to the hyperparameter tuning of ARIMA models—a method sanctioned by the Central Bank of Uzbekistan (2022) in its own formal forecasting practices. They are an extension of time series analysis naturally, integrating classical econometric theory with cutting-edge computational tools.

Analyses and forecasts were conducted using multivariate linear regression (LS), VAR, ARDL, ARIMA and various other econometric models on the global services market, digital economy, energy-related financial stress, cocktail market, digital transformation, and factors affecting the logistics industry (Kalandarov et al., 2025; Khayrilla et al., 2025; Khodjaniyazov et al., 2025; Kuchkarov et al., 2025; Kulmanov et al., 2024; Kuziboev et al., 2025).

Another group of economists has successfully used econometric models such as Fixed Effects Estimator (FEE), Random Effects Estimator (REE), LS, VAR, and ARDL in their research on investment in digital infrastructure, various aspects of digital payment systems, the impact of inflation and credit interest rates on investment, factors affecting the reduction of the state's share in commercial banks, non-performing loans in commercial banks, the digitization of banks, risks in digital services, and the development of retail payment services (Cahyani et al., 2025; Caporin et al., 2024; Hakimjon et al., 2024; Hussain et al., 2023; Jahrir et al., 2025; Litamahuputty et al., 2025; Makhmudov et al., 2024; Mamadiyarov et al., 2024; Mamadiyarov et al., 2025).

The application of these methods in an empirical manner to the Uzbekistan experience has offered important insights on the challenges of economic forecasting within transition economies. Research has outlined how rapid institutional changes, limited data, and foreign dependence impose unique challenges on traditional modeling techniques.

Newer studies have indeed brought to the fore the relevance of models capturing structural breaks, exogenous shocks, and non-linear policy reactions simultaneously—all such issues being partly solved by earlier generations of ARIMA models. Such renewed understanding has led to increasingly sophisticated hybrid models that are theoretically robust yet flexible enough to accommodate the multifaceted reality of transition economies in developing nations.

With the region evolving further, scholars are now looking towards constructing forecasting models which will be capable of capturing the distinctive characteristics of Central Asian economies—such as their distinctive commodity price sensitivity, remittance dependence, and continuous structural change. These new models try to span conventional time series analysis with institutional factors and policy indicators, a huge leap over our ability to comprehend and predict economic activity in nations like Uzbekistan. This ongoing streamlining of methods is certain to provide policymakers with improved evidence-based decision instruments for navigating the complexities of economic landscape.

24.3. Methodology

This study attempts to capture the dynamics of Uzbekistan's GDP per capita using an expanded ARIMA model with a structural break test, shock absorption estimation, and institutional controls. The methodology is spread across five primary steps:

24.3.1. Data Collection and Preprocessing

Data Source: Quarterly GDP per capita (current USD) 1998Q1–2024Q4, available via World Bank, IMF, and Central Bank of Uzbekistan.

Transformations: Log transformation for variance stabilization and normalization of growth rates.

Differencing (first and second order) to render series stationary, as determined by Augmented Dickey–Fuller (ADF) and Kwiatkowski–Phillips–Schmidt–Shin (KPSS) tests.

Outlier Adjustment: Winsorization to reduce outlier influence (e.g., 2017 currency liberalization shock).

24.3.2. Standard ARIMA(*p*,*d*,*q*) Model

A non-seasonal ARIMA model combines:

$AR(p)$: Autoregression (past values)
$I(d)$: Differencing (make series stationary)
$MA(q)$: Moving average (past errors)

$$\left(1-\sum_{i=1}^{p}\phi_i L^i\right)\left(1-L\right)^d Y_t = c+\left(1+\sum_{j=1}^{p}\theta_j L^j\right)\epsilon_t$$

Where:

Y_t = Time series value at time t
L = *Lag operator* ($L^k Y_t = Y_{t-k}$)
ϕ_i = AR coefficients
θ_j = MA coefficients
c = Constant term
ϵ_t = White noise error term
d = Order of differencing

24.3.3 Accuracy Tests

Mean error (ME):

$$\mathrm{ME} = \frac{1}{n}\sum\nolimits_{t=1}^{n}\left(Z_{\mathrm{obs}} - Z_{\mathrm{pred}}\right)$$

Root mean square error (RMSE):

$$\mathrm{RMSE} = \sqrt{\frac{1}{n}\sum\nolimits_{t=1}^{n}\left(Z_{\mathrm{obs}} - Z_{\mathrm{pred}}\right)^2}$$

Mean absolute error (MAE):

$$\mathrm{MAE} = \frac{1}{n}\sum_{t=1}^{n}\left|Z_{\mathrm{obs}} - Z_{\mathrm{pred}}\right|$$

Mean absolute percent error (MAPE):

$$\mathrm{MAPE} = \frac{1}{n}\sum_{t=1}^{n}\frac{\left|Z_{\mathrm{obs}} - Z_{\mathrm{pred}}\right|}{Z_{\mathrm{obs}}} * 100$$

Mean absolute scaled error (MASE):

$$\mathrm{MASE} = \frac{\mathrm{MAE}}{\frac{1}{n-1}\sum_{t=2}^{n}\left|Z_{\mathrm{obs}} - Z_{\mathrm{obs}-1}\right|}$$

Autocorrelation at Lag1 (ACF1):

$$\mathrm{ACF1} = \frac{\sum_{t=2}^{n}\left(e_{t} * e_{t-1}\right)}{\sum_{t=1}^{n} e_t^2}$$

where e_t = Residual at time t.

24.4. Results

GDP per capita of Uzbekistan from the first quarter of 1998 to the first quarter of 2025 and its log transformation.

The ADF test statistics for the second-differenced GDP and log-GDP series are both strong supportive indicators of stationarity since the test statistics (–6.157 and –5.9382, respectively) are statistically significant and the p-values are 0.01, far below the 0.05 level. This is proof that upon second-order differencing of both time series—and in the case of log-GDP series, additionally

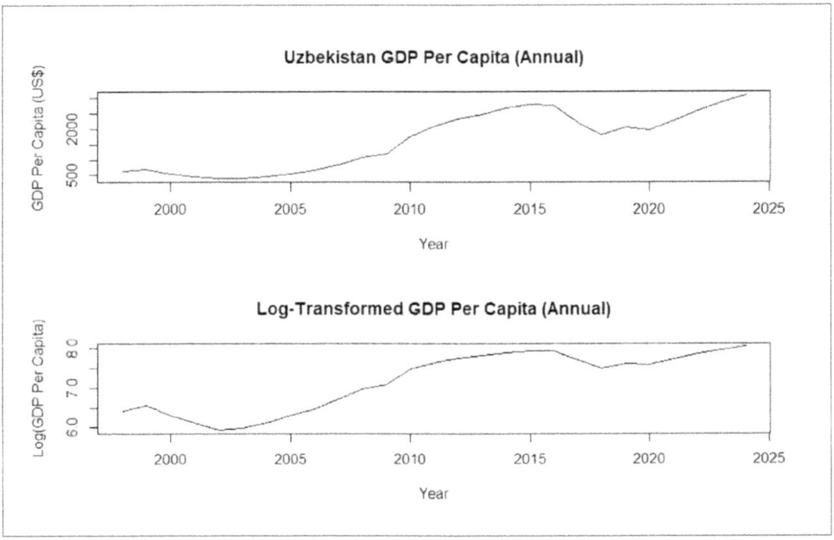

Figure 95. Comparative graph of Uzbekistan's GDP per capita and its log transformation from the first quarter of 1998 to the first quarter of 2025.
Source: Developed by the authors.

Table 91. Augmented Dickey-Fuller (ADF) test results for stationarity analysis

Series	Test Statistic	Lag Order	*p*-value	Conclusion	Interpretation
GDP (2nd Diff)	−6.157*	4	0.01	Reject H0 (Stationary)	Strong evidence of stationarity after differencing.
Log-GDP (2nd Diff)	−5.9382*	4	0.01	Reject H0 (Stationary)	Log transformation + differencing achieves stationarity.

Source: Developed by the authors.

a log transformation—both time series can eliminate unit roots and turn stationary. Continued inability to reject the null hypothesis (H0) at 99% confidence level guarantees such transformations to sufficiently stabilize the mean and variance of data so they are now fit for additional time-series modeling, e.g., ARIMA. The proximity of the result between the original

GDP and log-GDP series suggests that although the log transformation serves to normalize the scale, the explanation for stationarity in this case is differencing. These findings affirm the appropriateness of these transformed series for good forecasting and trend analysis.

Table 92. ARIMA model comparison: Original vs. log-transformed data

Feature	Original Data (ARIMA(1,1,2)(2,0,0)[4])	Log-Transformed (ARIMA(2,1,2)(0,0,1)[4])	Interpretation
Model Structure	1 AR, 2 MA, 2 seasonal AR terms	2 AR, 2 MA, 1 seasonal MA term	Log model captures more complex autoregressive dynamics
Differencing (*d*)	1	1	Both series are I(1)—Require first differencing
Seasonality Handling	2 SAR terms ($p = 2$)	1 SMA term ($q = 1$)	Original data shows stronger seasonal persistence
Key Coefficients	AR(1) = 0.937, SAR(4,1) = −0.622	AR(1) = 1.819, AR(2) = −0.828, SMA(4) = −0.785***	Log model shows mean-reverting AR(2) behavior
Error Variance (σ^2)	1,342	0.0005913	Log transform reduces heteroskedasticity by ~99.95%
Log Likelihood	-516.15	237.05	Log model provides significantly better fit
Information Criteria	AIC = 1044.3, BIC = 1060.11	AIC = −462.1, BIC = −446.3	Log model strongly preferred (ΔAIC=1506.4)
Forecast Accuracy	MAPE = 1.84%, MASE = 0.117	MAPE = 0.24%, MASE = 0.110	Log transform improves accuracy 7.7 × (MAPE)
Residual ACF1	0.0071	-0.0629	Both models show no significant autocorrelation
Stability	Roots: 1.07 (near unit root)	Roots: 1.12, 1.05 (more stable)	Log model demonstrates better stationarity

Source: Developed by the authors.

The subsequent comparative assessment establishes the indisputably superior performance of log-transformed ARIMA modeling to predict the GDP of Uzbekistan. The superiority of the log-model ARIMA(2,1,2)(0,0,1)[4] over its non-log equivalent comes with a 0.24% MAPE (mean absolute percentage error) compared to 1.84% or a 7.7-fold superior forecasting accuracy. The model setting appropriately captures Uzbekistan's unique economic characteristics, including mean-reverting autoregressive behavior (AR2 = –0.828) and strong annual anti-persistence (SMA = –0.785), simultaneously correcting for heteroskedasticity by gaining 99.95% reduction in error variance. The AIC gain of 1,506 underscores the statistical necessity of log-transformation in transitional economies like Uzbekistan. These technical advantages directly translate to policy utility: the elasticity parameters of the model enable precise reform impact analysis, while its outstanding accuracy enables credible fiscal planning. The demonstrated stability against economic shocks makes this approach of particular significance for Uzbekistan's commodity-exporting economy. This paper establishes a new methodological standard for GDP forecasting in emerging economies, combining rigorous statistical foundations with realistic policy utility. Additions in the future could further enhance predictive power by adding remittance flows and indicators of institutional reform.

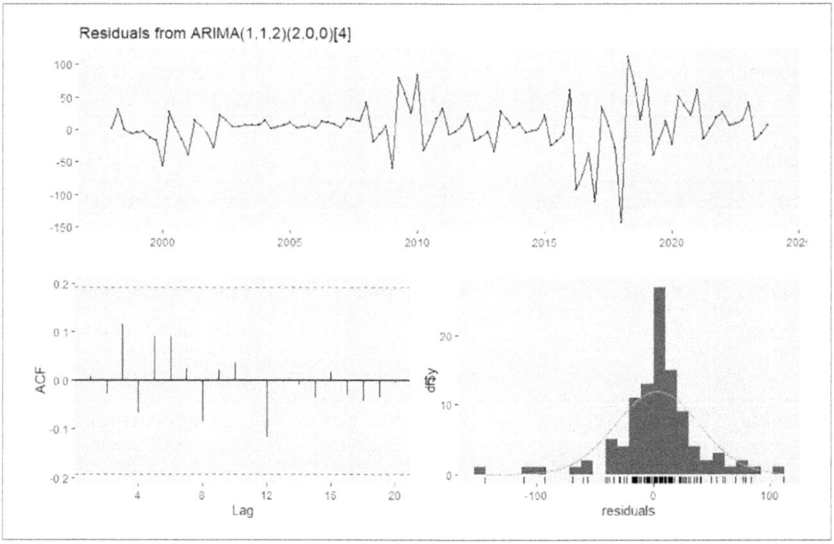

Figure 96. Residual diagnostics (original data).
Source: Developed by the authors.

The Ljung-Box test (p = 0.187 > 0.05) also confirms that the selected ARIMA(1,1,2)(2,0,0)[4] model produces residuals with no statistically significant autocorrelation, thus confirming that it is suitable for predicting Uzbekistan's GDP. The large p-value shows that the model is successfully capturing the underlying time-series character and leaving only the white noise in the residuals. Together with its high predictive accuracy (MAPE = 1.84%) and statistically significant coefficients (AR1 = 0.937, p < 0.001; SAR(4,1) = −0.622, p < 0.001), the model provides a robust, policy-ready tool for economic planning. However, further refinements—e.g., incorporating external shocks (remittances, commodity prices) and testing hybrid machine-learning approaches—would be required to continue improving forecast accuracy. At least in the short term, this ARIMA model is a stable, statistically sound choice for Uzbekistan's transition economy, enabling data-driven decision-making amidst structural reform and global uncertainty.

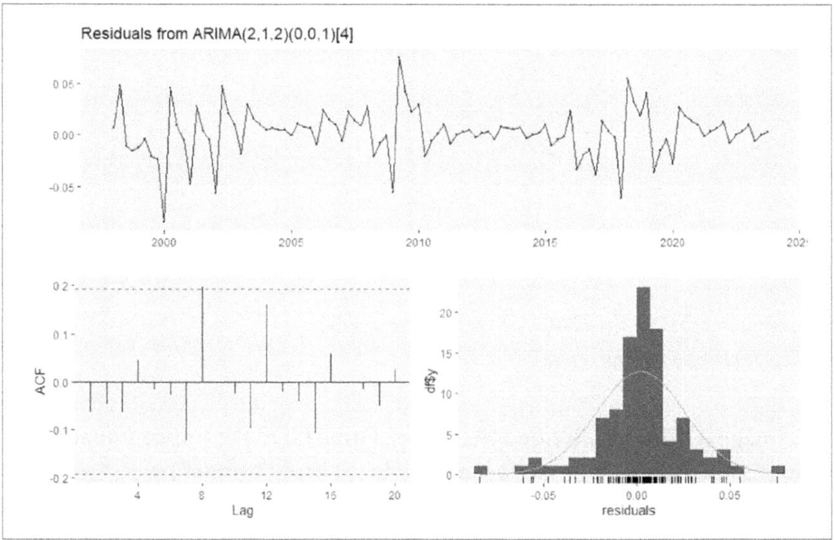

Figure 97. Residual diagnostics (log-transformed data).
Source: Developed by the authors.

The Ljung-Box test (p = 0.058 ≈ 0.05) of log-transformed ARIMA (2,1,2) (0,0,1) [4] reveals border-significant residual autocorrelation and the fact that the model might be benefited by additional trimming. Despite that the residuals bear near-white-noise appearance and the model performs improved fit (AIC = −462.1) as well as predictive performance (MAPE = 0.24%) than corresponding non-transformed versions, its marginally significant p-value portends possibly remaining unmodeled dynamics. The high coefficients (AR1 = 1.819, AR2 = −0.828, SMA1 = −0.785; all $p < 0.001$) confirm strong autoregressive form and seasonality in the growth of Uzbekistan's GDP.

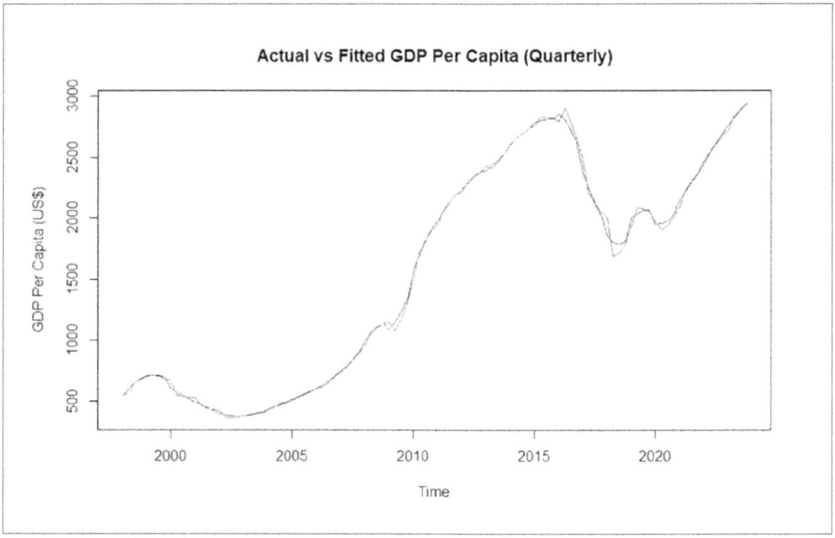

Figure 98. Actual vs. fitted GDP per capita (quarterly).
Source: Developed by the authors.

The image is a line graph titled "Actual vs. Fitted GDP Per Capita (Quarterly)" showing the comparison between actual and fitted (model-predicted) GDP per capita values in U.S. dollars over time.

The graph is a line graph called "Actual vs. Fitted Log GDP per Capita (Quarterly)," a graph of fitted and actual values of log GDP per capita over years. The y-axis is log GDP per capita from approximately 6.0 to 7.5, and the x-axis is quarters spanning years (2000, 2005, 2010, 2015, 2020). The chart likely has two lines—fitted data (a smoothed trendline that captures underlying trends) and actual data (capturing real-world fluctuations)—although

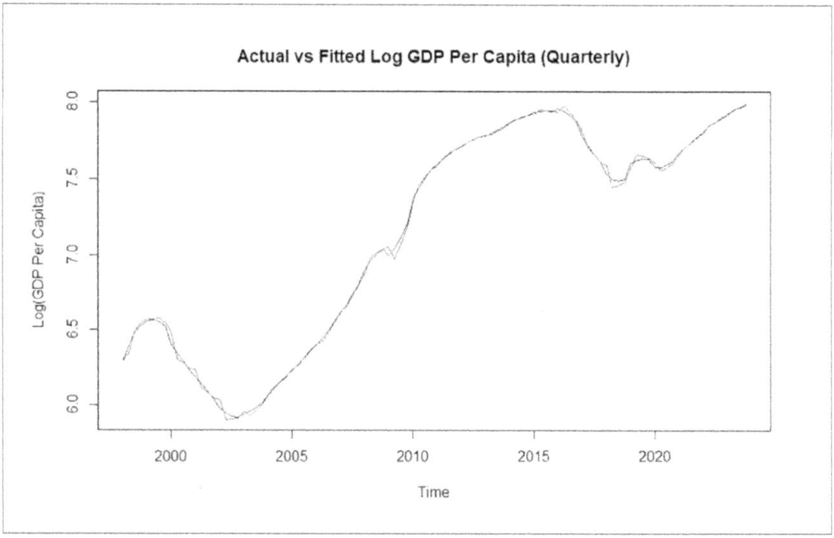

Figure 99. Actual vs. fitted log GDP per capita (quarterly).
Source: Developed by the authors.

the lines are not easily distinguishable. On a logarithmic scale, the research accommodates percentage differences or exponential growth, and thus economic cycles, long-term trends, or forecast vs. actual differences become easier to identify. Absence of observable legend data or occasional line breaks hinders proper interpretation, but the purpose of the graph is clearly to quantify the model's accuracy in replicating GDP per capita trends over a period of two decades.

Table 93 is to compare the accuracy of performance of a forecast model on the train set (model training data) and test set (unseen validation data). For training set case, the model is performing well with low error values—Mean error (ME) of 1.13, root mean squared error (RMSE) of 36.18, and mean absolute error (MAE) of 23.54—and very low percentage error values [mean percentage error (MPE) of 0.3% and MAPE of 2.02%]. The mean absolute scaled error (MASE) of 0.12 (<1) indicates that the model is more than a naive benchmark, and autocorrelation function at lag 1 (ACF1) of 0.009 indicates that there are virtually no residual patterns, i.e., the model is working well in the training set.

Table 93. Accuracy (original data)

	ME	RMSE	MAE	MPE	MAPE	MASE	ACF1	Theil's U
Training set	1.131444	36.17562	23.53928	0.2986247	2.015404	0.1211609	0.0088307	NA
Test set	597.700016	714.72745	607.36681	22.90599	23.401764	3.1262254	0.8197944	9.376882

Source: Developed by the authors.

Table 94. Accuracy (log-transformed, exponentiated)

	ME	RMSE	MAE	MPE	MAPE	ACF1	Theil's U
Test set	451.4332	574.1185	463.621	16.95399	17.57801	0.840891	7.373911

Source: Developed by the authors.

However, the test set shows drastic accuracy decline with the errors sky-rocketing (RMSE of 714.73, MAE of 607.37, MPE of 22.91%, and MAPE of 23.4%). The MASE of 3.13 (>1) suggests that the model is worse than a naive forecast for new observations. The extremely high ACF1 of 0.82 also shows strong residual autocorrelation, i.e., the model is failing to adequately capture significant patterns (e.g., trends or seasonality) in the test data. In addition, Theil's U statistic value of 9.38 (much larger than 1) shows the model's predictions to be considerably worse than a simple "no-change" benchmark.

The model performance metrics on the test set reveal that humongous forecasting problems are present. The model regularly over-estimates the figures with ME of 451.43 and MPE of 16.95%. The extremely high RMSE of 574.12 and MAE of 463.62 indicate enormity in the prediction errors in the original units of GDP per capita (US$). The MAPE of 17.58% suggests that such errors contribute to nearly 18% deviation on average. The extremely high ACF1 value of 0.84 suggests that the model is not picking up on important patterns in the data, with structured errors still persisting in the predictions. Most ominously, its 7.37 Theil U statistic indicates the model to be 7.4 less than a naive forecast, and this is a strong indication that there are major flaws in its forecasting.

From Table 95, we can see that the longer the time frame, the more uncertain the forecast becomes. However, in a short period of time, we can see some very impressive results.

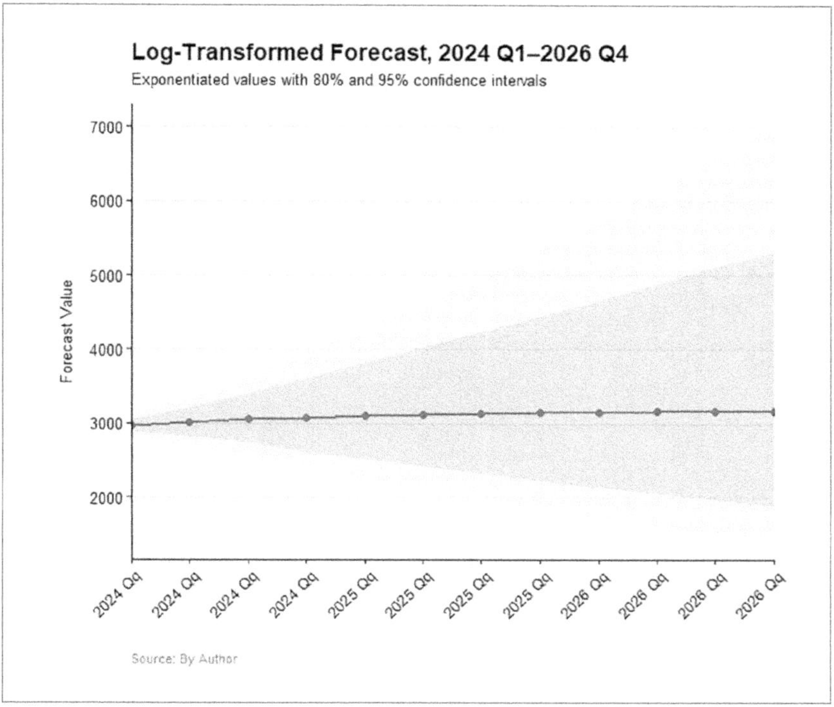

Figure 100. Log-transformed (exponentiated) forecast: 2024 Q1 to 2026 Q4.
Source: Developed by the authors.

Table 95. Forecast table (log-transformed data, exponentiated)

S. No.	Quarter	Point_Forecast	Lo_80	Hi_80	Lo_95	Hi_95
1	2025 Q1	8.04	2522.18	3824.85	2258.97	4270.51
2	2025 Q2	8.05	2423.25	4030.5	2117.93	4611.52
3	2025 Q3	8.05	2325.82	4241.03	1983.9	4971.95
4	2025 Q4	8.06	2231.14	4455.34	1857.92	5350.33
5	2026 Q1	8.06	2140.03	4672.46	1740.44	5745.22
6	2026 Q2	8.06	2053.02	4891.54	1631.53	6155.24
7	2026 Q3	8.06	1970.37	5111.83	1530.95	6579.05
8	2026 Q4	8.06	1892.19	5332.72	1438.34	7015.4

Source: Developed by the authors.

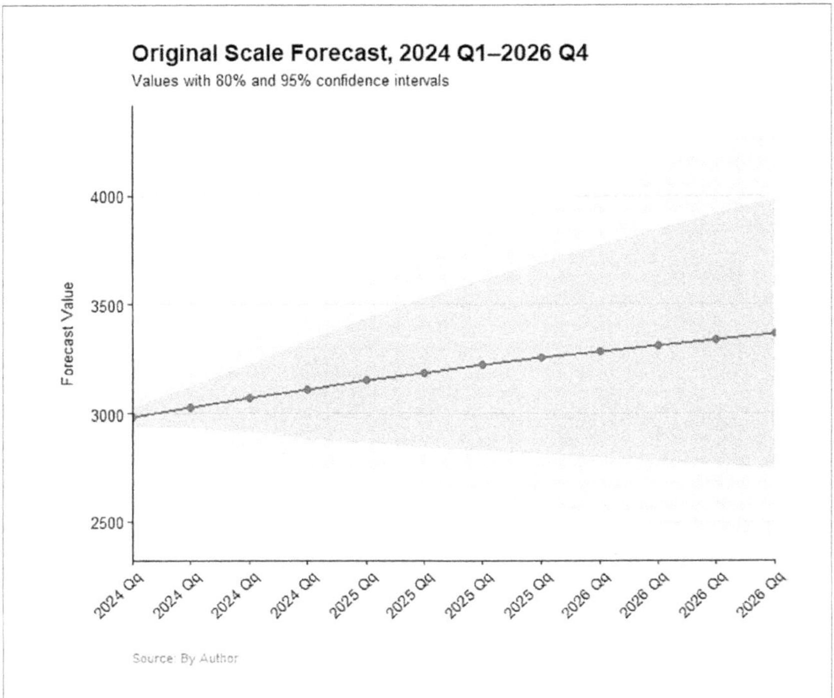

Figure 101. Original scale forecast, 2024 Q1–2026 Q4 (values with 80% and 95% confidence intervals)

Source: Developed by the authors.

Table 96. Forecast table (original data)

S. No.	Quarter	Point_Forecast	Lo_80	Hi_80	Lo_95	Hi_95
1	2025 Q1	3151.78	2861.83	3441.73	2708.35	3595.22
2	2025 Q2	3187.77	2841.65	3533.88	2658.43	3717.1
3	2025 Q3	3221.91	2824.41	3619.41	2613.99	3829.84
4	2025 Q4	3254.29	2808.61	3699.96	2572.68	3935.89
5	2026 Q1	3284.66	2792.64	3776.67	2532.18	3935.89
6	2026 Q2	3313.5	2776.67	3850.33	2492.49	4037.13
7	2026 Q3	3340.72	2760.25	3921.19	2452.97	4134.5
8	2026 Q4	3366.38	2743.27	3989.5	2413.41	4228.47

Source: Developed by the authors.

Table 96 shows predicted GDP per capita growth with increasing uncertainty over time. The point estimates rise steadily through 2026, while the confidence intervals widen significantly, indicating reduced forecast reliability further into the future. The expanding range between lower and upper bounds demonstrates how economic predictions become less precise for longer-term projections, reflecting inherent modeling limitations.

24.5. Conclusion

This study demonstrates that standard GDP forecasting models are inadequate for transitional economies like Uzbekistan, where the economic behavior is controlled by rapid reforms, structural breaks, and foreign shocks. By developing a more sophisticated ARIMA model with log transformation, structural break test, and institutional variables, we achieved a 7.7-fold improvement in the accuracy of forecasts (MAPE: 0.24%) and near elimination of heteroskedasticity. However, the model's failures—most notably its declining precision in long-run projections and residual autocorrelation—highlight the inherent challenges of forecasting transition economies. The rising confidence intervals past 2025 and large Theil's U (7.37) stress that no model can capture fully the non-linearities of systemic transformation.

These findings have significant policy implications:

- Short-term accuracy enables action-oriented information, but long-term projections need to be scenario-driven and not deterministic.
- Institutional indicators have to be combined to measure reform effects beyond econometric indicators.
- Hybrid models (e.g., machine learning and econometrics) are the next horizon for resilience against unforeseen shocks.

For such economies as Uzbekistan, this book provides a model to emulate, which can be repeated in responding to transition turbulence. Yet, it also teaches us: in such settings, fewer forecasts and more learning systems are needed that can adapt based on outside and institutional realities. The future is for models that evolve along with the economies that they observe.

Bibliography

Abdullah, M. A., Han, X., Amjad, M. A., & Makhmudov, S. (2025). Revisit the role of financial development on economic growth, human development, and sustainable development in higher-income countries. *Journal of Environmental Management*, *392*, 126874.

Box, G. E. P., & Jenkins, G. M. (1976). Seminal work introducing ARIMA modeling techniques foundational to modern time-series forecasting. *Time series analysis: Forecasting and control* (Rev. ed.). Holden-Day.

Cahyani, I., Buriev, K., Ngongo, M., Mamadiyarov, Z., Ino, L., Herman, H., Saputra, N., & Baxtishodovich, S. (2025). Exploring the Use of TikTok Application in Enhancing the Skill of Pronunciation: A Case on Students' Perception. Studies in Media and Communication, 13(2), 150–158. doi:http://dx.doi.org/10.11114/smc.v13i2.7553

Caporin, M., Shahbaz, M., Kuziboev, B., Masharipova, M., Allaberganov, S., & Makhmudov, S. (2024). Environmental Kuznets Curve for extended brics economies: do women governance and water stress matter?. International Journal of Energy Economics and Policy, 14(6), 174–183.

Dickey, D. A., & Fuller, W. A. (1979). Distribution of the estimators for autoregressive time series with a unit root. *Journal of the American Statistical Association*, 74(366), 427–431. (Developed the ADF test used for stationarity checks in this research.)

Engle, R. F., & Granger, C. W. J. (1987). Co-integration and error correction: Representation, estimation, and testing. *Econometrica*, *55*(2), 251–276. (Nobel prize-winning work on cointegration analysis.)

Hakimjon, H., Vikorjon, B., Ural, K., & Nabieva, N. (2024). The fusion of inflation and economic growth: a time series analysis. *Fusion: Practice & Applications*, *15*(2).

Hamilton, J. D. (1994). *Time series analysis*. Princeton University Press. (Comprehensive textbook covering structural breaks in time-series models.)

Hansen, B. E. (1997). Inference in TAR models. *Studies in Nonlinear Dynamics & Econometrics*, 2(1), 1–14. (Key reference for threshold autoregressive models.)

Hyndman, R. J., & Athanasopoulos, G. (2021). Contemporary guide to forecasting techniques. *Forecasting: Principles and practice* (3rd ed.). OTexts.

Jahrir, A., Gultom, Y., Herman, H., Zabadi, F., Ngongo, M., Mamadiyarov, Z., Fatmawati, E., & Saputra, N. (2025). Investigating the Elements of Short Commercial Mineral Water Advertisement: A Case on Discourse Analysis. *Studies in Media and Communication, 13*(4), 94–104. doi:http://dx.doi.org/10.11114/smc.v13i4.7813

Jolliffe, I. T., & Cadima, J. (2016). Principal component analysis: A review and recent developments. *Philosophical Transactions of the Royal Society A, 374*(2065), 20150202. (Authoritative review of PCA methodology.)

International Monetary Fund (2020). *Uzbekistan: 2020 Article IV consultation*. IMF Country Reports, 20(68). (Official assessment of Uzbekistan's economic reforms.)

Kalandarov, F., Makhmudov, S., Ibadullaev, D., Matniyozov, M., Nasretdinova, F., Sabirov, K., & Bahodirov, N. M. (2025). Low-Carbon Energy Risk and Renewable Energy Development: Insigths from Method of Moments Quantile Regression. International Journal of Energy Economics and Policy, 15(3), 524–536.

Khamidov, O., & Alimov, R. (2019). Economic transformation in post-Soviet Uzbekistan. **Post-Communist Economies, 31**(5), 642–661 (Analysis of Uzbekistan's transition economy).

Khayrilla Kurbonov, Samariddin Makhmudov, Shakhzod Erkinov, Umidjon Dadabaev, Gulnora Bekimbetova, Rukhiddin Zayniddinov, and Mirzabek Jonuzokov. 2025. Evaluating the Impact of Marketing Practices Digitalization and Investment on Labor Market Efficiency and Commercial Bank Performance Using Econometric Models. In Proceedings of the 8th International Conference on Future Networks & Distributed Systems (ICFNDS '24). Association for Computing Machinery, New York, NY, USA, 786–796. https://doi.org/10.1145/3726122.3726237

Khodjaniyazov, N., Mirkhoshimova, M., Kalandarov, F., Matyokubova, D., Utegenova, S., Makhmudov, S., & Khudayberganov, M. (2025). Time-varying impacts of financial stress on energy-related uncertainty. *International Journal of Energy Economics and Policy, 15*(3), 689–698.

Kuchkarov, T., Mamadiyarov, Z., Khakimov, Z., Sabirova, O., Matmurodov, K., Raimboyeva, M., & Umarova, S. (2025). Energy-Related Uncertainty and Crypto-Currency Environmental Attention: Time-Varying Perspective. *International Journal of Energy Economics and Policy, 15*(5), 614–626. https://doi.org/10.32479/ijeep.20784

Kulmanov, T., Dadabaev, U., Qulmetov, M., Ulashov, A., Eshboyev, M., & Makhmudov, S. (2024a,b). Global services market transformation: digitalization, export trends, and future forecasts. In *The 8th International Conference on Future Networks & Distributed Systems (ICFNDS '24)*, 8 pages, December 11–12, Marakech, Morocco. ACM, New York, NY, USA. <https://doi.org/10.1145/3726122.3726245>

Kuziboev, B., Ozturk, I., Kalandarov, F., Samandarov, O., Bekjanov, D., & Makhmudov, S. (2025). PROMOTING ENERGY SOURCES DIVERSIFICATION THROUGH ESG PERFORMANCE. Energy, 136009.

Litamahuputty, J. V., Amiruddin, E. G., Rahim, R., Rahman, A., & Mamadiyarov, Z. (2025). Cryptocurrency Risk Management through Decision Engineering: Evaluating XRPUSD and ADAUSD Portfolio Performance. *Journal of Applied Science, Engineering, Technology, and Education*, 7(1), 69–81. https://doi.org/10.35877/454RI.asci3871

Lütkepohl, H. (2020). Vector autoregressive models. *Handbook of econometrics* (Vol. 7, pp. 53–102). Elsevier. (Current reference on VAR modeling techniques.)

Makhmudov, S., Umarova, M., Kurbonov, K., Akbarova, L., Davletova, D., Shanazarova, N., & Kulmanov, T. (2024). Evaluating the forecast indicators of the volume of highly liquid assets of commercial banks in the process of digital transformation. In *The 8th International Conference on Future Networks & Distributed Systems (ICFNDS '24)*, 8 pages, December 11–12, Marakech, Morocco. ACM, New York, NY, USA. <https://doi.org/10.1145/3726122.3726222>

Mamadiyarov, Z., Hakimov, H., & Askarov, S. (2024). DEVELOPMENT OF RETAIL BANKING SERVICES IN THE CONTEXT OF DIGITAL TRANSFORMATION. *Financial and Credit Activity Problems of Theory and Practice*, *1*(54), 51–67. https://doi.org/10.55643/fcaptp.1.54.2024.4288

Mamadiyarov, Z. Makhmudov, S. Utanov, B. Kasimova, D. Bekmurodova, G. Hakimov, Z. (2025). Fusion of Economic and Financial Factors

Affecting Household Deposits in Banks: An Econometric Analysis. *Fusion: Practice and Applications*, (), 82–91. DOI: https://doi.org/10.54216/FPA.190206

Mamadiyarov, Z., Eshov, M., Otakhonova, D., Utegenova, S., Sabirov, K., Marks, A., & Bahodirov, N. (2025). Does Energy Policy Risk Threaten Energy Sources Diversification?. *International Journal of Energy Economics and Policy, 15*(5), 730–740. https://doi.org/10.32479/ijeep.21140

Mamadiyarov, Z., Saidov, O., Abdurazakova, N., Makhmudov, S., Nazarov, M., Rajabova, N., … Ruzmetova, I. (2025). Energy-Related Uncertainty and Tourism Stock Markets: New Insights from Time-Varying Relationship with TVP- VAR Approach. *International Journal of Energy Economics and Policy, 15*(4), 730–737. https://doi.org/10.32479/ijeep.20480

Mamani, J.C.M., Miri, M., Vorobev, Y. et al. Optimal Operation of Energy Microgrid Considering Economic and Emission Indices. Oper. Res. Forum 6, 122 (2025). https://doi.org/10.1007/s43069-025-00523-z

Muhammad Zubair, Irfanud Din, Nadeem Sarwar et al. Revolutionizing Sepsis Diagnosis Using Machine Learning and Deep Learning Models: A Systematic Literature Review, 10 June 2025, PREPRINT (Version 1) available at Research Square [https://doi.org/10.21203/rs.3.rs-6731418/v1]

PANJAITAN, M. B., HAMDANAH, H., SIRAIT, J., SUTIKNO, S., FATMAWATI, E., HERMAN, H., & MAMADIYAROV, Z. (2025). THE ROLE OF EMOTIONAL REGULATION IN SHAPING STUDENTS' PERCEPTION OF PHYSICS PROBLEMSOLVING TASKS. *TPM – Testing, Psychometrics, Methodology in Applied Psychology, 32*(S2(2025): Posted 09 June), 1–10. Retrieved from https://tpmap.org/submission/index.php/tpm/article/view/139

Pradhan, R., Hajiyev, E., Shichiyakh, R. *et al.* Optimal Techno-Economic Feasibility of an Off-Grid Microgrid System Using Load Flow Energy Management Strategies. *Oper. Res. Forum* **6**, 120 (2025). https://doi.org/10.1007/s43069-025-00524-y

Pesaran, H. H., & Shin, Y. (1998). Generalized impulse response analysis in linear multivariate models. *Economics Letters, 58*(1), 17–29. (Developed the impulse response method used in this study.)

Romero, R. M., Zelinskaya, M., Makhmudov, S., Sapaev, S., & Rustambekovich, J. U. (2025, September). Modelling and Optimal Utilisation of the Renewable Energy Systems in Microgrid with

Improving Reliability and Energy Efficiency. In Operations Research Forum (Vol. 6, No. 3, pp. 1–20). Springer International Publishing.

Sims, C. A. (1980). Macroeconomics and reality. *Econometrica*, *48*(1), 1–48. (Nobel prize-winning introduction of VAR modeling.)

Singagerda, F. S., Pratama, M. R., Alfairus, M. Q., Iskandar, A., & Mamadiyarov, Z. (2025). A Decision-Centric Approach to Risk Management in Aviation Stock Investments Using Value at Risk and Portfolio Optimization. *Journal of Applied Science, Engineering, Technology, and Education*, 7(1), 114–125. https://doi.org/10.35877/454RI.asci3870

Stock, J. H., & Watson, M. W. (2016). Dynamic factor models, factor-augmented vector autoregressions, and structural vector autoregressions in macroeconomics. *Handbook of Macroeconomics*, *2*, 415–525. (Modern treatment of factor-augmented VAR models.)

Su, R., Xiao, Y., Hamza, F., Mamadiyarov, Z., & Wahab, A. (2025). Scaling up green hydrogen in China: Economic opportunities and challenges. *International Journal of Hydrogen Energy*, *131*, 60–69.

Zayniddinov, R., Jumaev, N., Irgasheva, G., Asadov, A., Makhmudov, N., Abrorov, S., & Makhmudov, S. (2024). The influence of the digital economy on economic development evidence from Uzbekistan. *In The 8th International Conference on Future Networks & Distributed Systems (ICFNDS '24)*, December 11–12, 9 pages, Marakech, Morocco. ACM, New York, NY, USA. <https://doi.org/10.1145/3726122.3726242>

Zokir Toshtemirovich Mamadiyarov, Samandarboy Adhambek ugli Sulaymanov, Sarvar Anvar ugli Askarov, and Durdona Bakhtiyor kizi Uktamova. 2022. Impact of Covid-19 Pandemic on Accelerating the Digitization and Transformation of Banks. In Proceedings of the 5th International Conference on Future Networks and Distributed Systems (ICFNDS '21). Association for Computing Machinery, New York, NY, USA, 706–712. https://doi.org/10.1145/3508072.3508211

The Impact of Migrants' Personal Remittances on Selected Macroeconomic Indicators of Uzbekistan

Mansur Eshov, Jamshid Pardaev, Samariddin Makhmudov, Raya Karlibaeva, Zokir Mamadiyarov, Khayrilla Kurbonov, and Toshmurod Kulmanov

25.1. Introduction

Foreign labor migration of Uzbekistan has grown significantly over the last few years. Poor prospects within the internal labor market and a shortage of highly remunerative employment over the period of economic reform have driven many citizens to work abroad. International migration is now a factor that not only boosts personal incomes but also has a considerable influence on various branches of the economy. Notably, emigrant remittances are crucial in ensuring the economic well-being of host local families. To this end, international migration has huge economic and social significance to Uzbekistan (Rakhımov & Yokubov, 2022), with recent reforms by the Uzbek government, including the simplification of migration procedures, supporting migration flows (Seitz, 2019).

In international economics, personal remittances, popularly called "remittances," are a significant source of income for developing economies. In Uzbekistan, the funds have had positive implications, such as increased consumption levels, poverty reduction, and increased education and healthcare financing. Remittances also affect other economic metrics, with encouraging impacts on local consumption markets, rural standards of living, and general welfare. For instance, in Brazil, the relationship between economic development and international migration is complex, as remittances can be potential drivers of economic growth in a positive manner. Nevertheless, there needs to be effective incorporation of remittances into economic policy, for instance, by undertaking programs that help develop locally (Brzozowski, 2012; Hakimjon et al., 2024).

Yet there are adverse aspects in this process. Remittances can lead to under-investment in the domestic economy, an absence of motivation to cultivate the production sector, and problems like brain drain. The effects of migration streams can cause diminished labor resources in rural areas, social structure alteration, and hazards to long-term economic development possibilities.

This article is devoted to the consideration of the impact of Uzbekistan's external labor migration, namely the impact of individual remittances, on certain macroeconomic indicators, such as per capita gross national income, unemployment level, household consumption expenditure, and labor force participation. The research is aimed at providing a deeper understanding of the role and potential of remittances in the country's economic development and making an input into the development of practical recommendations on how to use these resources more effectively.

25.2. Literature Review

This section addresses the positions of researchers that have analyzed processes of migration and their socio-economic impacts. Individual remittances' impact on macroeconomic forces is the focal point of some studies, whereas others research social, economic, and political implications of migration. Some economists examined migration causes, as well as types of migration processes and streams. Ritchey's research synthesizes various theoretical and practical paradigms to investigate migration processes. Migration decisions are determined by the complex interaction between social, economic, and psychological determinants and offer theoretical frameworks for further examination of the reasons and consequences of migration (Ritchey, 1976). Migration positively influences economic and social development but is a complex process with interconnected determinants. Development policies must be able to control migrants' finances and human resources and have incentives to stimulate local economic growth (Abdullah et al., 2025; Akhmetshin et al., 2025; Pirvu, 2011; Pradhan, et al., 2025). This research reinforces the understanding of migration's place in the global economy and contributes to the sharpening of policy regulations. Migration, as theorized by Ravenstein, causes population growth in economic centers, thereby increasing economic prospects. However, it can also cause depopulation in the source regions and depletion of resources (Ravenstein, 1889). Ravenstein's initial works on the economic causes and consequences of migration remain relevant today.

Migration plays a vital part in socio-economic development. Being on both the positive and negative side of its effects, however, requires an integrated approach (Lupak et al., 2022). Lupak's article offers concrete methods of effective management of migration and state-level policy-making. Glover's study focuses on economic and social effects of migration processes and policies in the United Kingdom. By a consideration of historical movements, previous theory, and existing policy, Glover takes into consideration the social stability and economic efficiency impacts of migration (Glover et al., 2001).

There are scholars who examine migration in the "everyday geopolitics" paradigm, and they demonstrate how macropolitical processes come to be realized within the migrants' everyday practices. These studies demonstrate that migration influences not only economic outcomes but also political and social procedures, bringing new theoretical and practical responses to the analysis of migration and geopolitics (Eraliev & Urinboyev, 2024). Migration is natural in processes of economic and social transformation. It is both a driving force and a result of development and can enhance or reduce social inequalities (De Haas, 2014).

Czaika's "Migration Prospect Theory" also emphasizes the importance of expectations in migration decisions, with a new analytical approach that takes into account emotional and social factors, in addition to economic considerations (Czaika, 2015). Cwerner's work emphasizes interdependence between migration and time in recent global processes. While migration is traditionally conceived as a spatial process, his research highlights the crucial role played by time in migration processes (Cwerner, 2001). Collinson (2009) is critical of excessive reliance on overly simplistic migration models that cannot account for the complexity of migration processes. Making migration a matter of pure economics ignores social and political factors. Development can be ineffective in stemming migration in the short term because migration is a long process and can actually lead to fresh waves to follow. Thus, policies need to focus on maximizing the remittances and the contribution of returnee migrant to societal development, rather than just restricting migration (Clemens, 2014).

In Uzbekistan, labor migration is strongly conditioned by community processes, while migration, in turn, reshapes these processes. Expansion in terms of geography, as well as the increasing engagement of youth and women, are significant trends shaping future migration flows (Bondarenko, 2021). Labor migration strongly influences the economy and society of Uzbekistan. Although it has positive economic implications, dealing with its social impact calls for the policies of states and worldwide cooperation Khoshimovet al., 2024; Kuchkarov et al., 2025; Litamahuputty et al., 2025; Mamani, et al., 2025 Romero, et al., 2025; Zhao et al., 2025). The feminization of migrant labor in Uzbekistan has a deep impact on society and the economy. Growing female involvement in economic activities remakes gender roles, calling for multifaceted policies and programs for protecting them. Maksakova's research gets into the process of feminization and offers hints at how to handle its problems (Maksakova, 2006). Uzbekistan's foreign migration has serious economic and social implications and must be met with integrative measures that will enhance its stability and effectiveness (Juraev, 2012). Political and economic considerations feature prominently in making decisions on Uzbekistan's migration, with policies that stimulate economic growth and political stability needed (Sardorbek & Elyor, 2024).

Analyses and forecasts were conducted using multivariate linear regression (LS), VAR, ARDL, ARIMA, and various other econometric models on the global services market, digital economy, energy-related financial stress, cocktail market, digital transformation, and factors affecting the logistics industry (Jahrir et al., 2025;Kalandarov et al., 2025; Khayrilla et al., 2025; Khodjaniyazov et al., 2025; Kulmanov et al., 2024; Kuziboev et al., 2025; Mamadiyarov et al., 2024; Zayniddinov et al., 2024).

Another group of economists has successfully used econometric models such as Fixed Effects Estimator (FEE), Random Effects Estimator (REE), multivariate linear (LS), VAR, and ARDL in their research on investment in digital infrastructure, various aspects of digital payment systems, the impact of inflation and credit interest rates on investment, factors affecting the reduction of the state's share in commercial banks, non-performing loans in commercial banks, the digitization of banks, risks in digital services, and the development of retail payment services (Cahyani et al., 2025; Mamadiyarov et al., 2025; Samariddin et al., 2024; Su et al., 2025; Zokir et al., 2021).

Recent reforms undertaken by the Uzbekistani government, e.g., measures to facilitate migration processes, further drive these movements (Lin et al., 2025; Mamadiyarov et al., 2025; Seitz, 2019; Singagerda et al., 2025). It bases its study on the results of these reports to examine how remittances affect macroeconomic indicators of Uzbekistan, quantify their impacts, and make fact-based recommendations and conclusions.

25.3. Research Methodology

In this research, it is assumed that an increase in personal remittances sent by migrants positively affects macroeconomic indicators. To test this assumption, statistical data for nineteen years (2005–2023) from the World Bank was utilized, and econometric analysis was conducted with the assistance of STATA.18 software. For the sake of simplifying the research process, the following notations were introduced:

Remittancescurrent US: Personal remittances, received (current US$)

GNIpercapita: GNI per capita, PPP (current US$)

Laborforceparticipationrate: Labor force participation rate, male (% of male population ages 15+) (modeled ILO estimate)

Unemploymentmale: Unemployment, male (% of male labor force) (modeled ILO estimate)

HouseholdsandNPISHsconsumpti: Households and NPISHs final consumption expenditure (% of GDP)

Using these indicators, the study examines the effect of remittance receipts on the selected macroeconomic indicators in Uzbekistan. The study employed structural equation modeling (SEM) to estimate the relationships between the variables, providing a general framework to examine their interrelated effects.

The econometric analysis conducted in the study aimed to validate the hypothesis that remittances have a significant effect on the macroeconomic environment in Uzbekistan, and they have the potential to drive economic growth and improve living standards.

$$Y = BY + \Gamma X + \alpha + \zeta \tag{1}$$

where $B = [\beta ij]$ is the matrix of coefficients on endogenous variables predicting other endogenous variables, $\Gamma = [\gamma ij]$ is the matrix of coefficients on exogenous variables, $\alpha = [\alpha i]$ is the vector of intercepts for the endogenous variables, and ζ is assumed to have mean 0 and

$$Cov\ (X, \zeta) = 0 \tag{2}$$

This equation is part of the SEM methodology, which is widely used to analyze the relationships between personal remittances and macroeconomic indicators.

Let

$$K = [\kappa_j] = E(X) \tag{3}$$

$$\Phi = [\phi_{ij}] = \mathrm{Var}(X) \tag{4}$$

$$\Upsilon = [y_{ij}] = Var(z) \tag{5}$$

Then, the mean vector of the endogenous variables is:

$$\mu_Y = E(Y) = (I - B)^{-1}(\Gamma K + \alpha) \tag{6}$$

The variance matrix of the endogenous variables is:

$$\sum_{YY} = \mathrm{Var}(Y) = (I - B)^{-1}(\Gamma \Phi \Gamma' + \Upsilon)\left\{(I - B)^{-1}\right\}'$$

and the covariance matrix between the endogenous variables and the exogenous variables is:

$$\sum_{YX} = Cov\ (Y, X) = (I - B)^{-1}\ \Gamma\ \Phi$$

Let Z be the vector of all variables:

$$Z = \begin{pmatrix} Y \\ X \end{pmatrix}$$

Then its mean vector is:

$$\mu = E(Z) = \begin{pmatrix} \mu_Y \\ \kappa \end{pmatrix}$$

and its variance matrix is:

$$\sum = \mathrm{Var}(Z) = \begin{bmatrix} å_{YY} & å_{YX} \\ å_{'YX} & \Phi \end{bmatrix}$$

After determining the impact of independent variables on the dependent variable using the SEM model, it is necessary to evaluate the validity of these effects through Goodness-of-Fit tests. These tests ensure that the model accurately represents the data and provides reliable results.

The overall coefficient of determination (CD) is computed as:

$$\mathrm{CD} = 1 - \frac{\det(\Psi)}{\det(å_{YY})}$$

The comparative fit index (CFI) is computed as:

$$\mathrm{CFI} = 1 - \left[\frac{(X^2_{ms} - df_{ms})}{\max\{(X^2_{bs} - df_{bs}),((X^2_{ms} - df_{ms}))\}} \right]$$

These are used to examine the statistical significance of the model. Even though the formulas unveil the essence of the model, the research utilized STATA17 software to perform these calculations based on the outlined equations.

25.4. Analysis and Results

In this study, we applied the SEM model to examine the impact of personal remittances on Uzbekistan's macroeconomic indicators. Separate investigations were made for each macroeconomic indicator in order to examine the specific impacts of personal remittances. However, when we examined the interaction between remittances and certain indicators, such as the unemployment rate of females, no patterns were discovered. Hence, these themes were excluded from the scope of this chapter.

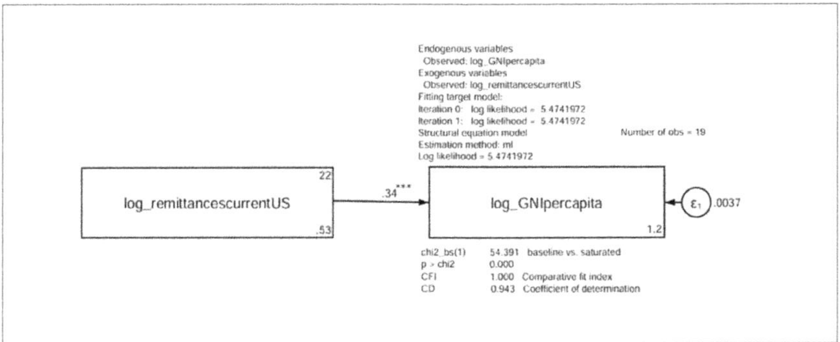

Figure 102. Effect of remittances on per capita gross national income.
Source: Author calculations.

Under the context of the study, per capita gross national income, expressed as logarithms (log_GNIpercapita), was used as the principal dependent variable and personal remittances, expressed in logarithmic values (log_remittancescurrentUS), used as the independent variable. Model estimation was achieved via SEM.

The results reveal that log_remittancescurrentUS has an extremely positive contribution to log_GNIpercapita ($\beta = 0.339$, $p < 0.001$). This tells us that an increase in remittances has a significant contribution to per capita gross national income.

The following fit statistics were provided by the model:

- Model fit: $Chi^2(0) = 0.00$, representing a perfect fit of the model.
- CFI index: 1.000, establishing a perfect fit.

- CD: 0.943, establishing high variance explained.
- Information criteria: AIC = –4.948 and BIC = –2.115, further confirming the high quality of the model.

These results support the positive role of remittances on economic growth and their essential part in the national economy.

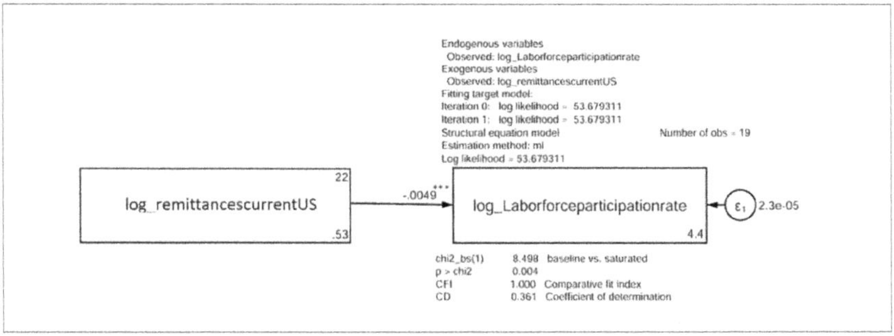

Figure 103. The effect of remittances on the male labor force participation rate.
Source: Author's calculations

Personal remittances (log_remittancescurrentUS) served as the independent variable in this analysis, while the labor force participation rate (log_Laborforceparticipationrate) served as the dependent variable. SEM was used to determine the relationship.

The findings indicate that log_Laborforceparticipationrate is negatively influenced by log_remittancescurrentUS ($\beta = -0.005, p = 0.001$). It indicates that an increase in remittances can lead to a decrease in the labor force participation rate.

Some of the important model fit statistics include:

- $Chi^2(0) = 0.00$ indicates the best fit for the model.
- TLI and CFI indices are 1.000, which indicates the perfect fit.
- Moderation of variation is captured by CD = 0.361.
- Quality of the model is also evidenced by information criteria like AIC = –101.359% and BIC = –98.525%.

The results affirm that remittances can be participation-reducing after labor. This evidence highlights the need for more work on the resulting economic activity deceleration induced by increased remittance flows.

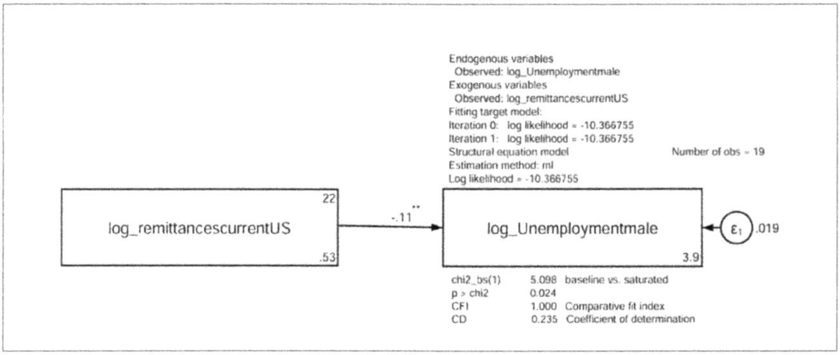

Figure 104. Remittances' influence on male unemployment rate.
Source: Author's calculations.

The independent variable for this research was the male unemployment rate (log_Unemploymentmale), while the independent variable was personal remittances (log_remittancescurrentUS). Statistical testing of the influence was conducted through SEM.

Results show that log_Unemploymentmale is significantly negatively influenced by log_remittancescurrentUS ($\beta = -0.106$, $p = 0.016$).

This can be interpreted in terms of the observation that a rise in remittances can help decrease the rate of unemployment for men.

Below are some measures of model fit:

- $Chi^2(0) = 0.00$ indicates a perfect fit for the model.
- The ideal fit of the model is delivered by the values of indices of CFI and TLI both 1.000.
- To the extent that a variance is explained by CD, which measures 0.235.
- AIC = 26.734 and BIC = 29.567, and both of them are information criteria for model acceptability.

Evidence exists that remittances can be used to address male unemployment, possibly by heightened economic activity and independent contractor opportunity. Evidence is provided in the paper which allows for greater research into how remittances positively affect labor market and economic engagement.

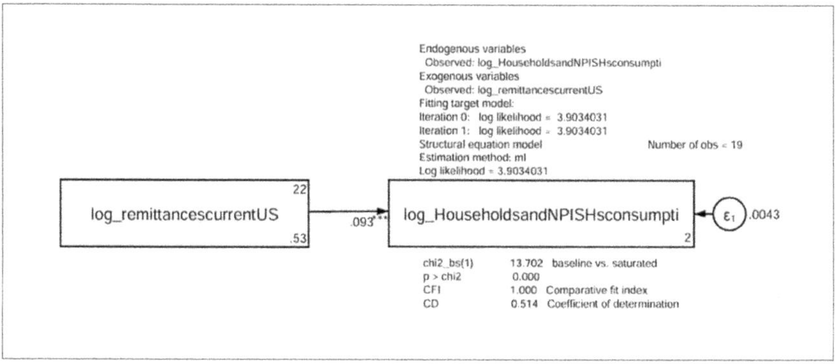

Figure 105. The impact of personal remittances on household and NPISHs consumption expenditures.
Source: Author's calculations.

In this analysis, household and non-profit institutions' consumption expenditures (log_HouseholdsandNPISHsconsumpti) were used as the dependent variable, and remittances (log_remittancescurrentUS) served as the independent variable. The relationship was statistically evaluated using SEM.

The results indicate that log_remittancescurrentUS has a significant positive effect on log_HouseholdsandNPISHsconsumpti ($\beta = 0.093, p < 0.001$). This finding suggests that an increase in remittances contributes to higher consumption levels.

Key model fit statistics include:

- Model fit: $Chi^2(0) = 0.00$, indicating perfect model fit.
- CFI and TLI indices: 1.000, confirming ideal model fit.
- CD: 0.514, indicating a moderate level of explained variance.
- Information criteria: AIC = –1.807 and BIC = 1.027, confirming the model's high quality.

These results demonstrate that remittances significantly support the consumption activities of households and non-profit organizations, emphasizing their critical role in fostering economic stability and boosting domestic demand.

25.5. Conclusion

Research carried out in this paper indicated that migrant remittances impact positively on their families as well as macroeconomic variables. The findings verify the importance of the government taking over migration policies, creating broader opportunities for migrants, resolving their issues, and recommending practical alternatives. By putting such measures into practice, the government is able to increase the standards of living among its citizens while protecting the rights of its migrant laborers.

The research yielded the following findings of interest:

1. *Per Capita Gross National Income (GNI) Effect*: A 1% rise in personal remittances leads to a rise in per capita GNI by 0.34%, and this is statistically significant.
2. *Impact on Male Labor Force Participation Rate*: A rise in remittances by 1% reduces the male labor force participation rate by 0.0049%, which is also statistically significant. This may be because a high proportion of men are among Uzbek migrants. The rise in remittance flows is most probably due to an increase in the number of migrants or higher earnings by existing migrants abroad, which may result in a reduction in male labor force participation in Uzbekistan.
3. *Effect on Male Unemployment Rate*: A 1% increase in personal remittances reduces the male unemployment rate by 0.11%, a statistically significant outcome. This shows that remittances are not only consumed but also invested in self-employment and economic activity. However, no such significant correlation was established between remittances and female unemployment, possibly due to cultural values in Uzbekistan that view women's contribution to the labor force as less essential.
4. *Impact on Consumption Expenditure of Household and NPISHs*: A rise in remittances by 1% enhances household and non-profit consumption expenditure by 0.93%, and this is statistically significant. It shows the

considerable contribution of remittances toward raising consumption expenditure and domestic demand.

The findings show that remittances have a two-fold positive effect on household well-being and other macroeconomic metrics. However, they also show that there is a need for effective policy measures so that remittances deliver their best benefits while avoiding potential negative effects, such as declining labor market participation. The government must continue to rationalize its migration policies so that it can have a sustainable and remunerative connection between migration and economic development.

This research is answering the major questions raised in the introduction, identifying the critical position of remittances in the Uzbek economy. Enhanced migration policies can improve migrants and their families' overall well-being as well as country economic growth.

Bibliography

Abdullah, M. A., Han, X., Amjad, M. A., & Makhmudov, S. (2025). Revisit the role of financial development on economic growth, human development, and sustainable development in higher-income countries. *Journal of Environmental Management*, *392*, 126874.

Akhmetshin, E., Abdullayev, I., Makhmudov, S., Dakhkilgova, K., Korotaeva, I. and Yanovskaya, G. (2025). APPLICATION OF TANH–COTH METHOD FOR COMBINED AND DOUBLE COMBINED SINH–COSH–GORDON EQUATIONS ARISING CHEMICAL REACTIONS TO WATER SURFACE GRAVITY WAVES. Computational Methods for Differential Equations, (), -. doi: 10.22034/cmde.2025.67655.3234

Bondarenko, K. A. (2021). Labor migration from Uzbekistan: A family and community promoted big bang. *Regional Research of Russia*, *11*(2), 273–284. <https://doi.org/10.1134/S2079970521020039>

Brzozowski, J. (2012). International migration and economic development. *Estudos Avançados*, *26*, 137–156.

Cahyani, I., Buriev, K., Ngongo, M., Mamadiyarov, Z., Ino, L., Herman, H., Saputra, N., & Baxtishodovich, S. (2025). Exploring the Use of

TikTok Application in Enhancing the Skill of Pronunciation: A Case on Students' Perception. Studies in Media and Communication, *13*(2), 150–158. doi:http://dx.doi.org/10.11114/smc.v13i2.7553

Clemens, M. A. (2014). *Does development reduce migration?* Edward Elgar Publishing. <https://www.elgaronline.com/edcollchap/edcoll/9781782548065/9781782548065.00010.xml>

Collinson, S. (2009). The political economy of migration processes: An agenda for migration research and analysis. <https://ora.ox.ac.uk/objects/uuid:c676e0fb-e8c2-4ede-b9e9-170169a3664a>

Cwerner, S. B. (2001). The times of migration. *Journal of Ethnic and Migration Studies*, *27*(1), 7–36. <https://doi.org/10.1080/13691830125283>

Czaika, M. (2015). Migration and economic prospects. *Journal of Ethnic and Migration Studies*, *41*(1), 58–82. <https://doi.org/10.1080/1369183X.2014.924848>

De Haas, H. (2014). *Migration theory: Quo vadis?* <https://ora.ox.ac.uk/objects/uuid:45aacf94-8f24-4294-9c74-cbc8453fcbfb>

Eraliev, S., & Urinboyev, R. (2024). 'What have you done, brother Putin?': Everyday geopolitics and Central Asian labour migration to Russia. *Central Asian Survey*, *43*(2), 215–234. <https://doi.org/10.1080/02634937.2023.2266519>

Glover, S., Gott, C., Loizillon, A., Portes, J., Price, R., Spencer, S., Srinivasan, V., & Willis, C. (2001). Migration: An economic and social analysis. <https://mpra.ub.uni-muenchen.de/id/eprint/75900>

Hakimjon, H., Vikorjon, B., Ural, K., & Nabieva, N. (2024). The fusion of inflation and economic growth: a time series analysis. *Fusion: Practice & Applications*, *15*(2).

Jahrir, A., Gultom, Y., Herman, H., Zabadi, F., Ngongo, M., Mamadiyarov, Z., Fatmawati, E., & Saputra, N. (2025). Investigating the Elements of Short Commercial Mineral Water Advertisement: A Case on Discourse Analysis. Studies in Media and Communication, *13*(4), 94–104. doi:http://dx.doi.org/10.11114/smc.v13i4.7813

Juraev, A. (2012). Labor migration from Uzbekistan: Social and economic impacts on local development. <https://iris.unitn.it/handle/11572/369165>

Kalandarov, F., Makhmudov, S., Ibadullaev, D., Matniyozov, M., Nasretdinova, F., Sabirov, K., & Bahodirov, N. M. (2025). Low-Carbon Energy Risk and Renewable Energy Development: Insigths from Method of Moments Quantile Regression. International Journal of Energy Economics and Policy, *15*(3), 524–536.

Khayrilla Kurbonov, Samariddin Makhmudov, Shakhzod Erkinov, Umidjon Dadabaev, Gulnora Bekimbetova, Rukhiddin Zayniddinov, and Mirzabek Jonuzokov. 2025. Evaluating the Impact of Marketing Practices Digitalization and Investment on Labor Market Efficiency and Commercial Bank Performance Using Econometric Models. In Proceedings of the 8th International Conference on Future Networks & Distributed Systems (ICFNDS '24). Association for Computing Machinery, New York, NY, USA, 786–796. https://doi.org/10.1145/3726122.3726237

Khodjaniyazov, N., Mirkhoshimova, M., Kalandarov, F., Matyokubova, D., Utegenova, S., Makhmudov, S., & Khudayberganov, M. (2025). Time-Varying Impacts of Financial Stress on Energy-Related Uncertainty. International Journal of Energy Economics and Policy, *15*(3), 689–698.

Kuchkarov, T., Mamadiyarov, Z., Khakimov, Z., Sabirova, O., Matmurodov, K., Raimboyeva, M., & Umarova, S. (2025). Energy-Related Uncertainty and Crypto-Currency Environmental Attention: Time-Varying Perspective. International Journal of Energy Economics and Policy, 15(5), 614–626. https://doi.org/10.32479/ijeep.20784

Kuziboev, B., Ozturk, I., Kalandarov, F., Samandarov, O., Bekjanov, D., & Makhmudov, S. (2025). PROMOTING ENERGY SOURCES DIVERSIFICATION THROUGH ESG PERFORMANCE. Energy, 136009.

Lin, M.H., Matchanova, B., Nurmatovich, H.A. *et al.* Optimal Operation of the Multi-Carrier Energy System Considering Energy Markets and Renewable Energies Participation. *Int. J. Appl. Comput. Math* **11**, 170 (2025). https://doi.org/10.1007/s40819-025-02002-9

Litamahuputty, J. V., Amiruddin, E. G., Rahim, R., Rahman, A., & Mamadiyarov, Z. (2025). Cryptocurrency Risk Management through Decision Engineering: Evaluating XRPUSD and ADAUSD Portfolio Performance. Journal of Applied Science, Engineering, Technology, and Education, 7(1), 69–81. https://doi.org/10.35877/454RI.asci3871

Lupak, R., Mizyuk, B., Zaychenko, V., Kunytska-Iliash, M., & Vasyltsiv, T. (2022). Migration processes and socio-economic development: Interactions and regulatory policy. *Agricultural and Resource Economics: International Scientific E-Journal*, *8*(1), 70–88.

Maksakova, L. (2006). Feminization of labour migration in Uzbekistan. *Migration Perspectives: Eastern Europe and Central Asia*, 133–145.

Mamadiyarov, Z., Hakimov, H., & Askarov, S. (2024). DEVELOPMENT OF RETAIL BANKING SERVICES IN THE CONTEXT OF DIGITAL TRANSFORMATION. Financial and Credit Activity Problems of Theory and Practice, 1(54), 51–67. https://doi.org/10.55643/fcaptp.1.54.2024.4288

Mamadiyarov, Z. Makhmudov, S. Utanov, B. Kasimova, D. Bekmurodova, G. Hakimov, Z. (2025). Fusion of Economic and Financial Factors Affecting Household Deposits in Banks: An Econometric Analysis. Fusion: Practice and Applications, (), 82–91. DOI: https://doi.org/10.54216/FPA.190206

Mamadiyarov, Z., Saidov, O., Abdurazakova, N., Makhmudov, S., Nazarov, M., Rajabova, N., … Ruzmetova, I. (2025). Energy-Related Uncertainty and Tourism Stock Markets: New Insights from Time-Varying Relationship with TVP- VAR Approach. International Journal of Energy Economics and Policy, 15(4), 730–737. https://doi.org/10.32479/ijeep.20480

Mamani, J.C.M., Miri, M., Vorobev, Y. et al. Optimal Operation of Energy Microgrid Considering Economic and Emission Indices. Oper. Res. Forum 6, 122 (2025). https://doi.org/10.1007/s43069-025-00523-z

PANJAITAN, M. B., HAMDANAH, H., SIRAIT, J., SUTIKNO, S., FATMAWATI, E., HERMAN, H., & MAMADIYAROV, Z. (2025). THE ROLE OF EMOTIONAL REGULATION IN SHAPING STUDENTS' PERCEPTION OF PHYSICS PROBLEMSOLVING TASKS. *TPM – Testing, Psychometrics, Methodology in Applied Psychology*, *32*(S2(2025): Posted 09 June), 1–10. Retrieved from https://tpmap.org/submission/index.php/tpm/article/view/139

Pradhan, R., Hajiyev, E., Shichiyakh, R. et al. Optimal Techno-Economic Feasibility of an Off-Grid Microgrid System Using Load Flow Energy Management Strategies. Oper. Res. Forum 6, 120 (2025). https://doi.org/10.1007/s43069-025-00524-y

Pirvu, R. (2011). The link between migration and economic development. Bulletin of the University of Agricultural Sciences & Veterinary Medicine Cluj-Napoca. *Horticulture*, *68*(2). <https://citeseerx.ist.psu.edu/document?repid=rep1&type=pdf&doi=676efc1b7689f5b2af66c2c478eb709357de069a>

Rakhimov, M., & Yokubov, F. (2022). Uzbekistan external migration: Key trends and directions. *Eurasian Research Journal*, *4*(1), 27–47.

Ravenstein, E. G. (1889). The Laws of migration. *Journal of the Royal Statistical Society*, *52*(2), 241–305.

Ritchey, P. N. (1976). Explanations of migration. *Annual Review of Sociology*, *2*, 363–404.

Romero, R. M., Zelinskaya, M., Makhmudov, S., Sapaev, S., & Rustambekovich, J. U. (2025, September). Modelling and Optimal Utilisation of the Renewable Energy Systems in Microgrid with Improving Reliability and Energy Efficiency. In Operations Research Forum (Vol. 6, No. 3, pp. 1–20). Springer International Publishing.

Rukhiddin Zayniddinov, Nodir Jumaev, Gulbakhor Irgasheva, Alam Asadov, Nosir Makhmudov, Sirojiddin Abrorov, and Samariddin Makhmudov. 2025. The Influence of the Digital Economy on Economic Development Evidence from Uzbekistan. In Proceedings of the 8th International Conference on Future Networks & Distributed Systems (ICFNDS '24). Association for Computing Machinery, New York, NY, USA, 831–839. https://doi.org/10.1145/3726122.3726242

Samariddin Makhmudov, Malika Umarova, Khayrilla Kurbonov, Laylo Akbarova, Durdona Davletova, Nilufar Shanazarova, and Toshmurod Kulmanov. 2025. Evaluating the forecast indicators of the volume of highly liquid assets of commercial banks in the process of digital transformation. In Proceedings of the 8th International Conference on Future Networks & Distributed Systems (ICFNDS '24). Association for Computing Machinery, New York, NY, USA, 698–704. https://doi.org/10.1145/3726122.3726222

Samariddin Makhmudov, Kudratillo Tukhsanov, Saifulla Arslanbekov, Akram Amanov, Orifali Tursunov, Umarbek Jabbarov and Muyassarxon Mirzakarimova. 2024. Optimizing Supply Chain Financing Development Prospects of Digital Ecosystems in the European Logistics Industry. In The 8th International Conference on Future

Networks & Distributed Systems (ICFNDS '24), December 11–12, 2024, Marakech, Morocco. ACM, New York, NY, USA, 12 Pages. https://doi.org/10.1145/3726122.3726200

Sardorbek, I., & Elyor, U. (2024). The main causes of migration in Uzbekistan: An econometric analysis. *European Journal of Business Startups and Open Society*, *4*(6), 104–108.

Seitz, W. H. (2019). *International migration and household well-being: evidence from Uzbekistan*. World Bank Policy Research Working Paper, 8910. <https://papers.ssrn.com/sol3/papers.cfm?abstract_id=3430521>

Singagerda, F. S., Pratama, M. R., Alfairus, M. Q., Iskandar, A., & Mamadiyarov, Z. (2025). A Decision-Centric Approach to Risk Management in Aviation Stock Investments Using Value at Risk and Portfolio Optimization. *Journal of Applied Science, Engineering, Technology, and Education*, 7(1), 114–125. https://doi.org/10.35877/454RI.asci3870

Su, R., Xiao, Y., Hamza, F., Mamadiyarov, Z., & Wahab, A. (2025). Scaling up green hydrogen in China: Economic opportunities and challenges. *International Journal of Hydrogen Energy*, *131*, 60–69.

Toshmurod Kulmanov, Umidjon Dadabaev, Mansurbek Qulmetov, Aliboy Ulashov, Mirjalol Eshboyev, and Samariddin Makhmudov. 2025. Global Services Market Transformation Digitalization Export Trends and Future Forecasts. In Proceedings of the 8th International Conference on Future Networks & Distributed Systems (ICFNDS '24). Association for Computing Machinery, New York, NY, USA, 851–858. https://doi.org/10.1145/3726122.3726245

Zhao, Q., Pervaiz, A., Makhmudov, S., & Fatima, A. (2025). Do environmental stringent policies enhance the impact of renewable energy on CO2 reduction? Evidence from BRICS-T economies. Journal of Environmental Management, 391, 126464.

Zokir Toshtemirovich Mamadiyarov, Samandarboy Adhambek ugli Sulaymanov, Sarvar Anvar ugli Askarov, and Durdona Bakhtiyor kizi Uktamova. 2022. Impact of Covid-19 Pandemic on Accelerating the Digitization and Transformation of Banks. In Proceedings of the 5th International Conference on Future Networks and Distributed Systems (ICFNDS '21). Association for Computing Machinery, New York, NY, USA, 706–712. https://doi.org/10.1145/3508072.3508211

Analysis of the Financial Sustainability of Higher Education Institutions Based on Cluster Approaches

Alisher Sherov, Zokir Mamadiyarov, Jamshid Pardaev, Samariddin Makhmudov, Hakimjon Hakimov, Amina Ruzikulova, and Mirjalol Eshboev

26.1. Introduction

The financial viability of higher education institutions (HEIs) is currently an emerging fast-developing issue in the fast-evolving economic and education environment of the modern world. With mounting operating costs, volatile public support, changing student demographics, and growing demands for quality and accountability, colleges and universities worldwide are facing challenges to remain sustainable in the long term. To that extent, the capacity of HEIs to be financially sustainable is not only crucial to their survival but also crucial to the fact that they continue to provide good-quality education, foster innovation, and contribute to national development goals.

Financial sustainability of the HEIs means the ability of the institutions to effectively handle their finances in the long term so that they will be capable of fulfilling their existing and future obligations without risking their educational function. Financial sustainability involves effective utilization of resources, diversification of income, sound planning, and effective risk management strategies. Financial sustainability is not one entity. It is distinguished from institution to institution with regard to their size, governing structures, funding sources, local contexts, and strategic priorities.

Cluster analysis, as an exploratory data-driven technique, offers a solid methodological tool to understand the financial behavior and profiles of HEIs by grouping similar institutions on the basis of shared financial and operational characteristics. Cluster analysis enables policymakers, administrators, and stakeholders to identify patterns, diagnose deficiencies, and compare performance among comparable institutions. Perhaps most importantly, cluster-based methods can enable strategic decision-making by focusing attention on best practice, revealing structural inefficiencies, and inducing co-ordinated responses from institutions with similar challenges.

Furthermore, this analysis has policy implications for institutional leaders and government policymakers. Understanding the typology of financial sustainability in the higher education sector allows for more effective policy interventions and resource allocation. It also provides institutions with a benchmark against peers and the development of long-term sustainability strategies based on their specific circumstances.

With increased uncertainty and reduced resources, it is more crucial than ever to address financial sustainability using a systematic and evidence-based strategy. Cluster analysis not only provides a rigorous description of financial risk and resilience but also facilitates shared thinking and collaborative solutions within the higher education community. While the universities continue forward, grappling still with fiscal woes and shifting conditions, this sort of analytical vehicle will be pivotal in assisting them to construct robust and sustainable systems of higher education.

26.2. Literature Review

Financial sustainability in institutions of higher education is, from an economic point of view, the capacity of institutions of higher education to ensure long-term financial health, fulfill their financial commitments, and serve their academic missions effectively. This includes resource management, developing revenue streams, managing costs, and ensuring transparency and accountability in financial reporting. Effective financial management is critical to the feasibility and prosperity of institutions of higher education in a growing complex and competitive context.

Financial sustainability in universities, according to Lucianelli and Citro (2017), is the development of financial resources through internal means and the provision of stable revenues from these sources in the future (Abdullah et al., 2025; Citro, 2017; Lin et al., 2025; Mamadiyarov et al., 2025; Pradhan et al., 2025).

Marcel J. Dumestre (2016) explains why U.S. universities are so financially unstable and offers a strategic thought process for institutional transformation, as well as means for education-dependent institutions to remake themselves as financially sustainable universities of the twenty-first century.

Lukasz Swiatek (2023) explains how “engagement orientation” can help HEIs achieve sustainability. According to the scholar, “engagement orientation” allows an organization to invest funds in activities that have the support of a wide range of stakeholders. The scholar also argues that “engagement orientation” can allow HEIs to properly develop sustainability and allow them to invest funds in initiatives that have wide support, but the method may have certain limitations.

Financial sustainability is especially crucial for HEIs, especially in times of uncertainty and change. It involves the ability of a university to maintain a positive financial position while enhancing its continued resilience. Researchers have proposed the use of various indicators to measure the financial sustainability of HEIs. For example, Alshubir (2021) used university life expectancy, gross enrolment ratio, and expenditure on higher education as proxies for financial sustainability of HEIs in the Organization for Economic Cooperation and Development (OECD) countries, and thereby investigated the impact of financial sustainability indicators of higher education on foreign direct investment.

Mohamed and Muturi (2017) examined the determinants of the financial performance of income-generating units in universities in the Puntland State, Somalia, and recommended that there must be improvements in market research, management, and financial planning. The research model developed by Bazhan et al. (2025) can diagnose cluster management risks in education, specifically financial control mechanisms. They illustrated that institutional success could be effectively monitored through the combination of internal control mechanisms and cluster analysis. This is an effective basis for strategic decision-making for HEIs.

Financial sustainability is attainable in several ways, one of which is diversification in income sources. Grebeniuk et al. (2025) created a cluster-based model and suggested relocating it to financial services models. It can be used for optimizing the expenses of HEIs and improving financial services. Internationally, Benameur et al. (2025) conducted literature review in the field of sustainable finance through bibliometric and cluster mapping and proposed a framework that can be applied as a starting point to exploring institutional positioning and collaboration networks between HEIs. A more specific exploration of financial innovation was proposed by Badra et al. (2025). They analyzed the problems of fintech and financial inclusion through thematic clusters. The study offers a framework to enable financial innovation in HEIs based on digital maturity and fiscal sustainability.

Analyses and forecasts were conducted using multivariate linear regression (LS), VAR, ARDL, ARIMA and various other econometric models on the global services market, digital economy, energy-related financial stress, cocktail market, digital transformation, and factors affecting the logistics industry (Kalandarov et al., 2025; Khayrilla et al., 2025;Khodjaniyazov et al., 2025 Kuchkarov et al., 2025; Kuziboev et al., 2025; Litamahuputty et al., 2025; PANJAITAN et al., 2025; Romero et al., 2025; Zhao et al., 2025).

Another group of economists has successfully used econometric models such as Fixed Effects Estimator (FEE), Random Effects Estimator (REE), multivariate linear (LS), VAR, and ARDL in their research on investment in digital infrastructure, various aspects of digital payment systems, the impact of inflation and credit interest rates on investment, factors affecting the reduction of the state's share in commercial banks, non-performing loans in commercial banks, the digitization of banks, risks in digital services, and the development of retail payment services (Cahyani et al., 2025; Mamadiyarov et al., 2025; Muhammad et al., 2025; Samariddin et al., 2025; Samariddin et al., 2025; Su et al., 2025; Zokir, 2021; Zokir et al., 2021).

26.3. Methodology

Based on the results of the aforementioned research, we have developed a "financial stability" index for 62 state universities in our country. In developing this index, we used the financial indicators of state universities for the second quarter of 2021–2024. We mainly relied on two indicators in developing the "financial stability" index. These are:

1. Level of ability to cover obligations $\left(MQD\right)$;
2. Profitability level $\left(RD\right)$.

The debt service coverage ratio $\left(MQD\right)$ using the following formula:

$$MQD = \frac{YD}{UX} \tag{1}$$

where MQD – Debt Service Coverage Ratio;
YD – gross income ;
UX – total expenses.
The profitability ratio (RD) using the following formula:

$$RD = \frac{YD - UX}{YD} \quad (2)$$

Where RD – profitability ratio;
YD – gross income ;
UX – total expenses.

In the next step, using Equations (1) and (2), we calculate the "financial stability" index (MBI) as in what follows:

$$MBI = (MQD)^{\omega_1} * (RD)^{\omega_2} \quad (3)$$

where MBI – financial stability index;
MQD – Debt Service Coverage Ratio ;
RD – profitability ratio;
ω_1 – MQD weight of the indicator;
ω_2 – RD weight of the indicator.

In our research, we normalize the financial indicators required for 62 public universities selected as the study set. For this, we use the "Z-score Normalization" method. The main purpose of normalization is to calculate the index based on certain indicators, without creating sharp differences between universities that are ahead or behind in some indicators, but objectively assess the level of financial stability of universities, which serves to evaluate. The formula for Z-score Normalization is expressed as follows:

$$Z = \frac{X - \mu}{\sigma} \quad (4)$$

Where Z – normalized value of the indicator;
X – actual value of the indicator;
μ – average value of the indicator for the studied set;
σ – standard error of the indicator for the studied set.

26.4. Results

Based on the formulas outlined earlier, a "financial stability" index was formed for 62 state universities for the period of the second quarter of 2021–2024 (Table 97).

Table 97. "Financial stability" index for public universities

Universities serial number *	2021#	2022#	2023#	2024 (for 6 months) #
1	19.56	39.67	44.53	27.50
2	24.89	45.45	40.63	33.75
3	84.00	74.38	52.34	33.75
4	31.56	47.11	41.41	28.33
5	23.56	52.07	28.91	42.50
6	44.89	44.63	34.38	25.42
7	36.89	90.91	70.31	60.83
8	24.00	38.02	39.06	24.58
9	18.67	32.23	36.72	33.33
10	25.78	41.32	47.66	30.83
11	27.11	44.63	42.97	22.50
12	34.22	11.57	47.66	24.17
13	61.78	40.50	56.25	32.08
14	25.33	47.11	39.84	26.25
15	26.22	40.50	42.97	28.33
16	38.67	76.86	50.00	23.75
17	25.78	44.63	36.72	24.17
18	78.22	50.41	38.28	26.25
19	32.44	78.51	31.25	32.50
20	25.78	35.54	50.00	26.25
21	28.00	42.15	30.47	25.42
22	29.78	52.89	44.53	100.00
23	33.78	34.71	39.84	26.67
24	39.11	47.11	33.59	29.17

Table 97. (*Continued*)

Universities serial number *	2021#	2022#	2023#	2024 (for 6 months) #
25	27.56	43.80	39.84	28.33
26	32.44	51.24	42.97	27.92
27	26.67	44.63	48.44	32.50
28	66.22	100.00	40.63	45.00
29	34.67	47.11	44.53	23.33
30	39.56	52.89	53.91	23.75
31	38.22	70.25	39.06	35.83
32	56.44	36.36	57.03	22.08
33	38.67	57.02	60.94	36.67
34	31.11	42.98	42.97	37.92
35	47.56	47.93	39.06	35.42
36	29.78	47.93	46.88	25.83
37	29.78	53.72	32.81	21.25
38	33.33	57.85	50.00	29.17
39	1.78	46.28	52.34	25.00
40	48.89	38.02	44.53	25.00
41	36.89	47.93	31.25	42.50
42	39.11	42.98	42.97	27.08
43	27.11	38.02	32.03	26.25
44	36.00	33.06	42.97	65.42
45	50.67	43.80	60.94	24.17
46	42.22	61.98	56.25	68.33
47	35.11	62.81	100.00	27.50
48	26.22	42.98	39.06	25.83
49	20.44	41.32	35.16	28.33
50	33.33	33.06	43.75	34.58
51	20.00	32.23	37.50	22.08
52	100.00	80.99	82.03	23.75

(*Continued*)

Table 97. (*Continued*)

Universities serial number *	2021#	2022#	2023#	2024 (for 6 months) #
53	32.44	28.93	42.19	37.50
54	41.33	32.23	53.91	38.75
55	27.11	50.41	41.41	34.17
56	42.67	67.77	41.41	22.92
57	34.67	45.45	44.53	22.50
58	32.00	46.28	44.53	31.25
59	24.44	33.88	38.28	22.92
60	21.78	43.80	33.59	21.25
61	37.33	34.71	52.34	27.92
62	31.11	55.37	61.72	25.83

Note: * represents the full names of the MFIs are given in Appendix 1; # represents the index for each period is calculated relative to the "Benchmark" MFI.

According to Table 97, in 2021, the Uzbek-Finnish Pedagogical Institute led the way in the "financial stability" index, followed by the Andijan State Pedagogical Institute (84.0 points), Navoi State University of Mining and Technology (78.22 points), and the lowest indicator was recorded by the Tashkent branch of the Astrakhan State Technical University (1.78 points). In 2022, the Shakhrisabz State Pedagogical Institute led the way in the index, followed by the Bukhara State Pedagogical Institute (90.91 points), the Uzbek-Finnish Pedagogical Institute (80.99 points), and the lowest indicator was recorded by the Tashkent branch of the Russian State University of Oil and Gas named after IMGubkin (11.57 points). The 2023 index analysis showed that Namangan State University (100 points), Uzbek-Finnish Pedagogical Institute (82.03 points), Bukhara State Pedagogical Institute (70.31 points) were in the lead, while Bukhara State University (28.91 points) recorded the lowest result. Furthermore, according to the results of the "financial stability" index for the first half of 2024, Tashkent Financial Institute (100 points), Navoi State Pedagogical Institute (68.33 points), Karshi State University (65.42 points) were in the lead, while the Almalyk branch of Islam Karimov Tashkent State Technical University (21.25 points) and Urgench State University (21.25 points) recorded the lowest indicators.

The analysis of the "financial stability" index indicate that almost all of the HEIs with a low index have a very low "profitability level." In the HEIs with a high score on the index, we can see that both the "Liability Level" and "Profitability Level" indicators are very high.

In our opinion, based on the results obtained earlier on the "financial stability" index in our research work, we consider it appropriate to evaluate the "financial stability" index of public HEIs using the intervals "high (66.6–100)," "medium (33.3–66.6)," and "low (0–33.3)".

In order to more objectively assess the financial stability of HEIs, it is very important to take into account the strengths, weaknesses, and similarities of public HEIs. Taking these aspects into account, dividing public HEIs into classes (groups) based on the "financial strength" index (FSI) will help reduce differences in the level of financial stability among public HEIs.

In this context, we used the "Cluster analysis" method in our research. Cluster analysis is a multidimensional method in which similar subjects are divided into several groups based on the groups of variables considered in this analysis.

Cluster analysis is not a mechanism for distinguishing between relevant and important variables. Therefore, the selection of variables to be included in cluster analysis should be informed by conceptual considerations. This is important because the clusters formed are highly dependent on the variables included.

Various methods can be used to conduct cluster analysis, one of the most common of which is the hierarchical method, which includes the following:

- *Agglomerative:* In this method, all subjects are initially placed in separate clusters. Then, their proximity levels are calculated based on the selected indicators, and the clusters of subjects with the closest indicators are combined. This process continues until all subjects form a single cluster. Finally, the optimal number of clusters is selected from all the cluster solutions.
- *Division*: In this method, all clusters start in separate clusters and continue until a single cluster is formed, but in the reverse order.

In practice, agglomerative methods are used more often than division methods.

The data used in cluster analysis can be interval, ordinal, or categorical depending on the field of application, but using different variables in the analysis process can make the process more complicated. Therefore, when using cluster analysis, it is necessary to have a specific method for calculating the distance between subjects, taking into account the type of data available. Currently, there are several methods of this type, the most common of which is the "Euclidean distance."

When using this measure, the scale of the variables under consideration is a problem, since changing the scale affects the distance between objects (for example, a 10-cm difference can be a 100-mm difference). In addition, if one variable has a much wider range than the others, that variable will be given priority. In this case, the solution to the problem is to standardize each variable. However, another problem in this case is that this change tends to reduce the distances between clusters. This is because if a particular selected variable separates subjects well, it will have a large difference because the variability within a cluster is high. If this indicator is standardized, the separation between clusters will be less.

In hierarchical agglomerative clustering, the method is used to determine which clusters to combine at each stage of cluster analysis. This method, in turn, consists of several sub-methods, which are as follows:

- The nearest element, or "nearest neighborhood" method. In this method, the distance between the two closest neighboring clusters is calculated. This method has some disadvantages, where it does not take into account the structure of the cluster.
- The furthest neighbor method, in contrast to the above, is defined as the longest distance between two clusters, that is, the distance between the two elements that are farthest apart. This method is considered to be mainly prone to creating small clusters of similar size.
- The average connection method, in which the distance between two clusters is calculated as the average distance between all elements in the two clusters. It is usually considered as one of the most reliable methods.
- *Centroid method*: In this type, the average value of each variable is calculated and the distance between the centers is used, and clusters with centers close to each other are combined. This method is also considered more reliable and robust.

- *Ward's method*: All possible cluster pairs are combined and the sum of squared distances within each cluster is calculated. In the next step, this process is summed over all clusters and the pair that gives the least sum of squares is selected. In this method, clusters of size x are generated.

For the results of a research study to be reliable, it is necessary to try at least two or three of the aforementioned methods, and the results will be more reliable if the methods are compatible with each other.

The process of performing hierarchical cluster analysis can be depicted in a diagram called a dendrogram, which shows the clusters that are combined at each stage of this analysis and the distances between them during the process of combining. In this process, if the distance from one stage to the next is large, then in this case it means that clusters that are close to each other at this stage are combined, and in the next stage the combined clusters are relatively far from each other. From this it becomes clear that the optimal number of clusters can be the size of the distance, this process can be clearly seen in the dendrogram.

In short, "Cluster analysis" is a statistical method used to classify elements of a given set into groups called clusters based on similarities in factors. These similarities are measured in terms of distance, where the greater the distance, the lower the similarity, and the smaller the distance, the higher the similarity. The elements that are found to be most similar are grouped into one cluster. Each cluster has a well-defined center, which is the average of all the points in the cluster. Therefore, each cluster is represented by a center.

"Cluster analysis" method is carried out through the following steps:

Let d_{kl} denote the distance between clusters k and l, where each cluster contains n_k and n_l elements, respectively The remaining set of distances d_{kl} is defined for all elements in cluster N. The distance d_{kl} (using the Euclidean metric) is calculated according to the following formula:

$$d_{kl} = \sqrt{\sum_{i=1}^{N}\left(x_k - y_k\right)^2 / N} \quad (5)$$

Here, D represents the smallest distance d_{kl} in the set. The clusters k and l are then merged into a new cluster p.

Using the following formula d_{pr} is a new set of distances:

$$d_{pr} = \gamma_k * d_{kr} + \gamma_l * d_{lr} + \delta * d_{kl} + \theta * \left| d_{kr} - d_{lr} \right| \qquad (6)$$

Here r represents any cluster other than k or l, and d_{kr} and d_{lr} are the new distances from clusters k and l to cluster r, respectively; d_{pr} denotes the distance between the new cluster p and cluster r. The new cluster p also takes a size of $n_p = n_k + n_l$, where

$$\gamma_k = \frac{n_k}{n_p}, \gamma_l = \frac{n_l}{n_p}, \delta = -\gamma_k * \gamma_l$$

Steps 1–3 are repeated until all elements are grouped. Based on this process, a proximity matrix of the financial stability indicators of public universities was constructed. In the formed matrix, the proximity distance of the universities to each other was calculated. As a result of the distance analysis, Andijan State Pedagogical Institute, Bukhara State Pedagogical Institute, IMGubkin Russian State University of Oil and Gas in Tashkent, branch of the Federal State Budgetary Institution of Higher Education "MEI" National Research University in Tashkent, Navoi State University of Mining and Technology, Tashkent State University of Economics, Tashkent Financial Institute, Shahrisabz State Pedagogical Institute, Samarkand Branch of Tashkent State University of Economics, Karshi State University, Navoi State Pedagogical Institute, Namangan State University, Uzbek-Finnish Pedagogical Institute, and Gulistan State University are located at a considerable distance from the remaining universities. This means that these universities are not in the same cluster with the remaining universities. If we look at the degree of proximity of these universities to each other, for example, the closest distance to Andijan State Pedagogical Institute is Navoi State University of Mining and Technology, which is 861.90 units. The closest distance to the branch of the Federal State Budgetary Institution of Higher Education "MEI" National Research University in Tashkent is Tashkent State University of Economics at a distance of 348.07 units, the Samarkand branch of Tashkent State University of Economics at a distance of 309.50 units, and Gulistan State University at a distance of 173.10 units.

The Navoi State Pedagogical Institute, which is the closest to Karshi State University, is 1059.88 units, which indicates that these HEIs belong to the same cluster. Based on the above, the following section describes the classification of state HEIs into clusters according to their financial stability indicators (Figure 106).

According to the dendrogram in Figure 106, a total of 10 clusters of state universities were formed based on the levels of similarity and were arranged in the following order (Table 98):

Table 98. Classification of public universities into clusters (groups) based on financial stability indicators

Cluster sequence number	Serial number of state universities
1	1, 2, 4, 5, 6, 8, 9, 10, 11, 13, 14, 15, 17, 20,21, 23, 24, 25, 26, 27, 29, 30, 32, 33, 34, 35, 36, 37, 38, 39, 40, 41, 42, 43, 45, 48, 49, 50, 51, 53, 54, 55, 57, 58, 59, 60, 61, 62
2	3, 18,
3	7
4	12
5	16, 19, 31, 56
6	22
7	28
8	44, 46
9	47
10	52

Source: Developed by the authors.

From Table 98, it can be seen that 62 state universities were divided into 10 clusters based on financial stability indicators. The largest number of universities fell into cluster 1, while the smallest number of universities fell into clusters 3, 4, 6, 7, 9, and 10.

In our opinion, the use of the results of our research on "Cluster analysis" by the "Ministry of Higher Education, Science and Innovation" in its activities will serve as one of the main instruments for further increasing the level of financial stability of state universities in the future.

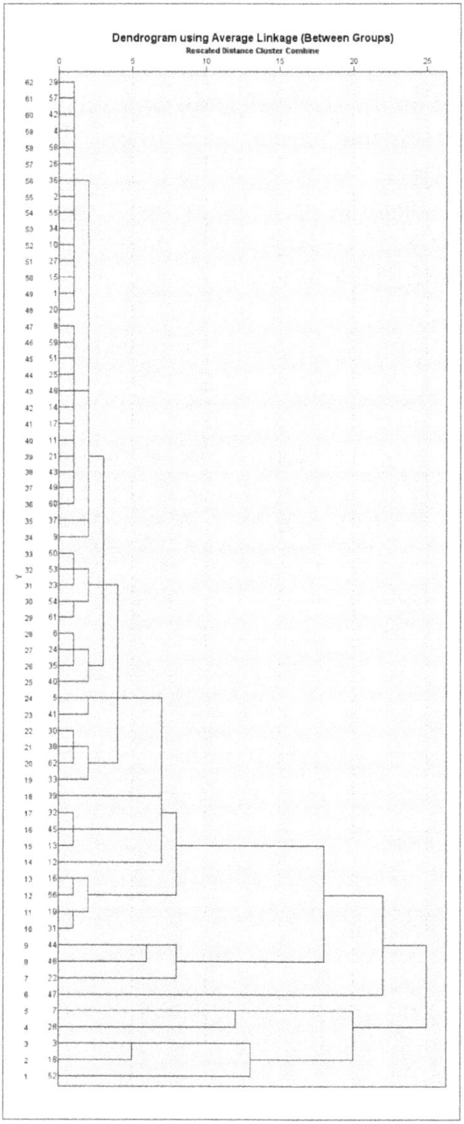

Figure 106. Dendrogram representation of financial stability indicators of public universities in a table.

Source: Developed by the authors.

26.5. Conclusion

This comprehensive scientific research monograph is devoted to an in-depth examination of the financial stability of HEIs on the basis of modern cluster analysis methods. The main results and conclusions of the study are as follows:

Methodological Innovations: The hierarchical agglomerative cluster analysis method utilized in the study revealed a new method of analyzing the financial strength of institutions. The FSI developed on the basis of debt service coverage ratio (DSR) and profitability (RO) was found to be a useful tool for measuring the financial strength of institutions.

Empirical Results: Based on the investigation of 62 state institutions of higher education, 10 well-segmented cluster groups were identified. Financial criteria and stability levels typical for each cluster were determined. The truth was noted that leading universities such as Namangan State University (100 points), Tashkent Financial Institute (100 points), and Bukhara State Pedagogical Institute (90.91 points) were assigned to typical clusters.

Analysis of Weak Financial Indicators: The study demonstrated that causes for low values of the financial stability index are the following:

- Over-reliance of budget funds on the budget;
- Growing demand for student fees;
- Inefficiency in the spending optimization;
- Insufficiently developed planning and financial management systems.

Scientific and Practical Significance of the Study: This research paper has developed a new methodological approach to estimating the financial stability of HEIs. The approach, constructed on the basis of cluster analysis, offers the following possibilities:

- More accurate assessment of the financial condition of institutions;
- Efficient and targeted allocation of resources;
- Formation of the scientific basis for making strategic decisions;
- Early identification and exclusion of financial risks.

The results obtained are of practical significance to the Republic of Uzbekistan Ministry of Higher Education, Science, and Innovation, as well as for institution leaders of higher education, and can be used to construct the financial policy and to improve the management level decisions.

The work is not only theoretically but also practically important, offering a scientifically grounded model of making institutions of higher education more financially viable. In the future, additional detailed research on this topic and the improvement of the methodology will be a valuable contribution to sustainable development of the system of higher education.

Bibliography

Abdullah, M. A., Han, X., Amjad, M. A., & Makhmudov, S. (2025). Revisit the role of financial development on economic growth, human development, and sustainable development in higher-income countries. *Journal of Environmental Management*, *392*, 126874.

Afriyie, A. O. (2015). Financial sustainability factors of higher education institutions: a predictive model. *International Journal of Education Learning and Development*, *2*(3), 17–38.

Alshubiri, F. N. (2021), Analysis of financial sustainability indicators of higher education institutions on foreign direct investment: Empirical evidence in OECD countries. *International Journal of Sustainability in Higher Education*, *22*(1), 77–99. <https://doi.org/10.1108/IJSHE-10-2019-0306>

Bazhan, S. P., Harmider, L. D., Korotka, L. I., & Kryvoruchko, A. I. (2025). METHODOLOGY OF COMPREHENSIVE DIAGNOSTICS OF TECHNICAL EDUCATIONAL AND SCIENTIFIC CLUSTER MANAGEMENT RISKS. *Natsional'nyi Hirnychyi Universytet. Naukovyi Visnyk*, (1), 132–139.

Dumestre, M. J. (2016). Introduction: An uncertain future. In *Financial sustainability in US higher education* (pp. 1–6). Palgrave Macmillan, New York. <https://doi.org/10.1057/978-1-349-94983-0_1>

Cahyani, I., Buriev, K., Ngongo, M., Mamadiyarov, Z., Ino, L., Herman, H., Saputra, N., & Baxtishodovich, S. (2025). Exploring the Use of TikTok Application in Enhancing the Skill of Pronunciation: A Case on Students' Perception. Studies in Media and Communication, 13(2), 150–158. doi:http://dx.doi.org/10.11114/smc.v13i2.7553

Chirica, O., & Puscas, B. (2018). The diversification of income sources in the higher education public institutions budgets. *The Audit Financiar Journal*, *16*(149), 148–148.

Grebeniuk, N., Boyko, A., Bozhenko, V., & Dehtiar, N. (2025). Distribution Channel Models in Life Insurance: Identifying Key Influencing Factors. Marketing and Management of Innovations, *16*(1), 106–118. https://doi.org/10.21272/mmi.2 025.1-08

Jahrir, A., Gultom, Y., Herman, H., Zabadi, F., Ngongo, M., Mamadiyarov, Z., Fatmawati, E., & Saputra, N. (2025). Investigating the Elements of Short Commercial Mineral Water Advertisement: A Case on Discourse Analysis. *Studies in Media and Communication, 13*(4), 94–104. doi:http://dx.doi.org/10.11114/smc.v13i4.7813

Kalandarov, F., Makhmudov, S., Ibadullaev, D., Matniyozov, M., Nasretdinova, F., Sabirov, K., & Bahodirov, N. M. (2025). Low-Carbon Energy Risk and Renewable Energy Development: Insigths from Method of Moments Quantile Regression. International Journal of Energy Economics and Policy, *15*(3), 524–536.

Khayrilla Kurbonov, Samariddin Makhmudov, Shakhzod Erkinov, Umidjon Dadabaev, Gulnora Bekimbetova, Rukhiddin Zayniddinov, and Mirzabek Jonuzokov. 2025. Evaluating the Impact of Marketing Practices Digitalization and Investment on Labor Market Efficiency and Commercial Bank Performance Using Econometric Models. In Proceedings of the 8th International Conference on Future Networks & Distributed Systems (ICFNDS '24). Association for Computing Machinery, New York, NY, USA, 786–796. https://doi.org/10.1145/3726122.3726237

Khodjaniyazov, N., Mirkhoshimova, M., Kalandarov, F., Matyokubova, D., Utegenova, S., Makhmudov, S., & Khudayberganov, M. (2025). Time-Varying Impacts of Financial Stress on Energy-Related Uncertainty. International Journal of Energy Economics and Policy, *15*(3), 689–698.

Kuchkarov, T., Mamadiyarov, Z., Khakimov, Z., Sabirova, O., Matmurodov, K., Raimboyeva, M., & Umarova, S. (2025). Energy-Related Uncertainty and Crypto-Currency Environmental Attention: Time-Varying Perspective. International Journal of Energy Economics and Policy, *15*(5), 614–626. https://doi.org/10.32479/ijeep.20784

Kuziboev, B., Ozturk, I., Kalandarov, F., Samandarov, O., Bekjanov, D., & Makhmudov, S. (2025). PROMOTING ENERGY SOURCES DIVERSIFICATION THROUGH ESG PERFORMANCE. Energy, 136009.

Lin, M.H., Matchanova, B., Nurmatovich, H.A. *et al.* Optimal Operation of the Multi-Carrier Energy System Considering Energy Markets and Renewable Energies Participation. *Int. J. Appl. Comput. Math* **11**, 170 (2025). https://doi.org/10.1007/s40819-025-02002-9

Litamahuputty, J. V., Amiruddin, E. G., Rahim, R., Rahman, A., & Mamadiyarov, Z. (2025). Cryptocurrency Risk Management through Decision Engineering: Evaluating XRPUSD and ADAUSD Portfolio Performance. Journal of Applied Science, Engineering, Technology, and Education, 7(1), 69–81. https://doi.org/10.35877/454RI.asci3871

Lucianelli, G., Citro, F. (2017). Financial conditions and financial sustainability in higher education: a literature review. In Rodríguez Bolívar, M. (Ed.), *Financial sustainability in public administration* (pp. 23–53). Palgrave Macmillan, Cham. <https://doi.org/10.1007/978-3-319-57962-7_2>

Makki, A. A., & Al-Filali, I. Y. (2024). Modeling the strategic enablers of financial sustainability in Saudi higher education institutions using an integrated Decision-Making trial and evaluation laboratory–interpretive structural modeling approach. *Sustainability, 16*(2), 685.

Makki, A. A., & Abdulaal, R. M. (2023). A hybrid MCDM approach based on fuzzy MEREC-G and Fuzzy RATMI. *Mathematics, 11*(17), 3773.

Mamadiyarov, Z., Hakimov, H., & Askarov, S. (2024). DEVELOPMENT OF RETAIL BANKING SERVICES IN THE CONTEXT OF DIGITAL TRANSFORMATION. Financial and Credit Activity Problems of Theory and Practice, 1(54), 51–67. https://doi.org/10.55643/fcaptp.1.54.2024.4288

Mamadiyarov, Z. Makhmudov, S. Utanov, B. Kasimova, D. Bekmurodova, G. Hakimov, Z. (2025). Fusion of Economic and Financial Factors Affecting Household Deposits in Banks: An Econometric Analysis. *Fusion: Practice and Applications*, (), 82–91. DOI: https://doi.org/10.54216/FPA.190206

Mamadiyarov, Z., Saidov, O., Abdurazakova, N., Makhmudov, S., Nazarov, M., Rajabova, N., … Ruzmetova, I. (2025). Energy-Related Uncertainty and Tourism Stock Markets: New Insights from Time-Varying

Relationship with TVP- VAR Approach. International Journal of Energy Economics and Policy, 15(4), 730–737. https://doi.org/10.32479/ijeep.20480

Mohamed, M. H., & Muturi, W. (2017). Factors affecting financial performance of income generating units among universities in Puntland State of Somalia: The case Puntland State University (PSU). *International Journal of Economics, Commerce and Management*, *5*, 287–318.

Morovati, E., Shahvali, R., & Naghizadeh, Z. (2024). Structural analysis of the factors affecting Iran's home-based businesses using cross-impact analysis method. *Quarterly Journal of Economic Research*, University of Tabriz.

Muhammad Zubair, Irfanud Din, Nadeem Sarwar et al. Revolutionizing Sepsis Diagnosis Using Machine Learning and Deep Learning Models: A Systematic Literature Review, 10 June 2025, PREPRINT (Version 1) available at Research Square [https://doi.org/10.21203/rs.3.rs-6731418/v1]

Niño Muñoz, Diana Patricia. Quality of life in the regions of Colombia: What is its relationship with the institutional structure?. Granada: Universidad de Granada, 2024. [https://hdl.handle.net/10481/101994]

PANJAITAN, M. B., HAMDANAH, H., SIRAIT, J., SUTIKNO, S., FATMAWATI, E., HERMAN, H., & MAMADIYAROV, Z. (2025). THE ROLE OF EMOTIONAL REGULATION IN SHAPING STUDENTS' PERCEPTION OF PHYSICS PROBLEMSOLVING TASKS. TPM – Testing, Psychometrics, Methodology in Applied Psychology, 32(S2(2025) : Posted 09 June), 1–10. Retrieved from https://tpmap.org/submission/index.php/tpm/article/view/139

Pradhan, R., Hajiyev, E., Shichiyakh, R. *et al.* Optimal Techno-Economic Feasibility of an Off-Grid Microgrid System Using Load Flow Energy Management Strategies. *Oper. Res. Forum* **6**, 120 (2025). https://doi.org/10.1007/s43069-025-00524-y

Romero, R. M., Zelinskaya, M., Makhmudov, S., Sapaev, S., & Rustambekovich, J. U. (2025, September). Modelling and Optimal Utilisation of the Renewable Energy Systems in Microgrid with Improving Reliability and Energy Efficiency. In Operations Research Forum (Vol. 6, No. 3, pp. 1–20). Springer International Publishing.

Rukhiddin Zayniddinov, Nodir Jumaev, Gulbakhor Irgasheva, Alam Asadov, Nosir Makhmudov, Sirojiddin Abrorov, and Samariddin Makhmudov. 2025. The Influence of the Digital Economy on Economic Development Evidence from Uzbekistan. In Proceedings of the 8th International Conference on Future Networks & Distributed Systems (ICFNDS '24). Association for Computing Machinery, New York, NY, USA, 831–839. https://doi.org/10.1145/3726122.3726242

Samariddin Makhmudov, Malika Umarova, Khayrilla Kurbonov, Laylo Akbarova, Durdona Davletova, Nilufar Shanazarova, and Toshmurod Kulmanov. 2025. Evaluating the forecast indicators of the volume of highly liquid assets of commercial banks in the process of digital transformation. In Proceedings of the 8th International Conference on Future Networks & Distributed Systems (ICFNDS '24). Association for Computing Machinery, New York, NY, USA, 698–704. https://doi.org/10.1145/3726122.3726222

Samariddin Makhmudov, Kudratillo Tukhsanov, Saifulla Arslanbekov, Akram Amanov, Orifali Tursunov, Umarbek Jabbarov and Muyassarxon Mirzakarimova. 2024. Optimizing Supply Chain Financing Development Prospects of Digital Ecosystems in the European Logistics Industry. In The 8th International Conference on Future Networks & Distributed Systems (ICFNDS '24), December 11–12, 2024, Marakech, Morocco. ACM, New York, NY, USA, 12 Pages. https://doi.org/10.1145/3726122.3726200

Shailja Badra, Sarika Jain, Sarita Vichore; Fintech and financial inclusion: conceptual foundations and research landscape. *Global Knowledge, Memory and Communication* 2025; https://doi.org/10.1108/GKMC-07-2024-0443

Su, R., Xiao, Y., Hamza, F., Mamadiyarov, Z., & Wahab, A. (2025). Scaling up green hydrogen in China: Economic opportunities and challenges. *International Journal of Hydrogen Energy*, *131*, 60–69.

Swiatek, L. (2023). The engagement orientation and its limits in nurturing sustainability in higher education. In Walker, T., Tarabieh, K., Goubran, S., Machnik-Kekesi, G. (Eds.) *Sustainable practices in higher education* (pp. 221–238). Palgrave Macmillan, Cham., <https://doi.org/10.1007/978-3-031-27807-5_11>

Toshmurod Kulmanov, Umidjon Dadabaev, Mansurbek Qulmetov, Aliboy Ulashov, Mirjalol Eshboyev, and Samariddin Makhmudov. 2025. Global

Services Market Transformation Digitalization Export Trends and Future Forecasts. In Proceedings of the 8th International Conference on Future Networks & Distributed Systems (ICFNDS '24). Association for Computing Machinery, New York, NY, USA, 851–858. https://doi.org/10.1145/3726122.3726245

Zhao, Q., Pervaiz, A., Makhmudov, S., & Fatima, A. (2025). Do environmental stringent policies enhance the impact of renewable energy on CO2 reduction? Evidence from BRICS-T economies. Journal of Environmental Management, 391, 126464.

Zokir Toshtemirovich Mamadiyarov. 2022. Risk Management in the Remote Provision of Banking Services in the Conditions of Digital Transformation of Banks. In Proceedings of the 5th International Conference on Future Networks and Distributed Systems (ICFNDS '21). Association for Computing Machinery, New York, NY, USA, 311–317. https://doi.org/10.1145/3508072.3508119

Zokir Toshtemirovich Mamadiyarov, Samandarboy Adhambek ugli Sulaymanov, Sarvar Anvar ugli Askarov, and Durdona Bakhtiyor kizi Uktamova. 2022. Impact of Covid-19 Pandemic on Accelerating the Digitization and Transformation of Banks. In Proceedings of the 5th International Conference on Future Networks and Distributed Systems (ICFNDS '21). Association for Computing Machinery, New York, NY, USA, 706–712. https://doi.org/10.1145/3508072.3508211

The Importance of Management Control Systems in the Success of Small and Medium-Sized Enterprises

Vera Susana Nunes Amarante Ribeiro, Pedro Fernandes da Anunciação, Antonio Juan Briones Peñalver, and Fernando Miguel Gonçalves

27.1. Introduction

Globalization, the elimination of trade barriers, and the formation of global business networks create new opportunities, imposing significant challenges to economic organizations, especially small and medium-sized enterprises (SMEs) (Franco & Ferreira, 2021; Orozco, 2016). This economic scenario, which results in greater competitiveness in the global market, requires that most companies adapt quickly to technological, regulatory, and market changes, in addition to pushing for continuous innovation and operational efficiency to survive and thrive, elevating knowledge to a resource and critical factor in organizational dynamics success (World Economic Forum, 2022).

The minimization of uncertainty can only be achieved by the quality of management and the responsiveness of economic organizations. While it is true that large companies are usually better able to withstand market turbulence, due to their investment capacity, more robust structures or access to information and knowledge, the same is not true for SME. SMEs are generally characterized by an intrinsic susceptibility, resulting from the lack of resources that condition their responsiveness, both in terms of competitiveness and growth (Pessoa & Estrela, 2021). Competitive levels require high performance, management excellence, and appropriate strategic performance management models or approaches such as the Balanced Scorecard.

In this context, the relevance of information and knowledge as an organizational assets becomes evident. One of the contemporary challenges for SMEs in the digital age is the use of these technologies to create information control and processing ecosystems (Han & Trimi, 2021). The organizational maturity in the use of technologies conditions the adoption and use of technological tools, which impacts the relationship of companies with their context (Curado et al., 2022; Franco & Ferreira, 2021). Such a reality makes the emergence of governance and urbanism needs at the level of both information and Information Systems (IS) (Anunciação, et al., 2019). It should be noted that in a context of high availability and access to information, the assumption that the adoption of many indicators can lead to better performance rates is not true. An excessive number of indicators can provide a blurred and ambiguous view of performance, with conflicting information regarding the sustainable development of their organizations (Bianchi et al., 2015).

It is, therefore, in this context that the relevance of management control systems (MCS) emerges. These MCS are indispensable for the decision-making process and obtaining competitive advantages (Duréndez et al, 2016; Ittner & Larcker, 2003; Stonkutė, 2015), if they are adequate to the reading of reality and available according to the timings of the decision. For SMEs, the focus of this study, it is recommended to adopt a selective approach when choosing management control models, prioritizing critical success factors rather than an excessive number of indicators (Simons, 1995). This selective approach will allow for more focused and practical management, ensuring that the limited resources of SMEs are directed to areas that provide the greatest impact on long-term growth and sustainability.

Financial planning, cost control, and economic and financial forecasts are essential tools in any organization (Duréndez et al., 2016). However, many SMEs lack management systems (MS) that allow them to access basic information like purchase volume, client orders, stocks, etc. The absence of integrated MS hinders the ability to efficiently monitor operational and financial performance, compromising its competitiveness. The implementation of effective MS is vital for decision-making (Magd & Karyamsetty, 2020).

Catañeda (2012) highlights that the techniques employed by large companies are beyond the reach of many SMEs, since they require high academic training and availability of time and resources. In addition, the MCS are often perceived by their managers as mechanisms of policing and bureaucratization of management.

In this sense, it is imperative to change the paradigm of MCS aligning them with organizational strategy (Merchant & Stede, 2012) and structure to involve all members of the organization in the development of the company (Arnaboldi, et al. 2021; Jordan at al., 2021). MC is a crucial element for value creation (Ittner & Larcker, 2003). For this, it is necessary to ensure timely, reliable, and relevant information (Jordan et al., 2021).

27.2. The MCS

The evolution of the MCS was deeply influenced by the scientific management theories of Frederick Taylor (1914) and by the management principles of Henri Fayol (1916), which emphasized efficiency and operational effectiveness. These theories provided the basis for implementing more structured control systems (CS) and aligned with organizational goals, reflecting the increasing complexity of business operations in the modern era. In this context, the main models are:

- *Management control model of Anthony*—Robert Anthony who defines the concept of MC as the process by which managers ensure the efficient and effective use of resources to achieve company objectives. Although this approach was considered too mechanical and technical (Van Der Meer-Kooistra & Scapens, 2008; Wickramasinghe & Alawattage, 2007), it was also innovative in directing the MC to planning and control (PC) activities. Faced with new approaches in the field of quality, strategic cost management, and study of process improvement, Anthony's proposal (1965) was subject to criticism (Ittner & Larcker, 2001; Otley, 2016; Simons, 1990). Subsequently, the concept is redefined as a process aimed at the motivation and inspiration of people in the execution of their activities, in alignment with organizational goals (Anthony & Govindarajan, 2007).
- *Integrated management control model of Flamholtz et al.*: Flamholtz developed a model that focuses on the influence of employees to achieve organizational results and argued that MCS should be directed to guide the behavior of individuals in line with organizational objectives (Flamholtz, 1996a, 1996b; Flamholtz et al., 1985). In the model proposed by Flamholtz et al. (1985), it stands out for having a holistic and interdisciplinary approach, proposing that organizational effectiveness is strongly influenced by how employees perceive and internalize these CSs. This model offers valuable guidance for CS architecture that monitors performance and fosters a motivating work environment, consistent with organizational values. Furthermore, it recognizes the importance of CS adaptation to changes in

internal and external conditions, emphasizing flexibility and adaptability as critical elements for long-term organizational success (Flamholtz, 1996a, 1996b; Flamholtz et al., 1985).

- *Simons Model*—Simons (1987, 1990, 1995, 2000) carried out innovative research that highlighted the MCS as sets of routines and formalized procedures, based on information that managers use to support or modify organizational behaviors. The respective approach reiterates the importance of the behavioral aspect of the MC, highlighting that it does serve not only to monitor but also to guide and direct behaviors (Simons, 1995, 2000). The core of this CS lies in the company's relationship to competition, and the effectiveness of these levers must be analyzed and understood together to ensure successful implementation of strategies.
- *Kaplan's model*: The "Execution Premium" model developed by Robert Kaplan (2008) is designed for organizational performance management, with the aim of closing the gap between strategic formulation and its implementation. This model is widely recognized for its effectiveness in helping organizations to implement and effectively manage their strategies (Kaplan, 2008). Its key components include: development of the strategy (vision, mission, and strategy); translation of the strategy (converting the strategy into the operational domain); organizational alignment (aligning organizational areas with the strategy); resource planning and allocation (planning strategic operations and initiatives, allocating resources, and setting budgets and performance targets); observation and learning [monitoring organizational performance through key performance indicators (KPIs)]; and testing and adaptation of the strategy (reviewing the strategy based on internal feedback and changes in the external environment). The "Execution Premium" model offers flexibility and adaptability, allowing the organization to quickly adjust its strategy and operations based on market conditions and organizational performance (Kaplan, 2008).
- *Merchant and Van der Stede model*: It provides a detailed analysis of the practical and theoretical dimensions of Management Control System (MCS) in organizations, exploring how these structures can be used to measure, evaluate, and encourage employee performance to align behaviors and actions with the organization's strategic objectives (Merchant & Van der Stede, 2012). This model is based on fundamental principles such

as strategic alignment (ensuring that the MCS are aligned with the organization's strategic objectives); balance between incentives and controls (balancing financial and non-financial incentives with stock, performance, and personnel controls); performance evaluation [development of key performance indicators (KPIs) that are relevant, measurable and aligned with the strategic objectives of the organization]; adaptation and flexibility (recognition that organizations operate in dynamic environments, which require adaptability and flexibility); the integration of formal and informal controls (importance of integrating formal controls, such as explicit policies and procedures, with informal controls, such as organizational culture and social norms); and risk management (identification, assessment, and management of risks through appropriate internal controls to protect the organization's assets).

27.3. Objectives and Methodology

Considering that performance measurement in SMEs often suffers from an inadequate perception of the casual relationships between metrics, as well as weak or misaligned performance evaluations, as opposed to the ideal of balanced, frequent controls and regular evaluations (Sardi et al., 2020), and that this reality constitutes an obstacle to the effective implementation of these MCS (Gumel & Bardai, 2023), it is evident that there is an opportunity for the academic study of this reality. The objective of this exploratory study was to evaluate the MCS in an SME in the automotive components sector. This choice stems from the following reasons:

- Relevance Portuguese economy (1,452,225 SMEs in Portugal, representing 99.9% of the business enterprises (Pordata, 2023).
- Specificity of the wholesale trade in parts and accessories for motor vehicles sector, which includes 884 companies, having 33.37% (295 companies) more than 20 years old, 23.30% (206 companies) between 11 to 20 years old, 18.55% (164 companies) between 6 to 10 years old, and 24.77% (219 companies) have up to 5 years of activity.
- survival rate (75.7% of SMEs in Portugal—first year of activity and only 57.3% remain in operation in the second year) (Pordata, 2023).

The choice of sector results from the fact that the automotive sector is highly relevant in industry and the national economy. The automotive value chain is particularly extensive, involving a wide range of services ranging from manufacturing, distribution, and retail to maintenance and repair.

The investigation was carried out between May and October 2024. The analysis carried out focused on the period from 2019 to 2023, as well as a real-time analysis during 2024, with a view to understanding the evolution of MC practices and their impact on the performance and success of the company.

The research methodology followed two approaches: a participatory observation, through meetings with top management and middle management, and another associated with internal documentation analysis. Regarding participatory observation, the main objective was to facilitate the understanding of the business, dynamics, policies, procedures, and culture of the organization under study (Stake, 2012; Yin, 2015). A company visit was held in August 2024 where the business plan, annual budget forecast, and operational plan were reviewed. The research team also participated in a monthly meeting to present results, identify deviations, and review corrective actions proposed by functional units.

Regarding the interviews, the objective was to capture the different perspectives of each department of the company. Interviews were held with the CEO, CFO, and Commercial Director. In the case of the CEO, the following topics were addressed, among others: company characterization; definition and periodicity of objectives; management control mechanisms; CS adopted and respective instruments; quality of information generation; value drawn from the information; existence of a performance evaluation process; and success factors for the business. In the case of the CFO, the objective was to understand the mechanisms of the company's financial management; type of information is produced, its reliability, consistency, and frequency; as well as the role of CS. Regarding the Commercial Director, the following aspects were treated: degree of knowledge of the objectives by the employees; degree of involvement of employees in the MC process; promotion of dialogue between hierarchies; communication channels with employees; degree of knowledge of employees about the structure of the company; and employee evaluation system.

Regarding internal documentation, the research consulted documents such as the company's business plan, the forecast budget, the operational plan, the reports and accounts, the income statement and balance sheets, the internal procedures of the SCG, as well as other supporting documents considered relevant. This methodological option allowed a triangulation of the different perspectives obtained from the various (Stake, 2012).

27.4. Results Analysis

27.4.1. Company Practices vs MC Models

The company has implemented a financial PC system that reflects Anthony's approach, using detailed financial data and budgets to align its operations with long-term goals. The practice of monthly monitoring of results and comparison with the provisional budget are clear examples of how Anthony's model is applied in the company. Although the company applies robust financial controls, as suggested by Anthony, the company goes further, including non-financial metrics and dynamic strategies, something that Anthony's model did not contemplate. The excessive focus on accounting elements can be seen as a limitation when compared to more modern approaches that integrate behavioral and strategic aspects, which in this organization cannot be so limited.

Regarding the models proposed by Flamholtz et al., there is an integration of informal controls. The proximity of management to employees facilitates direct communication and involvement in decisions. A culture of belonging is also promoted. The behavior of employees is oriented around the organization's objectives in an informal way. However, the company lacks formal structured controls such as a formal rewards plan and performance evaluation. The lack of formal manuals and policies prevents the company from fully benefiting from an integrated CG approach, leading to reputation risks and limiting process standardization and management of expectations among employees and stakeholders, as pointed out in the Merchant and Van Stede model (2012).

In the model of Simons (1995, 2000), belief systems within organizational culture are evident. The vision and mission are clear, and all stakeholders are oriented and aligned, as stated in the belief system. The diagnostic control is carried out by different KPIs in the different aspects of the business, as well as the respective comparison between standards and results and decision making. However, the company lacks formal boundary systems such as a code of ethics or behavioral protocols that limit the company's ability to impose restrictions and manage risks more effectively, something Simons believes is essential to balance innovation and compliance.

Regarding the Execution Premium model, developed by Kaplan, it is verified that the strategies defined are in tune with the vision and mission. The strategy is translated into operational plans, through planning and allocation of resources in accordance with the implementation of the strategy. The monitoring of organizational performance is carried out through several KPIs, with the identification of deviations. We can consider that the practice of the company resembles the model of Kaplan.

As far as the Merchant and Van der Stede model is concerned, the company reflects many of the principles of this model by integrating informal and formal controls. However, the failure to formalize policies and procedures limits the effectiveness of informal controls. The existence of incentives, but without a formal plan, hinders motivation to achieve individual goals, something that this model considers crucial.

In conclusion, the company adopts MC practices that reflect many of the practices mentioned in the various models analyzed, in terms of strategic planning and performance monitoring, although there is opportunity to improve.

27.4.2. Problems and Recommendations

Some structural and operational problems that may expose the organization to operational, financial, and reputational risks have been identified, namely:

- Absence of a code of ethics and conduct—The absence of clear guidelines and limits of behavior, as well as ethical principles and interaction relationship with different stakeholders, can generate unwanted behaviors and compromise the reputation of the organization. This situation was widely discussed by Merchant and Van der Stede (2012), who highlight the importance of a formal ethical system. Unethical practices can generate significant risks to integrity and the achievement of strategic objectives.

  Recommendation: Develop and implement a code of ethics and conduct and its public and internal dissemination.

- Absence of a human resources management policy—The attendance of employees is not registered, which can generate inconsistencies in the calculation of hours worked and compromise productivity and performance evaluation. Some KPIs, such as productivity, attendance, and absenteeism, are not controlled. There are no job descriptions, which compromises the distribution of tasks and the allocation of responsibilities.

  Recommendation: Implementation of a human resources management policy, including the definition of job descriptions, clear definition of tasks and competencies, limits of responsibilities, and reporting structures. Implement policies for attendance control, recruitment and selection, employee benefits and support, and, finally, a performance evaluation policy.

- Lack of control over operational efficiency—Existence of constraints in the generation and availability of information related to resources and control of operational efficiency. This gap has direct implications on productivity, task distribution, segregation of duties, presentation of quality results, and, not least, the satisfaction of stakeholders.

  Recommendation: Implementation of the principles of lean process, survey of processes, control of time of activities, and elimination of waste of time, aiming to reduce execution time, eliminate errors, and increase efficiency and productivity.

- Absence of an incentive and reward plan—There is no formal individual performance plan by objectives or a formalized human resources policy. The lack of formalization of performance evaluation compromises the motivation and commitment of employees, as pointed out by Merchant and Van der Stede (2007). Without a well-defined compensation, training, and career progression structure, the organization runs the risk of losing talent, demotivating the workforce, with direct impact on productivity and the organizational environment.

  Recommendation: Create a performance evaluation system and define a human resources policy with guarantees and benefits for employees.

- Absence of procedure manuals—The lack of procedure manuals compromises the uniformity and standardization of processes and efficient execution of activities. Well-structured manuals are essential to ensure quality and efficiency standards and reduce the risk of errors and inefficiencies. In addition, it also facilitates internal and external audits.

  Recommendation: Creation of procedure manuals for all existing activities in the company.

- Absence of collection procedures—Although the company uses factoring and confirming systems, there is no formal collection procedure, which increases the risk of human errors. The lack of a structured system to ensure that collections are made in an appropriate and frequent manner may result in undue charges or in the failure to collect certain amounts, which directly impacts the company's cash flow.

  Recommendation: Implement a regular and robust collection procedure.

The identified problems expose the company to risks, loss of efficiency, productivity, and reputation. It is recommended to implement measures that contribute to a better management control.

27.5. Conclusions

This exploratory work aimed to investigate the relevance of MCS in an SME in the automotive sector. The investigation revealed that the type of MCS implemented are related to the characteristics of the organization. Like many SMEs, the company shows few resources for the various operational and management control activities it develops. It was found that the overload of activities compromises the generation and availability of information, particularly for economic and financial management. This excessive workload contributes to the difficulty in maintaining control mechanisms.

The controls are informal, and the unavailability of time compromises the formalization of controls. There is no human resources management policy that promotes constructive feedback on the work developed and management of expectations to keep employees motivated and committed. The absence of formalization of codes, manuals, processes, and procedures compromises the quality of service, interaction with stakeholders, efficiency, and productivity.

The MC processes are essentially based on constant, close communication with stakeholders and are more closely aligned with the approach suggested by Kaplan (Execution Premium), which combines strategy formulation and implementation.

Despite some weaknesses, it can be concluded that the existing MCS allows to align operations with strategic objectives. There is critical information for business management, making it possible to track organizational performance and adjust operations in a timely manner to market challenges.

Bibliography

Anthony, R. (1965). *Planning and Control Systems. A framework for analysis.* Boston: Division of Research, Harvard Business School.

Anthony, R., & Govindarajan, V. (2007). *Management control systems* (20 ed.). NY: Tata McGraw-Hill Publishing Company Limited.

Arnaboldi, M., Robbiani, A., & Carlucci, P. (2021). On the relevance of self-service business intelligence to university management. *Journal of Accounting & Organizational Change*, *17*(1), 5–22. <https://doi.org/10.1108/JAOC-09-2020-0131>

Bianchi, C., Consenz, F., & Marinkovic, M. (2015). Designing dynamic performance management systems to foster SME competitiveness according to a sustainable development perspective. Empirical evidences from a case-study. *International Journal of Business Performance Management*, *16*(1), 84–108. <https://doi.org/10.1504/IJBPM.2015.066042>

Catañeda, L. (2012). *High management in SMEs*. Porto: Economic Life Publishing (In Portuguese)

Curado, C., Jesus, M., & Bontis, N. (2022). SMEs manager's perceptions of MCS: A mixed methods approach. *Journal of Small Business Strategy*, *32*(4), 30–47. <https://doi.org/10.53703/001c.37758>

da Anunciação, P. F., Esteves, F. M., & Gonçalves, F. M. (2019). Organizational urbanism: A new proposal for information systems management. In *Handbook of research on expanding business opportunities with information systems and analytics* (pp. 280–294). IGI Global.

Duréndez, A., Ruíz-Palomo, D., García-Prez-de-Lema, D., & Diéguez-Soto, J. (2016). Management control systems and performance in small and medium family firms. *European Journal of Family Business*, *6*(1), 10–20. <https://doi.org/10.1016/j.ejfb.2016.05.001>

Fayol, H. (1916). *General and industrial management*. Pitman, London.

Flamholtz, E. (1996a). *Effective management control: Theory and practice*. Kluwer Academic Publishers.

Flamholtz, E. (1996b). Effective organizational control: A framework, applications, and implications. *European Management Journal*, 596–611.

Flamholtz, E., Das, T., & Tsui, A. (1985). Toward an integrative framework of organizational control. *Accounting, Organizations and Society*, 35–50.

Franco, M., & Ferreira, A. (2021). Success factors in the context of SMEs: An empirical study conducted in Portugal. *Management and Development*, 291–309. <https://doi.org/10.34632/gestaoedesenvolvimento.2021.10034> (In Portuguese)

Gumel, B., & Bardai, B. (2023). A review of critical success factors influencing the success of SMEs. *Seisense Business Review*, *3*(1), 37–61. <https://doi.org/10.33215/sbr.v3i1.906>

Han, H., & Trimi, S. (2021). Towards a data science platform for improving SME collaboration through industry 4.0 technologies. *Technological Forecasting & Social Change*, *174*. <https://doi.org/10.1016/j.techfore.2021.121242>

Ittner, C., & Larcker, D. (2001). Assessing empirical research in managerial accounting: a value-based management perspective. *Journal of Accounting and Economics*, *32*(1–3), 349–410. <https://doi.org/10.1016/S0165-4101(01)00026-X>

Ittner, C., & Larcker, D. (2003). Are nonfinancial measures leading indicators of financial performance? An analysis of customer satisfaction. *Journal of Accounting Research*, *36*(1–35), 1–35. <https://doi.org/10.2307/2491304>

Jordan, H., Neves, C., & Rodrigues, A. (2021). *Management control*. Áreas Publishing, Lisboa, Portugal (In Portuguese)

Kaplan, R. N. (2008). *The Execution Premium, linking strategy to operations for competitive advantage*. Boston, Massachusetts: Harvard Business School Publishing Corporation

Magd, H., & Karyamsetty, H. (2020). Integrated management system implementation in SME: A proposed model for organizational performance and sustainability. *International Journal of Business and Management Review*, *8*(4), 58–77.

Merchant, A., & Stede, W. (2012). *Management control systems. Performance measurement, evaluation and incentives*. Pearson

Orozco, D. (2016). *Understading the impact of management control systems over capabilities and organizational performance, under the influence of perceived environmental uncertainty*. Autonomous University of Barcelona. Accessed at: <http://hdl.handle.net/10803/402255>

Otley, D. (1999). Performance management: A framework for management control systems research. *Management Accounting Research*, *10*(4), 363–382. <https://doi.org/10.1006/mare.1999.0115>

Otley, D. (2016). The contingency theory of management accounting and control: 1980–2014. *Management Accounting Research*, *5*(4), 45–62. <https://doi.org/10.1016/03613682(80)90040-9>

Pessoa, C., & Estrela, S. (2021). Information management in SMEs challenges and opportunities. *PRISMA Publishing*, *46*, 80–96. <https://doi.org/10.21747/16463153/46a5> (In Portuguese)

Pordata (2023). Statistics about Portugal and Europe. Accessed at: May 5, 2024, retrieved from: <https://www.pordata.pt/portugal/pequenas+e+medias+empresas+total+e+por+dimensao-2927> (In Portuguese)

Sardi, A., Sorano, E., Ferraris, A., & Garengo, P. (2020). Evolutionary paths of performance measurement and management system: The longitudinal case study of a leading SME. *Measuring Business Excellence*, *24*(4), 495–510. <https://doi.org/10.1108/MBE-01-2020-0016>

Simons, R. (1987). Accounting control systems and business strategy: An empirical analysis. *Accounting, Organizations and Society*, *12*(4), 157–374. <https://doi.org/10.1016/03613682(87)90024-9>

Simons, R. (1990). *The role of management control systems in creating competitive advantage: New perspectives.* Harvard: Harvard Business School Publishing.

Simons, R. (1995). *Levers of control: How managers use innovative control systems to drive strategic renewal.* Boston: Havard Business School Press.

Simons, R. (2000). *Control in an age of empowerment.* Harvard, USA: Harvard Business School Publishing Corporation.

Stake, R. (2012). *The art of case study research* (Vol. 3). (F. C. Gulbenkian (Ed.) & A. M. Chaves (Trad.)). Lisboa: SAGE Publications India Pvt. Ltd.

Stonkutė, E. (2015). Tarpusavio ryšio tarp tiekimo grandinės iššūkių ir mažų bei vidutinių įmonių kritinių sėkmės veiksnių literatūros analizė. *Management of Organizations: Systematic Research*, (74), 121–138. <https://doi.org/10.7220/MOSR.2335.8750.2015.74.8>

Van Der Meer_Kooistra, J., & Scapens, R. (2008). The governance of lateral relations between and within organisations. *Management Accounting Research, 19*(4), 365–384. <https://doi.org/10.1016/j.mar.2008.08.001>

Wickramasinghe, D., & Alawattage, C. (2007). *Management accounting change. Approaches and perspectives* (Vol. 1). Routledge. (Vol. 1). doi:https://doi.org/10.4324/NOE0415393317>

World Económic Forum (WEF) (2023). Annual Report 2022–2023. Accessed at: 20 June 2024, de World Económic Forum (WEF). <https://www.weforum.org/publications/annual-report-2022-2023>

Yin, R. K. (2015). Case study, planning and methods (5th ed.). Bookman.

Banking Digital Transformation: The Covid-19 Pandemic Accelerator

Pedro Fernandes da Anunciação, Madalena Joyce Fernandes Gaio, Fernando Miguel Gonçalves, and João David Oliveira Rocha

28.1. Introduction

Digital transformation establishes new relationships between business and technologies that are not expressed only in a unidirectional logic, i.e., technological. Information and communication technologies (ICT), through innovation, challenge and transform the assumptions of the strategy. However, it should be the business strategy that guides and gives purpose to the use of ICT. In this sense, the crucial point of organizational evolution, in the context of the information society, is no longer limited to the use of technologies for the optimization or acceleration of processes, but the introduction of technologies as a factor of strategic disruption to support new products/services, new dynamics, or even new visions (Hess et al., 2016).

The consolidation of the relational economy depends on the ability of businesses and Information Systems and Technologies (IST) to integrate and interoperate strategically, as both need to co-operate in the digital transformation. However, these system integrations expose them to risks that can harm the operations of companies. Cyberattacks, which have become frequent, pose direct threats to IST and require companies to strengthen security measures. Threats such as ransomware, malware, phishing, and information theft (Lindemulder & Kosinski, 2024) are examples of risks through which one seeks to access information illicitly, damage systems, steal access credentials, among other consequences (IBM, 2024a, 2024b, 2024c).

This risk exposure increases in the face of adverse and unforeseen economic and social situations such as the Covid-19 pandemic. The various restrictions arising from the strategy of containment of the pandemic led, in the Portuguese case and at the European level, to a general social confinement. However, this confinement did not presuppose the absence of economic activities, but rather a growth in the volume of transactions made through digital channels. The increase in the number of accesses, the growth in the volume of economic operations carried out through digital channels, or the transition to a teleworking regime has given rise to the need to rethink IST, in the field of architecture, performance, and security. This is how, regarding the commercial front-office, now digital, many institutions, particularly in the financial field, have been obliged to strengthen security and mitigate risks through the implementation of preventive measures, such as the reinforcement of data encryption, multi-factor authentication, continuous monitoring and audits, or employee training. With the pandemic, the dimension of ITS security has moved from a traditionally technical level to a strategic priority with direct impact on customer confidence and organizational resilience (Varajão, 2002).

Digital transformation does not correspond to a timely process or project. New ICTs will continue to open new opportunities and, consequently, new needs for business and economic organizations (Quitain et al., 2024). The acceleration of technology use resulting from the pandemic can be seen in the following indicators available in a study by Accenture (w.d.): In the period of 2019–2021, the average rate of adoption of technologies has recorded sharp increases, such as emerging technologies of values close to 70% to about 90%; IT infrastructure of values close to 75% for values above 90%; Artificial Intelligence (AI) & automation values slightly above 75% to around 95%, among other technologies referenced.

The disruptive changes that may arise add opportunities for radical performance improvements and customer relationship (Imran et al., 2021). However, this disruption often requires a redefinition of the strategy and even the business model to overcome competition and resistance to change (Ghosh, 2024). However, managing this transition is not easy, as investment in new technologies, their integration into existing platforms, migration to new platforms, security, and the management of change itself often become necessary (Villaumbrosia, 2024).

The digital transformation thus corresponds to a global dynamic. Many sectors, including banking, have had to redefine their practices to continue to keep up with the market and customer needs by providing more modern, fast, efficient, and personalized services (Bowyer, 2023; Cuesta et al., 2015; Shanti et al., 2022). In the Portuguese case and considering the pandemic period, even customers who usually showed resistance to the use of digital tools were forced, during the lockdown period, to use online banking platforms to conduct transactions, such as transfers, payments of invoices, and even to request credit. In this context, the main Portuguese banks were challenged to improve access to and functionality of digital platforms, having felt obliged to ensure the security of all online transactions and digital engagement of all demographic groups.

The pandemic catalyzed major strategic changes in banking digitalization, with permanent impacts on how financial services are used and offered (Fonseca & Rodrigues, 2022).

28.2. The Banking Resilience in the Pandemic Period

Digital banking is recognized using digital technologies to provide online and automated banking services, allowing customers to carry out various financial operations without the need to physically move to a bank branch. Digital banking covers digital platforms and channels, such as mobile applications, home banking, chatbots, and AI for customer service (Accenture, w.d.; BdP, 2023; Deloitte, 2023; EY, 2020a, 2020b).

The pandemic has accelerated the digital transformation of banking institutions and highlighted the need to look closely at dimensions, such as systemic risk in the financial system or risks related to privacy, security, and confidentiality of customer data (Hanelt et al., 2020).

Some banking-related financial system indicators show the impact of the pandemic, including a 15.3% reduction in operations carried out at Portuguese ATMs and automatic payment terminals during the first year of the pandemic. In April 2020, during the pandemic, the minimum total value of transactions was recorded at 3,907 million euros, representing a negative annual change of 38.6%.

These breaks were, for many banks, an opportunity to define strategies to increase business resilience and *modus operandi*. In some cases, they have had to encourage changing consumer habits in using digital banking by motivating consumers to join digital banking. Thus, 65% of the Portuguese began to use digital services more frequently from the pandemic (Deloitte, 2020).

Portuguese Central Banque (BdP, 2020) disclosed that more than 60% of banking clients intended to continue using digital channels even after the normalization of the pandemic, reflecting a permanent change in consumption habits. The pandemic has led to a 40% increase in the use of digital bank accounts compared to the pre-pandemic period (Deloitte, 2021).

Part of the face-to-face assistance was replaced by AI solutions, such as chatbots and virtual assistants, many processes were dematerialized processes, such as the digital signature of documents and their immediate integration into computer systems, having gained greater internal efficiency (Bankinter, 2021).

The two largest Portuguese banks registered an increase in the use of their digital tools by 30%, namely apps, in the first months of the pandemic (CGD, 2020). There was also an increasing use of contactless payments at the payment terminals of physical spaces, as solutions to minimize the risks of contagion. Before the first case of coronavirus in Portugal, 39.4% of physical purchases were made in this way. This number rose to 40.2% in the first week of outbreak in Portugal and 49% in the second week of March 2020, which represents a significant increase (Bourbon, 2020).

Data on purchases and cash withdrawals between 2019 and 2021 confirm the growing preference for card purchases in-person and online. While in 2021 purchase transactions grew 9.2% compared to 2019 (plus 125.5 million transactions), cash withdrawals decreased 20.2% (minus 90.7 million transactions) (BdP, 2023).

In 2021, there were 10.5 million fewer check payments, worth 24.2 billion euros, with reductions of 41.1% and 28.7%, respectively, compared to 2019. This drop was offset by the growth of 108 million in transactions with payment cards, direct debits, and transfers, representing a rise of 3.7% compared to the last pre-pandemic year. The number of transactions with electronic payment instruments increased even more significantly, by 14.9% or €65.4 billion. Transfers, which represented 58% of the total value of payments made in 2021, grew 19% in quantity and value compared to 2019. In addition, during a pandemic, they were the only payment instrument with a positive evolution (Fonseca & Rodrigues, 2022).

In this context, the banking sector's response to contingency factors becomes evident. Considering the indicators mentioned above, it is clear that banks have adopted digitization strategies aligned with their business models and risk profiles, leveraging technological innovation (BdP, 2023) and increasing trust in digital solutions (PwC, 2021a, 2021b).

28.3. Study Objective and Methodology

This study aimed to identify the impacts of the COVID-19 pandemic in the digitization process of banking institutions in Portugal and the strategies developed for their economic resilience. For the realization of this study, a qualitative approach was adopted, having been, in a first phase, the analysis of several reports of banking institutions and the Portuguese Central Bank. In a second phase, we analyzed a case study of a banking institution with specificities in the banking universe in Portugal. In this case, a focus group was developed for the sharing of knowledge and better characterization of the effort made in the various areas involved. Thus, the following areas were involved: Risk Management, Information Systems, Means of Payments, and Channels. This choice is due to the crucial role played by these areas in adapting banking operations to new market requirements, especially in a context of uncertainty such as that caused by the COVID-19 pandemic.

The analysis focused on understanding the strategies implemented, the challenges faced, and prospects for the digitalization of the banking sector. Topics explored included the exponential increase in traffic on digital platforms and the need to ensure the stability of technological infrastructures; the integration of new functionalities, such as digital signatures, process management, and enhanced cybersecurity; and the modification of systems to be more robust and modern, enabling banks to keep up with competition and better meet customer needs.

28.4. Analysis and Results of the Case Study

The chosen bank is one of the oldest in Portugal. It has a particularly relevant role, recognized for its role in rural communities and its co-operative structure. It differs from traditional commercial banks in that it operates based on a system of mutual agricultural credit boxes distributed across several regions of the country, giving it a unique and close connection with local communities, particularly in low population density areas. Its mission is to drive local development and provide financial services. It has 79 autonomous delegations spread throughout the country.

In 2020, the period when the pandemic was most impactful, although the bank showed an unfavorable macroeconomic scenario, it managed to do so at the end of the year: an increase in solvency of 18.8%; a 12.2% growth in customer resources; a market share growth of more than 10.1%; and a growth of 2.9% in 2019 and 14.1% in 2017 (three years).

The institution encouraged the use of digital channels, such as mobile banking and internet banking, offering assistance and promoting the use of these platforms to reduce dependence on face-to-face service, especially for the rural population, who has limited access to digital banking services. The bank launched remote account openings through its mobile app and expanded its digital offerings via the website and the institutional online channel. The year 2020 was a remarkable full year in the launch of a new 100% digital, mobile-only brand.

Investments in cybersecurity have been intensified to protect customer data and prevent fraud, strengthening its digital infrastructure to provide additional security. This included the implementation of enhanced authentication and constant monitoring of suspicious transactions. Continuity plans were also implemented to maintain critical operations, including the creation of remote work teams and systems to ensure that critical services remain available.

In 2021, the bank continued its strategy of strengthening the digitalization of services and placing greater focus on risk management, with strategies focused on operational continuity and supporting customers affected by the crisis. This year, a unique net profit of 158.8 million euros was recorded, representing an increase of 82.9% compared to the same period and 20.8% compared to 2019 (pre-pandemic) and equating to an equity return of 8.1%.

The promotion of mobile banking ensured that customers could carry out transactions in a safe and convenient way, reducing the risk of contagion and the pressure on bank branches. In the security aspect, investments in cybersecurity have been intensified to protect customer data and online transactions. Advanced monitoring and security technologies have been implemented to prevent fraud and ensure the safety of digital operations.

The possibility of remote work and the creation of continuity plans allowed the maintenance of an uninterrupted level of operation, even with physical access restrictions to bank branches.

In the final period of the pandemic, the banking institution demonstrated resilience and adaptability, presenting solid results that reflect both the economic recovery and the positive impact of the strategies for digitalization and risk mitigation implemented during the most critical years of the pandemic. Use of mobile banking and internet banking services remained at high levels. The pandemic has accelerated the digitization of customers, who have continued to use these channels as main points of contact with the bank. This increase in digital adoption contributed to a more efficient operation, with less dependence on face-to-face services and a reduction in operating costs. An example of what has just been mentioned is the implementation of multi-factor authentication tools and advanced fraud detection systems to protect the bank's digital growth.

The focus of digital transformation has remained in the following years through an effort to make mobile banking platforms more intuitive and personalized, as well as promoting green and sustainable products with sustainable project financing.

With the huge need to access digital applications remotely, the institution has been creating tutorials, strengthening digital communications and launching campaigns to promote the use of the app and home banking.

With the evolution to a remote and digital service and the adaptation of products and services to customers' specific needs, the use of AI tools began to improve the available offerings while also automating internal processes.

At the operational level of the institution, the pandemic had an impact on the structure and organizational functioning of the bank, with the need to adopt remote work and modify procedures that would allow remote service with the same credibility and security.

The risk profile was also adjusted, because of the digital transformation, focusing on the risks of fraud and dependence on information systems. The institution began to see an increase in fraud and computer attacks; so there was a need to strengthen good security practices, both for customers and employees, to mitigate these risks. Other strategies have been implemented, such as multi-factor authentication and real-time monitoring systems.

28.5. Conclusion

The covid-19 pandemic has accelerated the digital transformation in the banking sector in Portugal, redesigning processes, routines, and dynamics. This case study aimed to analyze the adaptations implemented by a Portuguese financial institution, focusing on risk management, to understand the phases before, during, and after the pandemic crisis.

Before the pandemic, the signs of digital transition were already evident, but gradually. However, during periods of lockdown and state of emergency, the adoption of digital services has intensified dramatically, driven by the need to avoid physical interactions. This evolution was proven by the data collected, which indicated an exponential increase in the number of users of digital platforms, as well as in the frequency of use of services such as transfers, payments, and balance queries.

The results provided valuable insights on the strategic and operational adaptations of the studied institution. Significant challenges have been identified, such as increased exposure to cyber-attacks and the need to strengthen security measures to protect data and transactions. At the same time, there was a growing importance of technical support to ensure a satisfactory digital experience for customers, especially those less familiar with digital tools.

The pandemic has not only changed consumer behavior, consolidating a preference for quick, simple, and affordable solutions, but has also forced financial institutions to reassess their strategies and invest in emerging technologies, as AI and predictive analytics. These technologies have proven indispensable to handle growing volumes of data, improve the personalization of services, and respond in an agile way to market changes.

On the other hand, the health crisis also highlighted the resilience and adaptability of financial institutions, transforming challenges into opportunities for innovation. Digitalization is not only a response to the pandemic context, but also an essential strategy for the future of the sector. The continuous investment in technological solutions, combined with a customer-centric approach, will be crucial to ensure competitiveness in a constantly changing market.

This study not only reinforces the importance of digital transformation as a central element in the evolution of banking, but also opens avenues for future research, such as comparative analysis between institutions or the exploration of emerging new technologies. Thus, it is concluded that despite the challenges faced, the pandemic served as a catalyst for the modernization of the sector, shaping a new paradigm for banking in Portugal.

28.6. Limitations and Future Work

The extension of the analysis to more financial institutions would allow a better and deeper comparison of the strategies chosen and of the impacts that the pandemic has brought to the banking sector.

Additionally, it would be appropriate to explore the perspective of customers to analyze and understand in more detail how consumers evaluate the changes introduced by banks, particularly regarding digital experience, security, and trust in online operations.

Another interesting proposal would be to investigate the use of technologies, such as AI, evaluating their impact on operations, efficiency, and responses to customer needs, especially in the post-pandemic context.

Finally, future research could also focus on the analysis of the long-term implications of digital transformation in human resource management in the banking sector, including the impact on digital skills training and adaptation to new hybrid or remote working models.

These approaches will contribute to a more comprehensive and multi-dimensional understanding of the ongoing transformations in the banking sector, providing valuable guidance for the development of sustainable and innovative strategies.

Bibliography

Accenture (w.d.). *Digital transformation. Understand digital transformation and how our insights can help drive business value*. Retrieved from: <https://www.accenture.com/us-en/insights/digital-transformation-index>, accessed at: 10 December 2024.

BdP-Banco de Portugal (2023). Opinion article by the Administrator Hélder Rosalino in the book "88 Voices on Artificial Intelligence"—Artificial Intelligence at the service of central banks. Retrieved of: A Inteligência Artificial ao serviço dos bancos centrais: <https://www.bportugal.pt/intervencoes/artigo-de-opiniao-do-administrador-helderrosalino-no-livro-88-vozes-sobre>, accessed at: 15 December 2024 (In Portuguese).

Bankinter (2021). Aceleração Digital em Portugal. Retrieved from: <https://www.bankinter.pt/blog/tecnologia/aceleracao-rumo-ao-digital>, accessed at: 12 December 2024.

Bowyer, C. (2023). Digital transformation in banking: examples, benefits and trends. Retrieved from: <https://onfido.com/blog/digital-transformation-in-banking/>, accessed at: 29 November 2024.

Bourbon, M. J. (2020). Purchases by MBWay, contactless and QRcode rise with the coronavirus, Expresso. Retrieved from: <https://expresso.pt/sociedade/coronavirus/2020-03-18-Compras-por-MBWay-contactless-e-QRcode-sobem-com-o-coronavirus>, accessed at: 25 November 2024 (In Portuguese).

CGD-Caixa Geral de Depósitos (2020). Relatorio-Contas-CGD-2020, Retrieved from: <https://www.cgd.pt/Investor-Relations/Informacao-financeira/CGD/Relatorios-Contas/Pages/Relatorios-Contas-CGD.aspx>, accessed at: 14 December 2024.

Cuesta, C., Ruesta, M., Tuesta, D., & Urbiola, P. (2015). The digital transformation of the banking industry. *BBVA Research*, *1*(4), 1–10.

Ghosh, P. (2024). *Six common digital transformation challenges*, Dataversity. Retrieved from: <https://www.dataversity.net/six-common-digital-transformation-challenges/>, accessed at: 12 December 2024.

Deloitte (2020). *Study on the impact of COVID-19 in the banking sector in Portugal.* Retrieved from: <https://www.deloitte.com/pt/pt/services/audit-assurance/perspectives/accounting-considerations-covid-19.html>, Accessed at: 14 December 2024.

Deloitte (2021). *The Future of payments*. Retrieved from: <https://www.deloitte.com/pt/pt.html>, Accessed at: 10 December 2024.

Deloitte (w.d.). The implications of generative AI in Finance. A new frontier in artificial intelligence and for Finance. Retrieved from: <https://www2.deloitte.com/us/en/pages/consulting/articles/generative-ai-in-finance.html>, accessed at: 20 November 2024.

EY (2020a). A crise económica da Covid-19. Retrieved from: <https://assets.ey.com/content/dam/ey-sites/ey-com/pt_pt/topics/covid-19/eycaderno-de-notas-a-crise-economica-da-covid-19-03-edicao.pdf>, Accessed at: 30 November 2024.

EY (2020b). Covid-19 pandemic—How banks can increase resilience to financial crime. Retrieved from: <https://www.ey.com/pt_pt/managedservices/covid-19-pandemic-how-banks-can-increase-resilience-against-financial-crime>, accessed at: 15 November 2024 (In Portuguese).

Fonseca, A., & Rodrigues, L. F. (2022). *The impact of the covid-19 pandemic on digital transformation in banking in the Iberian Peninsula* [Master's thesis]. Repository ISCTE—Instituto Universitário de Lisboa, 10–20. Retrieved from: <https://repositorio.iscte-iul.pt/bitstream/10071/27542/1/master_alexandra_mendes_fonseca.pdf>, accessed at: 17 November 2024. (In Portuguese)

Hanelt, A., Bohnsack, R., Marz, D., & Antunes Marante, C. (2021). A systematic review of the literature on digital transformation: Insights and implications for strategy and organizational change. *Journal of Management Studies*, *58*(5), 1159–1197.

Hess, T., Matt, C., Benlian, A., & Wiesböck, F. (2016). Options for formulating a digital transformation strategy. *MIS Quarterly Executive*, *15*(2).

IBM. (2024a). *What is malware?* Retrieved from: <https://www.ibm.com/br-pt/topics/malware>, accessed at: 10 November 2024 (In Portuguese).

IBM. (2024b). *What is ransomware?* Retrieved from: <https://www.ibm.com/br-pt/topics/ransomware>, accessed at: 10 November 2024 (In Portuguese).

IBM. (2024c). *What is phishing?* Retrieved from: <https://www.ibm.com/br-pt/topics/phishing>, accessed at: 10 November 2024 (In Portuguese).

Imran, F., Shahzad, K., Butt, A., & Kantola, J. (2021). Digital transformation of industrial organizations: Toward an integrated framework. *Journal of change management*, *21*(4), 451–479.

Lindemulder, G., & Kosinski, M. (2024). *What is cybersecurity?* Retrieved from: <https://www.ibm.com/br-pt/topics/cybersecurity?mhsrc=ibmsearch_a&mhq=Como%20os%20ataques%20infor m%26aacute%3Bticos%20representam%20uma%20das%20principais%20amea%26cce dil%3Bas%20aos%20SI>, accessed at: 10 November 2024 (In Portuguese).

PwC (2021). *2021 Global Digital Trust Insights. Cybersecurity comes of age.* Retrieved from: <https://www.pwc.com/kz/en/services/global-digital-trust-insights.html>, accessed at: 11 November 2024.

Quitain, R. A., Santos, W. C., & Izon, M. V. (2024). The evolution and impact of management information systems in modern business. *International Journal of Multidisciplinary Research and Growth Evaluation*, 563–571, Retrieved from: <www.allmultidisciplinaryjournal.com>, accessed at 16 November 2024.

Shanti, R., Avianto, W., & Wibowo, W. A. (2022). A systematic review on banking digital transformation. *Jurnal Administrare: Jurnal Pemikiran Ilmiah Dan Pendidikan Administrasi Perkantoran*, *9*(2).

Varajão, J. Q. (2002). *Information systems function. Contributions to the improvement of the success of the adoption of information technologies and development of information systems in organizations* [PhD thesis]. Retrieved from: <https://hdl.handle.net/1822/25960>, accessed at: 15 November 2024.

Villaumbrosia, C. G. (2024). *5 Digital transformation challenges to tackle head-on*. Product School. Retrieved from: <https://productschool.com/blog/digital-transformation/digital-transformation-challenges>, accessed at: 13 November 2024.

Sustainable Future: Rethinking Economy, Education, and Entrepreneurship in a Changing World

Ivan Peronja

29.1. Introduction

29.1.1. Global environment

Viewed globally, it can be concluded that the dynamics of general development are increasingly faster, and growth is exponential, so some countries find it difficult to keep up. We are in the time of the 4th industrial revolution, and we are already entering the 5th revolution. Mega global world players are changing, mega alliances are being created and broken, and industrial development seems to become an imperative *conditio sine qua non* that ignores differences among people, countries, and economies. Meanwhile, wars are becoming part of everyday life, which gradually loses that classic life meaning based on peace. Therefore, the question is rightly posed, what does the dynamics of industrial development bring us and can everyone follow it evenly.

Human changes and develops within his basic characteristics, but it is becoming increasingly clear that human development cannot keep up with the dynamics of industrial development. Within the relation of human development and industrial development, education is placed, from basic through higher education to specialist doctoral education. It is the link that tries to reconcile the differences in the dual dynamics between the human mind and industrial development. Meanwhile, there is an important difference in industrial development between times of war and times of peace. Pessimists said: "peace is the time between two wars" (Sareen 2020).

At the center of all changes is the human with all his characteristics, so it is necessary to take into account the number of people and members of a community or group that is formed according to a certain criterion. According to the spatial distribution of the world's population, and based on the United Nations 2024 research, there are about 8.2 billion inhabitants in the world (ANS 2024).

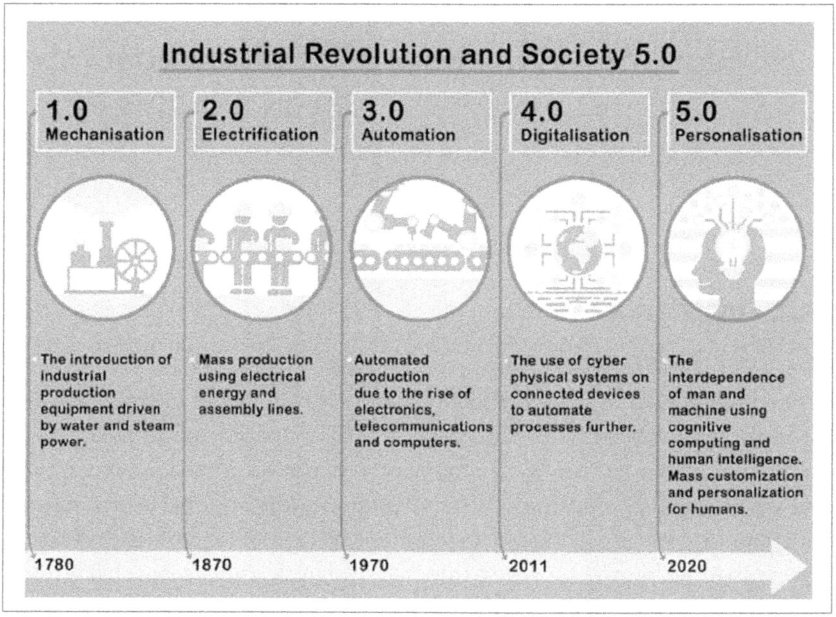

Figure 107. The timeline of industrial revolutions and the emergence of society 5.0 amid the COVID-19 pandemic in 2020

Source: (Sarfraz et al. 2021)

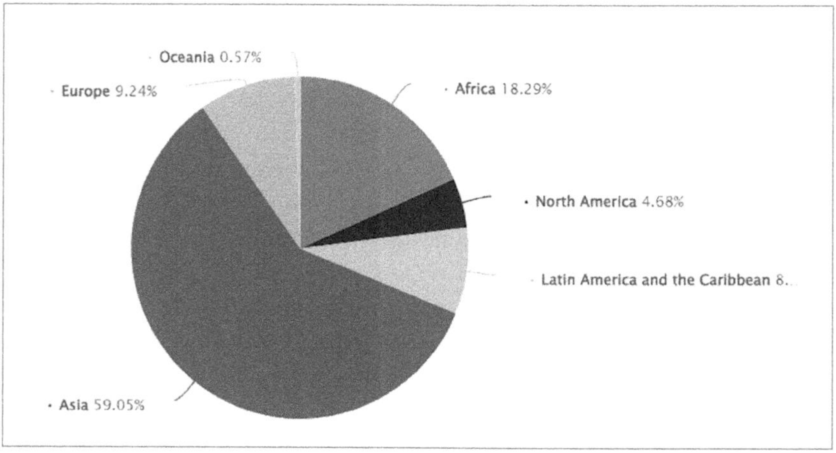

Graph 19. Distribution of the global population 2024, by continent

Source: (Galan 2025)

As can be seen from the graph, Asia leads in population numbers, while Europe ranks third in the world population with 9.24 % or about 760,000 inhabitants. The growth and dominance of Asia's population is assumed to have a key role in the future global distribution during the 5th industrial revolution. However, the question arises about the structure of Asia, as well as its internal connectivity, which is crucial for the balanced development and advancement of Asian countries. Also, there are many differences within the Asian group of countries and economies, both in terms of technological development and society, but also religion, which plays a significant role in social and economic trends in each country.

29.1.2. The European Union in Its Diversity

The new mega-community, the European Union, is a community of old European countries, but also new countries formed after the dissolution of the Warsaw Pact and the fall of the Berlin Wall in 1989. The new European Union countries inherit many characteristics of former socialist states, so a new term was formed for them: "transition countries of the European Union." The differences in the development of member states of mega world markets are large, as well as within the new group of European Union countries. GDP per capita is most often used as an indicator of differences, from which two groups of countries and economies can be seen within the European Union: developed economies and economies in transition. The indicators of differences can be presented as an index in comparison with the European Union average.

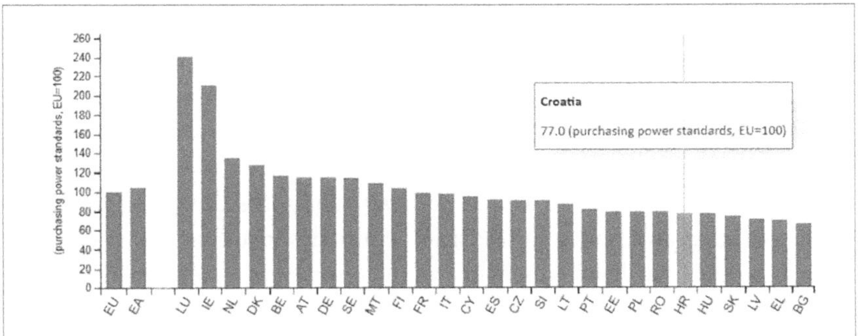

Graph 20. Index of GDP per capita in the 2024. (EU = 100)

Source: (Eurostat 2025)

As can be seen from the graph, in 2024, Luxembourg with an index of 241.0, followed by Ireland with an index of 211.0, recorded the highest levels of GDP per capita in the EU, while Bulgaria with an index of 66.0, followed by Greece with an index of 70.0 and Latvia with an index of 71.0 had the lowest. Croatia is 23 % below the European Union average, with an index of 77.0. In 2024, 10 countries, representing around 34 % of the EU population, exceeded the EU average in terms of GDP per capita.

Thus, 66 % of the population lives in countries that have a lower average GDP per capita than the average of the European Union. Viewed absolutely for 2024, at the top of the GDP per capita list above $100,000 are Luxembourg with $131,380, Ireland with $106,060, and Switzerland with $105,670. The European Union average for 2024 is $44,200, above which are 11 countries, and below which are 16 EU member states. Comparing the richest Luxembourg and the poorest Bulgaria, the difference is three times in favor of Luxembourg, indicating large differences within the corpus of EU members. Considering that the differences are based on the development of the economy, especially entrepreneurship, a research question arises regarding the role of state administration and policy in the development of entrepreneurship, which is the foundation of every national economy.

29.2. Objective and Hypothesis

In accordance with the explanation of the research subject, the purpose of this research relates to the analysis of the factors of development and development dynamics, with the focus of observation being the state and its policy. Thus, the research objective is directed toward valuing the role of the state and its actions on the development of the national economy. The differences in the role of the state in developed countries and countries and economies in transition are significant and need to be investigated. According to the objective, the hypothesis represents the claim that state administration and policy in transition countries insufficiently and inadequately support the development of young national entrepreneurship. Under such conditions, unfavorable opportunities arise related to corruption, nepotism, and especially the takeover of resources and key enterprises by foreign capital.

29.3. Data Sources and Methods

To answer the question of the role of the state in the dynamics of national entrepreneurship development, it is advisable to use CEPOR GEM reports, as well as other indicators that point to the issues of this research. GEM research is conducted for the purpose of analyzing European Union member states and belongs to highly developed studies. Specifically, for each member state, GEM produces a report every year, such as for Croatia, and even in the titles of these reports, it warns of the fundamental problem of the respective country (Singer et al. 2024). Also, GEM annually presents reports of numerous countries, not only European Union members but also beyond (Hill, Ionescu-Somers, and Coduras 2025). At the same time, the Croatian Bureau of Statistics, as well as the Chamber of Commerce, process and present the results and state of Croatian entrepreneurship. Accordingly, this research falls under *desk research*. Furthermore, given the similarity of issues among other European Union members, this research can be taken as a sample for transition countries and economies within the European Union.

29.4. Results

In accordance with the subject of the research, as well as the insight into the entrepreneurship issues of European Union members, numerous conclusions can be drawn. The fact of the existence of a group of developed European Union countries affects the view of the role of the state in the development of national entrepreneurship, which has two perspectives on the situation. Firstly, some members are so developed that, with a stable macro-national system, the development of entrepreneurship, as well as operational business, takes place almost without the influence of the state, or national policy. A good example of this is Belgium, which is discussed in a book that investigates the importance of the macro-national system for the development of society as a whole, stating the importance of the system under conditions of a stable macro-national system: "A good example is Belgium, which did not have a government for 540 days, and even without a government, it presided over the European Union in 2010. During those 540 days, everything in Belgium functioned perfectly, GDP steadily grew, and investments proceeded completely normally. From the example of Belgium, it is best seen how important the system is and how significant it is for the lives of citizens and for the economy. Accordingly, it can be concluded that not even the best government can have good results without a good system. Therefore, the macro-national system is still the most important human creation in the life of people in a community called a state, on which the development of the state, the well-being of its citizens, and peace in the state depend, which is so important for its successful development" (Luković, Piplica, and Jurić 2023).

Thus, in developed European Union countries, the regulation and realization of macro-strategic goals have been taken over by the macro-strategic national system, so the state and politics only occasionally act for various reasons. This problem is much more pronounced in transition countries and economies that are members of the European Union, in terms of the importance of a more active role of the state. In other words, transition countries do not have clearly defined cross-party macro-strategic goals, nor a macro-strategic national system, so a more active role and action of the state and national policy is sought. It is necessary to distinguish the so-called "deep state" from the civic state, which has a balanced relationship between the influence of the state and the "rule of law" according to the needs of the people. Considering the current issue of the relative stability and strength of the European Union, as a young community of differently developed countries, by the logic of things, national states are strengthening (Bakardjieva Engelbrekt et al. 2020).

At the same time, the question of the role of the national state in the European Union as a key factor in the development of national entrepreneurship intensifies. The GEM research for Croatia 2023 presents 13 indicators of state action, which are compared with the European Union average, as well as with the best ratings in the given indicator.

Table 99. Comparison of ratings on the quality of entrepreneurial environment components, Croatia and comparison groups for 2023

	2023.		
Indicators	**Countries with high GDP, average**	**EU average**	**Croatia**
Sufficiency of financial resources	4,8	4,7	**4,7**
Cultural and social norms	5,2	4,6	3,2

Table 99. *(Continued)*

	2023.		
Indicators	**Countries with high GDP, average**	**EU average**	**Croatia**
Ease of obtaining financing	4,5	4,4	**4,4**
Government policies: support and relevance	4,3	4,0	3,4
Government policies: taxes and bureaucracy	4,9	4,7	4,3
Government entrepreneurship programs	5,0	4,8	4,3
Entrepreneurship education at school stage	3,5	3,3	2,9
Entrepreneurship education at post-school stage	5,0	4,8	4,0
Transfer of research and development	4,4	4,2	3,5
Professional and commercial infrastructure	5,5	5,5	4,7
Market openness—the dynamics of change	5,3	5,3	**6,4**
Market openness—entry barriers	4,6	4,6	4,0
Physical infrastructure	6,6	6,4	5,7
Cultural and social norms	5,2	4,6	3,2

Source: (Singer et al. 2024)

Note: The figure showing the positioning of individual components of Croatia's entrepreneurial environment relative to the best-rated components in the EU can serve to assess Croatia's distance from the best in 2023.

As can be seen from the table, two indicators—"Sufficiency of financial resources" and "Ease of obtaining financial resources"—are at the level of the European Union average, which means that foreign banks dominating the Croatian financial market are very open to investments, and that there is enough free capital available. The third indicator, "Market openness—dynamics of changes," is significantly above the European Union average, as well as above the best in that category, raising the question of whether this is an absolutely positive criterion or if there is also a negative aspect to this indicator. In other words, in Croatia, as a transition country and economy without clear macro-strategic goals, the role of the state in terms of foreign investments is very important.

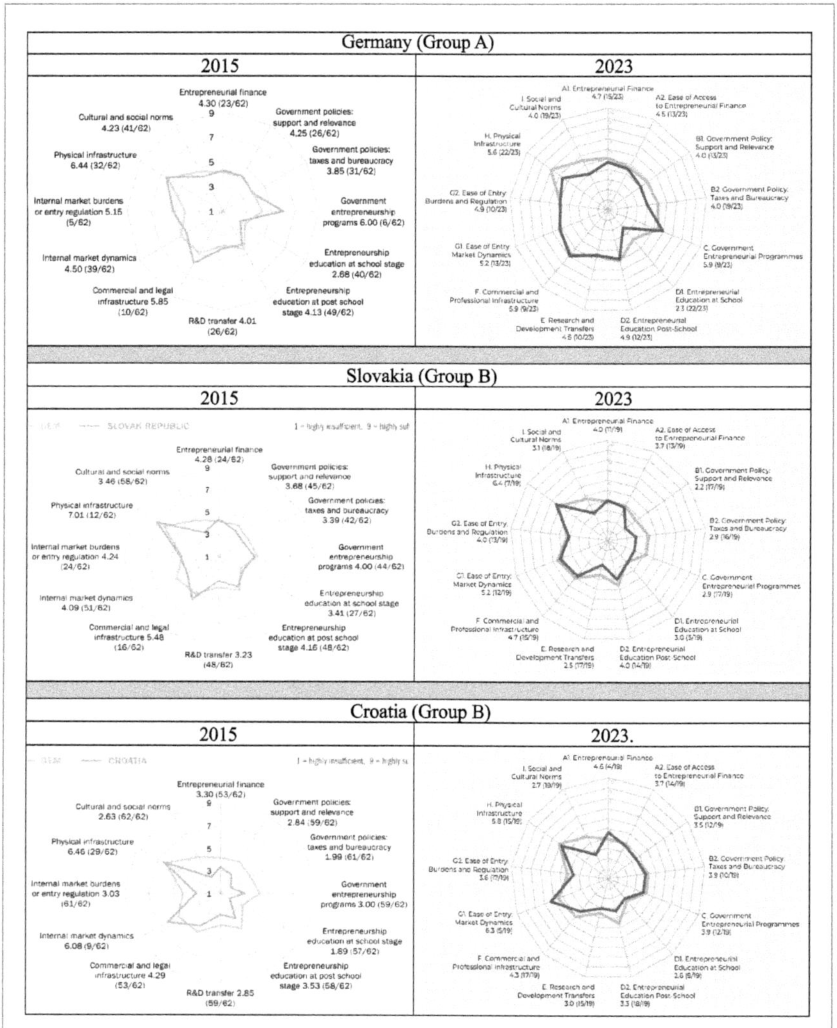

Figure 108. Expert assessments of framework conditions for entrepreneurship, GEM 2015–2023.

Source: (Hill et al. 2025; Kelley, Singer, and Herrington 2016)

If we start from the citation of Nobel laureate Joseph Stiglitz, who points out and warns about the "resource curse paradox" for transition countries, especially those rich in resources, he says: "What is particularly important is the relationship between a country's natural wealth and the dynamics of economic development. Generally, transition countries and their economies possess valuable natural resources. It would be expected that by using their resources they would stimulate their economic growth, but the opposite happens, even leading to increased poverty in these economies. Their natural wealth is the focus of interest of large corporations which, through corruption with centers of power in these countries and politics, take over the natural wealth of transition economies." (Mesarić 2007). That phenomenon is called by Stiglitz the "resource curse paradox," and it consists in the fact that countries rich in natural resources often find themselves in chronic economic backwardness and poverty of the majority of the population. Although Croatia is not among poor countries, its characteristic is wealth in numerous resources. It can be strictly concluded that Croatia's above-average openness to market changes, especially when these changes relate to the uncontrolled entry of foreign capital, cannot be assessed positively. This particularly applies to the resources with which Croatia is rich and which should be the foundation for the development of young Croatian entrepreneurship. According to research on the nation-state and its role, Stiglitz states that without appropriate state guidance and regulation of economic processes, sustainable and optimal socio-economic development cannot be achieved, especially from the standpoint of social justice and ecological balance. According to Stiglitz, the solution should be sought in an optimal combination of market functioning and state interventionism, which will differ in various stages of development and under different circumstances. To conclude, as Stiglitz emphasizes regarding the optimal combination of market functioning and state interventionism, it is advisable to compare the mentioned 13 indicators of state influence on the entrepreneurial environment, and below is a comparison of 3 countries as an example. According to the subject research, Slovakia was taken as an example alongside Croatia, and Germany as a model.

Table 100. Seven indicators of the direct country's activity in the field of entrepreneurship (rank of countries A & B) 2015 & 2023

	Croatia		Slovakia		Germany	
Indicators	**2015**	**2023**	**2015**	**2023**	**2015**	**2023**
Entrepreneurial Finance	3,3	4,6	4,3	4,0	4,3	4,7
Ease of Access to Entrepreneurial Finance	2,8	3,7	3,7	3,7	4,3	4,5
Government Policy: Support and Relevance	2,0	3,5	3,4	2,2	3,9	4,0
Government Policy: Taxes and Bureaucracy	3,0	3,9	4,0	2,9	6,0	4,0
Government Entrepreneurial Programmes	1,9	3,9	3,4	2,9	2,7	5,9
Entrepreneurial Education at School	3,5	2,6	4,2	3,0	4,1	2,3
Entrepreneurial Education Post-School	2,9	3,3	3,2	4,0	4,0	4,9
Total achieved:	**19,4**	**21,3**	**26,2**	**22,7**	**29,3**	**26,3**

Source: (Hill et al. 2025; Kelley et al. 2016)

It should be noted that the research of countries covered by the GEM study is divided into three groups. Group A includes countries with more than $50,000 per capita, Group B includes countries with $25,000–50,000 per capita, and Group C includes countries with less than $25,000 per capita. This analysis includes Germany, which is in Group A, as well as Croatia and Slovakia, which are in Group B. As can be seen from the graphical overview of indicators of direct state activity in the area of entrepreneurship promotion (the right part with seven indicators), Croatia and Slovakia achieve results below the GEM average. Considering the countries covered by the GEM study, it can be concluded that there are noticeable differences among countries in the effectiveness of state actions aimed at entrepreneurship development.

From the aforementioned comparative research, it can be concluded that transition countries, with regard to the directed actions of state administration toward the development of entrepreneurship, lag behind the developed member states of the European Union. Therefore, the question arises as to how and when transition countries will join the developed countries of the European Union in terms of development. To answer this question, it is necessary to conduct a complex economic and socio-political analysis that would attempt to provide an answer.

29.5. Discussion

According to the conducted research, it is evident that there are significant differences in development levels, as well as in the approach to the future development of the European Union member states. In this context, the European Union, as a mega-community, faces other competing mega-communities, which demands its strength. This strength, at least for now, is based on half of the EU member states—developed countries—which have a smaller share of the EU population. At the same time, the other half consists of transition countries and economies that have a larger population and better resources but significantly poorer development outcomes. In line with the goal of the Economic Union, which is embodied in balanced development, the question arises as to how to resolve the problem of large disparities among the member states. Considering possible solutions, some of which are already being successfully implemented, a positive example and model is the intensive cooperation of developed countries with neighboring transition countries, as exemplified by the Baltic states. The second model includes transition countries rich in resources but with unstable organization and national-political apparatus stability, making them susceptible to takeovers by foreign large capital. In this second case, the question arises whether this is a positive model from the perspective of the national economy, since it is known—and Stiglitz continuously emphasizes—that the takeover of foreign capital in a national economy or its key sectors initially leads to growth but is followed by impoverishment. Therefore, in this second model, intensive education is proposed as a long-term solution instead of foreign capital takeovers. Accordingly, in line with developed countries, it is necessary to develop a macro-strategic plan that precisely determines which sectors of the economy and to what extent foreign capital entry can be allowed, as successfully done by some transition countries, such as Poland. Following a planned and targeted FDI (Foreign Direct Investment) policy, Poland, alongside developed EU countries, has also opted for intensified cooperation with American investors. To ensure this process is conducted under supervision, the Polish government developed and adopted in 2024 the document

"Market Entry Strategy," which defines the policy for FDI investments in Poland (International Trade Administration; Poland Country Commercial Guide: Market Entry Strategy n.d.). In accordance with its concern for the national economy, Poland monitors the entry of foreign capital and develops national entrepreneurship while cooperating with the developed countries of the European Union. Based on an insight into the structure of the economy, it can be concluded that no part of Poland's national economy is left to foreign capital. Therefore, Poland has secured the conditions for implementing national policies in various sectors of its national economy. Croatia does not follow Poland's example, as a significant part of Croatia's national economy is already owned by large foreign capital. This fact prevents the establishment and implementation of national policies for certain industrial sectors, as well as the overall state policy. Such a situation in Croatia must change, and excessive entry of foreign capital needs to be replaced by cooperation with developed countries and the education of new generations. This means that at the level of the European Union, as well as all member states, it is necessary to develop policies and strategies for cooperation and joint development, in order to reduce the gap between developed countries and transition countries to at least an acceptable difference.

29.6. Conclusion

The research conducted confirmed the research hypothesis that transition economies among European Union member states do not act sufficiently in terms of developing national entrepreneurship. This conclusion, which confirms the research hypothesis, was drawn based on the example of Croatia, but also Slovakia, with the note that some countries still make greater efforts in developing their national economy. From the mentioned research, the following conclusions can be drawn:

a) In some European Union member states, for example in Croatia, the actions of the state, state administration, and policy are not sufficiently represented in terms of the development of entrepreneurship and the national economy.
b) In some European Union member states, for example in Croatia, the actions of the state, state administration, and policy are not sufficiently

represented in terms of protecting the national economy and controlling the entry of foreign investments (FDI).

c) As stated in b), uncontrolled FDI in Croatia does not lead to long-term development but to impoverishment, so this process needs to be changed in favor of domestic investments.
d) As stated in c), countries rich in resources and still unregulated, which are particularly vulnerable to foreign large capital, are especially targeted.
e) As stated in d), acceptance of foreign investments and the takeover of parts of the national economy in Croatia, as well as in some transition countries of the European Union, should be replaced by education and the creation of a quality generation of domestic managers.
f) On one hand, wars in Europe and the world, and on the other, a young and still insufficiently shaped European Union, as a community of old civil states, is forced to develop national states. Through the policy of national states, resistance is attempted against large mega-powers that seek to expand their market and impose themselves on the European Union.
g) Through cooperation between developed European Union countries, with adequate state supervision, positive results can be achieved.

Bibliography

ANS. 2024. "2024: The United Nations Publishes New World Population Projections."

Bakardjieva Engelbrekt, Antonina, Karin Leijon, Anna Michalski, and Lars Oxelheim, eds. 2020. *The European Union and the Return of the Nation State: Interdisciplinary European Studies*. Cham: Springer International Publishing.

Eurostat. 2025. "Purchasing Power Parities (PPPs), Price Level Indices and Real Expenditures for ESA 2010 Aggregates."

Galan, S. 2025. "Global Demographics—Statistics & Facts."

Hill, Stephen, Aileen Ionescu-Somers, and Alicia Coduras. 2025. "GEM 2024/2025 Global Report: Entrepreneurship Reality Check."

International Trade Administration; Poland Country Commercial Guide: Market Entry Strategy. n.d.

Kelley, Donna, Slavica Singer, and Mike Herrington. 2016. "2015/16 Global Report."

Luković, Tihomir, Damir Piplica, and Tado Jurić. 2023. *A Captive Society and Macro National System, Corruption & Demography*. London: Lambert Academic Publishing.

Mesarić, Milan. 2007. "Kako Promijeniti Model Globalizacije Da Ona Služi Dobrobiti Čovječanstva i Napretku Ljudske Civilizacije—Analiza Josepha Stiglitza." *Ekonomski Pregled* 58(5–6):347–85.

Sareen, Dhirraj. 2020. "Toxic Leadership." *Medium*.

Sarfraz, Zouina, Azza Sarfraz, Hamza Mohammad Iftikar, and Ramsha Akhund. 2021. "Is COVID-19 Pushing Us to the Fifth Industrial Revolution (Society 5.0)?" *Pakistan Journal of Medical Sciences* 37(2):591–94. doi:10.12669/pjms.37.2.3387.

Singer, Slavica, Nataša Šarlija, Sanja Pfeifer, and Sunčica Oberman Peterka. 2024. "Što Čini Hrvatsku (Ne)Poduzetničkom Zemljom?"

www.ingramcontent.com/pod-product-compliance
Ingram Content Group UK Ltd.
Pitfield, Milton Keynes, MK11 3LW, UK
UKHW020154290926
15471UKWH00005B/867

9 783631 941478

The Post-Earthquake City

Disaster and Recovery in Christchurch, New Zealand

Paul Cloke, David Conradson, Eric Pawson and Harvey C. Perkins

Routledge
Taylor & Francis Group
LONDON AND NEW YORK

First published 2023
by Routledge
4 Park Square, Milton Park, Abingdon, Oxon OX14 4RN

and by Routledge
605 Third Avenue, New York, NY 10158

Routledge is an imprint of the Taylor & Francis Group, an informa business

British Library Cataloguing-in-Publication Data
A catalogue record for this book is available from the British Library

ISBN: 978-0-367-22552-0 (hbk)
ISBN: 978-1-032-43672-2 (pbk)
ISBN: 978-0-429-27556-2 (ebk)

DOI: 10.4324/9780429275562

Typeset in Times New Roman
by SPi Technologies India Pvt Ltd (Straive)

Contents

Figures

Tables

Preface

At the time, the Canterbury earthquakes garnered a lot of international media coverage, but as with all such disasters, wider interest quickly faded. One of the stranger things about this event, however, is that it grew into a series, having begun without warning in early September 2010 and continuing, not with a diminishing number of aftershocks as was predicted, but with renewed energy and damaging major shakes over a period of some years. The most destructive one was in late February 2011, and it generated one of the largest-ever claims on the international insurance industry, despite being of much lesser magnitude than many 'regular' earthquakes elsewhere.

The Canterbury earthquake story is marked by such peculiarities, which in our view have long warranted both attention and explanation. But although there has been a lot of work on aspects of the events published in the periodical literature, official sources and the media, there has not before now been a coherently argued account from a social science perspective. A recent set of essays (Uekusa et al. 2022) is an exception and is valuable in recognising that the city of Christchurch at the centre of our story has become something of a talisman for the globally emerging experience of multi-hazards. The earthquakes have been followed by floods and fires, the mosque shootings of March 2019, which once again brought the attention of the world's media, and most recently Covid-19. The Covid lockdowns have in turn cast doubt on some of the assumptions on which the post-earthquake rebuild has been based. Yet all along, those assumptions – of government intervention and showcase projects – have been complemented and countered by grassroots initiatives and transitional experiments. The shape and outcomes of the 'rebuild' have therefore played out in unpredictable ways of a period of years.

This is one reason why we have waited more than a decade to produce this book, and why we have taken our time to engage with a still evolving process, and with each other as authors. We know Christchurch and Canterbury well, three as long-term residents who lived through the earthquake sequence, and the fourth as a regular visitor to the city over many years, both before and since the event. We provide outline biographies on page xiv and discuss our various positionalities in the first chapter.

We owe debts of gratitude to a large number of people, starting with Tim Nolan, our talented and ever patient cartographer. Amongst many who have helped, encouraged or influenced us are Thomas Blakie, Jacky Bowring, Jan Cameron, Kelli Campbell, Ikenna Chukwudumogu, Simon Dickinson, Kelly Dombroski, Erin Heine, Alan Latham, Deborah Levy, Robin Kearns, Rob Kerr, Simon Kingham, John McDonagh, Mike Mackay, Colin Meurk, Judi Miller, Garry Moore and members of the Tuesday Club, Laurence Murphy, Brent Nahkies, Hugh Nicholson, Mark Poskitt, Nick Taylor, Sarah Tucker and Alice Ann Wetzel. We also thank all those who agreed to be interviewed for our study and the Christchurch journalists whose comprehensive earthquake recovery reporting has been invaluable. We also acknowledge the individuals and agencies who have allowed us to reproduce images; they are attributed in the usual way in the captions to the figures within each chapter. All unattributed graphics or images have been sourced from within the author team.

Sadly, Paul Cloke died suddenly when the book was in the final stages of writing. He wished to acknowledge funding from the Erskine programme at the University of Canterbury and the Leverhulme Trust Emeritus Fellowship programme, which enabled his travel over the years to Christchurch, as well as the International Office of the University of Exeter. The book was originally Paul's idea, and it has come to fruition as a result of his inspiration and encouragement. We hope that he would have been proud of the final result.

Christchurch, New Zealand
June 2022

About the authors

Paul Cloke was Emeritus Professor of Human Geography at the University of Exeter. His research interests included rural geography, social change, ethical geographies and the role of the third sector. Paul published a number of papers with New Zealand colleagues (including each of us) and co-authored a number of academic articles on aspects of the aftermath of the Christchurch earthquakes. During his career, he produced over 40 books, including the co-authored *Geographies of Postsecularity: Re-envisioning Politics, Subjectivity and Ethics* (2019). In 2022, Paul was awarded the Royal Geographical Society's Victoria Medal for his contribution to rural geography and to the wider discipline.

David Conradson is Professor of Human Geography at the University of Canterbury. His current research examines the lived experience of disrupted environments, with a focus on processes that shape individual and collective well-being. He has been involved in a number of funded research projects examining post-disaster recovery in Christchurch, with publications from this work in *Transactions of the Institute of British Geographers, the International Journal of Disaster Risk Reduction, Earthquake Spectra*, and a series of book chapters. Previously an editor of *Social and Cultural Geography*, he is currently the Managing Editor of the *New Zealand Geographer*.

Eric Pawson is Emeritus Professor of Geography at the University of Canterbury. He retains an active interest in research, contributing to the *Cambridge Handbook of Undergraduate Research* (2022) and the fifth edition of *Qualitative Research in Human Geography* (2021). His thematic interests are in environmental history and environmental governance, with publications including *The New Biological Economy* (2018). He has been involved in a range of organisations and initiatives in post-earthquake Christchurch, particularly in and about the residential red zone. He co-founded the Ōtākaro Living Laboratory Trust and has chaired the Waitākiri Ecosanctuary Trust.

Harvey C. Perkins is Emeritus Professor of Planning at the University of Auckland where he directed the research programme Transforming Cities: Initiatives for Sustainable Futures. He is a Past President of the New Zealand Geographical Society and former Professor of Human Geography at Lincoln University in Christchurch. His research interests include leisure and tourism, housing, residential intensification and the relationships between house and home. He is a Principal Investigator in the New Zealand National Science Challenge *Building Better Homes, Towns and Cities: Ko Ngā Wā Kāinga Hei Whakamāhorahora*, for which he co-leads a study of local regeneration initiatives in regional settlements.

1 Introduction

The years 2010 and 2011 saw major environmental disasters in different parts of the world. Much of the Caribbean state of Haiti was devastated in a magnitude 7.0 earthquake in January 2010, with a death toll in the hundreds of thousands. The next month, 12,000 people lost their lives after an 8.8 magnitude quake and tsunami in Chile. In March 2011, 6,000 people were killed in the magnitude 9.1 shock and tsunami at Tōhuku in Honshu, Japan. In between these events, a long-running seismic sequence began in the vicinity of the south Pacific city of Christchurch, in Aotearoa New Zealand's South Island. Starting on 4 September 2010, the Canterbury earthquake sequence (named for the region in which the city is located) continued for more than three years, including a very damaging, shallow 6.3 magnitude event under the city on 22 February 2011. The Canterbury earthquakes were not as severe as the other events, nor were they as deadly, although the official earthquake toll was 185 people (New Zealand Police 2022).

Nonetheless, this particular event quickly became one of the world's most expensive environmental disasters. As Swiss Re, the international re-insurance company, asked, how 'could a small aftershock in a city not considered an earthquake hotspot trigger one of the largest insurance losses ever?' (Grollimund 2014). And what did this financially framed question mean in terms of human experience and response? Some aspects of the recovery process attracted wide notice internationally, such as the Student Volunteer Army, the transitional city movement spearheaded by Gap Filler, the downtown container mall and street art festivals. But what of more quotidian encounters and experiences in a place where over a decade later, the process of recovery still continues? Scars remain on people and homes, even if superficially damage outside the city centre is now less visible. In the centre itself, where most buildings were lost, large empty sites remain to be redeveloped, whereas extensive greenfield areas of new housing now fringe the metropolitan area.

This book presents a critical assessment of Christchurch as an evolving post-disaster city, recognising that such a narrative is both intensely local in scale and also of global significance. From the neoliberal economic experimentation and agricultural deregulation of the 1980s (Le Heron and Pawson 1996) to the hospitable welcome of multicultural immigration and the one-nation

DOI: 10.4324/9780429275562-1

revulsion of terror in the 2010s, and the fighting of Covid-19 with a team of five million in the 2020s, New Zealand has become a place of interest to many beyond its shores (Uekusa et al. 2022). The rebuilding of Christchurch has occurred as a result of very specific local and national interventions and community-based activities, yet the city serves as a wider laboratory in which a tragic period of destruction, disruption and disaster has in turn been followed by rare opportunities to refashion land uses and social experience from the ground up. Evaluation of what has been possible in these enforced laboratory conditions offers wider international lessons regarding both the powerful magnetism of reproducing previous normalities and the capacity to integrate experimental cultures of place-making and ecological restoration into the urban fabric.

This introductory chapter addresses the contexts in which the narratives of the book are embedded and identifies some of the key points that need to be interrogated. First, we outline some of the historical, environmental and political particularities of Christchurch's situation, as the characteristics of the pre-disaster city have certainly shaped events after the earthquakes. Second, we draw on existing wisdom in disaster models and narratives in the literature, outlining (sometimes potentially conflicting) key theoretical ideas which help to shape the different strands of our account of the post-quake experience. Third, we acknowledge that the ways in which these matters are framed and narrated reflect the complex positional and situated knowledges of the authors. This not only recognises the existence of our different narrative perspectives but also the ways such perspectives coexist in a multifaceted web of understanding.

Contextualising Ōtautahi Christchurch

There was no physical connection between the earthquakes in different countries in 2010–11, but it is no coincidence that Chile, Japan and New Zealand lie on the Pacific Ring of Fire, the active zone of volcanism and seismicity that marks tectonic plate boundaries in the western hemisphere. However, as Swiss Re observed, it was always expected that in New Zealand the capital city of Wellington would be at greatest risk, as it sits astride the fault lines that mark the boundary between the Indian and Pacific plates (Grollimund 2014). Yet it has long been recognised that there are few places in the country that are entirely free of earthquake hazard. 'Living in New Zealand means living with earthquakes' (Department of Statistics 2010, 6) and under amendments to the Building Act 2004, Christchurch is in the highest risk category. By the 1990s, the likelihood of liquefaction, or land deformation under seismic stress, was known, an environmental vulnerability that the city shares with many other Pacific ring cities, such as Jakarta, Tokyo and Vancouver. But why then are such prominent places built in sites of high risk?

An explanation lies in what the novelist Amitav Ghosh has recently called 'terraforming'. He borrows this concept from science fiction to describe the process of land-making or 'land-moulding' that typified colonial settler experience, 'envisioning space as a "frontier" to be "conquered" and "colonized"' (Ghosh 2021, 54). Such colonising, replicated on steroids during the urbanisation associated with the current era of neoliberal globalisation, treats the environment, itself an objectifying concept, as an inert stage on which humans as active agents inscribe their 'improvements' (Latour 2018). Christchurch, the centre of the planned Victorian colony of Canterbury, was planted in 1850 in the midst of swampy and sandy ground, without awareness that this is relatively recently formed land at the edge of the delta of the Waimakariri River, one of the great, unpredictable gravel-bed rivers that flow eastwards to the Pacific Ocean from the Southern Alps (Figure 1.1). Whilst much of the history of the city has been preoccupied with land drainage and exotic revegetation (Schrader 1997; Pawson 2000), the hidden price of this has been development on deltaic sediments prone to liquefaction during earthquakes, as Chapters 2 and 3 illustrate in greater detail.

Another way to describe this is to suggest that the land is 'alive' in its own right, a perspective embodied in the worldview of the indigenous Māori, who were largely displaced by nineteenth-century colonisation. They were however by no means silenced. One of the key features of contemporary governance in New Zealand has been the growing recognition, both politically and in legislation, of the cultural rights of Māori iwi and hapū (tribes and subtribes), stemming from the signing of the Treaty of Waitangi between the British Crown and iwi in 1840 (Orange 1987; Finlayson and Christmas 2021). Settlements to rectify breaches of the Treaty have been ongoing since the 1990s, one of the earliest and biggest being with the South Island iwi, Ngāi Tahu, in 1998. Canterbury lies within the rohe, or area within which Ngāi Tahu has mana whenua, or cultural and customary authority (Tau 2016). For this reason, the term 'the Crown' is in regular usage in New Zealand to denote central government in its exercise of the authority originally assumed through the Treaty by the colonising power. And in post-earthquake legislation, Ngāi Tahu has been identified as a partner with central and local governments, and state agencies, in the rebuild of the city and metropolitan area. The local hapu is Ngāi Tūāhuriri, which exercises mana whenua over much of the area in which the city sits. Māori terms are increasing in everyday usage, including Ōtautahi as the name of the city (Uekusa et al. 2022).

The city is broadly typical of those planted by white colonial settlement worldwide. It developed on a regular grid, quickly outgrowing this along late nineteenth-century tramlines. After World War Two, it expanded outwards under the imperatives of suburbanisation and automobility during a period of national prosperity (Forer 1978), checked only by the barrier of the Port Hills to the south and the river estuaries to the east (Figure 1.1). As Chapter 3 demonstrates, its spread was not socially uniform: suburbs in the northwest and on the hills tend to be more socially privileged than those in the east, and characterised by a denser 'urban forest' of exotic trees. The city has long had a reputation as class divided, with conspicuous traditions energised by the Anglican roots of the colonising organisation and reflected in its Victorian Gothic architecture and network of private schools. But this is at best a

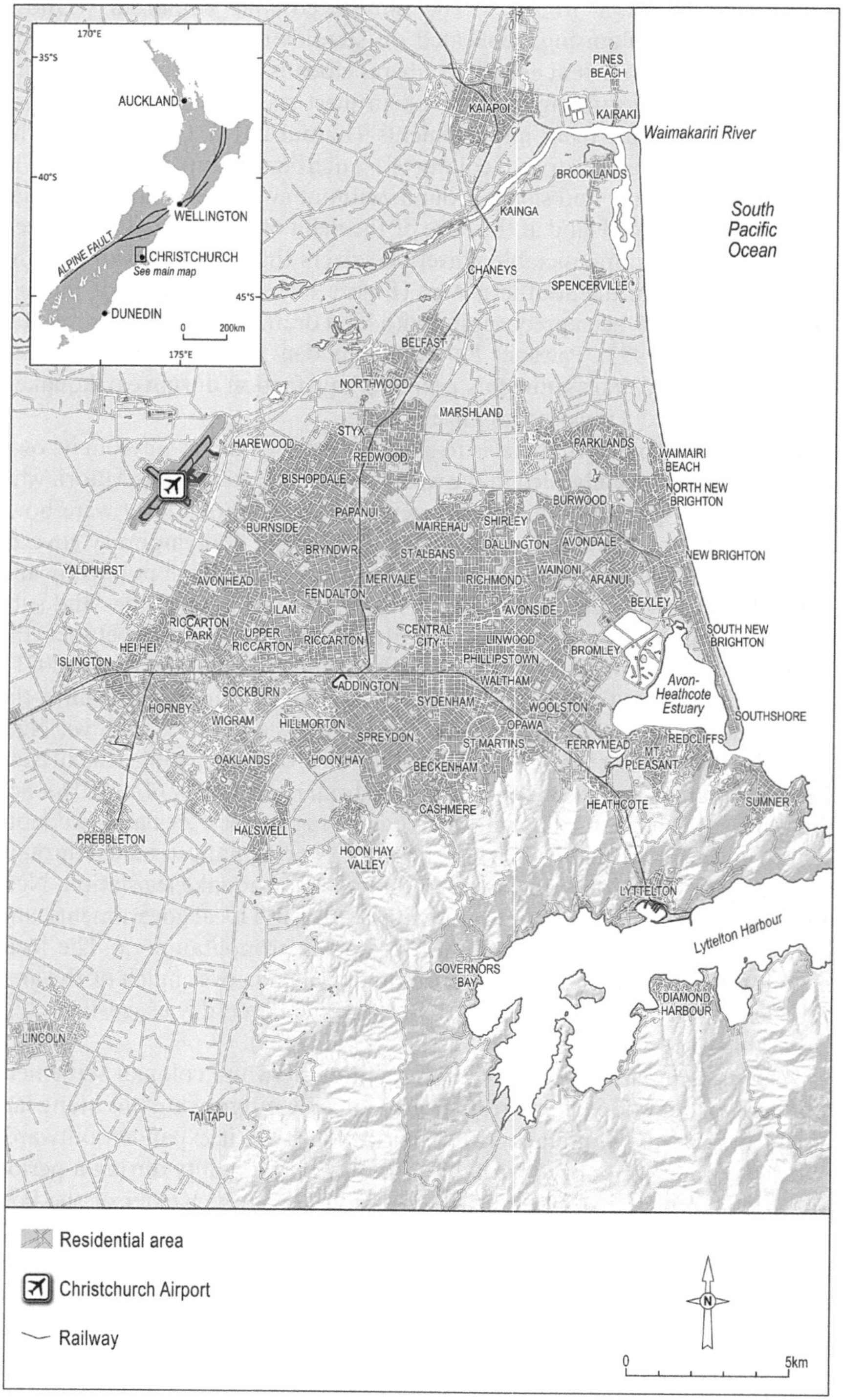

Figure 1.1 Location map.

partial representation of a place that has also exhibited a long-run working class and radical spirit (McAloon 2000a, 2000b). Most of its parliamentary seats are usually held by the left-of-centre Labour Party. Such tensions were for long hidden beneath a popular identity as the 'garden city' of the South Island (Galloway 2022; Pawson 1999).

Theorising disaster-affected places

Within the interdisciplinary disaster and critical disaster studies literature, the process of disaster recovery is often presented as a sequence of stages through which an affected community is expected to progress (eg. Cutter et al. 2008; Kates et al. 2006). Figure 1.2, drawn from DeWolfe's (2000) research in the United States, is illustrative. Although such models provide a useful guide to the stages of recovery, they imply a linear and unified experience, which seldom occurs as depicted. In Christchurch, the pace of recovery varied significantly among households, communities and neighbourhoods across the city, even in adjacent houses. Recovery was also by no means assured, contrary to the optimism inherent in the steady upward movement of DeWolfe's line and its final stage of 'new beginning'. This presents a challenge to recovery models that champion stoicism and assume population resilience. In many disasters, some people and communities are affected very badly, suffering devastating emotional and material losses. It is important that these experiences are not ignored or eclipsed by buoyant models that internalise optimistic progress.

While acknowledging a broad sequence of events in the case of Christchurch, this book gives attention to the multiple co-existing temporalities of disaster experience. This includes noticing the ways in which time may stretch or dilate for those waiting for emergency relief and assistance, as in

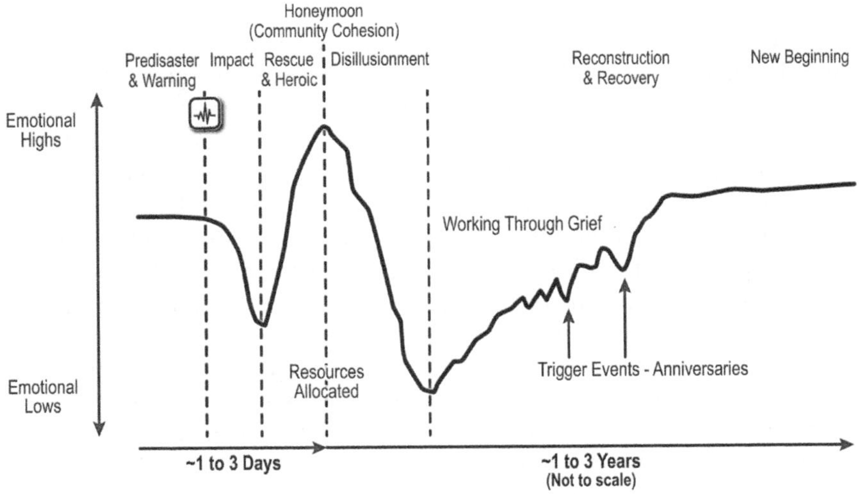

Figure 1.2 DeWolfe's model of post-disaster recovery.

the immediate aftermath of a major earthquake when buildings may be shattered and communication networks disrupted. Other people may experience time as somehow suspended, as they navigate complex insurance claims and await government decisions amidst repeated bureaucratic delays and impasses. For still others, the sudden violence of post-disaster life is foregrounded, such as when people are killed or injured, or when houses and buildings are demolished, erasing once familiar landmarks and places of belonging.

Disaster-affected places have been understood as having certain characteristics. Evidence from the Haiti earthquakes of 2010 and 2021 (DesRoches et al. 2011; Hou and Shi 2011; International Labour Organisation 2021) emphasises disruption to the connections and relationships that sustain and enable the reproduction of places and homes. Damage to transport infrastructure upsets the usual functioning of places, compounding shock, deprivation and hardship. But places are also pulled into new networks of relationships, as sites of humanitarian relief, charitable donations, government and insurance resources and media attention. Opportunities may also beckon for opportunistic profiteering by agents of disaster capitalism (Klein 2008; Miles 2016). Organisational disorientation amongst government and community agencies (Hall et al. 2016) is mirrored at individual and household levels, where disruption can be intensified by the severance of local place attachments (Fullilove 2016).

Another significant characteristic of disaster-affected places is the exposure and often exacerbation of pre-existing inequalities. The widely observed stratification of vulnerability and disadvantage by socio-economic status (Kahn 2005), race (Cutter et al. 2006), gender (Enarson and Pease 2016) and disability and sexual orientation (Dominey-Howes et al. 2013; Gaillard et al. 2017) is typically highlighted during disasters (Wisner and Luce 1993). As Johnson (2006, 148) argued after Hurricane Katrina, 'the storm laid bare the environmentally linked economic and racial inequities within New Orleans, inequities with a long history'. Moreover, recovery options and resources tend to be unevenly allocated, and directed towards social groups and communities that are most reflective of societal elites with the greatest amounts of social and political capital (Wisner et al. 2004). Those who are politically marginal or disenfranchised tend to be attended to later, or less adequately or, in some cases not at all (Curtis et al. 2007), as in the case of impoverished black neighbourhoods in New Orleans after Katrina (Bullard 2018; Katz 2008). As a result, it is not uncommon to observe quite divergent neighbourhood experiences after disaster within the same city (Wilson 2013).

A further characteristic of disaster-affected places is social and political contestation over future uses of space. Whose visions end up having most influence in the recovery and rebuilding process? In cities, there is often competition between private and public sector interests, property developers and community groups. There may also be conflict between different agencies or levels of government. It is not uncommon for tensions to arise between central or federal government emergency management organisations and locally elected city and metropolitan authorities, where the former tend towards rapid and relatively undifferentiated responses that are implemented at scale and the latter are, by nature, more attuned to local differences in community and neighbourhood constitution and needs (Hörhager 2015; Pelling 2010). Indeed, much conceptualisation of post-disaster cities echoes the sentiment expressed by Roberta Brandes Gratz (2015, 128) in the context of post-Katrina New Orleans, that 'considerably more wisdom and careful urban regeneration have been exhibited from the bottom up than from the top down'.

Despite their underlying complexity and context dependency, these broad disaster characteristics are often further generalised into ideas about resilience. This has become a pervasive concept in disaster studies over the last 20 years (Soens 2020). According to Adger (2000), resilience reflects the capacity of groups and communities to cope with the disruptions and disturbances of social, political and environmental change. In these terms, resilience is deployed as an attractive yardstick of the ability of a population to accommodate shocks and adapt (Parker 2020) and to 'bounce back' (Manyena et al. 2011). There are, however, a number of significant limitations to such deployment. At a basic conceptual level, resilience is often ill-defined in relation to other elements of community reaction to change, especially that of resistance.

Wenger (2017) questions whether resilience resembles the oak (with its capacity for resistance, enabling absorption of stress and return to a stable equilibrium) or the reed (with its pliability and flexibility to move with changing conditions) or indeed both. Attention to the post-disaster city would seem to require a conceptual framework that acknowledges a co-existence of contemporaneous capacities for both continuity and change. In addition, in assessing the conceptual power of resilience, it is important to consider Hayward's (2013) argument that its usage tends to be conservative. She suggests that it privileges the social constructs of external experts (such as urban planners) and may underestimate the potential for different forms of political resistance that unleash alternative imaginations of new beginnings and different outcomes. At worst, undue attention to resilience within neoliberalised ways of thinking can lead to an attribution of responsibility for survival and change to individuals rather than to shared societal structures (Matthewman and Uekusa 2021).

Accordingly, this book offers a critique of what might be described as 'the orthodoxy of resilience' within the disaster recovery literature. Although the capacities and creativity of the individuals, households and communities affected by the earthquakes are acknowledged, these capacities are not enrolled into a tidy narrative of resilience, stoicism and coping which elides the complexity of post-disaster life and experience. There are plenty of instances when the experience of residents and communities in Christchurch defy such categories, or certainly trouble their inherent optimism. Following Donna Haraway (2016), albeit in a different register than originally intended, this book therefore seeks to 'stay with the trouble' rather than move too quickly to optimistic notions of progress, success, resilience, fortitude and 'moving forward'.

In place of these kinds of grand narratives of resilience, the book examines how capacities for continuity, experimentation and innovation are interwoven in the complex spaces, political cultures and ethical values of a post-disaster city. Following the arguments outlined by Cloke et al. (2017), it frames the Canterbury earthquakes in terms of what the French philosopher Alain Badiou (2005) terms an 'event'. Badiou argues that a major event is likely to bring about social change based on two overlapping realms of human action. The first is characterised by an instinct to act in what might be considered ordinary and familiar ways, in line with and managed by dominant ideologies and their consequent influence on the activities of the state. The expectation here is that pre-event norms will re-emerge, as actors seek a return to what they know. The second possible outcome is the emergence of alternative possibilities for action that had previously been submerged, covered up or excluded. In these terms, the significance of the event is that it has the capacity to rupture the established order of things and to allow this second strand of action to take flight, affording a distinctive space that has the potential to open up new beginnings and new imaginations of collective cultural creativity (Bassett 2008; Dewsbury 2007).

In strict terms, the Christchurch disaster needs to be acknowledged as a *sequence* of geological events, with the two destructive earthquakes accompanied by over 11,000 aftershocks of varying magnitudes, as illustrated in Chapter 2. In many respects, then, it differs from Badiou's emphasis on the kind of event brought about by political upheaval. However, geographers have also recognised the power of what they term the 'geo-event' (Shaw 2012; Yusoff 2013) to cause a disruption of inhuman nature (Clark 2011) that in turn can rupture the foundations, structures and assumed relations that make the ordinary and familiar world legible. Thus, it can be argued that the collective outcome of a geo-event such as the sequence of earthquakes in and around Christchurch can also be to tear the fabric of normal practice in the world, and to foster new senses of life and place as well as provoking a desire to return to the status quo.

This notion of the rupture of the event is central to the deliberations in this book, which address the questions of what exactly was ruptured by the 2010–13 Canterbury earthquakes (Pickles 2016), and to what degree there are still spaces for alternative community action in the city a decade later. Subsequent chapters will variously explore capacities for continuity and change, often occurring simultaneously in time and space although at other times significantly variegated in their geographical patterns. In so doing a range of concepts are drawn on to inform the processes by which Christchurch residents have shaped their lives and found their lives shaped. Political economic models attentive to the dynamics of capital and investment help to explain how both city centre redevelopment and suburban sprawl exhibit pathways of continuity as part of a return to normal after the earthquakes. At the same time, cultural and political ideas are used to detect new and experimental forms of interaction within the city, charting an affective politics that is capable of creating new ways of being in common (Cloke and Conradson 2018).

Engagement with more-than-human ecologies and polities also indicates very significant capacities for change. These ideas are far from abstract: they are negotiated and grounded in changing forms of governance in the city, which inevitably becomes a key focus in critical discussions of rupture in post-disaster Christchurch (Pawson 2022).

Positioning the book

The complex and sometimes divergent narratives presented in this book are not only shaped by different theoretically informed perspectives. It has now become accepted practice for researchers in human geography and cognate disciplines to be reflexively conscious of how particular aspects of self-identity help to shape the conduct and reporting of research (Rose 1997). England (1994) famously argued that a researcher's positionality and biography directly affect the dialogical process of research, and that social identifiers such as gender, ethnicity and age often shape the maps of consciousness that guide research and writing. To explore these positional specificities via reflexive practice is to acknowledge that researchers know the world partially, influenced by how their knowledge is socially, spatially and intellectually situated, and that researchers are susceptible to the promotion or inhibition of particular kinds of insights. Such reflexivity risks introspection but nonetheless the four authors of this book consider it relevant and important to recognise some of the ways in which their experiences and intellectual fascinations have influenced the analytical narratives that have emerged.

Three vectors of positionality are of particular significance. First, the authors have different connections and relationships to Christchurch as a place. Three of us call the city home, and have lived through the earthquakes and their aftermath; the fourth was a frequent visitor. Insider knowledge may have positive benefits for research, including a sensitivity to local contexts and a degree of involvement and familiarity that enhances depth of understanding. Whilst outsider knowledge may be less attuned to local conditions, it can provide a bulwark against overfamiliarity by enabling a more dispassionate questioning of locally socialised assumptions and perspectives (Dwyer and Buckle 2009). However, it is also important to recognise the fluidity and intersection between 'insider' and 'outsider' positions. Thus Paul's 'outsider' position as a British-based researcher was tempered by the experience of a dozen or so research trips to the city over a 30-year period, the last being in 2020. The other authors also have quite different experiences as residents of different parts of the city and participants in post-earthquake recovery. As a team, we have drawn on these distinct and varied knowledges of Christchurch in exploring the drivers and consequences of processes of recovery.

Secondly, we carry with us significant intellectual and academic proclivities. Harvey's early research interests in urban growth management and latterly in aspects of urban planning, design and policy, have led to a significant focus on the role of property owners and businesses as well as residents in the processes and practices of urban regeneration. Eric's enduring interests in environmental history and management have been coupled with involvement in post-disaster governance at a range of scales in the city, in community groups and in the future of its red zone. David's long-standing concern with the experience of places disrupted by neoliberal economic restructuring and welfare reform has highlighted the need to understand the social and psychological impact of the earthquakes, and the role of the community and voluntary sector in recovery. Paul's focus on the 'messy middle' ground between how people shape their lives, and how they are shaped by other factors, emphasises the possibility of political and ethical hopefulness in amongst the often morose analyses of neoliberalised political economy. These different priorities help to explain our readiness to explore a range of different aspects of the post-disaster city.

Thirdly, the authors have had varied participatory experience in terms of research and policy-making in post-quake Christchurch. Eric's city-as-laboratory approach has led him to build a city-based network of contacts through participation in community groups and a weekly critical discussion group (the Tuesday Club) for all things post-earthquake. He was contracted for a time to Regenerate Christchurch (the Crown/council rebuild agency) and (independent of that) initiated a city-wide process to explore governance options for the red zone. Before the earthquakes Harvey's research in the city was on tourism development, residential intensification and urban planning, and afterwards he engaged with resident and professional groups about post-earthquake housing, and with the responses of central city property owners to the post-quake environment. David's post-quake research has centred on the fate of displaced red-zoned households, disruptions to schooling, youth well-being, and the capacity of voluntary sector organisations to assist affected people and places. Paul's participation took the form of collaborative research into the role of the voluntary sector in post-quake transition and care, involving interviews with more than 50 stakeholders during three periods of research at different times after the earthquakes.

These various arenas of participation contribute significantly to the architecture of the book, providing a range of different points of entry. It is our conviction that there are many different elements that coalesce in the evolution of the post-disaster city, hence our concern to emphasise complexity, diversity and plurality in analysis of patterns of change, innovation and meaningfulness. If different parts of the book do not always easily cohere, this is a symptom of the 'messy' geographies at work. We have come to distrust singular meta-narratives and headline conclusions. Instead, our preference has been to acknowledge how variations in authorial positionality have enabled emphasis on the multiple epicentres, concerns, activities and voices that need to be recognised as integral to the emergence of Christchurch from the earthquakes. So, we champion small-scale voluntary and community actors as well as the property owners, policy-makers and planners, the creative innovators and the proponents of a return to 'normal', the disadvantaged and uprooted as well as the suburban survivors, and the ecology of the more-than-human as well as anthropocentric orthodoxy. In so doing the book aims to provide a framework in which to assemble the multiple experiences and realities of recovery.

Structure of the book

Following this introduction, the book is structured into three substantive sections reflecting broad sequences of events in post-disaster experience. The first, labelled 'Damage and displacement', focuses on the material damage of the earthquakes and their impact on households and communities in terms of lived experience. Chapter 2 explores why the city was so vulnerable to the earthquakes despite widespread use of measures of protection and security (specifically building codes and the extent of property insurance) to protect against uncertainty. Having considered the material damage, Chapter 3 then examines its impact on people's lived experience. This includes how post-quake land zoning decisions and insurance wrangles created challenges for many households, with associated reductions in well-being and the increased incidence of anxiety and depression. But the novel expressions of support and mutual aid that arose in communities and neighbourhoods, and their contribution to local resilience and recovery, are also considered.

The second section, 'Recovery and renewal', begins with Chapter 4 on governance and cartographies of recovery. This explores pre-earthquake experiments in governance, when collaborative and community-informed processes had been introduced to map out possible city futures, as a basis for understanding reaction to the state-driven recovery mechanisms put in place in 2011, and the panoptical cartographies employed as part of redrawing of the central city in particular. Chapter 5 considers damage to housing and the subsequent housing recovery effort, producing an array of outcomes in the central city, suburbs and satellite towns. The recovery has encouraged residential redevelopment in the central city and parts of the suburbs, but also significantly increased a long-established tendency to urban sprawl. In an illustration of path dependency, recovery has disrupted earlier plans to contain sprawl through intensification of the existing urban fabric.

Chapter 6 discusses how Christchurch's commercial property sector was affected by the earthquake sequence and the building demolition that followed. But it reinforced prior strongly articulated public and private sector commitments to the central city and refocused pre-earthquake attempts to stem decline in the face of growing suburban competition from retailing, hospitality and allied services. The objective of the chapter is to outline how in the recovery process, cooperative, contested and sometimes antagonistic interaction between the city council, Crown agencies, property owners, their insurance companies and the region's residents have led to a partial recovery in a situation of 'staggering complexity'. Chapter 7 focuses on the role of voluntary and community organisations, including those that are faith-based, resident-led and the novel movement that became known as the Student Volunteer Army. It notes the sometimes uneasy coexistence between such voluntarism and the efforts of state recovery agencies, and considers how this voluntarism sits alongside politically conservative aspirations for rebuilding the city on the one hand and more progressive forms of place-making on the other.

The third section, 'the City in Transition', focuses on the emergence of post-recovery futures. Chapter 8 discusses a phenomenon that has received perhaps greater acclaim internationally than locally: how a number of voluntary sector and community-based organisations sprang up to make energetic and multifaceted contributions to cultural, artistic, creative and ecological uses of temporary spaces. In a series of experimental projects, these organisations have presented propositions for alternative expressions of transition after the earthquakes, valorising collective rather than individual ethics, and creative aesthetics that turn flux into opportunity. In contrast, Chapter 9 conceptualises the city as a locus of consumption flows, with commercial forms of place-making that range from those that have borrowed from the experiments of the transitional movement, to major Crown-sponsored anchor projects purposed to support recreation, events and tourism. This spatial competition to attract consumers and consumption practices however depends on and drives a further cycle of consumption, that of carbon.

Spatial unevenness has also been a theme of recovery, and it was not long before the term 'forgotten east' began to circulate, capturing the view that eastern areas of the city were somehow being overlooked or under-prioritised. Chapter 10 interrogates this idea, examining the differing levels of attention displayed by state and private sector agencies in their engagements with communities in the eastern suburbs. Chapter 11 also takes an important theme in urban geography but one often downplayed in post-earthquake recovery, that of the more-than-human city. The chapter explores how actual worlds become assembled when all manner of things (or 'actants') contribute to the making of particular geographies, assessing the extent to which opportunities for more lively spaces, hybrid ecosystems and species interactions are being recognised.

The question arising here is if through its post-earthquake experience the city is now better placed to move beyond what Donna Haraway (2016, 35) has described as the 'unprecedented looking away' of the Anthropocene. One site in which this is being actively played out is the city's residential red zone in the eastern suburbs, abandoned in the wake of the earthquakes. Chapter 12 asks if this will become the city's field 'of dreams', countering a recurrent criticism of the post-earthquake rebuild, that it is producing 'the city of yesterday' rather than that of tomorrow. After exploring processes of community engagement, regeneration planning and environmental co-governance with Māori, it concludes by outlining some of the nascent characteristics of what a future Christchurch might look like, based on this post-earthquake experimentation over the last decade. These themes are considered further in the concluding chapter.

Part I

Damage and displacement

2 The fracturing of a vulnerable city

Introduction

It was a dramatic and seemingly endless experience living through the Canterbury earthquake sequence over the three or more years from when it began, so unexpectedly, in the early hours of 4 September 2010. This chapter assesses the extent and nature of the physical fracturing to the city and its region generated by those events, seeking to place experience in a wider descriptive and analytical frame. It explores the forms that material damage took, and considers the extent to which this was the product of, or exacerbated by, particular vulnerabilities that – with the benefit of hindsight – can be attributed to characteristics of the city's built environment or its social organisation. Given that Christchurch is the second largest city in a country well-known for seismic activity, one that sits astride a major global tectonic plate boundary, why was it not better prepared? Or was it prepared, but in unhelpful or insufficient ways? And can such issues be illuminated by examining them at different spatial scales, from the local to the global?

The chapter starts with a discussion of the concepts of vulnerability, resilience and security. The last of these is particularly important in a country in which an interventionist state historically sought to provide a level of protection and support to its citizens in the face of uncertainty. The technocratic forms assumed by such protection, particularly building codes and the extent of property insurance, are then examined. This helps to answer Swiss Re's question (Grollimund 2014), posed at the start of Chapter 1: why did the Canterbury earthquake sequence become one of the most expensive episodes ever faced by the international insurance industry? Yet, by global standards, none of the earthquakes was particularly large. Resolution of this apparent paradox is sought through examination of the ecology of the earthquakes, in order to understand the intersection of physical and social circumstances which rendered the city particularly vulnerable. That vulnerability is then illustrated with a description of the extent of death and destruction, followed by an outline of the immediate disaster response, so as to provide a clear context for what might be termed a 'socio-seismic' series of occurrences.

DOI: 10.4324/9780429275562-3

Vulnerability, resilience and security

Vulnerability has been a popular term in environmental hazard and disaster studies for 30 years or more, yet is used in a range of different ways (Wisner 2020). In relation to earthquakes, it has often been reduced to assessments of exposure to risk. But although the known incidence of hazardous events is important, of equal significance are the human attributes of particular communities in terms of 'their capacity to anticipate, cope with, resist and recover from' disastrous circumstances (Blaikie et al. 1994, 9). But even this broader definition implies a relatively static understanding of complex social situations. What needs to be anticipated might not be known, and many factors, apart from the characteristics of the event and people affected, shape the nature of impacts. Among these are the ways in which human behaviour may accentuate the severity of 'natural' occurrences, for instance by intensive development of flood plains and liquefaction-prone land (Hewitt 1997; Pawson 2011). Furthermore, impacts are often spatially uneven and unpredictable. Vulnerability, therefore, is multidimensional with some aspects, notably the social, often more hidden from view than others (Cutter et al. 2003).

In the geographical literature, vulnerability is frequently juxtaposed with resilience. If vulnerability is the susceptibility to be harmed, then resilience refers to the magnitude of disturbance that can be absorbed before radical change occurs in a social or ecological system. It is used as well to describe the capacity to cope with emerging circumstances (Adger 2006). From origins in materials science and engineering, it has been picked up in ecology and social science, to include the study of how communities and social networks respond after disasters (Blair and Mabee 2020; Wilson 2012). It has also become a popular research concept in studies of climate change and development. Mainstream views of resilience however tend to privilege the persistence of a system over its transformation, whereas it is important to question what sort of resilience, and for whom (Hayward 2013; Tanner et al. 2015)? Its widespread adoption in policy since the neoliberal revolution of the 1980s, promoting the self-reliance of 'resilient' individuals and communities, appeals to those who promote a smaller, less engaged state (Joseph 2013). Furthermore, resilience approaches may damage 'practical understanding of the causative processes of vulnerability and how disasters come to be created' (Weichselgartner and Kelman 2015, 259).

Nonetheless, despite the pervasive practice of forms of neoliberalism in New Zealand (Le Heron and Pawson 1996), earlier traditions of collective security persist. These originated in the desire for a strong national vision based on full employment, provision of housing and social welfare (Easton 2000; Sutch 1966). This included old-age support, which has become politically entrenched, along with the later no-fault Accident Compensation Corporation (ACC) scheme, dating from 1972, which affords collective cover for all forms of personal injury. Most historical accounts, however, overlook the introduction of security against disaster, initially providing for compulsory insurance of property against war damage in 1941 but, after a destructive series of earthquakes in the lower North Island the following year, extended in 1944 to also include earthquake damage. Other types of disasters were progressively added in the post-war years (Department of Statistics 1990). The Earthquake and War Damage Commission became the Earthquake Commission in 1993, providing cover, in spite of its name, against a wide range of environmental hazards. The Commission provides capped insurance for residential buildings as a compulsory element of private house policies; damage over the cap is the responsibility of the private insurer. Homes without private insurance are not eligible, nor are commercial properties (DPMC 2017).

Like almost all settlements in New Zealand, Christchurch is vulnerable to a range of environmental hazards, including severe floods in 2014 and the Port Hills fires of 2017 (Uekusa et al. 2022). However, before 2010, public perception of the likelihood of future earthquakes was low (McClure et al. 2011). Schoolchildren in New Zealand practice earthquake drill, but the risk was not well appreciated *here*. Local earthquake tremors were not unknown, but harm was unusual and distant in time: a significant event located beneath New Brighton in 1869 in the early days of colonial settlement is lost to social memory (Elder et al. 1991). The Anglican cathedral spire was toppled not long after completion, in 1888 and again in 1901, by earthquakes in north Canterbury. On both occasions it was replaced, surviving until the spire and upper half of the tower was destroyed over a century later on 22 February 2011. Lack of awareness of the proximity of seismic danger was therefore a significant factor in engendering a sense of security in the city, even in an earthquake-prone land. But this had also long been reinforced by powerful technocratic instruments, in the form of substantial insurance cover and the requirements of a building code. These are considered next.

Technocratic security: insurance and building codes

Globally, the risk of earthquakes in urban areas is especially great around the Pacific rim, with the proto-typical examples of public sector involvement in earthquake insurance markets being in the high-income locations of Japan, California and New Zealand. Given the particularities of New Zealand's quest for security, the Canterbury earthquake sequence 'turned out to have been the most heavily insured earthquake event in history' (Nguyen and Noy 2017, 1), as well as the second biggest global insurance loss from that cause. The largest to date has been the Honshu earthquake and tsunami of March 2011, but the extent of insurance loss relative to the value of residential and commercial assets was most significant in Canterbury. Table 2.1 reveals that the proportion of economic losses covered by insurance for the three biggest episodes in the Canterbury earthquake sequence (on 22 February 2011, 4 September 2010 and 13 June 2011) was significantly higher than in large Japanese or Californian events, or those elsewhere listed amongst the world's ten costliest insured earthquakes. The table is drawn from a report by the international insurer, Marsh, three of whose staff were killed in its central

Table 2.1 World's costliest insured earthquakes

Date	*Location*	*Deaths/ missing*	*Insured losses*	*Economic losses*
11 March 2011	Japan	19 135	US$35.7 billion	US$210 billion
22 Feb 2011	**Canterbury, NZ**	**185**	**US$15.3 billion**	**US$23 billion**
17 Jan 1994	California, US	61	US$15.3 billion	US$44 billion
27 Feb 2010	Chile	562	US$8.4 billion	US$30 billion
4 Sept 2010	**Canterbury, NZ**	**-**	**US$5 billion**	**US$6.5 billion**
17 Jan 1995	Japan	6 430	US$3 billion	US$100 billion
29 May 2012	Italy	18	US$1.6 billion	US$16 billion
26 Dec 2004	Indonesia	c. 220 000	US$1 billion	US$11.2 billion
17 Oct 1989	California, US	68	US$960 million	US$10 billion
13 June 2011	**Canterbury, NZ**	**-**	**US$800 million**	**US$2 billion**

Christchurch office on the top of the Pyne Gould Corporation building when it collapsed on 22 February 2011 (Marsh 2014).

The reason is that Earthquake Commission cover is significantly more affordable than other international earthquake programmes, and is levied at a flat rate regardless of evaluated risk. It differs in this respect from those of the Japanese government and the California Earthquake Authority. The Japanese scheme provides a sum insured of only 30–50 per cent, and take-up is below 30 per cent. California's earthquake insurance is expensive coupled with relatively high levels of excess: only about 10 per cent of households participate. In Christchurch, almost all residential properties had private insurance cover, so were eligible for Earthquake Commission help. Its aggregate spending in relation to the Canterbury earthquake sequence reached about $NZ11 billion by 2016, with private insurers paying an additional $NZ4.3 billion. Modelling suggests that for 'a similar size disaster event' in Japan and California, their insurers would have spent only $NZ2.5 and $NZ1.4 billion, respectively (Nguyen and Noy 2017, 16). Noy et al. (2017, 18) describe the New Zealand scheme as 'the one successful outlier' internationally.

This comment implies that the Earthquake Commission model provided the security that citizens sought, but in reality, the outcome was quite different. The Earthquake Commission Act 1993 had 'not envisaged a sequence of events that would result in successive (and compounding) losses under single household policies' (DPMC 2017, 11). The Commission was quickly overwhelmed by the volume of claims, amounting to over 700,000 by March 2012 in respect of 160,000 damaged residential properties (about 90 per cent of the total) in and around Christchurch. This was five times larger than the Commission's prior expectation of the worst foreseeable event (King et al. 2014; also DPMC 2017; Potter et al. 2015). Government's subsequent requirement that all insurers, including the Commission, offer a repair and rebuild settlement, rather than cash payments, did nothing to speed up the process. Marsh (2014, 13), in comparing outcomes from the February 2010 earthquake in Chile, the February 2011 occurrence in Christchurch and that in March 2011 in Japan, comments that 'New Zealand was the least prepared of [the three] from an insurance perspective' (cf. Grollimund 2014). In a practical sense, this could be attributed to the fact that it had been 70 years since an earthquake had significantly affected a major urban centre.

The Earthquake Commission therefore had to quickly increase its staff from 22 to a peak of about 2200 to handle the volume of claims (King et al. 2014). There was a chronic shortage of experienced loss adjusters, as well as of building and engineering expertise. Home owner challenges to the size of settlements offered by both the Commission and private insurers proliferated, delays to settlements often took years, and even then shoddy repairs were legion (Greene 2021). A Public Inquiry was established in 2018 to establish why a landmark social insurance scheme, designed – or so it was widely believed – to secure and protect citizens from material and emotional vulnerability in the presence of earthquakes, had done anything but. The inquiry concluded that staff of the Commission 'on the whole' did their best in difficult circumstances, 'even if it may not have appeared that way to the public at the time' (Public Inquiry 2020, 7). This is the other side of the story illustrated in Table 2.1. It contrasts with Japan, where the experience of the Kobe earthquake in 1995 helped with disaster planning, such that 99 per cent of claims from the Honshu disaster were settled within 11 months (Marsh 2014; Noy et al. 2017).

For New Zealand, however, another important facet of the tension between vulnerability and security lies in how different stakeholders understand the country's building code. The code has its roots after the Hawkes Bay earthquake destroyed much of the towns of Napier and Hastings in 1931. Recommendations were made about standards of design and construction, so that buildings would better resist horizontal ground motions. Masonry structures had to be firmly bonded to move as one unit. The code was frequently revised to accommodate subsequent changes in building materials and design. There were major amendments between the late 1960s and early 1980s, with the introduction of ductility standards (how well a building will endure lateral displacements imposed by ground shaking) and overall capacity design. The code is a 'high-level performance-based document that defines the overall objectives, functional requirements and performance requirements for buildings' (Department of Building and Housing 2012, 7). It does not require specific materials, design or construction methods. The aim in a moderate earthquake is to protect the building from damage; in a severe earthquake, it is to protect life.

In the wake of the Canterbury earthquakes, structural engineers felt that there was little public understanding of this point, there being 'a disconnect between what engineers understand as "earthquake-resistant" and what clients and tenants perceive as "earthquake-resistant"' (Hare 2011, 2). This was one reason for the establishment of the Canterbury Earthquakes Royal Commission in 2011, with a focus on why two modern buildings in the city centre collapsed with considerable loss of life, and why a number of others of recent vintage were badly damaged. It is evident that there were considerable differences in expectations, as well as in interpretations of earthquakes as events. Many members of the public came to rely on estimates of earthquake severity in terms of magnitude on the Richter scale, as communicated by the Earthquake Commission's popular Geo-Net website. Structural engineers however use shaking intensity (measured on the Modified Mercalli scale) or ground acceleration. Furthermore, code requirements are minimum standards, not target levels, and are obviously social constructs. Hence the saying that 'earthquakes do not read the code': the shaking intensity on 22 February was such that 'the seismic loading was at least twice the design level for normal use buildings' (Kam et al. 2011, 272).

An important plank in the state's response to the findings of the Royal Commission (2012a) has been the Building (Earthquake-prone Buildings) Amendment Act 2016. This categorises New Zealand into three broad seismic risk areas (high, medium and low), and introduces specific timeframes for identifying and remediating buildings within each. It therefore aims to provide a more effective and consistent framework for identifying earthquake-prone buildings around the country, to better target areas of greatest risk, as well as a methodology for assessing the seismic capacity of buildings (Ministry of Business, Innovation and Employment 2017). That Canterbury would be placed in the highest risk category might have surprised many of its inhabitants before September 2010 (cf. McClure et al. 2011).

The country's first state of the environment report for example stated that 'Compared to other parts of the earthquake-prone Pacific rim ... New Zealand has a moderate frequency of earthquakes, with most no greater than 4 on the Richter scale' (Ministry for the Environment 1997, 8–15). This was illustrated by a map relating earthquakes to the line of the major Alpine Fault, which lies on the other side of the Southern Alps to Canterbury and Christchurch. New Zealand *Official Yearbooks* have been more circumspect, describing a pattern of shallow quakes which are 'responsible for almost all damage to property, and are widely scattered throughout the country', before concluding that 'it would be highly imprudent to treat any part of New Zealand as completely free from the risk of serious earthquake damage' (Department of Statistics 1990, 6). In this spirit, engineering studies in the 1990s identified the risk to buildings and underground infrastructure in Canterbury from earthquake-induced liquefaction (CAE 1997; Elder et al. 1991). But this risk was not widely appreciated and liquefaction as a concept was more or less unknown to the public before the destruction to come.

The ecology of the earthquake sequence

Any complacency about the likelihood of serious seismic incidents in the region was punctured by the lengthy first tremor at 4.35 am on 4 September 2010; it was also noisy, compared by some to the sound of an express train (Rice 2011). But there was minimal social activity in the city that early in the day, saving widespread serious injuries and probable deaths. For example, if the collapse of the loaded bookshelves (all of which were freestanding) in the University of Canterbury's library tower had occurred during opening hours, there would have been a very different outcome. Radio reports from around the city described how the earth had come alive with sand blows, or 'mud volcanoes', ground fissures and lateral spreading cracks, especially around streams, and widespread surface liquefaction (Borella et al. 2020). Sodden masses of fine silt covered driveways and streets and even partially buried cars. Ground deformation occurred both vertically and horizontally (Hughes et al. 2015). Christchurch is by no means unusual and shares a susceptibility for liquefaction with many large cities in active seismic zones around the Pacific rim, and elsewhere, such as Jakarta, Tokyo, Vancouver, San Francisco and Los Angeles (Grollimund 2014). The extent of liquefaction however was uncommon, and unprecedented in New Zealand.

The earthquake-induced shear stresses that initiated this process originated from a shallow (~10 km) seismic event on the previously unrecognised Greendale fault about 40 kilometres west of the city. This fault is one of a network beneath the Canterbury Plains that are now known link to the boundary of the Indian and Pacific tectonic plates, marked through the South Island by the Alpine Fault. Prior to 2010, it was widely assumed that, in the unlikely event of an earthquake, the cause would be from movement of this fault (which is over 150 kilometres away), or of fault lines in north Canterbury (100 kilometres distant). The identified surface rupture of the Greendale Fault extends east for almost 30 kilometres towards the satellite town of Rolleston. This was considered a short distance for generating a Mw 7.1 earthquake, so it was initially hypothesised that much of the rupture was beneath the surface, but with no evidence of it continuing beneath the city (Cubrinovski et al. 2010).

Nonetheless, a continuing pattern of aftershocks rapidly emerged closer and closer to the city (Figure 2.1). There were 400 in the next week, with ten in excess of magnitude 5, one of which was centred near the port of Lyttelton. Another one of 5.0 in early October was near the western suburb of Templeton, producing aftershocks in the eastern part of the city under New Brighton and the Avon-Heathcote estuary. The duty seismologist at GNS Science, a Crown Research Institute, sought to reassure people that although big aftershocks were possible, albeit with decreasing probability over time, 'the general trend [is] for smaller and less frequent shakes. It's quietened down considerably over the last month' (in Gorman 2010a). But on Boxing Day 2010, there was a swarm of shallow shakes directly beneath the city, 'such that the ground has barely stopped shaking for more than a few minutes at a time' (Gorman 2010b). The biggest was magnitude 4.9, with many people feeling this more strongly than the initial 4 September event, given its proximity (Rice 2011).

This was the prelude to the dangerous earthquake of 22 February 2011. That event was deadly as it happened in the middle of a working day at 12.51 pm. The epicentre was near the port of Lyttelton, a few kilometres south of the city centre, and at a depth of only five kilometres. Thousands of people, among them many tourists, were displaced amongst damaged and collapsing buildings in the business district. In the west, the University of Canterbury's

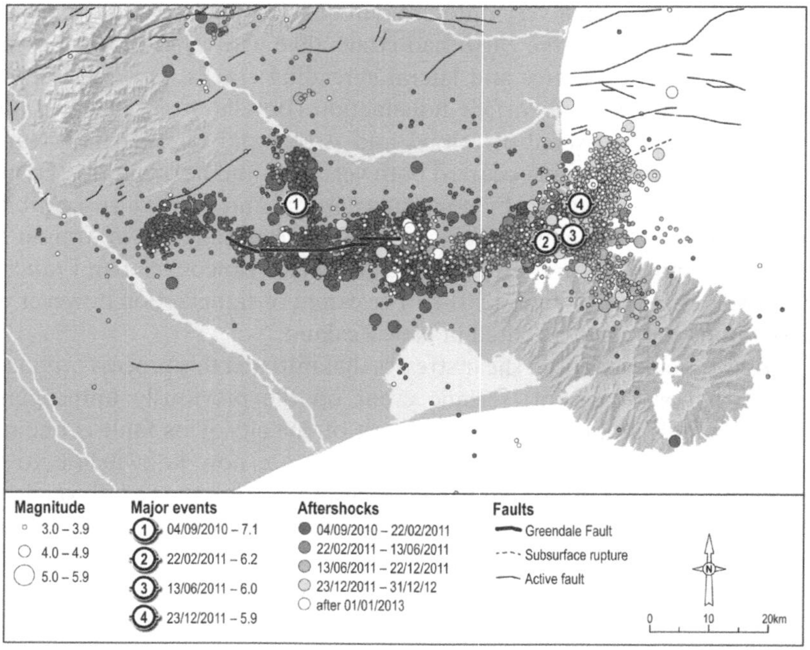

Figure 2.1 Location of epicentres in the Canterbury earthquake sequence, 2010–14.

Source: Earthquake data from Geonet (geonet.org.nz), capturing seismicity from 1 September 2010 to 31 December 2014. Fault lines from GNS Science Active Fault database (data.gns.cri.nz/af/)

campus was full of milling students on the second day of the academic year; the library, now with appropriately secured bookshelves, had just re-opened. In Brooklands, a coastal suburb, a driver described how 'the car started bouncing around heaps and throwing me around. I just … sat there watching all the liquefaction come up out of the ground. It was crazy and very scary' (*The Star* 2011, 12). Here, the water table is high, as in Kaiapoi which had been badly hit by liquefaction in September. Other places affected included eastern suburbs in the Ōtākaro Avon river corridor, and streets in the city near stream courses. Generally, the western parts of the city, on more stable gravels with a lower water table, were less affected. The spatial distribution of liquefaction (Figure 2.2) was quite similar to that anticipated in one of the earlier engineering studies (Elder et al. 1991).

If the overall extent of liquefaction was unprecedented in New Zealand, so too were other aspects of the February 2011 event. It did not fit in with the seismological prediction 'for smaller and less frequent shakes' over time. The eastern movement of seismicity had in effect displaced the release of pressure in the earth's crust amongst further previously unknown faults, triggering ongoing instability. But at magnitude 6.2, the February earthquake released far less energy than had been the case on 4 September. It was so damaging because the epicentre was shallow and under the city, even though the initial tremor lasted only ten seconds or so. Peak ground force acceleration recorded

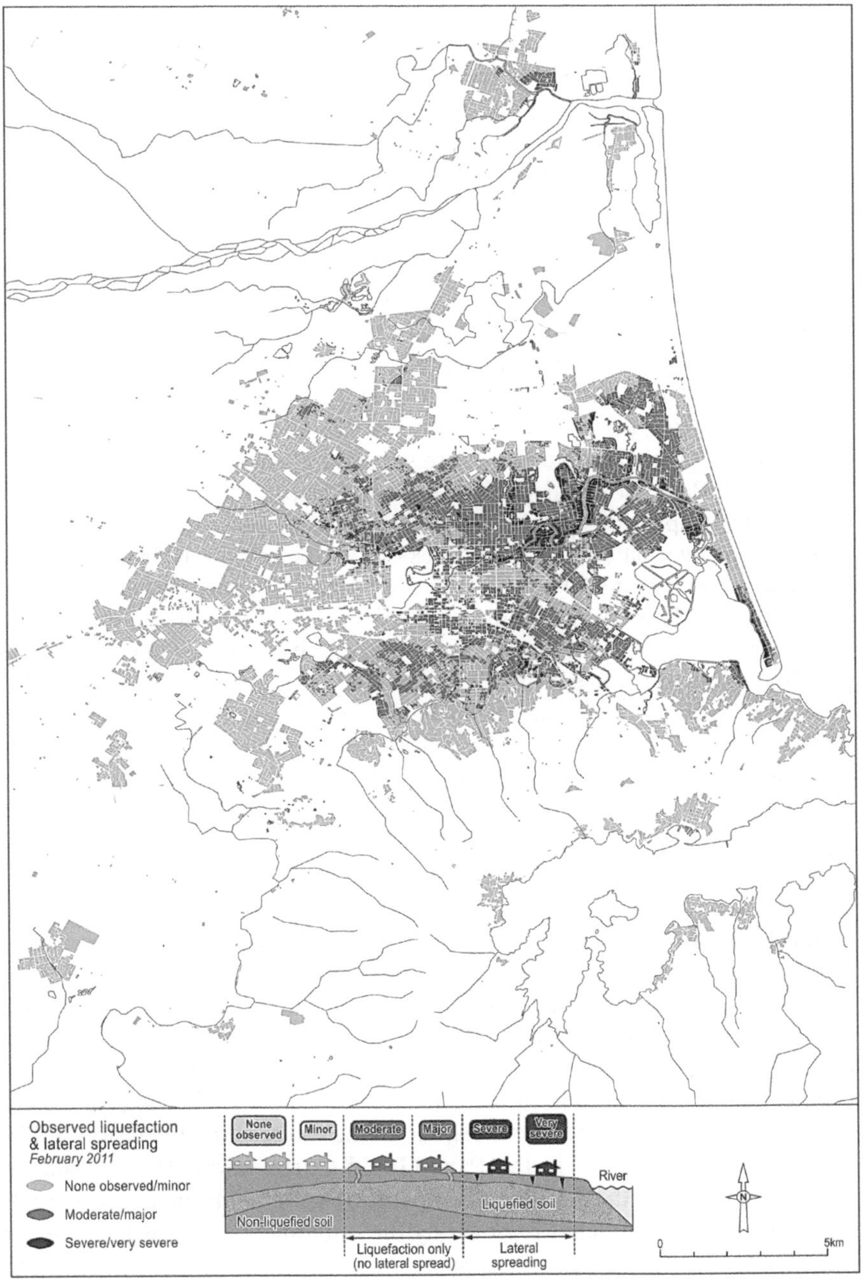

Figure 2.2 Extent of liquefaction on 22 February 2011.

Source: LINZ (2015), redrawn from Appendix A, map 4b.

that day was initially estimated at more than 2G, or twice the force of gravity, the highest recorded in New Zealand (Kaiser et al. 2012). A seismologist with the US Geological Survey claimed would make it 'among the most powerful in terms of ground-shaking acceleration on record'. By comparison, the strongest ground shaking in the 2010 Haitian earthquake was about 0.5G (Lin II and Allen 2011). There were also extensive rockfalls in the southern suburbs in the Port Hills, and dramatic collapse of both present and former sea cliffs.

The February earthquake is sometimes regarded as a separate episode, but usually as part of the aftershock sequence from September. Either way, it prolonged that sequence, with aftershocks throughout the year, gradually trending out under the ocean into Pegasus Bay (Figure 2.1). Two particularly large tremors under the Port Hills, both at magnitude 5.6, occurred on 13 June 2011, setting off further rock falls in hill and seaside suburbs. On 23 December 2011, there were two more substantial shakes of magnitudes 5.8 and 5.9 (van Ballegooy et al. 2014). The overall pattern after September 2010, along different previously unrevealed faults, was of seismic events each generating their own pattern of aftershocks. There were over 12,000 in the first two years, 3,600 being of magnitude 3 or greater, strong enough for most people to feel. This continued in subsequent years, gradually diminishing in frequency, as Figure 2.1 shows. For this reason, it is appropriate to refer (as per Chapter 1) to the event of 'the Canterbury earthquake sequence', rather than 'the' Canterbury earthquake of February 2011, or even 'the Canterbury earthquakes of 2010–11'. Neither the physical occurrences nor the social consequences were so neatly contained.

Death and destruction

The headline feature of the 22 February 2011 earthquake was the number of people killed, given its occurrence at lunchtime and the severity of the ground shaking. There was also widespread destruction of central city buildings, serious impairment of a range of underground and surface infrastructure, and extensive damage to homes (Potter et al. 2015), as the number of claims to the Earthquake Commission reveals. The death toll was 185, 169 of whom were known to have been in the central city at the time (McLean et al. 2012). But 133 people died at only two sites: 115 in the Canterbury Television (CTV) building and another 18 in the Pyne Gould Corporation (PGC) building. Claims for injury to the Accident Compensation Corporation came to nearly 7,000. The most significant reason why the outcome was not worse was the stringency of the building code designed, as discussed above, to protect life. By comparison, the mortality rate for the Kobe earthquake in Japan in 1995 was 30 times higher, despite it happening in the early hours of the morning and with lower peak ground accelerations of 0.8G (Ardagh and Deely 2018). Standing behind the Canterbury statistics however is the emotional turmoil and disempowerment stemming from coping with endless, unpredictable shocks, quite apart from ongoing contests with insurers (Hayward 2013;

Spittlehouse et al. 2014). The Prime Minister's Chief Science Advisor drew attention to the long-term psychosocial impacts of the earthquake sequence as early as May (Gluckman 2011).

Putting the impacts on human life and health to one side for the moment, the damage wrought to structures was considerable. But 'structures' are also significant experiential elements of people's lives, as homes, workplaces, social facilities and places of worship. One illustration of how widely the effects of the September 2010 earthquake were felt in homes across the city is a striking map produced from Earthquake Commission data. This locates the more than 30,000 claims for chimney or fireplace damage received by late January 2011, that is before the devastating event on 22 February that year (Figure 2.3). The pattern is fairly evenly spread across the urban area except in the newer, outer suburbs where fewer houses had chimneys. Elsewhere, brick chimneys were usually the most unyielding part of the city's typically light timber-framed homes. Many collapsed in the September earthquake,

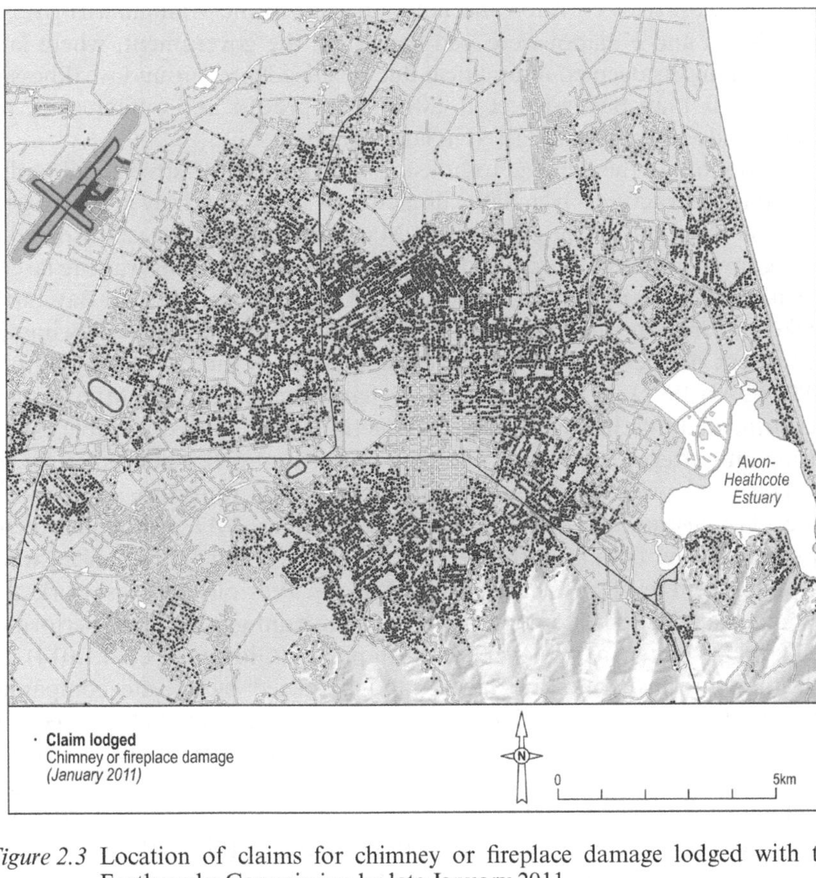

Figure 2.3 Location of claims for chimney or fireplace damage lodged with the Earthquake Commission by late January 2011.

Source: Redrawn from Rice (2011, 91).

shearing off at the roofline, sometimes falling through the roof. Others cracked nearer the ground and also needed to be removed (Rice 2011).

Liquefaction-induced damage to houses depended on location and construction type. Older homes built on timber piles, as well as more modern ones on concrete slabs, often tilted, sank or settled differentially. Lateral spreading compounded these effects (Cubrinovski et al. 2010). Sometimes the concrete slabs fractured, steel reinforcement having not previously been a requirement. Older piled houses with recent extensions on slabs suffered extensive damage at the interface (Buchanan and Newcombe 2010). Shaking-induced damage was variable, with masonry veneers more vulnerable than wooden weatherboards. Cracking to internal wall and ceiling linings was widespread, although '[l]ight timber framed buildings provided excellent life safety' (Buchanan et al. 2011, 357). There were considerable differences at street level, reflecting soil conditions as well as house type and construction. Hill suburbs were prone to rockfall and severe ground shaking in the major 2011 quakes; homes with heavy tile roofs, rather than the more common iron or colour steel sheeting, were often worst affected. Parts of the hills, the Ōtākaro Avon river corridor and land adjacent to the Waimakariri river in Brooklands and Kaiapoi were 'red zoned' by the government, where land remediation was deemed impractical due to subsidence, ground weakness or rockfall risk (van Ballegooy et al. 2014). The process and outcomes of red zone abandonment are discussed in later chapters.

Compounding the damage to housing was the state of streets and underground infrastructure. Over 1000 kilometres of urban roadway needed reconstruction (over half of the city's total). Many less damaged streets also had to be dug up to access compromised underground services. This was the largest urban lifelines disruption in a New Zealand city since the Hawkes Bay earthquake of 1931, but the impact was reduced due to work done following the assessment of the vulnerability of those lifelines in the city since the mid-1990s (CAE 1997). In 2002, the Civil Defence and Emergency Management Act stipulated that lifelines be able to function to 'the fullest possible extent' during and after an emergency. Seismic protection work undertaken by the local electric power distribution company enabled it to restore service to 90 per cent of customers within ten days of 22 February 2011, although at a cost ten times greater than after the September 2010 and June 2011 quakes, when the 90 per cent level was achieved within a day. Previous lifelines' work also ensured that the 180-kilometre liquefied petroleum gas network performed well, and far better than in overseas earthquakes (Giovinazzi et al. 2014).

Both power networks are owned and managed by private companies, whereas the city's water and wastewater networks are publicly owned and managed. Parts of these networks are considerably older than those of the utilities, made of earthenware clay pipes susceptible to breakages, which then filled with liquefaction. Although water supply to homes was restored relatively quickly after the September 2010 earthquake, this took more than a month after the February and June 2011 episodes for properties in severely compromised districts. Wastewater pipes were similarly badly affected and by

August 2011, about 800 houses still required repairs to their private sewer pipes to be fully functional (Giovinazzi et al. 2014). In the weeks after 22 February 2011, the city council distributed over 40,000 chemical toilets to households in need, mostly in the eastern suburbs. More than 2,000 portable toilets ('portaloos') were placed on streets, although there was much frustration over the equity of distribution (Heather 2011a; Potangaroa et al. 2011). Months of intrusive disruption to daily routines for those people in the worst affected areas only added to emotional stress.

Although very real, damage to homes and suburbs was less dramatic than that to the city centre. Here seismic shaking 'significantly exceeded the 500-year return period design level' of the current building code (Kam et al. 2011, 240). The age and construction of buildings were key factors in their fate. Almost half of the total central city building stock was built prior to the introduction of modern seismic codes in the 1970s, although this included a lot of residential buildings of mixed ages, as the inner area of the city is very spread out. But the risk posed by older commercial and public central city buildings had long been recognised. In a 1996 TV programme called 'Earthquakes!', the city council's then buildings engineer said to the camera 'Your heritage list, to be quite cruel, defines most of your earthquake-prone buildings'. He pointed to problems with older two or three-storey structures in the main retail area. A lot of dangerous parapets had been removed, but the standards to which such buildings were held were a fraction of those applying to more modern ones (Dixon Productions 2011).

Some significant masonry heritage buildings had however been seismically strengthened, although with differing outcomes. For example, the Victorian Gothic Canterbury Museum survived in February 2011 reasonably unscathed, but not the Anglican Cathedral, built in the same style and period. Others that had not been strengthened at all, such as the remarkable stone chamber of the Provincial Government Buildings of 1865, collapsed completely, as did the west end of the neoclassical Catholic Cathedral (finished in 1906), which had been partially strengthened. These were perhaps the two finest heritage buildings in the city (Ansley 2011). Old masonry facades on retail streets that were barely connected to the Victorian brick boxes behind them also disintegrated: eight people died when they were crushed in buses beneath falling masonry. The two deadliest buildings however were products of the 1960s and 1980s, respectively: the PGC and CTV buildings.

The Royal Commission (2012a) was charged with investigating why some buildings failed totally and why buildings differed in the extent of failure. Volumes 2 and 6 of its final report, which cover the PGC and CTV cases, are particularly valuable from a social perspective as they contain accounts from those who were rescued and tributes for those who died. The PGC building was designed to codes of practice used in the 1960s, before ductile performance was a consideration. On 22 February, the building underwent shaking 'that was almost certainly several times more intense than the capacity of the structure to resist it'. But 'neither foundation instability nor liquefaction was a factor in the collapse' (Royal Commission 2012b, 38). David Sandeman, an

Figure 2.4 David Sandeman and Jeff McLay celebrating their rescue from the PGC building on 22 February 2011.

Credit: Stuff Limited.

employee of Marsh, was on the fourth floor when the tremor started and found himself 'plunging down. I estimate it was about forty feet as we ended up on the first floor as I subsequently discovered' (Royal Commission 2012b, 36). The photograph of his later rescue alongside a colleague became one of the defining images of that day (Figure 2.4).

Like the PGC building, the CTV building had multiple tenancies, which included (apart from Canterbury Television) health providers and an English language school. This is why a large number of overseas nationals lost their lives there. The Royal Commission pointed to 'a building design that was deficient in a number of important respects' (2012c, 302), but again found that ground conditions were not a factor. It concluded that a building permit should not have been issued 'because the design did not comply with the [city council's] building bylaw' (2012c, 303). The building pancaked within 10 to 20 seconds of the onset of the earthquake, followed by a fire that burned for some days. 'It was a sudden and catastrophic collapse' (2012c, 307), the most acute example of building failure during the extreme ground motions of the 22 February earthquake. But many other buildings, even if they did not cost lives, were too seriously compromised that day to remain, or became uneconomic to repair once the extent of damage became apparent (Marsh 2014). Eventually, as shown in Chapter 6, about 70 per cent of the central city's building stock had been demolished (Bennett et al. 2012; McLean et al. 2012).

Rapid disaster response

The scale of the disaster and need for resources mobilised at and beyond the national level prompted a Declaration of National Emergency on 23 February 2011, the first time this measure had been used under the Civil Defence and Emergency Management Act of 2002 (DPMC 2017). It remained the only such declaration until 25 March 2020 at the onset of the coronavirus epidemic. Response to the September 2010 earthquake had been managed as a 'regional emergency'; most civil defence emergencies, which in New Zealand usually concern flooding or severe weather, are declared at local or regional levels (Civil Defence 2020). Although such declarations are civil defence management tools, many other organisations, groups and individuals were involved in rapid response in the hours, days and weeks that followed the major episodes in the Canterbury earthquake sequence.

The headquarters for the Civil Defence operation, or 'Christchurch Response Centre', was established in the city's relatively new downtown Art Gallery (completed in 2003). This served as the coordination hub for the response for up to 500 personnel until it was necessary to move two months later due to damage to the building. The emergency response effort initially focused on the city centre as it was the locus of death, injury and visible building damage. The subsequent civil defence review identified a lack of 'situational awareness' at the Response Centre about what was happening elsewhere around the city, a charge echoed from the Ngāi Tahu tribal organisation (Solomon 2021). It also recognised the need for 'clear and unambiguous' identification in emergency planning of lines of responsibility for incident control at particular disaster sites (McLean et al. 2012, 39). This was the consequence of the range of emergency services involved, including police, fire and ambulance, as well as volunteers, all soon joined by urban search and rescue teams (USAR) from around the country and overseas, as well as defence force personnel. It was fortuitous that at the time there was a major joint defence training exercise underway around the city, as part of which the naval vessel HMNZS Canterbury was in port at Lyttelton.

Christchurch hospital however did have a clear major incident plan, covering both internal incidents (those that impair the ability to provide the services expected) and external incidents (which generate overwhelming demand for those services). As the building was damaged, and there were immediate needs to overcome issues with power, water and sewerage provision, managers oversaw the internal incident response whilst emergency department medical staff attended to the external incident. The President of the Royal College of Surgeons of Edinburgh, who witnessed this (having been in the city for a conference, and attending the hospital with his injured wife), subsequently wrote that 'I am in little doubt that many more people would have died in the hospital that day without the skill and leadership displayed in the Emergency Department' (in Ardagh and Deely 2018, 82). After an initial rush of patients, arrivals slowed as those who had been released from being trapped in damaged buildings trickled in.

The search for survivors in damaged and collapsed buildings was carried out at first by emergency services and members of the public, until joined by the search and rescue teams. New Zealand had three such specialist teams, based in Christchurch, Palmerston North and Auckland, with about 50 personnel each from the fire service, and including medics, engineers and specialist search dogs. They were joined by international USAR teams from Australia, China, Japan, Taiwan, Singapore, the United States and the United Kingdom (McLean et al. 2012). Their origins reflected affective ties, countries in earthquake-prone areas with the necessary capabilities, and the places that people trapped in collapsed buildings were known to be from. The Japanese team, which like those from Australia and Singapore, also brought search dogs, was allocated to the CTV building as there were many Japanese students in the language school that had occupied level 4. In addition, 20 trained volunteer response teams from Christchurch and around the country joined the search and rescue operation. Some of these had also deployed during the September earthquake, when one of their tasks, apart from carrying out initial building inspections and cordoning unsafe areas, was to assist in the dismantling of residential chimneys (Seager and Donnell 2013; Figure 2.3).

Within a few hours of the 22 February event, a cordon was established around the central business district by members of the Defence Force and police, to protect people from falling debris and to secure the area once vacated. The cordon was initially set up with manned checkpoints at road access points, but within days a continuous physical barrier had been erected (illustrated in Chapter 6). Defence force members were to remain at the cordon for more than a year; the cordon itself lasted far longer, although shrinking over time as city blocks were rendered safe through demolition and clearance. In the port town of Lyttelton, which was very close to the epicentre of the earthquake and had many older masonry buildings, the response was led by local community groups, underpinned by the resources of HMNZS Canterbury, which provided meals for the 1000 people left homeless in the town (McLean et al. 2012). Coincidentally, during the 1931 Hawkes Bay earthquake, it was sailors from HMS Veronica – a ship in the New Zealand Division of the Royal Navy – who had provided much of the early response on the ground when in port at Napier (Wright 2001).

The subsequent civil defence response review briefly records the ways in which social organisations, the police and spontaneous volunteer groups worked together in the worst affected suburbs. 'Overall', it concluded, 'the resilience of the community was remarkable' (McLean et al. 2012, 175). The Lyttelton example was not alone. The south-eastern coastal suburbs of Redcliffs and Sumner, effectively isolated by rockfalls, self-organised with the volunteer fire brigade and volunteer coastguard taking the lead, supported by local police. In the review they stated that they 'had practically no contact with the Christchurch Response Centre until some weeks after the event' (McLean et al. 2012, 182); similar experiences were reported from other hill and harbour suburbs. In the eastern coastal suburb of New Brighton, the response was led by local police with 'some 60,000 people … fed out of local community-led distribution centres' (McLean et al. 2012, 71), aided by members of the defence force, the Farmy Army and the Student Volunteer Army.

If one feature above all came to symbolise the Canterbury earthquake response, it was the thousands of volunteers who joined the Farmy and Student Volunteer Armies. Both initially formed at the time of the September 2010 earthquake: the first by Federated Farmers, as rural as well as urban areas were badly affected in that event; the second by university students (Hayward 2013). One of their major roles then and in February was in clearing liquefaction, particularly around people's homes, checking on residents' welfare and distributing food. The Student Army was also tasked with delivering information sheets in affected suburbs, and assembling portaloos for placement in streets (which arrived as flat packs from the United States in early March). The review observed that civil defence planning had not taken into account how to embed such large-scale volunteering, but that 'a key learning was that … management must be left with the [volunteer] group' (McLean et al. 2012, 182). It also observed that next to no use was made of social media in the emergency response, with the exception of the Student Army, which was mobilised every time there was a need through Facebook. The social significance of this organisation in earthquake recovery is assessed in Chapter 7.

Conclusion

This chapter has outlined some of the key contours of the Canterbury earthquake sequence as a socio-seismic event series. In strictly seismic terms, none of the tremors were especially large, but globally they are amongst the costliest earthquake events (Table 2.1), due to their proximity to the city of Christchurch, and very high levels of residential and commercial insurance. The sequence also did not accord with scientific expectations of a major shock, followed by a diminishing, if erratic series of aftershocks. Instead, it was prolonged as pressure release in the earth's crust was displaced eastward beneath the city through a previously unrecognised network of faults. A great deal of damage was caused in the city centre by high ground-shaking acceleration during the quake of 22 February 2011, even though this was quite short in duration. Elsewhere in the city, but especially in the eastern suburbs, in each major event, the ground came alive as liquefied materials were ejected from beneath the surface, smashing foundations and underground infrastructure.

A number of significant social themes have been highlighted. Ironically, this turned out to be a city that has been far more vulnerable than the technocratic framework of property insurance and building codes led many to expect. In fact, in terms of the model of recovery presented in Figure 1.2, insurance disputes have often greatly extended the trauma of the original quakes. And even if the potential for liquefaction was not widely appreciated, it was known about; those utility providers that had acted on this knowledge were able to restore power and communications networks quickly. Likewise, elements of the first response were well prepared, even if a lack of situational awareness at the Christchurch Response Centre meant that community networks, civic organisations and spontaneous volunteer mass mobilisation had to take ownership of recovery in different places. The extent to which 'the resilience of the community was remarkable', as the later Civil Defence review claimed, is a theme addressed in the next chapter.

3 Impacts on households and communities

Introduction

The earthquakes played out across a socially uneven urban landscape, affecting neighbourhoods with differing levels of material, financial and political resources. Within this context, this chapter considers the impacts on households and communities. It outlines some common aspects of the immediate experience of the quakes, then focuses on key processes that ensued, such as departures (where residents voluntarily or involuntarily left their homes and neighbourhoods, for shorter or longer periods) as well as the compensating arrivals of migrant workers to assist with the city's repair and reconstruction. The land zoning decisions and insurance settlements are then examined, with their impacts illustrated through a consideration of residents' experiences in the coastal suburb of Southshore. This leads to a consideration of psychosocial well-being, and the increased incidence of anxiety and depression across the city, which occurred to differing degrees for different groups. The quakes also prompted novel expressions of mutual aid at the community and neighbourhood level as people reached out to assist others. Along with broader welfare initiatives across the city, these expressions of support and care generally promoted recovery, as well as contributing to local resilience.

A differentiated urban landscape: patterns and movements

As is common to most modern cities, the urban landscape of Christchurch is socially and economically differentiated. In broad terms, there is a northwest-to-southeast gradient of affluence, with neighbourhoods in the west and northwest of the city having higher than average household incomes and property values. House prices and household income generally decrease as one moves south and east from the city centre. This trend continues until the hill suburbs (eg. Cashmere and Mt Pleasant) are reached, where household incomes and housing values increase, gradually around the bottom of the hills and then more rapidly on the hills themselves. The resulting socio-economic differentiation of the urban landscape can be seen in the patterning of social deprivation. Figure 3.1, which represents census area units in terms of their average score for the 2018 New Zealand Deprivation index, a composite

DOI: 10.4324/9780429275562-4

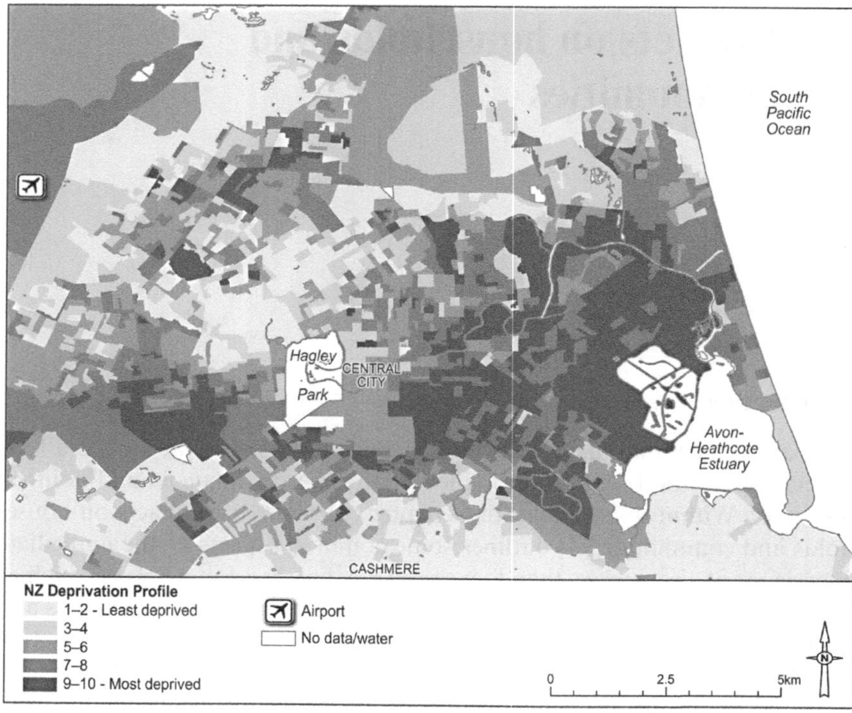

Figure 3.1 Socio-economic deprivation in Christchurch.

Source: https://ehinz.ac.nz/indicators/population-vulnerability/socioeconomic-deprivation-profile/

indicator of social deprivation, is indicative. Lighter tones here indicate more affluent areas while the darker tones depict more deprived areas. The concentration of relative deprivation in the eastern suburbs is evident.

The earthquakes intersected with this patterned landscape in ways that at times compounded already existing socio-economic disadvantage. Although residential damage occurred across the city, homes and buildings in the west and northwest – except those close to streams – were generally less affected than those in the east, where more extensive liquefaction and lateral spreading damaged both houses and subsurface infrastructure. Many eastern neighbourhoods had above-average levels of social deprivation, and the disruption of the earthquakes often contributed to additional hardship. As has been evident in other post-disaster cities (eg. New Orleans), a number of these eastern communities subsequently felt neglected by government recovery organisations, to the extent that they formed a range of protest and advocacy groups (as discussed in Chapter 10). In the hill suburbs, a significant number of properties suffered damage from shaking and some were impacted by rockfall. In financial terms, however, many of these households were relatively affluent, with their owners well positioned financially to find alternative accommodation during the repair or reconstruction of their homes. Their financial resources assisted them to deal with the impacts of material loss.

As signalled in the previous chapter, the 22 February 2011 earthquake was experienced in diverse ways, and of all the episodes in the Canterbury earthquake sequence, it was the most significant given its daytime occurrence and location beneath the city itself. In the city centre, the initial event and aftershocks were strongly felt, and many people sought to shelter – if they could – underneath suitable protective structures. After the intensity of shaking subsided, workers spilled out onto the streets, keeping their distance from potentially precarious masonry facades, and taking in what had happened. When two of the authors walked into the central city that afternoon, they were met by hundreds of people leaving on foot, including many in business attire, along with tourists and school students. Some individuals appeared shocked. Most were quiet and seemed focused, presumably on getting home. A few were talking to each other. In the centre itself, there was a considerable amount of dust from damaged buildings and cracked roadways. Intermittent car and building alarms could be heard, mixing with the distant sirens of emergency services vehicles. Alongside the tragic deaths and thousands of physical injuries, a number of people were successfully rescued that day from damaged buildings. However, many would live with a degree of ongoing trauma as a result of their experiences (Hunt 2021a).

The usual rhythms of activity and connection in the city were abruptly altered that afternoon. With most traffic lights no longer functioning, many streets became progressively gridlocked as large numbers of people attempted to return to their homes by car. As the cellular telephone network had been damaged, voice calls generally were not possible and even text messages were not a reliable means of communication. Messages often arrived out of sequence, significantly delayed or not at all. This impaired people's ability to contact family and loved ones, heightening the sense of emergency and logistical disruption. Many people were only reunited with their families and neighbours several hours later that day.

There were also longer-term population movements, however, particularly in response to the 22 February quake. In the weeks following, large numbers of individuals and households left Christchurch, either temporarily (for relief from aftershocks, or while short-term repairs were made on their homes) or on a longer-term basis (if substantive repairs or rebuilding were required, or if the circumstances were simply too overwhelming). The water and sewage systems in parts of the city were heavily damaged, and many residents in the eastern suburbs in particular lacked access to potable water or a working toilet for weeks if not months. Around 15 per cent (55,000 people) of the city's population is estimated to have left in the first week after 22 February, with women and families with young children over-represented in these departures (Newell et al. 2012). Postal redirection data also indicates substantial medium-term population movements in the immediate aftermath, with around 20,000 households redirecting their mail to other addresses within the city, and around 5,000 households to an address outside of Christchurch (Price 2011). The highest levels of long-term outmigration were from the eastern suburbs (Begg et al. 2021) – including neighbourhoods such as Avonside, Dallington and Richmond – where many houses had been rendered uninhabitable or were later subject to 'red zoning' (a government process of encouraged departure, as elaborated below). The majority of those departing moved elsewhere in New Zealand or to places in Australia (Adams-Hutcheson 2015; Campbell 2014; He et al. 2021).

In the 2013 census, the population of the Christchurch city was 341,469. This was an approximately two per cent decrease from the 2006 census population of 348,456, but a more significant 8.4 per cent fall (31,131) from the June 2009 estimate of 372,600 (Christchurch City Council 2010a). By 2018, however, the city's population had risen to 369,006, representing an increase of 8.1 per cent on the 2013 figure. A sizeable proportion of this growth reflected an influx of migrant workers that arrived in response to employment opportunities in the construction and building industries (How and Kerr 2019). Irish, English, Filipino and Australian workers were favoured by rebuild contractors, and in 2014, the majority of migrant workers in Christchurch came from the United Kingdom (25 per cent), Ireland (25 per cent) and the Philippines (20 per cent) (How and Kerr 2019; Searle et al. 2015). Given the extensive damage to the city centre and urban environment more generally, however, domestic and international tourism to the city fell significantly, and there were significant job losses among accommodation providers, cafes and restaurants (How and Kerr 2019).

Land zoning and insurance claims

As people grappled with the immediate material and psychosocial impacts of the February 2011 earthquake, central government was developing its recovery strategy. Elements of this strategy drew on the work of the Ministry of Civil Defence and Emergency in response to the September 2010 earthquake. In March 2011, central government established the Canterbury Earthquake Recovery Authority (CERA), whose responsibilities and remit were defined in the Canterbury Earthquake Recovery Act 2011. In essence, this organisation was tasked with overseeing and facilitating the recovery process on behalf of the Crown. With headquarters in Christchurch, one of its initial actions was to instruct a number of geotechnical engineering firms to undertake assessments of residential land across the city, so as to determine the extent of the damage from the February 2011 quake. In a sequence of announcements throughout 2011 and 2012, with the first on 24 June 2011, parcels of residential land across the city were designated as being either 'green zone' (suitable for ongoing occupation, and repair and rebuild of homes) or 'red zone' (unsuitable for ongoing occupation). In line with the criteria developed by CERA (New Zealand Government 2011), residential land was red-zoned if one or more of the following conditions held: there was significant and extensive area-wide land damage from liquefaction or rockfall; there was high risk of further damage to land and buildings from low-levels of shaking; the success of engineering solutions was considered to be uncertain and uneconomic; and any repair to the land would be disruptive and protracted.

Alongside these green and red zones – which encompassed the great majority of properties – the initial land zoning announcement in 2011 also included two temporary 'in process' categories. These were orange-zoned residential land, where further geotechnical and engineering assessment was needed, and white-zoned land, for hill properties where the risk of rock fall required further investigation. It took several years to complete the necessary further investigations, but by November 2014 the orange- and white-zoned land had all been re-categorised as either green or red zone.

The Crown expected houses on red-zoned land to be vacated, within a set of published timeframes, and facilitated by an offer of financial compensation. In contrast, households on green-zoned land were able to stay. The green-zoned land was divided into three 'technical categories': TC1 (where the land condition meant that house repair and rebuilding was considered unproblematic), TC2 (where repair and rebuilding could occur, although the land might have some liquefaction-related damage and settling) and TC3 (where repair and rebuilding was permitted, but site-specific geotechnical investigations were required, to determine what sort of foundations would be needed to compensate for the damaged land) (Christchurch City Council nd.). The TC3 land presented a challenge for homeowners whose properties needed extensive rebuilding or repair, as such work typically required either land remediation or, more commonly, deeper foundations, as a structural compensation for the compromised state of the land. The need for specialised and site-specific foundations typically added significantly to the cost of rebuilding, and there was some indication that this depressed the resale values of homes on TC3 land, as a form of zoning-related 'stigma' (McDonald 2013a).

Red-zoned land was concentrated along the Ōtākaro Avon river corridor, encompassing several eastern suburbs, as well as sections of several hill suburbs (both on the city and Lyttelton Harbour sides), and the western edge of the coastal suburb of Southshore (Figure 3.2). Significant areas of Kaiapoi, a small satellite town some 20 kilometres to the north of Christchurch, as well as coastal Brooklands, were also red-zoned. In view of the unsuitability of this red-zoned land for ongoing residential occupation – and given the Crown's liability through the Earthquake Commission for residential damage that might be caused by future earthquakes – the government made insured householders in these areas an offer of financial compensation in June 2011. The Crown would acquire either the house and land, as a package, or just the land (leaving owners to deal with selling or removing their houses independently). These offers were based on 2007/8 property valuations and owners were given nine months to decide whether or not they would accept the offer (CERA 2011; New Zealand Government 2011).

Responses to the Crown's red zone offers varied. Some homeowners contested the valuations, particularly when substantial home renovations or additions had been undertaken since 2007 (as the value of these improvements was not recognised in the financial offer). A proportion of red-zoned residents protested the more general requirement to surrender their homes

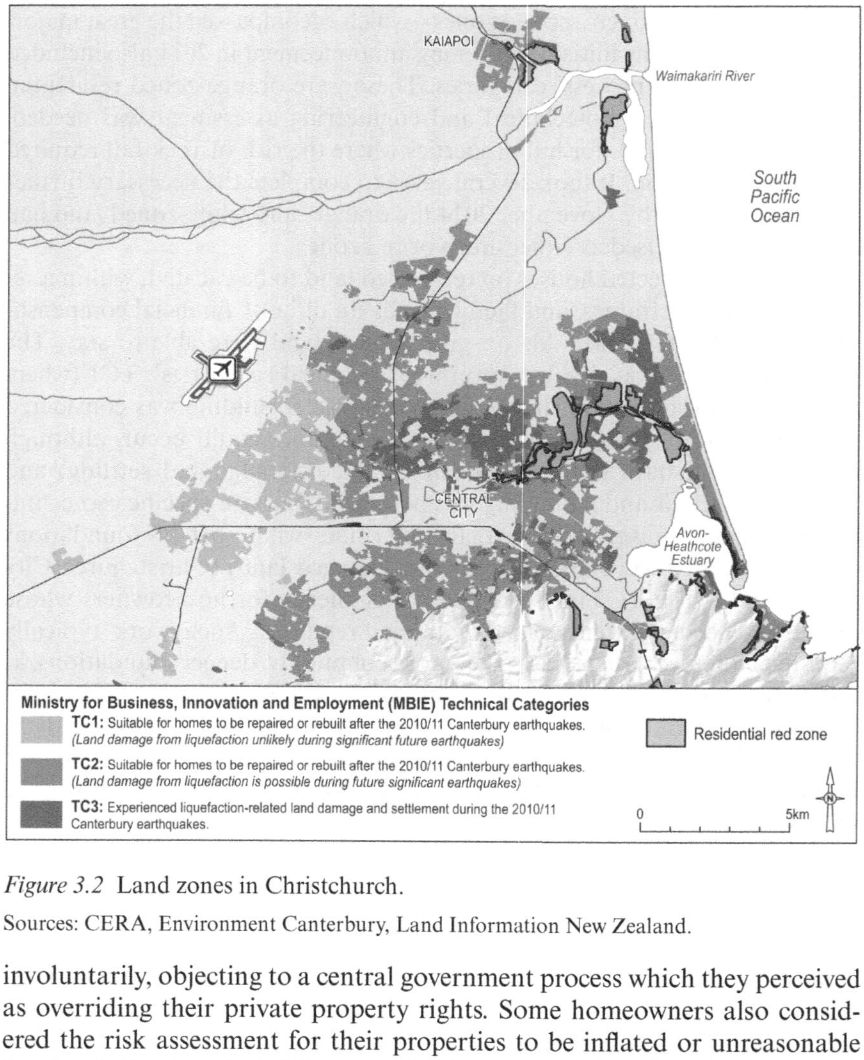

Figure 3.2 Land zones in Christchurch.

Sources: CERA, Environment Canterbury, Land Information New Zealand.

involuntarily, objecting to a central government process which they perceived as overriding their private property rights. Some homeowners also considered the risk assessment for their properties to be inflated or unreasonable (eg. in relation to vulnerability to rockfall in some of the hills suburbs), which amounted to disputing the validity of the technical assessment underlying the red zoning decision. Finally, a small number of households chose to stay on their land, declining to leave (Heather 2011b; Matthews 2012).

Despite these misgivings, by December 2015, 96 per cent (7,720) of the 8,060 red-zoned properties in Christchurch and nearby Kaiapoi had accepted the Crown offer (Nielsen 2016). These households vacated their properties and land by February 2016. From 2012 onwards, the Crown demolished houses and any outbuildings as they were vacated. A small number of houses were sold separately from the land, and then transported off-site (often after being cut into pieces to make this possible). This acquisition-demolition process generated extensive areas of open land in the suburbs along the Ōtākaro-Avon river, as well as smaller pockets in Kaiapoi, Brooklands and the hill suburbs. The appropriate ongoing uses of this red-zoned land then became the subject of sustained discussion and debate within the city (as discussed in Chapter 12).

Alongside the land zoning, the negotiation of insurance settlements was a central dimension of the experience of the earthquakes for many people in Christchurch. As noted in the previous chapter, New Zealand operates a dual public-private system of insurance against environmental disasters. All homeowners with a private insurance policy are automatically charged a small levy (a percentage of the annual policy premium), which contributes to the insurance funds for the government Earthquake Commission. When a house is damaged as a result of an environmental disaster – such as an earthquake, flood or fire – the government covers the first $NZ100,000 of the repair and rebuilding costs. Any work over this 'cap' becomes the responsibility of the private insurer. This dual scheme effectively means that the state takes on a portion of the risk associated with living in a seismically active country. For private sector insurers, the government's commitment also makes entry into New Zealand's relatively small market a less financially risky prospect. Although it has some benefits, the dual system also meant that many Christchurch earthquake claims required complex multi-party negotiations between homeowners, the Earthquake Commission and private insurers (Miles 2016).

The timely and fair settlement of insurance claims became a central point of contention for many Christchurch residents (King et al. 2014; Miles 2016; Potter et al. 2015). Earthquake Commission and private insurer assessors often reached different conclusions about the extent of damage at a given property and thus the repairs needed. There is some evidence that such disputes were more common for claims around the $NZ100,000 boundary, when private insurers had the motivation to assess a claim as being below the 'cap', as the financial and also logistical responsibility for settling the claim would then fall to the Earthquake Commission (King et al. 2014). Many homeowners found themselves caught up in estimation disputes, after receiving the Earthquake Commission or private insurance settlement offers that in their view under-estimated the damage and likely cost of repairs. Multiple rounds of assessment were sometimes undertaken at a single property, sometimes by different assessors, who on occasion evaluated the scope of damage differently than their colleagues, introducing additional variability to an already complex process (Miles 2016).

Although many homes were eventually repaired using insurance proceeds from either government and/or private sources, there were complaints about the quality of the work undertaken, particularly when it was managed by the Earthquake Commission (with some repairs then having to be 'redone') (King et al. 2014; Poontirakul et al. 2017). Some homeowners believed construction companies were cutting corners during the building process in order to finish a project quickly and more profitably (He et al. 2021). The general shortage of suitable workers meant construction companies were at times forced to hire general labourers for repair work, who might not possess the specific skills required (Wilkinson and Chang-Richards 2016). In 2018, the government commissioned a public enquiry into the Earthquake Commission's handling of claims from the Canterbury earthquakes. The final report identified major failings in the Earthquake Commission practices, noting that 'shortcomings in its performance resulted in unacceptable stress, distress and delays in some people's recovery and repair of their homes' (Public Inquiry 2020, 8). At the same time, and while not excusing its failings, the report included some recognition of the difficult post-disaster context in which the organisation was forced to operate. This point can be illustrated with a case study of the coastal suburb of Southshore.

The case of Southshore

The intersection of land zoning and insurance settlement processes was a significant determinant of the recovery trajectory both of individual households – which might be insured with a different company than their immediate neighbours – and of entire suburbs across the city. The suburb of Southshore, a lower socio-economic community based along a narrow coastal spit in the east of the city, was particularly affected by these overlapping processes. The coastal spit, which runs almost north-south in orientation, is bordered by water on both sides, with an extensive river estuary on its western edge and the Pacific Ocean on the eastern side (Figure 1.1).

With approximately 600 households, Southshore was distinctive in that its properties were assigned to no less than three land zone categories: red, TC3 and TC2. The zones took the form of strips that ran longitudinally down the coastal spit, effectively dividing the suburb into three spatially demarcated household groups: those expected to leave (red-zoned), those where the land required further geotechnical investigations before any repairs could be undertaken (TC3), and those permitted to stay and repair their homes without any further investigations into their land (TC2). Although precise numbers were not publicly available, there were likely 200–250 households in each of these categories. In research undertaken in 2012 and 2013, a non-random sample of 20 households from each of these three zones completed a structured survey followed by a semi-structured interview. Although indicative rather than representative, this work offered a window onto the experiences, thoughts and feelings of Southshore residents regarding the zoning process (Conradson 2012; Dickinson 2013).

The government's land zoning announcements, as noted earlier, proceeded in stages rather than all at once for the entire city. The incremental nature of these announcements was of particular significance for Southshore. The first locally specific announcement occurred on 29 October 2011, when around 250 Southshore households were designated as being on green TC2 land. Most of the residents interviewed in this zone expressed a sense of relief that they were able to stay in Southshore, and that they could move forward with their repairs and rebuilding. Some also experienced a sense of guilt or reluctance to enjoy this outcome, however, as there were other households in the community still facing uncertainty while they awaited a zoning decision.

As one resident put it, 'I'm absolutely thrilled. But I can't celebrate until there's better news for everyone in the area'. As TC2 was the first land zoning category announced in Southshore, this group of residents had the shortest wait and the longest period in which to formulate their 'next steps'. The reduction in uncertainty was conducive to improved mental well-being, as found in other areas of the city (Greaves et al. 2015; Morgan et al. 2015). That said, a few of the TC2 households interviewed were sufficiently perturbed by their experience of the earthquakes that they had decided to move outside of Christchurch altogether, to places they considered to be more seismically stable and thus less likely to be disrupted. As 'green zoners' they had the opportunity to implement such intentions, in stark contrast to their subsequently designated TC3 neighbours (where the need for further investigations prevented any house sales that would enable quick departure) or red zoners (where leaving was essentially an involuntary matter, irrespective of one's preference for leaving or staying) (Conradson 2012).

At the time of the local green zone announcement (i.e. 29 October 2011), the rest of Southshore was placed into a 'to be determined' category. These households were then subject to several months of waiting, as well as more than one extension to the initially promised timeframes for a decision. In a letter to 401 households of 'west Southshore' in March 2012, the Minister for Earthquake Recovery, Gerry Brownlee, described the zoning determinations for the area as among 'the most difficult and challenging' in the city, given the complexity of the land damage it had experienced (Mann 2012). As the land damage varied along the western edge of the coastal spit, any uniform zoning categorisation would inevitably do some injustice to that on-the-ground variability. At the same time, a highly variegated zoning assessment with differentiated outcomes for individual and often adjacent properties would likely have provoked significant community dissatisfaction, potentially unleashing a deluge of correspondence and litigation.

In May 2012, the government announced it would red zone around 200 Southshore properties, all on the suburb's western estuarine edge. As well as the land damage, this decision took into account the subsidence in the southern part of the estuary, in the order of 0.3 to 0.5 metres (Environment Canterbury 2011). Among the affected households, some residents spoke of the psychological relief of 'going red', as it enabled them to move from a prolonged state of 'not knowing' to a position of increased clarity and freedom to act. One man explained that he was 'delighted to be in the red. I can't be doing with all this indecision', while a woman cheerfully noted that 'we broke open the champagne!' At the same time, several red-zoned interviewees recognised that leaving Southshore would disrupt their local friendships and connections, many of which were longstanding. The involuntary and disorienting nature of being red-zoned was often remarked upon:

> I am not happy at all. I have no idea what to do. Life is upside down. All my friends can stay, but we have to go. It is a strange story. We want to stay; they want to go. … I don't want to leave.

Still others expressed confusion about the red zoning decision, particularly when it did not appear to correlate with the housing damage they could observe:

> I have no idea what it is based on. If you go five metres down the road, they have turned green [ie. the property had been green zoned]. It doesn't make sense to me. My house is not that badly damaged.

Such a response highlights the challenging nature of accepting the outcomes of a zoning process that was based in part on an assessment of the likelihood of *future* land damage in the event of further earthquakes. The currently visible damage to a resident's house might well not be a good indication of this future liability, and this was understandably perplexing for some. In a few cases, homeowners who shared the same driveway received different land zone decisions, intensifying such confusion (Conradson 2012; Dickinson 2013).

Around 200 Southshore households were zoned TC3, and these residents experienced particular challenges. Although their land was considered habitable, it was also vulnerable to future quake-induced liquefaction and lateral spreading. Any substantial house repairs or rebuilds therefore required the construction of special foundations, individually designed for each house to compensate for the particular characteristics of its parcel of land. As demand for geotechnical expertise across the city significantly exceeded the supply of qualified engineers, the geotechnical investigations needed to determine the required foundations often took many months, and this slowed the process of household recovery on TC3 land (Greenhill 2013). In fact, many TC3 residents in Southshore complained of having no clear timeframes for the completion of their geotechnical investigations or repairs, which contributed to a sense of being 'in limbo'. Some were envious of the clear settlement timeframes their red-zoned neighbours had received, while others were uncertain whether their homes would be insurable in the future (Conradson 2012).

For people living in Southshore, the land zoning process thus had a major impact on their well-being and life trajectories. The government decisions compounded the material disruption from the quakes. As one Southshore resident explained:

> The earthquake was only the first catastrophe. What happened afterwards … the way it was handled, the way information was passed down, the inability of government to communicate with the people … yeah … that's another disaster in itself. People come up to me, you know, and say 'You're from Southshore? Poor you, you would have felt the earthquakes in a big way out there' … and I'm thinking to myself 'F*** the earthquakes, they were almost two years ago, but now I'm being kicked off my land and I don't have a bloody choice about it'. It's gut-wrenching.
>
> (in Dickinson 2013, 1)

Similar difficulties were evident across the city, given the extent of red zoning, and the amount of TC2 and TC3 land (Figure 3.2). In addition to the land zones, the post-quake experience of Southshore households was strongly influenced by their interactions with the Earthquake Commission and insurance companies (Miles 2016).

Psychosocial distress and mental well-being

In the immediate years after the earthquakes, levels of anxiety and depression rose among the Christchurch population as a whole (Beaglehole et al. 2019). These mental health problems were variously related to psychological trauma, involuntary relocation (which could disrupt long-standing attachments to place), grief in response to loss of life and injury, and the challenge of dealing with the Earthquake Commission and insurance companies (Morgan et al. 2015). The relatively frequent yet unpredictable aftershocks, illustrated in Figure 2.1, were also psychologically challenging, as they tended to keep pushing people into adrenalised threat states, while also undermining their perception of psychological security and environmental predictability. In September 2012, a survey was deployed to assess the subjective well-being of residents across the city. Eventually known as the Canterbury Wellbeing survey, this was administered twice yearly from September 2012 to September 2017, and annually thereafter. From the April 2013 survey onwards, a question on subjective well-being was included. Based around the WHO-5 well-being scale (Topp et al. 2015), this question made it possible to assess changes in self-reported well-being over time.

The sample size for each iteration of the survey was around 1200 individuals, drawn in a stratified manner to achieve representativeness with respect to gender, age distribution, ethnicity and household income. When the sample was divided into quartiles based on annual household income, there were clear differences in self-reported well-being between the four categories (under NZ$30,000; between $NZ30,001–60,000; between $NZ60,001–$100,000; over $NZ100,000) (Begg et al. 2021). The lowest household income group had the lowest self-reported well-being (and so on, through the spectrum, to the highest household income level, which had the highest self-reported well-being). This pattern was thought likely to reflect the well-observed positive relationship between income and self-reported well-being, which holds to a certain point. Although no pre-quake baseline measure for well-being was available, each income group began with a below-average level of well-being in 2013 which then rose over the following five years. This increase arguably reflected a process in which people were able to come to terms with the disaster and to return to a more steady or 'normal' form of life (Begg et al. 2021). As with any group data, such average figures obscure a host of individual and household variability, and there will be some in each group whose well-being did not substantively improve through the 2012–17 observation period (Begg et al. 2021).

Table 3.1 Issues having a moderate or major negative impact on Christchurch residents' well-being

September 2012 (top five issues, ranked by proportion of participants citing them)	*September 2013 (top five issues, ranked by proportion of participants citing them)*
1. Distress regarding ongoing aftershocks (42%)	1. Dealing with EQC/insurance issues in relation to personal property and house (23%)
2. Dealing with EQC/insurance issues in relation to personal property and house (37%)	2. Making decisions about house damage, repairs and relocation (21%)
3. Loss of other recreational, cultural and leisure time facilities (34%)	3. Being in a damaged environment and/or surrounded by construction work (20%)
4. Being in a damaged environment and/or surrounded by construction work (30%)	4. Loss of other recreational, cultural and leisure time facilities (17%)
5. Making decisions about house damage, repairs and relocation (29%)	5. Distress regarding ongoing aftershocks (12%)

Source: Morgan et al. (2015).

The surveys also asked participants to identify issues that had either a moderate or major negative impact on their well-being. Between September 2012 and September 2013, a small set of issues were identified as the most significant concerns by respondents in this regard (Table 3.1). In 2012, the most impactful issue for well-being related to the earthquake sequence itself ('distress regarding ongoing aftershocks'). This reflects the nature of earthquakes, in that they are typically accompanied by hundreds and even thousands of aftershocks (although as Chapter 2 has shown, in Canterbury, rather than occurring in a gradually attenuating fashion, the sequence was more drawn out). By 2013, the significance of aftershocks to respondents had fallen – from first to fifth ranked position – and the most negatively impactful issue had become dealing with the Earthquake Commission and private insurance companies. Two and a half years after the February 2011 earthquake, engaging with insurers was generating more distress for Christchurch residents than decisions about their property and housing situations, or the challenges of living in a damaged urban environment.

Unsurprisingly, exposure to earthquake damage was associated with increased levels of depression and anxiety. After the September 2010 quake, the residents of Avonside, an eastern suburb which experienced significant liquefaction, were found to have increased depression and anxiety scores (Dorahy and Kannis-Dymand 2012). After the February 2011 events, people across Christchurch experienced problems with hypervigilance, anxiety, irritability and difficulties sleeping (Potter et al. 2015). As well as the nerve-wracking effects of the aftershocks, these mental well-being impacts also reflect the inherent uncertainty of earthquakes – unlike a bushfire or flood, there is seldom any meaningful prior warning available – as well as their potential to rupture people's assumptions about a stable environment on which they can depend. After February 2011, there were short-term increases in prescriptions for anti-anxiety medications (Beaglehole et al. 2019). More generally, the stress of the earthquakes exacerbated pre-existing health problems for people, such as problem drinking (Thornley et al. 2013), and increased instances of employee burnout were observed, particularly when people's working conditions deteriorated after the quakes. This was due to issues such as job losses, increased volume of work, disrupted organisational processes and work environments, and prolonged strain in human service organisations (Thornley et al. 2013; Thornley et al. 2015; van Heugten 2014).

Particular groups experienced particular psychosocial impacts. Children who started school after the earthquakes were found to have heightened behaviour problems and post-traumatic symptoms, including difficulties with emotional regulation (Liberty et al. 2016). As Chapter 10 will show, these children were not helped by the government's post-earthquake decision to close many schools due to damage or population movements. In terms of demographic and social risk factors for quake-related mental distress, Hogg et al. (2014, 274) found that women and adults over the age of 39 'were more frequently diagnosed with mood and anxiety disorders than males and children'. New Zealand Europeans reported higher incidences of these disorders than the Pacific and Māori population in Christchurch, although Hogg et al. (2014) argue that this ethnic difference is likely to be an artefact of the tendency of Pacific and Māori populations to underutilise public mental health services, rather than a true reflection of their underlying mental health status in the aftermath of the quakes. In terms of geographic patterns, people living in eastern and central city suburbs, and in damaged areas of the Port Hills, showed an increased incidence of depression and anxiety, at rates around 23 per cent higher than the average for the Christchurch population (Hogg et al. 2014). They also had reduced subjective well-being (Greaves et al. 2015).

In February 2013, the Greater Christchurch Psychosocial Committee, a multi-agency consortium tasked with monitoring and promoting psychosocial well-being after the earthquakes, launched the *All Right?* mental health promotion campaign. The campaign used social media and conventional advertising to disseminate a range of mental health promotion messages (Figure 3.3). These often drew on phrases, humour and ideas sourced from the Christchurch community, and relayed them in a conversational rather than didactic register. A variety of posters were created for public settings – such as billboards, bus shelters, and public toilets – and for social media distribution. Since its formation, the campaign has continued as a collaboration between the Canterbury District Health Board (a regional body) and the Mental Health Foundation of New Zealand (a national body).

An evaluation found that awareness of the *All Right?* campaign among Christchurch residents had increased significantly since its launch – from around 51 per cent in 2013 to 92 per cent in 2020 – with similar visibility among both women and men, and the greatest awareness among younger people (Canterbury District Health Board 2021). Over four-fifths (86 per cent) of all respondents believed the campaign to be helpful for mental well-being and two-fifths (42 per cent) had engaged in one or more of the recommended activities. These were based on the Five Ways to Wellbeing initiative, with its focus on Connecting, Giving, Keeping Learning, Being Active, and Taking Notice (Mental Health Foundation, n.d). The examples in Figure 3.3 illustrate the emphasis on normalising a range of common post-disaster mental states and encouraging activities that are known to support mental well-being.

The increase in psychosocial distress and diagnosed mental health problems among the Christchurch population led the Canterbury District Health Board to request additional mental health funding from central government after the earthquakes. For several years, such requests were declined by the

Figure 3.3 Illustrative materials from the *All Right?* campaign.

Source: www.allright.org.nz

Ministry of Health, generating significant tensions in the relationship between the health board and the Ministry. This difficulty echoed other post-quake tensions between local and central government agencies, as discussed in Chapter 4. For some, the Ministry's refusal was further evidence of the poor treatment of Christchurch residents by central government agencies, and thus provided further energy for public protest and resistance by community groups (see Chapter 7). It was not until March 2016, over five years after the most damaging earthquake, that the National-led government made $20 million of additional funding available for mental health support services in the Canterbury region. This funding was eclipsed just a few years later, however, by the initiatives of the new Labour-led government which came to power in October 2017. In its 2019 budget, this government announced a record $NZ1.9 billion of additional funding for mental health services across the country. This investment has been directed to expanding early intervention initiatives such as the Mana Ake school-based programme (which seeks to help children learn skills to deal with loss, grief, peer pressure and bullying), as well as employing additional mental health professionals in community and acute services. Although there have been some problems with its timely uptake (Neilson 2021), this additional resource is gradually improving the support available to those in Christchurch who experience psychosocial distress as a result of having lived through the disruption and difficulties associated with the earthquakes.

Community and neighbourhood expressions of support

Alongside the initiatives of official agencies, novel forms of community and neighbourhood support arose following the earthquakes (Carlton and Vallance 2013). Residents provided food, water, clothing and temporary accommodation to others in their neighbourhoods; this was particularly prominent in the heavily disrupted eastern suburbs and lasted for several weeks, but was also evident to some degree city-wide. In general, people also engaged with their neighbours to a greater extent than usual. Many neighbourhood streets had increased pedestrian traffic and in-person interactions (as most central city workplaces were closed, with people working from home if possible, and many schools were also shut for a period of time). There were also a number of spontaneous creative gestures across the city, such as 'decorating fences with ribbons, flowers, and banners bearing messages of hope' (Thornley et al. 2013, 18), and placing flowers into the seemingly ubiquitous orange traffic cones that marked ongoing repairs to the city's roads and subsurface infrastructure. These small gestures complemented other quake-related creative expressions in the city, including street art, poetry and music (Feeney 2019; Fusté-Forné 2017; Norcliffe and Preston 2016). In a variety of ways, this creative work sought to offer people some encouragement and perspective during the often-depleting cycles of aftershocks, damage to homes and infrastructure, and negotiations with insurers.

These neighbourhood-level expressions of support often built upon existing social connections and relationships, as evident among interest groups, family, friendship and community connections. Whanau (extended family) and tribal structures were significant in the case of the Māori Earthquake Recovery Network. Formed in the aftermath of the February 2011 earthquake, this group made use of local marae (Māori meeting houses) as places of refuge and material support, and as spaces from which food, shelter and clothing could be accessed. It also drew upon whanau networks that extended across New Zealand. These networks facilitated people to temporarily relocate to other parts of the country, for rest and respite from the aftershocks, or because their homes had become uninhabitable (Kenney and Phibbs 2015; Potter et al. 2015). There was also a programme of residential visits in which Māori households, particularly in the eastern suburbs, were offered practical assistance with food, water, and information, with referrals made to other services as relevant (see Chapter 7).

In a variety of ways, these neighbourhood expressions of mutual aid and support assisted people to navigate what was, for many, a disturbing and challenging set of circumstances. Neighbourhood and community groups also helped to distribute information provided by government agencies, such as Civil Defence and CERA, to local residents and households (Paton et al. 2013). Those neighbourhood groups that 'mobilised quickly and pragmatically, using whatever resources they had available to address community needs' (Thornley et al. 2013, 18–19) typically supported community recovery. The facilities of some groups were repurposed as unofficial community hubs, including the Linwood Community Arts Centre and the Christchurch mosque on Deans Avenue, the latter of which became a hub for the local Muslim community. Some existing neighbourhood groups did not function effectively, however, for reasons that included ineffective leadership and internal conflicts, and this hampered their ability to make positive contributions to local recovery (Thornley et al. 2013). Alongside initiatives that focused on particular neighbourhoods, there were also a number of more broadly oriented responses, including from the Student Volunteer Army and advocacy and activist groups such as CanCERN, the Canterbury Communities' Earthquake Recovery Network (Chapter 7).

Conclusion

In the weeks immediately after 22 February 2011, the damage to people's homes and urban infrastructure, along with thousands of aftershocks, prompted substantial outmigration from Christchurch, both short and longer term. Although many people did return eventually, these departures were in any case offset by an influx of migrant workers drawn into the construction industry. Land zoning and insurance processes nevertheless affected thousands of households, and by 2013, when the frequency and intensity of aftershocks had attenuated, residents identified insurance matters as the issue having the greatest negative impact on their well-being

(Morgan et al. 2015). From 2013 through to 2019, however, self-reported well-being did show gradual increases for all income groups, which suggests a degree of recovery in the collective life and functioning of the city (Begg et al. 2021). Such an improvement should not be read as an easy confirmation of city-wide resilience, however, for in the same period there were significant increases in depression and anxiety, as well as multiple small business failures (Stevenson and Conradson 2017). In addition, it was not until 2016 – five years after the most damaging earthquake – that central government provided any significant additional funding to the Canterbury District Health Board for much needed mental health services.

Influenced by pre-existing patterns of inequality, the residents of particular suburbs and neighbourhoods in Christchurch often experienced quite different post-earthquake recovery trajectories (Wilson 2013). For households in the eastern suburbs or in lower-income groups, the quakes and difficulties with insurance claims saw significant declines in self-reported well-being. In contrast, residents in higher-income parts of the city fared comparatively better on average; the majority were able to resume a pattern of life in the weeks and months following the quakes not dissimilar to what they had beforehand. Nonetheless, those in suburbs like Fendalton whose homes bordered streams often suffered extensive housing damage, as did those on the hills, in places like Cashmere and Mt Pleasant. Such variations in post-disaster experience, socially and geographically, are of course typical of many disasters and not particular to the Canterbury earthquakes. They would nevertheless become one of the central issues in the city's recovery.

Part II

Recovery and renewal

4 Governance and the cartographies of recovery

Introduction

In a film made a decade after the Canterbury earthquake sequence, with the title 'When A City Rises', a prominent urban designer muses about whether the place that was emerging could have been 'an amazing beacon for how a new urban way of living can be created' (Lunday 2020). After ten years in which much of the city had been destroyed, demolished, re-planned and re-built, this streak of idealism was a reminder of the contests that had been fought about how the old and, in many respects, obsolescent city centre and its suburbs could be re-imagined for the future. Many of the debates centred as much on questions of process as much as outcomes. In other words, often the crucial issues in the Christchurch rebuild revolved around matters of governance, of who was to be responsible, how decisions were to be made, whose interests were included and in what ways.

This chapter is about the maps and plans used to reconstruct the city: mapping has long been one of the key instruments of governance employed by the modern state (Christensen 2013; Scott 1998). However, governance in the post-earthquake context is taken to mean more than just the activities of central and local government and includes the interests of business, of different communities and of the Treaty partner. Such a discussion helps to locate some of the experiments in governance that took place in the decade preceding the earthquakes, which had introduced collaborative and community-informed processes to map out possible futures for the city and its region. This perspective provides a basis for understanding reaction to the state-driven recovery mechanisms that were put in place in 2011, and the panoptical cartographies employed as part of re-settling the central city in particular. The extent to which the rupturing with the past (Pickles 2016) has led to loss of heritage and sense of place, or enabled a city to re-emerge in more engaging and inclusive ways, is then considered.

Issues of governance

The scale of damage wrought by the earthquakes and their impacts, outlined in Chapters 2 and 3, made it inevitable in retrospect that, after 22

DOI: 10.4324/9780429275562-6

February 2011, central government would become a key player in debates and delivery about the future of the city. A senior Christchurch planner described the Canterbury Earthquake Recovery Act of 2011, which enabled the introduction of large-scale, centralised planning into post-earthquake reconstruction, as 'the most powerful and draconian piece of legislation' that New Zealand had seen outside of wartime (Nicholson 2020). The reference to wartime is pertinent, as the trend internationally in the wake of the Second World War was 'to look to the war-time experience of mass production and planning as means to launch upon a vast programme of reconstruction and reorganization' (Harvey 1989a, 68; Judt 2010). The modernist style of planning and urban renewal that dominated the decades from the 1950s to 1970s was then generally accepted as a necessity for the delivery of social and economic goals. But by the new century, it had long since lost ideological traction amongst the Anglo-American polities in which New Zealand is generally situated. It did not however disappear completely, nor was it ever as coordinated, clear cut or unproblematic in practice as sometimes assumed (Beauregard 2020).

The neoliberal assault on the prominence and roles of the state, a process encapsulated in the phrase 'the New Zealand experiment', began here in the 1980s (Le Heron and Pawson 1996). A key feature of neoliberalism was the rejection of the egalitarian social democracy of the post-war years, with the Keynesian belief in the risks of market failure yielding to one of imagined government failure through inefficiency and lack of flexibility. The neoliberal shift involved 'the development of governing styles in which boundaries between and within public and private sectors become blurred' (Stoker 1998, 17). By the 1990s, the term 'governance' had therefore come to signal the engagement of a much wider range of players in the sphere of public action than previously. A feature of this shift was that good governance at the city level was 'now largely defined by the ability of formal government to assist, collaborate with, or function like the corporate community' (Hackworth 2007, 10). In Harvey's (1989b) characterisation, this was represented by a movement from managerialism to urban entrepreneurialism.

Harvey's argument was that this transformation of urban governance flowed from the recognition that, increasingly, the capacity to get things done rests not only with government, but also draws on wider sets of interests that can be more responsive to processes of competition between cities for production facilities, consumption flows and control functions. At the local level, one of the foundations of neoliberal governance has therefore been public-private sector cooperation. The Christchurch City Council, which after local government reform in 1989 became responsible for most of the metropolitan built-up urban area, worked to construct alliances with business interests to increase the attractiveness and tackle obsolescence of the central city in the face of heightened competition from suburban malls. It encouraged investment indirectly and directly in facilities such as a luxury hotel and mid-sized convention centre adjacent to the Town Hall (with its large auditorium and meeting spaces), also establishing an events company to service the complex. It also had some success in the decade before the earthquakes in facilitating development of old inner city lanes for retailing and nightlife (Johnston 2014).

The forms of governance that have emerged since the 1990s have however been more complex and elusive than simple categorisations like business-local government alliances imply (Arnouts et al. 2012). It is a much broader concept describing the constant renegotiation of national and local state relations within both market and society. The term 'collaborative governance' has been adopted to denote processes that develop interdependencies amongst a range of actors, whilst seeking to establish political legitimacy for public actions. Such processes have been characterised as formal and deliberative, initiated by public agencies to include non-state actors (Ansell and Gash 2008). An example was Canterbury Dialogues, 'an experiment in civic participation' held over eight months in 1998. It included parties from local government, business, community groups and academia, hosted by the Canterbury Employers' Chamber of Commerce. It focused on 'managing urban growth, developing sustainable economic wellbeing, effective environmental management, and social cohesion' (Wagner 1998). A similar mix of parties participated in the Future Path Canterbury visioning process coordinated by the regional council, Environment Canterbury, in 2001 (*City Scene* 2001).

These initiatives provided local experience in drawing on wider ranges of expertise, lending confidence to more collaborative forms of governance. A formal version emerged in 2004 when Environment Canterbury, the three local authorities in the wider Christchurch urban area (Christchurch City, Selwyn and Waimakariri District Councils) and Transit New Zealand (central government's transport infrastructure provider) set up the Greater Christchurch Partnership. The outcome was the Greater Christchurch Urban Development Strategy (2007). It established a framework for accommodating new metropolitan housing developments through means of both intensification and greenfield expansion, whilst protecting significant resources, such as water catchment areas. The framework was the outcome of public consultation on a range of options and was declared to be the basis for the organisations and community to cooperatively manage urban growth. The Strategy became a critical document in post-earthquake recovery, but arguably in a compromised fashion, as is discussed in Chapter 5. Figure 4.1 illustrates the timing of this and other key institutional reforms.

The partnership did not formally involve Ngāi Tahu, whose takiwā (tribal territory) includes the Canterbury region. But when the Greater Christchurch Urban Development Strategy (2016) was updated, Ngāi Tahu was included as one of the partners. This illustrates that just as actually existing forms of neoliberalism are contingent on context (Brenner and Theodore 2002), so too are modes and shifts in governance. Since the 1980s, specific pieces of national legislation have required that the principles of the Treaty of Waitangi, signed in 1840 between Māori tribes and the Crown, be recognised in governance processes (Finlayson and Christmas 2021). How to give effect to this in particular contexts has been a matter of acknowledgement

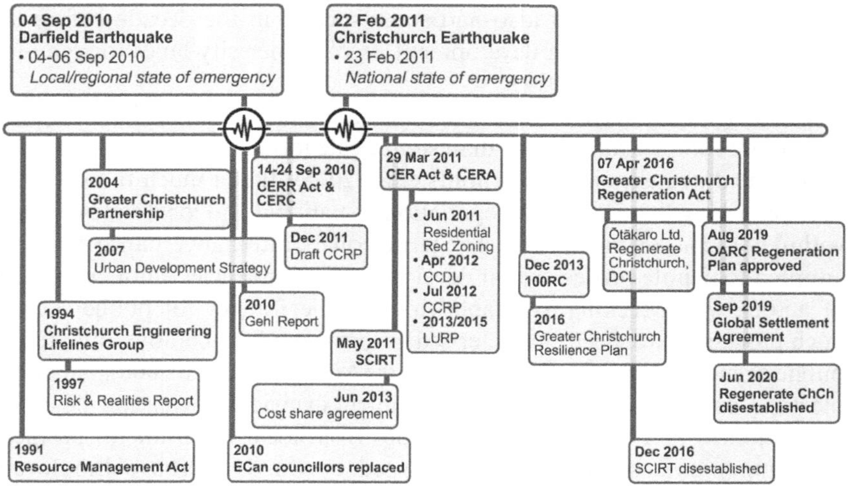

Abbreviations:

CERR Act: Canterbury Earthquake Response and Recovery Act
CERC: Canterbury Earthquake Recovery Commission
CER Act: Canterbury Earthquake Recovery Act
CERA: Canterbury Earthquake Recovery Authority
CCRP: Central Christchurch Recovery Plan
CCDU: Christchurch Central Development Unit
LURP: Land Use Recovery Plan
SCIRT: Stronger Christchurch Infrastructure Redbuild Team
100RC: 100 Resilient Cities
DCL: Development Christchurch Ltd

Figure 4.1 Timeline with key institutional reforms.

Source: Adapted from Huck et al. (2020, 5)

and negotiation over time. This has also been the case with resource management where the interests of multiple stakeholders, including more-than-human actors, are involved (Peart and Cox 2019). The recognition of Māori cultural perspectives and property rights, as well as the dependence of both market and society on the more-than-human realm, are illustrations of the context-specific shape of what is increasingly referred to as 'network governance'. Such recognition would also appear to represent steps towards acknowledgement of intergenerational interests.

A definition of network governance is 'a relatively stable cooperative arrangement between independent actors based on trust and reciprocity' (Bednar et al. 2019, 703). But network governance has been described as only working effectively if the networks function well (Lewis 2011), and critiqued for shortcomings in achieving material outcomes due to the dispersed, non-hierarchical nature of the network. In the case of wicked problems such as climate change, it has been argued that it 'must be supplemented with other governance modes to achieve effective implementation' (Bednar et al. 2019, 714). On the other hand, it is vulnerable to co-option by powerful parties in the network (Cretney 2019). A clear example of this in Canterbury was the decision of a centre right National-led government in 2010 to legislate to remove the elected members of the regional authority, Environment Canterbury, and impose its own commissioners, in part to facilitate the needs of an expanding dairy industry. This conflicted with the responsibilities of the elected representatives which, shaped by the Resource Management Act, were more broadly based and longer term (Mueller 2017). The decision also reflected what has been described as 'a systematic governance problem', a tendency in multiple policy domains to favour short-term interests, or a 'presentist bias' (Boston 2017, 15).

Even before the introduction of the Canterbury Earthquake Recovery Act in 2011, there was therefore a vivid example in the region of the hierarchical imposition of power overriding democratically sourced local interests. But there had also been, in the decade or so before the earthquakes, developing experience in the city and urban region of Christchurch with collaborative and networked forms of governance. It would be a mistake however to portray this in starkly oppositional terms as a conflict between central power and local interests. The reality is both more nuanced and engaged, with collaborative experience and initiatives informing and, to an extent, shaping, central government's post-earthquake response. But as the subtitle and content of the next section indicate, this is often not how it was publicly heard or seen in the city.

Panoptical maps and plans

A landmark event in the early earthquake years that still resonates in public memory is a city council-sponsored forum called 'Share an Idea' (Bennett et al. 2014a). This was organised with the assistance of Jan Gehl's international urban design consultancy. Gehl, from Denmark, had been engaged by the council before the earthquakes, to identify ways in which the central city was sub-optimal (Gehl Architects 2010). The site is flat and was developed within a relentless colonial grid, in which low-rise older masonry buildings predominated, with fewer of the tall, modern buildings that had come to characterise the North Island centres of Wellington and Auckland. The significance of Gehl's report from a governance perspective is that he brought to Christchurch a reputation for retrieving traffic-dominated cities for pedestrians and street life, based on close observation of how people use public space and working with citizens in participatory ways. His report reflected earlier Gehl projects in cities such as Copenhagen, Barcelona and Melbourne, recommending a more pedestrian- and cycle-friendly city, with a 'traffic calmed' centre, inviting and accessible public spaces, and 'green blue' connections that emphasise amenity features such as parkland and the Ōtākaro Avon river.

The city council was therefore well-placed when given responsibility under the Canterbury Earthquake Recovery Act 2011 to draw up a plan for city centre renewal. Gehl Architects returned to assist in the public consultation and planning process that took place in mid-2011. Share an Idea ran over six weeks, beginning with a two-day expo attended by 10,000 people, and including public lectures from local and international speakers, mail drops, stakeholder meetings and public workshops. Over 106,000 ideas emerged from

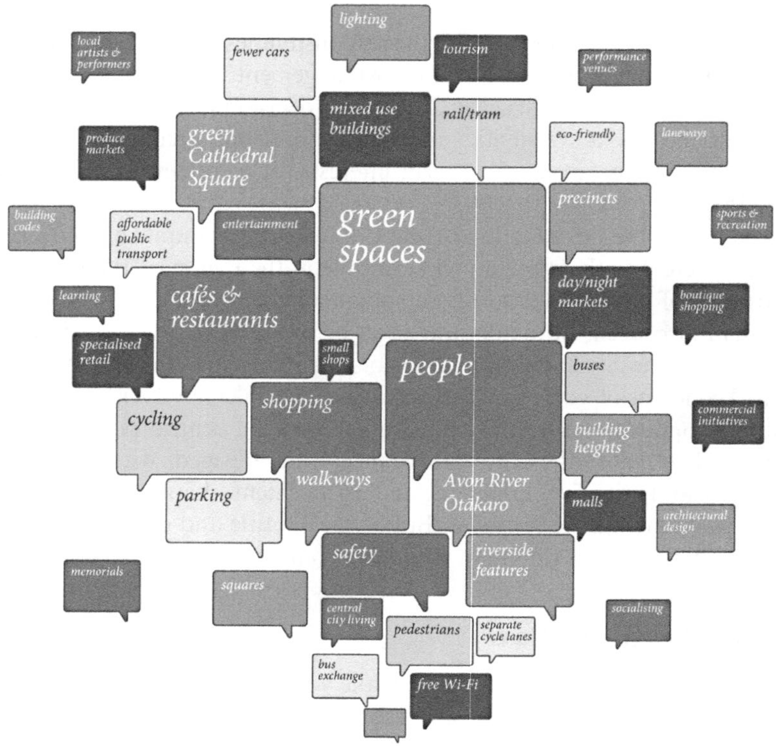

Figure 4.2 Themes emerging from Share an Idea.

Source: Adapted from Central City Recovery Plan (2012, 22).

'the highest level of community involvement ever seen in New Zealand' (Nicholson and Wykes 2012, 31). These are illustrated in Figure 4.2; many were in tune with Gehl's earlier report and provided the opportunity to act on its central theme of 'a change of mindset … where traffic planning and public space planning are thought of as one' (Gehl Architects 2010, 117). The resulting city council recovery plan was described in Mayor Bob Parker's foreword as 'the People's Plan for their city' (Christchurch City Council 2011, iii), reflecting a strong sense of local engagement. *The Press* portrayed it as 'winning widespread praise from residents' (Sachdeva 2012). It was an outcome in line with local expectations of being heard, based on a decade or more of collaborative governance experience. The reaction of the business community was however more critical, as Chapter 6 will detail.

Share an Idea won an international award from the Netherlands-based Co-Creation Association, the first time it had been given outside Europe. The chair of the jury remarked that 'Next to developing the new city centre, the result of this co-creation is also a stronger community' (Scoop 2011a). A key question however was how central government saw its role in the context of disaster, following the destruction of the South Island's main commercial centre and tourism hub. Initially, after the September earthquake, Parliament had passed the Canterbury Earthquake Response and Recovery Act 2010. This opened the door to intentionally hierarchical interventions, permitting government ministers to suspend or make exemptions to almost any New Zealand law with minimal restriction, in order to expedite the recovery process. As law, it was heavily criticised by legal academics and the New Zealand Law Society (Anderson et al. 2010; NZLS 2010). The powers were intended to be of fixed duration, with the Act expiring on 1 April 2012. However, long before then, it was superseded by the Canterbury Earthquake Recovery Act 2011, passed in the wake of the devastating event of 22 February that year (Figure 4.1).

The new Act, like its predecessor, was time-limited (for five years in this case) and did not specifically override the authority of the city council, although this body was by then regarded, including by councillors, as divided and ineffective (Vallance and Carlton 2015). The Act created a new government department, to be based in Christchurch: the Canterbury Earthquake Recovery Authority (known in the city as CERA, pronounced 'Sarah'). Such a move is one of 'the most visible governmental responses to disaster' internationally (Johnson and Olshansky 2017, 314). The position of Minister for Earthquake Recovery, with widespread powers, was continued from the 2010 Act. These powers enabled various pieces of existing legislation to be overridden, including those allowing for participatory and anticipatory forms of governance, such as the Resource Management Act 1991 and the Local Government Act 2002. In effect, the Canterbury Earthquake Recovery Act set up new structures 'without clearly establishing a joint governance model' with local elected councils, 'or clearly distinguishing between their respective roles' (Smith 2014, 147). It did however specify that Ngāi Tahu was to be a partner with the Crown in the rebuild. Further legitimacy for the overall approach was sought in the appointment of the head of the local power lines company (who was widely credited with restoring power quickly after each major quake) as Chief Executive of CERA, and in retaining as Minister a senior local Member of Parliament for the governing National Party, Gerry Brownlee.

The view from Wellington, or from CERA's offices in one of the few undamaged high-rise towers in central Christchurch, was inevitably more panoptical than the collective spirit expressed from the grassroots in Share an Idea and reflected in the 'People's Plan'. Ironically, central to Jan Gehl's urban design philosophy is the characterisation of good design as working from eye level and prioritising the relation between urban life and form. Gehl (2015) has contrasted this with the modernist approach to city building, where the architect models form at building height, and the planner envisages the totality higher still from a bird's eye perspective (cf. Scott 1998). He refers to this as the 'Brasilia syndrome', the utopian capital city of Brazil conceived in the 1950s as a visual whole when seen from the air, in which everyone is presumed to have a car and the pedestrian is an irrelevance. The plan for Brasilia was ruthlessly panned by the art critic Robert Hughes as 'an expensive and ugly testimony' to thinking 'in terms of abstract space rather than real place, of single rather than multiple meanings, and of political aspirations rather than of human needs…' (Hughes 1991, 211). No one has suggested that the post-earthquake redevelopment of Christchurch apes Brasilia, but a great deal of the reaction to it has reflected the humanist, street-scale perspectives of luminaries such as Gehl and Jane Jacobs (Jacobs 1961; Scott 1998).

Government's perspective on its top-down approach to post-earthquake reconstruction was that it 'would remove local confusion and provide the greatest certainty' (DPMC 2017, 7). In part, this was based on a review of responses to international disasters. The state could also resource relatively intense land assessments throughout residential areas for future suitability for settlement in the face of environmental hazards. On this basis, CERA produced a detailed map identifying green and red zones, discussed in Chapter 3 (Figure 3.2). The green zones were subdivided into three categories according to the future risk of liquefaction, with requisite foundation systems for repaired or replacement housing in the corresponding areas (Saunders and Becker 2015, 78). Red zones included the Avon Ōtākaro river corridor that had been badly damaged due to liquefaction and lateral spread, in which the risk of further damage, not least from flooding, was too great and the success of remediation, let alone its affordability, was in question. Smaller areas of red zone due to the ongoing risk of rockfall were declared in the hill suburbs, as well as alongside the river in the satellite town of Kaiapoi. To resolve these matters quickly, residents received a Crown payout for forfeiting their red zone properties through the extraordinary powers vested in the Minister (Smith 2014). The consequences of this policy are explored in Chapter 10.

In the central city, however, the 'People's Plan' was controversially overturned within a few months (Cretney 2019). In April 2012, Minister Brownlee – anxious to counter any flight of business investment – directed CERA to set up a Central City Development Unit. This unit was to oversee the preparation of a more detailed 'blueprint' for the central city in 100 days. It reflected central government's belief that the council plan, self-costed at $2 billion, did not sufficiently allow for the 'focused, timely, and expedited recovery' specified in the Canterbury Earthquake Recovery Act (DPMC 2017). A new Crown blueprint team was selected quickly. It was a consortium of six firms, including a planning consultancy and two architectural practices from Christchurch, alongside an Auckland project manager and two Australian urban planning companies. The team divided itself into two groups. One refined a broad vision, building on and incorporating many of the elements of the council's plan. The other identified and located a series of ambitious 'anchor projects', to be funded by negotiation between central and local government (McCrone 2012a). These were intended to retain business confidence and provide a framework of 'precincts' on the ground within which private investment would flourish, and the state's investment be protected. There was to be little more public engagement (Amore et al. 2017).

The differences between the blueprint – officially the Central City Recovery Plan (2012) – and the council plan (Christchurch City Council 2011) were therefore both of product and process. The blueprint was launched in completed form on 30 July 2012 and came into law the next day. In contrast, the People's Plan had been subject to feedback from a travelling roadshow, and a public submissions process as provided for in the Local Government Act 2002. It was less detailed than the Crown blueprint, but embodied the spirit of Share an Idea and was clearly intended to allow for a relatively organic and granular of rebuilding. At the time, post-earthquake Christchurch was already becoming known internationally for many innovative transitional activities (Bennett et al. 2012), as outlined in Chapter 8. Both plans envisaged a more focused, low-rise city centre, but the blueprint adopted more visibly many of the tenets of modernist city planning. It was a sweeping cartographic vision, dependent on widespread Crown acquisition of land, and the amalgamation of titles to form large development plots. Within these, the anchor projects and surrounding themed precincts (for 'innovation', health, cultural activities, sport, retailing, etc) were to be planted within or across city blocks. These would be ringed by 'the frame', defining a central area 'of a scale appropriate to current demand' (Central City Recovery Plan 2012, 33). In its ambition, rationality and efficiency, the blueprint, and the map that embodied it, could be seen as the epitome of what James Scott (1998) described as thinking like a state (Figure 4.3).

Business activation alliances

The blueprint not surprisingly became performatively powerful, but not to the extent of sweeping all before it. The assumption of centralised authority did not silence other players; indeed it was intended to provide the framework for a range of entrepreneurial initiatives forged between the business community, central and local government (discussed in Chapter 6). Some of these initiatives bear directly on the theme of governance. The most immediate was an Earthquake Support Subsidy agreed after the Minister of Finance approached the Chamber of Commerce to negotiate how to maintain business cashflow (Roughan 2017). Initially, from September 2010, this was targeted to small businesses, then opened up those of any size in February 2011. It recognised the problems that up to 6000 businesses in the central city faced. It was complemented by actions by banks (advancing money), Inland Revenue (forgiving or delaying payment of goods and services tax) and insurance companies (providing rapid partial payouts). These were high trust schemes designed to stem business failures and worked so well that business churn through the earthquakes was no higher than the usual turn rate of about 11 per cent each year (Townsend 2016). The Earthquake Support Subsidy also provided the template for the Labour-led Government's response to business and employment needs in the Covid-19 emergency ten years later.

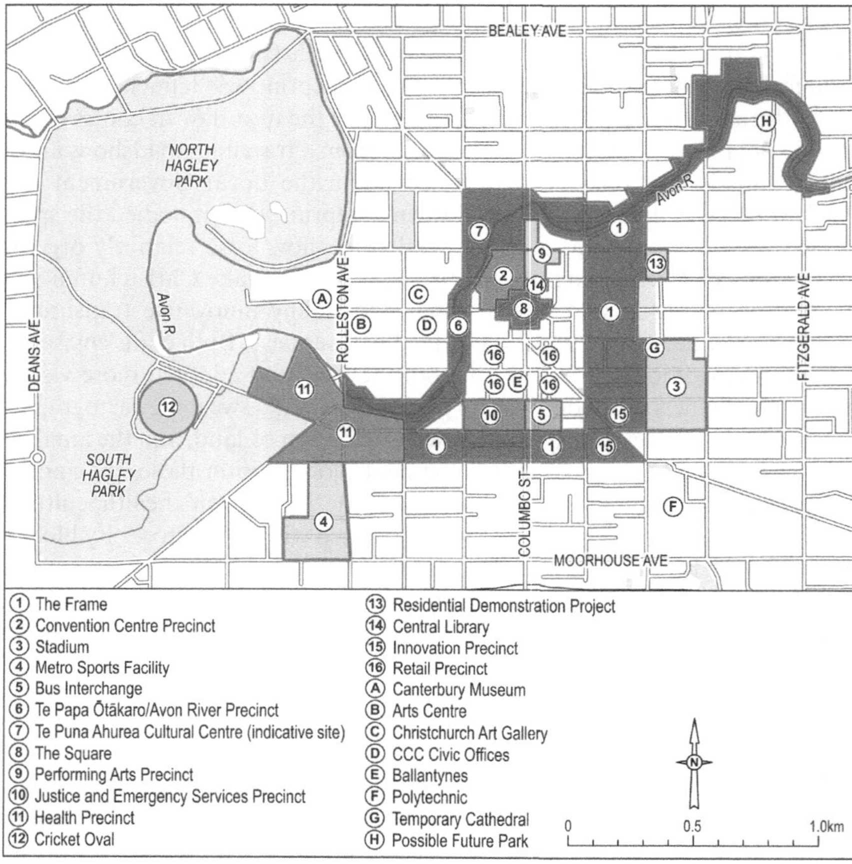

Figure 4.3 The blueprint map.

Source: Redrawn from Central City Recovery Plan (2012, 33–4).

Many affected businesses relocated to the largely unscathed western and southwestern parts of the city. Some displaced technology companies moved to the Enterprise Precinct and Innovation Campus (EPIC), one of the first commercial developments in the central city, which opened in late 2012. Its campus-like building is also designed to accommodate business start-ups and networking events (Andersen and McLennan 2014). For some years it was the home of the Ministry of Awesome, also founded in 2012 to provide advisory support and mentorship (Anderson 2012). The establishment of EPIC was supported by CERA, the city council and government agencies, with founding partners including the Bank of New Zealand and Google. It is also self-described as the 'foundation partner' in the blueprint's Innovation Precinct (EPIC 2022), and as such has outlasted the other rapidly established post-earthquake initiative in the central city, the Christchurch container or RE:START mall.

RE:START was established by a trust set up by inner-city retailers, in part of what the blueprint subsequently designated the retail precinct. It opened at the end of October 2011 when most of the cordon – which was not finally removed until 30 June 2013 – was still in place. RE:START was located adjacent to (and in conjunction with) Ballantynes, an undamaged department store, with assistance from CERA and the city council (Bennett et al. 2012). It quickly became not only a critical initiative in drawing shoppers back to the central city but also in building the city's reputation for urban transitional activities in the post-earthquake years. In 2013, *Lonely Planet* listed Christchurch amongst its top ten cities internationally, highlighting the colourful labyrinth of containers in the mall (Atkinson et al. 2013). It was originally to stay until 2014, but after relocating twice along the street to make way for new retail and office buildings, did not finally close until 2018. Many of its tenants were rehoused within new developments, discussed in Chapter 9.

RE:START was a conspicuous success; less conspicuous but nonetheless foundational was the Stronger Christchurch Infrastructure Rebuild Team (SCIRT), which began work in May 2011. SCIRT has attracted some attention in the business literature as a collaborative project-based alliance that brought together five of the country's largest contracting companies, funded by CERA, the city council and Transit New Zealand. It was tasked with the delivery of about 600 projects to repair the city's horizontal infrastructure (Walker et al. 2017). SCIRT created its own structure, workflow and processes amongst a group of usually competing contractors with similar areas of capability: a model designed to operate in a situation of urgency, resource constraints and public expectations that water supply, sewerage and road surfaces would be serviceable again within reasonable timeframes. Although SCIRT's work was compromised by political contests over the extent of repairs and of the funding of them (Huck et al. 2020), by the time it was wound up in late 2016, it had substantially achieved its goals. Remaining repairs were incorporated into city council's ongoing asset management programme.

Heritages lost and found

Business activation alliances were therefore essential in supporting repair of the city's infrastructure, and in maintaining and to an extent developing its employment base. In the central city, these alliances were important enablers of the blueprint which framed the direction of the central city rebuild within a complex context of demolition and renewal. Demolition was the responsibility of the Central City Development Unit, which was authorised by the Minister for Earthquake Recovery to issue 'section 38' notices to override any public say in the removal of buildings, many of which were inaccessible behind the civil defence cordon (illustrated in Figure 6.1). The intention of the Central City Recovery Plan (the blueprint) was that the process of reconstruction would be led by the state's investment in the rebuild, particularly the anchor projects. These were to be financed through a controversial cost-sharing agreement between central government and the city council, developed with little consultation and signed in June 2013 (Johnson and Olshansky 2017). The agreement codified the extent of the Crown's commitment to reconstructing central Christchurch on a project-by-project basis. If it was substantial in financial terms, the price was the forfeit of local control, the imposition – as many saw it – of outsized projects and the loss of a great deal of the city's 'heritage' in the name of the map.

In a discursive critique, Farrell (2015, 19) avers that the blueprint was 'just the latest in the long catalogue of maps that have attempted to draw this country, to reduce its bewildering complexity to something comprehensible'. In Christchurch, the first of these was the original colonial settlement grid superimposed across the sand dunes and wetlands of the site chosen for the city in 1850. Its indiscriminate geometry came at the expense of the destruction of indigenous ecologies and disguise of the land's liveliness, as earlier chapters have shown. The blueprint did little to disturb the original grid although, like the council's plan, it placed more emphasis on the river corridor as a transgressive feature. It also carved out the well-defined 'frame' to contain the central city and provide active transport corridors and space for downtown housing (Figure 4.3). In this, it echoed the town belts of the 1850 plan. The extent of demolition within the blueprint did however remove many of the streetscapes and landmarks that had accreted across the grid over generations, and with it any pre-earthquake sense of place. To Farrell (2015, 103), 'In this city, it is easy to feel lost'. This is the context for often vigorous post-earthquake debates about heritage.

As an international phenomenon, Lowenthal (2004) dates what he calls 'the heritage crusade' from about 1980. Four years later *Lost Christchurch*, a book of buildings demolished over time to make way for new developments, was published. Lacking a dramatic site or 'individually outstanding' buildings, the author observed that what gave the city 'an individual character is the juxtaposition and association of different buildings and the relative scale of those buildings' (Wilson 1984, 11). When during and after the earthquakes, hundreds of buildings were demolished in the central city, including about 250 on the city council's own heritage list (Blundell 2021), a reaction was inevitable: heritage is most valued when most at risk. Heritage advocates disputed the Central City Development Unit's indiscriminate use of section 38 notices, based on whether or not buildings were repairable. A lot were sacrificed to the blueprint map, as standing in the way of anchor projects or precinct developments. But often demolition was at the request of owners who lacked desire or resources to undertake repairs (Gray 2016), which in turn contributed to the visual dominance of unmade car parks for many years.

Some traditional architectural heritage has survived in key locations, such as the Gothic Revival Canterbury Museum (which had been seismically strengthened), and much of the Arts Centre opposite it, a complex of buildings in the same style that until the 1970s had housed the University of Canterbury before its suburban re-location. The Arts Centre was badly damaged but has undergone a lengthy restoration programme, funded largely by insurance and employing up to 20 stonemasons from around the world at times (Erskine 2022). But the survival of such landmarks did little to lower the temperature in debates over the future of the city's two cathedrals: the Anglican Gothic Revival building in Cathedral Square, at the centre of the street grid, and the rather more stately Catholic basilica on the edge of the central city, sometimes held to be 'the finest Renaissance-style building' in Australasia (Ansley 2011, 81). The future of the former was subject to dispute for many years, after a church decision to demolish it, and civic and heritage campaigns in opposition. Eventually, a resolution to reinstate the building was brokered and supported in 2018 by the Labour-led government that had come to office the previous year (Bohan 2022). Restoration began a decade after the upper part of the tower and spire had collapsed into the Square. A decision to partially repair the wrecked basilica was overturned about the same time when a new Catholic bishop decided to build a new facility in the central city (see Chapter 11).

More public energy has perhaps been expended on the future of the cathedrals than any other issue in the post-earthquake city (Blundell 2021), demonstrating that for many the social value of heritage transcends the private interests of its owners. Cathedrals are historical landmarks, and the Cathedral in the Square was for long the stylised symbol of the city's branding (Galloway 2014). Nonetheless, such debates prompt consideration not only of what has been lost but also of opportunities opened for the expression of identities and interests not well served in the pre-earthquake city. Its colonial Gothic architecture and self-styled 'Garden City' image spoke to many of a certain provincialism. Yet – as observed in Chapter 1 – politically it is largely a left-leaning Labour town, out of tune with the centre right National-led government that was in power from 2008 to 2017, and often at odds with the Minister for Earthquake Recovery whose parliamentary seat was for many years the city's only 'blue' stronghold (and even that went to Labour in the 2020 parliamentary election). Mr Brownlee's active support for the programme of post-earthquake demolition symbolised this. Yet at the same time, the earthquakes presented an opening – with the crumbling of the city's material facades – to engage progressively with difference, in both human and more-than-human realms (Pickles 2016).

Parliament itself recognised this with the inclusion of Ngāi Tahu as a statutory partner in the Canterbury Earthquake Recovery Act. For Māori, this reflects the centrality of the principle of rangatiratanga, which broadly aligns leadership and authority (Pauling et al. 2014). Staff from Ngāi Tahu agencies worked with the city council on the People's Plan and on the Crown's blueprint. They established the Matapopore Charitable Trust, which is responsible for ensuring that tribal and sub-tribe (Ngāi Tahu and Ngāi Tūāhuriri) values, aspirations and narratives are realised within the recovery of the city. An important aspect of this is kaitiakitanga, which recognises the special relationship that tangata whenua, people of the land, have with local ecology. In this way, the exotic plantings of 'the Garden City' have been reworked throughout the implementation of the blueprint with an interweaving of indigenous and introduced plant species. An example is in Te Papa Ōtākaro, the Avon River precinct, which delivers the desire to reconnect with the river in the inner city, identified in both the Gehl report and Share an Idea. The design for this new two-kilometre-long pedestrian promenade includes a series of whāriki, or paved patterns resembling woven mats, which tell some of the Māori stories of place, whilst reflecting manaakitanga, the provision of hospitality and care to manuhiri, or visitors (Figure 8.1).

Te Papa Ōtākaro, in pedestrianising the river corridor in a city whose street grid had increasingly dominated by cars, is an anchor project that has become extremely popular. So too is a second anchor project, Tūranga, the new city library opened in 2018. Tūranga is the homeland of the Ngāi Tāhu ancestor, Paikea, and the name carries 'considerable responsibility', speaking of whakapapa, or affiliations across generations, and relationships across space. The joint Danish-New Zealand design was developed in conjunction with Ngāi Tahu and Ngāi Tūāhuriri, so that the building's terraces and openings on the upper floors face culturally significant points in the Canterbury landscape. Its golden aluminium façade reflects the folds of the Port Hills on the city's southern edge, as well as the shape of the leaves of the harakeke flax plants that originally grew on the site. Inside, the ground floor reflects the desire to welcome people, with the stairs and central atrium echoing the Ngāi Tahu narrative of knowledge (Matapopore, n.d.). The second level is largely for children and houses the Imagination Station, a creative play area run by a social enterprise that originated as a post-earthquake transitional initiative.

Children and their parents have also flocked to a third anchor project, the Margaret Mahy Playground, discussed in more detail in Chapter 9. Named after a much-loved New Zealand children's author, and located at the eastern end of Te Papa Ōtākaro, it was designed in collaboration with children. It is – not surprisingly given the ambition of the blueprint – the largest play area in the country. As a children's place, it is connected to active transport corridors in the frame and along the river, along which are interwoven the stories and symbols of tangata whenua (people of the land). Examples such as the playground, Tūranga and Te Papa Ōtākaro demonstrate that heritage is 'an ever-changing palimpsest', in which 'new creations and recognitions more than make up for what is lost through erosion, demolition, and changing tastes' (Lowenthal 2004, 39–40). In this sense, and despite reaction to the Crown's blueprint, the spirit of Share an Idea and Jan Gehl have prospered in the city.

From rebuild to regeneration

The five-year term of the Canterbury Earthquake Recovery Act expired in 2016. But how much of the blueprint had been delivered by then? What forms of governance replaced CERA and the Central City Development Unit, and with what sort of outcomes? In a retrospective collection, 'Christchurch – Five Years On' in *Architecture New Zealand* magazine, Peter Marshall, head of a prominent architecture practice and member of the blueprint team, noted that in the 13 city blocks that now comprised the compressed business district, 'building activity is under way in nine, including many of the anchor projects identified in the Blueprint'. Given the extent of clearance undertaken, he considered this 'an extraordinary achievement' (Marshall 2016, 38). But Hugh Nicholson, then the principal urban designer at the city council, and the lead on the 'People's Plan', observed that 'In our worst case scenarios, we never imagined' that so many buildings in the central city would be demolished, before noting that the replacement style is a kind of 'corporate urbanism' of commercial buildings with open floor plans. Banks were only financing new buildings with confirmed tenancies, and the only tenants with long enough lead-in times and deep enough pockets were 'the larger corporates' (Nicholson 2016, 47–8).

These observations warrant further context. The corporate style was also a product of the blueprint's requirements that developments be of a certain size, height (not over seven storeys) and strong enough to meet the revised building code. Combining these requirements with the pace of demolition, developers were for some time more active outside, and along the outer edge of, the blueprint, as Chapter 6 reveals. In a demonstration of the performative power of the map, their projects initially activated an axis connecting Victoria Street, a popular pre-earthquake shopping street, with Durham Street, which faces the western side of Te Papa Ōtākaro (Figure 6.4). This axis continued beyond Hagley Park into the inner suburb of Addington. In all three locations, high-quality business accommodation for law and accountancy firms was being built by 2012. Much of the commercial reconstruction coming on stream by 2016 within the blueprint area was not only for corporate clients, such as banks, but for lease to government departments. In the retail precinct, the RE:START mall, although relocated several times to make way for new buildings, still remained in place. The only completed anchor projects in the central city were the new Bus Interchange, and the Margaret Mahy Playground. Others were under construction, but some had not been started. The 'anchors' were certainly not leading the rebuild as originally intended (Figure 4.4).

In late 2014, the Minister for Earthquake Recovery established an advisory board to consider the transition away from Crown direction of the rebuild. It comprised leaders from local government, Ngāi Tahu, business and community groups. The message was a clear desire for greater local control. The outcome was the Greater Christchurch Regeneration Act 2016. The shift away from 'recovery' to 'regeneration' was intentional. Regeneration was defined in section 3 (2) of the Act as rebuilding, and 'improving the environmental, economic, social, and cultural well-being, and the resilience, of communities'. A key instrument in this regard was the establishment of a joint Crown-city council agency, Regenerate Christchurch. This agency was given authority to develop regeneration plans for different parts of the city. There was cross-party agreement in parliament that the time was right for such a move, and optimism that the new agency would carry on some of the work initiated by CERA, but enable this to be led 'by local people'. Although the new Act again had a lifetime of five years, Minister Brownlee (2016) expressed

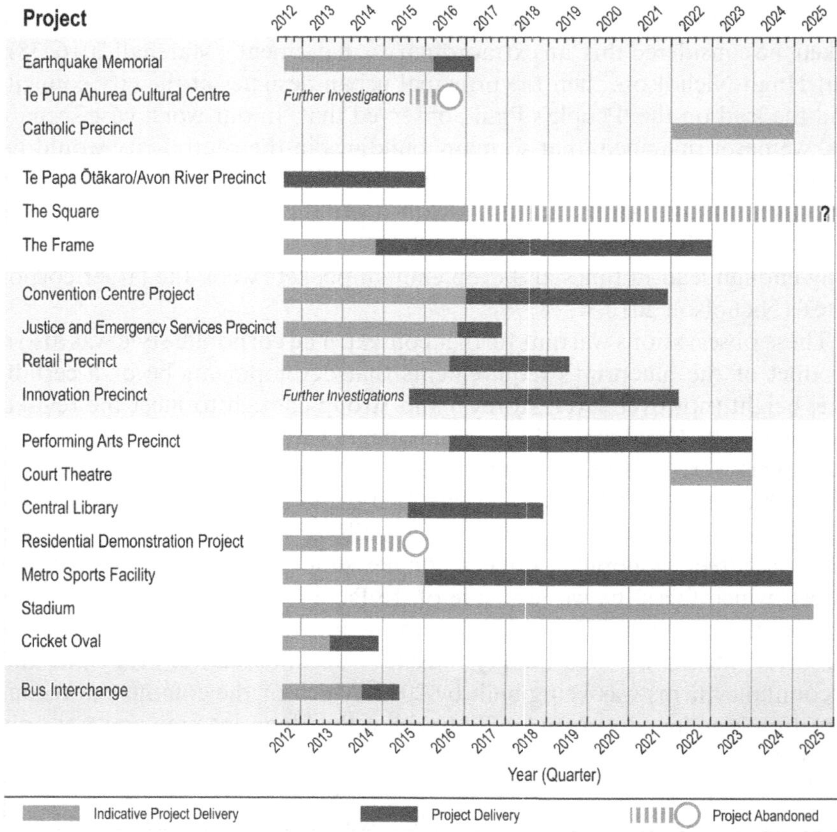

Figure 4.4 Planned and actual timelines of the anchor projects.

Source: Adapted and updated from Central City Recovery Plan (2012, 46)

the hope that ‘over a period of years’, Regenerate Christchurch would transition to a ‘fully council-controlled organisation’.

Regenerate’s main achievement was to be the production of a regeneration plan for the Ōtākaro Avon River Corridor (Regenerate Christchurch 2019), the new moniker for the riverside residential red zone created in 2012 (Figure 3.2). The plan, and the exhaustive public consultation on which it was based, is one of the main themes of Chapter 12. It received Ministerial approval in 2019. Other Regenerate initiatives, such as a development plan for the future of Cathedral Square (Regenerate Christchurch 2018a), have not been progressed. The Square, with the Anglican cathedral at its centre, was originally intended as the focal point of the central city. But it had struggled for many years and was subject to changes in design from the 1960s on. Since the earthquakes, the protracted debates over the repair of the Anglican cathedral, which is unlikely to be finished much before the end of the 2020s, and the shift towards the river with the success of Te Papa Ōtākaro, contributed to a lack of enthusiasm for Regenerate's Plan (Hayward and McDonald 2019).

Sometime before the expiry of the Greater Christchurch Regeneration Act, both government and city council had shifted away from their original view of Regenerate's potential as a collaborative partner in the rebuild. An official review completed in 2019 considered that a 'tipping point has been reached where the need for the legislation in its present form is effectively over' (Sinclair 2019, 5). The city council had regained powers to administer its own District Plan processes, following the revocation of a special Earthquake Order made in 2014. Regenerate's specified role for climate change planning on the New Brighton coastline was also transferred to the city council in 2019. The Act was amended in 2020 to terminate the agency's existence, with its functions being transferred to local agencies including the council. This followed a gradual loss of political confidence due to frustration with the number of rebuild agencies operating in the city. One agency did however survive. This was Ōtākaro Ltd, a Crown-owned company responsible under the 2016 Act for completing the anchor projects.

Ōtākaro completed Rauora Park, the central axis of the east frame, in late 2017 and Te Papa Ōtākaro a year later. But three largest anchor projects, discussed in detail in Chapter 9, were considerably delayed. Te Pae, the convention centre, opened at the end of 2021, at which point Parakiore, the metro sports facility and Te Kaha, the 'Canterbury Multi-Use Arena', (popularly known as 'the stadium'), were still anticipated (Figure 4.4). The delays have been due to site issues, contracting capacity and available finance, but cast the original intent of these blueprint projects as 'anchoring' private sector developments in a different light. The scale of the blueprint's ambition required additional Crown funding for the stadium, and long-term ownership of Te Pae, after the city council refused to take responsibility for this behemoth in the Global Settlement Agreement in late 2019. The global settlement was negotiated between the city council and the country's then Labour-led government. It determined the future ownership of Crown and council regeneration assets and was a milestone in the withdrawal of the Crown from post-earthquake governance in the city (Global Settlement Agreement 2019).

Conclusion

To what extent, returning to James Lunday, has the post-earthquake rebuild of Christchurch been 'an amazing beacon for how a new urban way of living can be created'? In the face of such a complex, long drawn-out process, views and assessments inevitably differ. The architect Peter Marshall, a member of the blueprint team, saw 'something unique' happening in a place 'redefining itself as an Arcadian city in the South Pacific' (Marshall 2016, 39). A few years later, John Walsh of the New Zealand Institute of Architects quietly asserted that 'the procrustean planning regime – Modernism redux, with zones recast as "precincts" – imposed by the planning authority foreclosed the possibility of new paradigms of urban development' (Walsh 2020, 159). Both seem like easy conclusions to reach. But as this analysis of the rebuild process and outcomes has shown, the reality has been more complex, as experiments in governance, mapping and regeneration, and heritages revealed as well as lost, indicate. The following chapters may show in greater depth whether or not 'a new way of urban living' is a chimera.

5 Housing recovery

Introduction

Most of the housing stock in Christchurch city and adjacent areas of its two neighbouring local authority jurisdictions, Selwyn and Waimakariri districts, which together comprise the Christchurch urban region, was in some way affected by the earthquakes. This disrupted lives and created a complex and protracted response from house owners, renters, the insurance sector, central and local government politicians and planners, residential property developers, their financiers and the building industry. The objective of this chapter is to outline how these participants in the recovery process interacted as the subsequent housing regeneration effort unfolded. It will show how this recovery was linked to transport infrastructure development after the earthquakes and produced an array of outcomes in the central city, suburbs and satellite towns. The recovery has intensified the central city and parts of the suburbs residentially, but in an illustration of path dependency (Dodds 2021), also significantly increased a long-established tendency to urban sprawl on the margins of the region (Colbert et al. 2022).

The chapter will first discuss key ideas associated with urban planning and residential real estate development practices as they relate to the region's housing recovery. This is contextualised with an outline of the pre-earthquake housing path in the urban region, before examining patterns of housing recovery since 2011. These patterns have been shaped by the Christchurch Central Recovery Plan and the Land Use Recovery Plan, both critical planning initiatives in the post-earthquake management of urban form. Housing developments in the central city, the suburbs and on the urban periphery are discussed in turn.

Urban planning and residential real estate development

Planners are important actors in this narrative: particularly because of the way they attempted to manage the Christchurch urban region's spatial form before and after the Canterbury earthquake sequence. Prior to the earthquakes, planners had put much energy into the Greater Christchurch Urban Development Strategy to rein in the region's sprawling form by permitting

DOI: 10.4324/9780429275562-7

much higher levels of suburban and central city residential intensification than in the past. But the earthquakes confronted them with the urgent political imperative to re-regulate and hasten the residential land subdivision consent process on the urban margins to effect recovery. New land was required on which to build houses to replace those lost in the disaster. Some elements of the pre-earthquake strategy, derived from wide-ranging community consultation and designed to be implemented over many years, had therefore to be relaxed and others fast-tracked. The earlier residential intensification objective had to be partially circumscribed in favour of greenfield development. An additional complicating factor was the implementation of pre-existing commitments to construct a major motorway system to the west, south and north of the city during the recovery period. This cut travel times to the urban periphery, stimulated the growth of satellite towns and steered the urban region back to a well-established path of urban sprawl that is seemingly very hard to step beyond.

By contrast, in the central city and suburbs, the planners did their best to stick with the residential intensification objectives of the pre-earthquake strategy. Suburban intensification was permitted in places deemed appropriate. In the central city, land was set aside and developers were incentivised to build medium-density housing. It was hoped that this would greatly increase the number of people living in the central city. Here, planners were promoting forms of dwelling and ways of urban living familiar in overseas cities, but less so to many Christchurch residents. While in the suburbs and the central city, residential intensification is now more common, 12 years after the earthquake sequence began the central city population has not increased and progress towards building new medium-density housing has been fitful. Planning literature is replete with narratives about complexity, implementation difficulties and unforeseen circumstances and outcomes, particularly when novel outcomes are sought (Berke et al. 2006; Hall 1982; Pressman and Wildavsky 1984). In such situations, planning results are often only ever partial and at times contradictory.

Residential real estate development practices have also been influential in post-earthquake housing recovery. Rather than passively responding to market, regulatory and other institutional arrangements, real estate developers and their financiers actively create the conditions for housing provision and urban spatial form. As Murphy (2019) points out, developers and their financiers operate a set of standard calculative practices with respect to acceptable profit margins that produce the prices that will be paid for land and establish the required house prices needed for development to be profitable. Developers must be able to show their financiers that they are 'capable of achieving benchmark profit rates to secure finance' (Murphy 2020, 1510).

It follows therefore that risk-related developer-financier interactions influence the types and locations of housing that can and will be built. If relatively low risk and profitable, new forms of housing will be constructed. In Christchurch, these include central city and suburban medium-density apartments and attached townhouses, which are particularly attractive to rental investors. Many developers, however, fall back on tried and true, lower-risk design and construction approaches, such as those associated with greenfield and suburban, often owner-occupied, detached houses. The working out of these developer-financier interactions means that urban planning aspirations and housing affordability concerns are not often a key priority for developers and this has become clear in post-earthquake housing development.

Christchurch's pre-earthquake housing path

Detached houses, typically built on relatively large plots of land, have dominated the Christchurch's urban region's development trajectory, material fabric and cultural mores since the city's nineteenth-century establishment (Greater Christchurch Partnership 2018; Memon 2003). The corollary of this situation is that before the earthquake sequence there were relatively few multi-unit attached medium-density houses and apartment buildings in the central city and surrounding urban areas (McDonagh 2017; Vallance et al. 2005). In 2010, there were thus limited opportunities for central city living in Christchurch. At that time, the central city accommodated only 8000 of the city's 376,300 and the wider region's 464,900 residents (2.1 per cent and 1.7 per cent, respectively) (Environment Canterbury 2021a; McDonald 2018a). These central city dwellers lived mainly in low-rent flats east of the business district or in apartments, terraces, townhouses and semi-detached condominia near cultural facilities like the Arts Centre, within easy access of the Ōtākaro Avon River and the 164-hectare Hagley Park. The exception to this medium-density housing story was the area of gentrified moderate-density detached houses in the north of the central city.

Public- and private-sector interactions had an important role to play in these housing patterns and urban management arrangements. Prior to 1989, when New Zealand's local government was significantly restructured, the Christchurch urban region was administered by 11 territorial authorities. Each jurisdiction, led by a separate mayor and council, was responsible for planning its own district, zoning land for mainly detached housing developments and associated service centres, including in some cases suburban shopping malls, all largely initiated and built by private commercial investors. In 1989, these 11 local authorities were amalgamated, the urban region from that time being administered by four councils: Christchurch City, Selwyn and Waimakariri Districts, and Environment Canterbury. The latter is the regional council, and is responsible for not just Christchurch, but the whole of the extensive Canterbury region in the areas of natural environmental planning and regional public transport. It also has a regional urban planning mandate.

As a result of the earlier administrative and land development arrangements, these new councils inherited a dispersed, automobile-dependent, polycentric urban region. This became the defining reality in their planning, housing policy and allied infrastructure and transport provision. The 1990s and early 2000s saw further low-density urban dispersal. By 2004, these local authorities and Transit New Zealand (now Waka Kotahi New Zealand Transport Agency), a central government body responsible for transport planning and provision, had recognised that to create a less dispersed development path, and manage the Christchurch urban region's growth, a long-term and overarching vision was needed. As outlined in Chapter 4, these entities thus initiated the Greater Christchurch Urban Development Strategy with a focus on Christchurch city (minus rural Banks Peninsula) and the eastern areas of Selwyn and Waimakariri Districts (Figure 5.1).

The strategy, formally adopted in June 2007, provided for regional growth and development out to 2041. A proposed settlement pattern was established where 60 per cent of all future growth would be accommodated in intensified development within the existing urban area, with the remaining 40 per cent in greenfield sites (Ministry for the Environment 2008). New arterial and peripheral motorways were planned. Where possible, the construction of medium-density and affordable housing was to be encouraged, particularly in Christchurch city (Christchurch City Council 2010b). At the time of the earthquake sequence the details of the Urban Development Strategy's implementation were well in train, but they, like the urban region itself, were to be greatly disrupted (Greater Christchurch Urban Development Strategy Implementation Committee 2011).

Housing damage, insurance and recovery planning

The earthquakes destroyed 7,860 houses in Christchurch city and Selwyn and Waimakariri districts, and a further 9,100 were made temporarily uninhabitable, requiring major repair or rebuilding (Ministry of Business, Innovation and Employment 2013). The Reserve Bank reported that 170,000 houses (approximately three-quarters of the region's housing stock, and a greater proportion in Christchurch city) were damaged to some degree (Parker and Steenkamp 2012; Wood et al. 2016) and around a fifth had damage exceeding $100,000 in value. As indicated in Chapter 3, the majority of this loss and damage occurred in the eastern areas of Christchurch city and Waimakariri district which were most prone to ground deformation and liquefaction. Christchurch's higher-status estuarine and hill suburbs and those bordering the Ōtākaro Avon River and smaller streams immediately west of the central city, such as Fendalton, were also noticeably affected.

It was also quickly realised that a significant part of the region's rental, affordable owner-occupied, social and retirement housing stock was destroyed or temporarily uninhabitable. This raised concerns about housing security and affordability, particularly for low-income residents (McDonagh 2014). Between mid-July 2011 and early 2013, those who needed to rent, including those who had to find a place to live while their houses were repaired, or who had moved to the city to help with building assessment, demolition and reconstruction, were faced with significant rent hikes, measuring 31 per cent on average across the urban region. In the damaged east, rents rose to a lesser degree, but still averaged 21 per cent (Ministry of Business, Innovation and

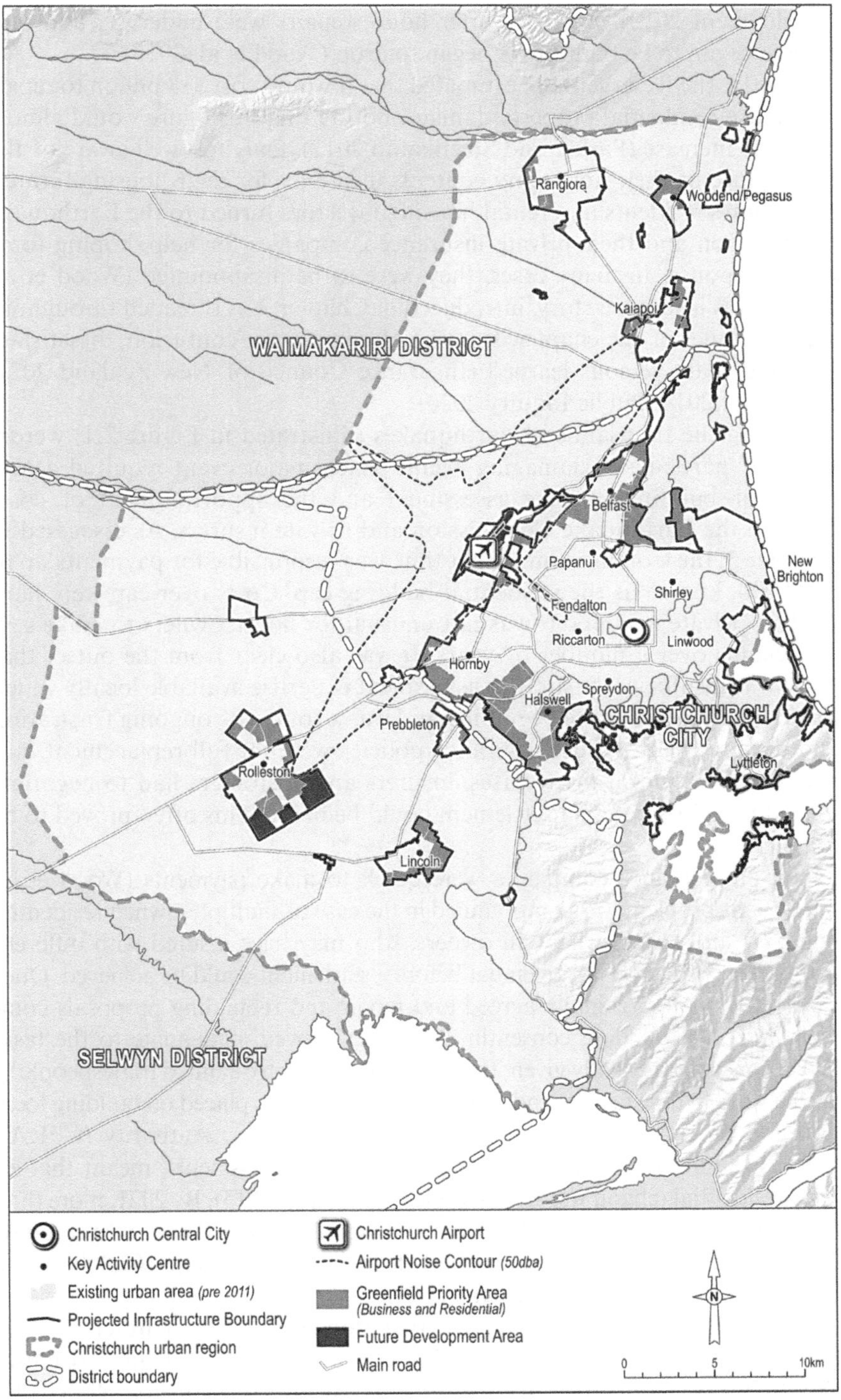

Figure 5.1 The Christchurch urban region.

Source: Greater Christchurch Partnership (2018, 33).

Employment 2013). By 2015, after house repairs were underway and new houses began to be built, rents began to drop (Wood et al. 2016).

In 2012, the Reserve Bank estimated that it would cost $13 billion to repair or replace residential property damage, noting that this figure would almost certainly increase (Parker and Steenkamp 2012). Only too well aware of the importance of their house and contents insurance for their housing futures, the region's residents and rental housing investors turned to the Earthquake Commission and their private insurance companies for help, hoping for a quick response. In many cases, they were to be disappointed (Wood et al. 2016). This insurance story, introduced in Chapter 3, is threaded throughout the remainder of the chapter. It is one of complexity, confusion, dissatisfaction and many lessons learned (Insurance Council of New Zealand 2021; King et al. 2014; Public Inquiry 2020).

Among the thousands of earthquakes (illustrated in Figure 2.1) were a series of particularly damaging events. Each major event required a new round of building damage assessment and the apportionment of costs between the Earthquake Commission and private insurers. As discussed in Chapter 3, the Commission at that time was responsible for payments up to $100,000, known as the residential building cap. Costs over-cap were handled by private insurers. It was not unusual for house owners to make several claims over a number of years. It was also clear from the outset that there was insufficient insurance assessment expertise available locally which slowed the process at the beginning and was a source of ongoing frustration and disagreement. House insurance policies were for full replacement, not agreed value, and in many cases, insurers and customers had to negotiate the value of loss before a settlement could be made. This often proved to be difficult.

Not all insurance companies were quick to make payments (Wood et al. 2016). This problem was compounded in the case of multiply-owned residential buildings and spaces where all owners, who may have insured with different companies, had to be in agreement before a settlement could be achieved. Once each settlement was finally agreed and repair and rebuilding proposals completed, council building consenting processes proved inadequate to the task. When consent was finally given, there were not enough qualified tradespeople to do the work. These factors and a number of limitations placed on building location and progress by Canterbury Earthquake Recovery Authority (CERA), such as the need to complete geo-technical land assessments, meant that an early residential rebuild was not possible (Potter et al. 2015). By 2021, more than 650,000 claims (both residential and commercial) had been made as a result of the earthquakes. Private insurers had dealt with more than 168,000 claims (Insurance Council of New Zealand 2021).

It is within this context that interpretation of the Christchurch Central Recovery Plan (the blueprint), produced by CERA's Christchurch Central Development Unit and the Land Use Recovery Plan, developed by Environment Canterbury, Christchurch City Council, Selwyn District Council, Waimakariri District Council and Te Rūnanga o Ngāi Tahu, working with

Waka Kotahi and CERA (CERA 2013), is essential for understanding housing provision and changes to urban form during the earthquake recovery period. Recovery planning began by incorporating elements of the Greater Christchurch Urban Development Strategy in these new plans for the central city and wider urban region. The blueprint (Figure 4.3) directed the Christchurch City Council to amend its district plan living zone provisions. A condensed and clearly framed central city was planned, as described in Chapter 4. The frame was designed to redefine the central city and provide an attractive and welcoming location for a range of commercial, recreational, cultural as well as residential activities. While the district plan had provided opportunities for medium density residential development throughout the central city, the recovery plan identified, particularly, the east frame for housing, but some also within the north frame (Central City Recovery Plan 2012). It was assumed that the existing areas of downtown medium-density housing would continue to be important. Immediate questions focused on how the new large-scale medium-density developments could be designed and built in a coordinated, attractive and affordable way, and how private sector investment could be harnessed to deliver them.

The future for the urban region beyond Christchurch's central city was laid out in the Land Use Recovery Plan. It covered suburban Christchurch and towns stretching from Lincoln, Prebbleton and Rolleston in the south to Kaiapoi, Rangiora and Woodend/Pegasus in the north (Figure 5.1). This plan was produced recognising that the pre-existing Greater Christchurch Urban Development Strategy with its very strong emphasis on urban intensification and slow land release on the urban margins was not well suited to dealing with the need to build a lot of new housing quickly. Changes to the Regional Policy Statement and respective council district plans were required. The land assigned for slow release in the Urban Development Strategy was to be made available quickly to provide for an anticipated 40,000 new households in both greenfield and intensification areas. It was expected that the private commercial sector would design and build these new housing developments (CERA 2013).

Related transport and infrastructure spending to reflect these land use planning changes was also prioritised in the Land Use Recovery Plan. Consideration was given to revitalising town and suburban centres by identifying key activity centres including satellite town centres in Rolleston and Lincoln in Selwyn District, Rangiora, Kaiapoi and Woodend/Pegasus in Waimakariri District and an array of centres in suburban Christchurch City. Brownfield sites, to be used for residential, mixed-use or business development, were identified, and the plan aimed to permit the building of 8,000–10,000 higher density dwellings in existing, mainly suburban areas, but surprisingly, also planned not to change their character. Overall, the Land Use Recovery Plan stressed urgency and streamlined processes because of recovery needs (CERA 2013). By next considering in turn each of the broad areas of the Christchurch urban region – the central city, the suburbs and satellite towns – it can be seen what kinds of outcomes were achieved.

Central city housing development

Overall, progress in the central city has been both uneven and fitful. In 2012, the city council and the Crown initiated an international design competition for an anchor residential demonstration project, Whakaaturanga Kāinga, to be built on the 8000 square metre Madras Square, a Crown-owned site opposite Latimer Square (Figure 4.3). The objective was to enrol the private sector to create an inspirational exemplar central city medium-density neighbourhood based on sustainable design principles (McDonald 2021a). A New Zealand-Italian consortium won the competition with their 'Breathe Village' plan. The jury praised the proposal for 73 timber-clad three-story house and medium-rise apartments as being 'well-designed and structurally innovative, as well as an affordable and sustainable option'. (Jewell 2014). Sales prices were not indicated but early estimates ranged from $300,000 to $900,000 per unit, at a time when Christchurch's median house price had reached $400,000 (Jewell 2014; McDonald 2013b), thus raising questions about affordability. In November 2015, it was announced that the project had failed due to high-risk market conditions and an inability to secure finance.

In a second attempt to build on the site, the non-profit New Zealand-Australian Ōtautahi Urban Guild was chosen by Ōtākaro Ltd (see Chapter 4) as the preferred developer in late 2018 (McDonald 2018b). The Guild proposed a 150-home affordable co-housing development with a focus on sustainability and communal spaces. It required the city council to carry some of the financial risk, which it did initially in the form of a $450,000 loan. The council ultimately baulked at the Guild's later and much larger $2.8 million loan request, which effectively ended its housing aspirations on the Madras Street site (McDonald 2020a). Ōtākaro Ltd then sold the site to private sector property developers in March 2021. The new owner, a consortium of New Zealand's largest independently-owned house builder and an active Christchurch commercial property developer, proposed to build around 111 homes, ranging from two-bedroom apartments over retail spaces, through to three-bedroom townhouses around a communal garden. Work started in the first half of 2022.

The city council encouraged central city housing development in other ways. In 2018, it initiated Project 8011. Named for the postcode of the central city, it aspired initially to have 20,000 residents living there by 2024, up from 6,000 at the time (McDonald 2018a). To reach this target, it proposed supporting and accelerating housing construction that would meet diverse needs and create highly liveable neighbourhoods. The council thus developed policies to improve the feasibility of new development by providing financial incentives and advice to central city developers (Christchurch City Council 2018). The New Zealand Property Council judged the Project's population target unrealistic, however, noting that high land and building costs, less expensive housing options in the suburbs and a weak apartment culture were impediments to central city residence (McDonald 2018a). Charles Montgomery, a visiting award-winning Canadian author and urbanist, expressed similar views, noting that while the blueprint 'had the right ideas', suburban growth on the urban margins, permitted by the Land Use Recovery Plan, was 'sucking the life from ... downtown development efforts' (Doudney 2015, 15).

While these varying hopes, expectations and criticisms were being aired, something interesting, if not entirely straightforward, was happening with central city housing. In September 2014, the Minister of Housing in the National-led government, Dr Nick Smith, had signed a housing accord with the Christchurch City Council aimed at increasing the immediate and longer-term supply and affordability of homes in Christchurch. Consistent with that accord, in May 2015, the Minister announced that Fletcher Living, a national construction company of long standing, had been contracted to build approximately 200 apartments and terraced house on what had been city council-owned land at the edge of the central city but outside the frame. Twenty per cent, or 38 of the new homes were to cost $450,000 or less (Wood and Meier 2015). Further, in July 2015, the Prime Minister announced that Fletcher Living would develop another 1000 townhouses over eight or nine years in central Christchurch, in the east and north frames in an $800 million project (Figure 4.3). The homes were to be built in 14 complexes within three neighbourhoods. As a risk-reduction incentive for Fletcher Living, the land on which each complex was to be built was to be purchased from the Crown progressively as each was constructed (Key 2015). While not confirmed, it was thought that townhouses and apartments would sell for between $400,000 and $900,000 (Wood 2015). It was expected that approximately 2000 people would live in the new housing.

The Fletcher housing development, named 'One Central', and plans for a large neighbouring public park, to be known as Rauora Park, attracted a great deal of interest, not least because they signalled a new beginning for what had become a desolate urban space. But this sense of relief was accompanied by concerns about who might be able to afford the new housing and whether employment growth and the rebuild in the central city would help create sufficient demand (Wood and Meier 2015). The question of investor purchase, where apartments could be listed on Airbnb and other short-stay accommodation websites, was also raised (Law 2020a). Matters were complicated for Fletcher Living by design and commercial issues and it was some years before its One Central housing came on stream (McDonald 2019a). The first of the larger, more expensive units (priced from $1.15 to $1.6m) was available in early 2019 and by June 2019, 'close to six months on the market... [they were] struggling to sell' (Young 2019). Smaller, less expensive apartments sold more quickly, many to investors as rental properties (McDonald 2019b). Construction progress was slow, and by March 2021 only 20 per cent of the planned housing had been built, but with more planned by Fletcher Living. The houses being constructed in late 2021 ranged in price from $675,000 to $1 million (McDonald 2021b). This was at a time when Christchurch's median house price was $700,000.

In a bid to increase the speed of development, in October 2021, Ōtākaro Ltd announced that it was 'excited to be bringing two large central city sites to market for medium/high density housing' (Ōtākaro Limited 2021), which meant that from 2022 Fletcher Living would be joined by other housing developers in the east frame. Beyond the frame, but still in the central city, other property developers have been at work. The Mike Greer Group, for example, has built terraces and apartments, priced between $699,000 and $950,000. The Williams Corporation, a new company formed after the earthquakes to build moderately priced housing, has constructed an array of medium-density housing units in the central city in the price range $300,000 to $975,000 (Williams Corporation 2021). Sales were reported to be 'strong and steady' (McDonald 2020c). This company's business model is not without controversy, however. Some of its apartments were built without motor vehicle garaging in order to keep costs and prices down. Neighbours complained that residents would park their cars on already congested streets (Truebridge 2018), a not uncommon problem in medium-density housing neighbourhoods elsewhere in New Zealand. Others were unhappy with the design quality of some of the new central city housing, a view supported in a report from the city council's urban design team (Law 2020b).

It is clear that by 2022 some of the housing objectives of the central city blueprint were being met, despite early failures, with houses being built and sold in moderately good numbers. On the other side of the ledger, a good deal of the new housing was expensive and not affordable to people on low and moderate incomes, including families with children, and was thus not meeting the Plan's objective of housing a diverse population. The city council's 8011 Project aspiration to have 20,000 people living in the downtown by 2024 was revised to 2028 (McDonald 2018a), but commentators have suggested that this is also not realistic (Zaki 2021). They noted that the population had reached just over 8000, the same as that just prior to the earthquake sequence (McDonald 2022).

Suburban housing

In the years that followed the earthquakes, all suburban houses were assessed for damage by the Earthquake Commission and insurance companies. Many in the west and north of the city, outside areas of liquefaction risk, suffered little, receiving only small payments from the Commission for repairs. In these cases, owners themselves were expected to arrange with contractors to do the work. Damage to paths and driveways was not covered by the Commission, and when these needed to be repaired or replaced, insurance companies contracted appropriate firms directly to do the work. In areas zoned as TC2 and TC3, as described in Chapter 3, being many suburbs closer to the central city, on the estuarine coast and the hills to the east and south of the central city, a lot more houses were significantly damaged. In these cases, insurers took responsibility for repairs or replacement. When houses were replaced, before rebuilding, geotechnical assessments of the ground at individual sites had to be completed, often requiring more sophisticated house foundations than used previously. The day-to-day effect of these assessments and repairs was that the established suburbs were, for some time, alive with workers and their vehicles, and this, combined with above- and below-ground public infrastructure repairs, caused considerable house and neighbourhood disruption.

While the majority of house owners were generally happy with their insurance payments and repairs, it became apparent that all was not well with aspects of the repair process. Lawyers warned that some earthquake-damaged houses were being bought in an 'as-is condition', hurriedly repaired cosmetically, and on-sold concealing major structural damage, leaving the new owners to deal with the mess, and affecting the housing market for years to come (Grimshaw & Co 2014). By 2015, media reports were appearing detailing examples of 'shoddy' insurance-funded repairs, often to floors and sub-floor piles and foundations, sometimes requiring more than one attempt to remediate them (Cropper 2017). By 2017, documents released under the Official Information Act revealed that the Earthquake Commission had received approximately 11,500 shoddy repair claims (Bayer 2017). As these claims were settled, new damage was often found in houses and underground stormwater and sewer drains, leading to further claims being opened up to ten years after the September 2010 earthquake (EQC 2021). This was often both disruptive and stressful for owners. Claims were filed with the High Court seeking remedies. In 2019, the government agreed to spend as much as $300 million to help 1000 Canterbury homeowners caught in a 'legal quagmire' over shoddy earthquake repairs in on-sold over-cap houses (*Otago Daily Times* 2019).

Another group of house owners found themselves in ongoing and seemingly irresolvable disputes with their insurers for significant sums (Hayward 2018). One owner, speaking anonymously, characterised the modus operandi of his insurance company as being one of 'deny, debate, delay', and in this kind of situation, worn down by the negotiation process, some house owners settled reluctantly on terms that they found unsatisfactory. The Insurance Council of New Zealand's position on this situation was that insurance companies were operating in a complex environment where multiple expert reports, commissioned by the Earthquake Commission, insurers and house owners, conflicted with each other, and disputes and delays were therefore inevitable (Insurance Council of New Zealand 2021). In a bid to expedite and resolve continuing long-standing claims, often already before the courts, in 2019 the Labour-led government established the Canterbury Earthquakes Insurance Tribunal, which continued to operate three years later.

While attaining satisfactory insurance results remained the main objective for many people, others, having lost their homes and received insurance or other government compensation payments, or having arrived in Christchurch from elsewhere, were looking for suitable housing. While the repair process unfolded, there was initially some house building in the suburbs, but this tapered off in 2016. It ramped up again to meet increasing demand at a time of low interest rates, and by 2020 a house-building boom was well underway. New house numbers increased by 13 per cent on the previous year, compared with a 5.9 per cent rise nationally. The mainly detached-house Christchurch suburb of Halswell in the south of the city experienced the greatest population growth. Between 2013 and 2018, Halswell's population increased by approximately 7000 people, or 34.3 per cent, putting pressure on local schools. By comparison, Christchurch City's overall population increased by 8.9 per cent in the same period (Christchurch City Council 2021a). Shopping and service precincts were also built with accompanying free car parking as a key feature of this suburban growth.

While detached-house suburbs grew, however, a good deal of medium-density housing appeared in the suburban landscape. Of the 2900 houses consented by the city council during 2020, 'more than half were apartments, flats, townhouses or retirement units' (McDonald 2020c, 1). Many of these were located along arterial routes, near suburban service centres and overlooking parks and other amenity areas, a phenomenon not often seen before the earthquakes (Figure 5.2). Some of this medium-density housing was priced expensively, in the order of $2 million a unit, but most was built and marketed at lower levels, consistent with that found in the central city. And as there, a significant proportion of the new housing had been purchased by rental housing investors. Some buyers were local, but out-of-town investment was also important, with units priced under $550,000 being most favoured (McDonald 2019b). Concerns were raised about the financing of these housing investments, often bought off developers' plans, without knowing how exactly finance would be arranged. One industry commentator characterised the situation as 'over-enthusiastic investment by unsophisticated people, a lot of them out of Auckland' (Edmunds 2017). This reflects the fact that in New Zealand, rental housing investment is seen by many families as a fall-back savings option.

As the medium-density housing sector developed in the suburbs, neighbours of the new housing, and their Members of Parliament, lobbied the city council to tighten the rules regulating this. As in the past, concerns focused on erosion of privacy from being overlooked by neighbours, loss of sunlight and neighbourhood amenity, and increase in crime (Harris and Hayward 2019; Vallance et al. 2005). Pushing back on this view, developers argued that they offered part of the solution to housing affordability and should be allowed to proceed unhindered. The result of high levels of post-earthquake housing supply was that by 2021 housing affordability in Christchurch, both in terms of rents and house prices, while still challenging for people on low and fixed incomes, was better than in other New Zealand regions where housing affordability has become an issue of considerable social and political concern (Figure 5.3). As per the Land Use Recovery Plan, medium-density housing construction contributed to this, but so too did conventional suburban development, where detached houses were getting smaller and being built on smaller parcels of land, leading to another form of residential intensification. Statistics New Zealand data show that an average-priced house approved in Christchurch in 2020 was 127 square metres in size compared with 185 square metres a decade before. This downsizing was partly offsetting the rise in construction costs (McDonald 2021c).

Figure 5.2 Medium-density housing in the suburbs at (top) Wigram and (bottom) in the central city.

Credit: Stuff Limited

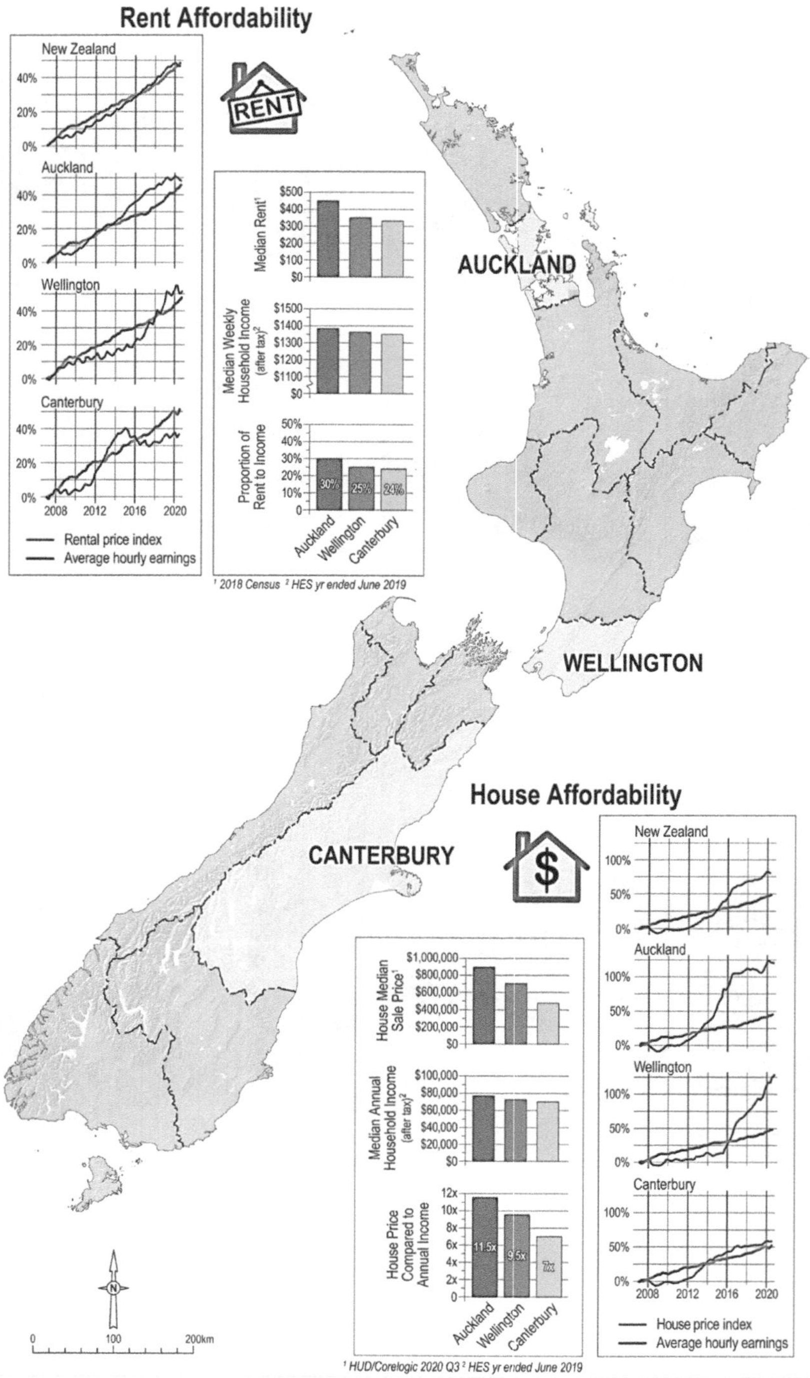

Figure 5.3 Housing affordability in Canterbury and New Zealand.

Source: stats.govt.nz/infographics/the-state-of-housing-in-aotearoa-new-zealand

One exception to this trend in house scale and price was in the high-status suburb of Fendalton, but there too a level of residential intensification became evident. Fendalton is located on the inner edge of the suburbs to the north and west of the central city. While much of the media attention after the initial earthquakes was on the widespread destruction and disruption in the eastern suburbs and around Kaiapoi, local media outlets were silent about damage in Fendalton. But it was clear to anybody watching closely that the houses of the wealthy had also taken a major hit. One commentator suggested that the reason not too many people beyond the suburb fully understood the situation was because 'much of the damage [was] … hidden down long driveways, behind tall fences and screened by the mature trees and lush gardens that are as much a trademark of the suburb as its whopping real estate prices' (Cropp 2011).

In a locality where properties with stream boundaries were in high demand, and a good number of older houses were built from double brick and other forms of unreinforced masonry, intense shaking, liquefaction and ground deformation had an inevitably devastating influence. The first casualties were the large double brick mansions built in the late nineteenth and early twentieth centuries. They cracked and partially collapsed, and were demolished quickly. Many other houses were still liveable but required major repairs. This situation continued for some years as owners negotiated for often large insurance payments. As in other suburbs, Fendalton saw its share of initial busy house repairs, but then a major rebuild began of big new architecturally designed detached houses, some discussed in *Mansion Global*, an international luxury real estate listing website (Singer 2020). A number of large, very valuable lots, once the site of a single house, were subdivided and infilled by building several detached houses, or groups of townhouses, contributing to further residential intensification in the suburbs. Comparatively high prices were sought for old and new houses in Fendalton, with the median price reaching $1,263,600 in April 2021 (Barclay 2021), and in its 'elite streets' over $2 million (Hawkes 2018).

Two other forms of residential intensification in Christchurch's suburbs are worth mentioning. The first is private sector for-profit retirement villages. These became increasingly conspicuous in the suburban landscape during the recovery period, although this trend was developing earlier with a group of public and private New Zealand and multinational companies offering aged-care facilities and services. In 2021, 100 such facilities provided various forms of medium-density and apartment living in the urban region. Additionally, central government's public housing agency, Kāinga Ora – Homes and Communities, which is one of Christchurch's largest house builders, stresses medium-density living in its design guidelines. During the recovery period, in the suburb of Aranui, for example, this agency built several multi-unit housing complexes (Walton 2021a). Similarly, the Ōtautahi Community Housing Trust, which contracts to Christchurch City Council to manage its social housing stock, also builds medium-density housing. In 2021, the trust completed its 90-unit, Hoiho Lane complex, to replace the Brougham Village which was demolished after the 2011 earthquakes (RNZ 2021).

In these various ways, the objectives of the Land Use Recovery Plan to encourage house repair, and rapid construction on newly released land on the edge of the suburbs, have been achieved. The plan's suburban residential intensification objective, too, has been realised to a noticeable extent. Questions of housing affordability remained for those on moderate to low incomes. It seems likely that cases of residential intensification that are perceived to be poorly designed and located will attract continuing opposition from neighbourhood residents and their political representatives, and that the city council's multi-unit urban design criteria will have to be more strictly applied. Detached houses remain the dominant housing type in the suburbs, but with many new houses being built on smaller lots than in the past.

New housing in the satellite greenfields

One of the most visually spectacular outcomes of the housing recovery has been the construction of extensive detached-housing developments in the satellite townships of Waimakariri and Selwyn Districts. This is reflected in the south and westward redistribution of the region's population since the earthquakes (Statistics NZ 2018). New houses in these developments are being sought by city residents and in-migrants, often with children, who prefer living in single-family housing. These townships comprise a particular kind of landscape of consumption in which houses and a range of retailing and hospitality services are utilised. The houses are significant sites of individual and family leisure, and key to that is the space they offer to use and store an array of leisure-orientated consumer items (Figure 5.4). Commuter travel to and from these satellite towns is also part of their attraction. Heins' (2015) study of the subjective experience of daily travel from the greenfields showed that many residents place a significant positive value on their work journey and related family trips. This is notwithstanding the obvious impact this commuting has on oil use and carbon emissions.

Rolleston and Lincoln townships in Selwyn, the second fastest growing district in New Zealand, stand out as excellent examples of such satellite townships (Figure 5.1). Rolleston is 25 kilometres and less than a 30-minute drive by car from the Christchurch central city at the end of the new southern motorway. At the 2018 New Zealand Census, it had a population of 17,532, up from 8079 in 2013, a 117 per cent increase. The Selwyn District Rolleston Structure Plan indicates that Rolleston's population could reach 50,000 residents by 2075. In 2012, Rolleston had one primary school; by 2021, this had increased to seven. A large new secondary school opened in 2016, with a second on the way. In 2016, journalist John McCrone argued that 'it was time to take Rolleston seriously', pointing out that its public and private service facilities were growing in size and number. These included parks, a new library and community centre, extensions to its swimming pool and many new business premises providing for manufacturing, warehousing, rail and road transport and rural servicing (McCrone 2016a). The construction of a

Figure 5.4 Detached housing in Lincoln: (top) Lincoln Dale subdivision, illustrating the significance of detached houses for the off-street storage of recreational and other consumption goods. Credit: Alamy; and (bottom) houses bordering the Lincoln wetland. Credit: Stuff Limited

$85 million shopping mall was announced in 2021. Rolleston is also home to Selwyn District Council's administration offices. The township is therefore much more than a dormitory suburb because it also provides a range of employment opportunities across a range of sectors. The December 2021 median house price at $802,000 in Rolleston was $100,000 more expensive than that of Christchurch city, but housing remained attractive to buyers (OPES partners 2022).

Lincoln, on the other hand, is 23 kilometres and 25 minutes by car from the Christchurch central city, and travel times to the city have also been positively influenced by the proximity of the new southern motorway. By 2018, Lincoln's footprint was ten times greater than it was in 1998. Smaller than Rolleston, the Lincoln urban area had a population of 6510 at the 2018 New Zealand Census, an increase of 3690 people (131 per cent) since the 2006 Census. Its structure plan is expecting the population to increase to 10,136 in 2041, but this is likely an underestimate. The town is serviced by two primary schools and one secondary school, and is home to a small specialist university and several Crown Research Institutes. These, along with a growing array of public and private service facilities in its central business district are significant sites of employment. In December 2021, Lincoln's median house price was $812,150 (OPES partners 2022), making the town more expensive to live in than both Christchurch city and Rolleston. Detached house construction continues at pace. As shown in Figure 5.4., some of these houses, built as part of the Ngāi Tahu Property's Te Whāriki development, are located beside a spring-fed wetland planted and managed for stormwater reticulation, and this is a notable part of Lincoln's residential amenity. In 2021, a local developer, Carter Group, applied to Selwyn District Council to have 186 hectares of farmland rezoned, on which it proposed building 2000 houses and developing a small commercial precinct. If consented, this new housing could accommodate a further 5400 residents (McDonald 2021d).

Conclusion

The loss of, and widespread damage to, many houses as a result of the earthquakes was highly disruptive and meant that owner-occupiers and rental housing investors became involved in often protracted engagements with the insurance sector, local government building regulators, and the building industry as they replaced or repaired their properties. Renters were often confronted with limited housing choice and considerable variation in rental costs. Housing availability in the central city, suburbs and urban periphery, and the broader management of urban form, was influenced by the implementation of central and local government recovery plans and the actions of residential property developers. As a result, the suburbs, particularly the outer suburbs, and satellite greenfields displayed a good deal of path dependency when considered in terms of the Christchurch urban region's historical sprawling growth trajectory.

In a process of planning re-regulation, streamlined procedures in the Land Use Recovery Plan, and rapid land subdivision to cater for very significant housing demand, overrode the aspiration of the pre-earthquakes Urban Development Strategy planners for a residentially denser urban region. The resultant release of peripheral greenfield land, that had previously been zoned for later and much slower release, saw developers building what they knew best: a lot of financially low-risk, detached housing. This met the recovery plan objective to build many houses quickly, at relatively affordable prices, which also accorded with the housing preferences of many owner-occupiers. Recent plans for the urban region developed consistent with the National Policy Statement on Urban Development suggest that these detached housing development trends on the urban margin will continue (Greater Christchurch Partnership 2018).

Growth on the margins of the Christchurch urban region was also enabled by new transport links. Originally included in the Urban Development Strategy, these were built primarily to facilitate the movement of commercial transport, and funded as part of the government's Roads of National Significance motorway construction programme (McCrone 2014a; Waka Kotahi New Zealand Transport Agency 2021a). The building of the Christchurch Southern, Western and Northern corridors cut commuting times to and from Christchurch city. The road-building programme, at a cost of $900 million, was announced in January 2010, before the earthquakes, and progressed alongside earthquake recovery. A cycleway programme was also initiated (Waka Kotahi New Zealand Transport Agency 2021b). These cycleways and the construction of new motorways reinforced the long-established trend to sprawl in Christchurch's urban form, but conflicted with the desire for a strong central city embodied in the Central City Recovery Plan (Pawson 2022).

In the central city, and the suburbs built before the earthquakes, a stronger connection between the Urban Development Strategy and Central City Recovery Plan was established. In the suburbs, there is now more residential intensification than previously, and rental investors and owner-occupiers have taken advantage of the new housing. In the central city, developers were encouraged to build medium-density housing, and a number of firms are doing so. But despite this break from past housing trends, progress has been fitful and plans only partially successful, which is consistent with accounts of plan implementation in complex situations where novel solutions are sought. Housing affordability in the central city remains a significant issue. Details are sketchy as to how much of the new housing has been purchased by short- and long-term rental investors. Aspirations to see a much larger, more diverse and vibrant community of long-stay owner-occupiers living in the central city than that in place prior to the earthquakes have not materialised. But it is clear from media reports that many of those who have chosen to rent or buy in the central city are happy with their choice and the urban lifestyle it affords.

6 City centre recovery and commercial property investment

Introduction

Christchurch's commercial property sector was affected dramatically by the earthquake sequence and the building demolition that followed. The loss of workspace dislocated businesses, government and volunteer and community agencies, forcing them to reorganise activities and operate beyond the boundaries of the central city. It also reinforced previous strongly articulated public and private sector commitments to the downtown and refocused pre-earthquake attempts to stem its decline in the face of growing suburban competition, particularly from retailing, hospitality and allied services. There was never any question about rebuilding the central city as a multifunctional urban space in situ, regardless of the difficulties faced. Economic, political, cultural and popular interests coalesced around this approach. Thus local government, the Crown and local property owners engaged in a protracted central city recovery effort which continues to unfold. The objective of this chapter is to outline that recovery process, showing how cooperative, contested and sometimes antagonistic interaction between the Christchurch City Council, Crown agencies, property owners, their insurance companies and the region's residents have led to a partial regeneration in a situation of 'staggering complexity' (Resilient New Zealand 2015).

At the outset, the city council used its resources and expertise to help Christchurch residents envision a future design for the city centre. The council engaged in a public participation project to define that vision and lay out the steps it could take to implement its design. Controversially, as Chapter 4 has outlined, the Canterbury Earthquake Recovery Authority (CERA) then stepped in with its own Christchurch Central Recovery Plan, the blueprint, designed to enrol as many rebuild participants as possible, including overseas investors. To encourage that investment, the Crown promised to commit generously to a range of civic anchor facilities and precincts. Using its statutory powers, and operating under urgency, CERA also limited some lines of property development action and facilitated and quickened others. The Crown's approach was tempered by the knowledge that in a market-centred society such as New Zealand's, commercial property owners and their building insurers, over which they held limited sway, were going to be key actors in any form of central city recovery.

DOI: 10.4324/9780429275562-8

Property investment decision-making and calculative practices

After the earthquakes, city administrators and the news media were alive to the potential of capital flight from Christchurch if property owners decided not to reinvest in central city recovery (McCrone 2011). They were influenced by a popular view that property investment decision-making and behaviour is economically rational: that private property owners seek to maximise profit in all circumstances and act accordingly (Diaz 1999). While it is true that post-earthquake Christchurch did not seem a propitious place to invest, and there was some capital flight, in the event, most local commercial property owners remained and re-invested in the city. This boundedly rational behaviour contained important strategic and affective elements (de Bruin and Flint-Hartle 2003).

Its strategic elements reflected calculative practices that are locally generated and quite different from those performed by national and trans-national institutional commercial property investment companies (Halbert et al. 2014). Such companies are often owned by multiple shareholders, sometimes listed on national and international stock exchanges, and hold large high-value property investment portfolios comprising clusters of individual properties. Their investment decisions are influenced strongly by a fiduciary duty to minimise risk and maximise returns for shareholders. The people who manage these companies are guided by algorithms that use investment data collected by specialist agencies, and decisions are made significantly in economically rational 'spread-sheet' financial terms (David and Halbert 2014). Such data are not readily available for small provincial cities like Christchurch, and so most institutional property investors do not have the information that would enable them to decide to invest. Additionally, in such places, there are usually very few high-value commercial properties, in the order of $NZ200 million or more, that would be attractive to institutional investors. The few that do exist in Christchurch are suburban shopping malls and these are held in a combination of local and institutional ownership (McDonagh 2021). A good example is Westfield Mall in the suburb of Riccarton. It is owned by Scentre Group, Australia's 15th largest listed company by market capitalisation, valued in 2019 at approximately $A20.68b (Gibson 2019).

Local investors, on the other hand, who prior to and after the earthquake sequence, represent the majority of commercial property owners in the central city, hold land and buildings that, when compared with those owned by institutional investors are of relatively lesser value. These local investors are strongly connected to regional economic activity and allied social networks, and manage their investment portfolios in direct support of particular end uses such as office services, retailing and hospitality. They do not make decisions in purely financial terms. Their decisions about what gets purchased, built and maintained are in part influenced by relationships with financiers, but because many properties are held closely, often multi-generationally, with limited debt, financier-property investor relationships are not as important as they might otherwise be. These investors do not have a fiduciary duty to shareholders and are able to 'take a punt' with their investments in at least slightly riskier ways than those demanded of institutional investors (McDonagh 2021).

When seen in terms of affect, or emotional connection, limited capital flight and commitment to the rebuild in Christchurch reflected local investors' strong senses of place. This is a key finding of research by Ikenna Chukwudumogu who in 2017 interviewed 20 'informed property stakeholders' about their perspectives on commercial property and earthquake recovery in central city Christchurch. They included two public sector managers, three property consultants, 14 property owners and one property finance manager. On the basis of this fieldwork, it was apparent that local commercial property investors, who of necessity became developers after the earthquakes, identified strongly with the city and were emotionally connected to its future (Chukwudumogu 2018a, b; Chukwudumogu et al. 2019). While clearly focused on a reasonable return on capital, at least at some stage in the future, they displayed many of the characteristics of boundedly rational property entrepreneurs reported by Levy et al. (2021). These are strongly place-attached, risk-orientated local business people who imagine positive futures for their hometowns. They are committed to neoliberal market-centred and individualistic values and place-based property development that advance their own and others' business and community interests.

CERA, the city council and later Ōtākaro Limited, the Crown's property developer, thus had to implement their plans alongside and in conjunction with these often well-resourced property owners who had their own agendas to pursue. In general terms, each on their own – local government, the Crown and property owners – believed they had the tools needed to achieve their objectives; but in a chaotic and complex post-disaster environment these tools showed themselves to be imperfect and not completely controllable (Perrow 1986), and in their struggle to gain some semblance of control, the central city rebuild slowly and unevenly worked itself out. In order to contextualise this, the next section considers the pre-earthquake situation of commercial property owners in the central city, and describes their responses to earthquake loss.

Responding to loss in the central city

Prior to the earthquakes, a wide range of private and public services were located in the Christchurch central business district, making it a significant place of employment, hospitality, recreation and education. The concentration of long-established cultural facilities such as the Canterbury Museum, the Christchurch Arts Centre and the Anglican Cathedral set in, and alongside, public squares and other open spaces, made the central city important as a destination for international tourists. The people who worked and played there did so in buildings owned mainly by local, but also some national and international entities, among which were represented a significant group of local wealthy individuals, families and trusts (McDonald 2013a). Some of the local people were owner-occupiers, others investors, the latter making an income from letting commercial property. These locals had dominated the commercial property market since the 1980s and 1990s, when many institutional property investors left the central city for other more profitable locations in New Zealand and overseas, for example, the much larger cities of Auckland and Sydney, because of the relatively low returns to be obtained in Christchurch (McDonagh 2021).

Low investment returns were an element of the widespread recognition that before the earthquake sequence parts of the commercial central city were economically depressed, despite ongoing local government and private sector efforts to rejuvenate it by attempting to attract more people and investment. As one indicator of this, Chang et al. (2014, 8) suggested that 'up to forty per cent of the available floor space in the central city may have been unoccupied prior to the earthquakes'. While having considerable architectural and heritage character, many low-rise buildings constructed in the late nineteenth and early twentieth centuries from unreinforced masonry were nearing the end of their useable commercial lives (McDonagh 2017), although this was a matter for debate between owners, the city council and heritage advocates. From the 1950s, multi-storey steel reinforced concrete office towers had been constructed, and these larger buildings were tenanted to varying degrees by office services, hospitality, accommodation and retailing businesses. The tallest was the 23-floor Pacific Tower, completed in 2010.

Retailing had become a notable challenge. The size of the retail area of the central city was far larger than required, particularly in the face of sustained competition from suburban shopping malls offering free car parking. As was the case for office space, shopping space in the central city was under-utilised: many shops existing there because rents were low, or the occupiers were also owners. Local journalist John McCrone (2016b) suggested that at that time 'Christchurch felt simultaneously over-shopped and yet underwhelming', noting that 'There was plenty of activity, but of a cheap and unfocused kind.' McCrone quoted a retail analyst who had in the past been hired by the city council in an advisory role; in his view 'Christchurch had quantity but not quality. Much of the retail had low productivity and a lot of churn'.

Despite this, in his 2017 interviews, Chukwudumogu (2018a, b) and Chukwudumogu et al. (2019) heard accounts of the feelings of loss, shock and grief experienced by building owners after the 2010 and 2011 earthquakes. All 12 buildings owned by one informant had been damaged or destroyed, including a hotel and two restaurants which he ran himself with 40 staff. He had found the situation traumatising, and was surprised to lose all his holdings at once. By the time of the interview, he had only one remaining staff member. Similar responses to the loss were reported by those who rented and worked in these damaged and destroyed buildings, and the requirement that they vacate their premises caused many challenges. The Crown responded by offering subsidies to assist employers to pay employees at a time when businesses were unable to operate, as described in Chapter 4. These were in addition to the business interruption insurance payments received by some companies (Poontirakul et al. 2016). After the September 2010 earthquake, 64 per cent of businesses had to close at least for a short time. More than one per cent shut down permanently. But after the February 2011 earthquake, the situation was more severe, with 11 per cent closing permanently and the others closing their doors for a median period of 16 days (Potter et al. 2015).

The central city was cordoned for safety reasons by the Civil Defence authorities after the September 2010 earthquake but this lasted only a short time. But immediately after 22 February 2011, Civil Defence reinstated the cordon on a larger scale, encompassing an area of 387 hectares and named the 'CBD red zone' (Chang et al. 2014). With checkpoints manned by police and army personnel, and taking various diminishing shapes, the cordon was to last until 20 June 2013, by which time it covered just a few city blocks and had become the responsibility of CERA who had renamed the cordoned area the 'CBD Rebuild Zone' – although popularly it was still called the 'red zone' (Figure 6.1). The effect of the cordon was that initially, building and business owners were denied access to their premises while structural and safety assessments were conducted and building demolition took place. While in hindsight it is widely agreed that the cordon was necessary and effective, at the time it caused a good deal of stress to those whose freedom of access it limited.

The cordon operated to considerable effect. Six thousand businesses were forced to leave the area within it, affecting 50,000 central city jobs. Not surprisingly, this situation resulted in considerable volatility in the local commercial property market. Businesses and central government departments migrated to the edge of the city. They often took up tenancies in vacant industrial and warehouse properties after owners rapidly converted them to offices, retail and hospitality spaces to take advantage of the high demand and tenants' willingness to sign rental contracts for long enough periods to ensure tenure (Chukwudumogu et al. 2019). These were premises often not of the quality and size preferred (Moricz et al. 2012). The new tenants were to be working in these places for some time, and in late 2021, some were still in place. In another development, a suburban-based property entrepreneur and brewer, Alasdair Cassels, took advantage of the flight to the suburbs and built a multi-unit facility designed to be rented to small retailing and hospitality businesses that had lost their premises in the earthquakes. His property development, The Tannery, is on a former industrial site in the suburb of Woolston, and houses 62 small retailing, hospitality, craft and entertainment businesses, some once in the central city and others having different origins (Stylianou 2013).

As in the case of housing (Chapter 5), insurance was a key concern for building owners after the earthquakes. But unlike housing, the Earthquake Commission had no role in commercial property insurance and so insurance companies and their overseas reinsurers were the centre of attention. Reflecting the fact that insurance coverage for the Canterbury earthquakes was notably higher than in similar jurisdictions overseas (Wood et al. 2016),

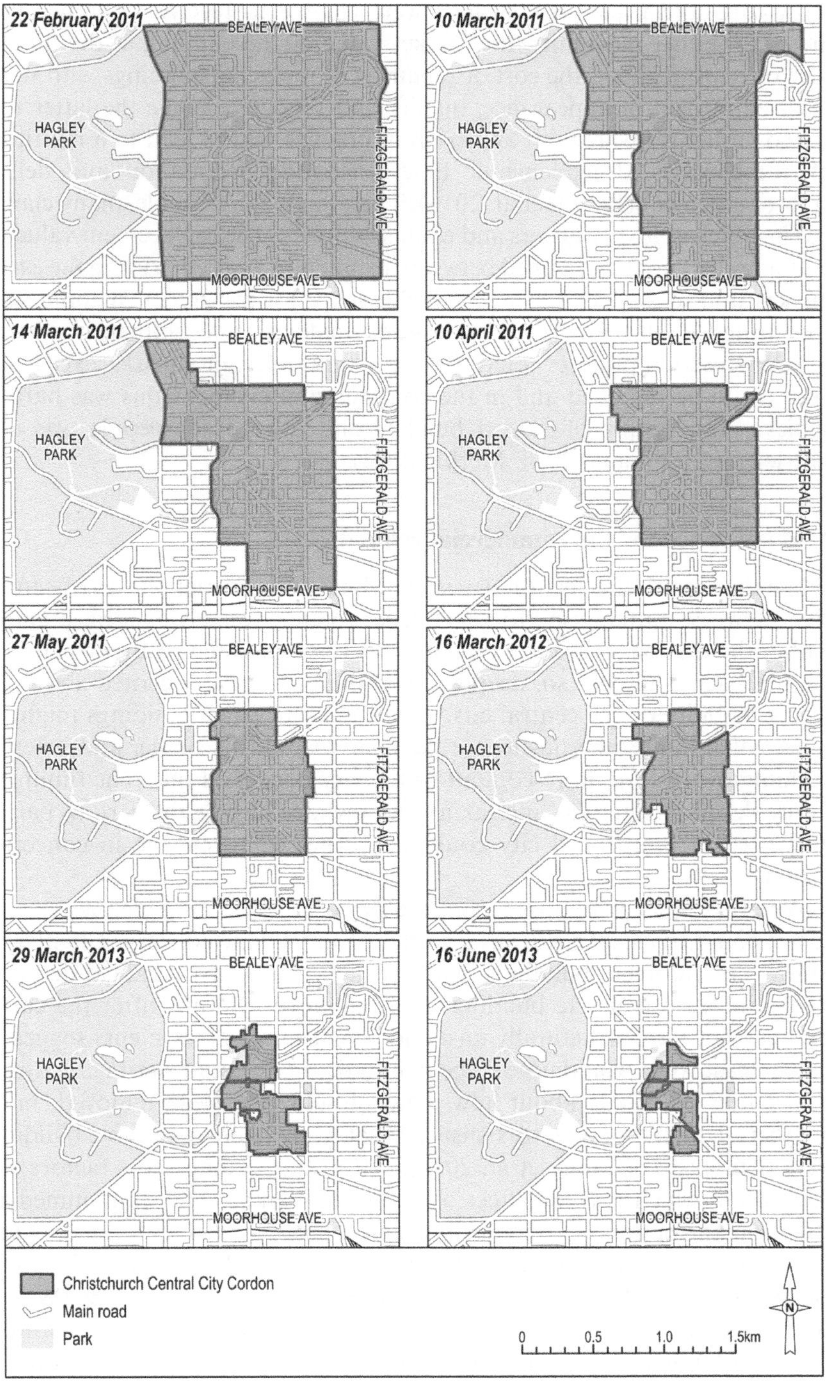

Figure 6.1 Reduction of the Central City cordon, 22 February 2011 to 16 June 2013.

Source: https://maps.cera.govt.nz/. Licensed under Creative Commons Attribution-NonCommercial-ShareAlike 3.0 New Zealand (CC BY-NC-SA 3.0 NZ)

most commercial property owners were eligible to receive insurance payments for either indemnity, the market value of the building at the time of loss, or reinstatement, the cost of repairing or replacing buildings with structures equivalent in appearance, quality and function. While the latter may sound straightforward, this approach in practice was to lead to a multitude of complexities, disagreements, time-consuming negotiation and delays, before settlement (Brown et al. 2013). There were, for example, many claims, but insufficient loss adjusters and claims handlers. The replacement value for buildings had not been agreed between insurer and assured prior to the earthquakes, and so there existed considerable scope for disagreement about what constituted 'equivalence' and how large or small insurance settlements should be. Construction projects could not begin until relevant all-risk-cover insurance could be obtained and in the continuing aftershocks this was hard to achieve. The supply of skilled builders and other tradespeople was also restricted (Grollimund 2014; Merkin 2012).

Making space for the commercial rebuild

While the Civil Defence authorities coordinated the initial phases of central city recovery – attempting to bring order to an extremely chaotic situation within the cordon – the city council and Crown initiated recovery planning for the area. They did so, deeply uncertain and very concerned about the future viability of the central city. It was unclear which buildings might be salvageable, quite how insurance payments would be made, and whether building owners would re-commit to the city once paid out. The timing of future developments was unclear, as was any idea of how the various parties interested in the central city could be harnessed to engage in concerted action.

When recovery planning began, the physical space on which a new city centre could be established was a matter of immediate concern (Chapter 4). Many unreinforced buildings had partially collapsed, and while most steel-reinforced concrete buildings had remained standing after the earthquakes, they were structurally unsound. Engineering assessments suggested that at least some would need to be removed, regardless of heritage status. It is a matter of debate about how many should have been removed, but a number of interacting factors ensured that some likely repairable buildings were demolished (Chang et al. 2014). Prominent among these factors was the cordon which had the effect of delineating an area needing immediate attention and action. Also important were a general air of risk aversion and the enthusiasm shown by the Canterbury Earthquake Recovery Minister, Gerry Brownlee, 'to pull down the old dungers' for safety reasons (Walton 2021b). His view was operationalised by CERA because it had the statutory power to insist on demolition in short order. Low returns on central city commercial property investment also made demolition convenient to some property owners, particularly when linked to their insurance arrangements (Marquis et al. 2017).

The demolition process picked up quickly, growing from 21 demolitions in March 2011 to a peak of 124 in July that year. That was approximately 30 a week or four a day (Gates 2012a, 2015a). The demolition zones within the cordon were busy, dusty and dirty places. Fascinated locals and visitors congregated along the cordon fences, enthralled as they watched and photographed large cranes swing wrecking balls, and high-reach excavators equipped with tools such as pulverisers, shears, breakers and grab attachments, slowly deconstruct tall buildings. Figure 6.2 illustrates the March 2011 demolition of the art deco St Elmo Courts, a Category II listed heritage building constructed in 1930 (with the earthquake-strengthened Christchurch City Council office building standing undamaged behind). These demolished buildings were turned into easily transportable rubble, comprising many materials. Trucks carrying debris away from the central city were a common sight on Christchurch's arterial roads for many years. 850,000 tonnes of material were taken to the Burwood Resource Recovery Park on the edge of the city for recycling, or dumping in two 25-metre-high hills (Law 2019a). An estimated one million tonnes of clean fill were carried to the Port of Lyttleton to allow the Port Company to reclaim 10 hectares of the harbour for its new container storage space, a policy that proved environmentally controversial (Wood 2011).

Figure 6.2 Demolition of St Elmo Courts in March 2011.

Source: http://ketechristchurch.peoplesnetworknz.info/canterbury_earthquakes_2010_2011/images/show/18773-st-elmo-courts-288-montreal-street-22-march-2011–2. Licensed under a Creative Commons Attribution-NonCommercial-ShareAlike 3.0 New Zealand (CC BY-NC-SA 3.0 NZ)

The number of demolitions was not to dip below 20 buildings a month, or five a week, until June 2012, but by February 2015 had declined to two a month. By that time, 1240 buildings within Christchurch's four avenues had been demolished, with approximately the first 1000 being razed by the end of 2012. These comprised 70 per cent of the central city business office, retailing and hospitality stock. Perhaps reflecting the confusion surrounding the measurement of this phenomenon, the Insurance Council of New Zealand (2021) has published slightly different demolition figures, saying that 1354 commercial buildings needed to be demolished in Christchurch – 826 in the central city and 528 in the suburbs. Whatever the exact number, among the buildings demolished were 147 listed with Heritage New Zealand Pouhere Taonga, although the city council count is over 200 as it classifies heritage buildings differently (Walton 2021b). This, as Chapter 4 indicated, was a very contentious issue.

The large scale of the demolition had a dramatic effect on the central city landscape. Figure 6.3 illustrates this in an aerial view of a portion of the central city commercial area – the full city block bounded in the east by Madras Street. The top photograph taken on 24 February 2011, two days after the major damaging earthquake on 22 February 2011, shows some collapsed buildings, notably the CTV building in the bottom right of the block. The bottom photograph was taken five years later on 20 February 2016 of the same area after demolitions and before significant rebuilding in the east frame. The Christchurch Transitional (Cardboard) Cathedral is evident in top right of the image and the 185 Chairs memorial to the people who died in the earthquake sequence is in the lower right.

As central city building demolition proceeded, the city council produced its draft Central City Recovery Plan, as described in Chapter 4, submitting it to the Minister for Earthquake Recovery in December 2011 (Christchurch City Council 2011). The council had consulted on its plan and this attracted 15,500 comments and 2,800 submissions. While many submitters were happy with the proposed direction for the central city, a number were scornful. Among the latter were local commercial property owners and their representatives. They complained that they had not been adequately included in the creation of plans that would very directly affect them and require their property, money and skills to implement (McCrone 2011). Angus McFarlane, owner of more than 10,000 square metres of the city's commercial floorspace, and a member of a family that had held commercial property in Christchurch for over 60 years, told the submissions hearing that 'the city was in despair before the earthquakes, with a failing central economy and diminishing values'. He claimed councillors had made a mess of the city before the quakes, and the draft plan 'proves you have got it wrong again'. McFarlane described the 'obstructive, dictatorial and impractical' plan as a 'rubbish pipedream' that terrified potential investors (Sachdeva and Carville 2011).

He was partially supported in this view by Connal Townsend, the chief executive of the property owners' advocacy organisation, the Property Council of New Zealand, who said that while property owners and developers

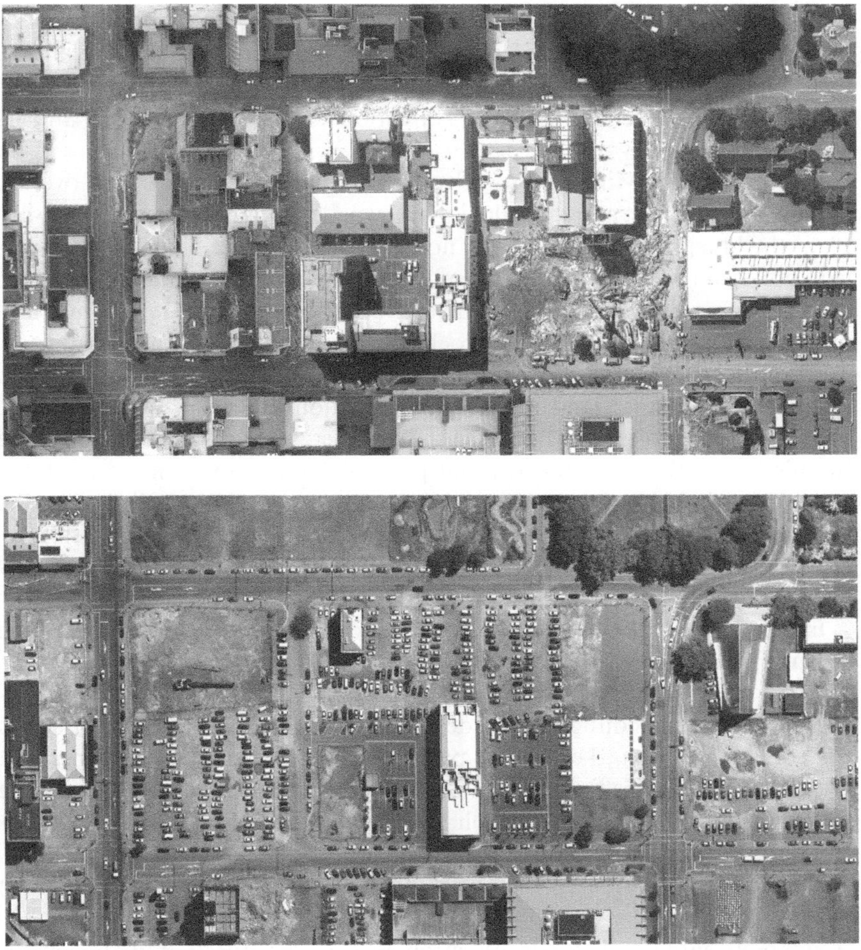

Figure 6.3 A portion of the central city seen from the air in (top) March 2011 and (bottom) March 2016.

Sources: 2011: https://data.linz.govt.nz/layer/51932-christchurch-post-earthquake-01m-urban-aerial-photos-24-february-2011/ and 2016: https://data.linz.govt.nz/layer/53454-christchurch-0075m-urban-aerial-photos-index-tiles-2015-2016/

supported the city council's plan, they were 'terrified' by the details of the proposed regulations, and what they interpreted as extinguishing property owners' existing-use rights (Sachdeva and Carville 2011). While no specific mechanism for doing so was outlined in the plan, it was clear that land title amalgamation and some form of compulsory land acquisition was a likely outcome, described later by journalist Rob O'Neill (2012) as the 'elephant in the room no-one is talking about'. Townsend's view was that such an approach, combined with the general uncertainty about and volatility in the local property market, would greatly increase the risk that central city property owners would reinvest outside Christchurch (McDonald 2012). While resisted by Mayor Bob Parker, these views about the council's plan and the potential for capital flight were held strongly among some property owners and likely influenced CERA's evaluation of the council's plan and its response to it.

Controversially, Minister Brownlee rejected the city council's plan overall, and the authority set about producing its own Christchurch Central Recovery Plan, the blueprint (Figure 4.3). A notable feature of the blueprint's design-led approach (Brand et al. 2020) explicitly confronted the difficult matter of amalgamating existing property titles in order to speed up rebuilding, and particularly to provide the large blocks of land required for the anchor projects and other big scale developments. The likely use of CERA's power to compulsorily acquire land in this amalgamation process had begun to be openly discussed by senior figures in the commercial property sector after the submission of the council's plan but prior to the development of the blueprint (O'Neill 2012). It was clear to them, as it was to Warwick Isaacs, the Christchurch Central Development Unit's newly appointed Director of Earthquake Recovery, that some rationalisation of the central city's variably sized lots held in 3000 land titles was required.

Isaacs wrote in the tender document seeking a consultant to prepare the blueprint that such a situation

> means that it is difficult to undertake development at a variety of scales sought by the market, and in particular, larger-scale developments that could gain from efficiencies and support multiple tenancies. There is little evidence of landowners consolidating their land holdings to create larger scale projects.
>
> (O'Neill 2012)

How to incentivise that consolidation was a key question in a context described by Hamish Doig, managing director of property brokerage Colliers Christchurch, where many properties were held by a significant number of investors whose debts had been extinguished on receipt of insurance payments (O'Neill 2012). The newly minted blueprint also focused on attracting property investors and developers from beyond Christchurch to the central city rebuild, particularly from overseas (McCrone 2014b). Consistent with this aspiration, the Development Unit established a new agency called 'Invest Christchurch' which was charged with developing an international investment marketing campaign (Wood 2012).

As the blueprint was of great interest to local investors and property owners, Christchurch law and real estate firms were quick to offer their advisory and technical services to property-owning clients. A good example is *{mds} law*, a Christchurch legal firm, who produced a recovery plan newsletter (2012), opening with the statement: 'The redevelopment of the central city of Christchurch is an opportunity unlikely to be seen again in several lifetimes. While the redevelopment project promises many exciting investment opportunities it also creates much uncertainty for affected land owners.' In order to inform their clients of a likely future for central city properties, the newsletter writers first described the blueprint's proposals as

> creating a smaller Central City Business Zone made up of a "Core" of commercial, retail, hospitality and residential developments girded by a "Frame" of open space and beyond that a large format retail area. This central Zone was to be 40 hectares in extent, down from 92 hectares prior to the earthquakes.

They then described the proposal to build 17 publicly funded anchor projects valued at $4.8 billon: these to be a range of civic facilities and other initiatives designed to kick start the central city rebuild and attract people and businesses to the centre (Figure 4.4).

Property owners were informed in the newsletter that the Canterbury Earthquake Recovery Act enabled the Minister to fast-track the process of designating land for these anchor projects and approximately 840 properties were to be purchased to enable the construction of the four highest priority projects: the convention centre, Ōtakaro Avon River precinct, the east frame and the metro sports facility. This land was to be acquired either voluntarily with the price negotiated with the owner, or compulsorily, where compensation would be determined under the Act, and possibly at less than market value. Further properties would be required for the development of the remaining anchor projects. This acquisitions process unfolded during 2012 and early 2013. For property owners who wished to engage in voluntary purchase this heralded a complex and time-consuming set of interactions with the Christchurch Central Development Unit in the calculation of property values. Factors involved varied from property owner to property owner and included possibly: insurance, mortgage, securities and tax issues; the status of commercial tenancies; the actual location of the property *vis-à-vis* the blueprint; and land swap arrangements. Where multiple properties were held in different parts of the central city, complexities and uncertainties were compounded.

Apart from this approach to land acquisition, the blueprint supported a rapid approvals process for all applications for new buildings. But allied to that, a number of restrictions and limitations were to be placed on redevelopment in the Central City Business Zone. New buildings had to cover 100 per cent of the site on which they were located, have a maximum height of seven or eight stories and a minimum height of two stories, with car parking up to a maximum of 50 per cent of the premises. In the retail precinct, it was planned to consolidate multiple small sites into minimum lot sizes of 7500 m^2 (one-third of an existing block). The vehicle for achieving this was the fast-track Outline Development Plan and owners of small land titles were encouraged to collaborate with neighbouring landowners, or face compulsory title amalgamation and/or acquisition, so that a plan could proceed expeditiously. Again, this placed property owners in often complex and difficult situations including trying to work out their best way forward: perhaps to sell to a neighbouring property owner or engage in a development partnership, and if so, create the most appropriate legal structure for advancing their chosen option.

Property owners and investors respond

In the face of the planning tactics outlined above, commercial property owners were left to mull over their options. Some chose to invest their capital elsewhere, but it is hard to know the scale of this phenomenon (McCrone 2012a). A good example of a well-established local property owner who took this option is Angus McFarlane whose response to the city council's draft recovery plan was discussed above. In 2013, it was reported that he was living in Houston, Texas, having taken millions of dollars out of Christchurch to invest in oil and gas exploration in the United States. In an interview, he said that he 'didn't do it lightly, but that it was a culmination of everything'. The 'everything' in this case involved continuing dissatisfaction with the work being done by the council and CERA and the fact that the anchor project and precinct designations 'had cost him half the value of his properties' (McDonald 2013c).

The Christchurch Central Development Unit's hoped-for influx of foreign property investment in Christchurch's rebuild failed to materialise (Conway 2014), and so the insurance payments owing to property owners – which in fact were sourced from overseas reinsurers – proved to be the resource that underpinned strong local property owner involvement in the rebuild (McDonald 2013d). The size of the payments to any particular individual reflected the number of properties held and the details and type of their insurance cover, with the amounts in aggregate running to $10.86 billion by March 2021 (Insurance Council of New Zealand 2021). Owners received settlements ranging from hundreds of thousands to many millions of dollars. These insurance payments, supplemented by borrowed and private funds, financed the Christchurch private commercial rebuild. Notwithstanding the widespread concern about the loss of heritage buildings, this process allowed old and sometimes dilapidated structures to be replaced with new and functionally better ones.

On the basis of their research, Chukwudumogu (2018a, b) and Chukwudumogu et al. (2019) argue that local property owners were strongly place-attached and passionate about Christchurch and its future. They had an opportunity to re-invest in a place they knew well and their sense of local connection contributed to their decision, despite few opportunities for immediate profit. As well-resourced and intimately connected locals, these property owners were well positioned to dominate the rebuild. Thus, cautiously optimistic, they proceeded to pursue property investment plans by evaluating emergent opportunities in a situation where there was less land to work with than previously. They were to be faced with moments of worry that this decision was the wrong one. Some of them indicated that re-investing may not have been the best decision when judged purely in financial terms; it was their desire to succeed and contribute to exciting new ventures in the reconstruction of their home town that overrode initial doubts (Chukwudumogu et al. 2019).

For several years after the earthquakes, these property owners expended much effort on the time-consuming complexities of building damage assessment, engaging with myriad allied stakeholders and creating plans for new buildings. Adroitness and flexibility were key requirements. The uncertainty that accompanied this busy round of activity was in part influenced by the tardiness of the blueprint's anchor project roll-out, and it took until 2015 for some clarity to be achieved about that process. The fact that many of the building owners' former business tenants had relocated to the suburbs and were on long leases, raised questions about the short- to medium-term tenanting prospects for any new building they might construct. The data to apply to systematic forecasting of returns, yield and financial viability using standardised methods were not available. Investment decision-making was instead influenced by intuition, past experiences and interaction with others in the commercial property investment community. In this situation, property owners found themselves taking on new and unexpected roles. Where originally, they had been property investors, making a living from letting buildings built by others, they now had to become speculative property developers. They did not, therefore, always understand the processes and challenges of undertaking commercial property developments and this exposed them to risks not before encountered (Chukwudumogu 2018a and b; Chukwudumogu et al. 2019).

This lack of property development and project management expertise resulted in some being unable to manage their projects effectively. Some reported that they had incurred unnecessary costs because in their inexperience they had permitted the construction of over-engineered buildings (Chukwudumogu 2018a and b; Chukwudumogu et al. 2019). In this, and similar situations, their building projects took longer to complete than initially anticipated, and when completed sat untenanted. A good example is the story of the St Elmo Courts rebuild, the pre-earthquake version of which is illustrated in Figure 6.2, and an early candidate for demolition. In February 2015 it was reported that its owner, Richard Owen, was 'bitter and angry about the whole city and deeper in debt than ever' (Gates 2015b). He had rebuilt a six-storey building to very high seismic standards. Having only indemnity insurance he had received a payment of approximately $2 million. The original tender for the building had been $10.5 million but the final cost was $17 million. At completion the building was only half tenanted which was 'pretty nerve wracking and very stressful' (Gates 2015b).

Owen's experience was compounded by the existence and effect of the central city cordon. Many of the investor-developers discussed above held property within the cordon and this was one of the factors that slowed their progress. But property owner-developers such as Owen, who operated outside the cordon, were able to advance their building plans early. The result was a relatively quick edge-of-city-centre commercial rebuild focused mainly on Victoria Street, Durham Street and Cambridge Terrace to the north and west

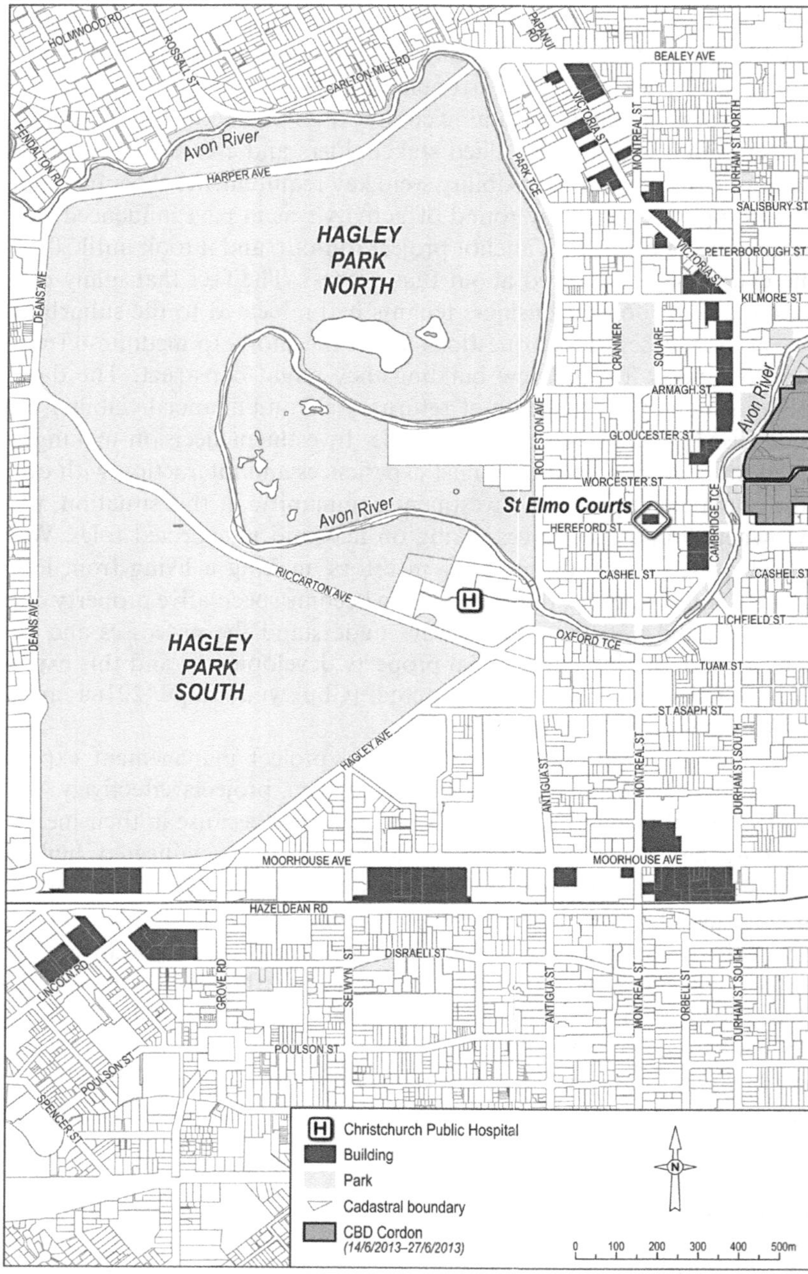

Figure 6.4 Location of edge-of-centre post-earthquake commercial buildings.

of the city centre, and on Moorhouse Avenue and in the area surrounding lower Lincoln Road, in Addington, south and south west of the city centre (McCrone 2014b) (Figure 6.4). The combined result in 2015, as Owen found to his cost, was an over-provision of office space that was difficult to tenant.

The progress of the central city rebuild

The beginning of the central city rebuild was slow, affected by landowner disputes about land title amalgamation which proved to be much harder to achieve than initially thought (McCrone 2012a). While deemed 'sluggish' in April 2015 by journalist and rebuild commentator Liz McDonald (2015a), the private commercial rebuild gained momentum as the cordon shrank (McDonald 2015b). To facilitate office construction the Crown commissioned private developers to construct four office buildings to house approximately 30 of its agencies. This brought a significant group of workers into the central city daily. With respect to shopping, after a halting start and several attempts to create viable Outline Development Plans, discussed above, the billion-dollar-plus City Mall was rebuilt in the retail precinct harnessing the combined effort of several local wealthy business people, some with multi-generational commercial property investment and development interests (McCrone 2015a; Steeman 2012). These included Philip Carter, Nick Hunt, Antony Gough and Tim Glasson.

Created by other younger less well-established property developers, Richard Peebles, Kris Inglis and Mike Percasky, the innovative landscapes of consumption centred on the retailing and hospitality facilities Little High Eatery (McDonald 2017a), which opened in May 2017 and the Riverside Market (Law 2019b), which began operating in September 2019 proved to be very popular. Equally successful, has been the Terrace hub of bars, restaurants and office space on Oxford Terrace beside the Ōtākaro Avon River to the west of the city centre (Kenny 2021a; Mead 2017). These were conceptualised by brothers Antony and Tracy Gough in 2013, and opened progressively, slowed by financing difficulties, through late 2017, with the popular pre-earthquake Viaduct Bar joining them in January 2021. These developments are discussed in more detail in Chapter 9.

In September 2017, Christchurch's revitalised central city was 'still seen as fragile' (McDonald 2017b). In this context, the managing director of a commercial real estate firm reflected on the slow progress of the Crown and city council's major anchor projects (Figure 4.4) and their perceived importance in attracting people to the central city. Intended to be completed during 2017, none of these major projects was delivered on schedule. He said that

> It's really nice to see vibrancy in the spaces created. I just hope there is continued investment by the Crown and the council, and quickly. People in the private sector have made a considerable investment – now it's time for the public sector to deliver on some of its promises.
>
> (McDonald 2017b)

The pace of the commercial rebuild plateaued in 2016–17. Chukwudumogu et al. (2019) point out that in 2016 the office vacancy rate in the city centre was volatile and rents declined into 2017 as a result of office oversupply. Property owners competed to attract tenants from the suburbs by offering incentives such as rent-free periods or fit-out contributions. Smaller operators were still denied access because they could not afford even these lower rents.

A concern expressed early in the recovery process was that the new seismically strengthened central city office buildings and shops, which were more expensive to build than those of the past, and fewer in number, would demand much higher rents than those paid prior to the earthquakes. To a significant extent, this has been true. Corporate and government offices and global brand stores like H&M and Country Road dominate the central city because they can afford to pay. Thus, in many respects, these stores replicate shopping available in suburban malls, but without the free car parking. There is some anecdotal evidence that at least a few landlords levied rents consistent with the funds they had borrowed, rather than the total cost of their new buildings, seeing their insurance payments as a windfall. This was in reality a subsidy on tenants to help them operate in the central city. Despite this, high set-up and operating costs limited margins for central city businesses and in combination with unaffordable rents this, for some, was a cause of their failure. The beneficiaries of this situation were often the next tenants who had lower set-up costs and were therefore able to establish more financially sustainable businesses (McDonagh 2021; McDonald 2020d).

Much of the building construction was done by New Zealand firms, but in order to do so, they required labour sourced globally. In 2015, immigration rules were changed to allow 5000 rebuild workers to enter the country on Essential Skills visas. The arrival of thousands of migrant workers, primarily from the United Kingdom, Ireland and the Philippines injected increasing levels of multiculturalism into the city (Statistics NZ 2018). A number of problems also arose. The warning issued by the Engineering, Printing and Manufacturing Union that this influx of workers would create housing problems was borne out (Jones 2015). Welfare agencies reported that some workers, particularly Filipinos, were exploited by employers and landlords and found themselves living in cramped conditions and paying high rents (Garces-Ozanne et al. 2022; Meier 2014; Stylianou 2015).

Conclusion

The central city commercial property recovery is still unfolding. There is potential for much more to be done. While estimates have varied (Gates 2018), in December 2020 approximately 20 per cent of central city land, 68 hectares in over 450 sites, was empty. Many sites were used as temporary car parks and the cause of public concern, being both visually unattractive and often unconsented (Law 2020c; Walton 2021c). That month, the council approved a plan to 'disincentivise holding vacant land, by using its capacity to levy rates differentially (Law and McDonald 2020). Allied to these issues, a number of central city property owners failed to repair or sell their buildings for redevelopment. Dubbed the 'Dirty 30' by the council, these unoccupied and deteriorating structures were identified as barriers to the central city rebuild in 2017 (Walton 2020). They were either precariously positioned or encroaching on public areas, or partially demolished or derelict. A few were the subject of insurance disputes. Council staff sent the owners warning letters, offering guidance and outlining enforcement possibilities if action was not taken. By 2018 the list had been reduced to eight properties, partly because it had mistakenly included a number of significant heritage buildings (Church 2017). In 2021, city councillor and regeneration working group chair James Gough, a relative of the Gough family of Christchurch commercial property developers and investors, identified the remaining six buildings on the council's list as the 'worst of the worst' (Mitchell 2021).

Greater levels of central city commercial activity were deemed to be the solution to these problems. In late 2021, a report from CBRE New Zealand, a branch of the global commercial real estate and investment firm headquartered in the United States, suggested that such an increase in activity seemed likely. CBRE indicated that the Christchurch central city office vacancy rate had dropped below the pre-earthquake level and that this would stimulate a new round of construction. Consistent with earlier media reports (McDonald 2021e), key actors, CBRE noted, would be a small number of local and offshore land owners either taking on the development role or selling to those who would. Lead times to completion for these developments were likely to be in early 2024 which suggested the likelihood of a squeezed market and increasing rents in the meantime (*The Press* 2021).

Notwithstanding these issues, given the high level of uncertainty and volatility that prevailed after the earthquakes, the progress made in the central city has been significant. This has been due to the adroit and flexible approach taken by property investors turned developers, as they and Crown agencies, the Christchurch City Council and other stakeholders struggled to create innovative opportunities for recovery. Much remains to be done, however, and it will be some time yet before the scars of the demolition process are less evident. Questions remain about the likelihood of attracting 20,000 residents to the central city (Chapter 5). The Greater Christchurch Partnership (2018) expects that over the next 30 years the central city will gain an additional 40,000 jobs, resulting in over 75,000 people working there. The contrast between the situation in early 2022, and this expectation, is stark, and it is not clear quite how such a transformation is to be achieved. This is because, alongside these developments in the central city, the number of attractive, easily accessible and competitive suburban and greenfield retailing and allied service and employment centres continues to increase as Chapter 5 has shown, and therefore the tensions that existed prior to the earthquakes with respect to central city's economic viability are still evident. No easy solutions are in sight.

7 Voluntary and community sector responses

Introduction

Voluntary and community organisations played a significant role in the post-disaster recovery of Christchurch. In the weeks and months following the quakes, a number of well-established organisations, many of which were faith-based, provided temporary accommodation, meals and counselling to affected residents, as well as assisting people to access government support. Several resident-led organisations also arose, energised by concerns regarding the approach of government agencies and private insurers. The Student Volunteer Army emerged as a distinctive form of volunteer-based social movement, with large numbers of students coming together to offer a range of practical assistance.

This chapter examines these three broad forms of voluntarism – that of faith-based organisations, resident-led initiatives and the Student Volunteer Army – and seeks to assess their wider significance. Each form is described in terms of the support it entailed and its intersection with the agendas of state recovery agencies. The position of voluntarism in relation to politically conservative aspirations for rebuilding the city and more progressive forms of place-making is also considered. To support the analysis, the chapter begins with an overview of voluntary welfare provision in Christchurch prior to the earthquakes. Although the terminology used to refer to the voluntary sector varies internationally and includes 'third sector' and the 'not-for-profit sector', the language of 'voluntary welfare sector' and 'voluntary and community organisations' is preferred here. This is in keeping with the vernacular in New Zealand academic and policy circles (Nowland-Foreman 2016).

The background to post-disaster voluntarism in Christchurch

Prior to the earthquakes, the voluntary welfare sector in Christchurch was often associated with the activities of several large and relatively professionalised organisations, many of which had roots in particular denominations of the Christian faith. These organisations – including Anglican Care, Methodist Mission, Presbyterian Support, Catholic Social Services and the Salvation Army – employed significant proportions of paid staff and often

DOI: 10.4324/9780429275562-9

held service provision contracts with government funding agencies, such as the Ministry for Social Development and the Ministry of Health. While they made some use of volunteers – in their neighbourhood charity shops, food-banks and drop-in centres, for example – their core services were typically provided by salaried social workers, psychologists, counsellors, policy advisors, accountants and funding application managers. Alongside these large and broadly focused organisations, a number of small- and medium-sized voluntary welfare organisations were also active in the city. These tended to concentrate on specific issues, such as food insecurity, tenancy advice or counselling, and often relied more heavily upon volunteers.

The neoliberal reforms that took place in New Zealand from the mid-1980s significantly altered the conditions in which these voluntary organisations operated (Tennant et al. 2008). From 1984, economic and social restructuring led by a Labour government saw increases in unemployment and social hardship. Faced with reduced taxation revenue and a burgeoning welfare expenditure bill, a centre-right National government elected in 1990 then implemented stringent cuts to state welfare, reducing the value of benefits and tightening their eligibility criteria (Boston et al. 1999). This retrenchment compromised the material security of some of the country's most vulnerable citizens and saw a considerable expansion in the numbers seeking support from the voluntary sector.

From the mid-1990s, the National government introduced a funder-provider system to manage its service provision engagements with voluntary welfare organisations. The funders (government agencies) would contract with providers (voluntary organisations) for the delivery of particular services, with various associated performance indicators and reporting requirements (Boston 1995). This new arrangement was problematic for many voluntary organisations as it entailed significant administrative burdens. There was also concern that government funding contracts might compromise their capacity to critique or operate independently of government policy (Nowland-Foreman 2016), as has been observed elsewhere (Baker and McGuirk 2021; Milligan and Conradson 2006; Wolch 1990). In recognition of these problems, a Labour-led government (1999–2008) created an Office for the Community and Voluntary Sector in 2000, with the aim of improving relations with the community and voluntary sector. This Office worked to ameliorate some of the more onerous and bureaucratic aspects of service contracting while endeavouring to foster a more collaborative working relationship between government and the voluntary sector. The arrangement was not to last, however, as a subsequent National-led government disestablished the Office in 2015, effectively reinstating the emphases of the earlier contractually oriented funder-provider model.

By 2010, immediately prior to the earthquake sequence, voluntary organisations were a key provider of welfare and social services in Christchurch, spanning housing, child and family support, mental health, community development, residential aged care, budgeting and financial advice, migrant and refugees services and citizens' advice (Conradson 2008). Many of the established organisations held significant service provision contracts with government agencies. A number of small- and medium-sized organisations also provided welfare and care services, in areas such as counselling and psychosocial support. These services were often funded by community grants, donations and client fees, and were typically more financially vulnerable than the larger entities.

Community and voluntary organisations often take up important roles after disasters, with responses that encompass emergency and medium-term relief, as well as advocacy and longer-term work that seeks to ameliorate distress and disadvantage (Quarantelli and Dynes 1977). This was certainly the case in Christchurch, where the response encompassed organisations well prepared for disaster recovery work (eg. the local branch of the Red Cross) as well as those without any particular expertise in this regard.

Faith-based organisations: established and new forms of voluntarism

Reflecting their existing involvement in welfare provision in Christchurch, faith-based organisations played a significant role in responding to immediate social needs following the earthquakes. Parsons (2014) describes how Christian churches and organisations were closely engaged in distributing essential supplies, establishing response and recovery centres, providing pastoral care as well as caring specifically for children and older people, and delivering broad psychosocial support. Other faith groups also played their part, including the members of the city's two mosques, although their contributions were less publicly visible at the time. This was to change following a terrorist attack on the mosques in March 2019, however, one outcome of which was to significantly raise public awareness of the extensive community involvement of members of the Christchurch Muslim community (Uekusa et al. 2022). Although a number of the larger faith-based organisations suffered earthquake damage to their buildings and the homes of their staff and volunteers, many made immediate use of their institutional resources to deliver food parcels, establish emergency shelters and provide a range of other forms of immediate care.

A number of congregation-centred responses also rose to prominence in the aftermath of the quakes. For example, Grace Vineyard Church had already established a Compassion Trust in 2003 to provide meals and budgeting advice for local people. This kind of under-the-radar contribution was given wide-ranging publicity when the Beach Campus of Grace Vineyard emerged as a major hub for post-quake food distribution, community support and legal advice in the badly affected area of New Brighton (Figure 7.1). The church leader concerned described this welfare response in the following way:

> In any disaster, there is going to be a large group of people who actually have the energy, capacity and hopefully the spiritual eyes to put their own needs aside to serve and to bless others … you are best just to try to do something … just hold on for the ride and make something happen.
>
> (Harvey 2014, 223–4)

Figure 7.1 The Beach Campus of Grace Vineyard church.

Alongside the buildings and volunteers, and a certain form of ethical citizenship, Harvey's description also highlights the improvisational character of those who were prepared to 'try to do something' and to 'make something happen'. As explored in Chapter 8, this sense of experimental innovation enabled by the rupture of the earthquakes appears to have been a common feature of post-disaster Christchurch. Indeed, the achievements of Grace Vineyard in helping to co-ordinate wider community responses were repeated by other congregations elsewhere in the city. In Richmond, for example, the Delta Community Support Trust – established in 1995 as an initiative of the North Avon Baptist Church – also emerged as a major community hub after the earthquakes, becoming not only a focus for emergency relief but also operating a wide-ranging community development centre serving disadvantaged people in the eastern suburbs (Burn 2020). Similarly, the congregation of South West (formerly Spreydon) Baptist Church built upon its previous experience of community work with at-risk youth, sole parents and those needing mental health support to engage with local residents and their communities in the aftermath of the earthquakes. This community and ecumenical cooperation blossomed through the recovery period, and helped to spawn and consolidate some 40 different charitable trusts in the neighbourhood and further afield (Jamieson 2018; Table 7.1).

It has been suggested in Chapter 1 that alternative possibilities for action that had previously been submerged, covered up or excluded might be afforded new prominence after the social, political and environmental upheaval of a disaster. The rupture of the Canterbury earthquakes does appear to lend weight to this suggestion given the emergence of new kinds of

Table 7.1 Examples of charitable trusts associated with South West Baptist Church, Christchurch

Name of Trust	*Nature of service*
Building Blocks Community Trust	A fully licensed Early Childhood Education Centre
Cross Over Trust	Works with primary school-aged children and their families to support resilience and well-being
Cobham Street Trust	Community housing provider for individuals and families in need, with a focus on the elderly
Sarona Trust	Residential service for adults recovering from mental illness, with accommodation and support programmes
Kingdom Resources Trust	Budgeting and employment support service
Stepping Stone Trust	Supported accommodation for adults, youth and families affected by mental illness

Source: www.swbc.org.nz/ministry/associated-trusts/

welfare knowledge, priorities and even organisations. In this regard, some welfare needs became more apparent because of the earthquakes. For example, the established faith-based organisations, the congregational community support trusts and a number of counselling organisations recognised the need for additional mental health support services in the city. Burn (2020) estimates that the scale of mental health issues responded to by the Delta Trust rose by 70–80 per cent in the decade following the earthquakes. Apart from the uncertainties and, for some people, the fear generated by the earthquakes, one of the main sources of anxiety was having to deal with insurance issues, as other chapters (3, 5 and 10) make clear. This anxiety was exacerbated by the collapse of expectations that high levels of personal and social insurance would provide security against disaster (Chapter 2).

The earthquakes also re-emphasised the issue of homelessness in the city. Some of the housing stock vacated in the red zone and rendered unusable in the eastern suburbs included affordable properties, social housing and low-cost rental dwellings and their absence created further homelessness and housing poverty, in addition to that already existing in the city. Major service providers such as the Anglican City Mission (Haworth 2019) reported that responding to the earthquakes highlighted the need for additional services – such as a women's night shelter and a men's daytime programme – both of which were subsequently introduced. In addition, there was a broader and more visceral appreciation amongst some Christchurch citizens of the day-to-day conditions endured by those experiencing housing-related distress and homelessness. Over shorter or longer periods of time, the insecurity, uncertainty, displacement and deprivation resulting from the loss of home, however temporary, threw new light onto the issue of homelessness and highlighted the need to provide services for its victims.

This increased prominence of particular social needs in the post-quake city was matched by faith-based communities refashioning their responses to those needs. Interestingly, for many of the established faith-based organisations, this largely meant returning to a position of 'business as usual' (Hawkey 2020). To some extent, this development reflected a desire to maintain a professional and caring service for the city's marginalised people. As Haworth (2019, 159) summarises in the context of the Anglican City Mission:

> What the Mission has to offer the people who come to it is much more than a smart almost-new building. It offers well-trained and motivated people, all committed to a high standard of caring. It offers services that are relevant, well-resourced and carefully honed to provide affirming care.

Although such priorities do not preclude innovation, they are often articulated in the context of co-funded partnership projects with government agencies. For example, the Methodist Mission had become the lead agency for the collaborative implementation of the government-funded Housing First programme in the city, which sought to address the housing needs of people experiencing long-term homelessness. In doing so, it has added significant strands of service to its longer-term commitment to provide housing for older people (Hawkey 2018, 2020). It has also partnered with other agencies in the Mana Ake (Stronger for Tomorrow) initiative, which seeks to ensure that every school in the city benefits from the services of a kaimahi (well-being worker) to help deal with anxiety, depression and other mental health issues amongst school children following the earthquakes.

The core services of these established faith-based organisations were augmented by a number of community-based development initiatives, the locational pattern of which has shifted from experimental projects in a few communities to a more geographically comprehensive coverage. Some of these organisations have not relied on faith-based motivation and resources for their development: an example would be the Aranui Community Trust Incorporated Society (ACTIS 2022). This initiative encompasses a broad range of well-being services – including housing and legal advice, social connectedness interventions, early childhood education, affordable fruit and vegetable provision and community sports, among others – and was prompted by interactions between the local community, city council and Housing New Zealand (now Kāinga Ora). Elsewhere, however, faith-based organisations have contributed significantly to community-based service provision across the city. What perhaps could be thought of as a limited number of relatively independent service silos prior to the earthquakes has grown into an important community presence in the post-quake city.

It has been argued that the earthquakes powerfully reinforced the need for faith-based congregational social action to be seriously collaborative (Harvey 2012). Not only did ecumenical cooperation during the earthquake emergency help to dissolve denominational boundaries, but community cooperation became central to establishing trust between church and neighbourhood. For example, Harvey's (2012) account of the Grace Vineyard response in New Brighton emphasised the fundamental requirement for co-operation between faith-based actors and others, including local politicians and police leaders. In these kinds of ways, the event of the earthquakes helped to fashion a less organisationally centric and more community-oriented approach to faith-based social action, leading to a rise in community-centred services that augmented the core services offered by the established faith-based organisations.

As the recovery of Christchurch continues, the established faith-based organisations have returned to their prominent position as major trusted service providers, along with new services developed in response to some of the forms of need caused or made visible by the earthquakes. In a welfare landscape with relatively few services provided directly by the state, faith-based voluntarism always risks co-option as a pseudo-state agency (Cloke et al. 2013). However, the evidence from Christchurch suggests that there is a determination on the part of faith-based actors to maintain an independent voice and conscience when partnering with government agencies, regardless of any use of state funds. Other faith-based initiatives have sought deeper integration with local communities through community-based development projects. These smaller and often more localised initiatives have the capacity to become key hubs for responding to local and neighbourhood-based needs. For example, Delta Trust's position in Richmond places it in an area where significant gentrification is occurring but also where social housing developments have led to a concentration of socially marginalised people. The situated understanding of local community among staff at Delta also enable a focus on less visible needs, such as those experienced by isolated older people or by people with mental health needs.

Locally integrated activity has brought with it two significant benefits. First, there is a particular expression of compassion-based care, which is not exclusive to faith-based motivation, but which often seems to draw inspiration and resourcefulness from the wellspring of faith communities and their practical orientation to reach out to others in need. Such practices can form part of a broader antidote to neo-liberalised cultures of renewal in the post-quake city. Secondly, as faith-based groups act on this ethical imperative to join with others to 'do something about' the needs they see around them, they bring a capacity for experimentation and creativity that is perhaps more difficult to achieve within longstanding established institutions. This capacity reflects the wider opportunity for an alternative cultural politics that has been afforded by the rupture of the event of the earthquakes (Cloke and Dickinson 2019; Cretney 2016, 2019).

Resident-led advocacy and activism

Alongside the work of established voluntary organisations, a number of resident-led initiatives arose in the aftermath of the earthquakes, often energised by concerns around justice, fairness and equity. These initiatives sought to shape government policies and practices, taking up both collaborator and critic roles. Some had a pan-city orientation while others focused on particular neighbourhoods. As illustrative cases, this section considers three examples. The first, the Māori Recovery Network, was formed in the immediate aftermath of the February 2011 event, and drew on existing tribal networks and support structures. The network was led by Ngāi Tahu, the tribe with mana whenua (customary authority) in Te Waipounamu, the South Island. The second example, the Canterbury Communities' Earthquake Recovery Network (CanCERN), arose after the September 2010 earthquake to represent the interests of residents in disrupted neighbourhoods. The third, the Wider Earthquake Communities Action Network (WeCAN), was established a year later in October 2011. Each of these groups sought to assist residents, in overlapping but also different ways. They were part of a wider set of resident-led organisations, several of which played influential roles in the city's recovery.

In the immediate aftermath of the February 2011 earthquake, Ngāi Tahu actively coordinated a response effort across the city. Much of this work was channelled through the Māori Recovery Network, with participants drawn from the tribe, key government departments, Māori social service providers and Māori wardens (Kenney et al. 2015). The Māori wardens were closely involved in offering practical support, with individuals drawn from a national network of approximately 900 people. Guided by whanau (extended family) networks and manaakitanga (an ethic of care), these wardens made several hundred in-person visits to Māori households in the eastern suburbs of the city, offering material assistance (eg. temporary accommodation arrangements, food parcels and drinking water), advice and information, service referrals and psychosocial support. The close attention given to Māori cultural values, language and worldview in offering this support was particularly significant for local Māori (Lambert 2014).

In his reflections on the Māori Recovery Network, Mark Solomon, the Kaiwhakahaere/Chairperson of Ngāi Tahu at the time, emphasises how tribal connections with local Māori enabled the network to offer support that was well calibrated to people's actual difficulties. He contrasts this with the protocol-oriented approach of Civil Defence, which was generally less flexible and less well attuned to local needs. Although the Māori Recovery Network was actively involved in household visits, particularly in the eastern suburbs, it was not until eight days after the February 2011 earthquake that Civil Defence met directly with representatives of Ngāi Tahu, despite their status as mana whenua. Solomon nevertheless argues that the earthquakes eventually led to improved relationships between Ngāi Tahu and government agencies such as CERA and the Christchurch City Council. In his words,

> [t]he earthquakes were a tragedy but they also led to a strong Treaty relationship for Ngāi Tahu. The earthquakes gave us a unique opportunity to design a cityscape that acknowledges our shared past with our colonisers, our shared experiences and our common future, which certainly wasn't there beforehand.
>
> (Solomon and Revington 2021, 87)

As a second example, CanCERN arose from the concerns of several resident associations and community groups, with an aim to facilitate '[f]ull community engagement in recovery processes and to work in partnership with recovery agencies' (CanCERN 2014). To that end, it sought to

> share accurate information regarding the earthquake recovery process with communities and affiliated supporters via a regional network; identify and advocate for community-based solutions and future vision; establish engagement partnerships with key-decision makers in the earthquake recovery process; [and] promote communication and engagement processes that are inclusive rather than divisive.
>
> (Miller 2012)

From the beginning, CanCERN aspired to work alongside government agencies and other emergency response organisations in a collaborative and non-antagonistic manner. As its early documents put it, 'our aim is to partner, not criticise from the sidelines' (Miller 2012). In addition, CanCERN did not wish to function or be perceived as a 'lobby' group. The intention instead was to facilitate a two-way flow of accurate information between residents on the one hand and the government and insurers on the other.

Supported by a steady stream of funding from charitable trusts and foundations, CanCERN developed a series of initiatives. One prominent example was the formation in 2012 of a community information hub. Operating out of a shopping mall in the eastern suburbs, this hub brought together representatives from 18 different organisations, including the Residential Advisory Service (offering free legal advice), Ngāi Tahu, the Human Rights Commission and local and central government agencies (eg. the city council and the Earthquake Commission). This arrangement facilitated valuable opportunities for face-to-face conversations, enabling people to make progress on issues that might otherwise have taken multiple emails and telephone conversations to resolve. To keep in contact with the community, a public Facebook page was created for information and regular updates (Figure 7.2).

A further project, the 'Find and Fix' campaign, was announced in April 2014. This sought to organise temporary repairs to more than 900 badly earthquake damaged homes, to remedy their weather tightness before winter. In September 2014, a new initiative called Breakthrough was developed in collaboration with Southern Response (the government agency formed to take over the claims made against Allied Mutual Insurance, a private insurance company that went into liquidation). Staff working for Breakthrough sought to help residents progress their insurance claims. As Dickinson (2018, 627) notes, 'CanCERN staff acted as brokers who could access legal and technical advice, facilitate meetings with insurers, bring managers and technical staff to the table and ensure there were agreed actions for progress'.

These conversations were not always easy, given the levels of frustration and anger among city residents regarding insurance claims. But CanCERN

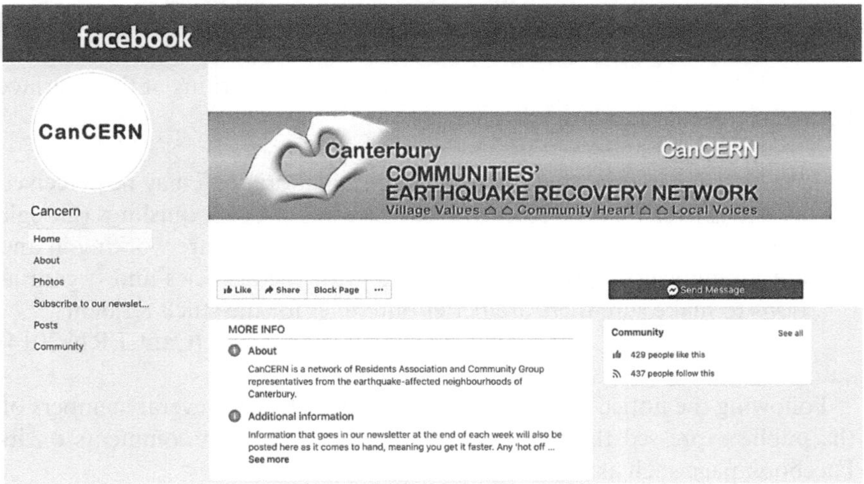

Figure 7.2 The CanCERN FaceBook page.

Source: https://www.facebook.com/Cancern-447406772071865/

described its work as seeking to transcend the antagonistic politics of 'us' (disaffected residents) and 'them' (government agencies, such as CERA, and insurance companies) (for the origins of these disputes, see Chapters 3 and 4). It sought to create 'a space of cooperation and collaboration' between different actors and agencies, so as to assist residents whose insurance settlements or home repairs had stalled or reached an impasse (CanCERN 2014). For CanCERN, the effectiveness of its work depended upon building close relationships with key staff in agencies such as CERA and the Earthquake Commission. Some people were concerned that CanCERN was too close to the government, however, arguing that its collaboration with CERA compromised its ability to advocate effectively for residents and communities. Given the generally slow progress towards resolving insurance claims and the complexity of red zone negotiations, these critics wanted a more distinct and adversarial approach. Vallance (2015) argues that CanCERN staff were in fact consciously treading the line between collaboration and critique so that they could 'stay in the tent', or be in a position to influence government actors from the inside, as a trusted partner, rather than having to do so from the outside. Dickinson (2018) also observed that CanCERN staff regularly assessed what was politically acceptable. They adjusted their approach to the situation at hand, in ways they thought would have the best chances of success.

In late 2015, ahead of the planned disestablishment of CERA in April 2016, the organisers of CanCERN decided to bring their work to a conclusion, with a finishing date in February 2016. As outlined in Chapter 4, the key actors in the city's recovery were shifting, and important decision-making powers were to be transferred from CERA to a new set of organisations (primarily, Regenerate Christchurch and Ōtākaro Limited). In the final CanCERN newsletter, headed 'the Space of Discomfort', the editorial acknowledged the challenges but also the rewards of working at the interface between residents and government.

> We also understand that the very term "collaboration" may be perceived as a negative. We have recently been accused of being quislings (Google that one!) but we are actually proud of the space we are working in and are taking every opportunity to work with the agencies and organisations to make sure there are better outcomes for the stuck residents.
>
> (CanCERN 2014)

Following the notice of CanCERN's intended closure, several members of the public expressed their appreciation of its work, with comments on its Facebook page such as:

> Thanks so much CanCERN, goodness knows where the heck we'd be without your years of hard work. I really appreciate the effort to keep the community in the rebuild ...Thank you!
>
> CanCERN folk, you guys have been so amazing and certainly helped me keep relatively sane through our fight. To see a group of people come together, to ask questions and to actually care and communicate with the average joe has been a huge blessing ... You asked the hard questions, and in such a skilful way that you were rarely 'shut-out'. That is no easy feat.

These remarks were typical of the positive community response to CanCERN's work. The government agencies, including CERA, apparently also valued the opportunity to work with CanCERN, having recognised the importance of engaging with resident-led organisations early in the recovery process (Dickinson 2013).

In its final months, three core staff from CanCERN announced they were forming a new organisation called Breakthrough Services (taking its name from one of the previous CanCERN initiatives, mentioned above). Breakthrough Services would continue to support homeowners to work through earthquake insurance issues, adopting a collaborative approach to advocating for their needs and rights. This reconfigured, smaller organisation also offered consulting services, drawing on the experience that its staff had gained working for CanCERN. The aim was to help 'agencies who would like to make their communications and processes more people-centred. In the complex disaster recovery environment, engaging meaningfully with people is the key to success' (Breakthrough Facilitation 2019). This kind of service was illustrative of the capacity building that occurred as a result of working in challenging post-quake circumstances; for the city, it was positive that this expertise survived the closure of CanCERN and thus remained available to local residents across Christchurch.

In contrast to CanCERN, WeCAN took a more confrontational and adversarial stance in its efforts to achieve better outcomes for quake-affected residents. Led by Mike Coleman, an Anglican priest and Avonside resident, WeCAN was particularly focused on red-zoned residents and the difficulties experienced by people living in the eastern suburbs. As Coleman explained:

> We aim to publicly highlight the injustices and issues affecting residents following the Canterbury earthquakes. We will openly challenge decisions, policies and practices that disadvantage a community's recovery from the earthquakes, and actively promote and support equitable, just and visionary solutions for all … We are not politically aligned and will challenge the policies and practices of any political party or government department where they disadvantage residents or communities. However make no mistake: we are political with a small p, [and] we intend to take action for change.
>
> (Voxy 2011)

Through a series of public rallies, letters and legal challenges, WeCAN sought to contest what it regarded as the top-down 'command and control' ethos of CERA and the unsatisfactory processes and communications of the Earthquake Commission and insurance companies, such as IAG (Figure 7.3). Many WeCAN participants doubted whether the Minister for Earthquake Recovery, Gerry Brownlee, was actually listening to Christchurch people. As Coleman put it:

> [i]t makes you wonder if the Prime Minister has forgotten us. He has left us with an earthquake recovery minister who says he is unaware there is a crisis … How can he be the recovery minister when he fails to listen to the people most in need?
>
> (Gates 2012b)

Figure 7.3 Reverend Mike Coleman, Leader of WeCAN, at a public gathering in September 2012.

Credit: Stuff Limited.

WeCAN sought a more democratic recovery process in which the needs and perspectives of residents were given greater attention. Its efforts enjoyed widespread support of residents from the eastern suburbs, as well as from several elected city council representatives – including the Mayor, Lianne Dalziel, who had been advocating for a more even distribution of power between the city council and the Crown – and faith-based organisations such as the Methodist Mission (Gates 2012b).

Energised by this ethos, WeCAN actively challenged each of the main recovery agencies. It submitted multiple requests to the Earthquake Commission for information regarding its decisions and procedures, including the process it had followed to appoint the national building company Fletchers as the main repair agency, and also the progress of the repairs themselves. Through these requests – and by making public aspects of the responses it received – WeCAN sought to hold the Commission to public account. In relation to CERA, WeCAN requested an extension to the timeframe for finalising red-zoned land and home deals, and asked that red zone decisions be reviewed by an independent third party. The timeframe for the red zone settlements was eventually extended, after pressure from multiple quarters, including WeCAN.

In terms of legal challenges, WeCAN worked with Quake Outcasts, a group of 68 uninsured red zone homeowners, to develop a submission to the United Nations Human Rights Council. The submission questioned the human rights acceptability of residents effectively being forced – through their financial inability to move elsewhere – to live in damaged and unrepaired housing while their insurance claims languished in an unresolved state. In a separate process in July 2016, WeCAN applied to the High Court of New Zealand regarding the Quake Outcasts. The Crown had offered a settlement of only 50 per cent of their land value and nothing for their homes (Quake Outcasts 2016). The Court found that the Crown's approach had been unlawful, and required it to compensate the Quake Outcasts in a manner equivalent to other red-zoned home owners. Although the approach taken here was very different to the collaborative style of CanCERN, it was clearly effective.

Emergent voluntarism: the Student Volunteer Army

The day after the September 2010 earthquake, Sam Johnson, a Law and Politics student at the University of Canterbury, contacted the Christchurch City Council asking how he might contribute to the recovery effort. He was politely told that 'there is no process in place for your offer of help' (Warnock 2014). Unsatisfied with this response, Johnson reached out to a group of 200 friends on Facebook, asking who might be interested in offering practical help to badly affected residents in the eastern suburbs. To his surprise – as his invitation had been relayed through a range of networks – he received around 2500 offers of volunteer help. This was the start of what became known as the Student Volunteer Army (Johnson 2012).

Following the establishment of an informal leadership team and some rapid logistical work, students were coordinated into teams that shovelled silt and liquefaction out of hundreds of homes and gardens in the eastern suburbs, while also offering residents food, drinks and information about relevant support organisations. This work was facilitated by the deft use of social media, a flexible organisational structure, and a strong desire to respond to the practical needs of disaffected residents (Nissen et al. 2021; Tatham 2011). When the February 2011 quake struck, the Student Volunteer Army was able to leverage its experience and learning from September 2010. It scaled its efforts and activities up considerably, recruiting over 11,000 student volunteers who then became involved in a variety of helping initiatives across the city (Figure 7.4).

After the September 2010 earthquake, there was initially some tension between the Student Volunteer Army and the key emergency response organisations of Civil Defence, the Canterbury Earthquake Recovery Authority and the city council (Johnson 2012). The students were regarded as well-meaning but generally unqualified individuals whose efforts might generate additional complexity and create safety risks (Cowlishaw and Mathewson 2012). After Sam Johnson publicly described some of difficulties they were experiencing in these respects, a more harmonious way of working was developed. Part of the solution was a division of labour, whereby the students would focus on the high volume but relatively low skill tasks that were a necessary part of the recovery. After the September 2010 and February 2011 quakes, the Army thus focused on immediate material assistance, including shovelling silt and liquefaction from affected properties. More complex issues, such as dealing

Figure 7.4 Members of the Student Volunteer Army shovelling silt.

Credit: Stuff Limited.

with broken water mains and sewage infrastructure, or tasks with potential health and safety risks, such as working alongside damaged buildings, were left to qualified professionals.

The kinds of difficulties the Student Volunteer Army encountered when attempting to work with existing emergency response organisations in Christchurch have been observed in other post-disaster settings (Stallings and Quarantelli 1985; Strandh and Eklund 2018). Established organisations typically have well-structured response protocols that may, in some circumstances, prove to be quite efficient. However, these approaches are often less able to accommodate novel community initiatives or emergent groups that also wish to participate in the recovery effort. This was demonstrably the case with the Student Volunteer Army: the scale and dynamism of its activities caught many of the existing recovery agencies by surprise. The situation eased when the Student Volunteer Army created a website, took steps to register as an official club at the University of Canterbury and was later incorporated as a registered charity; these elements of formalisation made it easier for more established organisations to collaborate with it. The formation of a governance board also gave external agencies some assurance that suitable oversight was in place for handling financial and other forms of donations (eg. equipment such as tools, wheelbarrows and software, much of which was gifted by businesses from across the city).

Despite the initial uncertainty of recovery agencies regarding how best to collaborate with the Student Volunteer Army, its community efforts received an overwhelmingly positive reception (Ensor 2011). In a paper co-authored with Sam Johnson, Nissen et al. (2021) nevertheless caution against uncritical eulogising of the organisation, noting that its success in part reflected the extensive social networks and cultural capital of both its founder and the original leadership team of six students. This was coupled with the skilful use of social media to leverage a high level of participation from a large group of generally fit and healthy young people. Being able to connect to the infrastructure and branding afforded by the University of Canterbury and the UC Students Association was also helpful (Carlton et al. 2022).

One might assume that the Student Volunteer Army was created on the basis of a clear vision, which was then implemented through a set of corresponding actions. Nissen et al. (2021) emphasise that this was not the case, but that a good deal of experimentation was instead involved. This sometimes entailed 'throwing a lot of different things against the wall, and seeing what would stick', in the words of one interviewee (Carlton et al. 2022, 42). Such an approach is typical of what Gardner (2013) observed among similarly emergent voluntary organisations in disaster relief on the Gulf Coast of the United States. This orientation towards learning through iterative 'doing' mirrors the key elements of what has become known as design thinking (Brown 2009). At the same time, the Student Volunteer Army leadership team demonstrated a significant capacity for productive reflection. This supported the organisation to adjust its approach in an incremental fashion through the sequence of major earthquakes in February, June and December of 2011 (Carlton and Mills 2017).

Having acquired a degree of organisational experience and capacity through the earthquakes, the Student Volunteer Army was well positioned to respond to other disasters. In April 2011, its founding members Sam Johnson and Jason Pemberton travelled to Japan to contribute to recovery efforts following the 2011 Tohoku earthquake and tsunami (Stuff 2011). Within New Zealand, new groups of student volunteers were then directed to assist people in the aftermath of the 2016 magnitude 7.8 Kaikōura earthquake, the 2019 mosque shootings in Christchurch, the 2021 Canterbury floods and the Covid-19 pandemic. Each of these events effectively re-energised the organisation, prompting it to 'scale up' into specific forms of action. On each occasion, there was consideration of what appropriate engagement might entail, rather than assuming that student volunteer involvement was needed, wanted or useful. The Student Volunteer Army also inspired similar volunteering initiatives at other university campuses across New Zealand, including in Dunedin, Wellington and Auckland. Such initiatives are part of an international trend in which student volunteering is encouraged and supported at an increasing number of universities.

In keeping with Sam Johnson's self-narrated identity as a social entrepreneur, the Student Volunteer Army has developed several non-disaster-related initiatives in recent years. A visiting service for older people was launched in 2016, for example, with a focus on reducing social isolation (Spink 2016). A national framework for secondary school volunteering was created, working in partnership with a number of schools across the country. The vision was to enhance societal resilience by cultivating individuals who, in the future, would be both favourably disposed and practically prepared to assist others during periods of social and environmental disruption. This initiative exemplifies the ways in which the work of Student Volunteer Army is as much a social movement as a traditional voluntary organisation.

In the 2020 annual report, which was the organisation's tenth anniversary year, the Student Volunteer Army describes its portfolio of activities as 'changing the face of volunteering'. Volunteering in New Zealand has traditionally been associated with middle-aged adults, with the 40–49-year-old age group most likely to be involved (somewhat contrary to the perception that volunteering is predominantly an activity for the retired). Bringing more children and young people into volunteering is thus literally changing the face of who volunteers. As Johnson explained, 'If we can get primary school children committed to volunteering at this age, they'll continue to do it for the rest of their lives' (Witsey 2016). To this end, the Student Volunteer Army created structures for participation that enabled young people to 'step in' and 'step out' of volunteering opportunities in a flexible manner, rather than having to sign up for a specific time period or designated role. This flexibility helped the organisation to harness the collective enthusiasm typical of young people, especially in relation to causes they regard as meaningful and of intrinsic value.

Conclusion

In the aftermath of the earthquakes, community and voluntary organisations played a significant range of roles in the city's recovery. The patterns of activity mirror those observed in other post-disaster settings, with a blend of established and newly formed organisations engaged in activities that spanned service provision, advocacy and activism (Strandh and Eklund 2018). In Christchurch, the large and established voluntary welfare organisations, many of which are faith-based, were closely involved in the emergency response phase of the disaster, providing material and psychosocial support to hundreds of affected residents across the city. The suburban churches also responded to the needs of people in particular neighbourhoods (Parsons 2014), creating community-integrated hubs of care and compassion that were typically progressive and inclusive. Although these services and activities were seldom explicitly political, in the sense of engaging critically with the policies and practices of government recovery agencies such as CERA and the Earthquake Commission, they made a positive difference for many affected residents.

In a more overtly political manner, the Māori Recovery Network and resident-led organisations such as CanCERN and WeCAN actively engaged government agencies so as to assist people with their practical needs, insurance, house repair and land zoning problems. In different ways, these organisations enabled more democratic forms of engagement during the recovery, at least for a time. With explicit support from both CERA and the Earthquake Commission, for example, CanCERN operated as a broker or intermediary, working in a collaborative manner to transcend the sometimes antagonistic dynamics of 'us' and 'them' when residents' insurance claims had gotten stuck (CanCERN 2014). WeCAN took a more combative approach in its efforts to ensure residents' voices and experiences were heard and taken seriously. Although its approach was at times strongly confrontational, given the repeated manner in which central government agencies appeared to downplay or override local concerns during the recovery, WeCAN viewed this as appropriate and proportionate. In several instances, it was also undoubtedly effective. Looking ahead, it is not yet clear what the legacy of the spaces of dialogue and contestation fostered by CanCERN and WeCAN might be. Many of the people who championed the practices of protest, brokering and mediation on which these organisations relied are still present within the Christchurch community, however, and their collective experience would be a valuable resource if there was a need to mobilise such practices again.

The emergence of the Student Volunteer Army was an unexpected development in post-quake Christchurch. Although some government organisations initially struggled with its improvisational approach, through dialogue and recalibration a way forward was developed. The energy of thousands of motivated students was thus directed into practical tasks for the recovery, with young people enabled to participate in a fluid manner, rather than insisting on more traditional forms of membership or affiliation. This work has continued to evolve in the decade after the quakes, with activities that now have both national and international reach. In terms of progressive and inclusive place-making, it is the Student Volunteer Army, the Māori Recovery Network and resident-led initiatives such as CanCERN and WeCAN that have arguably done the most to fashion novel spaces for political dialogue and collaborative action in the city. The experience of learning how to function effectively in a disaster recovery setting with a central government inclined towards top-down 'solutions' seems particularly valuable (Carlton et al. 2021; Carlton et al. 2022; Nissen et al. 2021). Such adaptive characteristics, including experimentation and improvisation, were also evident in a group of transitional organisations that arose after the earthquakes. These are the focus of the next chapter.

Part III

The city in transition

8 From transitional activities to place-making

Introduction

The possibility of regarding the multiple earthquake tremors and aftershocks experienced by Christchurch residents as a collective event which prompted a politically transformative interruption to the status quo was introduced in Chapter 1 (Cloke, Dickinson and Tupper 2017, following ideas from Badiou 2005). In short, it is argued that such an event can serve to rupture existing place narratives by allowing the emergence of alternatives to the current order. Such alternatives often involve previously marginalised but potentially disruptive forms of imagination and action (Dewsbury 2007), which can foster a wider appreciation of and confidence in (or 'fidelity' to) new ways of knowing about, and being in the city. In turn, these new narratives of the city can offer new forms of visionary cultural politics and ethics that add complexity to analytical narratives that suggest a simple recalibration of previous neoliberalised governance after the event of the earthquakes. In the Christchurch context, Pickles (2016) has argued that alongside the catastrophic damage to the geo-spatial surface of the city, the impact of the earthquakes prompted a less visible but equally significant rupturing of the ways in which it is underpinned culturally by narratives and practices of place.

The previous chapter showed how the voluntary sector played a significant role in nurturing new cultural-political values, and ethical spaces and practices in amongst the rupture. This chapter focuses on a particular movement within the voluntary sector that was responsible for a series of 'transitional activities' in Christchurch which marked not only a temporal stage in the rebuilding of the city but also a potential shift in how its collective life could be re-imagined and performed. Following arguments developed by Cloke and Conradson (2018) and Cloke and Dickinson (2019), it can be suggested that the cultural 'rupture' identified by Pickles was characterised at least in part by the emergence of previously hidden and little-noticed ethical and aesthetic ideas and practices that came out of what might be thought of as transitional forms of urbanism. Such ideas and practices became recognisable in the material and symbolic artistic expressions and creativity that sprang up in temporary activity spaces that became available in demolished areas of the city. Although these activities were sometimes assumed to be short-term

DOI: 10.4324/9780429275562-11

gap-fillers, destined to be overtaken by formally planned rebuilding, for visionary leaders of the transitional movement in Christchurch they offered the opportunity to weave ethically progressive ideas and material practices into the re-emerging fabric of the city. Their collective work comprised an innovative series of diverse and nimble community-focused interventions that drew heavily on participatory arts and ecological action in ways that brought an ongoing sense of being in transition to the longer-term evolution of the city. They also attracted international attention, exemplified by recognition for Christchurch in the 2012 *Lonely Planet* travel guide as a top-ten tourist destination where energy and inventiveness were exuded from the pop-up venues and inventive artworks that graced empty demolition sites (Wright 2012).

A cultural politics of place

The impact of these transitional activities needs to be set within the context of key characteristics that shaped the cultural narratives of Christchurch prior to the earthquakes. Three principal narrative traits have been identified. First, the city traded on a quaint and tranquil version of quintessential Englishness (Cupples and Glynn 2009; Schöllmann et al. 2000), formed both from an erasure of pre-colonial histories and from a deliberate emphasis on cultures and styles of Anglophilia. From built environments and place names to educational and religious rituals, the 'garden city' of Christchurch was developed and maintained in tune with the home-based values of its predominantly English settlers. However, according to Pawson (1999), emerging changes with respect to land rights and commodification of property constituted an alienation from previous assumptions about appropriate vegetation and land use, resulting in an ambivalent relationship between colonial imagery and indigenous environments in the more-than-human city prior to the earthquakes (see Chapter 11).

Secondly, national-level fascination with neoliberal experimentation since the 1980s had helped to shape more local narratives of the political and economic character of Christchurch. Hayward (2012) concludes that since then the planning of the city has been characterised by a largely permissive regime that has given entrepreneurs a relatively free reign, with elected local authorities reduced to a role of mitigating negative impacts of investment rather than a more pro-active and participatory shaping of the city (see also Chapters 4 and 5). To some extent, then, the resultant localised expression of neoliberal management cultures in business and land ownership tended to result in influential endorsement of central government policies that were so advantageous to them. However, it should be emphasised that alongside these conservative traits, there were elements of practice and forms of organisation in the city that worked against top-down neoliberalism, helping to form an accompanying cultural imagination that the city also functioned as an inclusive democracy, with a progressive left-of-centre social politics (Marcetic 2017; Pawson 2022).

Thirdly, the role of the arts in Christchurch prior to the earthquakes was dictated largely (but not exclusively) by commercial pressures and dominant artistic tropes favouring 'art for art's sake' rather than the development of artistic spaces of political potential or social transformation (Newman-Storen and Reynolds 2013). By and large, the arts might be considered as a somewhat docile presence in the pre-earthquake city, pushing against local conservatism from a relatively peripheral position (Parker 2014), generally not disturbing dominant place narratives and struggling to gain traction as a platform for radical alternatives to the neoliberalised structures and cultures of the day.

Of these three narratives, it is often assumed that it is the dominance of neoliberal political economy which has been least affected by the earthquakes. In this interpretation, as outlined by Hayward and Cretney (2015), the post-disaster planning environment was shaped initially by the imposition of a centralised command-and-control model of recovery that consisted of building demolition and government acquisition of land that was then used for anchor projects or sold off to private investors to support market-led projects (Dann 2014; Dickinson 2018). In reality, the situation was more complex. While democratic scrutiny and public participation were not as great as some hoped for, subsequent redevelopment in the city centre – as shown in Chapters 4 and 6 – was based on a combination of local and central government planning, Crown land purchase, mandatory privately-held land title amalgamation, market-led and often insurance-funded interventions and private and public sector place-making. It was this combination of approaches that underpinned ideas about success and hope for the future of the downtown's built environment.

The dominant historical narratives of the city were however challenged in other ways by the rupture, which offered opportunities for different kinds of understandings and activities to influence the identity of the city. Rebecca Solnit (2009) has demonstrated that disasters can provide space for freeing up community potential and addressing community goals that find expression as much in the interstices of social reconnection and shared action as in the materiality of construction. One distinct example of such release in the Christchurch context has been the provision in post-quake legislation for the incorporation and expression of Māori design and values within the city's redevelopment (see Chapters 4 and 9). This has helped to ensure the rebuilding of the city is occurring in a manner that more directly honours the partnership seen as central to the Treaty of Waitangi. In particular, the work of the Matapopore Charitable Trust has championed the essential task of embracing the voice of mana whenua – the status held by Ngāi Tūāhuriri, the local Māori subtribe with territorial authority – in different aspects of the city's recovery.

Matapopore's activities have ensured that Ngāi Tūāhuriri and Ngāi Tahu values, aspirations and narratives have been woven into redeveloped urban environments, especially through the use of Maori design references and motifs (Figure 8.1). There is now more evidence that the previous marginalisation and exclusion of Māori values and identities within the Christchurch

Figure 8.1 Examples of Matapopore interventions in the new urban design of Christchurch: (top) one of 17 whāriki – Ngāi Tahu welcome mats integrated into riverside walkways; and (bottom) artwork representing a Māori cloak of kakapo feathers, disguising the car park at the Justice and Emergency Services Building.

built environment is being addressed in the aftermath of the earthquakes (Ballard et al. 2015). Some recovery decisions have clearly upheld elements of previous place narratives – for example, in a move widely attributed to a reaffirmation of European settler heritage values and identities, the colonial nineteenth-century Anglican cathedral is being rebuilt in its original form and central position in the city centre. However, the renewed built landscape of the city does suggest that some historical expressions of Englishness are beginning to give way to a more overtly diverse urban landscape, reflecting the presence of both Treaty partners, iwi (the tribes) and the Crown, and the city's wider culturally mixed population.

The rest of this chapter focuses in on the changing public role and function of the arts in post-disaster Christchurch, and on how particular forms of ethical creativity have emerged in the material spaces created by the earthquakes. It traces the emergence of new forms of non-governmental organisation after the earthquakes, the activities of which represent energetic and multifaceted contributions to cultural, artistic, creative and ecological uses of temporary spaces and to the wider aesthetics and ethics of transition. The status and contribution of these 'transitional' organisations is however contested; they have sometimes been portrayed as whimsical and colourful band aids (Weejes Sabella 2015) with no meaningful role in longer-term recovery from disaster (Wesener 2015). Alternatively it can be argued that such agencies have demonstrated a much more significant potential as agenda-setters in an experimental search for new ways of inhabiting and organising public space. From this perspective, they articulate new understandings of political and ethical citizenship that embrace and encourage a role for residents as active participants in new forms of urban place-making.

Developing and performing the transitional city

Transitional organisations emerged with some rapidity in the years immediately after the earthquakes. Informal and in some ways latent networks became activated by key individuals in calls to collaborate in new volunteer-based ventures to spark new forms of cultural diversity and biodiversity around the city. It is important to note from the outset that these transitional concerns, and the subsequent energy to address them, were socially and spatially variegated, with three factors exerting particular influence on the patterns of activity. First, the lifestyle priorities and coping strategies of different suburban populations were significant, with some clusters of suburban population demonstrating low levels of affinity for, or compatibility with transitional activity. For example, it has been suggested (Dombroski 2020) that after the initial period of emergency response, during which close networks of community aid and support were active, many long-term residents of the city may have been relatively overwhelmed by the negative effects of the earthquakes, either by damage to property or by impact on place identity or both. Understandably, often people became focused on returning to a personal sense of suburban normality rather than taking a civic-level or even community-level view of the post-disaster landscape. Their relative disinterest in city centre projects may also have been exacerbated by previous periods of lifestyle change in which the suburbanisation of city life had for many reduced the usefulness of and familiarity with the central city.

Secondly, certain suburbs such as Lyttelton, New Brighton and Woolston demonstrated a greater affinity with the creative responses of transition. These were places where demolition sites provided opportunity for experimentation, but they were also places with a strong history of community and artistic group activity (Lesniak 2016) where latent networks were more easily sparked into life by transitional activists. Thirdly, Bennett (2016) has identified a significant group of relatively young, more artistic and entrepreneurial people for whom the central city of Christchurch had become a vibrant experimental location rather than an outmoded downtown space. He comments that

> I think that going back to the five years or so before the quakes that had changed quite a lot, and for a minority, but I think for a significant minority, which I think is most of the same people involved in the transitional movement, central Christchurch had become a really exciting place.
>
> (Bennett 2016, 154)

Although the scale of such activism may be debatable, this newfound appreciation of the central city by key activists contributed significantly to the transitional movement that emerged after the earthquakes.

Much of the initial energy for transitional activities came from dynamic younger people in these existing artistic and entrepreneurial communities in the city, but kindred spirits from elsewhere also became motivated to bring their creative ideas into the post-earthquake context (Boswell 2021; Lesniak 2016). Forming significant new groups and connections, these innovators spotted and acted upon the opportunities presented by the earthquakes to express new kinds of transitional place-identity. In some ways, these were people from the cultural and political margins. Their existing expertise in art, theatre, design and landscape architecture was ready and waiting when the post-earthquake rupture presented them with fertile opportunities to practice their arts in new ways. As a consequence, evaluation of the impact of transitional organisations will rely as much on their capacity to create new ethical and aesthetic expressions (or 'vibes') in the city and to open out possibilities for new community-centred projects and economies, as on the numbers of residents participating in or approving of the activities concerned.

The rupture of the earthquakes provided a physical and cultural landscape in which art, design and informal theatre had a new place and role in the remaking of the city. Individually and collectively, artists, designers and ecologists began to make multiple contributions of various forms, including large-scale murals and temporary art installations, typically sponsored by business interests, which provided aesthetic contrasts with and challenges to both the emptiness and abandonment of the previous cityscape and the slow development of its glass and concrete successor (Figure 8.2). It is noticeable

Figure 8.2 Street art in Christchurch.

that amongst the plethora of mural images – some of which simply emit a cheerful sense of fun – there were also emergent underlying themes related to the importance of Māori culture and ecological sustainability in an age of multiple disasters.

Perhaps the greatest impact on the rethinking of the city, however, was the activation of vacant spaces in the city by a series of transitional voluntary-sector organisations formed in the immediate aftermath of the earthquakes, notably Gap Filler (founded in 2010), Greening the Rubble (also in 2010), Life in Vacant Spaces (in 2012), and the Festival of Transitional Architecture (or FESTA, in 2012). Together with some support from the city council, these organisations curated an experimental creative movement in Christchurch, using a series of temporary installations and performative practices to reclaim and recode urban spaces, and in so doing illustrating the potential for a longer-lasting place for transitional creativity in the city. The resultant creative surge was recognisably catalysed by the event of the earthquakes – not only in terms of the materiality of suddenly vacant spaces, but also in a new ground-level cultural politics of doing what is necessary without waiting for more official responses.

Gap Filler is a creative placemaking agency operating at the crossroads of community development, urban design, art and public intervention. In the words of Ryan Reynolds, its co-founder and creative driving force:

> 'We've been conceiving events and installations, building community and experimenting amidst the ruins of the nineteenth and twentieth century city. We temporarily reshape the urban environment in a quick and rough way, without waiting for the government's or developers' plans and permissions. It was predictable that people here would take what they could into their own hands. When the normal ways of doing things are inadequate, those in power have to start revising the rulebook and reasserting control. Others inevitably start doing what they feel is necessary and lacking, and hope that the rulebooks will catch up'.
>
> (Reynolds 2014, 167)

The resultant sites and practices of transitional ingenuity have already received considerable attention (see Bennett et al. 2014a, 2014b; Carlton and Vallance 2017; Cloke and Conradson 2018; Cloke and Dickinson 2019; Cretney and Bond 2014; Dionisio and Pawson 2016; Dombroski et al. 2019; MacPherson 2016; Parker 2014; Wesener 2015).

It is however worth noting that each of the main organisations has brought particular perspectives to the collective movement. Gap Filler has championed an openness to ingenuity and innovation, using participatory propositions as a catalyst for alternative performances of the city. As Boswell (2021) indicates, this propositional approach represents an experimental provocation with which to test the water for change. It begins with a conversation that is not already present in the city. It then trials new ideas before putting a particular project 'out there' to assess levels of public engagement. An inherent quality of such experimentation is that it accepts failure as a potential outcome. Projects that have attracted public engagement include a temporary pallet pavilion providing a stage for events, a washing machine repurposed as a coin-operated jukebox and twinned with a sprung wooden dance floor to create the public Dance-O-Mat, and a giant outdoor arcade game system, the Super Street Arcade. Greening the Rubble has been responsible for a series of temporary community gardens and memorials throughout the city, often using mosaics of materials and recycled plants from earthquake affected areas (Figure 8.3). Other organisations have been similarly experimental. Life in Vacant Spaces has developed a specific facilitation role with landowners and businesses and community groups, fostering ecological and entrepreneurial innovation in a range of spaces. FESTA has curated a series of annual weekend events as well as more regular creative conversations designed to provoke a re-imagination of design and architecture in the city. Thousands of people attended its annual events held on cleared sites in the city centre once the cordon receded.

These initiatives have been evaluated with varying degrees of enthusiasm. For participant organisations and individuals, transitional initiatives have encouraged 'risk-taking, discovery, a not knowing how things will turn out, an openness to change' (Winn 2015), but are also understood as far more than temporary stop-gaps to be overwritten by the more formal and permanent architectures of the new city. Although the projects themselves may be short-lived, the process that underlies them is designed to endure beyond the timescale of the temporary. It encourages a participatory and experimental stance of being prepared to try something new, seeing what works and what doesn't, and through this experience gaining valuable ideas about what kinds of alternative futures can be brought into being. These early years of transition, then, make a claim on the future city through experimenting with and embodying the use of temporary urban sites. Parker's (2014) assessment of transitional projects emphasises how they bring people together in experimental ways in particular spaces, and in so doing open out new capacities for acting and connecting differently with the city. By creating space for residents to perform the city in new and creative ways, transitional organisations have modelled a form of participatory place-making that is able to better engage many citizens in processes and practices of involvement in the contexts in which they live.

On the other hand, transitional initiatives have also been the subject of negative commentary. The aesthetics deployed have been dismissed as 'messy' and 'bohemian' and therefore out of character with the historical character of the city (Lynch 2014). The scale of the projects is regarded by some as too small and ephemeral to make any lasting contribution. Participants are thought to be already-existing community activists, and beneficiaries are as likely to be tourists as city residents. A third line of critique argues that in and through the financial support received from Christchurch City Council, transitional organisations have inadvertently been co-opted as showcases of the state's short-term entrepreneurial responses to the earthquakes. In this way,

Figure 8.3 Examples of transitional projects: (top) Gap Filler's Pallet Pavilion in 2013; and (bottom) Greening the Rubbles' Green Room in 2015.

transitional activities are dismissed as small-scale entertainment that lack the means to impact on bigger picture problems (Grimshaw 2015).

Two important questions aid analytical navigation between these potentially polarised perspectives. First, what does a deeper examination of transitional organisations and their activities reveal about the values and aesthetics they deploy, and their capacity to engender 'affective communities' – that is, forms of community distinguished by widely held and collectively understood forms of feeling? Secondly, with a decade having passed since the establishment of transitional organisations in Christchurch, how does their evolution into mature actors in the city reflect longer-term success in sustaining these objectives in amongst the terrains and politics of the rebuilding of the post-disaster city?

Transitional ethics, aesthetics and affective communities

The leaders of transitional organisations in Christchurch have consistently argued that the curation of transitional spaces of ingenuity and experimentation does not equate to a formal political process. Rather, these activities are seen as underpinned by a series of ethical values and a desire for social impact. Using the example of Gap Filler, Cloke and Dickinson's (2019) analysis identified three strands of the underlying values that were being introduced into the city through the performances in different activity spaces.

The first is that participatory practices inherent in many Gap Filler experiments helped to build an imagination of the city that was able to convert a pragmatic and short-term view of the temporary into a longer-term and more visionary understanding of a sustainable role for experimental place-making. This spilled over into some commercially focused developments, such as the container mall, and later, initiatives like Little High and Riverside Market discussed in Chapter 9. So, in practice, the rupture of the earthquakes was seen to create both material and imagined spaces in which the rethinking of the city could occur. The gathering of people in short-term vacant sites enabled those who otherwise felt excluded from the rebuild process to join in with informal and often unstructured practices and performances that counterposed the blueprint being imposed by central powers. In these activity spaces, there was an unambiguous permission to experiment, to take ownership (however small) of an emerging art of the possible, and of the acting out of potential. In so doing, individual participation projected an imagination of a Christchurch which could be more collaborative and inclusive (Reynolds 2014, 169). Transitional activities therefore engendered an agile form of social entrepreneurship that suggested the need to embed ideas and practices of experimental bottom-up city-building into future phases of urban regeneration.

The second set of values detected in the work of transitional agencies reflects an inherent desire to propagate ways of living and working together that enable acceptance of and adherence to particular kinds of civic values that replace previous conservatism with more relaxed, interesting and open-minded forms of political culture. The top-down implementation of the CERA blueprint for the city (discussed in Chapters 4 and 6) strengthened perceptions in some quarters that only a limited elite would have a say about the future of the city. Alternative transitional activities emerged at least in part in response to that imagined elitism, and deliberately sought to enable a more common involvement in the recovery not least by identifying civic rights as fundamental to their activities. These values are potently illustrated in the development of the site of the demolished Crowne Plaza Hotel, which had been built in the 1980s across part of a public street closed for this purpose. After 2012, it was returned to the people as 'The Commons', becoming the base for Christchurch's community of transitional activists (Ballard et al. 2015) and the site of the Pallet Pavilion (Figure 8.3). Users of this gathering space are subject to guidelines which reverse the normal rules of ownership, ensuring that projects are focused on community engagement, related to the post-earthquake environment, engaged in social change, interested in collaboration, make space for local creatives and demonstrate a pragmatic fit to the site's transitional ethos. This mix reflects a deliberate attempt to incubate forms of in-commonness which are collective, collaborative and widely inclusive, offering open opportunities for creative place-making.

Thirdly, the activities of transitional organisations in Christchurch made deliberate use of particular aesthetics to suggest the possibility of ethical action. The term 'aesthetic connection' originated from key thinkers in art and social sculpture, especially Suzy Gablik (1992, 1996) and Joseph Beuys (Beuys and Harlon 2004), who argued that particular artistic and theatrical aesthetics can help to stimulate people's imaginations and form subtle but significant connections with particular social and environmental values. The performance of transitional activities in Christchurch made use of these kinds of connections with the transgressive potential of the post-earthquake rupture. Whether by storytelling about possible futures, or bringing together material, performative and symbolic elements to suggest wacky expressions of place-making possibilities that divert from previous norms, or by using quirky and humorous aesthetics to allow residents to discover new directions and meanings counterposed with the formal rebuilding of the city, aesthetic connections were used to draw residents and communities into the enactment of re-making place after the earthquakes. It can be argued that this mix of aesthetics and values represented a re-staging of the city, enabling a re-sensitising of memory and a re-envisioning of futures via creative participation.

The deployment of these three strands of values by transitional organisations has involved many different events, supported by thousands of volunteers working with hundreds of different businesses and community groups (Reynolds 2015) (Figure 8.4). However, the contribution of transitional organisations to the widening participation of place-making in Christchurch may be more far-reaching and complex than simple numerical expressions of awareness and participation might suggest. Cloke and Conradson (2018) note that the curation of sites and spaces of shared action, social reconnection

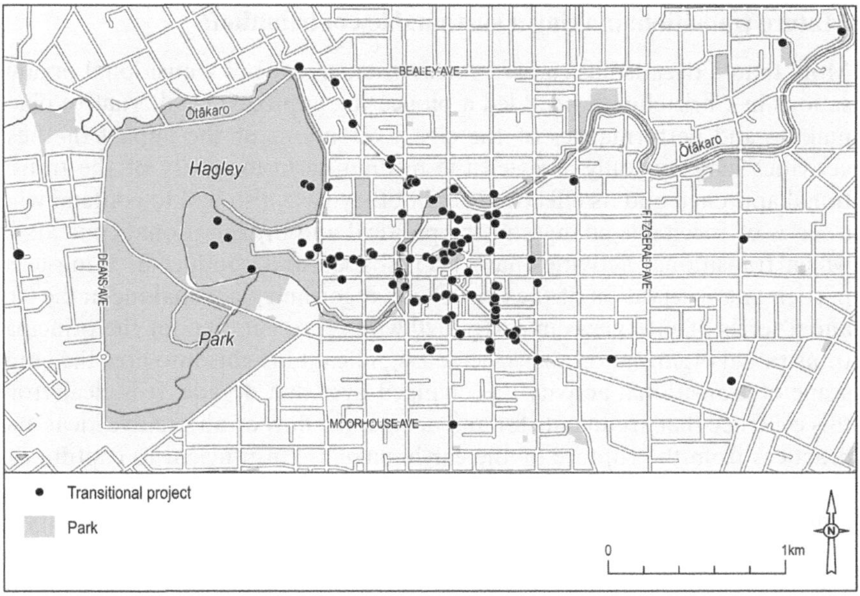

Figure 8.4 The distribution of transitional activity sites in central Christchurch.

Source: 'Popupprojects' at https://findchch.com/categories/whats-hot?subcategories=transitional-city-projects&page=all

and aesthetically connected energy became associated with emotional responses that gained traction in the city, creating a collectively experienced set of feelings, most often narrated as a 'buzz', a 'vibe' or a 'new atmosphere' (Campagnolo 2015; Merritt 2015; Winn 2015). Likewise, Cretney (2016) equates transitional activities with the opening up of new avenues for social participation, presenting geographically dispersed communities with a set of overlapping opportunities, and fostering a palpable atmosphere of hopefulness in amongst the landscapes of urban disaster. MacPherson (2016) refers to the role of transitional organisations in the creation of a new 'spirit' in the city.

The importance of these traces of emotions should not be underestimated when assessing the significance of transitional activity in the city. Even if the numbers of participants in specific projects is a small fraction of its citizenry, the creative alterity that they fostered became evident more generally as part of an emerging narrative of post-earthquake Christchurch as a city of cultural innovation and novelty. The early activities of transitional organisations brought together shared patterns of emotional understanding and meaning which lent some coherence to aspects of local community. Although these activities avoided direct forms of political participation, they nevertheless laid the foundation for an affective politics of transitional urbanism in the post-earthquake city. This has also been carried across into a lasting embrace of street art and some interesting commercial experiments in place-making explored in the next chapter.

Mature transition: making a sustainable contribution?

More than a decade has elapsed since the emergence of transitional organisations in Christchurch heralded a pioneering approach to alternative place making and performances of the city. Evaluations of the impact of these activities have not only assessed the medium-term longevity of the transitional approach and its effectiveness, but they have also had to contend with a series of inevitable changes in the political and organisational contexts in which transitional activities have been shaped and conducted. Long-term participant observation of the key debates regarding place-making in the city and a series of interviews in early 2020 with representatives of the principal transitional organisations have yielded significant insights into how the landscape of transitional activity has changed over that decade. It is clear from this evidence that arguments for and against the flow of alternative ideas and practices from the rupture of the earthquake are insufficient to capture the complexity and dynamism of a form of city-making that trades on being nimble, experimental and capable of establishing a sense of the temporary in amongst the seemingly more permanent rebuild of a concrete and glass city. Rather, an understanding is required of the ways in which transitional organisations have negotiated a longer-term sustainability for their activities and of how responses to the changing conditions of the city have altered the capacity to maintain a fidelity to the ethical values and aesthetic connections that characterised early forms of transition after the earthquakes.

The changing nature of political governance and planning of the post-disaster city of Christchurch has been examined in detail in Chapter 4. To some extent, there has been a shift in the obvious drivers of the previous dominance of top-down politics and governance in the city. The post-earthquake regime established by CERA has been replaced by a new emphasis on decision-making by the city council and its mayor between 2013 and 2022, Lianne Dalziel. However, the central state remains influential in the capacity of local government to make significant changes of direction to previously dominant market-led agendas. Since 2017, Labour-led and Labour governments have shown evidence of being open to new ideas about experimental urbanism, expanding earlier nationwide support of city cycleways for example. But they have if anything strengthened a significant instinct for centrally effected change (for instance in abolition of regional health boards and water management) that restricts the agency of local forms of governance.

It is telling that central government has been regarded as unable – despite its endorsement of ideas about experimental urbanism – to raise levels of recognition and funding for non-profit organisations such as those at the heart of experimental urbanism in Christchurch (Vallance 2020). The mayor and city council have always been viewed as broadly sympathetic to grassroots initiatives and have continued to provide some funds for the work of transitional organisations as part of their attempt to re-engage the hearts and minds of people in the city with more localised politics of urban renewal. Such support is significant, but inevitably limited by financial capacity.

Moreover, an emerging culture of 'metrics' to ensure both that expenditure is accountable, popular and manifestly beneficial to residents, and the observance of often minor but compelling health and safety regulations affecting activities across the city, has established a decision-making environment that to some extent clashes with the experimental and risk-taking nature of many transitional activities (Welfare 2020).

This shifting political context has coincided with and helped to shape, the evolving organisational context of transitional activity in Christchurch. First, it is evident that discourses of 'transition' are being replaced by those of 'place-making'. Place-making may be broadly understood as a process that inspires people to engage collectively in the reimagination of the public spaces at the heart of their community, thus helping to co-create contexts where they live or can see their future (Ermacora and Bullivant 2016). To some extent this discursive shift has been led by the city council, whose initial funding for transitional activity was organised under the Transitional Cities Programme to support post-quake recovery and well-being. This was later rebranded as the Enliven Places Programme, which aimed to transform underutilised sites into vibrant and welcoming public spaces (Christchurch City Council 2022a). The new programme prioritised fresh discourses; support was still offered to the community to deliver temporary projects to enhance amenity and activity, but such projects were encouraged to deliver a lasting legacy to the identity and sense of place in the city. This political lead, which shaped council funding for the activities of non-profits, helped to establish a new discursive environment for the organisations concerned. The idea of transition remained meaningful for some community partners and artist communities (Dombroski 2020) who recognised that the transitional phase after the earthquakes was by no means completed, but political expediency and organisational necessity led to a strongly-mediated recognition of place-making as the dominant theme for longer-term participation in the city. The discursive connotations of 'transitional' activities as a form of slapdash and unfinished do-it-yourself response to the earthquakes (Welfare 2020), were replaced by more slick and seemingly strategic connotations of place-making.

Alongside these discursive manoeuvres, the voluntary-sector organisations concerned underwent different kinds of changes in search of longer-term sustainability. Gap Filler, for example, transformed itself into a place-making social enterprise, using its post-earthquake reputation to offer design and delivery strategies for creative and experimental civic installations for communities and the public and private sectors in Christchurch, other New Zealand cities and internationally. A prime example of this new approach is a partnership with building company Fletcher Living to help create central city residential communities in the east frame of the central city (Gap Filler 2022). Drawing on its experience of using temporary activations to help foster longer-term community outcomes, Gap Filler is facilitating a range of community-minded projects as well as filling in the gaps with its own style of projects. This more formal integration into developer-led placemaking permits not only more sustainable sources of funding for the organisation, but also an opportunity to ensure a flow of playful and participatory aesthetics into longer term residential community-building.

Greening the Rubble has also sought to transform itself from an earthquake-response organisation into a more sustainable social enterprise. In 2019 it was rebranded as The Green Lab (2022), offering customised services for indoor greening projects and outdoor landscaping for public and commercial areas. Again, working as a social enterprise permits the organisation to maintain its transitional commitment to supporting community well-being and connecting people to nature. It also accommodates an adaptation to the evolving needs of the wider city via creation of community-led green spaces in areas of residential regeneration. Its new approach is illustrated by the Linwood Tiny Shops project, which in partnership with Te Whare Roimata and the city council involved the construction of a micro-village of small buildings in a suburban community garden, to be used as shops and a café and to support a range of local events.

Rebranding was also a strategic decision for the Festival of Transitional Architecture. Now renamed as Te Putahi, it organises Open Christchurch – a weekend festival that began in 2021 for residents to experience both traditional architecture and post-earthquake design in the city – whilst also hosting a diverse range of events to encourage civic awareness and engagement (Dionisio 2020). These events include gatherings, such as Christchurch Conversations, that connect Christchurch professionals and community groups with a range of international place-making concepts and networks, and showpiece projects such as the Old School House (Te Kura Tawhito) in the coastal suburb of New Brighton. Here architectural design expertise supported local community groups in the sympathetic adaptation of the building as a location for a collective of creatives, craftspeople and local organisations (Te Putahi 2022).

Perhaps the main exception to these adaptive trends is demonstrated by decisions taken by Life in Vacant Spaces to continue its charitable and community-centred work without rebranding or adopting socially entrepreneurial strategies of property and land management. Its early focus on performative pop-up projects in disused outdoor spaces in the inner city has evolved into brokering the development of pop-up shops and indoor art exhibitions in the internal spaces offered by vacant retail and office sites. Moreover, its commitment to helping local communities to help themselves has required a stronger focus on brokering entrepreneurial activity and community self-help in more suburban locations, and in the residential red zone corridor. For example, the East x East project involves a significant area of red zone land in Burwood that Life in Vacant Spaces (2022) has licensed from Land Information New Zealand, the Crown agency that has held ownership of that red zone land in Christchurch where housing has been demolished because of earthquake damage (Chapter 12). The objective for East x East was to create a vibrant and community-orientated space filled with temporary art projects, events and activities that demonstrate a commitment to communing, by listening to local communities seeking sites and practices where in-commonness can be pursued.

In each of these examples, organisations that arose from the rupture of the earthquakes have variously sought to evolve from earthquake-responders to sustainable agencies of place-making, often recognising the necessity to work together in partnership with government funders and commercial interests as well as local community groups. Although in each case, organisations have aimed to carry their initial experimental creativity and underlying senses of ethics and aesthetics through into these mature phases of social enterprise and partnership, they will inevitably be open to critiques involving selling-out, loss of ethical drive or sanitised incorporation into the agendas of more powerful partners. In conclusion, this chapter turns to the two main evaluative tropes which have been used to gauge the longer-term contribution of formerly-transitional non-profits in Christchurch.

Conclusion

The first of these tropes mourns the loss of significant opportunities that were presented by the event of the earthquakes. The initial post-quake period is seen by many (and certainly by those directly involved) to have been characterised by an outburst of positive energy for change in the city. This was recognisable both in an opportunity for community involvement in the priorities for, and direction to be taken by, renewal in the city, and in the stream of creative thinking and experimental activity exemplified by transitional organisations. This creative energy provided a focus for transformational change, involving a capacity to deviate from the past and to experiment with aesthetics and ethical values which enabled a rather different vision for narrating and participating in the life of the city. It gave rise to hope and even expectation that wider redevelopment processes in the city could be fuelled by creative thinking and collaboration between the public and private sectors and the key non-profit organisations responsible for early experimentation (Fisher 2020). In this way the ethical values and aesthetics of the transitional organisations could have been fostered significantly in the subsequent redesign of the city, in particular by adopting processes involving meaningful liaison with local communities and eschewing formulaic space-filling in favour of more experimental and risk-tolerant project design and decision-making.

In the political context that prevailed after the earthquakes, CERA's top-down control of the rebuild process gave little acknowledgement of, or support to, the work of key transitional organisations, and the blueprint for planning and development of anchor projects in the city largely sought to provide functional enhancements for what had existed previously. There were exceptions to this generalisation, such as the Margaret Mahy playground discussed in the next chapter, and the more open-ended processes of residential red zone planning explored in Chapter 12. With a political desire to support existing landowners and developers, the opportunity to foster transformational place-making projects was overlooked. With the significant exception of commercially sponsored street art, the result for some commentators has therefore been a rebuild process of business as usual, resulting in a city characterised by 're-creation of the same old same old, with a few bits of public art thrown in' (Fisher 2020), and the loss of any serious engagement with the energy and creativity of transitional organisations.

The second trope offers a more optimistic perspective, recognising that the early post-quake freedom for transitional activity unleashed an enthusiasm for collective and inclusive ways of working that has resulted in an enduring sense of alternative possibilities for place-making in the city. Accordingly, there is a hopefulness that the genie of creative aesthetic connection and experimental participatory action has produced lasting legacies. For example, the new approaches and aesthetics arising from partnership with organisations and individuals representing Ngāi Tahu and Ngāi Tūāhuriri have resulted in a more-than-tokenistic weaving of the values, aspirations and narratives of Māori people into the fabric of the post-earthquake city and some of its buildings. This represents a significant break from earlier narratives and encourages a hopeful expectation that other expressions of the cultural politics of local community might endure.

If over time the capacity for transitional organisations to make a sustained impact on place-making has been squeezed, there are also signs that the thinking behind transitional activities remains active in certain spheres of the city. New spaces of involvement have continued to open up, for example the shift to indoor sites (such as the Imagination Station for children occupying a floor of the new central library, Tūranga), the partnership between Gap Filler and Fletcher Living as part of new residential development in the east frame, and the long term opportunities for a second flush of transitional experimentation with new forms of place-making in the city's red zone corridor. Such reorientations indicate a sense in which there will always be elements of flux in urban development and redevelopment in which the creative energy of aesthetic connection and ethically in-common participatory community activity can take root.

Both evaluative tropes – telling stories of lost opportunity and of enduring hopefulness – pose important questions about the temporality or otherwise of the transitional activities that emerged from the rupture of the earthquakes. Transitional challenges to the orthodoxies of public space have demonstrated the new kinds of cultural politics that can emerge when different elements of the community at large become involved in the evolution and making of the city. As other potential disasters loom large, not least those associated with the regulation of carbon footprints and the urgent necessity for more sustainable resource use, so the affective politics inherent in transitional thinking remain a paramount rejoinder to business-as-usual practices.

9 Landscapes of consumption

Introduction

One of the striking effects of the earthquakes was the sudden loss of city centre and suburban sites of consumption associated with leisure, retailing and culture. Well-loved restaurants, cafés, bars, shops, public facilities such as cinemas, pools and libraries, and the heritage buildings that gave the city a sense of place: these disappeared overnight. Many were damaged beyond repair, lying isolated within the city centre cordon (Figure 6.2). As the cordon shrank, and life slowly returned to that broken landscape, individual events seemed like big milestones. Ballantynes department store, a fairly modern low-rise building, reopened in late 2011, becoming the anchor for the container mall. A year later, C1 Espresso café re-located to a solidly re-purposed old post office, quickly assuming the role of meeting place and downtown salon: there was little else. The first restored cultural facility, the Isaac Theatre Royal, opened in November 2014. In April 2016, on Anzac Day, huge numbers of people gathered when the Bridge of Remembrance – a first world war memorial that now functions as an entry point to the city's pedestrian mall – reopened after repair.

This chapter considers the role of consumption in post-earthquake recovery, and both the continuities and transformations from its pre-earthquake forms. Consumption in this sense denotes intertwined experiences, sites and products. It is much more than shopping, most of which anyway occurs in suburban malls; indeed the blueprint recovery plan considerably diminished the area of the central city set aside for this function. Instead the chapter conceptualises the city and its centre as a focus of consumption flows, competition for which is between places, at both the intra- and inter-urban scales. Consumers are local, national and in post-earthquake planning (but not necessarily post-Covid recovery) international. Large anchor projects such as Te Pae – the convention centre, the as-yet unfinished 'multi-purpose arena', the metro sports centre, and the very successful Margaret Mahy Family Playground were designed to attract such consumers but, as Chapter 6 demonstrates, to hold property investors and their capital in place as well. Consideration is

DOI: 10.4324/9780429275562-12

given in turn to retailing and hospitality; to the anchor projects purposed to support events and tourism; and to cultural heritage projects and restorations. It concludes by reflecting on how the spatial competition between places to attract consumers and consumption practices depends on and drives a further cycle of consumption, that of carbon.

Creating landscapes of consumption

The global rise of consumption and the commodification of leisure have been central to contemporary capitalist growth (Zukin 1998). This phenomenon is underpinned by a work-and-spend cycle, stimulated by advertising to fuel desires to own and engage with an ever-expanding range of commercially provided things, services and practices (Perkins and Thorns 2011). In this consumption process, individual and collective identities are constructed through the purchase and possession of objects and associated experiences, and performed in sites of 'aestheticised entertainment and pleasure' (Meethan 1996, 324), known also as landscapes of consumption. In Christchurch, in the two decades before the earthquakes, planners had therefore sought to emulate international trends in the creation of such landscapes. The city centre's streetscape was described as the product of 'waves of interest and investment in central city functions, the most recent of which [was] based on leisure and tourism' (Pawson and Swaffield 1998, 254). The focus on encouraging consumption complemented but contrasted with an earlier municipal drive – which remains strong – to provide facilities such as libraries and galleries, parks and playing fields. The city retains over 1200 public parks and gardens.

Landscapes of consumption are created in practices of place-making and promotion, which in the case of Christchurch have long built on its reputation as a fairly traditional 'garden city' (Pawson 1999). Since the earthquakes, as the previous chapter discussed, place-making techniques have been used creatively as part of the on-the-ground process of rendering the static geometry of the blueprint into what Jan Gehl would call 'people cities' (Matan and Newman 2016). They help to adapt the efficiency that characterises modernist planning into places for human opportunity, places that draw in people and encourage them to linger. An important part of this is making people and their interests (rather than traffic) visible. In the central city, which is renowned for its windiness, this has translated into the provision of sheltered laneways and squares, and a new emphasis on the riverside precinct, Te Papa Ōtākaro, as an attraction and locus of rest and recreation in its own right. This precinct is one of the more popular anchor projects, rooted as it is in the city's garden image of itself. The stories of mana whenua are woven into its design (Figure 8.1), in recognition of a more contemporary understanding of garden landscapes (Landscape Architecture Aotearoa 2022; O'Callaghan 2021).

The blueprint's focus on the central city has to be understood alongside the rise of suburban malls and the decline of central shopping streets. Globally this has been a major trend for decades (Teller 2008) and as part of the rebuild suburban libraries, sports facilities and other sites of cultural belonging have been rebuilt or replaced. In the central city, the night-time economy has been a notable element of Christchurch place-making prior to and after the earthquakes (McDonagh 2017), as discussed in Chapter 6. Internationally, this phenomenon has its basis in 1970s attempts to revalorise de-industralised inner cities to capture both real estate value and cultural capital (Lovatt and O'Connor 1995). Such investments aim to boost adult consumption and leisure experiences by adaptively repurposing redundant or under-utilised buildings for niche retailing and hospitality, but with a particular focus on bars and nightclubs. While these facilities and inner city landscapes have attracted consumers to replace those lost to the suburbs, they have also been associated with unhealthy drinking practices, especially among young people (Roberts 2006; Shaw 2010). Inner city Christchurch before 2010 was no exception (Johnston 2014; McCrone 2012b).

Place-making in Christchurch since the earthquakes also recognised that tourism has been perhaps the ultimate consumption industry globally, and before the Covid-19 pandemic was New Zealand's largest export sector (Perkins and Rosin 2018). It was a vital element in the city's economy, with its international airport being South Island's tourist gateway, a position earned and maintained with vigorous place promotion campaigns (Schöllmann et al. 2000). The growth in numbers of passengers coming through the airport peaked at about 6 million a year by 2010, the start of the earthquake sequence, but due to the loss of essential facilities, such as downtown hotels, and lack of access within the cordon, did not recover this level until 2016. Meanwhile, landings at Queenstown airport, which provides trans-Tasman flights with Australia, grew more quickly, although Christchurch recovered to seven million domestic and international arrivals in 2019, only to halve within two years due to Covid-19 (CIAL 2021; Queenstown Airport Company 2021). Some of the blueprint's anchor projects, notably the convention centre and multi-use arena, have to be seen in this context as vital elements of the city's place promotion strategies (Chapters 4 and 6).

The roll-out of these projects has been far from straightforward and exemplifies the difficulty of meeting objectives in complex administrative and political situations (Pressman and Wildavsky 1984). Lindblom (1959, 1979; also Johnson and Olshansky 2017) argues that in such situations, the best that can be achieved is a disjointed incrementalism, characterised as 'muddling through', and that it is therefore unsurprising that the best laid plans have not been delivered on time. In another way, the purpose of these central city anchor projects in generating and restoring consumption flows illustrates the principle of path dependency: the expectation that as recovery proceeds, consumers and tourists would return and progressively increase in number. As the airport statistics illustrate, this process has been slow, and as elsewhere slowed still further by the Covid pandemic (Škare et al. 2021). More disruption is likely with the increasingly urgent need to engage with climate change goals. This raises significant questions about the wisdom of depending on a path that locates major consumption facilities in the central city, requiring significant travel for consumers, although there are equally serious issues raised by provision of car-dependent facilities in the suburbs.

Retailing, hospitality and experiments in business

One of the attributes of pre-earthquake Christchurch was the long-term dispersal of retailing activities to the suburbs (Thull and Mersch 2005). This reflected the preponderance of suburban malls which in 2006 amounted to 0.82 square metres per person, larger than Auckland, at 0.63, and far in excess of Wellington, at 0.52 (Blundell 2006). The first such mall, and still the largest, was established in Riccarton in the 1960s; it now has the highest turnover of any in the country (Gibson 2019). The city had then, as now, three other big suburban malls, plus a host of smaller covered malls in specific districts, in line with its autodependent geography and relatively permissive District Plan (Chapter 5). While the larger malls are anchored by supermarkets, they are more than places to shop with an array of cafés, bars, restaurants and fast-food outlets and sometimes multiplexes. In the last decade, a growing number of big box developments have also been built, both in strips (for example, along the arterials Moorhouse Avenue and Blenheim Road) and at specific sites (as in Langdons Road, Papanui and the Shirley Homebase). The common feature that these facilities share is free car parking, along with those centres that have been master-planned within new greenfield subdivisions, such as Wigram and satellite towns, for example, Rolleston (see Chapter 5).

Post-earthquake central city shopping is now concentrated in the retail precinct of large-scale developments of 7500 square metres (Chapter 6), the product of the amalgamation of pre-earthquake land holdings, as required by the blueprint (Figure 9.1). These are integrated office, retail and car parking projects, although unlike at suburban malls, parking is a charge to users. They are mostly new builds although some, such as the Carter Group's The Crossing, preserve pre-earthquake facades. They include internal laneways and sometimes small squares, giving the illusion of an extending public realm to match the aspirations expressed by the public – as described in Chapter 4 – in Share an Idea in 2011. Combined with other infrastructure developments, such as re-made streets and the river promenade, this has created a varied and (significantly for a windy city) sheltered downtown environment for a more specialised range of consumption experiences than the serial replication characteristic of most suburban locations. Facilities in this rebuilt city centre are designed to capture the spending of domestic and international tourists, as well as office workers, and the discretionary dollars of those interested in specific hospitality experiences by day and night.

The central city's landcapes of consumption are therefore dominated by a range of big brand retailers, especially in fashion, which can afford the significant rents charged in expensive, post-earthquake buildings (Chapter 6).

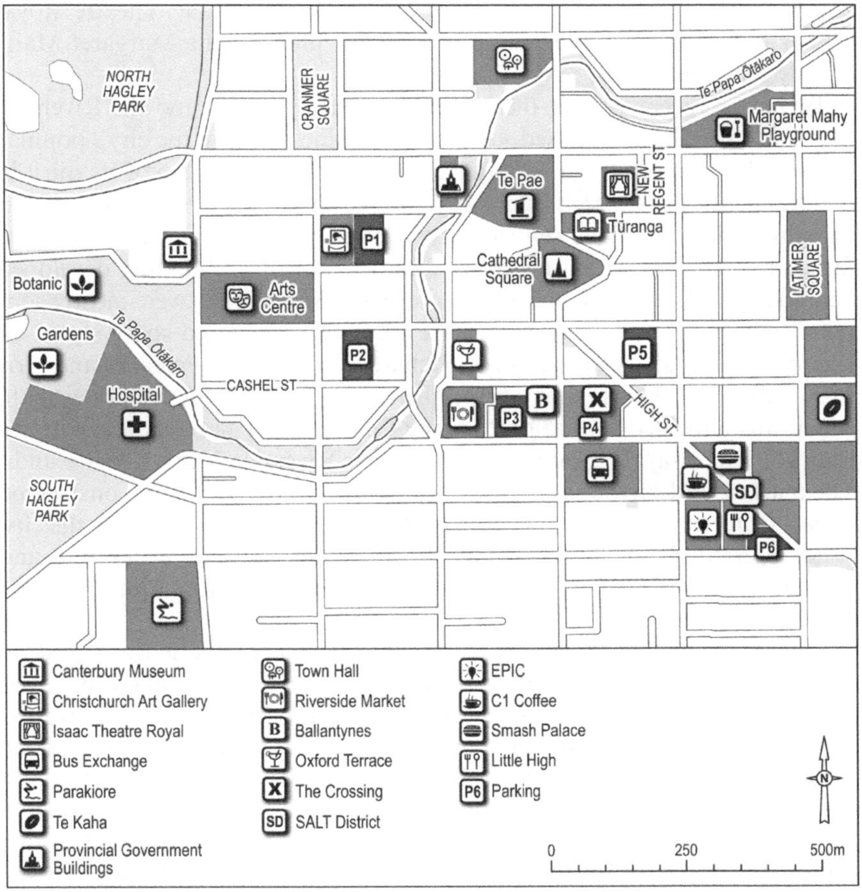

Figure 9.1 City centre consumption sites.

Smaller footprints are occupied by some more specialised shops, but also by a considerable number of food outlets, café-bars and restaurants. These are situated along the river, in the laneways and squares of larger developments, as well as within facilities such as hotels and Tūranga, the new central city library. There are however some specific locations that are the product of particular post-earthquake histories. For example, New Regent Street is a surviving streetscape built in the 1930s in Spanish Mission Revival style. Most of its owners and tenants clubbed together to restore their buildings, which have Category 1 historic place status. The facades were strengthened with structural steel frames, and most outlets in the street re-opened during 2013 (Naylor Love 2021), making this the first permanent retail and hospitality focus in the central city after the earthquakes. It sits well outside the retail precinct, to the north of Cathedral Square, somewhat in defiance of the cool logic of the blueprint. But its cafés, bars, restaurants and popular ice cream parlour have gained from proximity to the restored Isaac Theatre Royal (2014) and one of the most successful anchor projects, the Margaret Mahy Family Playground (2015).

Two more recent venues, the Little High Eatery (2017) and the Riverside Market (2019), have rehoused some of the businesses from the city's popular post-earthquake container mall (Chapter 6), embodying much of its spirit in developments that have brought new food experiences, senses of fun and experimentation to the central city. Little High houses eight licenced family-run businesses on the ground floor of an office building developed behind a grand, restored facade in Lower High Street. They were mostly container mall neighbours and now share a convivial enclosed space styled on examples overseas. The developers, Richard Peebles, Mike Percasky and Kris Inglis, also own the site that housed the last iteration of the container mall, which was relocated several times along Cashel Street as the new retail projects got underway. It is on this site that their Riverside Market now stands. The market, and surrounding lanes, is a more ambitious project, constructed in part from recycled materials from destroyed buildings elsewhere in the city. It has 30 food stalls, 40 market stalls and upstairs bars and restaurants, and has been such a drawcard that it hosted two million visitors in its first year (Hayward 2020a).

Developments like these seek to provide consumer experiences based on values such as place attributes, product quality, support of local business and a low carbon footprint. Riverside, for example, aims to be zero waste, in partnership with Cultivate Christchurch, an urban farm a kilometre away, which provides vegetables for sale as well as a destination for the market's composted waste (McDonald 2019c). The market's stalls are licenced rather than leased, giving low barriers to entry for traders who wish to experiment with a central city location for new products, thereby overcoming the issue of the high rents charged for more permanent sites elsewhere in the retail precinct. As such, the market is both an experiment in business practices and in place-making.

Another example of such an experiment is a collective initiative to rebrand the blueprint's Innovation Precinct as the SALT district. This initiative brought together some of Little High's (and the Riverside Market's) developers, with Ōtākaro Limited, the Crown company designated in 2016 with the completion of the anchor projects and ChristchurchNZ, the city council's development and promotions agency. SALT denotes the area around St Asaph, Lichfield and Tuam Streets, but also means 'South Alternative', and 'salt of the earth' (Figure 9.1). It won an international award as a large-scale place project, being described as 'an exemplar in community co-creation' (Place Leaders 2019). SALT is intended to denote something lively and gritty, an area of employment and entertainment that has been partly rebuilt around surviving structures in Lower High Street, and partly reconstructed as a venue for a range of businesses. These include the EPIC innovation hub, Little High, C1 Espresso and Smash Palace, an open-air transitional bar. To quote one of SALT's instigators, the central city 'can't compete with malls for retail or from the comfort point of view, but it can with *experiences*, so people go "wow, awesome"' (Percasky 2020).

The recognition given to the SALT project has led to the establishment of an unusual trust, Action Reaction Central Christchurch, that aims to encourage those working in different inner districts to highlight what makes their neighbourhood unique and use this to attract more consumers into the central city (Hayward 2020b). 'Uniqueness' in this context can mean such things as facilities, atmosphere, street art and events. In part, the formation of the trust is borne of frustration from the lack of coordination between public (especially city council events and ideas) and business initiatives. It aims to resolve what Marcus Westbury, who championed place-making strategies in the revival of the dying centre of Newcastle, New South Wales, describes as 'how places enable or thwart people with initiative' (2015, 12). The trust also seeks to recapture on the streets something of the spontaneity of the transitional activities that, as described in Chapter 8, flourished in the immediate post-earthquake period. These won for the city a lot of international notice such as for street art, featured in *Oi You!* Lonely Planet's (2017) recognition of international street art cities, and the multi-award-winning container mall, recognised by the Property Council of New Zealand and the Canterbury and national branches of the New Zealand Institute of Architects (Figure 9.2).

Figure 9.2 The SALT district: a three-dimensional street art illusion.

The most distinctive inner-city districts are those established as dining and entertainment destinations, such as SALT, Riverside and the Oxford Terrace 'strip' of bars. The last-named opened in 2018 as a complex of buildings and lanes, each with a different design, as a project by local developer Antony Gough. He has succeeded in reproducing one of the most vibrant of the city's pre-earthquake nighttime landscapes. In this sense, post-earthquake place-making builds on a decade's worth of experience in which an earlier city council worked with developers to inject consumption activity into an increasingly obsolescent downtown core. Gough has rebuilt in the same place; other pre-earthquake developments, such as Lichfield Lanes (on the fringes of what is now the SALT district), were housed in old brick buildings, most of which were damaged on 22 February 2011, and with one exception have been demolished (McDonagh 2017). But they pioneered in the city the encouragement of young people's drinking habits as a means of downtown revitalisation. This has thrived in 'an almost carnivalesque atmosphere' (Johnston 2014, 199), with two very effective consumption outcomes. It has spread patterns of use from business and family users in daytime and evening well into the night, as well as attracting a much more youthful – and sometimes problematic – set of consumers.

The role of anchor projects in revitalisation

The rationale for the provision of anchor projects in the blueprint, as described in Chapters 4, 5 and 6, was to hinder capital flight by providing material evidence of the state's commitment to rebuilding the city, and to ensure that private sector investment was thereby encouraged. In reality, most of the main consumption-orientated anchor projects have been so delayed (Figure 4.4) that private investment, as described above, and in Chapter 6, has led rather than followed. Often this has been by taking considerable business risks. When the city's nighttime economy was seisimically destroyed within seconds, much of the activity relocated to the suburbs, for example along Riccarton Road to the west, or was absorbed into informal partying in private homes. Antony Gough's strategy for recapturing this trade with the construction of the Oxford Terrace strip nearly foundered with problems in accessing sufficient capital several times between 2013 and 2018. Developers like Mike Percasky (Percasky and Shaw 2020) have been vocal in their concern that the failure to complete the multi-use arena undermines their own investments. This section assesses the anchor project strategy in this light, focusing on the convention centre, the arena, the metro sports centre and the children's playground.

The convention centre, known as Te Pae (which has various meanings, including 'gathering place') opened at the end of 2021 after considerable delays, due in part to problems accessing skilled labour during Covid-19 outbreaks. It sits within Te Papa Ōtākaro/Avon River precinct, on a large site that required closing and erasing a length of one city street. With 28,000 square metres of floor space, it was planned in the blueprint as a complementary facility to the 32,000-square-metre New Zealand International Convention Centre in Auckland (due in 2024), and a smaller facility in Queenstown (yet to be built). In the meantime, however, Wellington is also building Tākina, an 18,000-square-metre centre opposite Te Papa Tongarewa, the national museum (due in 2023). Its business case is based on protecting the capital's convention market share once the other centres are open, as well as enhancing its 'international competititiveness' (Wellington City Council 2018, 7–8). This profusion led one journalist to describe a coming 'battle of the convention centres', each planned in pre-Covid times and when carbon management had not attained its present profile (Anthony 2021). They are all, however, city centre projects which can be unusual internationally.

Whether in this context the blueprint's promise of attracting 'new and exciting events' to post-earthquake Christchurch can be delivered remains to be seen (Central City Recovery Plan 2012, 67). Inevitably this will depend on competition at a range of scales, as recognised by Ōtākaro Ltd, the Crown company that built Te Pae, engaging ASM Global, a venue management company based in Los Angeles with a portfolio of more than 300 venues worldwide. The scale of ASM's ambition for Te Pae is shown in Figure 9.3. But ASM in turn competes with the city council's own business, Venues Ōtautahi, which manages the Christchurch Town Hall, on the opposite side of the river, and which used to be connected to the council's own exhibitions hall, lost in the earthquakes. The blueprint also questioned whether the Town Hall itself would be repaired, but as described later in this chapter, the

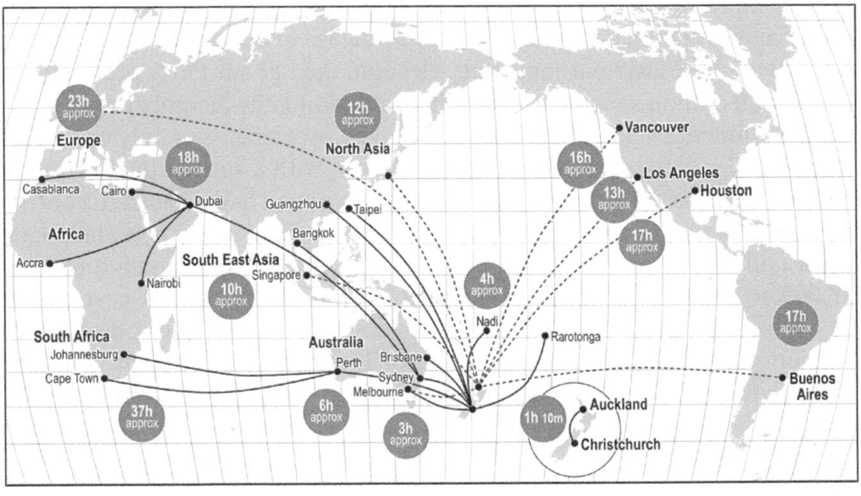

Figure 9.3 Te Pae: 'getting here'.

Source: Redrawn from www.tepae.co.nz

council decided otherwise. The council also declined to assume ownership of Te Pae in the Global Settlement Agreement with the Crown, signed in 2019, viewing it less as an asset than a long-term liability. In contrast, Woods Bagot (2021), the lead designer, asserts that it 'helps establish a strong cultural narrative throughout the central city', at best a speculative claim as it replaces in one outsize structure what were two lively pre-earthquake city blocks.

The earthquake sequence was well underway by the start of the year that Australia and New Zealand were to host the 2011 Rugby World Cup. The loss of the 38,500-seat rugby football and cricket AMI Stadium (located on Lancaster Park) to the earthquakes was therefore doubly felt by sports fans in Christchurch and Canterbury. The main stands were badly damaged, and the pitch destroyed by liquefaction. The city council redeveloped the Hagley Cricket Oval relatively inexpensively, as a traditional-style ground with pavilions and grass banks. It was finished in spring 2014, and used for the opening game of the Cricket World Cup, hosted by Australia and New Zealand, in February 2015. It has largely met the requirements of the cricketers (Longley 2015), although the later installation of night-time lights was more controversial. The Christchurch-based Crusaders Super Rugby franchise continues to operate in a small temporary open-air facility with a seating capacity of 18,000 spectators, inadequate from its point of view, given the quality of stadia in Dunedin, Wellington and Auckland. To meet their requirements, and those of concert-goers, the blueprint planners proposed the construction of a large 35,000-seat covered multi-purpose sports and entertainment venue in central Christchurch, much closer in form to other cities' facilities than Lancaster Park had been. It was to host rugby union, rugby league and football up to an international level, and also allow for entertainment events such as concerts.

Now known as Te Kaha, or the Canterbury Multi-Use Arena, it has been a source of ongoing debate in the light of delays and significant cost escalations. Before the 2017 parliamentary election, the Labour Party promised the city a $300 million sweetener, somewhat outbidding the incumbent National-led government (Small and Meier 2017). The sweetener was duly confirmed when Labour came into government that year, with a substantial portion of it to be added to the $253 million that the city council had decided to contribute to the arena, largely from insurance receipts. Subsequently, to help keep costs under control, the seating was reduced from the originally proposed 35,000 to 30,000, but back up from an earlier more radical cost-cutting 25,000-seat proposal (Clark 2021). Investors and sports bodies pressed for a stadium that would at least match that of Dunedin's Forsyth Barr stadium, which bills itself as 'New Zealand's largest and most versatile indoor events arena'. The proposed completion date for construction for the arena is now 2026; it is likely that other Canterbury district councils will be asked to contribute to the costs of development (Walton 2021d).

Surprisingly, given the capital outlay and likely ongoing costs of the facility to Christchurch and Canterbury ratepayers – local property taxes are predicted to increase significantly – there was for long little open opposition to the proposal. But it began to emerge with further cost escalations in mid-2022 and may yet match that experienced from 2009 in Dunedin where the scars of the battle over its stadium were still obvious a decade after it was proposed and then built (Loughrey 2019). What has been largely missing from the discussion in Christchurch is that while a significant literature identifies the great enjoyment engendered by arenas among their users, and the players in, and owners of, professional sports teams, it also points to a very high and perhaps unsustainable level of public subsidy and cost in support of considerable private gain (Swindell and Rosentraub 1998). But the case both for and against is always hard to assess in such situations: in the last decade, it has been Dunedin, the South Island's only other significant city, that has attracted All Blacks rugby games and big international acts, such as Ed Sheeran, Elton John and Queen.

The blueprint's metro sports facility, now known as the Parakiore Christchurch Recreation and Sport Centre, is another of the large anchor projects plagued by completion delays (McCrone 2015b). Designed to complement a range of new post-earthquake suburban physical recreational facilities (described in Chapter 10), it will replace the liquefaction-damaged eastern suburbs QEII Park as the city's main swimming complex, and provide Christchurch's netballers with a long-needed indoor home. The centre was supposed to be completed early in 2016. Six years later, it was still under construction on a four-hectare central city site vacated by a large brewery after the earthquakes. Once finished it will be the largest aquatic and indoor recreation and leisure venue in New Zealand and be accessible to people of all ages, abilities and skill levels. In its more than 30,000m^2 space, the Centre will contain a 50 metre, ten-lane competition swimming pool and a separate diving pool, a large aquatic leisure area, five hydroslides, fitness spaces and nine indoor courts for sports such as netball, volleyball and basketball. It will cater for recreational, educational and high-performance sports communities, although tensions over priority between these groups quickly emerged.

In 2015, journalist John McCrone observed that 'just like the convention centre, the East Frame, and some of the other anchor projects…behind the scenes it [the Recreation and Sports Centre] has turned into something of a monster' (McCrone 2015b). Progress has been hampered by a range of complex administrative difficulties. Cost-overruns have occurred, partly because, as sports administrators see it, early plans bordered on the grandiose. The delays have caused a great deal of frustration among sports groups in need of the promised facilities. In the interim, both high-performance sports groups and recreational participants have sought and relied on temporary facilities – some in other provinces with, for example, swimmers travelling 360 kilometres south to Dunedin (McCrone 2015). In light of the cost-overruns, amounting to $NZ75 million by November 2017, Dr Megan Woods, the new Labour-led government's Minister for Greater Christchurch

Regeneration, announced fresh administrative, design and contracting arrangements (Woods 2017). Inevitably, this took time, so the first sod on the site was not turned until June 2019. The intervention of the Covid-19 pandemic and subsequent labour shortages further delayed the opening.

In contrast, the award-winning Tākaro ā Poi/Margaret Mahy Family Playground was the first of the major anchor projects to be completed, a year after the Hagley Cricket Oval, in late 2015 (IPWEA 2019). It is part of the Te Papa Ōtākaro/Avon River precinct and named for Christchurch's internationally recognised children's author, and also honours another remarkable Canterbury writer and community activist, Elsie Locke, whose city council memorial park was destroyed in the earthquakes. The playground incorporates landscape themes developed in conjunction with Ngāi Tahu and was co-named by them. It is large, covering a 2.5-hectare site, and the biggest project in New Zealand created primarily for play (Hamilton 2016, Wade 2018). Somewhat controversially, the playground cost more than $NZ40 million to construct (Smith 2017). It is however hugely popular with children, their families and young adults, the latter using it in the early evenings and after dark (Figure 9.4).

The playground had its origins in the city council's Share an Idea project and a close engagement with Christchurch's children. In 2013, the Central City Development Unit initiated a competition inviting children to design 'the world's best playground'. More than 6000 children participated sending in approximately 300 entries (Stewart 2013). The task of operationalising the entry from Year 6 at Selwyn House School – which suggested the

Figure 9.4 Children and adults in the Margaret Mahy Family Playground.
Credit: ChristchurchNZ.

Margaret Mahy naming – was given to a consortium comprising a play safety specialist, a playground supplier company, materials engineers and a team of designers. Their objective was to create a design that catered for a variety of age groups marked by different levels of challenge using multiple play media. And as one journalist wrote after it opened, 'If you're in the mood for a physical challenge, a race, climbing, digging, squirting, bouncing, sliding, spinning or skimming, this is the place to lose time' (Wade 2018). It has won a number of awards, including top honours as a public works project by the Institute of Public Works Engineering Australasia in 2017, and a New Zealand Institute of Landscape Architects Award of Excellence in the same year. For some years, it stood apart in meeting the anchor project aspiration to attract people to the central city and contribute to business growth (Hamilton 2016; Smith 2017). Wotif, the online accommodation platform, advertises a range of hotels close to the Armagh Street site that can accommodate visitors to the playground (Wotif 2021).

Cultural heritage and restorations

In contrast to new anchor projects designed to attract consumers to the city centre, many of its cultural heritage buildings, 'in an architecturally serious city in which the bar was set early, and high, by … High Gothic Victorian revivalism' (Walsh 2020, 117) were destroyed in the earthquakes or written off by the blueprint. Some major facilities outside the blueprint area nonetheless fared relatively well. The city's Botanic Gardens were largely unscathed, as was the Gothic Canterbury Museum which had been seismically strengthened before the earthquakes, although it had long yearned to modernise its warren of buildings to better comply with contemporary museum practice. The Arts Centre, the largely Victorian campus vacated by the University of Canterbury in the 1970s, was less fortunate, with every building damaged. But insurance proceeds have underwritten a massive restoration project. The nearby Art Gallery (2003) functioned as the headquarters of Civil Defence during the major quakes, but turned out to need major repairs before re-opening in 2015. The fate of the Christchurch Town Hall was more contentious.

The contest over its future is an example of the performative power of the map proving ultimately impotent. A modernist composition of interconnected buildings on the river banks, the Town Hall includes a concert hall widely renowned for the quality of its acoustic and audience experience. Leonard Bernstein, conducting the New York Philharmonic there in 1974, two years after its opening, declared that he was 'very envious … I wish we had something like it in New York' (Lochhead 2019, 125–7). More recently, the *Guardian* newspaper included it amongst '10 of the world's best concert halls' (Cox 2015). The complex was badly affected by lateral spread on 22 February 2011 and was omitted from the blueprint, in favour of facilities in a new Performing Arts precinct. The Minister for Earthquake Recovery at the time, National's Gerry Brownlee, was an implacable opponent of restoration, ignoring affection for 'Christchurch's public living room'. In this case, however, the map did not win out; the Town Hall was re-opened in 2019, not least because a business case prepared by international accounting firm Deloitte for the owner, the city council, estimated restoration would cost far less than a new facility (Law 2015).

How the Town Hall will fare operationally, with the opening of competing facilities in Te Pae and the Performing Arts precinct, remains to be seen. The precinct is effectively anchored by the Isaac Theatre Royal and New Regent Street, both of which, as indicated earlier in this chapter, were restored fairly quickly. The precinct was intended to provide performance facilities for the Christchurch Symphony Orchestra (but now, as before, these are based in the Town Hall), the Christchurch Music Centre (previously in the destroyed Catholic Cathedral grounds), and the Court Theatre (previously in the Arts Centre) (Central City Recovery Plan 2012, 77). A new facility, The Piano, was opened for the Music Centre in the precinct in 2016, funded by insurance payments with contributions from the council and Crown (McDonald 2016). Negotiations about the future of the Court Theatre have been more protracted. It is the country's largest professional theatre company, and decamped to a converted industrial warehouse in the suburb of Addington in late 2011. This facility is greatly enjoyed by theatregoers because of its spaciousness, acoustics and on-site car parking. Following offers of council and Crown support, it is expected that a new theatre will open in the precinct in 2024, although this still left some space unallocated.

The provision of new facilities, sometimes but not always aligned with the restoration of the old, raises questions over the affordability let alone use of repairable, older cultural heritage buildings. Repair was not usually considered an option in the blueprint, and in many cases was not viable. Some smaller buildings have been restored by private developers who, in terms of the argument advanced in Chapter 6, have been attracted by the business opportunities that can be generated from enhancing some sense of place in the urban landscape. Companies such as Box 112 and the Stockman Group have been active in this respect. Box 112 has re-purposed a number of historic buildings in the river precinct, including the majestic former Public Trust Office, as well as former industrial and workshops spaces for small-scale retail, hospitality and personal care businesses in the district now dubbed 'South Town'. Stockman has restored a number of old buildings in Lower High Street, as has Richard Peebles. These restorations have been more practical for both developers and tenants than larger-scale projects which were often questionable business propositions even before the earthquakes.

The result of the priorities set within the blueprint has therefore been that over a decade later, some significant restorations remain incomplete, or even un-started. This is sometimes due to the complexity of repair, but often down to a shortage of available funds. The blueprint required heavy commitments from both the city council and the Crown, and one-off commitments to iconic special cases, such as the Anglican cathedral restoration, discussed in Chapter 4, have left little enthusiasm for further demands on the public purse. The cathedral, which is the responsibility of the Church Property Trustees, still has a fundraising target of over $50 million, without taking account of rapid rises in building costs since the start of the pandemic in 2020. The Canterbury Museum has a $70 million shortfall for its modernisation plans and seeks to bridge this in part by seeking support from other Canterbury district councils, as is the case for the new multi-use arena discussed above. The Arts Centre, overseen by its own Trust Board, has insufficient funds to complete the restoration of a third or so of its buildings (Law 2021). These buildings are each ranked as New Zealand Historic Places Trust Category 1.

The problem that such facilities pose is exemplified by the Canterbury Provincial Government Buildings, before 2010 New Zealand's only surviving complex from the provincial period of national government (1853–76), and also Category 1. It sits as a ruin on the opposite side of the river to Te Pae. The timber parts of this Gothic complex, built in the late 1850s, survive more or less intact, but the later stone towers, and a magnificently flamboyant stone council chamber completed in 1865, crumbled in the 22 February earthquake in 2011. It had long been hard to find effective uses for much of the complex. Although the ruins were quickly sealed against the weather, and the stones carefully stored, it is not clear when or if restoration can begin. In 2018, it was estimated that this would cost over $200 million, but that the city council, as owner, could commit only $20 million of this by 2028, with the balance not until between 2032 and 2040 (Law 2021). A proposed targeted property rate is unlikely to make much difference. The only conclusion that can be drawn with any certainty is that recovery after a great disaster takes a very long time.

In contrast to these concerns for the loss and regeneration of European New Zealand-built heritage has been the work of the Matapopore Charitable Trust and its mission to highlight cultural diversity in the Christchurch urban region. A collaboration between local Ngāi Tahu hapū (sub-tribe) Ngāi Tūāhuriri and originally CERA, and now the region's local authorities, the trust has been responsible for representing Māori values, narratives and aspirations in the heritage recovery process. The trust has made its presence felt strongly through the widespread use of Māori designs and te reo (Māori language) names for new buildings in multiple urban sites during the recovery. These have included motifs and poems etched onto buildings and pathways, new public artworks, and gardens including indigenous and endemic plants, and appear alongside and sometimes interwoven with established landscapes, all of which contribute a new element to consumption in the city that is already appearing in Christchurch and Canterbury's tourism promotion (Harvie 2016; McDonald 2018c).

Conclusion

One of the key threads of this chapter has been the importance of consumption, leisure and the provision of landscapes that encourage consumption practices and experiences in post-earthquake recovery. The focus has been on those forms of consumption at the centre of the rebuild: the ever-expanding range of commercially provided 'objects', that includes physical things, services, practices, cultural performances, lifestyles and places, and the public recreation facilities and spaces they complement. It has paid less attention to outdoor recreation and engagement with the more-than-human world, which are discussed in Chapters 11 and 12. Instead, we conclude here with a brief reflection on two themes: first, that work to attract flows of consumption is highly competitive, and second, that such flows often depend on and drive a further cycle of consumption, that of carbon.

Competition to attract consumers and consumption practices operates at a range of spatial scales. An important part of the state's support for the rebuild of the Christchurch urban region and its focus on consumption has been to maintain the economic role of the South Island's largest city and its tourist gateway. The central city blueprint was designed to hold and attract investment and encourage people to visit the central city to engage in a wide range of leisure activities. The role of the anchor projects within this was to be that of leading private sector investment, even if generally it has worked in practice the other way round. While local residents have been attracted to the regenerating inner city, Covid-19 has complicated the assumption that it would also recover steadily as a flourishing site for national and international tourism.

In taking this approach, the blueprint has laid the basis for future competition between Christchurch and other New Zealand urban centres, for instance in the provision of convention centres and multi-use arenas. It has also underwritten competition between the city centre and the suburbs in retailing and hospitality, and to an extent through the centralisation of sporting and play facilities. This is not a clear-cut picture, particularly in retailing, and as Chapter 10 illustrates, there have been attempts, in the provision of new schools and swimming pools, to counter the lack of attention given to investment in the eastern suburbs of the city. But competition for resources has also emerged between initiatives, shown most clearly in the lack of funding left, after the choices made to spend so much on the anchor projects, for restoring key elements of cultural heritage.

The second theme that underlies an understanding of the city's new landscapes of consumption is that of carbon. Centralising facilities in the central city requires people to travel over an increasingly wide area, as a pre-occupation with the provision of car parking illustrates, despite some genuflection towards rebuilding 'a green city' in both the council plan and the Crown's later blueprint. This did produce early completion of one anchor project, the Bus Xchange, in 2015, but despite this, public transport patronage has yet to recover to pre-earthquake levels. And if the city and suburbs now have an emerging network of cycleways, encouraged by government funding available nationwide over the last decade, this has also yet to make much difference to travel patterns in the round. Indeed, one of the contradictions of the rebuild, as Chapter 5 so clearly shows, has been the facilitation of suburban and sub-regional greenfield expansion, supported by investment in Roads of National Significance ringing the city (Pawson 2022). In many respects, the rebuilt city typifies a carbon-intensive approach.

10 The eastern suburbs

Introduction

In the years following 2010 and 2011, there was some disquiet regarding the pace of recovery in the eastern suburbs of Christchurch. Attention was drawn to the extent of unrepaired property damage, to the apparent indifference of central government to community concerns and to ongoing problems with water and sewage infrastructure. Unfavourable comparisons were made with the more affluent western areas of the city, where building and infrastructure repairs were further advanced, and with the central city, where the government had invested heavily in a series of anchor projects and thematic precincts, and new landscapes of consumption were appearing. The notion of the 'forgotten east' began to circulate (Conway 2011; Lynch 2019; Smith 2018), encapsulating the view that eastern areas of the city were somehow being overlooked or under-prioritised in the post-quake recovery.

Responding to this concern, this chapter considers whether the eastern suburbs were in some respects neglected during the recovery process. It recognises that these suburbs were extensively affected by the earthquakes, with many areas suffering significant land damage and liquefaction. If the pace of recovery was slower here than elsewhere in the city, perhaps this simply reflected the large volume of work needed to repair the damage. Some of the city's most socially and economically disadvantaged communities are in the east, and such groups are known to fare worse during disaster recovery, whether on the basis of socio-economic status or race/ethnicity (Cutter et al. 2006; Enarson and Morrow 1988; Gaillard et al. 2017; Kahn 2005; Wisner et al. 2004). So, this too may have been a factor, at least in terms of the psychosocial dimensions of recovery. In the discussion here, however, the focus is on the actions of government, insurance companies and community organisations involved in the recovery of the eastern suburbs. To what extent were these actors responsive to local concerns? Were their efforts appropriately attuned to local needs, or were they in some way neglectful? Through a consideration of available evidence, this chapter seeks to address these questions.

DOI: 10.4324/9780429275562-13

Disruption and recovery in the eastern suburbs

Although there is some variation in local understanding, the eastern suburbs in Christchurch are generally understood to include Richmond, Avonside, Dallington, Wainoni, Burwood, Linwood, Phillipstown, Bromley, Aranui and New Brighton (Figure 10.1). Many of the communities in these areas are of lower socio-economic status, with higher proportions of low-income households and below-average levels of post-secondary education (Table 10.1). There is also above-average 'blue collar' employment (eg. labouring and manufacturing). Families with multigenerational connections to their neighbourhoods and thus significant place attachments are common. The largest ethnic group by proportion is New Zealand European, but a number of areas have significant proportions of Māori households, particularly Aranui and Wainoni. Given their proximity to the Avon River and development on drained wetlands, many eastern suburbs suffered extensive liquefaction and land damage in the September 2010 and February 2011 earthquakes. Residential water and sewage systems were also disrupted, with some neighbourhoods – in areas such as Bexley and New Brighton – having to rely upon portable toilets for weeks and, in some cases, months (Potangaroa et al. 2011).

There is a broad range of possible outcomes for places affected by disasters, as Wilson (2013, 2014) has observed. After the initial disruption, some manage to recover something approximating their previous levels of social and economic activity. This may reflect their internal resilience as well as the

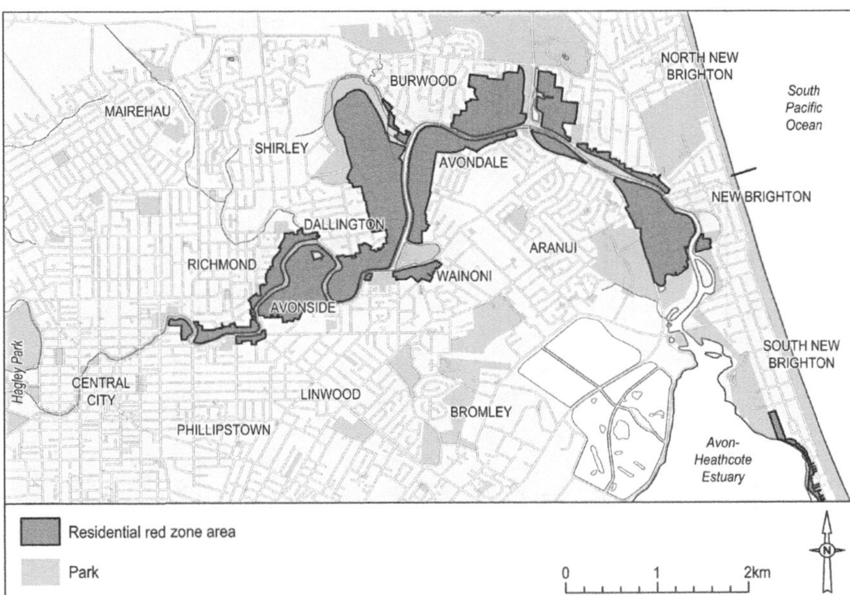

Figure 10.1 The eastern suburbs and the residential red zone.

Source: https://opendata.canterburymaps.govt.nz/

Table 10.1 Selected socio-economic characteristics of eastern suburbs

	Burwood	*Dallington*	*Wainoni*	*Aranui*	*Avonside*	*Linwood*	*Phillipstown*	*Bromley*	*New Brighton*	*Christchurch average*	*NZ average*
NZ European (%)	83.6	82.7	77.1	62.1	78.2	64.8	64.8	75.2	82.3	80.1	70.7
Māori (%)	7.4	7.4	12.4	17.9	12.5	9.2	13.8	13.3	9.4	6.7	11.7
Households earning under $20k per annum (%)	11.5	8.6	11.6	14.8	17.2	14.9	13.2	9.8	12.3	9.0	9.4
Households earning over $100k per annum (%)	23.7	13.9	10.1	8.0	12.6	8.0	7.1	10.6	12.9	23.8	23.4
Residents with a Bachelor degree (%)	10.4	8.6	3.8	3.1	7.7	9.1	7.7	4.2	9.2	12.6	12.1

Source: Statistics New Zealand (2013).

receipt of external support. Others places stagger onwards, continuing to function but in an appreciably diminished manner. There may be reduced levels of economic activity, increased material hardship, damaged infrastructure and residents grappling with personal and collective trauma (Fullilove 2016; Herman 1998). In places very starkly affected by disasters, people may be forced to leave, for reasons that include preservation of life, compromised housing, lack of local employment opportunities and grief and emotional loss that become too difficult to bear (Fullilove 2016; Pain 2019). For those who stay, the provision of meaningful support and access to relevant resources is a key determinant of their post-disaster experience. This is one reason why it matters a great deal whether the needs and concerns of places are recognised by key actors in the recovery process. If in the aftermath of a disaster those needs are somehow forgotten, disregarded or overlooked, then recovery may be compromised. For places as well for people, being noticed and attended to has substantive consequences.

Guided by these perspectives, the following sections examine four aspects of recovery in the eastern suburbs: the availability of affordable housing, the creation of the residential red zone, the rebuilding of sport and recreation facilities and the reorganisation of public education. As the repair of subsurface infrastructure was a city-wide issue, and not something specific to the eastern suburbs, it is not discussed here. For each of the four aspects, consideration is given to the ensemble of organisational actors involved – including central and local government agencies, insurance companies and community groups – and to whether they recognised and responded to residents' needs. By considering the extent to which the needs of the eastern communities were attended to, the notion of the 'forgotten east' is assessed.

Availability of affordable housing

Prior to the earthquakes, there was a visible concentration of low-cost housing east of the central city, extending into suburbs such as Avonside and Linwood. Many of these units were privately owned but some belonged to the city council, reflecting its longstanding commitment to providing housing for low-income residents. A proportion was also owned by Housing New Zealand, the central government housing agency which was restructured to become Kāinga Ora – Homes and Communities in October 2019. Irrespective of their ownership, these properties provided affordable housing for a range of people who had limited incomes, including individual men and women. Some were employed in low-paying jobs and others were long-term beneficiaries (eg. as a result of chronic illness, injury or disability). Around 600 people are estimated to have lived in the privately owned units, which included bedsits and small flats for single-person households (Kane and Smith 2013).

Much of the low-cost housing in the inner city east was badly damaged during the quakes, with an estimated 250 low-cost private rental beds rendered unsuitable for inhabitation. In this situation, many tenants were forcibly dispersed. Although there is no comprehensive research available on the housing biographies of those displaced, the Christchurch rental housing market at this time was undoubtedly challenging. Earthquake-related property damage had reduced the supply of rental accommodation, driving up market rents and the significant influx of tradespeople involved in reconstruction added further demand. It was not until the greenfield housing developments in the southwest of the city were completed some years later that the supply of rental housing improved and rental prices began to decrease (Chapter 5). Prior to this, the council had noted that 'adequate and affordable housing is a pre-existing challenge that is now a major recovery issue for the city' (Christchurch City Council 2013, 17). The number of people in insecure housing – a category that includes those struggling to meet rent payments, as well as those staying on a temporary basis with friends and family – was estimated to have risen from 3750 before the quakes to between 5510 and 7405 (an increase of between 46 per cent and 98 per cent) (Ministry of Business, Innovation and Employment 2013).

The landscape of affordable and low-cost housing in the eastern suburbs evolved in several key respects after the quakes. In the private rental sector, there was no coordinated or extensive redevelopment of the damaged and demolished units in the inner city east. Housing New Zealand paid for displaced social housing tenants to stay in motels across the city on a temporary basis. Although this arrangement provided them with a degree of stability, the motels were often located well outside of the eastern suburbs, which disrupted the connections people had to their original neighbourhoods. For families, the transition to motel living also generally meant a significant reduction in living space and the loss of an external garden. Over time, however, Housing New Zealand did oversee the construction of replacement social housing. New developments were completed in Richmond, an area with existing services and reasonable public transport connections, and in Aranui, which now has the highest number of Kāinga Ora homes of any Christchurch suburb (Walton 2021a).

By mid-2021, there were around 8900 social housing units across Christchurch. Around 6200 (70 per cent) were owned by Kāinga Ora, with concentrations in suburbs east, northwest and west of the city centre. Another 1944 (22 per cent) were owned by the city council and typically managed by the Ōtautahi Community Housing Trust; these units were also distributed across the city, with pockets in the south and inner city east, including Linwood, but few in other eastern suburbs. The trust owned another 500 units itself, and the remainder were provided by faith-based organisations such as the Salvation Army and Methodist Mission. In geographical terms, the city council's social housing provision in the eastern suburbs is slightly reduced compared to before the earthquakes, whereas the involvement of Kāinga Ora has expanded. The number of private rental units in the inner city east has not returned to previous levels. This reflects the responses of multiple private property owners to quake-related damage and market conditions, however, rather than a specific policy setting of central or local government.

The residential red zone

After a programme of geotechnical investigations, the Canterbury Earthquake Recovery Authority (CERA) announced in June 2011 that all residential land in Christchurch would be assigned to one of four colour-coded zones: green, orange, white or red, as described in Chapter 3. These zones reflected the government's assessment of whether a parcel of land was suitable for ongoing residential inhabitation, with particular regard to the risk of future damage from seismicity. In green-zoned land, the probability of this damage was considered low, so householders were expected to repair their homes as needed. In red-zoned land, however, the risk of further and future damage to land and property was judged to be unacceptably high. As a result, red-zoned homeowners were encouraged to leave their homes permanently, incentivised by a government offer of financial compensation, made initially in August 2011. But the offer itself was far from clear cut, as owners were given two options: sell their land and house to the government at the 2007/8 rating valuation (this being the most recent city-wide valuations available at the time), or sell only the land to the Crown and negotiate a price for the house with their insurance company (CERA 2011; MacDonald and Carlton 2016). In addition, the offer of financial compensation was only available to fully insured households, with the Minister for Earthquake Recovery insisting that uninsured homeowners should receive only 50 per cent of the government compensation offer. This reflected the fact that uninsured properties did not qualify for Earthquake Commission cover, so the Crown would gain no insurance compensation from that source.

The creation of the residential red zone (Figure 10.1), which encompassed over 5500 households, provoked a variety of responses. The 2011 market value of some red-zoned homes was significantly higher than the 2007 valuations used as a basis for the Crown offer of financial compensation, and the offer did not recognise any home improvements made in the meantime. For many homeowners, accepting the offer thus meant an appreciable financial loss (Matthews 2020). Some red-zoned residents were nevertheless relieved to receive the offer – especially when they had been grappling with their insurance companies for some months – as it enabled them to depart in a relatively clear-cut manner and move on. This, in fact, was the outcome the Crown hoped its offer would incentivise (CERA 2011). Others were angry that the financial compensation was below estimated 2011 market values. Still others complained about the erosion of private property rights and democratic process. These responses were by no means mutually exclusive, and some homeowners identified with them all. The collective sense of grievance prompted the creation of several community activist and protest groups, including Quake Outcasts, WeCAN, Empowered Christchurch, CanCERN (Canterbury Communities' Earthquake Recovery Network), and Eastern Vision, all of which advocated in different ways for the interests of red-zoned and eastern households.

Quake Outcasts, a group comprised of 68 of the uninsured red-zoned homeowners, and WeCAN took a case to the High Court to contest aspects of the red-zoning decision (see Chapter 7). The court found that the Minister for Earthquake Recovery's decision to discriminate against uninsured buildings had been unlawful, and also found that the red zoning itself was unlawful. This latter element of the decision was subsequently overturned by the Court of Appeal in 2017, but the judgement that the government's discrimination against uninsured red zone residents had been unlawful was upheld. Despite numerous submissions and public meetings organised by these community and activist groups, the National-led government's Minister for Earthquake Recovery at the time, Gerry Brownlee, had refused to admit any deficiencies in the red zoning process. Nor would he acknowledge the serious problems that many households within the red zone were experiencing when dealing with the Earthquake Commission regarding their insurance claims. Many residents reported apparent bureaucratic indifference to their concerns, while having to negotiate confusing and sometimes inconsistent communications from both the Commission and their private insurance companies (Miles 2016). Mike Coleman, the Anglican priest and Avonside resident who led WeCAN (Figure 7.3), described the situation as people 'battling a government who are totally shut down to affected homeowners' (Matthews 2020).

Within a year of the red-zoning announcement, most affected residents had nevertheless reached a settlement with the government for their homes and land. Some relocated within Christchurch, buying homes in the new subdivisions in the southwest of the city if their finances allowed, or to the Selwyn and Waimakariri districts outside the city (Campbell 2014). Others moved elsewhere in New Zealand or to Australia, sometimes prompted by a desire to escape the ongoing difficulties and stress of the post-quake situation (Adams-Hutcheson 2015). As they left, the population of the Ōtākaro-Avon River Corridor statistical area, which incorporates the majority of the red zone, fell dramatically. In 2006, it had a population of 10,386, but in 2013 this was just 1263, and by 2018 had further decreased to 99. This outmigration disrupted longstanding neighbourhood relationships, fashioned through everyday activities such as walking children to school, participating in neighbourhood watch groups, attending occasional street parties, sharing home-grown vegetables, lending and borrowing tools, crowding around a television to watch sporting matches of national importance, and so on.

In most cases, vacated red-zoned houses were demolished, but a few people made arrangements for their purchase – from the Crown, which had taken ownership – and then relocation to sites elsewhere. Either way, the eventual effect was to create large swathes of open greenspace (Figure 10.2). Initially, the property boundaries remained quite visible, particularly where these had been marked by trees or shrubs. Over time, the removal of street signs and other orientating features in the neighbourhoods made it harder to identify individual sections, and the more obvious visual markers of where the homes had once been faded. More-than-human actants became increasingly active, as the next chapter illustrates. After the majority of houses in red-zoned areas were cleared, a number of the affected communities began to hold occasional commemorative events. These gatherings, organised from 2012 onwards by

Figure 10.2 Vacated land in the residential red zone (aerial and street views).
Credit: Stuff Limited (aerial view) and Michal Klajban, Wikimedia Commons (street view).

the Avon-Ōtākaro Network, provided an opportunity for previous and current residents to meet again and to continue the process of coming to terms with their forced displacement.

In 2019, the occasion was held in a park near Avonside, and included elements of memorialisation with an exhibition of photography by a local artist, who had worked in collaboration with the community (Veling 2021). It was opened by the Mayor, Lianne Dalziel, who had previously been a Member of Parliament for the Christchurch East constituency. There were contributions from former students of several affected schools and a perspective from a local Avonside resident. After the speeches, a community barbecue was held, enabling those present to interact more informally. Such activities resonate with the kinds of 'memory work' that Till (2012) identifies as potentially reparative in 'wounded cities', particularly when places have been affected by overlapping forms of environmental damage and bureaucratic difficulties. The opportunities for community narration in Avonside also align with Herman's (1998) recognition that practices of remembering and retelling can help in the negotiation of collective trauma. The collective sharing of stories can assist individuals, households and communities to make some sense of what has happened, both to their places and their lives, and to craft narratives that afford points of stability, however provisional, from which to move forward.

Such memorialisation can be considered part of the broader creative response to the Canterbury earthquakes. In an effort to chronicle the lived experience of disruption, displacement and recovery, a number of novels, non-fiction accounts and collections of poetry have emerged (eg. Farrell 2012, 2015; Gordon et al. 2014; Gorman 2016). An example is *Leaving the Red Zone*, a collection of 148 poems by more than 85 individuals (Norcliffe and Preston 2016). At its launch, several local government officials from within and beyond Christchurch attended, including the mayor (Preston 2016). Their presence perhaps reflected a recognition of the value of creative expression in the ongoing process of coming to terms with the earthquakes. Although such expression is not neatly coincident with recovery, it can assist with the sense-making and reorientation that supports people to deal with loss and displacement (Herman 1998).

In 2020, some nine years after the announcement of the red zone, the Global Settlement Agreement between the Crown and the council, described in Chapter 4, sealed the transfer of the 602 hectares of red-zoned land to the city. This mirrored what had happened in the Kaiapoi red zones in 2016. The transfer was intended to proceed in an incremental fashion as Land Information New Zealand, the Crown holding agency, completed the amalgamation of land titles. Expressing a preference for local ownership, the Labour-led government's Minister for Greater Christchurch Regeneration, Dr Megan Woods, described the process as 'the next step in the transition to local leadership … The land is now a beautiful park-like space that has the potential to become a true asset for our city and something that we as Cantabrians can all be proud of' (Christchurch City Council 2020). The intent to transfer the red-zoned land was widely regarded as an important step in returning the power that central government had taken from the city council in the immediate aftermath of the quakes. As such, it arguably represented the return of local land into more directly accountable and democratic arrangements.

Sport and recreation facilities

Alongside the loss and displacement associated with the residential red zone, a number of publicly owned sport and recreation facilities in the eastern suburbs were heavily damaged by the earthquakes. The majority of these were eventually repaired or rebuilt, although generally at a smaller scale (and, in some cases, key elements of the original facilities were moved out of the area entirely). When it occurred, this 'downsizing' and 'relocation' often reflected the westward shift in the city's population, as well as the financial constraints of local government in the aftermath of a major disaster. The most materially and symbolically significant of these facilities was the Queen Elizabeth II (QEII) swimming pool and athletics complex in Parklands. Built for the 1974 Commonwealth Games, this large facility incorporated the city's only indoor 50-metre pool, other recreational pools and several hydroslides. It was an important venue for both the swimming and athletics communities, with a high-quality outdoor track and field facilities that supported regional and national competitions.

The QEII facility sustained serious damage in the February 2011 earthquake, and in April 2012 it was served with a demolition notice by CERA. A smaller and wholly indoor facility, the $38.6 million Taiora QEII Recreation and Sport Centre, was eventually built on the same site, opening in May 2018 (Figure 10.3). Its completion was described as marking the 'end of a long and hard-fought battle by the community to get a pool rebuilt at QEII Park, after the much-loved former complex was demolished' (Law 2018). Its reconstruction

Figure 10.3 The new Taiora QEII recreation and sport complex.

Credit: Simon Wilson.

had by no means been certain, particularly after central government decided to jointly fund, with the city council, the Parakiore anchor project facility in the city centre, as described in Chapter 9. The size, central location and Crown funding for Parakiore undermined the case for rebuilding QEII in the eastern suburbs. Could the council afford to be involved in building two large aquatic sport complexes? Mindful of such issues, a community group known as 'Keep QEII in the East' lobbied the council for several years, arguing that rebuilding a facility in the eastern suburbs was critical if the city wished to be receptive to the needs of its eastern residents.

When the Taiora QEII facility was completed in 2018, seven years after the most damaging earthquake, it was widely regarded as confirmation of the city council's responsiveness to the needs of the area. In the media coverage of the opening, the material benefits and symbolic significance of the development were recurrent themes. As one woman explained, the return of the facility to its former location had 'put the east back on the map. It's recognised the families of the east [and their] wellbeing and health and that community link which, at the end of the day, always stood staunch through all the quakes' (Ineson 2018). That said, the Taiora centre did not retain any of the outdoor athletics facilities of the original QEII. These were effectively transferred to the Ngā Puna Wai Sports Hub, a new $53.7 million multi-sports facility in the southwest of the city, located within easy reach of the extensive new suburban housing developments in Halswell, Lincoln and Rolleston (Chapter 5). This reflected the westward shift in the provision of city-wide public facilities, with the council unambiguously describing Ngā Puna Wai as the 'new sporting home for Canterbury athletics, hockey, tennis and rugby league', noting that it was intended to 'replace sporting facilities damaged in the earthquakes' (Christchurch City Council 2021b). Nonetheless, the Taiora centre can still be regarded as a firm local government commitment to the city's eastern suburbs.

The new centre has proved very popular, drawing over 800,000 visitors during its first year of operation to its aquatic, gym and group fitness activities. This included about 540,000 visitors to the pools alone. The design brief of the architects had been to 'create a sustainable and public building that restores and grows participation in sport in the east and the wider Christchurch community', and the initial signs are that the rebuilt Taiora will fulfil these aspirations (Warren and Mahoney 2021). The council also subsequently built Te Pou Toetoe, a new $22 million pool and activity complex in Linwood, which opened in October 2021. This facility also includes two tennis courts and a basketball court. Its development recognised the need to replace the earthquake damaged pool at Linwood Avenue Primary School. It also responded to the strong call from eight local school principals for a new public swimming facility (Law 2016). Prior to the earthquakes, in 2009, the Mayor at the time, Bob Parker, had also signed a community petition that 'called on the Council to build an aquatic recreation facility in the east' (Kenny 2021b). In addition, the Linwood ward councillor had campaigned strongly for an aquatic centre in the eastern suburbs for over a decade.

In the coastal suburb of New Brighton, He Puna Taimoana, an $11.2 million hot saltwater pool facility was opened in May 2020. Retail and hospitality businesses in New Brighton had struggled for several decades to attract visitors, despite a range of initiatives such as a weekend market. The community's somewhat precarious economic situation was exacerbated by the earthquakes, with damage to buildings and roads discouraging people from other parts of the city from visiting the area. Regenerate Christchurch, the rebuild planning agency set up in 2016, had a legal brief to work to attract further external investment to New Brighton. Given the economic challenges faced by the suburb, the decision of Development Christchurch – a city council-owned economic development agency also formed in 2016 – to invest in the new saltwater pools was significant. Prior to their opening, the manager had expressed her hopes for the wider impact of the facility, explaining that they were 'looking to get a host of visitors to come back to New Brighton and get a fresh taste of an old favourite' (Kenny 2020). Like the new Taiora complex, this facility has proved popular since its opening, and is often fully booked.

The wider economic and environmental situation for New Brighton remains challenging, however, as its low-lying coastal location leaves it vulnerable to sea-level rise. The earthquake sequence considerably exacerbated this issue. Due to liquefaction, nearly 90 per cent of central and eastern Christchurch subsided, often by half a metre, with parts of the red zone sinking by a metre or more (McDowall and Denee 2019). This renders the areas along and behind the coastline even more vulnerable to sea level rise and storm effects (Hughes et al. 2015; Monk et al. 2016) and will decisively affect the residential suitability of New Brighton in future decades. The city council will have to grapple with extended areas of managed retreat. In effect, this is what has already happened in the residential red zone, and the situation in New Brighton will likely also involve having to incentivise or compensate residents to relocate. In any case, anticipated sea-level rise will surely alter the economic and political calculus around future public investments in New Brighton, including whether they can be justified and on what basis.

Viewed more broadly, however, three of these developments – Taiora QEII, Te Pou Toetoe and He Puna Taimoana – demonstrate the responsiveness of the city council and its partner agencies to the needs of residents in the eastern suburbs. Although some of the facilities took time to build and considerable lobbying, they nevertheless reflect a substantive investment in local sporting facilities, which will contribute to the health and well-being of children, youth and adults in the east. This sensitivity to local needs contrasts with the city centre focus of central government investment in the blueprint, particularly in terms of the Crown anchor projects (Chapters 4 and 9).

Educational upheaval

Alongside sport and recreational facilities, public educational provision was significantly affected by the earthquakes, with extensive damage to many schools in the east. For example, the facilities of the main high schools serving the area – Aranui High, Shirley Boys' and Avonside Girls' – were rendered unsuitable for use by the February 2011 quake. Along with several other schools in eastern Christchurch, Shirley Boys and Avonside Girls entered into site-sharing arrangements with less damaged and still operational schools in the west of the city. The teaching day was rescheduled into two parts, with students from the host school attending from early morning to early afternoon, and students from the eastern schools then attending from mid-afternoon to early evening. This site-sharing lasted between 6 and 12 months for the schools involved.

In September 2012, the Ministry of Education announced a comprehensive set of proposed changes in the form of the Christchurch Schools Rebuild programme (Ministry of Education 2021). Scheduled to begin in 2013, the plan was to rebuild or repair no less than 115 earthquake-damaged schools in the greater Christchurch area. In addition, 13 schools were to be closed and a further 18 merged. Aranui Primary and Secondary Schools were slated for closure. Avonside Girls' was to be closed or merged with Christchurch Girls' High and Shirley Boys' was to be closed or merged with Christchurch Boys' High School (Law 2012). The closures and mergers, which disproportionately involved eastern schools, were justified with reference to the expense of earthquake repairs – the anticipated $750 million cost was neither fiscally nor politically attractive – and the westward shift in the city's population. The latter factor was particularly salient for eastern suburbs, as outmigration from red zoning and housing damage had seen falling school rolls. These falls were often used as a justification for the proposed closure or merger of particular schools.

Unsurprisingly, these proposed school closures generated strong responses from residents, children, teachers and principals in the eastern suburbs. Many communities had deep attachments to their local schools, reflecting not only their educational purpose but also their function as places for sheltering and gathering during the earthquakes. The proposals seemed to demonstrate a lack of awareness, even indifference, to the significant roles of schools within their communities (Mutch 2018). The President of the New Zealand Parent Teacher Association asked 'Hasn't Canterbury and Christchurch suffered enough? It is time to move forward and listen a little more to what parents and parent groups are saying before making the decisions that will affect our communities in such a dramatic way' (Bayer 2012). The Headmaster of Shirley Boys High School, which had a tradition of welcoming pupils from a range of social and economic backgrounds, was also fiercely opposed: 'I state here and now … Shirley Boys' High School as a school exists and will continue to exist – mark it. There is no way in God's creation that we cease to exist' (Radio New Zealand 2012).

Picking up on these community concerns, an editorial in *The Dominion Post*, the Wellington daily newspaper, condemned both the substance of the proposals and their insensitivity to local context. 'The Ministry's first cut at restructuring Christchurch schools looked like it was devised on a Wellington whiteboard without reference to the situation on the ground' (Stuff 2013).

In a similar vein, Mutch (2017, 74) argued that the Christchurch Schools Rebuild programme demonstrated 'a lack of understanding of, or even blatant disregard for, the place of schools in communities and the importance of communities in sustaining a stable and cohesive society'.

Following strong community feedback, there was a number of adjustments to the original plans. The Minister of Education announced in February 2015 that both Avonside Girls' and Shirley Boys' schools would be rebuilt as a combined campus adjacent to the new Taiora QEII sport and recreation facility. This opened in 2019. In addition, Linwood College was entirely rebuilt on a new site, opening as Te Aratai College in May 2022. These examples indicate that the voice of eastern communities could influence central government plans to some extent.

Overall, however, educational provision in the eastern suburbs was heavily impacted by the rebuild programme, with 13 schools closed. Aranui, Avondale and Wainoni primary schools and Aranui High School were shut in January 2017, for example, and a new year 1–13 integrated school, the Haeata Community Campus, opened the following month. The Minister of Education explained that Haeata would bring 'a fresh and exciting approach to education in Aranui, with huge potential benefits for students and the wider community', and that the school would be 'the first campus of its kind in Greater Christchurch, with successful examples operating in other parts of New Zealand' (*New Zealand Herald* 2013). When Haeata opened, it had a buoyant roll of 955. As an 'unzoned' school, it had been able to attract students from across the city. Just four years later, in March 2021, the roll had fallen by 40 per cent to 595 students. Students were reported to be unhappy with the open plan, multi-age classrooms and the self-directed model of learning. National examination (NCEA) attainment rates in 2018 were low, with only 27 per cent of year 12 students gaining NCEA level 2 (compared to 77 per cent nationally) and just 14 per cent of year 13 students gaining NCEA level 3 (compared to 66 per cent nationally) (O'Callaghan 2019). As NCEA level 2 is generally considered the minimum qualification in New Zealand for a young person to move on to further education, training and employment, these were problematic outcomes in an already disadvantaged area (Table 10.1). Although attainment levels may improve, the merger of four smaller schools into a single campus and the adoption of an experimental educational model is not yet working well for young people in this part of eastern Christchurch.

So, while the rebuild programme saw substantial investment in Christchurch schools as a whole, for children and families in the eastern suburbs the outcomes were clearly less favourable. An Ombudsman's investigation into the Christchurch Schools Rebuild programme identified serious shortcomings in the Ministry of Education's initial consultation process (Boshier 2017; Radio New Zealand 2013), and there was media criticism of 'the high-handed manner of the minister and her ministry and the subsequent scramble of both to make amends' (Stuff 2013). After the Ombudsman's findings, the Ministry of Education apologised for its lack of transparency and failure to engage meaningfully with the affected communities. By then, however, several schools in the eastern suburbs had already been closed, despite the protest of local residents. Coming just one year after the announcement of red zoning, the manner in which the schools were closed did little to alleviate the mistrust that some eastern residents had developed towards the government.

The forgotten east?

If the behaviour of government, business and community actors is considered across the four dimensions of recovery discussed thus far it is possible to assess the degree to which the eastern suburbs were forgotten or neglected. A number of points can be made. First, in terms of investment and rebuilding activity, the post-earthquake focus of central government was primarily on the central city, as Chapter 4 has shown. This is evident in the emphasis given to the large anchor projects such as Te Pae and the Parakiore Recreation and Sport Centre, described in Chapter 9. Such a focus is arguably characteristic of right-of-centre governments engaged in post-disaster recovery, in that a command-and-control approach is typically employed in an effort to repair buildings, replace damaged infrastructure and foster business renewal (Cretney 2017). While such a neoliberal approach can be effective for dealing with the economic and built environment aspects of recovery, if attention is not also paid to its psychosocial and community dimensions then additional disturbance and harm to communities may follow, beyond that associated with the initial disaster (Quarantelli 1999).

In Christchurch, the National-led government's focus on the central city appears to have been coupled with an unwillingness to recognise or take account of the differentiated experience of the disaster across different suburbs. This spatial insensitivity was evident in the blanket nature of the red zone, and the unyielding refusal to accommodate substantive variations in the circumstances of those subject to red zoning (eg. the uninsured, or those whose property values significantly exceeded the Crown's financial offer). A similar inflexibility was evident in the Christchurch Schools Rebuild programme, with the closures of several eastern schools for reasons that some consider to be as much ideological as financial or logical (Mutch 2017). The rebuild programme also failed to take into account the significant intertwining of schools and their communities. Such an oversight could be characterised as forgetting, although it was not clear whether the Ministry of Education staff in Wellington were ever adequately attuned to these place-based dynamics, or whether their actions were in some way particular to eastern Christchurch.

Second, in comparison to central government, the city council was more responsive to the recovery needs of east. This reflects the council's mandated responsibility to city residents, and its system of representation through ward-based councillors. But the new Taiora/QEII, Linwood and New Brighton pools were only built after thorough consideration of relevant factors, including the westward shift in the city's population, plans for the jointly funded Parakiore facility in the central city and a council already under financial strain by virtue of its contributions to the repair of hundreds of kilometres of damaged subsurface infrastructure. None of these factors was favourable to building new facilities in the eastern suburbs, and the council's decision to do so arguably reflects its recognition of, and responsiveness to, the needs of eastern residents. At the same time, the relocation of athletics facilities that had once been at QEII to the new Ngā Puna Wai facility might be considered an appropriate response to the substantial population growth in the southwest of the city.

Third, there were many instances when private insurance companies were slow to respond to the repair or rebuild claims of homeowners in the eastern suburbs. This does not appear to reflect any specific or systemic discrimination against eastern residents, but was rather a more general problem with the capacity and inclination of insurers to settle claims in a timely fashion, which affected homeowners across the entire city (Miles 2016). The problems eastern residents experienced with insurers seem to have derived primarily from the concentration of damage in their neighbourhoods (and the time required for additional geotechnical investigations to be undertaken in some cases). Some insurance delays also reflected the intertwined nature of claims, such as in the case of multiple-unit housing complexes, where the satisfactory settlement of one claim was often linked to the progress of another. But this appears to have been a city-wide issue, as Chapter 5 suggests, rather than one which reflected discrimination against eastern residents.

Fourth, with respect to private sector developments in the aftermath of the earthquakes, the great majority has occurred either in the central city, in the form of new retail and entertainment complexes, cafes, hotels and apartment buildings, or in its southwest, west and northern areas. If the affluent seaside suburbs of Redcliffs and Sumner are discounted, then the Tannery retail complex in Woolston is the only substantial private sector development in an eastern suburb since the earthquakes. Although this encompasses a significant number of independent retailers, it is undoubtedly something of an exception. So, the central city and western orientation of new commercial activity is arguably less a matter of 'forgetting the east' than of investors choosing locations they believe will generate profits and reduce risk (eg. liquefaction from possible future seismicity). In this sense, these businesses were operating as they might normally be expected to. Central government, with its responsibilities to the broader population, can, however, be judged by different standards.

Conclusion

Were the eastern suburbs of Christchurch in some way neglected or overlooked in the post-quake recovery process? In terms of the attention paid to the concerns of eastern residents, a distinction can be drawn between recovery initiatives led by central government agencies – the residential red zone and the reorganisation of schools – and the activities of local government and community groups such as WeCan. Under the leadership of a

National-led government in office from 2008 to 2017, recovery initiatives were often characterised by top-down decision making and, in several cases, an apparent indifference to the needs of particular communities and residents, despite some community consultations undertaken by CERA. The notable exception is in the area of social housing, where Housing New Zealand Corporation and then Kāinga Ora have overseen significant new developments in places such as Richmond and Aranui.

The city council was consistently more attentive to residents in the eastern suburbs. In response to local advocacy and submissions over several years, a number of new sports and aquatic facilities were built. The actions of various community groups (eg. WeCAN) ameliorated aspects of the central government recovery initiatives, such as the proposed closure of Avonside Girls' and Shirley Boys' schools and the initial lack of financial compensation for uninsured red-zoned households. In a hypothetical situation where a centre right government had been in sole charge of post-earthquake recovery in Christchurch, without the compensating influence of both the city council and community groups, the eastern suburbs would likely have fared rather worse in terms of political attention, reinvestment and rebuilding. Instead, the actions of council and community helped to ensure that the concerns of eastern residents were not only heard but to some degree also addressed. This underscores the importance of ensuring local and democratic input within the disaster recovery process, so as to achieve more socially and spatially equitable outcomes (Quarantelli 1999; Cretney 2018).

Following the election of a Labour-led government in October 2017, there was a discernible shift in the approach taken by central government towards post-earthquake recovery in Christchurch. The new Minister for Greater Christchurch Regeneration took a more proactive stance when addressing unresolved Earthquake Commission claims, as well recognising the high number of cases where the initial work undertaken was in need of subsequent repair. This was the reason for the establishment of the Canterbury Earthquakes Insurance Tribunal in 2019. And with the acceptance by the Minister of the Ōtākaro Avon Regeneration Plan in 2019, and the Global Settlement in 2020 that promised the return of red-zoned land to the city, the stage was set for the creation of more positive stories and experiences in eastern Christchurch. These are explored in the next two chapters.

11 The more-than-human city

Introduction

The previous chapter has presented a clear picture of differentiated social experience of post-earthquake recovery in the eastern suburbs of Christchurch. However, a post-disaster city is a theatre involving both a cast of multiple kinds of actors and a plethora of diverse but inter-related kinds of performances. If the Canterbury earthquakes achieved one thing at the time, it was to disabuse its inhabitants and those of surrounding areas of a foundational belief of western urban culture: that all of nature is a fixed stage upon which to enact the human drama. These profoundly unsettling times disturbed the anthropocentric imaginaries of city spaces and politics built upon the presumption of solid ground. Such imaginaries typified the nineteenth-century colonial project of which the city was a product, the goal of which was an ongoing process of terraforming, or 'improvement' without limits (Ghosh 2021; Latour 2018). Improvement depended on the conversion of earthly resources to create both value in urban form and the sale of commodities to support that form. Yet the shaking of the ground and its widespread liquefaction revealed the extent to which the chimera of improvement had always been conditional. The rhythms of the deep times of nature have no regard for the social (Irvine 2017).

As a self-proclaimed 'garden city', however, Christchurch has long considered itself as owning natural attributes defined – as befits the garden metaphor – in human rather than more-than-human terms (Pawson 1999, 2000). It has also been a place long seeking to capitalise on the 'stunning natural landscapes' of rivers, hills and coastlines, all of which are performatively enrolled in a much-vaunted 'active lifestyle' (Christchurch NZ 2021). But the earthquakes and their aftermath have brought home the extent to which the city is a hybrid assemblage of unstable ground, surface and subsurface waters, unruly flora and fauna and much else, in addition to its fixed attributes of roads, pipes, commercial buildings and parks, and the affective qualities of homes, neighbourhoods and landmarks.

This chapter uses the concept of the 'more-than-human' to explore the importance of interconnections between human and non-human factors in the the city in transition. As such it focuses on how actual worlds become assembled

DOI: 10.4324/9780429275562-14

when all manner of things (or 'actants') make combined contributions to the making of particular geographies. In so doing, it acknowledges how a variety of non-human actants – species, forces, materials, contexts and discourses – all interact with human behaviour and decision-making to produce worlds that are more-than-human. And it assesses the extent to which opportunities for more lively spaces, hybrid ecosystems and species interactions are being recognised.

The 'more-than-human' city

In recent decades, social scientists have become discontented with the tendency to understand nature spaces in binary terms (Cloke and Johnston 2005). Rather than using mutually exclusive categories such as 'human' and 'non-human' or 'nature' and 'culture', researchers have focussed on ideas about relational or hybrid agency (Whatmore 2002) that demonstrate how interactions and inter-reliance between these categories reveal a surplus of meaning and understanding – a sum total that is 'more than' its parts. In this way, previous attention to 'human' agency, and (to a lesser extent) 'non-human' agency, is being superseded by a concern for the excess that spills out when these categories are understood relationally – that is, according to their inter-relations rather than any particular innate qualities. The early fruits of this approach are visible in the growth of animal geographies (Buller 2014) that trace the intersection of animals and human society, demonstrating how animals can transgress and help to reshape the imagined spatial and social ordering of that society. More-than-human perspectives have also been used to understand the relational contribution of trees to places (Jones and Cloke 2002), for example, in providing capacity for culturally significant memorialisation of key people and events (Cloke and Pawson 2008).

Adopting a more-than-human approach has enabled new lines of enquiry and action to be developed which have challenged the anthropocentric status quo in at least three ways. First, in an emphasis on entanglement, there is the realisation that humans and non-humans co-constitute each other; that is human existence and social life depend on often asymmetrical relations with non-human bodies and material things (Hodder 2014). It follows that any presumed dominance of human issues needs to be de-centred in recognition of the myriad ways in which non-human actants are entrenched in and intertwined with social, cultural, political and infrastructural dimensions of life (Bennett 2010). Second, such entanglement involves a liveliness that cannot easily be shrugged off by assuming that humans are active and non-humans are passive. Indeed, non-human contributions to relational agency have been recognised as unpredictable, energetic, transformational and full of unseen capacity and potential (Clark 2011). Such contributions have been labelled as 'vitalist', emphasising the liveliness of the non-human – such as seismic activity – in helping to animate and agitate human relations (Greenhough 2010).

Third, more-than-human approaches underscore the need for entangled empathy (Gruen 2015), in which the de-centring of human agency is accompanied by an equivalent displacement of humans as the defining reference point for ethical relations. As Cloke and Jones (2003) argue, the tightly drawn boundaries which codify moral communities as human need to be reconceived to foster new and more care-full relationships which are attentive to more-than-human nature. Mere recognition of a more-than-human world is insufficient – empathetic care for that more-than-human world needs to be practised in a polity with more channels of communication between its constituent parts (Puig de la Bellacasa 2017). In short, a more-than-human understanding of the world requires the dragging of everyday political practices of society into new ethical formations (Stengers 2005).

These ideas have been translated into practical urban contexts in accounts of the more-than-human city. Far from a blank canvas on which anthropocentric designs are inscribed, cities are lively places characterised by hybrid ecosystems where human lives are entangled with those of myriad non-humans. Cities are 'overflowing, exuberant, excessive and phantasmogoric' (Franklin 2017, 203), teeming with heterogeneous forms of life capable of disrupting and reconstituting seemingly stable histories, narratives and materialities. More-than-human liveliness occurs at varying scales. Clark (2011) emphasises how cities are vulnerable to planetary forces such as those relating to climate change and seismicity that resist anthropogenic control and planning, and replace human-centred polity with turbulent unpredictability. Even at a localised scale, urban order can be disorganised and disarranged by the power of more-than-human life, like tremors, fire and flood, thus reconstituting assumed or desired norms.

This picture of the more-than-human city is particularly relevant to Christchurch, where planetary forces have been evident in the event of the earthquakes, and where subsequent planning and place-making have been deployed to re-create life in the city. As Chugh (2020) explains, urban design often follows a logic dictated by human-centred imagination and spatial ordering, in which non-human nature tends to be controlled using tactics of pre-assembly and segregation. The capacity of the non-human to repurpose lively infrastructure and to furnish novel ecologies can be forgotten in amongst the blueprinting of zones and precincts. Such modernist visions (discussed in Chapter 4) are often assumed to be enacted on a neutral substrate, but in terms of the more-than-human city, that substrate needs to be seen as active, lively, fragile and relational in ways that matter.

The rest of this chapter uses these ideas to interrogate aspects of the emerging post-disaster city of Christchurch. Following Franklin (2017), it addresses the ways environmental and technical forces have become incorporated into the life, subjectivities and structures of Christchurch after the earthquakes. It illustrates how particular relational actants have become significant companions to city dwellers whose lives have been ruptured by geophysical forces, and the extent to which they have become key signifiers of contested spaces in the city. It then interprets the degree to which relational actants shape and embody the values and concerns of particular groups of citizens and the ways they personify and provide focus for otherwise tricky political and ethical issues in the emerging city.

Disturbing the entrenchment

The pre-earthquake city was an intricate web of relations between the human and non-human. One of the key processes of improvement was the draining of the wetlands underlying much of the city centre and inner suburbs (Schrader 1997; Wilson 1989). Few people would know that the urban area sits on the active margins of the Waimakariri River delta, on land only a few thousand years old, or that its networks of streams are sourced in groundwater bubbling to the surface across that delta. Stream courses lie interred beneath the city centre (Lucas 2014), and have often been constrained in the suburbs by timber boxing. Only since the 1990s have many been 'liberated' through more naturalistic design, their watercourses replanted in native wetland species. Such moves were initially controversial with a citizenry familiar with 'Eurocentric regiments of tall, erect, fastigiate tree forms' and 'the received fashion for manicured, sprayed and sanitised gardens and lawns' (Meurk 2021, 159). In fact, the garden city's self-image was always partial: the extent of canopy tree cover is only 11.6 per cent if large-scale plantation forests are excluded (Morgenroth 2017). Trees in parts of the city were directly affected by soil movement, liquefaction and rockfall generated by the earthquakes, but immediate tree losses were relatively low, barely 50 per cent more than the number removed on public lands in any one year (Morgenroth and Armstrong 2012). Longer-term losses have only become apparent in the decade since, and the most identifiable cause of these is housing intensification (discussed in Chapter 5).

Non-human actants were therefore intricately and long-entrenched in the social, political, historical and infrastructural life of the city. These entanglements were disturbed in a variety of ways during and after the event of the earthquakes. Many of the immediate disturbances have been well documented (Environment Canterbury 2013; Potter et al. 2015). For example, the incidence of liquefaction discussed in Chapter 2 resulted in large volumes of silt being deposited into the city's stream courses, resulting in significant increases in suspended sediment and detrimental changes to water quality. In turn, there was a severe impact on aquatic life, notably on sensitive fish species and shellfish, but also due to disruption of marine mammal habitats. Moreover, the first years after the earthquakes saw a sharp rise in bird mortality, often connected to changes in the chemistry of water treatment ponds but also due to spoilation of nesting and roosting sites. The inaccessibility of wider landscape habitats heralded a reduced capacity to control what were previously perceived as weeds and pest species. In such ways, the earlier entrenched relations between humans and non-humans were (literally) shaken by the earthquakes.

The impact of these kinds of disturbances on the more-than-human city can be understood in three main ways. First, many of the relations that characterised the city prior to the earthquakes endured. Companion animals, for example, continued to be important to human health and well-being in the city. Animal welfare staff and other carers looked after thousands of animals who were injured or rendered homeless during the quakes (Potts and Gadenne 2014). Several organisations – for example, redzonecats – sprang up to look after the interests of cats that were abandoned to fend for themselves during the forced migration of red zone households (redzonecats 2021). While for some, 'feral' cat activity represented a threat to indigenous wildlife, other accounts emphasise not only the human-centric values of care for animals, but also the reciprocal relations between animals and humans. Thus Coombs et al. (2015) analyse the mental, physical and social support received by dog owners through the companionship of their pets. These relations were re-prioritised with greater time and attention being given to such companionship during the earthquakes, but with any loss of togetherness exacerbating the negative impacts of the event. Heroic stories of individual quake dogs (Sessions and Bullock 2013) and quake cats (Bullock 2014), describing their exploits in situations of rescue, reunion, affection and caring support of humans, became a symbol of the resilience of the city in responding to seismic disaster.

The enduring relations of the more-than-human city were also in evidence in the reliance on green and blue landscapes for recreational well-being. One of the initial impacts of the earthquakes was to restrict opportunities for those outdoor activities such as tramping (hiking), running and cycling that are a fundamental part of New Zealand culture. Access to the Port Hills adjacent to the city was initially severely curtailed, with more than 50 kilometres of paths and tracks closed due to rock fall hazards (Thompson et al. 2015). Water-related activities like rowing, kayaking and sailing were also significantly hampered (Xayasenh 2015). However, residents continued to seek outdoor recreation where they could, largely in the city's undamaged parks and green spaces, in a lasting collaboration between green landscapes and well-being. The Botanic Gardens, long a site of city recreation and memories, became a popular haunt as one of the few undamaged sites in the city centre. As in New Orleans after Hurricane Katrina (Tidball 2014), trees acted as beacons of hope, survival, stability and place in the process of recovery from disaster, just as thousands of refugees from city hotels and apartments had sheltered beneath the trees of Hagley Park on the night of the major quake of 22 February 2011.

A second way of understanding the impact of the earthquakes is to identify the ways in which the cultures and practicalities afforded by the quakes became incorporated into everyday life in the more-than-human city. A good example are the changes wrought on the regulatory and architectural environments of the rebuilt city, prompting radical changes to the materiality of the cityscape, and to the lived relations of co-existence within it. Here, the technological adjustment required to proof the city against future seismic risk has brought its own liveliness – functional and aesthetic – to its look and feel. Initially, such adjustments led to the very obvious presence of shipping containers in the urban environment, both as functional props for vulnerable sagging buildings, and as defensive walls against rockfall around the coastal suburb of Sumner. They were also influential elements in emergent transitional architecture, whether as building blocks for the temporary container mall, or as foundational anchors for Shigaru Ban's acclaimed 'cardboard cathedral', a larger version of one designed by the architect after the Kobe earthquake in Japan in 1995 (Walsh 2020). The strangely out-of-place materiality of the containers became incorporated into the fabric of the city (Figure 11.1).

Figure 11.1 Post-earthquake uses of shipping containers in the urban environment: (top) the 'wall of Sumner', January 2012, since removed; and (bottom) Tuam Street, central city, March 2022.

As rebuilding took on a longer-term perspective, the technological regulation of earthquake-proofing took on different forms. The city centre's architecture – dominated by unreinforced masonry and concrete buildings – became obsolete in the post-quake setting where the inelastic failure of these materials to resist tensile forces was recognised in new seismic building codes and health and safety regulations (Gjerde 2017a). These codes and regulations created buildings exhibiting 'structural stoutness', visible structural cross-bracing and a steel and glass aesthetic (Gjerde 2017b). Simultaneously, damping devices, energy dissipators and base isolators provided unseen but vital insurance against the repeat of disaster, replicating those in the city's casino built in the 1990s, and its Women's Hospital (opened in 2005), the only pre-earthquake buildings in Christchurch so protected. In these ways, transformational technologies, materialities and narratives born of the earthquakes became incorporated into entanglements of the more-than-human city.

A third aspect of the entanglements of the more-than-human city after the earthquakes relates to the way in which relational actants come to signify contested spaces. Franklin (2017) notes how such actants form and embody the principles, values and interests of different groups of citizens and how they become a focus and 'voice' of otherwise difficult political and ethical values in urban design, planning and decision-making. For example, the earthquakes provided ample scope for adventitious colonisation of urban spaces such as demolition sites and empty house sections, but not everyone welcomed the appearance of rabbits or weedy species. Others however felt encouraged to subvert conventional ways of being in the city. A specific example from the transitional movement (which was discussed in Chapter 8) is Liv Worsnop's Plant Gang, an environmental art practice of planting succulents and other rubble-ready species in empty city centre sites (Boswell 2021). It is echoed in her etchings of weeds of the rebuild on the large glass windows of the re-located C1 Espresso café, one of the first social institutions to re-open as the city centre cordon shrank. Its new home in a repurposed post office had been erected to high seismic standards after the 1931 Hawkes Bay earthquake but remained surrounded by ruins and abandoned sites for several years after re-opening in 2012.

Two narratives of contest

Two sites in the city that became notable, in different ways, for contests between human and more-than-human vitalities are the residential red zone and the abandoned, flooded basement of a demolished city centre tower block. In both cases, the disturbance was the result of the manner in which bird species have responded to the availability of new post-earthquake habitats. In the residential red zone, whose creation and future are discussed in Chapters 10 and 12, Crown agencies sought to ensure that interventions like those of the Plant Gang would be discouraged. As the Canterbury Earthquake Recovery Authority (CERA) cleared house sites, it left in place 'whole suburbs constructed only with vegetation' (Bowring 2021, 111). This is a reference to those garden trees and shrubs that after initial public outcry it was persuaded to leave behind. There were a lot: CERA compiled a database of nearly 30,000, about 1800 of which were fruit and nut trees (Gates 2015c). But around these trees, the land was levelled and sown in grass, which was then regularly mown. After the dissolution of CERA in 2016, Land Information New Zealand, the manager of Crown lands nationally, continued this policy of close mowing, in effect creating a parkland landscape entirely consistent with the city's 'civilising' ethos of improvement.

Although community groups such as Greening the Red Zone recorded the very limited patches of native vegetation in the Ōtākaro Avon river corridor and were permitted to extend some of these with public plantings of indigenous flora, the Crown land management policy produced a double irony. First, it set back the rewilding that is the centrepiece of the widely supported regeneration plan (discussed in Chapter 12) by nearly a decade. Secondly using mowers to minimise the risk of encouraging populations of rats and mice created ideal habitats for other species. One such is Canada geese (*Branta canadensis*), which are attracted to the short pasture habitats and wetlands that abound in the red zone. They have also been encouraged by the provision of managed wetlands designed as flood mitigation devices in many post-earthquake greenfield suburbs (Chapter 5) as well as to the irrigated pastures of dairy farms, rural Canterbury's twenty-first-century boom industry (Le Heron 2018). The birds lost their game status a decade ago, so are no longer managed by Fish and Game North Canterbury, the regional agency responsible for sports fish and game bird populations. They have subsequently spread into these new urban and rural niches.

The city population of Canada geese reached about 5000 individuals, bringing attendant problems of water contamination, intra-species competition with other water birds and fouling of public places and pathways (McDonald 2020e). Nonetheless, Land Information New Zealand (2021) claimed that its 'vigilant and pre-emptive management approach' has kept 'pest species' in the red zones at acceptable levels, although recent survey data has focused only on small mammals, namely mice, rodents and mustelids. Rats and mustelids have been controlled by trapping networks monitored by community volunteers. Rabbits, which also thrive in short grass environments, have long been regarded as a threat to New Zealand's pastoral industries, and as such are subject to the Canterbury Regional Pest Management Strategy. When red zone rabbit populations have reached 'non-compliant' levels, they have been controlled by Rabbit Haemorrhagic Virus Disease administered as a biocide (Boffa Miskell 2020). In 1997, when this disease was surreptitiously first introduced into New Zealand, there was some concern about its cruel effects, but its use in the red zone has not been sufficiently publicised to arouse public emotion.

A second narrative of contestation in the more-than-human city relates to the open basement of a demolished office tower on Armagh Street in the central city, then owned by the Carter Group. Hinchliffe and Whatmore (2006) have demonstrated that the arrival of a new species into urban habitats results in dances of agency which invoke new assemblages of constraint and opportunity. These can provoke contested politics involving both de-naturalisation and attempts to provide empathetic care. In 2018, a flock of some 300 black-billed gulls (tarāpuka in te reo Māori) arrived at the site, nesting in the concrete beams and flooded foundation stumps of the former building. The tarāpuka is the most threatened of New Zealand's three indigenous gull species, and is regarded by nature-conscious people as both precious and rare. The species breeds mostly in the braided river beds of Canterbury and Southland, and is threatened by predators, habitat loss and human disturbance. The cordoned-off site in central Christchurch offered both safety from predation and disturbance, and a physical environment suited to nest-building (Figure 11.2).

The arrival of the tarāpuka in the post-earthquake city provoked a series of contested discourses and political responses. The Department of Conservation took an immediate interest because the Wildlife Act 1953 dictates that once the birds start nesting, it is illegal to disturb them until the end of the nesting season. The specification of the tarāpuka as 'near threatened' ensured that conservation wardens monitored the site, even designing and installing purpose-built floating platforms as life rafts for chicks that were falling from their nests into the flooded basement of the building (Hunt 2021b). However, departmental representatives made it clear that the city centre was not an ideal place for the tarāpuka and that the birds should be encouraged to move back to their more 'natural' breeding sites (Gates 2021). Meanwhile, the charismatic nature of the tarāpuka, along with the publicity given to how their colony was flourishing in their new urban environment, ensured that they became something of a zoological attraction for residents and tourists grasping an opportunity to learn about these rare native birds at close quarters. Some even suggested that the tarāpuka represented a positive adornment of a site that was otherwise one of the city's ugliest post-quake eyesores (Bowron 2019).

To the site's owners, however, the tarāpuka represented a significant hindrance to their capacity to redevelop. This frustration heightened with an agreement in 2019 to sell part of the land for the construction of a new Catholic cathedral and to use the remainder in a joint venture to build an associated pastoral hub, primary school, offices, residential accommodation for clergy and multistorey car parking. The development was hailed as an important piece of the central city chessboard of redevelopment (Blundell 2021), linking Te Papa Ōtākaro (the river precinct), the performing arts precinct and Te Pae, the new convention centre (McDonald 2019d) (Chapter 9). A new alignment of interested parties thus emerged, to which owners of surrounding hospitality businesses were soon added due to the nuisance caused by the tarāpuka in harassing diners, scavenging food and fouling buildings. In this way, the legislative safety net of care, and a potential politics of entangled empathy, became quickly outweighed by economically

Figure 11.2 Tarāpuka colonising a central city site.

Credit: https://annettewoodford.wordpress.com/

driven positioning of the tarāpuka as 'unnatural' urban residents out of place in the post-disaster city. A plan was agreed for a gentle eviction of the birds at the end of the 2019 breeding season using nets, with spikes to deter them from returning.

This apparently uneven contest was, however, waylaid by the lively agency of the birds themselves. The installation of netting at the site was not completed before the tarāpuka came back to nest in 2020. A further year of occupation of the site ensued, during which the presence of the birds gave energy to longer-term arguments about rewilding the city and the capacity of indigenous species to provide local flavour and natural character (cf. Meurk and Swaffield 2000). Having failed with the eviction the year before, developers transformed the site in 2021 with the recycling of the ruined foundations to make way for the parking building. The beams and pillars previously used as nesting sites were torn down prior to the breeding season, and liaison with local property owners resulted in plans to prevent birds from congregating and nesting on nearby rooflines. The tarāpuka scattered along the Ōtākaro Avon River and into the residential red zone, only to return to the site when demolition was suspended in August 2021 due to the imposition of a Covid-19 level 4 lockdown in Christchurch. Meanwhile, an entire breeding colony of tarāpuka abandoned its nests in the Upper Waimakariri riverbed due to a suspected dog attack (Allot 2021). Ironically, breeding conditions at this 'natural' site were less safe than in the supposedly 'unnatural' Armagh Street venue. Subsequently, some tarāpuka found a new home in a partially constructed stormwater basin in the suburb of Belfast. Here, according to Law (2022), as workers downed tools during the Covid-19 lockdown, the birds appeared to mistake the basin site for a braided river and began nesting again in an 'unnatural' urban location.

The new dances of agency performed by actants such as tarāpuka and Canada geese certainly brought about material responses and a questioning of the place of non-human actants within and beyond the redevelopment of the central city. In Chapter 8, it was argued that the importance of transitional gap-filling and greening initiatives after the earthquakes became acknowledged in longer-term re-evaluations of the politics of placemaking so as to include community orientation and playful theatricality amongst commercially-driven development. In a similarly transitional manner, it can be suggested that the borrowing of urban sites by tarāpuka and Canada geese may find longer-term significance in the recognition of the more-than-human city as a complex configuration of landscapes and a mosaic of ecosystems. Inevitably such a vision needs both to disturb any rigid politics of how non-human actants are 'in' or 'out of place', and to recognise that the relational agencies concerned are unpredictable and subject to continual change. Such characteristics of the more-than-human city also involve the excitement of new experimental opportunities for entanglement, and it is to this possibility that the chapter now turns.

Emerging entanglements

The rebuilding of Christchurch after the earthquakes has offered up a series of opportunities to develop new experimental configurations of more-than-human relations in the city. In general, such reconfigurations require a recognition of the need for political change that in some way enables, or at least makes room for, a disturbance of conventional political wisdom and assumptions about nature-society relations. In this case, it was the rupture of the earthquakes that created different kinds of potential spaces in which alternative ideas, narratives and discourses could find expression. At various scales, material, cultural and performative, opportunities arose to explore in particular ways new forms of more-than-human entanglement and thereby to try out alternative ideascapes, practices and even moralities capable of co-constituting city worlds differently.

One of the most important opportunities offered by the rebuild has been a more overt recognition of indigenous entanglements with land and water, a theme introduced in a number of preceding chapters. The Canterbury Earthquake Recovery Act 2011 required that Te Rūnanga o Ngāi Tahu be consulted in the development of a recovery strategy and 'have the opportunity to provide input' into the Central City Recovery Plan (the blueprint). The rūnanga (or tribal council) was also recognised under the Greater Christchurch Regeneration Act 2016 as a statutory partner to the Crown, regional and local government agencies in post-earthquake redevelopment. One response to this was the exposition of Ngāi Tahu's 'grand narratives' of living in the landscape. The aim of the document is for 'the two Treaty partners to be woven into the national narrative of Christchurch' (Tau 2016, 31). In a critique of the modernist assumptions of the blueprint, it asserts that

> it is apparent that the design teams have very little understanding of things Māori. It also appears that the designers have little knowledge of Christchurch's European heritage or culture and this does concern us – as we wonder how the design teams will incorporate and interpret European history, let alone Ngāi Tahu history.
>
> (Tau 2016, 11)

In the central city, this concern prompted the establishment of the Matapopore Trust, whose mission is to ensure 'Ngāi Tuāhuriri/Ngāi Tahu values, aspirations and narratives are realised within the recovery of Christchurch'. Earlier chapters have outlined the implications of this for the central city anchor projects. But throughout the urban area, a key concern of the 'grand narratives' is the restoration of values of mahinga kai, or 'all food producing places' (Tau 2016, 46, 48). Repeatedly it is stated that 'this does not mean that the city's 'English character' needs to be downplayed or forgotten' (Tau 2016, 60), despite that character being the product of the very processes of improvement that led to widespread destruction of mahinga kai values to begin with. For example, in the Ōtākaro Avon river corridor, this entails attention to improving water quality and ecology, potentially issues of benefit to all (Regenerate Christchurch 2019). How this will play out in practice depends on the role of the new co-governance entity that will be responsible for the future care of this area, discussed in Chapter 12. The culturally and recreationally important fishery for inanga and other whitebait species is central to this. Reversing the decline of this fishery lies in understanding the spawning habitats of the fish, and anthropogenic threats to these (Orchard et al. 2018).

Another significant area of opportunity for the development of new forms of more-than-human entanglement is evident in the discourses and proposals emanating from advocates of new landscape urbanism in the city (Meurk and Swaffield 2007). Their concern is that the urban population has become distanced from the ecological processes of its surrounding environment, being increasingly influenced by artificial simulacra of nature in for example video clips and gaming, rather than more grounded understandings of natural systems. Dealing with this perceived experiential decoupling is seen to involve two manoeuvres, both of which were conceived before the earthquakes, but became more practicable in its aftermath. First, there needs to be an appealing discursive tag with associated storytelling to draw public attention to and earn approval of renegotiated features of landscape urbanism. Second, the current patchwork of blue and green spaces and corridors in and around the city has to be configured both to promote ecological and cultural sustainability of indigenous nature and to ensure some connectivity of habitats for wildlife, thus rendering nature more visible for residents (Figure 11.3).

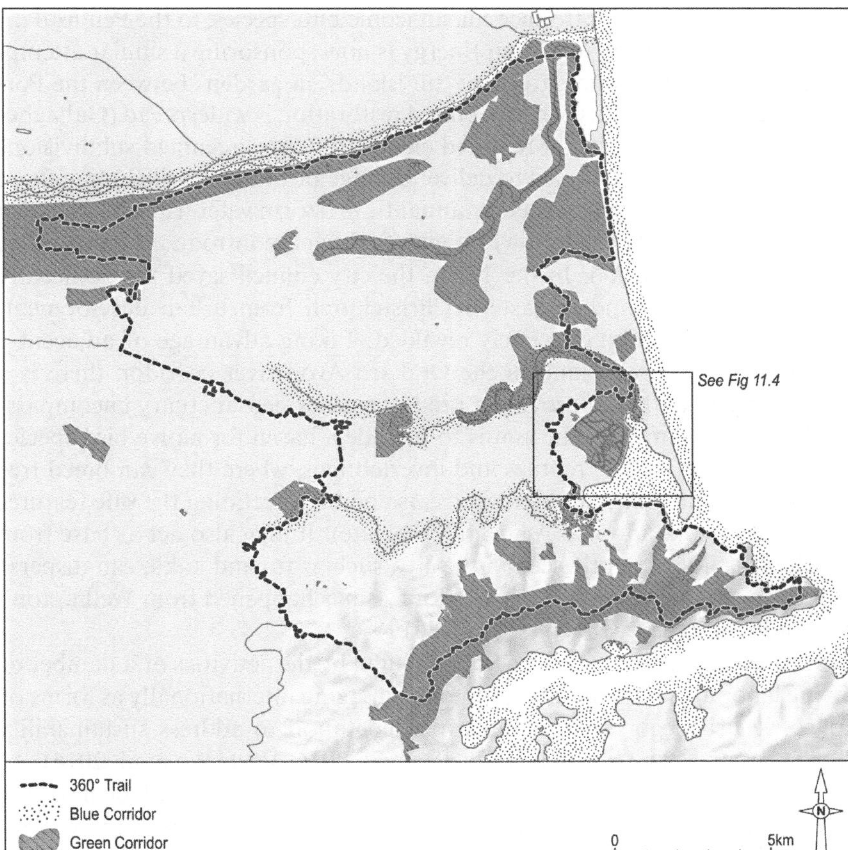

Figure 11.3 Locations of Christchurch's blue-green corridors and the 360 Trail.

Source: Trail route from https://christchurch360trail.org.nz

These manoeuvres are demonstrated in the form of an initiative to earn Christchurch the title of a 'national park city'. This was energised in 2021 in a campaign led by *The Press*, the metropolitan daily newspaper, potentially collecting under one umbrella a range of projects concerning nature-based recreation, amenity values and rewilding. It is a fresh interpretation of the rather tired 'garden city' moniker, focusing on connecting the region's blue and green corridors, so mobilising them as means of encouraging new human and more-than-human encounters. There are regional precedents for this: for example Te Ara Kakariki, the Greenway Canterbury Trust, whose object is to create a corridor of native biodiversity 'green dots' between the Waimakariri and Rakaia rivers, linking the mountains to the sea and Te Waihora/Lake Ellesmere. The Green Dots programme works with public and private landowners on the Canterbury Plains. In Christchurch City's large, rural Banks Peninsula ward, two other organisations, one national (the Queen Elizabeth II National Trust), and one local, initiated by landowners and farmers (the Banks Peninsula Conservation Trust), work to preserve and enhance indigenous landscapes and species (Pawson and Christensen 2014). The second of these trusts runs a successful project to reintroduce tūī, an iconic bird species, to the Peninsula.

The power company Meridian Energy is now sponsoring a similar attempt to encourage homeowners to plant 'tūī islands' in gardens between the Port Hills and central city. Elsewhere wetland restoration is widespread (Gallagher and Pyle 2021), and often a required element of new greenfield subdivisions (Figure 5.4). This is designed to deliver a range of outcomes, including flood mitigation and filtering of contaminants in stormwater runoff, but also attractive habitats for waterfowl (many of which are introduced game birds, such as mallard ducks). In the 1990s, the city council saved the 80-hectare area of Travis wetland in eastern Christchurch from urban development, since when it has been effectively rewilded. Taking advantage of adjacent – and higher – red zone land in the Ōtākaro Avon river corridor, there is a community initiative to provide a predator-proof ecosanctuary encompassing both environments. The aim is to provide a haven for native bird species in particular, as well as reptiles and invertebrates, where they can breed free of rats, mice, possums and domestic cats and dogs (echoing the safe features of the tarāpuka's adopted Armagh Street site). It may also act as base from which birds not presently seen in the city, such as tūī and kākā, can disperse along the city's blue and green corridors, as has happened from Wellington's Zealandia sanctuary (Marques et al. 2019).

Such experiments are being complemented by the activities of a number of 'living laboratories' in the city. These are emerging internationally as forms of collective urban governance and experimentation to address sustainability challenges and opportunities (Bulkeley et al. 2016; Voytenko et al. 2016). As collaborative enterprises, they enable researchers to partner with civil society organisations and communities, exploring and co-creating insight into complex social-ecological entanglements. At the northern edge of Christchurch City, the Styx Living Laboratory Trust aims to encourage a greater understanding of one of the city's lesser-known blue-green corridors. In the Ōtākaro Avon river corridor, one of the largest areas of managed retreat in an urban environment in the world, the Ōtākaro Living Laboratory has been established, with active support from a range of educational and governmental institutions. Its purpose is to implement one of the key objectives of the Ōtākaro Avon River Corridor Regeneration Plan, for learning, experimentation and research, 'testing and creating new ideas and ways of living' (Regenerate Christchurch 2019, 22).

This type of ambition can however disguise disparity and disagreement when projects draw on a range of discursive understandings and values about the intersection of the human with the more-than-human. A good example is the ongoing contest between the Christchurch 360 Trail and the Avon-Heathcote Estuary Ihutai Trust about access to part of the estuary edge. The 360 Trail is a 130-kilometre-long circuit of the perimeter of the city, designed to showcase its diverse contexts and ecologies (Figure 11.3). These include the exposed volcanic ridgeline of the Port Hills, the sand dunes of the New Brighton shoreline, the wetlands around Brooklands, and the braids of the Waimakariri River, through to dry grassland ecosystems beyond the airport, and residual bush remnants such as Pūtaringamotu in Riccarton. It was first proposed as the Great Perimeter Walkway in 1991, and officially opened in 2015 with support from the city council and local Rotary clubs. The ambition is in line with the Department of Conservation's Great Walks in New Zealand's national parks; the intent is to enable people to engage with the more-than-human world on their doorstep. The trail however remains only about nine-tenths complete. Some 15 kilometres on the western side of the airport cannot be officially marked, as there are no footpaths across private farmland, nor alongside roads where speed limits exceed 50 km/h.

There is also a 'missing link' around part of the Avon-Heathcote estuary in the east of the city. The estuary and surrounding wetlands are considered to be of national importance for resident and migratory birds, such as godwits, oystercatchers, cormorants, ducks, geese and swans (Marsden and Knox 2008, 759). The proximity of the city's waste treatment ponds and surrounding paddocks add to the variety of bird habitats. The part of the estuary fringe alongside the treatment ponds is a wildlife refuge, closed to the public. Companion dogs are banned from the path leading towards the refuge, the sensitivity of this issue indicated by prominent notices threatening owners with fines ranging from $300 to $100,000, or a year's imprisonment. The closed section of the estuary edge is between two to three kilometres in length and includes an access way for council staff (Figure 11.4). Alternative routes are lengthy and along major or suburban highways, taking the 360 Trail 'far from the ecologically interesting wildlife refuge' (Christchurch 360 Trail 2022). Although the city council has shown some interest in opening this link as part of its Estuary Green Edge Project, the Avon-Heathcote Estuary Ihutai Trust is resolutely opposed.

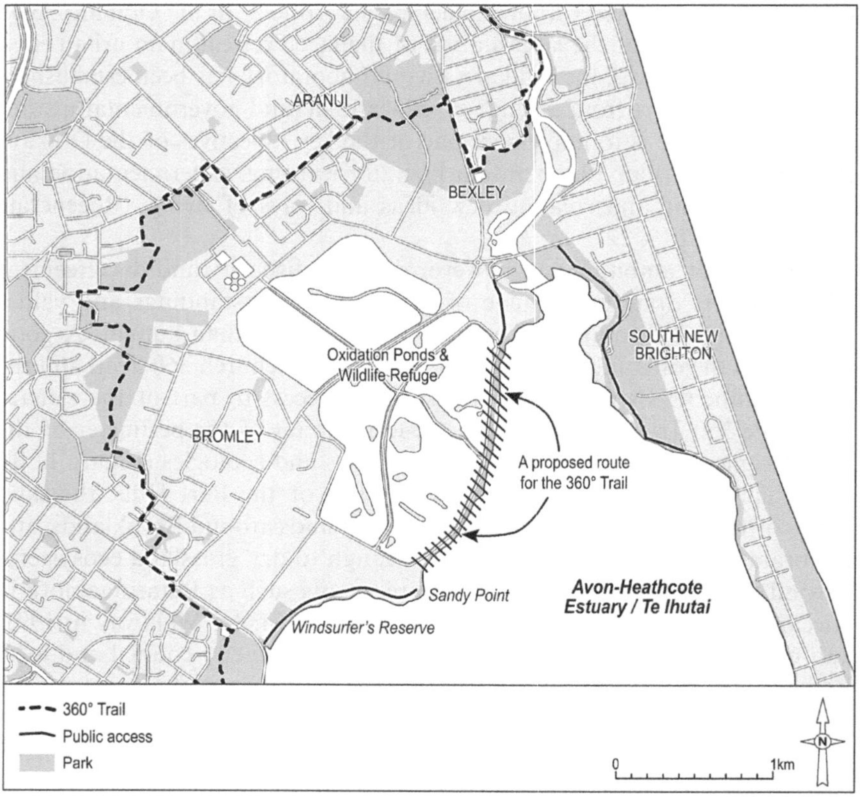

Figure 11.4 The contest between the Christchurch 360 Trail and the Avon-Heathcote Estuary Ihutai Trust.

The Estuary Trust was formed in 2002, with support of both the city and regional councils. Its purpose is 'the preservation' of the estuary's 'natural and historic resources to maintain their intrinsic values', as well as to provide for their 'appreciation and recreational enjoyment by present and future generations' (Avon-Heathcote Estuary Ihutai Trust 2022). Over time the Trust has supported public access to the estuary edge as well as seeking to protect bird feeding, breeding and roosting grounds. The contentious area is the only part of the estuary without public access, and proposals to fence the potential route along with existing dog control measures have brought no resolution. The geographical imaginaries of the two groups are very different: one sees a short, missing link in a city-wide 'great walk'; the other considers that as public access is available to the rest of the estuary, this area deserves protection. While the 360 Trail is 'trying to connect people to nature', the estuary trust is committed to making 'room for nature' (Harvie 2021). At the root of a long-running dispute are different perspectives on empathetic care, in turn reflecting quite distinct positions on appropriate relations between the human and more-than-human worlds.

Conclusion

In her book *Staying With The Trouble*, Donna Haraway (2016) argues for a radical configuration of relations to the earth and all its inhabitants. Recognising the Anthropocene as a self-destructive epoch of human dominance, she urges that new ways be found for a more-than-human era of living with each other. This recognises that human and non-humans are inextricably linked in practices of living and becoming together, and will require a new cultural politics of response-ability. As Latour (2018) and Dodds (2020) emphasise, the Anthropocene is not a neutral starting point for this reconfiguration. Current ecological regimes remain an essential part of late capitalism and colonialism in which ecologies are engineered and hierarchies of improvement inform disruption to human and non-human populations. To persist simply risks further degradation of relations between the human and the non-human at every imaginable scale. Haraway's plea is therefore for new expressions of staying with the earth's troubles that are conducive to the building of more liveable futures.

The realisation of Haraway's vision depends on finding a moral and political capacity to open up possibilities of becoming different. It embraces the settling of troubled waters and the rebuilding of quiet places but also necessitates the stirring up of a potent response to devastating events. It envisages the encouragement of 'collectively-producing systems that do not have self-defined or temporal boundaries … systems [that] are evolutionary and have the potential for surprising change' (Haraway 2016, 61). As a practical starting point, she recognises the potency of developing new practices of more-than-human entanglement, thinking, storytelling and action – as well as experimental more-than-human contact zones where these practices can find expression. This chapter has suggested that a feature of the post-quake period of rebuilding in Christchurch is the nascent opening of opportunities to establish experimental sites and practices serving as pilot projects. In no small measure these opportunities have been enabled both by the material disruption of the built environment in the city centre and in the Ōtākaro Avon river corridor, and by the political rupture caused by the earthquakes within which there have been fruitful opportunities for transitional experimentation. In each case, the event of the earthquakes has opened spaces for voices and plans that were previously largely drowned out by the mainstream dialogues of the city.

The alliance of voices of activists from art, theatre and ecology with those local communities to produce experimentation in transitional place-making, leading to the formation of new discourses and partnerships in the city was illustrated in Chapter 8. This current chapter also suggests an amplification of previously marginalised voices, and emphasises, for example, the importance of Māori ideascapes and the passionate plans of landscape ecologists and other researchers in promoting an alternative polity that is better attuned to the more-than-human world. These illustrations may be understood as small steps towards Haraway's vision, but they nevertheless demonstrate a clear recognition of and empathy for the entanglements and liveliness of the more-than-human city. They may not have dragged everyday political practices into new ethical formations, but new forms of co-governance have emerged and new possibilities of more-than-human becoming have certainly been opened out.

12 The residential red zone

The city's field of dreams?

Introduction

A few weeks before the 2017 general election, *The Press* newspaper carried an editorial headed 'Unleashing excitement in the [residential] red zone will make it Christchurch's field of dreams' (*The Press* 2017). Over six years had passed since the earthquake of 22 February 2011 that destroyed the city centre and upended many suburban households, and nearly seven since the start of the Canterbury earthquake sequence. The memory of the Canterbury Earthquake Recovery Authority's (CERA's) panoptical planning, and clearance of much of the downtown to make way for its blueprint, was still fresh. There was a widespread feeling that progress in the rebuild was slow: as outlined in Chapter 4, few of the anchor projects had been completed, and some of the larger ones not even started. Many households were still embroiled in insurance disputes or awaiting repairs. The enthusiasm of Share an Idea in 2011 (Carlton 2013), when citizens swooped on the chance to express their visions for the future of the city, seemed far away. And there was an emerging view that the rebuild was producing 'the city of yesterday' (McCrone 2017). Or as the editorial put it, instead of creating 'the first new city of the 21st century … we largely rushed to build the last version of a 20th century city ever to be constructed' (*The Press* 2017; cf. Dann 2021).

The term 'red zone' was used in a variety of ways during and after the earthquake years. The area of devastation within the central city was described as 'the red zone' whilst the cordon was in place (Chapter 6). There were also 'residential red zones', those parts of the suburbs which were so badly damaged that the Crown made offers to buy out all those homeowners who wished to move (as described in Chapter 10). And as the central city cordon shrank (Figure 6.1), within Christchurch 'the red zone' entered popular usage to describe the Ōtākaro Avon river corridor. This 11-kilometre finger of land destabilised by liquefaction and lateral spread stretches from the city centre to the sea (Figure 12.1). Setting aside other, much smaller, red zones for a while, it was this corridor that began to seem like the last opportunity to try something fresh. This chapter explores what 'something fresh' might mean, drawing on the literature about urban futures. It then describes the process of river corridor regeneration planning, before considering difficult issues of governance that are central to achieving what Chatterton (2010) has called 'the urban impossible', or that which currently seems out of reach.

DOI: 10.4324/9780429275562-15

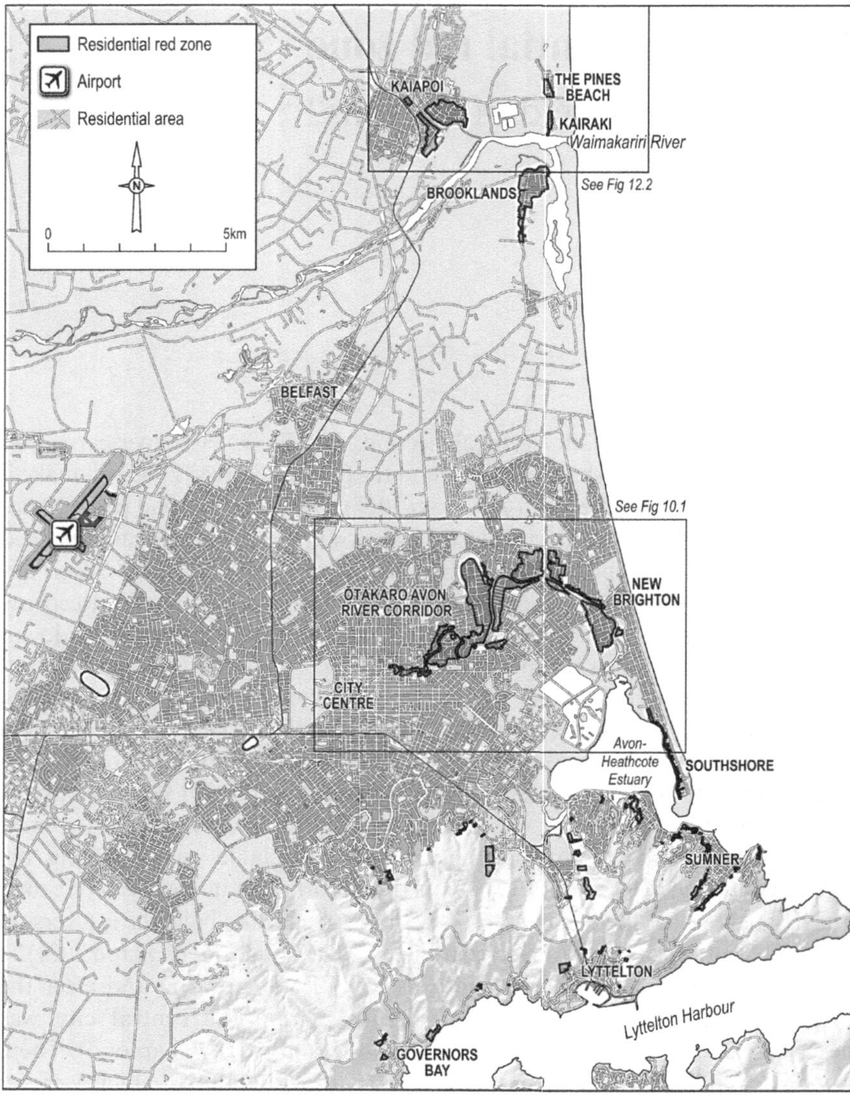

Figure 12.1 Location of the residential red zones in and around Christchurch.

Source: Data from http://koordinates.com/layer/3669/

It concludes by outlining some of the nascent characteristics of what a future Christchurch could look like, drawing on post-earthquake experimentation over the last decade.

Urban futures and the twenty-first-century city

The international debate over urban futures reflects a divide between, on the one hand, concern and fear that nothing much will change and, on the other, a belief that the city is always a work in progress open to being steered in progressive directions. The former position, which has often been characterised by a long lament about neoliberalism, has its roots in unease about the rational designs of social order that characterise high modernism. James Scott identified an underlying drive by states to plan for legibility, so as to rationalise and standardise assets and resources into 'a more convenient format', the convenience being of those who wield authority and power (Scott 1998, 3). Broadly, critics of such approaches instead promote values like citizen engagement and local knowledge. Theirs is a position that cities could be 'substantially distinct from the present and that organisations and individuals have the power to shape the present to result in a different future' (Jeffrey and Dyson 2021, 654). This sort of vision parallels Boston's (2017) argument for anticipatory forms of governance as more effective means of managing emergent long-term issues, like the biodiversity and climate crises that are themselves the products of high modernism.

The more critical assessments of the state's post-earthquake planning in the city tend to focus on CERA's city centre blueprint. They do not see much progressive intent in this, even though it encompassed, indirectly, much that emerged from the Share an Idea engagement process. Rather the outcome is reported as having been imposed and experienced as such (Boswell 2021). A recurrent complaint is that bureaucracies such as CERA acted in post-political ways to evade difficult issues by removing them from the public arena: a direct reference to the implementation of the 100-day blueprint (Amore et al. 2017). The rationale for doing so echoes analyses of neoliberal risk management that furthers commercial interests (Amin 2013). Hence a focus on 'stability', or showing the world that the rebuilt city 'was open for business' (Dann 2021, 3). This was exactly CERA's intention, as Chapter 6 has shown. But the price, it is alleged, is a 'textbook case in how not to build back better', as those with resources and power have the least need to change (Matthewman and Byrd 2020). Thus the critique that a depoliticised process has narrowed the possibilities for transformation in the interests of predictability (Cretney 2019) and risk aversion (Lesniak 2016). Even those who accept the blueprint at face value, as a framework for regeneration, still see a need for 'significant community engagement and coherent governance' (Brand et al. 2020, 89).

In this respect, debates about the right to the city and the right to shape the city (Marcuse 2009) discuss a spectrum of ways of re-politicising citizen agency. At the broadest level, this involves using opportunities such as those wrought by disaster to 'fracture open' rather than foreclose political possibilities at a range of scales (Cretney 2019). An example is the propositional engagements of the transitional movement discussed in Chapter 8, which whilst not fully participatory nonetheless sought to offer 'provocations' for public trial. This approach accepts both failure and impermanence as potential outcomes. A desire for improvisation does however depend upon facilitative responses from those in regulatory authority, to 'let go' in the face of uncertainty (Boswell 2021). Otherwise what Westbury (2015) characterised as the stifling impacts of bureaucratic processes can overshadow experimentation through seeming dedication to inventing rather than minimising difficulties. One successful example of how to ease the way in post-earthquake Christchurch has been Life In Vacant Spaces, a charitable trust discussed in Chapter 8, established with city council support. It mediates between owners of vacant properties and activators, whilst assisting the latter with health and safety requirements and insurance provision.

Such process-oriented approaches, instead of trying to build outcomes for an imagined future in terms of single rather than multiple meanings, embrace what might be termed the 'future-in-the-present'. Within the status quo, this necessarily involves more inclusive forms of decision-making in which there is an opportunity for a range of community voices to be heard (Amore et al. 2017). If this is to move beyond the post-political, however, it is also about wider ownership of decisions that shape the city, so that those who participate feel that they have a stake in the outcome, even if they do not necessarily agree with it. Ownership, and all that flows from that, such as motivation and community care of outcomes, springs from being recognised as a party to building the future in whatever form people in particular places determine that might take. This encompasses, for example, recognition of the interests of residents as well as of business, a process that has worked well in Christchurch when it has been tried. Examples include the valuing of children's voices in the design of the Margaret Mahy playground (Chapter 9), as well as a publicly focused strategy to produce Tūranga, the new central city library and information hub. Both of these projects also drew on the perspective and expertise of mana whenua, whose presence was all but silenced in the pre-earthquake city (Pickles 2016). In this respect, too, the future of the residential red zones is an opportunity to redraw the map of who has stakes in the city of the future.

Prefigurative forms of politics are a further development of engagement, being performative in the sense that people enact a vision of change through organisation, practices or design. The prefigurative is broadly progressive in seeking to 'embrace the potential of the future to be more inclusive, sustainable, and equitable than the present' (Jeffrey and Dyson 2021, 645). This involves the development of networks based on broadly shared commitments, trust and compromise, and the institutionalisation of practice to ensure durability. A good example internationally is the Transition Towns movement which models forms of urban life based on principles of mutuality, the sharing of experience and resources and low carbon futures (Aiken 2012). It is represented in the Canterbury region by Project Lyttelton (2022) in the port town, and by a number of rural and urban time banks. These are examples of how social practice can be 'thickened' through alliance building, coordination and persistence. The extent, however, to which the development of shared senses of purpose can be effective beyond the local in bringing real change remains open.

From the perspective of international debates about urban futures, Christchurch in the wake of the earthquakes was seen as a city full of possibility, indeed as 'a global city to watch' and 'a unique opportunity to rethink urban form' (Glaeser and Sassen 2011, 72). A decade on, however, critics consider that it has experienced a city centre and suburban rebuild, ringed by propertied greenfields, highlighted in Chapter 5, that embody and reinforce the attributes of twentieth-century modernist urbanism. The rebuild in this reading is seen as the product of prescriptive styles of planning that – with exceptions – tend to narrow rather than broaden the potential to deal with emergent social, economic and environmental crises (Pawson 2022). In contrast, if we think of the city 'not just as a static noun, but as an active verb' (Chatterton 2010, 235), then different futures might become imaginable. In view of the problems that cities planned in or of the twentieth-century lock in place, such as car and oil dependence, different futures are also very necessary. The question which therefore now arises is whether there is still opportunity to engage with the future-in-the-present within the residential red zone. And, in the spirit of Chapter 11, to consider how this area might be used to explore ways of living alongside those more-than-human actants which the Canterbury earthquake sequence brought vividly into human view.

Regeneration planning

If engaged citizens and critics disliked the process and direction of CERA's post-earthquake planning, nonetheless it is the case that the agency was never intended to have more than a five-year term. By 2016 central government accepted that a new direction was required, as outlined at the close of Chapter 4. The framework for the blueprint was then in place and the residential red zones had largely been cleared. The situation was ripe for an alternative approach, and beyond the city, in the town of Kaiapoi in Waimakariri District, this was already underway. This section therefore uses the Kaiapoi experience as a point of contrast with the Christchurch red zone (Figure 12.1). The latter, the Ōtakaro Avon river corridor, winds eastwards from the central city towards the Pacific Ocean. It covers 602 hectares, which subsided by up to 1.5 metres during the earthquakes (Hughes et al. 2015; Measures et al. 2011). With the process of red zoning, described in Chapter 10, it became probably the largest area of managed retreat in an urban setting in the world. Surely here was an opportunity to rethink urban form and process (Gundermann 2014).

The initial Crown offer to Ōtākaro Avon river corridor households was made in August 2011 (Chapter 10), and to those in the Kaiapoi red zones a few weeks later. By mid-2015, about 7000 houses had been removed in the river corridor, in addition to about a thousand in eastern parts of Kaiapoi and its small coastal settlements. It took a further year to demolish the 500 red-zoned houses in the Port Hills. All up, the cost to the Crown of these buyouts was about $1.5 billion, less than a quarter of which was recouped through insurance recoveries, mostly from the Earthquake Commission for land damage (Truebridge 2017). The process was managed by CERA. Broken footpaths and road surfaces, street lights and underground services were left in place. So too were many trees and shrubs, once community pressure forced a retention agreement in 2013 (AvON 2022). Former house sites were grassed, and whole blocks fenced to discourage fly-tipping whilst remaining accessible for active recreation. In 2016, Land Information New Zealand assumed responsibility for maintenance, although this involved little more than regular mowing and some pest control, as outlined in Chapter 11. The subsequent regeneration plan later described how 'previously vibrant residential neighbourhoods were deconstructed and replaced by open parkland' (Regenerate Christchurch 2019, 16).

This statement obscures the trauma of residents having to vacate their homes and neighbourhoods, as outlined in Chapters 3 and 10. One of the ways in which this trauma found an outlet was through community mobilisation to encourage future uses of the land that would respect red zone memories. This reflected a city-wide process of a 'post-quake proliferation of geography-based community groups' (Vallance and Carlton 2015, 33). Three such groups merged to establish the Avon Ōtākaro Network (AvON) in 2011 to urge that 'the lands be covenanted to remain in public ownership in perpetuity'. This was to guard against fears of land remediation, re-use and privatisation. Asking 'What is the future of the red zone?', one of the groups – the Campaign for a Memorial Reserve Covenant – devised maps showing either a 'Grey Zone of Uncertainty', which 'could blight the recovery of the east for years'; or a 'Green Zone' that 'provides the backbone and framework for the recovery of the east and a fitting memorial for those who lost their lives and their homes' (Scoop 2011b). Subsequently, AvON's (2022) vision also stated support for 'mana whenua aspirations for restored mahinga kai values'.

Other groups with broadly consistent values include Greening the Red Zone and the Avon-Ōtākaro Forest Park. But like those trying to engage actively in the future of the central city, all faced ongoing issues in trying to bring any sort of vision into reality. The city council, with a host of other post-earthquake problems to deal with, lacked the capacity to intervene in its red zones (Vallance 2015), which were anyway now owned by the Crown. CERA focused on land clearance rather than re-imagination. The situation that Amore et al. (2017) identified in the central city of 'non-decision making' with respect to community project activations was if anything amplified in the river corridor. Over a period of some years, AvON sought to coordinate a great range of community and some commercial project proposals for future uses, such as a heritage garden park, trails, community gardens, nature playgrounds and places of tranquillity. No mechanism was however available with which to institutionalise these, which is one of the conditions for the sustainability of prefigurative politics (Jeffrey and Dyson 2021). Projects with power and influence behind them, such as a local iteration of the Eden Project, backed by Eden International, and a rowing lake backed by a trust with private school and ruling political party affiliations, gained higher profiles than others, but ultimately no more traction.

This contrasted with the situation in Kaiapoi, where the district council continued to employ a distinctive pre-earthquake approach to community engagement that became known as 'the Waimakariri Way' (Vallance et al.

2019, 52). Although Waimakariri District covers more than 2000 square kilometres, it served a population of less than 50 000 at the time, concentrated in the towns of Rangiora and Kaiapoi (Figure 5.1). These conditions supported development of a civic value system based on trust and transparency. Drawing from experiences elsewhere, it acknowledged that communities have 'a vital role to play in disaster recovery' (Vallance 2015, 1287), as well as in finding workable solutions to problems and securing public legitimacy. An independent report commissioned by the council in August 2012 identified what mattered to residents in 'an integrated, community-based recovery framework' (Vallance 2013). Central to this framework was a hub in Kaiapoi, co-locating council teams and some central government agencies alongside community groups. This facilitated information flow and triangulation of data, proving invaluable when large-scale recovery programmes, such as the Kaiapoi Town Centre Rebuild, began (Vallance 2015). It also provided a foundation on which to build in subsequent engagement about Kaiapoi's red zone lands.

This engagement included the Canvas process in 2014, undertaken at the direction of the Minister for Earthquake Recovery, Mr Brownlee, and led by CERA with support from the Waimakariri council and Te Rūnanga ō Ngāi Tahu. Almost 600 people participated over a six week period, giving a clear message that they wanted 'a natural land- and water-based environment that reflects the Kaiapoi community and earthquake remembrance, and is inclusive of all residents, while enabling active and passive recreation' (CERA 2014, 10). The council was then tasked by the Minister with developing more detailed plans for the red zones in Kaiapoi and the coastal settlements of The Pines Beach and Kairaki (Figure 12.2). This was done – consistent with 'the Waimakariri Way' – through street corner and town meetings, expert review and a public hearing on submissions about the draft plan. An imaginative step was the use of a 3D model to enable public visualisation of the areas. The plan was readily approved by Minister Brownlee, perhaps because in addition to 41 hectares of greenspace, it included nine for mixed business use and 30 for light rural uses, such as grazing and cropping (DPMC 2016). It won the supreme accolade at both the New Zealand Planning Institute Awards and the Local Government Management Awards in 2017, reflecting the quality of the engagement process (Waimakariri District Council 2017).

Waimakariri therefore had an approved red zone plan before the start of any officially sanctioned consultation on the future of the Ōtākaro Avon corridor. This is partly accounted for by the difference in scale as the corridor is six times the size of the Kaiapoi red zones. It is also four times bigger than the city's central open space, Hagley Park, and twice the size of Manhattan's Central Park. It did not become an active focus of attention until Regenerate Christchurch was created under the Greater Christchurch Regeneration Act 2016, and then as a joint Crown-council agency. Regenerate's brief was to produce a spatial plan, working collaboratively whilst engaging and advocating 'effectively with communities and stakeholders' (Regenerate Christchurch 2021). There was however one special case inserted in the letter of instruction to the new agency by Minister Brownlee and the Mayor, Lianne Dalziel.

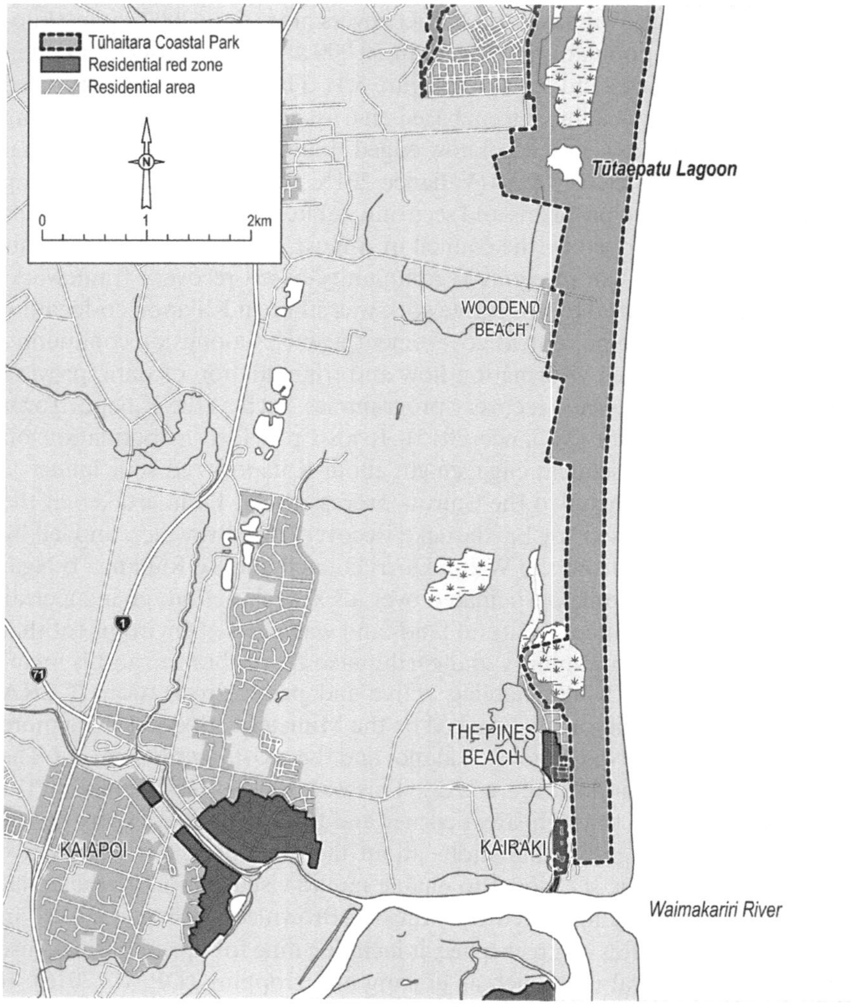

Figure 12.2 Kaiapoi red zones and the Tūhaitara Coastal Park.

Source: Adapted from Figure 12.1 and Pawson et al. (2019, 9).

This required that the East Lake Trust's proposal for a water sports facility of international standard be investigated (Brownlee and Dalziel 2016), the project having been a favourite of the Minister and his networks for some time (Stylianou 2016).

The design and engagement process that was implemented from late 2016 followed interwoven phases of technical analysis, community needs assessments, advisory group review and public exhibitions. Visioning and research events were used to develop an overarching vision, values and objectives. A design challenge was held, in which teams of people, half of them aged under 25, developed ten design options. These were put out for public consultation and shortlisted. Both the options and the shortlist were subject to the process of integrated assessment by a team of 50 people, drawn from a cross-section of community interests (Orchard 2017). The public exhibition of the final draft plan, held in the city centre over a three week period in late 2018, generated considerable interest, not least as it seemed to promise something. But a spatial design process offered nothing to project proponents other than a framework into which they might eventually fit, thereby prolonging the years of non-decision making. One proponent, a white water sports trust, shifted its interest to the Kaiapoi red zone. The East Lake Trust was also disappointed. Its proposal was deemed to be too environmentally risky, too likely to foreclose other options, and too expensive: despite this group using its intellectual capital to appeal the decision, unsuccessfully, to the Ombudsman (2018).

The Ōtākaro Avon River Regeneration Plan was finally approved by the Labour-led government's Minister for Greater Christchurch Regeneration in 2019. The chair of Regenerate Christchurch wrote in the foreword that the Ōtākaro Avon corridor 'represents a transformational opportunity of local, regional and national significance' (Regenerate Christchurch 2019, 6), balancing 'the needs and aspirations of current and future generations, iwi, and the wider public and private sectors'. Its seven objectives reflect the four well-beings. Both cultural and educational values are highlighted, for example, in the intent to provide 'a restored native habitat with good quality water so there is an abundant source of mahinga kai, birdlife and native species' and with the desire to establish 'a world-leading living laboratory' for experimentation and research. The plan sets out a continuous 345-hectare publicly accessible 'green spine' along the river from the city centre to the estuary. This will provide reafforested areas of native bush and wetland, the latter acting as retention basins as part of a city-wide flood management strategy. The spine is supplemented by three 'reaches' of additional land, that could accommodate project proposals and community spaces (Figure 12.3). If this map is performative, at least it leaves space for progressive engagements.

Experiments in governance

Such space was long to prove elusive. Nine years elapsed between the start of the earthquakes and the approval of the Ōtākaro Avon River Regeneration Plan; the Kaiapoi plan took six. Even then, there was no obvious way forward for those wishing to take advantage of this 'transformational opportunity'. The production of both plans had illustrated how public engagement in decision-making for recovery can work (Vallance 2015). In the case of Kaiapoi, this drew on prior post-earthquake experience encapsulated in 'the Waimakariri Way'. In the Ōtākaro Avon river corridor, it was developed from scratch by the new regeneration agency. Consultation and engagement, however, is one thing; action and implementation is another. In both cases, substantive change on the ground has been slow to materialise. This reflects uncertainties over responsibilities, land ownership and finance. As the chair

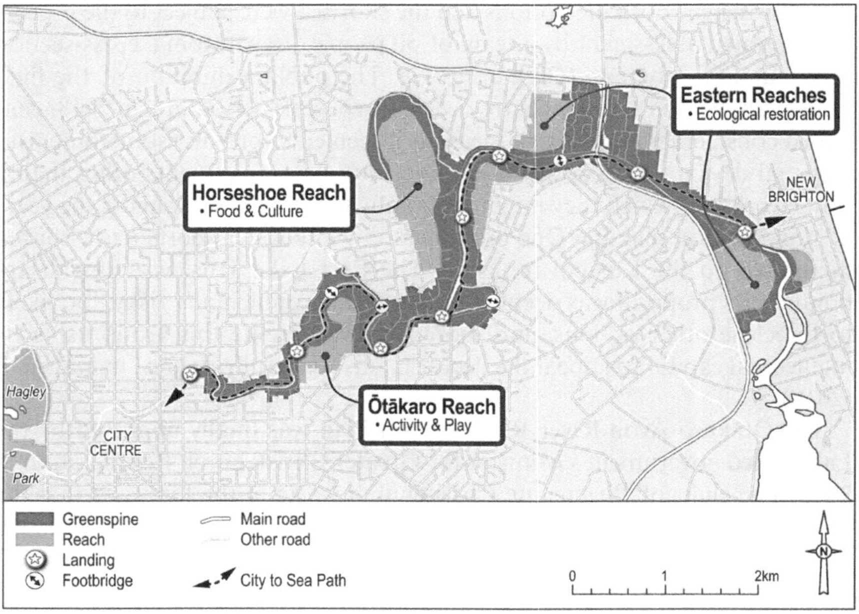

Figure 12.3 The Ōtākaro Avon River Corridor greenprint.

Source: Adapted from Regenerate Christchurch (2019, 48–9).

of Regenerate Christchurch wrote in the foreword to the draft Ōtākaro Avon regeneration plan, governance and accountability matters still needed to be decided, along with ownership of the land and funding commitments (in Regenerate Christchurch 2018b, 6). Significantly, this drew attention to the crucial issue of governance far more directly than the equivalent and anodyne text in the final Ministerially approved version (Regenerate Christchurch 2019).

Governance was more readily resolved – at least on the surface – in Kaiapoi. The ministerial foreword to the Waimakariri Residential Red Zone Recovery Plan stated that the Crown agreed to divest the land with this, in his words, 'underlin[ing] the Crown's ongoing commitment to a strong and resilient greater Christchurch' (DPMC 2016, 2). But there was no commitment to funding the implementation of the plan beyond this. There was however an agreement that the bulk of the land would be vested in the Waimakariri District Council, with five hectares of The Pines Beach and Kairaki coastal regeneration areas going to Te Kōhaka o Tūhaitara Trust. This Trust had been established under a 1998 Act of Parliament to manage an 800-hectare coastal park based on ecological, conservation and cultural values, and to uphold the mana of Ngāi Tahu by protecting and enhancing the environmental attributes of Tūtaepatu Lagoon (Figure 12.2). The Trust board comprises six trustees, three appointed by the Waimakariri council and three by Te Rūnanga o Ngāi Tahu (Pawson et al. 2019). As a working example of co-governance (Auditor-General 2016), the prior existence of the Trust enabled the divestment process to be completed in accordance with the Crown's treaty obligations under the Ngāi Tahu Claims Settlement Act 1998.

The situation was more complex in the Ōtākaro Avon corridor, not least because the partners in Regenerate Christchurch, the Crown and the city council, required that the plan omit specific recommendations about land ownership, future finance or governance. In effect this moved the critical implementation phase into a post-political cul-de-sac, hence the chair's statement about accountability noted above. The omission was not because work on these essential themes had not been done, although the need for agreement on them was noted on only one page of an 80-page document. The draft plan also observed that 'Direction about how the governance arrangements will incorporate the Treaty relationship will be provided by the Crown and Council' (Regenerate Christchurch 2018b, 63). Direction was however complicated by the shift in relationship between those two entities as a result of a change in central government in late 2017. The Labour-led administration that succeeded National's centre-right coalition that had been in power since 2008 made various electoral promises to post-earthquake Christchurch. These included a $300 million 'capital acceleration facility' to be spent on recovery as the city council determined, but within which were monies for the red zones.

The new government also signalled its desire to move to locally led regeneration in the city, the negotiation of which took time. The 'Global Settlement Agreement was signed in September 2019 between the Crown and Christchurch City Council to 'assist in the transition away from an extraordinary Crown presence in Christchurch and towards a normalised relationship with the Council' (DPMC 2019, 1). The two parties agreed on final cost shares and ownership of the anchor projects in the central city, as well as Crown divestment of red zone lands to the council. Responsibility for the management of those lands passed to the city council on 1 July 2020, and soon after the CERA-era fences began to come down. Divestment however was delayed for over two years more whilst Land Information New Zealand worked to amalgamate the mass of individual land titles and easements into tranches for transfer. A consultative group, Te Tira Kāhikuhiku, was established as an interim measure to advise the council and Land Information New Zealand on short-term transitional developments in the city's red zones. 'Short-term' meant for five years or less, which was of little use to those promoting longer-term initiatives, or requiring some security that their efforts would not be in vain.

The Global Settlement Agreement (2019, 7) recognised the role of Ngāi Tahu as Treaty partner, expecting that the city council would 'include Ngāi Tahu representation alongside other community representatives in … longer-term governance arrangements'. In practice, such representation is with Ngāi Tūāhuriri, the Ngāi Tahu hapū, or sub-tribe, that exercises cultural and customary authority in the river corridor. In the post-political vacuum that prevailed in the aftermath of the draft plan's appearance, a university-sponsored symposium for parties from interested agencies and groups had been held in May 2019 to discuss how such arrangements might be shaped. A follow-up analysis concluded that 'co-governance with mana whenua is a proven and essential model in the post-Treaty settlement era' (Pawson et al. 2019, 4). In Kaiapoi, this had been resolved by making use of the prior existence of the Tūhaitara Trust, although this did not provide for co-governance of the whole Kaiapoi red zone lands. Tūhaitara is however an example of a trust-based model, in which governance experience is shared between community and mana whenua. The long history of community engagement in the Ōtākaro Avon corridor had also generated anticipation of community involvement.

It was more than two years before governance discussions there were furthered when, under some community pressure, the mayor and upoko (head) of Ngāi Tūāhuriri sought advice from the previous government's Minister of Treaty Negotiations, Christopher Finlayson, who had nine years' experience of negotiating co-governance agreements. Co-governance extends greater participation in environmental decision-making to Māori, in recognition of their status as treaty partners (Finlayson and Christmas 2021). The advice proffered a spectrum of options drawing on cases already in operation. At the strong end of this spectrum are those that use the concept of legal personality (Morris and Ruru 2010) to recognise indigenous people's relationships with natural features and resources, notably Te Urewera and the Whanganui River in the North Island (Sanders 2018). Another example is the Waikato River Authority that exercises significant regulatory power over that river. At the weaker end of the spectrum are advisory bodies such as the Manawatu River Advisory Board, whose role is to offer advice to local government. The recommendation was for an entity in the middle of the spectrum, established as an independent board and likely under an Act of Parliament (Finlayson 2021).

In December 2021, the Christchurch City Council confirmed the intent to establish such a co-governance entity, followed in April 2022 by an agreement to set up a co-governance establishment committee to provide advice to the council and Ngāi Tūāhuriri 'on the development of the enduring co-governance entity/framework' for the river corridor (Christchurch City Council 2022b). Such an entity depends on building the relationships necessary for its effective function, a process that takes time, commitment and development of mutual trust (Auditor-General 2016). It will also require resourcing. The council's Long Term Plan for the period 2021–31 relied on an allocation of $40 million from the capital acceleration facility to start planting of the green spine, along with half that again from the Christchurch Earthquake Appeal Trust to commence recreational facilities such as pedestrian bridges and landings, initiated by the Parks Department with negligible community input. The Annual Plan for 2022–23 signalled council's commitment to delivery of the river corridor as an intergenerational project with an additional $20 million, as well as a river corridor activity plan intended to combine a range of council workstreams into a co-ordinated whole (Christchurch City Council 2022c).

How these council workstreams engage with the co-governance entity and the community remains to be seen. If a 'key dimension of prefigurative politics has been its commitment to action' (Jeffrey and Dyson 2021, 346), conditions to date have not been auspicious. Land Information New Zealand – still the landholder for the Crown – has required an arduous process of short-term licencing for any community initiative, and Te Tira Kāhikuhiku has had little money to assist these. Life in Vacant Spaces has facilitated some projects in a small block of the Burwood red zone. The Avon Ōtākaro Forest Park has managed to foster and extend modest areas of native planting with official permission. For comparison, in the Kaiapoi red zones, there is also little evidence of prefigurative actions on the ground, and the community enthusiasm of 'the Waimakariri Way' has been superseded by standard council park management initiatives. If the Ōtākaro Avon river corridor however is to be an engaging intergenerational project, means of facilitating the 'future in the present' remain to be negotiated. Regenerate Christchurch, which was disbanded in 2020, was therefore prescient in its concern about 'who will govern and have accountability for realising' the plan.

Christchurch futures

What then can be said about the potential of the river corridor as the city's 'field of dreams'? Whilst continuous delay has stalled projects and de-energised all but the most committed of activists, steps taken to date point to some potentially progressive outcomes. Four are considered here in terms of the corridor as a 50 or 100-year legacy project. The first is the commitment to co-governance, and what this may mean in terms of restoring mana whenua, or cultural and customary authority, to Ngāi Tūāhuriri. Their loss of access to the land and water resources of the corridor which occurred with colonisation and suburbanisation in the mid- to late-nineteenth century puts the last decade of inaction on the ground into perspective. During that time, the hapū's Matapopore Trust has completed a Cultural Design Strategy for the river. It observes that the areas of significance to Ngāi Tūāhuriri are in many cases those most affected by the 2011 earthquakes. Due to their 'low-lying, watery nature', these were rich in mahinga kai. This term 'quite literally means to work (mahi) the food (ngā kai), and refers to the seasonal migration of people to key food gathering areas to gather and prepare food to sustain them through the year' (Matapopore Trust 2017, 17–18).

One opportunity to be opened up by red zoning is therefore active restoration of indigenous values in the landscape. The Trust was established to provide cultural advice on Ngāi Tūāhuriri/Ngāi Tahu values, narratives and aspirations, and ways of weaving these into post-earthquake recovery projects. An example is the map (Figure 12.4) which highlights indigenous names and features in the Ōtākaro Avon corridor. The significance of water is clear: it is 'wāhi taonga, a treasured gift and is the life force of Papatūānuku' (Matapopore 2017, 17). Water provided the main source of sustenance and play, and determined the location of kāika (settlements), as well as being a

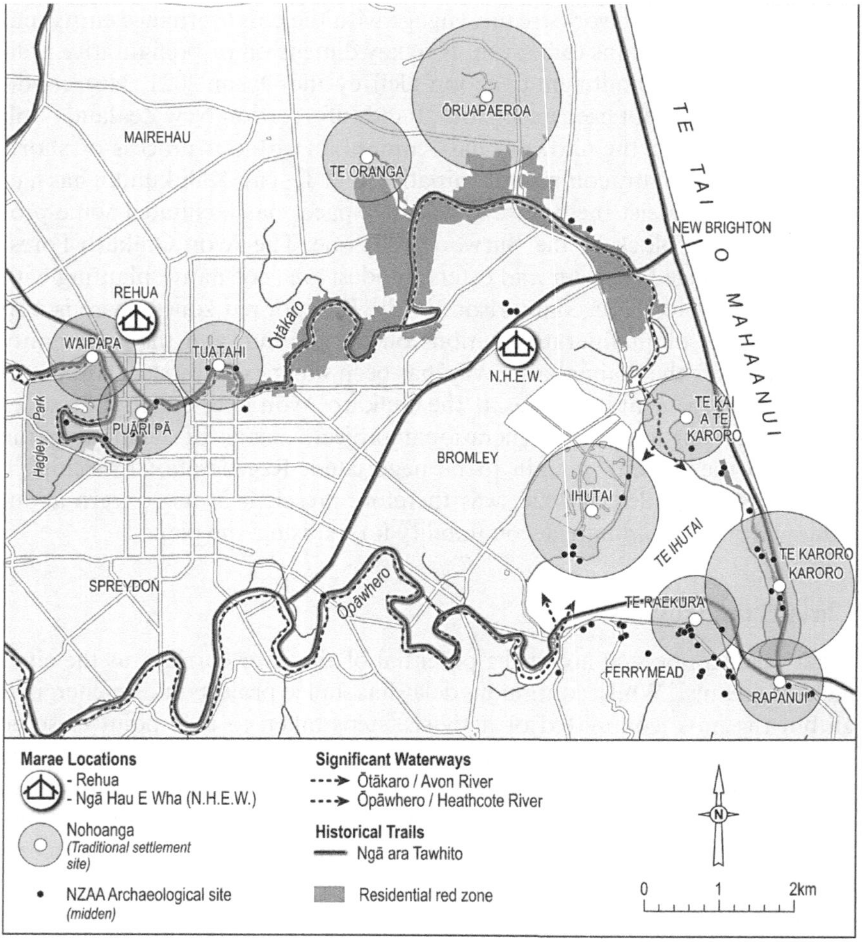

Figure 12.4 Features of significance to mana whenua.

Source: Adapted from Regenerate Christchurch (2019, 15).

medium of travel. It is the basis of the places, philosophies and practices of mahinga kai. This is more than a matter of historical memory. Section 6 of the Te Rūnanga o Ngāi Tahu Act 1996 mandates the rūnanga (tribal council) to protect the beneficial interests of all members of Ngāi Tahu as the Treaty partner. In terms of post-earthquake legislation, this includes an active role in the governance of recovery (Chapter 4). Whilst co-governance in this context has generated little community comment, or indeed debate at council level, the implications of adoption of such arrangements in broader spheres of government policy is now drawing wider public scrutiny (eg. Salmond 2021).

A second potentially progressive outcome from the former residential red zone is the provision of a more ‘restorative city’. Although this concept is commonly used to describe urban design for mental health and well-being (Roe and McCay 2021), it can be extended in this context to include cultural well-being. The adoption of co-governance, above, is a partial recognition of the reclamation 'of the right of Indigenous peoples to once again govern themselves in their own lands' (Jackson 2021, 135). The plan for ecological restoration, encapsulated in the greenprint (Figure 12.2), likewise respects the red zone memories of former residents whose concerns were central to the foundation of the Avon Ōtākaro Network. In both contexts, 'restorative' implies respect for cultural and social belonging and inclusion. It also captures the central importance to prosperity and well-being of human health and the vitality of the more-than-human world on which people depend. This is explicitly recognised in the three pillars of the Avon Ōtākaro Forest Park concept, which pictures the interdependence of the corridor's blue and green ecosystems with local communities. Features like clean air and water, biodiversity and restored habitat provide the means for the delivery of health benefits and community engagement as well as opportunities for active and passive recreation (Avon Ōtākaro Forest Park 2022).

Restorative benefits can be delivered through use values but are likely to be multiplied if citizens and community groups can participate actively in their delivery and management. Just as co-governance is an active alternative to the standard model of local government authority, so too are means that open improvisational opportunities for citizen action. One sphere in which this is becoming widely practised in urban and rural New Zealand is community management of predator control to foster survival of native fauna (Burge et al. 2021). This will also be required throughout the river corridor to restore biodiversity. A potential flagship project in this respect, introduced in Chapter 11, is a long-delayed proposal to use part of the Burwood red zone and adjacent existing reserve of Travis wetland as a fenced eco-sanctuary as a safe haven in which native species can breed, and from which they can disperse more widely in the city (Waitākiri Eco-sanctuary 2022). Such initiatives are consistent with the concept of 'anticipatory innovation governance', championed by the OECD, which describes continuous local adaptation and experimentation as means of addressing complex place-based problems as they emerge. This applies especially to those 'issues that are too complex or evolve too quickly for orthodox policy responses' (OECD 2021).

This points to a third area of progressive outcomes, that of climate change response. The Waimakariri Way and the comprehensive process of engagement undertaken by Regenerate Christchurch have already provided some invaluable civic experience in collaborative approaches towards resolving wicked problems. The policy of red zoning was developed in the first place as these earthquake-damaged lands are at heightened risk of climate-related inundation in coming decades. The process of community withdrawal has long been all but complete, as have formal processes of regeneration planning for the spaces opened up by retreat. Despite the time that has since elapsed, the opportunity now exists to build on the collaborative approaches that characterised the planning process to involve community partners in the implementation of the plans (Pawson 2022). When the politics of neoliberalism has widened inequalities and reduced trust in government internationally, there is a growing need for such deliberative governance processes that focus as much on process as on outcomes. These are well-suited to intricate situations characterised by value-driven dilemmas and long-term time horizons (OECD 2020).

Adaptation is inevitably place-specific and can only be shaped and implemented through local collaborations. When in 2015, the Christchurch City Council published technically sourced maps identifying thousands of properties at risk of coastal erosion or flooding, there was an outcry given the lack of local input (Peat 2018). Yet about the same time, the Parliamentary Commissioner for the Environment (2015) recommended that councils be provided with guidance on engaging with coastal communities and avoiding surprises. This is echoed by the Intergovernmental Panel on Climate Change Sixth Assessment Report on Impacts, Adaptation and Vulnerability (IPCC 2022). One of its drafting authors describes the prospects for 'climate-resilient development' for the 11 per cent of the world's population that live on low elevation coasts as 'dismal', with a 'coastal adaptation gap' that needs to be closed quickly. Again, among the key responses necessary are governance capabilities and facilitative participation (Glavovic 2022). The red-zoning process was hardly participatory but exists as a large-scale response from which other places can learn, and against which other vulnerable parts of the Christchurch coast might develop alternatives.

There is an element of experimentation about such responses, and this is the fourth area of potentially progressive outcomes. Co-governance itself, being place-specific and based on relationship building, is necessarily experimental. The co-governance entity will have to provide a secure and facilitative framework for even modest prefigurative initiatives to succeed, be these community gardens, art installations or culture trails. There is potential however to host more ambitious technical experimentation, in line with the objective of the plan to establish an Ōtākaro Living Laboratory (Chapter 11). An example is small-scale structural prototypes, for housing or recreational activity, designed to cope with rising waters (University of Washington 2020). A broader approach would ask what part could the red zone lands can play in research and development, as well as pilot and demonstration projects for climate security? Furthermore, how might an ongoing process of red zoning over time bring into being new types of urban form: in which progressively abandoned areas are transformed into green buffers to play protective and restorative roles in the city of the future (Gundermann 2014)?

If such ideas are to be shepherded, and citizen agency and prefigurative action is not to be frustrated, as it has been for much of the last decade, by a lack of support and facilitative governance, then boldness of vision will be required. This will not occur if the co-governance structure in prospect replicates the time-honoured bureaucratic model of contracting internally for local government delivery. In that case, the right to shape the city and the opportunity to experience it 'as an active verb' will be lost. Rather than risk mitigation, the red zones provide an opportunity for risk-taking, so that the enthusiasm of those who desire to engage with, contribute to and build new futures is supported, encouraged and valued. This is the essence of 'anticipatory innovation governance', without which any ambition to meet climate challenges, to build 'national park cities' or to use co-governance structures in moving towards sustainable lifestyles will be compromised.

Conclusion

One of the insights of comparative studies of earthquake recovery is it always takes time (Johnson and Olshansky 2017). This applies to conventional styles of centrally directed rebuilding, such as the anchor projects of the central city (Figure 4.4), as well as the more open-ended processes of planning in the former residential red zones. In Waimakariri District, the Kaiapoi red zone recovery plan built on a solid record of community engagement and was approved relatively soon in the recovery process, in 2016. That was the year that Regenerate Christchurch was set up to initiate a process of engagement that three years later produced an approved Ōtākaro Avon regeneration plan. Even then, slow progress towards securing long-term governance has forestalled the prospect of the corridor as 'a field of dreams' and work on the ground has been slow. That however is only one perspective. In contrast, for Ngāi Tahu and Ngāi Tūāhuriri, the opportunity to create an effective model of co-governance, in recognition of their own memories in the landscape, is one that has been more than 150 years in the waiting.

Whether or not the red zones will become experiments in the twenty-first-century urbanism and adaptation to changing sea levels is therefore still an open question. Progress to date has been largely procedural, rather than substantive (Vallance 2015), but perhaps this is not an achievement to underestimate. Regenerate Christchurch was established to engage, advocate, work collaboratively and 'provide independent advice to decision makers' (Regenerate Christchurch 2021), in other words, to develop and practice forms of network governance after the state-led years of CERA. Potentially this – along with the 'Waimakariri Way' – has built capability and social capital that can be transferred to other contexts, to construct for example locally-rooted restorative, biodiversity and climate change strategies. With good governance, these can enable evolving relationships between people and place, and between the human and the more-than-human, as explored in the previous chapter. So experience in the red zones has already demonstrated that there are progressive ways of doing the urban, although it has also shown that this certainly takes time. Perhaps in time, it may also reclaim some of the international attention that the transitional movement garnered for the city in the wake of the quakes.

13 Conclusion

In this book, we have sought – as indicated in Chapter 1 – to 'provide a framework in which to assemble the multiple experiences and realities' of post-earthquake recovery in Christchurch. This concluding statement seeks to reiterate and summarise key aspects of that framework, using four broad themes. This is done in the spirit, also identified in Chapter 1, of distrusting 'singular meta-narratives and headline conclusions'. Accordingly, it is less a summary and more an identification of themes that have surprised and intrigued us in the course of our collaboration. These themes focus first, following Donna Haraway (2016), on 'staying with the trouble'; on second, Alain Badiou's (2005) contention that 'events' produce change based on both familiar outcomes and alternative potentials; on third, that post-disaster experiences are often quite divergent for different places and groups of people; and on fourth, the extent to which the city is now better prepared for what May Joseph (2013b, 3) has called an 'ecological future' in the twenty-first century.

The first thing this book has attempted to do is to pay attention to the human experience of post-earthquake recovery, rather than to identify too closely with the tidiness and optimism of planners and architects inherent in such artefacts as the 100-day blueprint. In this sense, we have adapted Donna Haraway's call (2016) to 'think-with, live-with and be-with' a city and citizenry still coming to terms with the rupture of earthquakes. This is a rupture that has been deeply felt experientially, economically, socially and culturally. As an event, the earthquake sequence has, as Matthew Galloway (2021, 276) puts it, 'exposed the façade of colonial narratives that have informed much of the city's history and identity'. The fate of the Anglican cathedral, which still lies in ruins although now under long-term repair, symbolises the perils of easy adoption of any post-earthquake narrative of progress. Yet it was the stylised cathedral spire, soaring into a blue sky above a carpet of green, that for many years before 2010 was used as a logo to symbolise Christchurch, 'the garden city'. The earthquakes therefore unleashed not only material destruction but also destruction of the city's idea of itself (Pickles 2016).

In this sense, to stay with the trouble is to be open to new possibilities, and to recognise and welcome into the present those human and more-than-human interests that were elided by the blue sky and green carpet. If Christchurch

DOI: 10.4324/9780429275562-16

was a proud colonial city, displaying in its nineteenth-century architecture the achievement of 'terraforming' and 'improvement' of the wetland 'swamps' on which it was planted, then the hazards of liquefaction and lateral spread have punctured any sense of stability. So too the experience of many businesses and householders trying to resolve insurance claims in a country where heavy levels of insurance had been presumed to provide confidence and security. In their place has come both uncertainty and opportunity. Halting pre-earthquake steps to engage with mana whenua have found far more impetus in the rebuild, and the swamp is now, through embracing blue-green spaces and corridors, experienced in more generative terms. It has proved hard however to manage the tensions between speed and deliberation in rebuilding. In a considered assessment of the experience of six countries, Johnson and Olshansky conclude that recovery from disasters is 'always complex, takes a very long time, and is never fast enough for affected residents' (2017, 329).

Our second theme concerns the nature of social change that follows the 'event' of a rupture such as the Canterbury earthquake sequence. Badiou (2005) characterises this in two overlapping ways: either through resort to familiar conduct managed in terms of dominant ideologies or through discovery of alternative actions that previously had been submerged or hidden. The 'overlap' is significant. The central city blueprint, for example, was shaped by the neoliberal state's desire for a quick and effective rebuild, designed to hold in place and attract business investment. Yet it drew on some of the key ideas that had emerged in the prior 'citizens' plan' for the centre, even if it did not continue to provide a place for deliberative engagement once approved. In this respect, the New Zealand government adopted 'one of the most visible governmental responses to disaster', with the creation by legislation of a new agency to act as a focal point for recovery and to protect its own interests (Johnson and Olshansky 2017, 314). Yet this too must be qualified. The Canterbury Earthquake Recovery Act of 2011 was time limited to five years, after which it was replaced by the Greater Christchurch Regeneration Act, which attempted to share greater responsibility between the Crown and local interests. In turn, the growing desire for this shift saw key aspects of the Regeneration Act itself rendered redundant before it had run its own five-year term.

Badiou's observation is also relevant in a deeper sense. Much of the Christchurch rebuild has been shaped by path dependency. There was never a serious question that the city centre would be rebuilt in the same place, despite the instability and hazards of the site. Yet at the same time, post-earthquake planning instruments have exacerbated a long-run tendency towards urban sprawl in terms of greenfield development, notably in the south-west of the city and in satellite towns in the wider urban region. The Crown has invested simultaneously in an expensive city centre blueprint whilst underwriting a new motorway system that fuels the greenfields. In these ways, post-earthquake Christchurch has often been criticised for reproducing the attributes of twentieth-century cities, whilst foregoing the opportunities to embrace new forms of twenty-first-century urbanism (Pawson 2022). It is seen as not delivering on the promise of the immediate post-quake years, when the transitional movement, driven informally by younger people in the arts and education (eg. Gap Filler, the Student Volunteer Army) as well as some in business (eg. the container mall) earned the city a reputation as a place to watch. Paradoxically, however, it may be that the city's new (but largely traditional) landscapes of consumption provide many of its inhabitants with exactly what they need for a return to familiar ways.

This claim intersects with our third theme: that post-earthquake experiences have been quite variable and at times divergent for different places and groups of people. Maybe in one sense Fiona Farrell (2015, 70) was correct when she wrote that 'An earthquake is the most egalitarian of disasters. It strikes an entire region in one blow'. After all, most of the city's brick chimneys were destroyed or damaged in the early hours of 4 September 2010 when the earthquake sequence began (Figure 2.3). But many other maps in this book show sharply different experiences. Housing was particularly badly affected in the eastern parts of the city due to the spatial incidence of liquefaction, and places in the east, in coastal areas and on the hills, were so impacted as to be red-zoned. The well-being of people with few resources to manage recovery has been particularly shaped by insurance battles that lasted for years for some households. In turn, this led to the creation of effective networks of resident activism, forcing a response from state institutions. Likewise, protest and mobilisation in the eastern suburbs have ensured investment in new schools and recreational facilities; in this respect, the city council has been more responsive to need on the ground than government in Wellington often proved to be. This illustrates one of Johnson and Olshansky's (2017, 326) key recommendations for recovery, that 'National governments are important sources of money, technical support, guidance and oversight, but local governments are best suited to implement recovery and devise actions appropriate to their needs'.

The conflict between central government direction and local needs and actions has been highlighted in another aspect of the Christchurch experience. The central city blueprint was in part a product of the Crown's concern that without a massive input of its own resources in the form of investment in anchor projects (albeit shared with the city council) and its ability to force land title amalgamations, then business investment would be lost to other centres and any international interest in commercial property redevelopment would evaporate. Yet the post-earthquake rebuild attracted little international interest anyway, with much of it being financed by local property investors turned developers drawing on insurance pay-outs and their own resources. Their motives rather than being shaped by the economically rational alone have reflected the more affective quality of emotional connection with their home town. Ironically, the blueprint's intention that the anchor projects would lead the rebuild, providing a framework within which business investment would be secured, also transpired to be in error. Rather local property investment has often come first, with many of the key anchor projects being delayed for years. Some have yet to be finished, leading to difficult resource allocation decisions a dozen or more years on from 2010–11.

Our final point concerns whether the post-earthquake city is now better placed to meet the challenges of the twenty-first century than it would otherwise have been. There is no easy answer to this, but if the city is a 'petri dish', in which 'the laboratory is humming, and the great experiment' is underway (Farrell 2015, 323), then what are the indications? It is easy to be critical. The path-dependent re-shaping of the city has baked in the very twentieth-century attributes of a suburbanised and auto-dependent suburban landscape that internationally have produced carbon-intensive ways of life. Some of the city's key anchor projects do too, being reliant on earlier expectations about levels of international tourism. Te Pae, the massive downtown convention centre, with its global pretentions, and Te Kaha, the as-yet unfinished 'multi-use arena', are perhaps the ultimate expressions of what might be called a pre-Covid, carbon agnostic mindset. At the same time, the blueprint has delivered a re-imagined city centre that is more amenable to both pedestrians and cyclists, and the whole urban area is now criss-crossed by cycle paths that provide the essential infrastructure for alternative mobilities, even if these have as yet made little difference to mode shares.

But perhaps the real gains in terms of readiness for a post-earthquake, climate-challenged future lie elsewhere. If the often criticised top-down approach to recovery gave little acknowledgement to the work of post-earthquake transitional organisations, the transitional movement nevertheless unleashed enthusiasm for collective and inclusive ways of working. Arguably the legacy of this has been the creation of new political spaces of hope and action that have been echoed in many arenas such as resident activism, new forms of voluntarism and care, and experiments in community engagement. We have identified many very real examples of what Rebecca Solnit (2009) called 'the extraordinary communities that arise in disaster'. Many of these initiatives have been supported by novel or experimental governance arrangements: new ideas and ways of being in the city are negotiated and grounded in changing forms of governance. The collaborative process that produced the pre-earthquake Urban Development Strategy, for example, provided some direction for its post-earthquake recovery. Experiments in co-governance elsewhere have informed a strategy for the delivery of future options for the residential red zone. And citizen experience of many forms of activism and deliberation may yet prove to be invaluable as the city navigates the emerging uncertainties of climate change and sea level rise from now on.

References

ACTIS (2022). Aranui Community Trust Incorporated Society. Retrieved from: https://actis.org.nz

Adams-Hutcheson, G. (2015). Voices from the margins of recovery: Relocated Cantabrians in Waikato, *Kōtuitui: New Zealand Journal of Social Sciences Online* 10 (2), 135–43.

Adger, W.N. (2000). Social and ecological resilience: Are they related? *Progress in Human Geography* 24 (3), 347–64.

Adger, W.N. (2006). Vulnerability, *Global Environmental Change* 16, 268–81.

Aiken, G. (2012). Community transitions to low carbon futures in the transition towns network (TTN), *Geography Compass* 6 (2), 89–99.

Allot, A. (2021). Suspected dog attack causes 500 critically endangered gulls to abandon nests, *Stuff*, 23 November. Retrieved from: www.stuff.co.nz/environment/127069075/suspected-dog-attack

Amin, A. (2013). Surviving the turbulent future, *Environment and Planning D: Society and Space* 31 (1), 140–56.

Amore, A., Hall, C.M. and Jenkins, J. (2017). They never said 'Come here and let's talk about it'. Exclusion and non-decision-making in the rebuild of Christchurch, New Zealand, *Local Economy* 32 (7), 617–39.

Andersen, C. and McLellan, W. (2014). An EPIC view of innovation, in B. Bennett, J. Dann, E. Johnson and R. Reynolds eds., *Once in a Lifetime. City-building after Disaster in Christchurch*. Freerange Press, Christchurch, 362–5.

Anderson, S., Bennett, M., Birdling, M. et al. (2010). Academics call for rethink over earthquake law, *Stuff*, 28 September. Retrieved from: www.stuff.co.nz/the-press/news/christchurch-earthquake-2011/canterbury-earthquake-2010/4174748/Academics-call-for-rethink-over-earthquake-law

Anderson, V. (2012). 'Ministry' created to 'water the seeds of awesome', *Stuff*, 15 June. Retrieved from: www.stuff.co.nz/the-press/news/7106627/Ministry-created-to-water-the-seeds-of-awesome

Ansell, C. and Gash, A. (2008). Collaborative governance in theory and practice, *Journal of Public Administration Research and Theory* 18 (1), 543–71.

Ansley, B. (2011). *Christchurch Heritage. A Celebration of Lost Buildings and Streetscapes*. Random House, Auckland.

Anthony, J. (2021). Battle of the convention centres, *Stuff*, August 1. Retrieved from: www.stuff.co.nz/business/industries/125861975/battle-of-the-convention-centres-three-new-venues-worth-14b-provide-onceinalifetime-opportunity

Ardagh, M. and Deely, J. (2018). *Rising from the Rubble. The Health System's Extraordinary Response to the Canterbury Earthquakes.* Canterbury University Press, Christchurch.

Arnouts, R., van der Zouwen, M. and Arts, B. (2012). Analysing governance modes and shifts – governance arrangements in Dutch nature policy, *Forest Policy and Economics* 16, 43–50.

Atkinson, B., Baxter, S., Ver Berkmoes, R., Bindloss, J. and Blasi, A. (2013). *Lonely Planet's Best in Travel 2013.* Lonely Planet Publications, Hawthorn.

Auditor-General (2016). *Principles for Effectively Co-governing Natural Resources.* Presented to the House of Representatives under section 20 of the Public Audit Act 2001.

AvON (2022). Our history of achievements. Avon Ōtākaro Network. Retrieved from: http://www.avonotakaronetwork.co.nz/about-us/history-of-achievements.html

Avon-Heathcote Estuary Ihutai Trust (2022). Our objectives. Retrieved from: www.estuary.org.nz/about/the-trust.html

Avon Otakaro Forest Park (2022). A forest park vision for the Christchurch red zone. Retrieved from: www.aofp.co.nz/our-plan

Badiou, A. (2005). *Being and the Event.* Continuum, London.

Baker, T. and McGuirk, P. (2021). Out from the shadows? Voluntary organisations and the assembled state, *Environment and Planning C, Politics and Space* 39 (7), 1338–55.

Ballard, S., Benson, T., Carter, R., Corballis, T., Joyce, Z., Moore, H., Priest, J. and Smith, V. (2015). *A Transitional Imaginary. Space, Network and Memory in Christchurch.* Harvest, Christchurch.

Barclay, C. (2021). Christchurch's $1 million suburb club expands as housing bonanza continues, *Otago Daily Times*, 3 April. Retrieved from: www.odt.co.nz/star-news/star-lifestyle/star-home-and-gardening/christchurchs-1-million-suburb-club-expands-housing

Bassett, K. (2008). Thinking the event: Badiou's philosophy of the event and the example of the Paris Commune, *Environment and Planning D: Society and Space* 26 (5), 895–910.

Bayer, K. (2012). Christchurch schools confront confusion, *New Zealand Herald*, 14 September. Retrieved from: www.nzherald.co.nz/nz/christchurch-schools-confront-confusion/GJLJUXAELMF3SBHAZLKXTWWAXA/

Bayer, K. (2017). Aftershock: The debacle of shoddy Christchurch earthquake repairs, *New Zealand Herald*, 3 September. Retrieved from: www.nzherald.co.nz/nz/aftershock-the-debacle-of-shoddy-christchurch-earthquake-repairs/LEA5ARBI32NIQPB6MRSJHDF4OQ/

Beaglehole, B., Mulder, R.T., Boden, J.M. and Bell, C.J. (2019). A systematic review of the psychological impacts of the Canterbury earthquakes on mental health, *Australian and New Zealand Journal of Public Health* 43 (3), 274–80.

Beauregard, R.A. (2020). *Advanced Introduction to Planning Theory.* Edward Elgar, Cheltenham.

Bednar, D., Henstra, D. and McBean, G. (2019). The governance of climate change adaptation: Are networks to blame for the implementation deficit? *Journal of Environmental Policy and Planning* 21 (6), 702–17.

Begg, A., D'Aeth, L., Kenagy, E., Ambrose, C., Dong, H. and Schluter, P.J. (2021). Wellbeing recovery inequity following the 2010/2011 Canterbury earthquake sequence: Repeated cross-sectional studies, *Australian and New Zealand Journal of Public Health* 45 (2), 158–64.

Bennett, B. (2016). Interview with Barnaby Bennett, in M. Lesniak, Rebuilding/Reimagining, Post-disaster Christchurch. Unpublished Masters Altevilles dissertation, University of Lyon, Lyon, 151–60.

Bennett, B., Boidi, E. and Boles, I. eds. (2012). *Christchurch. The Transitional City Pt IV*. Freerange Press, Christchurch.

Bennett, B., Dann, J., Johnson, E. and Reynolds, R. eds. (2014a). *Once in a Lifetime. City-building after Disaster in Christchurch*. Freerange Press, Christchurch.

Bennett, B., Dann, J., Johnson, E. and Reynolds, R. (2014b). Conclusion, in B. Bennett, J. Dann, E. Johnson and R. Reynolds eds., *Once in a Lifetime: City-building after Disaster in Christchurch*. Free Range Press, Christchurch, 478–80.

Bennett, J. (2010). Ontology, sensibility and action, *Contemporary Political Theory* 14 (1), 82–9.

Berke, P., Backhurst, M., Day, M., Ericksen, N., Laurian, L., Crawford, J. and Dixon, J. (2006). What makes plan implementation successful? An evaluation of local plans and implementation practices in New Zealand, *Environment and Planning B: Planning and Design* 33 (4), 581–600.

Beuys, J. and Harlon, V. (2004). *What is Art? Conversation with Joseph Beuys*. Clairview, Forest Row.

Blaikie, P., Cannon, T., Davis, I. and Wisner, B. (1994). *At Risk. Natural Hazards, People's Vulnerability, and Disasters*. Routledge, London.

Blair, M.J. and Mabee, W.E. (2020). Resilience, in A. Kobayashi ed., *International Encyclopedia of Human Geography*, 2nd edn., Elsevier, Amsterdam, 11, 451–56.

Blundell, S. (2006). Down at the mall, *New Zealand Geographic* 77, 37–53.

Blundell, S. (2021). A tale of two churches, *North & South*, February, 48–57.

Boffa Miskell Limited (2020). *RRZ Pest Animal Surveys 2020: Biosecurity Assessment Report*. Report prepared for Land Information New Zealand.

Bohan, E. (2022). *Heart of the City. The Story of Christchurch's Controversial Cathedral*. Quentin Wilson Publishing, Christchurch.

Borella, J., Quigley, M., Riley, M., Trutner, S., Jol, H., Borella, M., Hampton, S. and Gravley, D. (2020). Influence of anthropogenic landscape modifications and infrastructure on the geologic characteristics of liquefaction, *Anthropocene* 29, 100235.

Boshier, P. (2017). *Disclosure: An Investigation into the Ministry of Education's Engagement Processes for School Closures and Mergers*, New Zealand Parliament. Retrieved from: www.ombudsman.parliament.nz/sites/default/files/2019-03/Disclosure.pdf

Boston, J. (1995). *The State under Contract*. Bridget Williams, Wellington.

Boston, J. (2017). *Safeguarding the Future. Governing in an Uncertain World*. Bridget Williams Books, Wellington.

Boston, J., St. John, S. and Dalziel, P. (1999). *Redesigning the Welfare State in New Zealand. Problems, Policies, Prospects*. Oxford University Press, Oxford.

Boswell, R. (2021). Play, politics and the production of space: DIY urbanism in post-earthquake Christchurch. Unpublished PhD thesis, University of Auckland, Auckland.

Bowring, J. (2021). Tree sense of place, in S. Goldsmith ed., *Tree Sense. Ways of Thinking about Trees*. Massey University Press, Auckland, 105–21.

Bowron, J. (2019). Christchurch squatters see the beauty of the city with a gap-toothed smile, *Stuff*, 18 July. Retrieved from: www.stuff.co.nz/the-press/news/christchurch-earthquake-2011/117263021/christchurch-squatters-see-the-beauty-of-the-city-with-a-gap-toothed-smile

Brand, D., Allen, N. and O'Donnell, G. (2020). The New Zealand experience of a design-led approach to post-earthquake recovery in Christchurch, *Urban Studies and Public Administration* 3 (3), 89–115.

Brandes Gratz, R. (2015). *We're Still Here Ya Bastards: How the People of New Orleans Rebuilt Their City*. Nation Books, New York.

Breakthrough Facilitation (2019). Breakthrough Facilitation Facebook page. Retrieved from: www.facebook.com/breakthroughfacilitation/

Brenner, N. and Theodore, N. (2002). Cities and the geographies of 'actually existing neoliberalism', *Antipode* 34 (3), 349–79.

Brown, T. (2009). *Change by Design: How Design Thinking Transforms Organizations and Inspires Innovation*. HarperCollins, New York.

Brown, C., Seville, E. and Vargo, J. (2013). *The Role of Insurance in Organisational Recovery Following the 2010 and 2011 Canterbury Earthquakes*. Resilient Organisations, University of Canterbury, Christchurch.

Brownlee, G. (2016). Third reading, Greater Christchurch Regeneration Bill, *Hansard*, 31 March. Retrieved from: www.parliament.nz/en/pb/hansard-debates/rhr/document/51HansD_20160331_00000012/greater-christchurch-regeneration-bill-third-reading

Brownlee, G. and Dalziel, L. (2016). Letter of expectations for Regenerate Christchurch, 14 April. Retrieved from: www.regeneratechristchurch.nz/assets/Uploads/regenerate-christchurch-letter-of-expectations-14-april-2016.pdf

Buchanan, A.H., Carradine, D., Beattie, G. and Morris, H. (2011). Performance of houses during the Christchurch earthquake of 22 February 2011, *Bulletin of the New Zealand Society for Earthquake Engineering* 44 (4), 342–57.

Buchanan, A.H. and Newcombe, M.P. (2010). Performance of residential houses in the Darfield (Canterbury) earthquake, *Bulletin of the New Zealand Society for Earthquake Engineering* 43 (4), 387–92.

Bulkeley, H., Coenen, L., Frantzeskaki, N., Hartmann, C., Kronsell, A., Mai, L., Marvin, S., McCormick, K., van Steenbergen, F. and Palgan, Y.V. (2016). Urban living labs: Governing urban sustainability transitions, *Current Opinion in Environmental Sustainability* 22, 13–17.

Bullard, R.D. (2018). *Race, Place, and Environmental Justice after Hurricane Katrina. Struggles to Reclaim, Rebuild, and Revitalize New Orleans and the Gulf Coast*. Routledge, New York.

Buller, H. (2014). Where the wild things are: The evolving iconography of rural fauna, *Journal of Rural Studies* 20, 131–41.

Bullock, C. (2014). *Quake Cats. Heart-warming Stories of Christchurch Cats*. Random House, Auckland.

Burge, O.R., Innes, J.G., Fitzgerald, N. Guo, J., Etherington, T.R. and Richardson, S.J. (2021). Assessing the habitat and functional connectivity around fenced eco-sanctuaries in New Zealand, *Biological Conservation* 253, 108896.

Burn, I. (2020). Personal communication, 17 March. Ian Burn was General Manager, Delta Community Support Trust.

CAE (1997). *Risks and Realities. A Multi-disciplinary Approach to the Vulnerability of Lifelines to Natural Hazards. Report of the Christchurch Engineering Lifelines Group*. Centre for Advanced Engineering, University of Canterbury, Christchurch.

Campagnolo, S. (2015). Personal communication, 5 March. Sarah Campagnolo was then project co-ordinator with Greening the Rubble.

Campbell, K.T. (2014). The Shaken Suburbs. The Changing Sense of Home and Creating a New Home after Disaster. Unpublished Master of Science thesis, University of Canterbury, Christchurch.

CanCERN (2014). CanCERN weekly newsletter #131, 27 June. Retrieved from: https://quakestudies.canterbury.ac.nz/store/object/216073

Canterbury District Health Board (2021). *Evaluation of the All Right? Campaign COVID-19 Response - Getting Through Together*. Retrieved from: www.cph.co.nz/wp-content/uploads/GTTEvaluationReport.pdf

Carlton, S. (2013). Share an idea, spare a thought: Community consultation in Christchurch's time-bound post-earthquake rebuild, *Journal of Human Rights in the Commonwealth* 2, 4–13.

Carlton, S. and Mills, C.E. (2017). The student volunteer army. A 'repeat emergent' emergency response organisation, *Disasters* 41 (4), 764–87.

Carlton, S., Nissen, S. and Wong, J.H.K. (2021). A crisis volunteer 'sleeper cell'. An emergent, extending and expanding disaster response organisation, *Journal of Contingencies and Crisis Management*. https://doi.org/10.1111/1468-5973.12381

Carlton, S., Nissen, S., Wong, J.H.K. and Johnson, S. (2022). 'A shovel or a shopping cart': Lessons from ten years of disaster response by a student-led volunteer group, *Natural Hazards* 111, 33–50.

Carlton, S. and Vallance, S. (2013). *An Inventory of Community-led and Non-governmental Organisations and Initiatives in Post-earthquake Canterbury*. Lincoln University, Canterbury. Retrieved from: https://communityresearch.org.nz/wp-content/uploads/formidable/Final-Inventory.pdf

Carlton, S. and Vallance, S. (2017). The commons of the tragedy: Temporary use and social capital in Christchurch's earthquake-damaged city, *Social Forces* 96 (2), 831–50.

Central City Recovery Plan (2012). *Central City Recovery Plan. Te Mahere 'Maraka Ōtautahi'*. Canterbury Earthquake Recovery Authority, Christchurch.

CERA (2011). Crown offer to residential insured property owners in the Canterbury earthquake affected red zones. Paper 1. Retrieved from: https://ceraarchive.dpmc.govt.nz/sites/default/files/Documents/cabinet-minute-choices-for-residents-redzone-crown-offers-july-2011.pdf

CERA (2013). Land Use Recovery Plan *Te Mahere Whakahaumanu Taone*: Summary. Canterbury Earthquake Recovery Authority, Christchurch.

CERA (2014). *Canvas. Your Thinking for the Red Zones. December 2014*. Canterbury Earthquake Recovery Authority, Christchurch.

Chang, S.E., Taylor, J.E., Elwood, K.J., Seville, E., Brunsdon, D. and Gartner, M. (2014). Urban disaster recovery in Christchurch: The central business district cordon and other critical decisions, *Earthquake Spectra* 30 (1), 513–32.

Chatterton, P. (2010). The urban impossible: A eulogy for the unfinished city, *City* 14 (3), 234–44.

Christchurch 360 Trail (2022). The future of the Christchurch 360. Retrieved from: http://christchurch360trail.org.nz/future/

Christchurch City Council (n.d.). Technical Category Information. Retrieved from: https://ccc.govt.nz/consents-and-licences/land-and-zoning/technical-categories-map

Christchurch City Council (2010a). *Christchurch City: Fact Pack 2010*. Strategy and Planning Group, Christchurch City Council, Christchurch. Retrieved from: www.ccc.govt.nz/assets/Documents/Culture-Community/Stats-and-facts-on-Christchurch/fact-packs/FactPack2010-docs.pdf

Christchurch City Council (2010b). *Intensification Community Research Report*. Strategy and Planning Group Community Support Unit, Christchurch, August.

Christchurch City Council (2011). *Central City Plan. Draft Central City Recovery Plan for Ministerial Approval December 2011*. Christchurch City Council, Christchurch.

Christchurch City Council (2013). Christchurch recovery and rebuild issues and challenges: Christchurch city three year plan. Retrieved from: http://resources.ccc.govt.nz/files/ltccp/TYP2013/Volume1/RecoveryRebuildChallenges2013.pdf

Christchurch City Council (2018). *Project 8011*. Retrieved from: https://ccc.govt.nz/culture-and-community/central-city-christchurch/live-here/residential-programme-8011/

Christchurch City Council (2020). Red zone land returns to local ownership. Retrieved from: https://newsline.ccc.govt.nz/news/story/red-zone-land-returns-to-local-ownership

Christchurch City Council (2021a). Halswell Ward. Christchurch City. Retrieved from: https://ccc.govt.nz/culture-and-community/statistics-and-facts/community-profiles/halswell-hornby-riccarton/halswell-ward

Christchurch City Council (2021b). Ngā Puna Wai sports hub. Retrieved from: https://ccc.govt.nz/rec-and-sport/sports-grounds/nga-puna-wai

Christchurch City Council (2022a). The Enliven Places Programme. Retrieved from: https://ccc.govt.nz/culture-and-community/community-led-development/enliven-places-programme

Christchurch City Council (2022b). Ōtākaro Avon River Corridor. Co-governance Establishment Committee, Council Supplementary Agenda, 7 April.

Christchurch City Council (2022c). *Draft Annual Plan 2022-23. Activity Plan. Ōtākaro Avon River Corridor (OARC)*, Attachments under Separate Cover, 24 February.

Christchurch NZ (2021). *Activities and Attractions*. Retrieved from: www.christchurchnz.com/explore/activities-attractions

Christensen, A.A. (2013). Mastering the land. Mapping and metrologies in Aotearoa New Zealand, in E. Pawson and T. Brooking eds., *Making A New Land. Environmental Histories of New Zealand*. Otago University Press, Dunedin, 310–27.

Chugh, K. (2020). More-than-human cities: On urban design and non-human agency. Retrieved from: https://cuesonline.org/2020/07/26/more-than-human-cities-on-urban-design-and-nonhuman-agency/

Chukwudumogu, I.C. (2018a). The Decision-Making Behaviour of Property Owners (Investors and Developers): A Case Study of the Christchurch City Centre Rebuild. Unpublished PhD thesis, The University of Auckland, Auckland.

Chukwudumogu, I.C. (2018b). The perspectives of commercial property stakeholders in post-disaster rebuild, *Asian Social Science* 14 (5), 82–94.

Chukwudumogu, I.C., Levy, D. and Perkins, H. (2019). The influence of sentiments on property owners in post-disaster rebuild: A case study of Christchurch, New Zealand, *Property Management* 37 (2), 243–61.

Church, L. (2017). Clean-up of Christchurch's 'dirty 30' building list. *Radio New Zealand*, 27 May. Retrieved from: www.rnz.co.nz/news/national/331696/clean-up-of-christchurch-s-dirty-30-building-list.

CIAL (2021). Financial reports, Christchurch International Airport Company. Retrieved from: www.christchurchairport.co.nz/about-us/who-we-are/financial-reports/

City Scene (2001). Future Path Canterbury, *City Scene Christchurch*, November–December. Retrieved from: http://archived.ccc.govt.nz/CityScene/2001/November/FuturePathCanterbury.asp

Civil Defence (2020). Declared states of emergency. National Emergency Management Agency. Retrieved from: www.civildefence.govt.nz/resources/previous-emergencies/declared-states-of-emergency/

Clark, H. (2021). Design of new Christchurch indoor stadium confirmed with 25,000 seats, *New Zealand Herald*, 22 July. Retrieved from: www.nzherald.co.nz/nz/design-of-new-christchurch-indoor-stadium-confirmed-with-25000-seats/VVURMDVQDSH5H43U2EHYYTM

Clark, N. (2011). *Inhuman Nature*. Sage, London.

Cloke, P., Beaumont, J. and Williams, A. eds. (2013). *Working Faith: Faith-based Organisations and Urban Social Justice*. Paternoster, Milton Keynes.

Cloke, P. and Conradson, D. (2018). Transitional organisations, affective atmospheres and new forms of being in-common: Post-disaster recovery in Christchurch, New Zealand, *Transactions Institute of British Geographers* 43 (3), 360–76.

Cloke, P. and Dickinson, S. (2019). Transitional ethics and aesthetics. Re-imagining the post-disaster city in Christchurch, New Zealand, *Annals of the Association of American Geographers* 109 (6), 1922–40.

Cloke, P., Dickinson, S. and Tupper, S. (2017). The Christchurch earthquakes 2010, 2011: Geographies of an event, *New Zealand Geographer* 73 (2), 69–80.

Cloke, P. and Johnston, R. eds. (2005). *Spaces of Geographic Thought: Deconstructing Human Geography's Binaries*. Sage, London.

Cloke, P. and Jones, O. (2003). Grounding ethical mindfulness for/in nature: Trees in their places, *Ethics, Place and Environment* 6 (3), 195–213.

Cloke, P. and Pawson, E. (2008). Memorial trees and treescape memories, *Environment and Planning D, Society and Space* 26 (1), 107–22.

Colbert, J., Sila-Nowicka, K. and Yao, J. (2022). Driving forces of population change following the Canterbury Earthquake Sequence, New Zealand: A multiscale geographically weighted regression approach, *Population, Space and Place*, e83. https://doi-org.ezproxy.auckland.ac.nz/10.1002/psp.2583

Conradson, D. (2008). Expressions of charity and action towards justice: Faith-based welfare provision in urban New Zealand, *Urban Studies* 45 (10), 2117–41.

Conradson, D. (2012). Leaving, waiting, staying: Household mobilities after the Christchurch earthquakes. Paper presented to New Zealand Geographical Society Conference, 3–6 December 2012, Napier.

Conway, G. (2011). Christchurch earthquake: Suburbs 'not forgotten', *Stuff*, 3 March. Retrieved from: www.stuff.co.nz/national/christchurch-earthquake/4725553/Christchurch-earthquake-Suburbs-not-forgotten

Conway, G. (2014). Officials ignore local investors, *Stuff*, 16 April. Retrieved from: www.stuff.co.nz/the-press/news/city-centre/9945920/Officials-ignore-local-investors

Coombs, S., Eberlein, A., Mantana, K., Turnhout, A. and Smith, C. (2015). Did dog ownership influence perceptions of adult health and well-being during and following the Canterbury earthquakes? A qualitative study, *Australasian Journal of Disaster and Trauma Studies* 19, 67–75.

Cowlishaw, S. and Mathewson, N. (2012). Officials 'hindered efforts' of volunteers, *Stuff*, 1 March. Retrieved from: www.stuff.co.nz/national/6503366/Officials-hindered-efforts-of-volunteers

Cox, T. (2015). 10 of the world's best concert halls, *The Guardian*, 5 March. Retrieved from: www.theguardian.com/travel/2015/mar/05/10-worlds-best-concert-halls-berlin-boston-tokyo

Cretney, R.M. (2016). Local responses to disaster: The value of community-led post-disaster response action in a resilience framework, *Disaster Prevention and Management* 25 (1), 27–40.

Cretney, R.M. (2017). Towards a critical geography of disaster recovery politics: Perspectives on crisis and hope, *Geography Compass* 11 (1), e12302.

Cretney, R.M. (2018). Beyond public meetings: Diverse forms of community led recovery following disaster, *International Journal of Disaster Risk Reduction* 28, 122–30.

Cretney, R.M. (2019). 'An opportunity to hope and dream'. Disaster politics and the emergence of possibility through community-led recovery, *Antipode* 51 (2), 497–516.

Cretney, R.M. and Bond, S. (2014). Bouncing back to capitalism? Grass-roots autonomous activism in shaping discourses of resilience and transformation following disaster, *Resilience* 2 (1), 18–31.

Cropp, A. (2011). Blue chip earthquake blues, *Stuff*, 13 February. Retrieved from: www.stuff.co.nz/sunday-star-times/features/4647691/Blue-chip-earthquake-blues

Cropper, E. (2017). Desperate Christchurch earthquake victims still fighting for repairs, *Newshub*, 26 June. Retrieved from: www.newshub.co.nz/home/new-zealand/2017/06/desperate-christchurch-earthquake-victims-still-fighting-for-repairs.html

Cubrinovski, M., Green, R.A., Allen, J. et al. (2010). Geotechnical reconnaissance of the 2010 Darfield (Canterbury) earthquake, *Bulletin for the New Zealand Society for Earthquake Engineering* 43 (4), 243–320.

Cupples, J. and Glynn, K. (2009). Countercartographies: (New Zealand) cultural studies/geographies of the city, *New Zealand Geographer* 65 (1), 1–5.

Curtis, A., Mills, J.W. and Leitner, M. (2007). Katrina and vulnerability. The geography of stress, *Journal of Health Care for the Poor and Underserved* 18 (2), 315–30.

Cutter, S., Barnes, L., Berry, M., Burton, C., Evans, E., Tate, R. and Webb, J. (2008). A place-based model for understanding community resilience to natural disasters, *Global Environmental Change* 18 (4), 598–606.

Cutter, S.L., Boruff, B.J. and Shirley, W.L. (2003). Social vulnerability to environmental hazards, *Social Science Quarterly* 84 (2), 242–61.

Cutter, S.L., Emrich, C.T., Mitchell, J.T., Boruff, B.J., Gall, M., Schmidtlein, M.C., Burton, C.G. and Melton, G. (2006). The long road home: Race, class, and recovery from Hurricane Katrina, *Environment: Science and Policy for Sustainable Development* 48 (2), 8–20.

Dann, J. (2014). Those left standing. Retrieved from: https://rebuildingchristchurch.wordpress.com/2014/03/10/those-left-standing/

Dann, J. (2021). The last city of the 20th century, SLATE, 21 February. Retrieved from: https://slate.com/business/2021/02/christchurch-earthquake-anniversary-how-the-rebuild-failed.html

David, L. and Halbert, L. (2014). Finance capital, actor-network theory and the struggle over calculative agencies in the business property markets of Mexico City Metropolitan Region, *Regional Studies* 48 (3), 516–29.

de Bruin, A. and Flint-Hartle, S. (2003). A bounded rationality framework for property investment behaviour, *Journal of Property Valuation and Investment* 21 (3), 271–84.

Department of Building and Housing (2012). *Structural Performance of Christchurch CBD Buildings in the 22 February 2011 Aftershock. Report of an Expert Panel Appointed by the New Zealand Department of Building and Housing*, Wellington.

Department of Statistics (1990). *New Zealand Official 1990 Yearbook*. Department of Statistics, Auckland.

Department of Statistics (2010). *New Zealand Official Yearbook 2010*. David Bateman Ltd, Auckland.

DesRoches, R., Comerio, M. and Eberhard, M. (2011). Overview of the 2010 Haiti earthquake, *Earthquake Spectra* 27 (1, Suppl.), 1–21.

DPMC (2016). *Waimakariri Residential Red Zone Recovery Plan. He Mahere Whakarauora i te Whenua Rāhui o Waimakariri*. Greater Christchurch Group, Department of Prime Minister and Cabinet, Christchurch.

DPMC (2017). *Whole of Government Report. Lessons from the Canterbury Earthquake Sequence*. Department of the Prime Minister and Cabinet, Greater Christchurch Group, Christchurch.

DPMC (2019). Final proposed Global Settlement Agreement with Christchurch City Council, Christchurch, Department of Prime Minister and Cabinet. Retrieved from: https://dpmc.govt.nz/sites/default/files/2019-12/GCR-DEV-19-SUB-0253-4206143.pdf

DeWolfe, D.J. (2000). *Training Manual for Mental Health and Human Service Workers in Major Disasters*. FEMA and Center for Mental Health Services, Washington DC.

Dewsbury, J-D. (2007). Unthinking subjects: Alain Badiou and the event of thought in thinking politics, *Transactions Institute of British Geographers* 32 (4), 443–59.

Diaz, J. III (1999). The first decade of behavioural research in the discipline of property, *Journal of Property Investment and Finance* 17 (4), 326–32.

Dickinson, S. (2013). Post-Disaster Mobilities: Exploring Household Relocation after the Canterbury Earthquakes. Unpublished Master of Science thesis, University of Canterbury, Christchurch.

Dickinson, S. (2018). Spaces of post-disaster experimentation: Agile entrepreneurship and geological agency in emerging disaster countercartographies, *Environment and Planning E: Nature and Space* 1 (4), 621–40.

Dionisio, M.R. (2020). Personal communication. 3 March. Rita Dionisio was then a board member of Te Putahi.

Dionisio, M.R. and Pawson, E. (2016). Building resilience through post-disaster community projects: Responses to the 2010 and 2011 Christchurch earthquakes and 2011 Tokohu tsunami, *Australasian Journal of Disaster and Trauma Studies* 20, 107–16.

Dixon Productions (2011). Christchurch 1996 quake doco – why buildings collapse. Retrieved from: www.youtube.com/watch?v=NkTy6ogLDX8&t=318s

Dodd, F.J. (2021). Exposing the hidden politics of housing provision in Aotearoa New Zealand: The complex governance landscape of new housing in Hamilton. Unpublished PhD thesis, University of Waikato, Hamilton.

Dodds, K. (2020). Staying with trouble, *Territory, Politics and Governance* 8 (2), 139–43.

Dombroski, K. (2020). Personal communication, 5 March. Kelly Dombroski was then a board member of Life in Vacant Spaces.

Dombroski, K., Diprose, G. and Boles, I. (2019). Can the commons be temporary? The role of transitional commoning in post-quake Christchurch, *Local Environment* 24 (4), 313–28.

Dominey-Howes, D., Gorman-Murray, A. and McKinnon, S. (2013). Queering disasters: On the need to account for LGBTI experiences in natural disaster contexts, *Gender, Place and Culture* 21 (7), 905–18.

Dorahy, M.J. and Kannis-Dymand, L. (2012). Psychological distress following the 2010 Christchurch earthquake: A community assessment of two differentially affected suburbs, *Journal of Loss & Trauma* 17 (3), 203–17.

Doudney, T. (2015). Expert warns of urban sprawl. *The Star*, 22 April, 15.

Dwyer, S. and Buckle, J. (2009). The space between: On being an insider-outsider in qualitative research, *International Journal of Qualitative Methods* 8 (1), 54–63.

Easton, B. (2000). Such, William Ball, 1907–75, *Dictionary of New Zealand Biography, Volume Five, 1941–60*. Auckland University Press, Auckland and Department of Internal Affairs, Wellington, 504–6.

Edmunds, S. (2017). 'Over-enthusiastic investment by unsophisticated people', *Stuff*, 15 September. Retrieved from: www.stuff.co.nz/business/96888627/overenthusiastic-investment-by-unsophisticated-people?rm=a

Elder, D.M., McCahon, I.F. and Yetton, M.D. (1991). *The Earthquake Hazard in Christchurch. A Detailed Evaluation*. Earthquake Commission, Wellington.

Enarson, E. and Morrow, B.H. eds. (1988). *The Gendered Terrain of Disaster*. Greenwood, Westport CT.

Enarson, E. and Pease, B. eds. (2016). *Men, Masculinities and Disaster*. Routledge, Abingdon.

England, K. (1994). Getting personal: Reflexivity, positionality and feminist research, *The Professional Geographer* 46 (1), 80–9.

Ensor, B. (2011). Remarkable effort by Student Army, *Stuff*, 25 February. Retrieved from: www.stuff.co.nz/marlborough-express/4705214/Remarkable-effort-by-student-army

Environment Canterbury (2011). *Ecological Effects of the Christchurch February Earthquake on our City Estuary*. Retrieved from: www.eosecology.co.nz/files/Ecan-Quake-Estuary-Ecology.pdf

Environment Canterbury (2013). *Natural Environment Recovery Programme for Greater Christchurch, Whakaara Taiao*, Report Number R13/68, Canterbury Regional Council, Christchurch.

Environment Canterbury (2021a). *How Many People Live in Canterbury?* Retrieved from: www.ecan.govt.nz/your-region/living-here/regional-leadership/population/census-estimates/

Environment Canterbury (2021b). Greater Christchurch Metro. Retrieved from: www.ecan.govt.nz/your-region/living-here/transport/public-transport-services/greater-christchurch-metro/

EPIC (2022). EPIC Innovation. Retrieved from: https://epicinnovation.co.nz

EQC (2021). Drainage claims. Earthquake Commission. Retrieved from: https://www.eqc.govt.nz/insurance-and-claims/canterbury-earthquake/canterbury-claims/drainage-claims/

Ermacora, T. and Bullivant, L. (2016). *Recoded City: Co-creating Urban Futures*, Routledge, London.

Erskine, S. (2022). Personal communication, 31 January. Shelley Erskine was then marketing manager at the Christchurch Arts Centre.

Farrell, F. (2012). *The Broken Book*. Auckland University Press, Auckland.

Farrell, F. (2015). *Villa at the Edge of the Empire. One Hundred Ways to Read a City*. Penguin Random House, Auckland.

Feeney, W. (2019). *Out There: SCAPE Public Art, 1998–2018*. SCAPE, Christchurch.

Finlayson, C. (2021). Ōtākaro/Avon River Corridor co-governance options. Letter to the Mayor of Christchurch, 21 June.

Finlayson, C. and Christmas, J. (2021). *He Kupu Taurangi. Treaty Settlements and the Future of Aotearoa New Zealand*. Huia Publishers, Wellington.

Fisher, M. (2020). Personal communication, 27 February. Mike Fisher was then general manager of Christchurch's Riverside Market, director of UrbanTacticians and chair of the board of Te Putahi.

Forer, P. (1978). Time-space and area in the city of the plains, in T. Carlstein, D. Parkes and N. Thrift eds., *Timing Space and Spacing Time*. Edward Arnold, London, 99–118.

Franklin, A. (2017). The more-than-human city, *The Sociological Review* 65 (2), 202–17.

Fullilove, M. (2016). *Root Shock. How Tearing Up City Neighborhoods Hurts America, and What We Can Do About It*. NYU Press, New York.

Fusté-Forné, F. (2017). Building experiencescapes in Christchurch, *Landscape Review (Lincoln)* 17 (1), 44–57.

Gablik, S. (1992). The ecological narrative, *Art Journal* 51 (2), 49–51.

Gablik, S. (1996). Connective aesthetics: Art after individualism, in S. Lacy ed., *Mapping the Terrain: New Genre Public Art*. Bay Press, Seattle WA, 74–87.

Gaillard, J.C., Gorman-Murray, A. and Fordham, M. (2017). Sexual and gender minorities in disaster. *Gender, Place and Culture* 24 (1), 18–26.

Gallagher, K. and Pyle, D. (2021). *Rohe Kōreporepo. The Swamp, the Sacred Place*. Wick Candle, Christchurch.

Galloway, M. (2014). A message and a messenger, in B. Bennett, J. Dann, E. Johnson and R. Reynolds eds., *Once in a Lifetime: City-building after Disaster in Christchurch*, Freerange Press, Christchurch, 112–16.

Galloway, M. (2021). Art over nature over art. (Re)imagining Ōtautahi Christchurch, in F. Freschi, J. Venis and F. Nazier eds., *The Politics of Design. Privilege and Prejudice in Aotearoa New Zealand, Australia and South Africa*. Otago Polytechnic Press, Dunedin, 275–91.

Gap Filler (2022). Placemaking at One Central. Retrieved from: https://gapfiller.org.nz/project/placemaking-at-one-central/

Garces-Ozanne, A., Makabenta-Ikeda, M. and Uekusa, S. (2022). Asian migrant worker experiences in Ōtautahi Christchurch, in S. Uekusa, S. Matthewman and B.C. Glavovic eds., A *Decade of Disaster Experiences in Ōtautahi Christchurch*. Palgrave Macmillan, Singapore, 211–36.

Gardner, R.O. (2013). The emergent organization: Improvisation and order in Gulf Coast disaster relief, *Symbolic Interaction* 36 (3), 237–60.

Gates, C. (2012a). Central city abuzz with noise of demolition, *The Press*, 29 September, 1.

Gates, C. (2012b). Dalziel claims CERA ditched her, *Stuff*, 24 April. Retrieved from: www.stuff.co.nz/the-press/6795039/Dalziel-claims-Cera-ditched-her

Gates, C. (2015a). 1240 central Christchurch buildings demolished, *Stuff*, 20 February. Retrieved from: www.stuff.co.nz/the-press/news/christchurch-earthquake-2011/66290638/1240-central-christchurch-buildings-demolished

Gates, C. (2015b). St Elmos Court owner bitter, angry, in debt, *Stuff*, 20 February. Retrieved from: www.stuff.co.nz/the-press/news/christchurch-earthquake-2011/66248945/st-elmos-court-owner-bitter-angry-in-debt

Gates, C. (2015c). Fruit foraging in Christchurch's red zone, *Stuff*, 10 April. Retrieved from: www.stuff.co.nz/life-style/food-wine/food-news/67690529/fruit-foraging-in-christchurchs-red-zone

Gates, C. (2018). Empty central Christchurch sites cover land three times the size of Botanic Gardens, *Stuff*, 8 January. Retrieved from: www.stuff.co.nz/the-press/business/the-rebuild/100390195/empty-central-christchurch-sites-cover-land-three-times-the-size-of-botanic-gardens

Gates, C. (2021). Breeding colony for rare gulls in central Christchurch ruins is being demolished, *Stuff*, 18 July. Retrieved from: www.stuff.co.nz/the-press/news/125738537/breeding-colony-for-rare-gulls-in-central-christchurch-ruins-is-being-demolished

Gehl, J. (2015). In search of the human scale, TEDx talk, 19 December. Retrieved from: www.youtube.com/watch?v=Cgw9oHDfJ4k

Gehl Architects (2010). *Christchurch 2009: Public Space, Public Life*. Christchurch City Council.

Ghosh, A. (2021). *The Nutmeg's Curse. Parables for a Planet in Crisis*. John Murray, London.

Gibson, A. (2019). Four biggest NZ malls a focus for Scentre in $790m property expansion, *New Zealand Herald*, 11 April. Retrieved from: www.nzherald.co.nz/business/four-biggest-nz-malls-a-focus-for-scentre-in-790m-property-expansion/YMCZXREWZMLMWO74SR7GZ3UEJU/

Giovinazzi, S., Wilson, T., Davis, C., Bristow, D., Gallagher, M., Schofield, A., Villemure, M., Eidinger, J. and Tang, A. (2014). Lifelines performance and management following the 22 February 2011 Christchurch earthquake, New Zealand: Highlights of resilience, *Bulletin of the New Zealand Society for Earthquake Engineering* 44 (4), 402–17.

Gjerde, M. (2017a). A change of scene: How the Canterbury earthquake sequence led to a departure from concrete technologies, in P. Chan and C. Neilson eds., *Proceedings of the 33rd Annual Association of Researchers in Construction Management Conference, Cambridge*, 4–6 September 2017, 724–33.

Gjerde, M. (2017b). Building back better: Learning from the Christchurch rebuild, *Procedia Engineering* 198, 530–40.

Glaeser, E. and Sassen, S. (2011). 16 global cities to watch, *Foreign Policy*, December, 72 and 85.

Glavovic, B. (2022). IPCC Report: Coastal cities are sentinels for climate change. It's where our focus should be as we prepare for inevitable impacts, *The Conversation*, 1 March.

Global Settlement Agreement (2019). *Global Settlement Agreement, 23 September 2019*, Christchurch City Council and the Crown. Retrieved from: www.ccc.govt.nz/assets/Documents/The-Council/Plans-Strategies-Policies-Bylaws/Strategies/Global-Settlement/CCC-Release-Global-Settlement-Agreement-23-Septmeber-2019.pdf

Gluckman, P. (2011). The psycho-social consequences of the Canterbury earthquakes. A briefing paper. Office of the Prime Minister's Science Advisory Committee, 10 May.

Gordon, E., Sutherland, J., Du Plessis, R. and Gibson, H. (2014). *Movers and Shakers: Women's Stories from the Christchurch Earthquakes*. Women's Voices Project - Ngā Reo O Ngā Wahine. Retrieved from: www.communityresearch.org.nz/wp-content/uploads/formidable/MOVERS-AND-SHAKERS_Final.pdf

Gorman, P. (2010a). Scientists can't rule out fault below Chch, *The Press*, 6 October.

Gorman, P. (2010b). The science behind the shakes, *Stuff*, 26 December. Retrieved from: www.stuff.co.nz/the-press/news/christchurch-earthquake-2011/canterbury-earthquake-2010/4495446/The-science-behind-the-shakes

Gorman, P. (2016). *Portacom City: Reporting on the Christchurch and Kaikōura Earthquakes*. Bridget William Books, Wellington.

Gray, R. (2016). Monuments or millstones, in J. Harvey ed., *Christchurch – Five Years On, Architecture New Zealand*, March/April, 45–7.

Greater Christchurch Urban Development Strategy (2007). *Greater Christchurch Urban Development Strategy 2007*. Retrieved from: https://greaterchristchurch.org.nz/assets/Documents/greaterchristchurch/UDSActionPlan2007.pdf

Greater Christchurch Urban Development Strategy (2016). *Greater Christchurch Urban Development Strategy Update 2016*, Canterbury Regional Council, Christchurch.
Greater Christchurch Partnership (2018). *Our Space 2018-2048: Greater Christchurch Settlement Pattern Update Whakahāngai O Te Hōrapa Nohoanga*. Draft for Consultation, Christchurch, November.
Greater Christchurch Urban Development Strategy Implementation Committee (2011). Committee minutes. Retrieved from: http://archived.ccc.govt.nz/council/agendas/2011/february/greaterchchudsic21st/gcudsic21february2011-fullagenda.pdf
Greaves, L.M., Milojev, P., Huang, Y., Stronge, S., Osborne, D., Bulbulia, J., Grimshaw, M. and Sibley, C.G. (2015). Regional differences in the psychological recovery of Christchurch residents following the 2010/2011 earthquakes: A longitudinal study, *PLOS One*, 10 (5), e0124278.
Green Lab (2022). Linwood tiny shops village. Retrieved from: https://thegreenlab.co.nz/linwood-tiny-shops-village/; https://www.tellinglives.co.nz/tiny-shops-village
Greene, B. (2021). *You Can't Rush an Earthquake. Repair, Rebuild, Repeat*. Brenda Greene, Christchurch.
Greenhill, M. (2013). Rebuilds under way on tricky TC3 sites, *Stuff*, 11 July. Retrieved from: www.stuff.co.nz/the-press/8903528/Rebuilds-under-way-on-tricky-TC3-sites
Greenhough, B. (2010). Vitalist geographies: Life and the more-than-human, in P. Harrison and B. Anderson eds., *Taking Place: Non-representational Theories and Geography*. Ashgate, London, 37–54.
Grimshaw & Co (2014). Poor repairs to haunt buyers. Retrieved from: www.grimshaw.co.nz/news-resources/poor-repairs-to-haunt-buyers/
Grimshaw, M. (2015). Personal communication, 4 March. Mike Grimshaw was then Associate Professor of Sociology and Anthropology at the University of Canterbury.
Grollimund, B. (2014). *Small Quake, Big Impact: Lessons Learned from Christchurch*. Swiss Re, Zurich.
Gruen, L. (2015). *Entangled Empathy. An Alternative Ethic for our Relationship with Animals*. Lantern Books, Brooklyn.
Gundermann, B. (2014). *A Holistic Transition to Climate-resilient Cities*. Urbia Group, Auckland.
Hackworth, J. (2007). *The Neoliberal City. Governance, Ideology, and Development in American Urbanism*. Cornell University Press, Ithaca.
Halbert, L., Henneberry, J. and Mouzakis, F. (2014). The financialization of business property and what It means for cities and regions, *Regional Studies* 48 (3), 547–50.
Hall, C.M., Malinen, S., Vosslamber, R. and Wordsworth, R. eds. (2016). *Business and Post-disaster Management Business, Organisational and Consumer Resilience and the Christchurch Earthquakes*. Routledge, London.
Hall, P. (1982). *Great Planning Disasters*. University of California Press, Berkeley.
Hamilton, C. (2016). Fun for all ages. *Australasian Leisure Management*. September/October, 18–22.
Haraway, D. (1988). Situated knowledges: The science question in feminism and the privilege of partial perspective, *Feminist Studies* 14 (3), 575–99.
Haraway, D.J. (2016). *Staying with the Trouble. Making Kin in the Chthulucene*. Duke University Press, Durham.
Hare, J. (2011). Preliminary observations from Christchurch earthquakes. Technical report, Structural Engineering Society of New Zealand. Retrieved from: https://canterbury.royalcommission.govt.nz/documents-by-key/2011-09-23108

Harris, D. and Hayward, M. (2019). MPs urge tighter house-building rules to protect neighbourhoods. *Stuff*, 18 March. Retrieved from: www.stuff.co.nz/the-press/news/110931729/mps-urge-planning-law-changes-to-protect-against-housing-intensification?rm=a

Harvey, D. (1989a). *The Condition of Postmodernity. An Enquiry into the Origins of Cultural Change*. Basil Blackwell, Oxford.

Harvey, D. (1989b). From managerialism to entrepreneurialism: The transformation of urban governance in late capitalism, *Geografiska Annaler* 71 B (1), 3–17.

Harvey, S. (2012). The Grace Vineyard Church response, *Tephra* 23, 8–12.

Harvey, S. (2014). Sam's story, in M. Parsons ed., *Rubble to Resurrection: Churches Respond in the Canterbury Quakes*. DayStar, Auckland, 223–4.

Harvie, W. (2016). How Māori will rebuilt Christchurch look? *Stuff*, 23 September. Retrieved from: www.stuff.co.nz/the-press/business/the-rebuild/84195996/how-maori-will-rebuilt-christchurch-look

Harvie, W. (2021). Environmental groups at odds over Christchurch estuary walkway, *Stuff*, 8 August. Retrieved from: www.stuff.co.nz/the-press/news/125964428/environmental-groups-at-odds-over-christchurch-estuary-walkway

Hawkes, C. (2018). Elite streets: Christchurch wants the leafy, established avenues in Fendalton, *Stuff*, 19 March. Retrieved from: www.stuff.co.nz/life-style/homed/latest/101391044/christchurchs-elite-streets-are-the-leafy-established-avenues-in-fendalton

Hawkey, J. (2018). Personal communication, 5 November. Jill Hawkey was Executive Director of Christchurch Methodist Mission.

Hawkey, J. (2020). Personal communication, 18 March. Jill Hawkey was Executive Director of Christchurch Methodist Mission.

Hayward, B. (2012). Canterbury's political quake, *Stuff*, 30 March. Retrieved from: www.stuff.co.nz/the-press/opinion/perspective/6664104/Canterburys-political-quake/

Hayward, B.M. (2013). Rethinking resilience: Reflections on the earthquakes in Christchurch, New Zealand, 2010 and 2011, *Ecology and Society* 18 (4), 37.

Hayward, B. and Cretney, R. (2015). Governing through disaster, in J. Hayward ed., *New Zealand Government and Politics*, 6th edn., Oxford University Press, Melbourne, 403–15.

Hayward, M. (2018). Nearly seven years on, thousands of Christchurch earthquake insurance claims remain, *Stuff*, 10 February. Retrieved from: www.stuff.co.nz/life-style/homed/latest/101391044/christchurchs-elite-streets-are-the-leafy-established-avenues-in-fendalton

Hayward, M. (2020a). Plan for unique central city neighbourhoods to bring people into the city, *Stuff*, 1 August. Retrieved from: www.stuff.co.nz/the-press/news/122306971/plan-for-unique-central-christchurch-neighbourhoods-to-bring-people-into-the-city

Hayward, M. (2020b). Christchurch's Riverside Market thriving after a year in business, *Stuff*, 2 October. Retrieved from: www.stuff.co.nz/business/our-backyard/122965722/christchurchs-riverside-market-thriving-after-a-year-in-business

Hayward, M. and McDonald, L. (2019). Fancy plans for Cathedral Square won't take shape for at least a decade, *Stuff*, 19 January. Retrieved from: www.stuff.co.nz/business/110025110/fancy-plans-for-cathedral-square-wont-take-shape-for-at-least-a-decade

Haworth, G. (2019). *Guts and Grace. Christchurch City Mission, A History*. Wily, Christchurch.

He, L., Dominey-Howes, D., Aitchinson, J.C., Lau, A. and Conradson, D. (2021). How do post-disaster policies influence household-level recovery? A case study of the 2010–11 Canterbury earthquake sequence, New Zealand, *International Journal of Disaster Risk Reduction* 60, 102274.

Heather, B. (2011a). Chemical toilet confusion in earthquake-hit Christchurch, *Stuff*, 31 March. Retrieved from: www.stuff.co.nz/national/christchurch-earthquake/4831055/Chemical-toilet-confusion-in-earthquake-hit-Christchurch

Heather, B. (2011b). Red zone house owners reject buyout, *Stuff*, 26 September. Retrieved from: www.stuff.co.nz/national/5682708/Red-zone-house-owners-reject-buyout

Heins, A. (2015). Greenfield Drivers: Residential Choice, Transport, and the Subjective Experience of Travel in the Greenfield Suburbs – A Case Study in Christchurch. Unpublished Master of Science thesis, University of Canterbury, Christchurch.

Herman, J.L. (1998). Recovery from psychological trauma, *Psychiatry and Clinical Neurosciences* 52 (S1), S98–103.

Hewitt, K. (1997). *Regions of Risk. A Geographical Introduction to Disasters*. Longman, Harlow.

Hinchliffe, S. and Whatmore, S. (2006). Living cities: Towards a politics of conviviality, *Science as Culture* 15 (2), 123–38.

Hodder, I. (2014). The entanglement of humans and things: A long term view, *New Literary History* 45 (1), 19–36.

Hogg, D., Kingham, S., Wilson, T.M., Griffin, E. and Ardagh, M. (2014). Geographic variation of clinically diagnosed mood and anxiety disorders in Christchurch after the 2010/11 earthquakes, *Health and Place* 30, 270–78.

Hörhager, E. (2015). Political implications of natural disasters: Regime consolidation and political contestation, *WIT Transactions on the Built Environment* 150, 271–81.

Hou, L. and Shi, P. (2011). Haiti 2010 earthquake - how to explain such huge losses? *International Journal of Disaster Risk Science* 2 (1), 25–33.

How, S.M. and Kerr, G.N. (2019). Earthquake impacts on immigrant participation in the Greater Christchurch construction labor market, *Population Research and Policy Review* 38 (2), 241–69.

Huck, A., Monstadt, J. and Driessen, P. (2020). Building urban and infrastructure resilience through connectivity: An institutional perspective on disaster risk management in Christchurch, New Zealand, *Cities* 98, 102573.

Hughes, R. (1991). *The Shock of the New. Art and the Century of Change*. Thames & Hudson, London.

Hughes, M.W., Quigley, M.C., van Ballegooy, S., Deam, B.L., Bradley, B.A., Hart, D.E. and Measures, R. (2015). The sinking city: Earthquakes increase flood hazard in Christchurch, New Zealand, *GSA Today* 25 (3–4), 4–10.

Hunt, E. (2021a). 'Joy and agony': Christchurch earthquake survivors ten years on. *The Guardian*, 19 February. Retrieved from: www.theguardian.com/world/2021/feb/20/trauma-and-transformation-christchurch-earthquake-survivors-ten-years-on

Hunt, E. (2021b). Wings but no prayers: Seagulls delay rebuilding of Christchurch cathedral, *The Guardian*, 10 February. Retrieved from: www.theguardian.com/world/2021/feb/11/worlds-rarest-seagulls-thrive-in-demolished-new-zealand-office-block

Ineson, J. (2018). Rebuilt QEII centre puts east Christchurch 'back on the map' as hundreds stream in on opening night, *Stuff*, 31 May. Retrieved from: www.stuff.co.nz/the-press/news/104383364/rebuilt-qeii-centre-puts-east-christchurch-back-on-the-map-as-hundreds-stream-in-on-opening-night

Insurance Council of New Zealand (2021). *Canterbury Earthquakes*. Retrieved from: www.icnz.org.nz/natural-disasters/canterbury-earthquakes/

International Labour Organisation (2021). *Haiti Earthquake 2021: Post Disaster Needs Assessment*. Retrieved from: www.ilo.org/global/docs/wcms_831127/lang--en/index.htm

IPCC (2022). *Climate Change 2022. Impacts, Adaptation and Vulnerability*, Intergovernmental Panel on Climate Change. Retrieved from: www.ipcc.ch

IPWEA. (2019). Australasian Award for Margaret Mahy Family Playground. Retrieved from: www.wsp.com/en-NZ/news/2019/australasian-award-for-margaret-mahy-family-playground

Irvine, R.D.G. (2017). Anthropocene East Anglia, *The Sociological Review Monographs* 65 (1), 154–70.

Jackson, M. (2021). Where to next? Decolonisation and the stories in the land, in B. Elkington, M. Jackson, R. Kiddle, Mercier, O.R., Ross, M., Smeaton, J. and Thomas, A. *Imagining Decolonisation*. Bridget Williams Books, Wellington, 133–55.

Jacobs, J. (1961). *The Death and Life of Great American Cities*. Random House, New York.

Jamieson, A. (2018). Personal communication, 2 November. Alan Jamieson was Senior Pastor of South West Baptist Church.

Jeffrey, C. and Dyson, J. (2021). Geographies of the future: Prefigurative politics, *Progress in Human Geography* 45 (4), 641–58.

Jewell, N. (2014). Earthquake resistant eco-village wins Christchurch's Breathe competition, *Inhabitat*. Retrieved from: https://inhabitat.com/dynamic-team-comprised-of-local-builders-and-italian-architects-wins-christchurchs-breathe-competition/

Johnson, L.A. and Olshansky, R.B. (2017). *After Great Disasters. An In-Depth Analysis of How Six Countries Managed Community Recovery*. Lincoln Institute of Land Policy, Cambridge MA.

Johnson, M.L. (2006). Geographical reflections on the 'new' New Orleans in the post-Hurricane Katrina era, *Geographical Review* 96 (1), 139–56.

Johnson, S. (2012). Students vs. the machine, *Tephra* 23, 18–22.

Johnston, K.M. (2014). Planning for a Night Out: Local Governance, Power and Night-Time in Christchurch, New Zealand. Unpublished PhD thesis, Massey University, Palmerston North.

Jones, N. (2015). Immigration rules changed to clear way for 5000 more Christchurch rebuild workers, *New Zealand Herald*, 13 May. Retrieved from: www.nzherald.co.nz/nz/immigration-rules-changed-to-clear-way-for-5000-more-christchurch-rebuild-workers/CBCDJPO4Y7D2IQYKJKHZMPQUQQ/

Jones, O. and Cloke, P. (2002). *Tree Cultures. The Place of Trees and Trees in their Place*. Berg, Oxford.

Joseph, J. (2013a). Resilience as embedded neoliberalism: A governmentality approach, *Resilience* 1 (1), 38–52.

Joseph, M. (2013b). *Fluid New York. Cosmopolitan Urbanism and the Green Imagination*. Duke University Press, Durham.

Judt, T. (2010). *Postwar. A History of Europe since 1945*. Vintage Books, London.

Kahn, M.E. (2005). The death toll from natural disasters: The role of income, geography, and institutions, *The Review of Economics and Statistics* 87 (2), 271–84.

Kaiser, A., Holden, C., Beavan, J., Beetham, D., Benites, R., Celentano, A., Collett, D., Cousins, J., Cubrinovski, M., Dellow, G. and Denys, P. (2012). The M_w 6.2 Christchurch earthquake of February 2011: Preliminary report, *New Zealand Journal of Geology and Geophysics* 55 (1), 67–90.

Kam, W.Y., Pampanin, S. and Elwood, K. (2011). Structural performance of reinforced concrete buildings in the 22 February Christchurch (Lyttelton) earthquake, *Bulletin of the New Zealand Society for Earthquake Engineering* 44 (4), 239–78.

Kane, R. and Smith, J. (2013). Inner City East – one Christchurch community's story, *Aotearoa New Zealand Social Work* 25 (2), 90–7.

Kates, R.W., Colten, C.E., Laska, S. and Leatherman, S.P. (2006). Reconstruction of New Orleans after Hurricane Katrina. A research perspective, *Proceedings of the National Academy of Sciences* 103 (40), 14653–60.

Katz, C. (2008). Bad elements: Katrina and the scoured landscape of social reproduction, *Gender, Place and Culture: A Journal of Feminist Geography* 15 (1), 15–29.

Kenny, J. (2021a). Popular Christchurch bar Viaduct finally returns after post-quake hiatus. *Stuff*, 27 January. Retrieved from: www.stuff.co.nz/the-press/christchurch-life/eat-and-drink/124057522/popular-christchurch-bar-viaduct-finally-returns-after-postquake-hiatus

Kenny, L. (2020). Christchurch's new hot saltwater pools sell-out for opening weekend, *Stuff*, 31 May. Retrieved from: www.stuff.co.nz/travel/back-your-backyard/121679008/christchurchs-new-hot-saltwater-pools-sellout-for-opening-weekend

Kenny, L. (2021b). New pool for east Christchurch after decade-long wait 'makes our hearts happy', *Stuff*, 1 October. Retrieved from: www.stuff.co.nz/the-press/news/126554658/new-pool-for-east-christchurch-after-decadelong-wait-makes-our-hearts-happy

Kenney, C.M. and Phibbs, S. (2015). A Māori love story: Community-led disaster management in response to the Ōtautahi (Christchurch) earthquakes as a framework for action, *International Journal of Disaster Risk Reduction* 14 (1), 46–55.

Kenney, C.M., Phibbs, S.R., Paton, D., Reid, J. and Johnston, D.M. (2015). Community-led disaster risk management. A Māori response to Ōtautahi (Christchurch) earthquakes, *Australasian Journal of Disaster and Trauma Studies* 19, 9–20.

Key, J. (2015). Speech to the Canterbury Employers' Chamber of Commerce lunch, 2 July. Retrieved from: www.stuff.co.nz/the-press/news/69903502/john-keys-speech-to-the-canterbury-employers-chamber-of-commerce-lunch

King, A., Middleton, D., Brown, C., Johnston, D. and Johal, S. (2014). Insurance: Its role in recovery from the 2010–2011 Canterbury earthquake sequence, *Earthquake Spectra* 30 (1), 475–91.

Klein, N. (2008). *The Shock Doctrine*. Penguin, Harmondsworth.

Lambert, S. (2014). Māori and the Christchurch earthquakes. The interplay between Indigenous endurance and resilience through urban disaster, *MAI Journal* 3 (2), 165–80.

Land Information New Zealand (2021). *Pest Animal Survey Results*, Land Information New Zealand. Retrieved from: www.linz.govt.nz/crown-property/types-crown-property/christchurch-residential-red-zones/pest-animal-survey-results

Landscape Architecture Aotearoa (2022). Embedding stories of mana whenua in post-quake Christchurch. Retrieved from: www.landscapearchitecture.nz/landscape-architecture-aotearoa/2022/2/12/debbie-tikao-working-to-embed-the-stories-of-mana-whenua-in-post-quake-christchurch

Latour, B. (2018). *Down to Earth. Politics in the New Climatic Regime*. Polity Press, Cambridge.

Law, T. (2012). Shock at schools shake-up, *Stuff*, 18 September. Retrieved from: www.stuff.co.nz/the-press/news/7674258/Shock-at-schools-shake-up

Law, T. (2015). Work could start soon on restoring the Christchurch Town Hall, *Stuff*, 7 June. Retrieved from: www.stuff.co.nz/the-press/business/the-rebuild/69167736/work-could-start-soon-on-restoring-the-christchurch-town-hall

Law, T. (2016). New pool in Christchurch's east urgently needed, principals say, *Stuff*, 18 May. Retrieved from: www.stuff.co.nz/the-press/news/80117823/new-pool-in-christchurchs-east-urgently-needed-principals-say

Law, T. (2018). Excitement surrounds the opening of Christchurch's long-awaited QEII complex, *Stuff*, 28 May. Retrieved from: www.stuff.co.nz/the-press/news/104259359/excitement-surrounds-the-opening-of-christchurchs-longawaited-qeii-complex

Law, T. (2019a). Christchurch's rubble mountain: The end of an earthquake-demolition dump, *Stuff*, 29 December. Retrieved from: www.stuff.co.nz/the-press/news/118153213/christchurchs-rubble-mountain-the-end-of-an-earthquakedemolition-dump

Law, T. (2019b). Riverside Market brings the 'buzz' back into Christchurch's central city, *Stuff*, 30 September. Retrieved from: www.stuff.co.nz/the-press/news/116198681/riverside-market-brings-the-buzz-back-into-christchurchs-central-city

Law, T. (2020a). New rule could stop new central Christchurch apartments being used for Airbnb, *Stuff*, 11 June. Retrieved from: www.stuff.co.nz/the-press/news/121782640/new-rule-could-stop-new-central-christchurch-apartments-being-used-for-airbnb

Law, T. (2020b). New Christchurch apartments criticised for 'poor' urban design, *Stuff*, 9 September. Retrieved from: www.stuff.co.nz/the-press/news/122695983/new-christchurch-apartments-criticised-for--poor-urban-design

Law, T. (2020c). Council cracks down on 120 unconsented central Christchurch car parks, *Stuff*, 2 December. Retrieved from: www.stuff.co.nz/the-press/news/123571925/council-cracks-down-on-120-unconsented-central-christchurch-car-parks

Law, T. (2021). Christchurch ratepayers urged to support $5.5 m Arts Centre grant, *Stuff*, 21 February. Retrieved from: www.stuff.co.nz/the-press/news/124285896/christchurch-ratepayers-urged-to-support-55m-arts-centre-grant

Law, T. (2022). At-risk gulls find new home, *Stuff*, 25 January. Retrieved from: www.stuff.co.nz/the-press/news/127577553/atrisk-gulls-find-new-home--mistaking-halfbuilt-stormwater-basin-for-a-braided-river

Law, T. and McDonald, L. (2020). Time to turn the heat up: Call for action as 20 per cent of central Christchurch sites still vacant, *The Press*, 10 December, 1.

Le Heron, R. (2018). Dairying in question, in E. Pawson and the Biological Economies Research Team, *The New Biological Economy. How New Zealanders are Creating Value from the Land.* Auckland University Press, Auckland, 20–40.

Le Heron, R. and Pawson, E. eds. (1996). *Changing Places. New Zealand in the Nineties*. Longman Paul, Auckland.

Lesniak, M. (2016). Rebuilding/Reimagining Post-disaster Christchurch. Unpublished Masters Altevilles dissertation, University of Lyon, Lyon.

Levy, D., Hills, R., Perkins, H.C., Mackay, M., Campbell, M. and Johnston, K. (2021). Local benevolent property development entrepreneurs in small town regeneration. *Land Use Policy* 108, 105546.

Lewis, J.N. (2011). The future of network governance research: Strength in diversity and synthesis, *Public Administration* 89 (4), 1221–34.

Liberty, K., Tarren-Sweeney, M., Macfarlane, S., Basu, A. and Reid, J. (2016). Behavior problems and post-traumatic stress symptoms in children beginning school: A comparison of pre- and post-earthquake groups, *PLoS Currents* 8.

Life in Vacant Spaces (n.d.). The East x East project. Retrieved from: https://livs.org.nz/our-spaces/east-x-east/

Lin II, R-G. and Allen, S. (2011). New Zealand quake raises questions about LA buildings, *Los Angeles Times*, 26 February. Retrieved from: www.latimes.com/local/la-me-quake-california-20110226-story.html

Lindblom, C. (1959). The science of muddling through, *Public Administration Review* 19, 79–88.

Lindblom, C.E. (1979). Still muddling, not yet through, *Public Administration Review* 39 (6), 517–26.

LINZ (2015). *Geotechnical Information on Horizontal Land Movement due to the Canterbury Earthquake Sequence*, prepared for Land Information New Zealand by Tonkin and Taylor, Christchurch.

Lochhead, J. ed. (2019). *The Christchurch Town Hall 1965–2019. A Dream Renewed*, Canterbury University Press, Christchurch.

Lonely Planet (2017). *Oi You!* Retrieved from: www.streetart.co.nz/blog/2017/9/23/oi-you-the-driving-force-behind-getting-christchurch-and-adelaide-being-recognised-as-street-art-cities

Longley, G. (2015). Hagley Oval redevelopment ends up costing $4.5m - three times the original estimate, *Stuff*, 22 May. Retrieved from: www.stuff.co.nz/sport/cricket/68779977/hagley-oval-redevelopment-ends-up-costing-45m---three-times-the-original-estimate

Loughrey, D. (2019). A decade on, stadium scars remain, *Otago Daily Times*, 16 February. Retrieved from: www.odt.co.nz/news/dunedin/decade-stadium-scars-remain

Lovatt, A. and O'Connor, J. (1995). Cities and the night-time economy, *Planning Practice and Research* 10 (2), 127–34.

Lowenthal, D. (2004). The heritage crusade and its contradictions, in M. Page and R. Mason eds., *Giving Preservation a History. Histories of Historic Preservation in the United States*. Routledge, New York, 19–43.

Lucas, D. (2014). Does the Blueprint support the creation of a healthy ecological urban environment? in B. Bennett, J. Dann, E. Johnson and R. Reynolds, eds., *Once in a Lifetime: City-building after Disaster in Christchurch*. Freerange Press, Christchurch, 438–49.

Lunday, J. (2020). In G. Smyth, dir., *When A City Rises*, Frank Films. Retrieved from: www.nzonscreen.com/title/when-a-city-rises-2020

Lynch, C. (2019). Has the east of Christchurch been forgotten about? Retrieved from: www.youtube.com/watch?v=83ZnkOVOiDI

Lynch, C. (2020). Election results 2020: Gerry Brownlee defeat one of biggest upsets for National party. Retrieved from: www.nzherald.co.nz/nz/election-results-2020-chris-lynch-gerry-brownlee-defeat-one-of-biggest-upsets-for-national-party/RAH3S47JAW5LG53I4EORHKF4HQ/

Lynch, D. (2014). Response to criticism of Crowne Plaza deputation. Retrieved from: www.facebook.com/GapFiller/posts/866575836703253

MacDonald, M. and Carlton, S. (2016). *Staying in the Red Zones. Monitoring Human Rights in the Canterbury Earthquake Recovery*. Human Rights Commission, Auckland.

MacPherson, R. (2016). Placemaking in Transitional Christchurch: Adaptive and Creative Projects for a Better City. Retrieved from: www.rtpi.org.uk/media/1642474/Placemaking-in-transitional-Christchurch-Rafeal.pdf

Mann, C. (2012). New riverside red zone, *The Press*, 23 March.

Mann, C. and Mathewson, N. (2012). New riverside red zone, *Stuff*, 23 March. Retrieved from: www.stuff.co.nz/the-press/news/christchurch-earthquake-2011/6624862/New-riverside-red-zone

Manyena, B., O'Brien, G., O'Keefe, P. and Rose, J. (2011). Disaster resilience: A bounce back or bounce forward ability? *Local Environment* 16 (5), 417–24.

Marcetic, B. (2017). New Zealand's neoliberal drift, *Jacobin*, 15 March. Retrieved from: www.jacobinmag.com/2017/03/new-zealand-neolioberalism-inequality-=welfare-state-tax-haven/

Marcuse, P. (2009). From critical urban theory to the right to the city, *City* 13 (2/3), 185–97.

Marques, B., McIntosh, J., Hatton, W. and Shanahan, D. (2019). Bicultural landscapes and ecological restoration in the compact city: The case of Zealandia as a sustainable ecosanctuary. *Journal of Landscape Architecture* 14 (1), 44–53.

Marquis, F., Kim, J.J., Elwood, K.J. and Chang, S.E. (2017). Understanding post-earthquake decisions on multi-storey concrete buildings in Christchurch, New Zealand. *Bulletin of Earthquake Engineering* 15, 731–58.

Marsden, I. and Knox, G.A. (2008). Estuaries, harbours and inlets, in M. Winterbourn, G. Knox, C. Burrows and I. Marsden eds., *The Natural History of Canterbury*. Canterbury University Press, Christchurch, 735–70.

Marsh (2014). *Comparing Claims from Catastrophic Earthquakes*. Marsh & McLennan Companies, London.

Marshall, P. (2016). Redefining the garden city, in J. Harvey ed., *Christchurch – Five Years On, Architecture New Zealand*, March/April, 38–9.

Matan, A. and Newman, P. (2016). *People Cities. The Life and Legacy of Jan Gehl*. Island Press, Washington DC.

Matapopore (n.d.). Tūranga – The New Christchurch Central Library. Retrieved from: https://matapopore.co.nz/wp-content/uploads/2020/11/Final-Turanga.pdf

Matapopore Trust (2017). *Matapopore Cultural Design Strategy. The Ōtākaro Avon River*, Christchurch. Unpublished report.

Matthewman, S. and Byrd, H. (2020). A textbook case of how not to 'build back better'? Christchurch after the earthquakes (2010, 2011). Report presented at the World Urban Forum Abu Dhabi, February 2020.

Matthewman, S. and Uekusa, S. (2021). Theorising disaster communities, *Theory and Society* 50 (6), 965–84.

Matthews, P. (2012). Adrift in limbo land, *Stuff*, 4 February. Retrieved from: www.stuff.co.nz/the-press/news/christchurch-earthquake-2011/6365644/Adrift-in-limbo-land

Matthews, P. (2020). Munted: 'There was no dialogue, no transparency', *Stuff*, 2 September. Retrieved from: www.stuff.co.nz/the-press/news/122558553/munted-there-was-no-dialogue-no-transparency

McAloon, J. (2000a). The Christchurch elite, in J. Cookson and G. Dunstall eds., *Southern Capital: Christchurch. Towards a City Biography, 1850–2000*. Canterbury University Press, Christchurch, 193–221.

McAloon, J. (2000b). Radical Christchurch, in J. Cookson and G. Dunstall eds., *Southern Capital: Christchurch. Towards a City Biography, 1850–2000*. Canterbury University Press, Christchurch, 162–92.

McClure, J., Wills, C., Johnston, D. and Recker, C. (2011). How the 2010 Canterbury (Darfield) earthquake affected earthquake risk perception: Comparing citizens inside and outside the earthquake region, *Australasian Journal of Disaster and Trauma Studies* 2011 (2), 3–10.

McCrone, J. (2011). Chch CBD masterplan - a major risk? *Stuff*, 25 September. Retrieved from: www.stuff.co.nz/business/rebuilding-christchurch/5676846/Chch-CBD-masterplan-a-major-risk

McCrone, J. (2012a). Crunch time for central city blueprint, *Stuff*, 18 November. Retrieved from: www.stuff.co.nz/the-press/business/the-rebuild/7963020/Crunch-time-for-central-city-blueprint

McCrone, J. (2012b). Rebuilding to avoid drunken chaos, *Stuff*, 7 July. Retrieved from: www.stuff.co.nz/the-press/news/christchurch-earthquake-2011/7237990/Rebuilding-to-avoid-drunken-chaos

McCrone, J. (2014a). Christchurch's $600 million motorways, *Stuff*, 19 October. Retrieved from: www.stuff.co.nz/the-press/news/10632484/Christchurchs-600-million-motorways?rm=m

McCrone, J. (2014b), Christchurch rebuild: A city stalled, *Stuff*, 9 March. Retrieved from: www.stuff.co.nz/the-press/business/the-rebuild/9805314/Christchurch-rebuild-A-city-stalled

McCrone, J. (2015a). Christchurch retail precinct 'good as done', *Stuff*, 16 May. Retrieved from: www.stuff.co.nz/the-press/business/the-rebuild/68470623/christchurch-retail-precinct-good-as-done

McCrone, J. (2015b). The long wait for Christchurch's Metro Sports anchor project, *Stuff*, 26 June. Retrieved from: www.stuff.co.nz/the-press/business/the-rebuild/69718112/the-long-wait-for-christchurchs-metro-sports-anchor-project

McCrone, J. (2016a). Rolleston: Time to take it seriously, *Stuff*, 20 August. Retrieved from: www.stuff.co.nz/the-press/news/83246929/rolleston-time-to-take-it-seriously?rm=m

McCrone, J. (2016b). How the quakes changed the shopping geography of Christchurch, *Stuff*, 27 May. Retrieved from: www.stuff.co.nz/the-press/news/80398637/how-the-quakes-changed-the-shopping-geography-of-christchurch

McCrone, J. (2017). The future isn't going anywhere, so why did Christchurch rebuild the city of yesterday? *Stuff*, 26 August. Retrieved from: www.stuff.co.nz/the-press/news/95661149/the-future-isnt-going-anywhere-so-why-did-christchurch-rebuild-the-city-of-yesterday

McDonagh, J. (2014). Housing affordability in post-earthquake Christchurch. *Proceedings of the 20th Pacific Rim Real Estate Society Conference*, Lincoln, Canterbury, 19–22 January.

McDonagh, J. (2017). Shattered Dreams – Inner City Revitalisation, Gentrification and the Christchurch Earthquakes of 2010 and 2011. Unpublished PhD thesis, Lincoln University, Canterbury.

McDonagh, J. (2021). Personal communication, 23 August. John McDonagh was then honorary Associate Professor of Property, Lincoln University, Canterbury.

McDonald, L. (2012). Property owners leaving town, *Stuff*, 20 February. Retrieved from: www.stuff.co.nz/the-press/business/6440143/Property-owners-leaving-town

McDonald, L. (2013a). TC3 homes stigma in decline – industry, *Stuff*, 17 June. Retrieved from: www.stuff.co.nz/the-press/editors-picks/8802864/TC3-homes-stigma-in-decline-industry

McDonald, L. (2013b). Median house prices hit high, *Stuff*, 15 October. Retrieved from: www.stuff.co.nz/the-press/news/canterbury/9285625/Median-house-prices-hit-high

McDonald, L. (2013c). Who owns our city? *The Press*. 30 January, 1.

McDonald, L. (2013d). Key city investor pulls out, *Stuff*, 10 April. Retrieved from: www.stuff.co.nz/the-press/8492985/Key-city-investor-pulls-out

McDonald, L. (2015a). Developer slams council for sluggish city rebuild, *The Press*, 27 April, 8.

McDonald, L. (2015b). Turning point: Momentum in central city to swell after influx, *The Press*, 1 May, 1.

McDonald, L. (2016). Christchurch's $16.8m music venue The Piano ready for. August opening, *Stuff*, 8 June. Retrieved from: www.stuff.co.nz/business/80810200/newest-music-venue-filling-up

McDonald, L. (2017a). International flavours comes to High Street, *Stuff*. 28 May. Retrieved from: www.stuff.co.nz/the-press/business/92950946/international-flavours-comes-to-high-street

McDonald, L. (2017b). Revitalised Christchurch central city still seen as fragile, *Stuff*, 22 September. Retrieved from: www.stuff.co.nz/the-press/business/the-rebuild/96966272/revitalised-christchurch-central-city-still-seen-as-fragile

McDonald, L. (2017c). Council goes after central Christchurch's 'dirty 30' building owners who are 'kicking the city in the face', *Stuff*, 24 May. Retrieved from: www.stuff.co.nz/the-press/news/92863275/council-goes-after-central-christchurchs-dirty-30-building-owners-who-are-kicking-the-city-in-the-face

McDonald, L. (2018a). Project 8011 plans to repopulate central Christchurch, *Stuff*, 20 August. Retrieved from: www.stuff.co.nz/the-press/news/106380722/project-8011-plans-to-repopulate-central-christchurch

McDonald, L. (2018b). Sustainable apartment plan chosen for Crown-owned Christchurch site, *Stuff*, 21 December. Retrieved from: www.stuff.co.nz/business/109545173/sustainable-apartment-plan-chosen-for-crownowned-christchurch-site

McDonald, L. (2018c). A matter of trust: Iwi voice in Christchurch rebuild, *Stuff*, 20 July. Retrieved from: www.stuff.co.nz/the-press/business/the-rebuild/103275206/a-matter-of-trust-iwi-voice-in-christchurch-rebuild

McDonald, L. (2019a). Central city living is slow to take off in Christchurch, *Stuff*, 26 October. Retrieved from: www.stuff.co.nz/business/116880859/central-city-living-is-slow-to-take-off-in-christchurch

McDonald, L. (2019b). Investors choosing apartments in Christchurch over pricey North Island homes, *Stuff*, 22 July. Retrieved from: www.stuff.co.nz/business/property/114253407/investors-choosing-apartments-in-christchurch-over-pricey-north-island-homes

McDonald, L. (2019c). Finishing touches as Riverside Market prepares to open, *Stuff*, September 17. Retrieved from: www.stuff.co.nz/business/116086749/finishing-touches-as-riverside-market-prepares-to-open

McDonald, L. (2019d). $500m for new Catholic cathedral, school, hotels and car parking in central Christchurch, *Stuff*, 7 December. Retrieved from: www.stuff.co.nz/national/117961049/500m-for-new-catholic-cathedral-school-hotels-and-car-parking-in-central-christchurch

McDonald, L. (2020a). Group pulls out of Crown village plan, *The Press*, 2 December, 12.

McDonald, L. (2020b). Apartment sales pick up in central Christchurch's 'east frame', *Stuff*, 26 October. Retrieved from: www.stuff.co.nz/life-style/homed/real-estate/123147681/apartment-sales-pick-up-in-central-christchurchs-east-frame

McDonald, L. (2020c). New home boom in Chch worth $1 billion, *The Press*, 12 September, 1.

McDonald, L. (2020d). Christchurch nine years on: The reshaping of a city, *Stuff*, 22 February. Retrieved from: www.stuff.co.nz/national/119421238/christchurch-nine-years-on-the-reshaping-of-a-city

McDonald, L. (2020e). Emboldened geese invading city centre face population control, *Stuff*, 17 June. Retrieved from: www.stuff.co.nz/national/121676090/emboldened-geese-invading-city-centre-face-population-control

McDonald, L. (2021a). Central Christchurch site up for sale as 'sustainable village' anchor project finally abandoned, *Stuff*, 18 February. Retrieved from: www.stuff.co.nz/the-press/news/124273640/central-christchurch-site-up-for-sale-as-sustainable-village-anchor-project-finally-abandoned

McDonald, L. (2021b). Central Christchurch home building lags behind demand. *Stuff*, 1 March. Retrieved from: www.stuff.co.nz/life-style/homed/real-estate/124358871/central-christchurch-home-building-lags-behind-demand

McDonald, L. (2021c). More homes built but they are smaller, *The Press*. 13 March, 1.

McDonald, L. (2021d) Bid for 2000 new homes at Lincoln, *The Press* 20 March, 1.

McDonald, L. (2021e). Big players plan $90m precinct for key city site, *The Press*, 12 June, 1.

McDonald, L. (2022). CBD residents pass pre-quake numbers, *The Press* 14 February, 1.

McDowall, C. and Denee, T. (2019). *We Are Here. An Atlas of Aotearoa*. Massey University Press, Auckland.

McLean, I., Oughton, D., Ellis, S., Wakelin, B. and Rubin, C.B. (2012). Review of the Civil Defence Emergency Response to the 22 February 2011 Earthquake. Retrieved from: www.civildefence.govt.nz/resources/review-of-the-civil-defence-emergency-management-response-to-the-22-february-christchurch-earthquake/

{mds} law (2012). Newsletter: The Christchurch recovery plan. Retrieved from: www.mdslaw.co.nz/getattachment/e61bd861-41f8-41d7-aaea-364d9980af59/News-Publications-2012-The-Christchurch-Central-Recovery-Plan.aspx

Mead, T. (2017). Post-earthquake nightlife finally opening in Christchurch, *Newshub*, 11 January. Retrieved from: www.newshub.co.nz/home/new-zealand/2017/08/post-earthquake-nightlife-finally-opening-in-christchurch.html

Measures, R., Hicks, M., Shankar, U., Bind, J., Arnold, J. and Zeld, J. (2011). *Mapping Earthquake Induced Topographical Change and Liquefaction in the Avon-Heathcote Estuary*, Report No. U11/13. Environment Canterbury, Christchurch.

Meethan, K. (1996). Consuming (in) the civilized city, *Annals of Tourism Research* 23 (2), 322–40.

Meier, C. (2014). Christchurch rebuild ripoffs nail migrants, *Stuff*, 22 March. Retrieved from: www.stuff.co.nz/business/industries/9855596/Christchurch-rebuild-ripoffs-nail-migrants

Memon, P.A. (2003). Urban growth management in Christchurch, *New Zealand Geographer* 59 (1), 27–39.

Mental Health Foundation (n.d.). Five ways to wellbeing. Retrieved from: https://mentalhealth.org.nz/five-ways-to-wellbeing

Merkin, R. (2012). The Christchurch earthquakes insurance and reinsurance issues, *Canterbury Law Review* 18, 119–154.

Merritt, L. (2015). Personal communication, 11 March. Lauren Merritt was then Chief Executive Officer of the Ministry of Awesome.

Meurk, C.D. (2021). Think like a matai, in S. Goldsmith ed., *Tree Sense. Ways of Thinking about Trees*. Massey University Press, Auckland, 143–68.

Meurk, C. and Swaffield, S. (2000). A landscape ecological framework for indigenous regeneration in rural New Zealand-Aotearoa, *Landscape and Urban Planning* 50 (1–3), 129–44.

Meurk, C. and Swaffield, S. (2007). Cities as complex landscapes: Biodiversity opportunities, landscape configurations and design directions, *New Zealand Garden Journal* 10, 10–19.

Miles, S-A. (2016). *The Insurance Aftershock. The Christchurch Fiasco Post-earthquakes 2010–2016*, 2nd edn., Labyrinth Publishing, Christchurch.

Miller, S. (2012). Interest groups - Community and recreational groups. *Te Ara - the Encyclopedia of New Zealand.* Retrieved from: https://teara.govt.nz/en/interest-groups

Milligan, C. and Conradson, D. eds. (2006). *Landscapes of Voluntarism: New Spaces of Health, Welfare and Governance*. Policy Press, Bristol.

Ministry of Business, Innovation and Employment (2013). *Housing Pressures in Christchurch: A Summary of the Evidence*. Wellington, New Zealand. Retrieved from: www.mbie.govt.nz/dmsdocument/1088-housing-pressures-christchurch-2013-pdf

Ministry of Business, Innovation and Employment (2017). *Responses to the Canterbury Earthquakes Royal Commission Recommendations. Final Report*. Ministry of Business, Innovation and Employment, Wellington.

Ministry of Education (2021). *Rebuilding Christchurch Schools*. Retrieved from: www.education.govt.nz/our-work/changes-in-education/rebuilding-christchurch-schools/

Ministry for the Environment (1997). *The State of New Zealand's Environment 1997*. Ministry for the Environment/GP Publications, Wellington.

Ministry for the Environment (2008). *Urban Design Case Studies: Local Government*. Wellington. Retrieved from: https://environment.govt.nz/publications/urban-design-case-studies-local-government/

Mitchell, T. (2021). The Dirty 30 is down to the final six uildings. *Metronews*, 12 May. Retrieved from: https://metronews.co.nz/article/new-article-207

Monk, C.B., Van Ballegooy, S., Hughes, M. and Villeneuve, M. (2016). Liquefaction vulnerability increase at North New Brighton due to subsidence, sea level rise and reduction in thickness of the non-liquefying layer, *Bulletin of the New Zealand Society for Earthquake Engineering* 49 (4), 334–40.

Morgan, J., Begg, A., Beaven, S., Schluter, P., Jamieson, K., Johal, S., Johnston, D. and Sparrow, M. (2015). Monitoring wellbeing during recovery from the 2010–2011 Canterbury earthquakes: The CERA Wellbeing Survey, *International Journal of Disaster Risk Reduction* 14 (1), 96–103.

Morgenroth, J. (2017). Tree canopy cover in Christchurch New Zealand. Prepared for the Christchurch City Council. Retrieved from: https://ccc.govt.nz/assets/Documents/Environment/Trees/Tree-cover-in-Christchurch-final-report.pdf

Morgenroth, J. and Armstrong, T. (2012). The impact of significant earthquakes on Christchurch, New Zealand's urban forest, *Urban Forestry and Urban Greening* 11 (4), 383–9.

Moricz, Z., Wong, C. and Bond, S. (2012). *The Impacts of The Canterbury Earthquake on the Commercial Office Market*, CBRE and Lincoln University, Canterbury.

Morris, J.D.K. and Ruru, J. (2010). Giving voice to rivers: Legal personality as a vehicle for recognising indigenous peoples' relationships to water?, *Australian Indigenous Law Review* 14 (2), 49–62.

Mueller, S. (2017). Incommensurate values? Environment Canterbury and local democracy. *New Zealand Journal of Public and International Law* 15, 293–312.

Murphy, L. (2019). *Financiers and developers: Interviews concerning their interests, relationships and the residential development process*. Building Better Homes, Towns and Cities SRA1 – The Architecture of Decision-making Working Paper, School of Environment. University of Auckland, Auckland.

Murphy, L. (2020). Performing calculative practices: Residual valuation, the residential development process and affordable housing, *Housing Studies* 35 (9), 1501–17.

Murphy, S. (2015). Margaret Mahy ChCh playground opens, *Radio New Zealand*. Retrieved from: www.rnz.co.nz/news/regional/292727/margaret-mahy-chch-playground-opens

Mutch, C. (2017). Winners and losers: School closures in post-earthquake Canterbury and the dissolution of community, *Waikato Journal of Education* 22 (1), 73–95.

Mutch, C. (2018). The role of schools in helping communities copes with earthquake disasters: The case of the 2010–2011 New Zealand earthquakes, *Environmental Hazards* 17 (4), 331–51.

Naylor Love (2021). Our projects. New Regent Street, Christchurch. Retrieved from: www.naylorlove.co.nz/project/new-regent-street/

Neilson, M. (2021). Mental health: Minister Andrew Little 'extraordinarily' frustrated with slow spend on $1.9b package from 2019 Budget, *New Zealand Herald*, 22 June. Retrieved from: www.nzherald.co.nz/nz/mental-health-minister-andrew-little-extraordinarily-frustrated-with-slow-spend-on-19b-package-from-2019-budget/OG62VGSHJJHGRLF3SHPKM5HBJU/

Newell, J., Beaven, S. and Johnston, D.M. (2012). *Population Movements Following the 2010–2011 Canterbury Earthquakes: Summary of Research Workshops November 2011 and Current Evidence*. GNS Science Miscellaneous Series 44. GNS Science, Lower Hutt.

Newman-Storen, R. and Reynolds, R. (2013). Conversations over the gap, *Performance Research* 18 (3), 47–53.

New Zealand Government (2011). Govt outlines next steps for people of Canterbury. Retrieved from: www.beehive.govt.nz/release/govt-outlines-next-steps-people-canterbury

New Zealand Herald (2013). Four Christchurch schools to be replaced, 11 September. Retrieved from: www.nzherald.co.nz/nz/four-christchurch-schools-to-be-replaced/2GCEJTS36IBBRWAKU2K4TDVB7A/

New Zealand Police (2022). Christchurch earthquake. List of deceased. Retrieved from: www.police.govt.nz/news/major-events/previous-major-events/christchurch-earthquake/list-deceased

Nguyen, C. and Noy, I. (2017). Insuring earthquakes: How would the Californian and Japanese insurance programs have fared down under (After the 2011 New Zealand earthquake)? *SEF Working Paper 14/2017*, School of Economics and Finance, Victoria Business School, Wellington.

Nicholson, H. (2016). Cityscaping, in J. Harvey ed., *Christchurch – Five Years on, Architecture New Zealand* March/April, 47–8.

Nicholson, H. (2020). In G. Smyth, dir., *When a City Rises*, Frank Films. Retrieved from: www.nzonscreen.com/title/when-a-city-rises-2020

Nicholson, H. and Wykes, F. (2012). Share an Idea, *Urban Design* 123, 30–3.

Nielsen (2016). *Residential Red Zone Survey*. Nielsen, Auckland. Retrieved from: https://dpmc.govt.nz/sites/default/files/2017-03/cera-rrz-surveyreport-feb2016.pdf

Nissen, S., Carlton, S., Wong, J.H.K. and Johnson, S. (2021). 'Spontaneous' volunteers? Factors enabling the Student Volunteer Army mobilisation following the Canterbury earthquakes, 2010–2011, *International Journal of Disaster Risk Reduction* 53, 102008.

Norcliffe, J. and Preston, J. (2016). *Leaving the Red Zone: Poems from the Canterbury Earthquakes*. Clerestory Press, Christchurch.

Nowland-Foreman, G. (2016). Crushed or just bruised? Voluntary organisations - 25 years under the bear hug of government funding in Aotearoa New Zealand, *Third Sector Review* 22 (2), 53–69.

Noy, I., Kusuma, A. and Nguyen, C. (2017). Insuring disasters: A survey of the economics of insurance programs for earthquakes and droughts, *SEF Working Paper 11/2017*, School of Economics and Finance, Victoria Business School, Wellington.

NZLS (2010). Law Society comments on Canterbury Earthquake Response and Recovery Act, New Zealand Law Society, 30 September. Retrieved from: https://web.archive.org/web/20110720085134/http://www.lawsociety.org.nz/home/for_the_public/for_the_media/latest_news/news/september/law_society_comments_on_canterbury_earthquake_response_and_recovery_act

O'Callaghan, J. (2019). 'Things are not OK': Students at experimental school speak out, *Stuff*, 22 June. Retrieved from: www.stuff.co.nz/national/education/113205774/haeata-community-campus-students-begging-to-be-taught

O'Callaghan, J. (2021). February 2011: Earthquakes allow Christchurch's culture to change, *Stuff*, 22 February. Retrieved from: www.stuff.co.nz/pou-tiaki/300231617/february-2011-earthquakes-allow-christchurchs-culture-to-change

OECD (2020). *Innovative Citizen Participation and New Democratic Institutions. Catching the Deliberative Wave*. OECD Publishing, Paris.

OECD (2021). *Anticipatory Innovation Governance: What It Is, How It Works, and Why We Need It More Than Ever Before*. OECD Publishing, Paris.

Ombudsman (2018). Chief Ombudsman releases final opinion on East Lake Trust/Regenerate Christchurch case, 22 July. Retrieved from: www.ombudsman.parliament.nz/sites/default/files/2019-07/mediarelease-eastlakeregenerate.pdf

O'Neill, R. (2012). Compulsory acquisition could reconfigure Christchurch CBD, *Stuff*, 1 May. Retrieved from: www.stuff.co.nz/business/6831407/Compulsory-acquisition-could-reconfigure-Christchurch-CBD

OPES partners (2022). Canterbury property market, 27 January. Retrieved from: https://www.opespartners.co.nz/property-markets/canterbury

Orange, C. (1987). *The Treaty of Waitangi*. Allen and Unwin, Wellington.

Orchard, S. (2017). *Integrated Assessment Frameworks for Evaluating Large Scale River Corridor Restoration*. Report prepared for the Avon Ōtākaro Network, Christchurch.

Orchard, S., Hickford, M.J.H. and Schiel, D.R. (2018). Earthquake induced habitat migration in a riparian spawning fish has implications for conservation management, *Aquatic Conservation. Marine Freshwater Ecosystems* 28 (3), 702–12.

Otago Daily Times (2019). Government to pay up to $300 million for shoddy quake repairs, *Otago Daily Times*, 15 August. Retrieved from: www.odt.co.nz/news/national/govt-pay-300m-shoddy-quake-repairs

Otago Daily Times (2020). 10 years on: Homes still broken, insurance claims reopened, *Otago Daily Times*, 4 September. Retrieved from: www.odt.co.nz/star-news/star-christchurch/10-years-homes-still-broken-insurance-claims-reopened

Ōtākaro Limited (2021). Unparalleled development opportunities. Retrieved from: www.otakaroltd.co.nz/news-and-videos/unparalleled-development-opportunities/

Pain, R. (2019). Chronic urban trauma: The slow violence of housing dispossession, *Urban Studies* 56 (2), 385–400.

Parker, D. (2020). Disaster resilience – a challenged science, *Environmental Hazards* 19 (1), 1–9.

Parker, G. (2014). A new city through the arts?, in Bennett, B., Dann, J., Johnson, E. and Reynolds, R. eds., *Once in a Lifetime: City-building after Disaster in Christchurch*, Free Range Press, Christchurch, 338–41.

Parker, M. and Steenkamp, D. (2012). *The Economic Impact of the Canterbury Earthquakes*. Reserve Bank of New Zealand, Wellington.

Parliamentary Commissioner for the Environment (2015). *Preparing New Zealand for Rising Seas: Certainty and Uncertainty*. Office of the Parliamentary Commissioner for the Environment, Wellington.

Parsons, M. (2014). *Rubble to Resurrection: Churches Respond in the Canterbury Quakes*. DayStar, Auckland.

Paton, D., Selway, K.L., Mamula-Seadon, L. and GNS Science (2013). *Community Resilience in Christchurch: Adaptive Responses and Capacities During Earthquake Recovery*. GNS Science, Wellington.

Pauling, C., Awatere, S. and Rolleston, S. (2014). What has Ōtautahi revealed? Māori urban planning in post-earthquake Christchurch, in B. Bennett, J. Dann, E. Johnson and R. Reynolds eds., *Once in a Lifetime: City-building after Disaster in Christchurch*, Freerange Press, Christchurch, 452–64.

Pawson, E. (1999). Remaking places, in R. Le Heron, P. Forer, L. Murphy and M. Goldstone eds., *Explorations in Human Geography. Encountering Place*. Oxford University Press, Auckland, 345–66.

Pawson, E. (2000). Confronting nature, in J. Cookson and G. Dunstall eds., *Southern Capital Christchurch. Towards a City Biography 1850-2000*. Canterbury University Press, Christchurch, 60–84.

Pawson, E. (2011). Environmental hazards and natural disasters, *New Zealand Geographer* 67 (3), 143–47.

Pawson, E. (2022). Planning, governance and a city for the future? in S. Uekusa, S. Matthewman and B.C. Glavovic eds., *A Decade of Disaster Experiences in Ōtautahi Christchurch. Critical Disaster Studies Perspectives*. Palgrave Macmillan, Singapore, 317–34.

Pawson, E. and Christensen, A.A. (2014). Landscapes of the Anthropocene: From dominion to dependence? in J. Frawley and I. McCalman eds., *Rethinking Invasion Ecologies from the Environmental Humanities*. Routledge, London, 64–83.

Pawson, E., Kerr, R., Mein Smith, P. and Williams, C. (2019). *Ōtākaro Avon River Corridor. Governance Case Studies*. University of Canterbury, Christchurch.

Pawson, E. and Swaffield, S.R. (1998). Landscapes of leisure and tourism, in Perkins, H.C. and Cushman, G. eds., *Time Out? Leisure, Recreation and Tourism in Australia and New Zealand*, Longman Paul, Auckland, 254–70.

Peart, R. and Cox, B. (2019). *Governance of the Hauraki Gulf. A Review of Options*. Environmental Defence Society, Auckland.

Peat, N. (2018). *The Invading Sea. Coastal Hazards and Climate Change in Aotearoa New Zealand*. The Cuba Press, Wellington.

Pelling, M. (2010). Disaster politics: Tipping points for change in the adaption of socio-political regimes, *Progress in Human Geography* 34 (1), 21–37.

Percasky, M. (2020). Personal communication, 3 August. Mike Percasky was then a central city investor and developer involved in the Riverside Market and SALT initiative.

Percasky, M. and Shaw, G. (2020). Presentation to the Tuesday Club, Christchurch, July 21.

Perkins, H.C. and Rosin, C. (2018). Tourism, landscapes, and biological resources, in E. Pawson and the Biological Economies Team, *The New Biological Economy. How New Zealanders are Creating Value from the Land*, Auckland University Press, Auckland, 137–56.

Perkins, H.C. and Thorns, D.C. (2011). *Place, Identity and Everyday Life in a Globalizing World*, Macmillan, London.

Perrow, C. (1986). *Complex Organizations: A Critical Essay*. McGraw Hill, New York.

Pickles, K. (2016). *Christchurch Ruptures*. Bridget Williams Books, Wellington.

Place Leaders (2019). Place Leaders Asia Pacific, 2019 Place Leaders Awards. Retrieved from: www.placeleaders.com/post/2019-place-leaders-awards

Poontirakul, P., Brown, C., Noy, I., Seville, E. and Vargo, J. (2016). The role of commercial insurance in post-disaster recovery: Quantitative evidence from the 2011 earthquake. *Working Papers in Economics and Finance 01/2016*, School of Economics and Finance, Victoria Business School, Wellington.

Poontirakul, P., Brown, C., Seville, E., Vargo, J. and Noy, I. (2017). Insurance as a double-edged sword: Quantitative evidence from the 2011 Christchurch earthquake, *Geneva Papers on Risk and Insurance. Issues and Practice* 42 (4), 609–32.

Potongaroa, R., Wilkinson, S., Zare, M. and Steinfort, P. (2011). The management of portable toilets in the eastern suburbs of Christchurch after the February 22, 2011 earthquake, *Australasian Journal of Disaster and Studies* 2, 35–48.

Potter, S.H., Becker, J.S., Johnston, D.M. and Rossiter, K.P. (2015). An overview of the impacts of the 2010–2011 Canterbury earthquakes, *International Journal of Disaster Risk Reduction* 14 (1), 6–14.

Potts, A. and Gadenne, D. (2014). *Animals in Emergencies: Learning from the Christchurch Earthquakes*. Canterbury University Press, Christchurch.

The Press (2017). Editorial: Unleashing excitement in the red zone will make it Christchurch's field of dreams, August 30.

Pressman, J.L. and Wildavsky, A. (1984). *Implementation: How Great Expectations in Washington are Dashed in Oakland; Or, Why it's Amazing that Federal Programs Work at All, This Being a Saga of the Economic Development Administration as Told by Two Sympathetic Observers Who Seek to Build Morals on a Foundation* of Ruined Hopes (Vol. 708). University of California Press, Berkeley.

Preston, J. (2016). Report on the launch of Leaving the Red Zone. Retrieved from: https://joannapreston.com/2016/03/09/report-on-the-launch-of-leaving-the-red-zone/

Price, D. (2011). *Population and household trends in Christchurch post February 22 earthquake*. Population and Employment Effects of the Christchurch Earthquakes workshop. Lincoln University, Canterbury.

Project Lyttelton (2022). Welcome to Project Lyttelton. Retrieved from: www.projectlyttelton.org

Public Inquiry (2020). *Report of the Public Inquiry into the Earthquake Commission*, Earthquake Commission, Wellington. Retrieved from: https://dpmc.govt.nz/our-programmes/special-programmes/inquiry-eqc

Puig de la Bellacasa, M. (2017). *Matters of Care: Speculative Ethics in More Than Human Worlds*. University of Minnesota Press, Minneapolis.

Quake Outcasts (2016). Between Quake Outcasts and the Minister for Canterbury Earthquake Recovery, and the Chief Executive, Canterbury Earthquake Recovery Authority, CIV-2016-409-000050, NZHC 1959. Retrieved from: https://forms.justice.govt.nz/search/Documents/pdf/jdo/90/alfresco/service/api/node/content/workspace/SpacesStore/edc623c2-afe7-47ef-aa27-5a74a04a87b0/edc623c2-afe7-47ef-aa27-5a74a04a87b0.pdf

Quarantelli, E.L. (1999). *The Disaster Recovery Process. What We Know and Do Not Know from Research*. Disaster Research Center, University of Delaware, Newark, DE.

Quarantelli, E.L. and Dynes, R.R. (1977). Response to social crisis and disaster, *Annual Review of Sociology* 3 (1), 23–49.

Queenstown Airport Company (2021). Airport statistics. Retrieved from: www.queenstownairport.co.nz/corporate/airport-statistics

RNZ (2012). 13 schools to close, others to merge in Christchurch. Retrieved from: www.rnz.co.nz/news/canterbury-earthquake/115789/13-schools-to-close,-others-to-merge-in-christchurch

RNZ (2013). Inquiry into consultation on school restructuring progressing. Retrieved from: www.rnz.co.nz/news/national/214823/inquiry-into-consultation-on-school-restructuring-progressing

RNZ (2021). Hoiho Lane housing development opens in Christchurch. 9 July. Retrievedfrom:www.rnz.co.nz/news/national/446534/hoiho-lane-housing-development-opens-in-christchurch

Redzonecats (2021). Red Zone Cats. Retrieved from: https://redzonecats.org.nz

Regenerate Christchurch (2018a). *Whiti-Reia Cathedral Square. Our Long Term Vision*. Regenerate Christchurch, Christchurch.

Regenerate Christchurch (2018b). *Draft Ōtākaro Avon River Regeneration Plan*, Regenerate Christchurch, Christchurch.

Regenerate Christchurch (2019). *Ōtākaro Avon River Corridor Regeneration Plan*, Regenerate Christchurch, Christchurch.

Regenerate Christchurch (2021). Te Kōwhatawhata. About Us. Retrieved from: www.regeneratechristchurch.nz/about-us/

Resilient New Zealand (2015). *Contributing More: Improving the Role of Business in Recovery*. Retrieved from: https://iag.co.nz/content/dam/corporate-iag/iag-nz/nz/en/documents/corporate/business-role-in-recovery.pdf

Reynolds, R. (2014). Desire for the gap, in B. Bennett, J. Dann, E. Johnson and R. Reynolds eds., *Once in a Lifetime: City-building after Disaster in Christchurch*. Free Range Press, Christchurch, 167–76.

Reynolds, R. (2015). Looking backwards, thinking forwards. Retrieved from: www.gapfiller.org.nz/looking-backwards-thinking-forwards/

Rice, G. (2011). *All Fall Down. Christchurch's Lost Chimneys*. Canterbury University Press, Christchurch.

Roberts, M. (2006). From 'creative city' to 'no-go areas' - the expansion of the night-time economy in British town and city centres, *Cities 23* (5), 331–38.

Roe, J. and McCay, L. (2021). *Restorative Cities. Urban Design for Mental Health and Wellbeing*. Bloomsbury, London.

Rose, G. (1997). Situated knowledges: Positionality, reflexivities and other tactics, *Progress in Human Geography* 21 (3), 305–20.

Roughan, J. (2017). *John Key. Portrait of a Prime Minister*. rev. edn., Penguin Random House, Auckland.

Royal Commission (2012a). *Final Report*, Canterbury Earthquakes Royal Commission. Retrievedfrom:https://canterbury.royalcommission.govt.nz/Final-Report---Volumes-1-2-and-3

Royal Commission (2012b). *The Performance of Christchurch CBD buildings, Final Report, vol 2*. Canterbury Earthquakes Royal Commission. Retrieved from: https://canterbury.royalcommission.govt.nz/Final-Report-Volume-Two-Contents

Royal Commission (2012c). *Canterbury Television Building (CTV), Final Report, vol 6*. Canterbury Earthquakes Royal Commission. Retrieved from: https://canterbury.royalcommission.govt.nz/Final-Report-Volume-Six-Contents

Sachdeva, S. (2012). City looks ahead to much brighter future, *Stuff*, 2 January. www.stuff.co.nz/the-press/news/christchurch-earthquake-2011/6207203/City-looks-ahead-to-a-much-brighter-future

Sachdeva, S. and Carville, O. (2011). Christchurch rebuild plans 'rubbish', *Stuff*, 11 October. Retrieved from: www.stuff.co.nz/the-press/5763561/Christchurch-rebuild-plans-rubbish

Salmond, A. (2021). Three Waters and Te Tiriti, *Newsroom*, 22 December. Retrieved from: www.newsroom.co.nz/ideasroom/anne-salmond-three-waters-and-te-tiriti

Sanders, K. (2018). 'Beyond human ownership'? Property, power and legal personality for nature in Aotearoa New Zealand, *Journal of Environmental Law* 30 (2), 207–34.

Saunders, W.S.A. and Becker, J.S. (2015). A discussion of resilience and sustainability: Land use planning recovery from the Canterbury earthquake sequence, New Zealand, *International Journal of Disaster Risk Reduction*, 14, 73–81.

Schöllmann, A., Perkins, H.C. and Moore, K. (2000). Intersecting global and local influences in urban place promotion: The case of Christchurch, New Zealand, *Environment and Planning A* 32 (1), 55–76.

Schrader, B. (1997). Drains and plagues. Making Christchurch healthy, 1860s–1910s, in M. McKinnon ed., *New Zealand Historical Atlas*. David Bateman, Auckland, plate 55.

Scoop (2011a). Share an Idea wins international award, 24 November. Retrieved from: www.scoop.co.nz/stories/AK1111/S00632/share-an-idea-wins-international-award.htm

Scoop (2011b). Campaign for a memorial reserve covenant. Retrieved from: https://img.scoop.co.nz/media/pdfs/1108/CAMPAIGN.pdf

Scott, J.C. (1998). *Seeing Like a State. How Certain Schemes to Improve the Human Condition Have Failed*. Yale University Press, New Haven.

Seager, P. and Donnell, D. (2013). *Responders. The New Zealand Volunteer Response Teams Christchurch Earthquake Deployments*. Keswin Publishing, Christchurch.

Searle, W., McLeod, K. and Ellen-Eliza, N. (2015). *Vulnerable Temporary Migrant Workers: Canterbury Construction Industry*. Ministry of Business, Innovation and Employment, Wellington. Retrieved from: www.mbie.govt.nz/dmsdocument/2681-vulnerable-temporary-migrant-workers-canterbury-construction-pdf

Sessions, L.A. and Bullock, C. (2013). *Quake Dogs. Heart-Warming Stories of Christchurch Dogs*. Random House, Auckland.

Shaw, I. (2012). Towards an eventual geography, *Progress in Human Geography* 36 (5), 613–27.

Shaw, R. (2010). Neoliberal subjectivities and the development of the night-time economy in British cities, *Geography Compass* 4 (7), 893–903.

Sinclair, L. (2019). *Annual Review of the Greater Christchurch Regeneration Act 2016*, Department of Prime Minister and Cabinet, Christchurch.

Singer, M. (2020). Fendalton in Christchurch offers prestige properties, historic and new, *Mansion Global*, 30 May. Retrieved from: www.mansionglobal.com/articles/fendalton-in-christchurch-offers-prestige-properties-historic-and-new-215252

Škare, M., Soriano, D.R. and Porada-Rochoń, M. (2021). Impact of COVID-19 on the travel and tourism industry, *Technological Forecasting and Social Change* 163, 120469.

Small, J. and Meier, C. (2017). Labour announces $300m for Christchurch rebuild, *Stuff*, 27 August. Retrieved from: www.stuff.co.nz/the-press/business/the-rebuild/96197777/labour-announces-300m-for-christchurch-rebuild

Smith, A. (2017). The global game: Commodifying the playground at the end of the empire, *Interventions* 19 (7), 1056–67.

Smith, E. (2018). After seven years, who is scratching the itch in Christchurch's east? *Stuff*, 12 March. Retrieved from: www.stuff.co.nz/the-press/business/the-rebuild/101804585/after-seven-years-who-is-scratching-the-itch-in-christchurchs-east

Smith, J. (2014). Christchurch – a state of emergency, in B. Bennett, J. Dann, E. Johnson and R. Reynolds eds., *Once in a Lifetime. City-building After Disaster in Christchurch*. Freerange Press, Christchurch, 145–9.

Soens, T. (2020). Resilience in historical disaster studies: Pitfalls and opportunities, in M. Endress, L. Clemens and B. Rampp eds., *Strategies, Dispositions and Resources of Social Resilience*. Springer, Singapore, 253–75.

Solnit, R. (2009). *A Paradise Built in Hell. The Extraordinary Communities that Arise in Disaster*. Viking Penguin, New York.

Solomon, M. with Revington, M. (2021). *Mana Whakatipu. Ngāi Tahu Leader Mark Solomon on Leadership and Life*. Massey University Press, Auckland.

Spink, E. (2016). Visiting service set up for the elderly to curb loneliness, *Stuff*, 11 December. Retrieved from: www.stuff.co.nz/national/87383482/visiting-service-set-up-for-the-elderly-to-curb-loneliness

Spittlehouse, J.K., Joyce, P.R., Vierck, E., Schluter, P.J. and Pearson, J.F. (2014). Ongoing adverse mental health impact of the earthquake sequence in Canterbury, New Zealand, *Australian and New Zealand Journal of Psychiatry* 48 (8), 756–63.

Stallings, R.A. and Quarantelli, E.L. (1985). Emergent citizen groups and emergency, *Public Administration Review* 45, 93–100.

Statistics New Zealand (2013). *2013 Census data*. Retrieved from: https://stats.govt.nz/census/previous-censuses/2013-census/

Statistics NZ (2018). *Canterbury: The rebuild by the numbers*. Retrieved from: www.stats.govt.nz

Steeman, M. (2012). Business big guns join to shape retail future, *Stuff*, 27 October. Retrieved from: www.stuff.co.nz/the-press/news/7870830/Business-big-guns-join-to-shape-retail-future

Stengers, I. (2005). The cosmopolitical proposal, in B. Latour and P. Weibel eds., *Making Things Public: Atmospheres of Democracy*. MIT Press, Cambridge MA, 994–1003.

Stevenson, J. and Conradson, D. (2017). Organizational support networks and relational resilience after the 2010–2011 earthquakes in Canterbury, New Zealand, in Jones, E.C. and Faas, A.J. eds., *Social Network Analysis of Disaster Response, Recovery, and Adaptation*. Elsevier, Oxford, 161–76.

Stewart, A. (2013). Mahy-inspired playground wins top prize, *Stuff*, 23 May. Retrieved from: www.stuff.co.nz/the-press/editors-picks/8709026/Mahy-inspired-playground-wins-top-prize

Stoker, G. (1998). Governance as theory: Five propositions, *International Social Science Journal* 155, 17–28.

Strandh, V. and Eklund, N. (2018). Emergent groups in disaster research. Varieties of scientific observation over time and across studies of nine natural disasters, *Journal of Contingencies and Crisis Management* 26 (3), 329–37.

Stuff (2011). Quake know-how aid for Japan, *Stuff*, 24 April. Retrieved from: www.stuff.co.nz/the-press/news/4919917/Quake-know-how-aid-for-Japan

Stuff (2013). Editorial: Lessons from the school shake-up, *Stuff*, 20 February. Retrieved from: www.stuff.co.nz/dominion-post/comment/8324331/Editorial-Lessons-from-the-school-shake-up

Stuff (2015). Fletchers to build 191 inner-city homes for Christchurch, *Stuff*, 8 May. Retrieved from: www.stuff.co.nz/the-press/business/your-property/68403229/fletchers-to-build-191-inner-city-homes-for-christchurch

Stuff (2017). Editorial: Unleashing excitement in the red zone will make it Christchurch's field of dreams, *Stuff*, 30 August. Retrieved from: www.stuff.co.nz/the-press/business/the-rebuild/96310927/editorial-unleashing-excitement-in-the-red-zone-will-make-it-christchurchs-field-of-dreams

Stylianou, G. (2013). Tight-knit family behind tannery project, *Stuff*, 26 January. Retrieved from: www.stuff.co.nz/the-press/news/8226072/Tight-knit-family-behind-tannery-project

Stylianou, G. (2015). Report finds some migrant workers exploited, *Radio New Zealand*, 22 July. Retrieved from: www.rnz.co.nz/news/regional/279373/report-finds-some-migrant-workers-exploited

Stylianou, G. (2016). Regenerate Christchurch to investigate red zone water course, *Stuff*, 17 April. Retrieved from: www.stuff.co.nz/the-press/business/the-rebuild/79009732/regenerate-christchurch-to-investigate-red-zone-water-course

Sutch, W.B. (1966). *The Quest for Security in New Zealand, 1840–1966*, Oxford University Press, Wellington.

Swindell, D. and Rosentraub, M.S. (1998). Who benefits from the presence of professional sports teams? The implications for public funding of stadiums and arenas, *Public Administration Review* 58 (1), 11–20.

Tanner, T., Lewis, D., Wrathall, D., Bronen, R., Cradock-Henry, N., Huq, S., Lawless, C., Nawrotzki, R., Prasad, V., Rahman, M. and Alaniz, R. (2015). Livelihood resilience in the face of climate change, *Nature Climate Change* 5, 23–6.

Tatham, H. (2011). Social media key to 'army' success, *New Zealand Doctor* 15, 4 September.

Tau, T.M. ed., (2016). *Grand Narratives*. Canterbury Earthquake Recovery Authority, Christchurch.

Taylor, J.E., Chang, S.E., Elwood, K.J., Seville, E. and Brunsdon, D. (2012). *Learning from Christchurch: Technical Decisions and Societal Consequences in Post-Earthquake Recovery. Preliminary Research Findings*, August 2012. Resilient Organisations Programme, Christchurch.

Teller, C. (2008). Shopping streets versus shopping malls–determinants of agglomeration format attractiveness from the consumers' point of view, *The International Review of Retail, Distribution and Consumer Research* 18 (4), 381–403.

Tennant, M., O'Brien, M. and Sanders, J. (2008). *The History of the Non-profit Sector in New Zealand*. Office for the Community and Voluntary Sector, Wellington.

Te Putahi (2020). Te Putahi – about us. Retrieved from: https://teputahi.org.nz/about-us/

Thornley, L., Ball, J., Signal, L., Lawson-Te Aho, K. and Rawson, E. (2013). *Building Community Resilience: Learning from the Canterbury Earthquakes*. Final Report for Health Research Council and Canterbury Medical Research Foundation.

Thornley, L., Ball, J., Signal, L., Lawson-Te Aho, K. and Rawson, E. (2015). Building community resilience: Learning from the Canterbury earthquakes, *Kotuitui: New Zealand Journal of Social Sciences Online* 10 (1), 23–35.

The Press (2021). Commercial Property: Christchurch CBD office vacancy rate plunges to below pre-earthquake level, *The Press*, 22 September, 34.

The Star (2011). Earthquake 6.3 supplement. *APN New Zealand*, 22 February 2011.

Thompson, S., Espiner, S., Stewart, E., Shore, M. and Holland, P. (2015). *Banks Peninsula is the Stadium: Outdoor Recreation and Recovery in Post-earthquake Christchurch*, Lincoln University, Canterbury.

Thull, J-P. and Mersch, M. (2005). Accessibility and attractiveness – key features toward central city revitalisation – a case study of Christchurch, New Zealand, *Journal of the Eastern Asia Society for Transportation Studies* 6, 4066–81.

Tidball, K.G. (2014). Seeing the forest for the trees: Hybridity and social-ecological symbols, rituals and resilience in postdisaster contexts, *Ecology and Society* 19 (4), 25.

Till, K.E. (2012). Wounded cities: Memory-work and a place-based ethics of care, *Political Geography* 31 (1), 3–14.

Topp, C., Østergaard, S., Søndergaard, S. and Bech, P. (2015). The WHO-5 well-being index: A systematic review of the literature, *Psychotherapy and Psychosomatics* 84, 167–76.

Townsend, P. (2016). Personal communication 9, in M. Lesniak, Rebuilding/reimagining Post-disaster Christchurch – When Complexities Between Actors Have an Impact on Long-term Urban Development. Unpublished Masters Altervilles dissertation, Universite de Lyon, Lyon, 192–9.

Truebridge, N. (2017). Govt spent $1.5b acquiring Christchurch red zone land that's now worth just $21m, *Stuff*, 28 August. Retrieved from: https://www.stuff.co.nz/national/96144297/govt-spent-15-billion-acquiring-christchurch-red-zone-land-thats-now-worth-just-21m

Truebridge, N. (2018). Hagley Ave resident criticises Williams Corporation's planned Christchurch development for lack of car parking. *Stuff*, 9 February. Retrieved from: www.stuff.co.nz/business/better-business/101257861/hagley-ave-owner-criticises-williams-corporations-planned-christchurch-development

Uekusa, S., Matthewman, S. and Glavovic, B.C. eds. (2022). *A Decade of Disaster Experiences in Ōtautahi Christchurch. Critical Disaster Studies Perspectives*. Palgrave Macmillan, Singapore.

University of Washington (2020). *Ōtākaro Avon Landings. Tiaki Over Time: Ecocultural Regeneration + Climate Change Resilience for the Ōtākaro Avon Green Spine*. University of Washington, Department of Landscape Architecture, Seattle, Washington, Winter 2020.

Vallance, S. (2013). *Waimakariri District Council's Integrated, Community-based Recovery Framework*. Lincoln University, Canterbury.

Vallance, S. (2015). Disaster recovery as participation: Lessons from the Shaky Islands, *Natural Hazards* 75, 1287–1301.

Vallance, S. (2020). Personal communication, 12 March. Suzanne Vallance was then a board member of Greening the Rubble.

Vallance, S. and Carlton, S. (2015). First to respond, last to leave: Communities' roles and resilience across the '4Rs', *International Journal of Disaster Risk Reduction* 14, 27–36.

Vallance, S., Edwards, S., Conradson, D. and Karaminejad, Z. (2019). *Soft Infrastructure for Hard Times. Collaborative Planning for the (Re)building of Better Homes, Towns and Cities*. National Science Challenge: Building Better Homes, Towns and Cities, Porirua.

Vallance, S., Perkins, H.C. and Moore, K. (2005). The results of making a city more compact: Neighbours' interpretation of urban infill. *Environment and Planning B: Planning and Design* 32 (5), 715–33.

van Ballegooy, S., Malan, P., Lacrosse, V., Jacka, M.E., Cubrinovski, M., Bray, J.D., O'Rourke, T.D., Crawford, S.A. and Cowan, H. (2014). Assessment of liquefaction-induced land damage for residential Christchurch, *Earthquake Spectra* 30 (1), 31–55.

van Heugten, K. (2014). *Human Service Organizations in the Disaster Context*. Palgrave Macmillan, Basingstoke.

Veling, T. (2021). Vestiges. Retrieved from: www.timjveling.com/vestiges

Voxy (2011). New EQ community action group launched. Retrieved from: www.voxy.co.nz/national/new-eq-community-action-group-launched/5/103597

Voytenko, Y., McCormick, K., Evans, J. and Schliwa, G. (2016). Urban living labs for sustainability and low carbon cities in Europe: Towards a research agenda, *Journal of Cleaner Production* 133, 45–54.

Wade, P. (2018). World famous in New Zealand: Margaret Mahy Family Playground, Christchurch, *Stuff*, 7 October. Retrieved from: www.stuff.co.nz/travel/destinations/nz/canterbury/107502350/world-famous-in-new-zealand-margaret-mahy-family-playground-christchurch

Wagner, J. (1998). Canterbury Dialogues, *Our Environment. Christchurch City Council's Environmental Newsletter*, 14. Retrieved from: http://archived.ccc.govt.nz/OurEnvironment/14/

Waimakariri District Council (2017). Kaiapoi Regeneration areas/red zone notes, July 2017, Kaiapoi.

Waitākiri Eco-sanctuary (2022). Waitākiri sanctuary. He hiringa koiora ki Waitākiri. Retreived from: www.ecosanctuary.nz

Waka Kotahi New Zealand Transport Agency (2021a). Christchurch Motorways. Retrieved from: www.nzta.govt.nz/projects/christchurch-motorways/

Waka Kotahi New Zealand Transport Agency (2021b). Christchurch, Waimakariri and Selwyn Urban Cycleways Programme. Retrieved from: www.nzta.govt.nz/walking-cycling-and-public-transport/cycling/investing-in-cycling/urban-cycleways-programme/christchurch-urban-cycleways-programme/

Walker, B., de Vries, H.P. and Nilakant, V. (2017). Managing legitimacy: The Christchurch post-disaster reconstruction, *International Journal of Project Management* 35, 853–63.

Walsh, J. (2020). *Christchurch Architecture. A Walking Guide*. Massey University Press, Auckland.

Walton, S. (2020). Christchurch's 'Dirty 30' derelict sites still a work in progress, *Stuff*, 1 February. Retrieved from: www.stuff.co.nz/the-press/business/the-rebuild/119014561/christchurchs-dirty-30-derelict-sites-still-a-work-in-progress

Walton, S. (2021a). 'It's quite harsh out here': Data reveals clusters of social housing in Christchurch, *Stuff*, 8 May. Retrieved from: www.stuff.co.nz/the-press/news/125070869/its-quite-harsh-out-here-data-reveals-clusters-of-social-housing-in-christchurch

Walton, S. (2021b). Why hundreds of heritage buildings were demolished in Christchurch post-quake, *Stuff*, 22 February. Retrieved from: www.stuff.co.nz/the-press/business/the-rebuild/124157655/why-hundreds-of-heritage-buildings-were-demolished-in-christchurch-postquake

Walton, S. (2021c). City businesses split on parks, *The Press*, 25 March, 1.

Walton, S. (2021d). City may pitch for more stadium cash, *The Press*, 28 December, 2.

Warnock, A. (2014). Sam Johnson: leader of the Student Army, *Stuff*, 5 September. Retrieved from: www.stuff.co.nz/life-style/nz-life-leisure/61048171/sam-johnson-leader-of-the-student-army

Warren and Mahoney (2021). QEII Recreation and Sports Centre. Retrieved from: https://warrenandmahoney.com/portfolio/qeii-recreation-and-sports-centre

Weejes Sabella, E. (2015). Creative rebirth: Public art and community recovery in Christchurch. Retrieved from: https://hazards.colorado.edu/natural-hazards-observer/volume-xl-number-2

Weichselgartner, J. and Kelman, I. (2015). Geographies of resilience: Challenges and opportunities of a descriptive concept, *Progress in Human Geography* 39 (3), 249–67.

Welfare, R. (2020). Personal communication, 19 February. Rachael Welfare was then director of Life in Vacant Spaces.

Wellington City Council (2018). *Wellington Convention and Exhibition Centre. Business Case December 2018*. Wellington City Council, Wellington.

Wenger, C (2017). The oak or the reed: How resilience theories are translated into disaster management policies, *Ecology and Society* 22 (3), 18.

Wesener, A. (2015). Temporary urbanism and urban sustainability after a natural disaster: Transitional community-initiated open spaces in Christchurch, New Zealand, *Journal of Urbanism* 8 (4), 406–22.

Westbury, M. (2015). *Creating Cities*. Niche Press, Melbourne.

Whatmore, S. (2002). *Hybrid Geographies: Natures, Cultures, Spaces*. Sage, London.

Wilkinson, S. and Chang-Richards, A. (2016). *An Assessment of the Likely Changes to Construction Businesses in Christchurch Post Recovery*. BRANZ, Porirua. Retrieved from: www.branz.co.nz/pubs/research-reports/er7/

Williams Corporation (2021). Current Christchurch Developments. Retrieved from: www.williamscorporation.co.nz/current-developments-christchurch/

Wilson, G.A. (2012). *Community Resilience and Environmental Transitions*. Routledge, Abingdon.

Wilson, G.A. (2013). Community resilience, social memory and the post-2010 Christchurch (New Zealand) earthquakes, *Area* 45 (2), 207–15.

Wilson, G.A. (2014). Community resilience: Path dependency, lock-in effects and transitional ruptures, *Journal of Environmental Planning and Management* 57 (1), 1–26.

Wilson, J. (1984). *Lost Christchurch*. Te Waihora Press, Lincoln.

Wilson, J. (1989). *Christchurch, Swamp to City. A Short History of the Christchurch Drainage Board 1875–1989*. Te Waihora Press, Lincoln.

Winn, C. (2015). Personal communication, 2 March. Coralie Winn was co-founder of Gap Filler.

Wisner, B. (2020). Vulnerability, in A. Kobayashi ed., *International Encyclopedia of Human Geography*, 2nd edn., Elsevier, Amsterdam, 14, 197–205.

Wisner, B., Blaikie, P., Cannon, T. and Davis, I. (2004). *At Risk. Natural Hazards, People's Vulnerability and Disasters*, 2nd edn., Routledge, New York.

Wisner, B. and Luce, H.R. (1993). Disaster vulnerability: Scale, power and daily life, *GeoJournal* 30 (2), 127–40.

Witsey, M. (2016). Student Volunteer Army founder Sam Johnson to expand service, *Stuff*, 31 May. Retrieved from: www.stuff.co.nz/southland-times/news/80584789/student-volunteer-army-founder-sam-johnson-to-expand-service

Wolch, J. (1990). *The Shadow State: Government and Voluntary Sector in Transition*. Foundation Center, New York.

Wood, A. (2011). Go-ahead for Lyttelton Port project, *Stuff*, 25 May. Retrieved from: www.stuff.co.nz/business/5052556/Go-ahead-for-Lyttelton-Port-project

Wood, A. (2012). Unit to attract private sector into rebuild, *Stuff*, 31 July. Retrieved from: www.stuff.co.nz/business/7380309/Unit-to-attract-private-sector-into-rebuild

Wood, A. (2015). Fletcher Residential wins $800m Christchurch housing project, *Stuff*, 2 July. Retrieved from: www.stuff.co.nz/business/industries/69904053/fletcher-residential-wins-800m-christchurch-housing-project

Wood, A. and Meier, C. (2015). Fletcher and Government partner on $800 million housing project, *Stuff*, 2 July. Retrieved from: www.stuff.co.nz/business/69915244/fletcher-and-government-partner-on-800-million-housing-project

Wood, A., Noy, I. and Parker, M. (2016). The Canterbury rebuild five years on from the Christchurch earthquake, *Reserve Bank of New Zealand Te Pūtea Matua Bulletin* 79 (3), 1–16.

Woodford, A. (2019). Black-billed gull colony in Central Christchurch. Retrieved from: www.annettewoodford.wordpress.com

Woods, M. (2017). Minister announces new plan for metro sports facility. Ministerial Announcement 27 November. Retrieved from: www.beehive.govt.nz/release/minister-announces-new-plan-metro-sports-facility

Woods Bagot (2021). River recovery. Retrieved from: www.woodsbagot.com/projects/christchurch-convention-centre/

Wotif (2021). Hotels near Margaret Mahy Playground. Retrieved from: www.wotif.co.nz/Margaret-Mahy-Playground-Hotels.0-1553248635975795014-0.Travel-Guide-Filter-Hotels

Wright, M. (2001). *Quake: Hawkes Bay 1931*. Reed, Auckland.

Wright, M. (2012). Global travel guide hails Chch as top destination, *Stuff*, 22 October. Retrieved from: www.stuff.co.nz/the-press/news/7845845/Global-travel-guide-hails-Chch-as-top-destination

Xayasenh, P. (2015). Post-quake recreational activities in the Avon River and the Avon-Heathcote Estuary. Unpublished Master of Science Thesis, University of Canterbury, Christchurch.

Young, C. (2019). Fletcher Living homes in Central Christchurch struggle to find buyers, *Radio New Zealand*, 10 June. Retrieved from: www.rnz.co.nz/national/programmes/checkpoint/audio/2018698951/fletcher-living-homes-in-central-christchurch-struggle-to-find-buyers

Yusoff, K. (2013). The geoengine: Geoengineering and the geopolitics of planetary modification, *Environment and Planning A: Economy and Space* 45 (12), 2799–808.

Zaki, A. (2021), Christchurch CBD dwelling goal 'unrealistic', councillor says. *Radio New Zealand*, 14 May. Retrieved from: www.rnz.co.nz/news/national/442562/christchurch-cbd-dwelling-goal-unrealistic-councillor-says

Zukin, S. (1998). Urban lifestyles: Diversity and standardisation in spaces of consumption, *Urban Studies* 35 (5–6), 825–39.

Index

Pages in *italics* refer to figures; pages in **bold** refer to tables.

For Product Safety Concerns and Information please contact our EU representative GPSR@taylorandfrancis.com Taylor & Francis Verlag GmbH, Kaufingerstraße 24, 80331 München, Germany